The First Department

A History of the Department of Agriculture

The First Department

A History of the Department of Agriculture

Mary E. Daly

INSTITUTE OF PUBLIC
ADMINISTRATION

Dublin

First published 2002
by the Institute of Public Administration
57–61 Lansdowne Road
Dublin 4
Ireland

British Library Cataloguing in Publication Data
A catalogue record for this title is available from the British Library

ISBN 1 902448 44 8

Cover illustration incorporates the Albert Power statue which is over the
parapet of the section of Government Buildings in Merrion Street where
the Department of Agriculture was housed. It is reproduced by kind
permission of the Office of Public Works.

Cover design by Butler Claffey Design, Dun Laoghaire
Typeset by Wendy A. Commins, The Curragh
Printed by Criterion Press, Dublin, Ireland

CONTENTS

CONTENTS

LIST OF TABLES

LIST OF ABBREVIATIONS

ACC	Agricultural Credit Corporation
ACOT	An Chomhairle Oiliúna Talmhaíochta
AFT	An Foras Talúntais
AI	Artificial insemination
APS	Aids to Private Storage
CAP	Common Agricultural Policy
CBF	Coras Beostoic agus Feola
CDB	Congested Districts Board
CDC	Central Development Committee
CSF	Community Structural Funds
CSO	Central Statistics Office
CTT	Coras Trachtála Teoranta
DATI	Department of Agriculture and Technical Instruction
EC	European Community
ECA	Economic Cooperation Administration (USA)
EEC	European Economic Community
EFTA	European Free Trade Area
EMS	European Monetary System
ERAD	Eradication of Animal Diseases Board
ERP	European Recovery Programme
ESRI	Economic and Social Research Council
EU	European Union
FAO	Food and Agricultural Organisation
FEOGA	European Agricultural Guidance and Guarantee Fund
GATT	General Agreement on Tariffs and Trade
IAOS	Irish Agricultural Organisation Society
ICA	Irish Countrywomen's Association
ICI	Imperial Chemicals Industries
ICMSA	Irish Creamery Milk Suppliers' Association
IDA	Industrial Development Authority
IFU	Irish Farmers' Union
IRA	Irish Republican Army
ITGWU	Irish Transport and General Workers' Union
MAFF	Ministry of Agriculture, Fisheries and Food (Britain)
MCA	Monetary Compensation Amount

MSA	Mutual Security Agency
NAC	National Agricultural Council
NDP	National Development Plan
NESC	National Economic and Social Council
NFA	National Farmers' Association (Ireland)
NFU	National Farmers' Union (Britain)
NIEC	National Industrial and Economic Council
NUI	National University of Ireland
OECD	Organisation for Economic Co-operation and Development
OEEC	Organisation for European Economic Co-operation
PDDE	Published Debates Dáil Éireann
PDSE	Published Debates Seanad Éireann
PLC	Publicly limited company
PPF	Programme for Prosperity and Fairness
PRO	Public Records Office (London)
RCVS	Royal College of Veterinary Surgeons
RDS	Royal Dublin Society
REPS	Rural Environment Protection Scheme
RIC	Royal Irish Constabulary
TB	Tuberculosis
TCD	Trinity College, Dublin
TUC	Trade Union Congress
UCC	University College, Cork
UCD	University College, Dublin
UCG	University College, Galway
VEC	Vocational Education Committee
WTO	World Trade Organisation

Conversion Tables

All measurements in the text are given in their original form. The following tables for weights, volume and area give the metric equivalents. The currency equivalents are based on the conversion rate at the time of the changeover to decimal currency; they do not take account of inflation.

WEIGHTS

1 ounce (oz)	= 28.35 grams
1 pound (lb)	= 0.4536 kilogram
1 stone	= 6.35 kilograms
1 hundredweight (cwt)	= 50.80 kilograms
1 ton	= 1,016 kilograms (1 tonne)

VOLUME

1 gallon = 4.546 litres

AREA

1 acre = 0.406 hectare

CURRENCY

Decimal

1p	= 2.4d (old pennies)
5p	= 1 shilling (12 old pennies)
£1	= £1 (240 old pennies)

Euro

£1	= €1.27

Acknowledgements

I would like to thank the Department of Agriculture, Food and Rural Development, and specifically the committee established to commemorate the centenary of the founding of the DATI, for asking me to write this book. Two former secretaries of the Department, Donal Creedon and Jimmy O'Mahony, read all the draft chapters, and I wish to thank them for their advice. Among the current staff of the Department of Agriculture, Food and Rural Development my thanks to the Secretary-General John Malone, and to Tom Arnold, Declan Coppinger, Jim Flanagan, John Gillespie, Seamus Healy, Martin Heraghty, Martin Heffernan, and Joe Shorthall.

My research assistant William Murphy made an enormous contribution to this book. Over two and a half years he worked through thousands of files and published reports. I am extremely grateful for his dedicated work and his intelligent observations on the material.

On my own behalf and on William's behalf I would like to thank the Librarian at the Department of Agriculture, Food and Rural Development, Mary Doyle, and Denise Duffy, Eilis Byrne, Marie Henchy, Martina Hickey and Ellen Leahy. The staff at the National Archives, most particularly Catriona Crowe, Frances Magee; Tom Quinlan, Paddy Sarsfield; Eamonn Mullally, Christy Allen, Pauline Dunne and Brendan Martin. The staff of the National Library – with special mention for Fran Carroll and Gerry Kavanagh. Tony Eklof and Anne Cooney in the Official Publications Section of UCD Library.

I also drew on the advice and assistance of various colleagues and friends: Dr Sighle Bhreathnach-Lynch; Professor Paddy Cunningham, Seán Donnelly; Professor Brigid Laffan; Colm Gallagher; Dr Michael Laffan; Dr Carla King; Barry Murphy; Dr Paul Rouse and Professor Seamus Sheehy.

At the Institute of Public Administration Jim Power took charge of production and Brigid Pike proved to be a demanding and intelligent copy editor. I would particularly like to thank Tony McNamara for producing a handsome book, and for his advice on many occasions during this project.

Finally, my thanks to Paul, Elizabeth, Nicholas and Alice Daly for their forbearance, and for assistance with various IT matters, and to P.J. for providing a sympathetic and at times a critical ear for my ideas.

This book is dedicated to my father Seamus Crowley, BAgrSc, who first made me aware of the existence of 'the Department'.

CHAPTER ONE

'A NATIONAL ASSET': THE DATI, 1899–1914

When the Department of Agriculture and Technical Instruction (DATI) opened its doors in Upper Merrion Street, Dublin, on 1 April 1900, it marked a new experiment in Irish administrative and economic history. The DATI was given responsibility for developing the most important branch of the Irish economy and it had much greater power than the British Board of Agriculture.[1] Because the DATI was partly financed by an endowment fund, it was not required to subject all its schemes for detailed scrutiny by the Treasury.

There were many other examples of government agencies that existed only in Ireland, or of programmes that were introduced in Ireland at an earlier date than elsewhere in the United Kingdom – for instance, the national schools, the dispensary system, the Land Commission and the Congested Districts Board.[2] However, there were several unique features about the founding of the DATI. Most other efforts to improve the condition of Ireland carried out the recommendations of some official body, commonly a royal commission, and the blue-print was drawn up in either Whitehall or Dublin Castle. The origin of the DATI was entirely different.

In August 1895 Horace Plunkett, a unionist MP for South County Dublin and a member of a distinguished Anglo-Norman landed family,[3] wrote an open letter to the leading Irish newspapers, inviting all who were interested to join a committee to explore non-contentious measures that would promote the economic welfare of Ireland. He suggested that the committee should meet while Parliament was in recess, and this led to its being known as the Recess Committee. Plunkett wanted it to investigate the merits of establishing a board of agriculture and introducing a technical instruction bill. The twenty-three men who formed the Recess Committee included unionist and nationalist politicians, landlords, clergymen, prominent businessmen and senior lawyers. Plunkett was the chairman; the secretary, T. P. Gill. Gill was a journalist, a former Home Rule MP and a veteran of the Plan of Campaign of the 1880s. Since the legislation establishing the DATI provided for a board and a council of agriculture, whose members would be partly elected, the DATI could not be condemned as yet another 'Castle board' that ruled Ireland without any reference to the views of the Irish people.

Despite this unprecedented co-operation between unionists and nationalists in the Recess Committee and the committee's efforts to involve other influential sectors of Irish society in drawing up an economic plan, it would be naive to assume that the DATI managed to escape the fault-lines inherent in Irish life – unionism and nationalism, catholicism and prot-estantism – during its formative years. Colonel Saunderson, the leader of the Irish Unionist Party, refused to serve on the committee, as did the anti-Parnellite majority of nationalist MPs, although the small Parnellite Party, which consisted of only twelve MPs, accepted Plunkett's invitation. Justin McCarthy, the leader of the anti-Parnellite MPs, accused Plunkett of an attempt at 'killing home rule by kindness'.[4] Plunkett did not deny this assertion. In the open letter inviting people to join the committee, he had stated that he was opposed to Home Rule 'because I do not think it would be good for Ireland'. He noted in his diary that John Dillon, a prominent figure among anti-Parnellite MPs, 'sees in it [the Recess Committee] the greatest danger home rule has yet to face. So do I.'[5]

THE NEED FOR A DATI

Irrespective of his political motives, Plunkett was correct in assuming that all the major political groupings in Ireland were concerned at the condition of agriculture. The total acreage under cultivation had declined almost continuously from the 1860s. Wheat acreage had fallen from 500,000 in 1851 to 150,000 by 1881, and continued to decline. The acreage under potatoes reached a post-Famine peak of 1.134 million in the early 1860s, but thirty years later it was little more than half that amount, 0.66 million acres. By 1900 'tillage was a lost art in some districts'.[6] In place of cultivated fields, there was a rise in the acreage devoted to hay and grass. Cattle numbers doubled between 1841 and 1900, as Irish farming increasingly concentrated on the export of live cattle to Britain. After the 1870s beef and store cattle not only superseded tillage; they also expanded at the expense of the dairy sector.[7] However, the expansion of livestock did not compensate for the decline in crops. On the eve of the Famine the produce of Irish farms could feed an estimated 9½ million to 10 million people.[8] This would have been impossible by the end of the nineteenth century. The volume of agricultural output reached its post-Famine peak in the late 1850s; by the late 1890s, on the eve of the founding of the DATI, it was approximately 20 per cent below that level.[9] Although no estimates of agricultural output were available in the 1890s, the annual statistics for crop acreages and livestock numbers, which were collected from 1847, documented the major changes that had taken place. The agricultural statistics, the census returns and statistics on emigration were regularly cited as evidence that the Irish economy was in decline.

Contemporaries were also aware of the changing market conditions for agricultural produce. From the late 1870s farmers throughout Europe faced falling prices and increased competition from producers in North and South America, Australia and New Zealand. The problem was most acute for grain farmers, who were forced to compete with imported wheat and maize (used to feed poultry and livestock) from North America, which could be transported cheaply by rail and steamship. Cattle farmers were also facing greater competition. Although frozen mutton and beef was inferior to the fresh meat produced by Irish and British farmers, many families bought it because it was cheap. Hard-tack American bacon, which was salty, of low quality but cheap, found a ready market among poorer Irish families. Dairy farmers faced two problems – competition from butterine (or margarine as it came to be known), a cheap and inferior subsitute for butter, and the threat to traditional farmhouse butter from butter produced in creameries. Farmhouse butter was of variable quality. On small farms it might take weeks to fill a barrel, and it was essential to salt the butter heavily to prevent its becoming rancid. The large number of small producers meant it was impossible to maintain uniform quality, despite the inspection procedures operated in places such as the Cork Butter Market. Creamery butter was able to command higher prices. If Irish butter was not to lose its share of the British market to countries such as Denmark, which had moved rapidly into creamery-produced butter, it was essential to establish creameries in Ireland

Although the story of Irish agriculture after the Famine seems to be one of unmitigated decline, recent research has presented a less bleak picture, calling into question the allegations that Irish farming was backward and productivity was low.[10] In the 1850s crop yields in Ireland were generally above those in Scotland,[11] although Scottish farming was frequently held up as an exemplar for Ireland. By the 1890s over 40 per cent of agricultural holdings were under fifteen acres, and these smaller farms were heavily concentrated on poorer land along the western seaboard. However, the declining numbers engaged in agriculture brought a rise in output per worker. Between the 1860s and World War I, Irish agricultural productivity per acre and per agricultural worker rose more rapidly than in Britain, at a rate that was somewhere in the middle of the European league table.[12] Such statistical insights were not available at the end of the nineteenth century, and even if they had been, it is doubtful whether they would have done much to mitigate the sense of crisis, particularly in the twenty years of falling prices from the mid-1870s to the mid-1890s. Many sectors of the Irish population, including an important element of Irish nationalists, regarded a prosperous cattle-exporting industry as contrary to the interests of both Irish agriculture and the wider economy.

If, as many assumed, Irish agriculture was in need of improvement, how should this be achieved? The proposals may be categorised under four headings:

1. reforming land tenure;
2. increasing the area under cultivation by taking land from graziers and giving it to smallholders and clearing waste land;
3. introducing tariff protection for agricultural produce;
4. raising the standard of farming through education and other means.

The first two remedies were popular among nationalists, although opinions were divided over the question of redistributing land. Most nationalists believed that the system of land tenure was responsible for poverty among farmers and the lack of investment in agriculture. They believed farmers had been deterred from investing in their farms and from working to achieve a higher output, because the fruits of their work would be confiscated by landlords, either in the form of higher rents, or by evicting the hard-working tenant. This line of argument suggested that no real improvement was possible until farmers had security, either in the form of the 3 Fs (fixity of tenure, fair rent, and freedom to sell their interest in the land), or by becoming owners of their land. In 1888 Murrough O'Brien, a Land Commissioner (the Land Commission was responsible both for setting judicial rents and for processing land purchase), told the Statistical and Social Inquiry Society of Ireland that the 'small French peasant proprietor working for himself' had survived and even thrived despite falling agricultural prices and the devastation of his vineyards by phyllhoxera.[13]

By the 1890s most tenant farmers in Ireland had security of tenure and their rents were set by the Land Commission. Thousands of farmers were in the process of buying their holdings with loans provided by the British government. The era of landlord authority was coming to an end. Yet these reforms did not seem to have brought any significant improvement in living conditions, although recent research suggests otherwise.[14] Farmers who had benefited from reduced rents in 1881/2 were demanding further reductions by 1886/7 to compensate for the continuing decline in farm prices. In 1890/1, 1894/5 and 1897/8 potato blight brought acute distress to the west of Ireland.[15]

Many families living on the western seaboard survived on holdings of less than five acres and they depended for their survival on outside sources of income, such as migratory work in England, fishing and domestic industry. In 1880 the Royal Commission on Agriculture (the Richmond Commission) recommended a programme of assisted emigration and the consolidation of farms into economic holdings as the solution to agrarian distress in the west of Ireland.[16] Assisted emigration was not politically acceptable, but in 1891 the Conservative government established the Congested Districts Board (CDB) with a remit to raise living standards in the west of Ireland and a goal of removing the need for short-term emergency relief schemes. Initially, the CDB concentrated on developing all possible sources of income outside agriculture, and on promoting various forms of intensive agriculture, such as poultry. By the late 1890s, however, the CDB was under increasing pressure from nationalist politicians to take over grazing land in western areas and to use it to resettle families from over-crowded areas along the coast.[17]

Protective tariffs were seen as another means of helping agriculture, and countries such as France and Germany had taken steps to protect their farmers from the flood of agricultural imports from non-European sources. Yet, when the Select Committee on Industries (Ireland) examined this issue in 1885, its report was inconclusive, perhaps because the members were aware that any decisions on free trade or protection would be taken in Britain.[18] The Act of Union meant that any decision on agricultural protection would be taken at Westminster, with British not Irish interests to the fore, and this would remain the case even under Home Rule. Moreover, since the 1840s Britain's economic policy had been based on free trade, and despite the growing support among British farmers for tariff protection, there was little immediate prospect that free trade would be abandoned.

Although the continental option of tariff protection was not possible, continental Europe offered other promising models. By the 1890s Danish, Dutch and French farmers were obtaining better prices and a higher share of the British market for eggs, butter and bacon because their produce was of a higher quality. The Recess Committee concluded that the higher quality of continental produce was due to government support. The committee's report gave details of government expenditure on agriculture and technical instruction in Holland, Belgium, Switzerland, France, Denmark and various German states.[19] In Belgium, France, Holland and Denmark, as in Ireland, most farms were small units that relied on family labour, whereas English agriculture was dominated by larger farms with landlords responsible for capital investment and most of the manual work being carried out by hired labour. There was obviously a greater need to provide state aid for small family farms than for larger holdings that were organised on a more capitalist basis.

THE FORERUNNERS OF THE DATI

There had been a long history of efforts to improve farming practices in Ireland prior to 1900, although it is difficult to determine whether or not they were effective. In the 1770s Arthur Young described how many Irish landlords had adopted modern practices of manuring and land reclamation.[20] Ayrshires, Herefords and Shorthorns were supplanting traditional breeds of cattle, such as the Kerry cow, in the decades before the Famine, and iron swing ploughs had replaced traditional wooden ploughs. The large number of local agricultural societies, agricultural shows and a lively farming press are further indications that Irish agriculture was responsive to change.[21] However, by the 1870s farmers' clubs seem to have been more interested in politics than in practical farming, with many clubs becoming branches of the Land League.[22]

The Royal Dublin Society (RDS), founded in 1731 'for improving Husbandry, Manufactures and other Useful Arts', was the most prominent national organisation involved in agricultural improvement.[23] Like most other eighteenth-century learned societies it was dominated by the landed class. In 1831 the RDS established the annual livestock show, the Spring Show, to improve the quality of livestock. It assisted in the founding of the Royal Agricultural Society in 1860. It worked to raise farming standards and spread practical information about agriculture throughout provincial Ireland, by working with local agricultural societies and organising an annual agricultural show in each province. The Royal Agricultural Society funded itinerant instructors and encouraged landlords and farmers to drain and reclaim land. In 1864 the Royal Agricultural Society and the RDS organised the first Dublin Horse Show to promote higher standards of bloodstock. The RDS encouraged the formation of societies of pig and cattle breeders and the registration of pedigree stock, and also carried out some of the first trials of experimental varieties of potatoes. In 1890 an instructor in agriculture in Swinford, County Mayo, appointed by the RDS, set up a series of experimental plots.[24] A similar scheme was later introduced by the CDB.

By the 1890s the RDS was receiving an annual state grant of £5,000, which accounted for more than one-quarter of its annual income of £18,000–£19,000. Yet in 1894 the *Fortnightly Review* suggested that the RDS had failed to effect 'any marked or permanent improvement in the methods of the Irish farmer', adding that 'it cannot be said to be in touch with, or representative of, the great mass of the agricultural classes of our country'.[25] It allocated £3,500 of its government grant for the improvement of horse-breeding and only £1,500 for cattle.[26]

The RDS depended on interested landlords to promote agricultural improvements. Many landlords provided tenants with lime, assisted with drainage schemes, or they might purchase a premium bull to improve the quality of livestock. Nevertheless, the share of rental that was devoted to investment was generally low.[27] Improving landlords were often unpopular because they consolidated farms, removed unsatisfactory tenants, or introduced Scottish tenants or a Scottish manager to teach new methods of farming to the existing tenants.[28] By the 1880s the power of Irish landlords was waning. The Land Act of 1881 had given tenants considerable security, and the transfer of land ownership to the tenant farmers was under way. Irish nationalists were replacing landlords as chairmen of the boards of guardians (the only democratic or quasi-democratic instrument of local government at the time).[29] Land reform meant that landlords were even less likely to invest in agricultural improvements than in the past.

Some landlords were determined to retain a prominent role in Irish society. Parnell believed that, if Irish landlords were to remain an important political élite, peasant proprietorship was the first step.[30] Horace Plunkett, the son of a prominent landlord, believed that co-operatives and agricultural improvement offered a new role for Irish landlords.[31] Given that the co-operative movement came into existence at the end of the 1880s, at a time when there was considerable bitterness between landlords and tenants over land reform and Home Rule, it is scarcely surprising that many nationalists were suspicious of the motives of landlords involved in the co-operative movement. Nationalist reservations were increased by the fact that co-operatives appeared to threaten the interests of shopkeepers and merchants, a group who were prominent supporters of the Irish Parliamentary Party. The committee of the Irish Agricultural Organisation Society (IAOS), the umbrella organisation of the co-operative movement, tried to keep a careful balance between unionists and nationalists, catholics and protestants. However, in 1894/5 the committee consisted of seven landlords, one land agent, one businessman, one politician, one Catholic bishop, and one farmer who was a large grazier and cattle breeder.[32]

During the 1890s the IAOS worked to spread the gospel of co-operation, citing the valuable contribution that the co-operative movement had made to agricultural development in continental Europe. In addition to organising creameries (its most successful activity), the IAOS attempted to provide farmers with cheaper and superior seed and fertiliser than that supplied by local traders. It also hired agricultural advisers to educate farmers in better farming practices and tried, with little success, to establish co-operative banks. However, while Irish farmers were keen on establishing creameries (and co-operatives often provided the best means of doing so), they were not necessarily committed to the principle of co-operation.[33] The IAOS was handicapped by a lack of finance, and it was difficult to raise money from the agricultural community. From 1891 the CDB provided farmers in western areas with cheap seed and fertiliser, new breeds of hens and ducks, Spanish asses, stud horses, quality bulls, fruit bushes and trees, sheep-dipping facilities, and advice from itinerant agricultural instructors – all at government expense.[34] Farmers in other areas were demanding similar services.

Other factors also made it probable that a department of agriculture would be established. In the year before the Recess Committee met, 1894, there was a new low in agricultural prices. In 1889 the British Board of Agriculture had been established and the British government increased the amount of public money provided for agricultural education in England and Wales. Agricultural colleges were established and several English and Welsh universities created departments of agricultural science.[35] In 1889 the amount of tax levied on British farming fell sharply, owing to the introduction of agricultural rates relief as part of the Local Government

Act of 1888. Agricultural rates relief was not extended to Ireland because Ireland was still without democratic local government.[36] However, in 1896 the Childers Commission revealed that since the 1850s the incidence of taxation had been much higher in Ireland than in Britain.[37] The simplest way of addressing this grievance was to increase government spending. The fact that the Conservative government was committed to peasant proprietorship was also an important factor. Otherwise, the decision to establish a department of agriculture would have been dismissed as a ploy to shore up landlord rule.

THE REPORT OF THE RECESS COMMITTEE

Plunkett's open invitation to join a committee to examine the feasibility of establishing a board of agriculture received a mixed reception. While there was general agreement on the need for some form of board for agriculture, Plunkett's proposal that the scheme should be devised by a committee representing all shades of Irish opinion was viewed with considerable scepticism. According to the *Freeman's Journal*, 'The most that could be hoped for from a committee as Mr Plunkett proposes is that it might do no harm'; the *Irish Independent* dismissed the proposal as 'an impossibility [which] might even lead to results the reverse of satisfactory'. The strongest opposition came from the *Belfast Newsletter*, which argued that it would be better to leave any decisions on a board of agriculture in the hands of the Conservative government. By contrast *The Irish Times* believed that the committee should have little difficulty in reaching agreement.[38] This last assessment proved correct, perhaps because the leading critics of Plunkett's proposal refused to join the committee, and because they were content to let Plunkett and Gill determine the contents of the report.

The Recess Committee recommended that a ministry of agriculture and industries for Ireland should be established. The outlines of this proposal can be found in a memorandum that T. P. Gill wrote for Plunkett in December 1895, one month before the first meeting of the Recess Committee on 7 January 1896. Gill had become acquainted with Plunkett when they were both Westminster MPs. When Gill lost his parliamentary seat, Plunkett found him a job with the IAOS, and he edited the co-operative newspaper, *The Irish Homestead*, for a brief period. In September 1895, when it was not yet certain that the Recess Committee would meet, the IAOS sent Gill to France and Denmark with instructions to examine 'the scope and relations with each other of Voluntary Associations of agriculturists and government departments of agriculture'. As Carla Keating notes, 'Many of the inputs into the planning of the Committee were Gill's, and it was he who finally wrote the Report, although Plunkett decided its content.' She adds:

> Although it is difficult to be certain, it appears that the proceedings of the Committee were more or less dominated by Plunkett's and Gill's conception of the Department they hoped to create, and the proposal that emerged was extremely close to Gill's memorandum of December 6. This helps to explain how the Committee managed to complete its task in such a short time. By late January 1896 they had agreed on the overall structure of the proposed Department; by the end of May the details had been fleshed out. The Report was published in mid-August.[39]

Gill claimed that Plunkett only wrote one short passage in the report – the passage about the Royal Dublin Society:

> With its great prestige, large membership including most of the leaders of thought in Ireland, its efficient staff, ample funds, and a government subsidy, it is capable of performing well its chief function, namely the advancement of agriculture, and yet its greatest admirers will not claim for it that it has succeeded in effecting any marked or permanent improvement in the methods of the Irish farmer.

The RDS had rejected a request from Plunkett in 1891 that it divert part of its government grant to support the co-operative movement, and Plunkett's biographer, Trevor West, has suggested that this passage was Plunkett's response. The RDS defended its record in a pamphlet, *Observations on the Reference in the Recess Committee's Report to the Royal Dublin Society, its Work and Position in Ireland*. In this pamphlet the RDS suggested that an Irish board of agriculture should be established as a branch of the English board.[40]

In contrast, the report of the Recess Committee praised the IAOS for giving effect 'to the system of agricultural organization which our evidence shows to be the most modern, beneficial, and widespread agency for agricultural and industrial progress on the Continent' and it referred to the 'rapid adoption by Irish farmers of agricultural co-operation'. The committee recommended that the new department should appoint travelling instructors, who would provide education and advice for farmers and oversee experimental plots; establish experimental stations and laboratories to investigate plant and animal disease and to determine the most effective fertilisers; and provide grant assistance to co-operative societies, which would promote agricultural improvement through self-help. It recommended that a consultative council should be established to act as an 'agricultural and industrial parliament'. Two-thirds of the members would be elected, one-third would be nominated by the Crown. The council, which would meet at least twice a year, would have the authority to draft and suggest 'such legislation as may be needed in the future for the protection or promotion of agriculture and industries'. It would report the views of the agricultural community on the administration of the department and its schemes, and on proposals for new measures.[41]

The concept of an advisory council was adopted from France; the recommendation that the department should work closely with voluntary societies followed the practice in Denmark.[42] Unlike the typical 'Castle boards', which were under the direct control of the Chief Secretary (in practice the Under-Secretary),[43] the new department should be headed by a minister, who would be a member of Parliament and responsible to Parliament for the work of the department. In addition to the consultative committee, there would be a five-man executive board, nominated by the Lord Lieutenant, simliar to the CDB. They would control all the monies allocated to the department.

The Recess Committee proposed establishing a joint department of agriculture and industries, which would absorb the CDB and the Irish functions of the British Department of Science and Art. The recommendations relating to industry anticipated many of the schemes introduced by government agencies in the 1960s and even later. It was suggested that the department identify a list of industries suited to Ireland; the skills, raw materials and capital equipment that would be needed; the best locations; and the names of people who would provide the necessary training. It urged that local communities should form committees to determine, in discussion with the minister, what industries were best suited to their area. These committees could apply for state grants to provide working capital or training, and the department would assist new and existing industries to identify potential markets. The Recess Committee tried to play down the radical nature of these proposals by suggesting that there was nothing inherently novel in the state's providing aid for industrial development; the CDB was already doing this. Yet there was a major distinction between assisting small craft industries in remote locations or a firm like the Foxford

11

Woollen industry, run on a philanthropic basis by the Sisters of Mercy, and assisting industrial development throughout Ireland. It is doubtful whether any British government at the time would have introduced such measures. When the DATI was established in 1899, it was restricted to assisting rural industries.

The Recess Committee also recommended a major expansion in technical education. Ireland had a strong claim to additional government money for technical education. In November 1895, before the first meeting of the Recess Committee, its two secretaries, Lord Monteagle and T. P. Gill, wrote to Gerald Balfour, the Irish Chief Secretary, suggesting that it would cost £120,000 per annum to put the provisions for technical education in Ireland on a par with those in England.[44] The Recess Committee recommended establishing two types of secondary school, one devoted to practical agriculture, the other to industry and commerce, with provision for night classes. It also suggested that local art schools should be established (at this time art and design were seen as very important to industrial development), and higher technical colleges for agriculture, industries and industrial art. Professors of agriculture and applied science should be appointed to Irish universities. These recommendations were only partly implemented.

Overall, the Recess Committee's report represented a compromise between the self-help co-operative principles beloved of the IAOS, and the nationalist belief that state aid was essential to achieve economic development.[45] Part One of the report, titled 'Past Action of the State', described the restrictions that had been imposed on Irish industry in the past by Westminster. It also quoted a statement by Arthur Balfour that many of the ills in Ireland were due to poverty, a poverty that was 'in part the work of England and Scotland'. While seeming to suggest that state aid was necessary to compensate for past ills, in reality the report adopted a more subtle line of analysis. In keeping with Horace Plunkett's belief that culture and character were the most important factors determining material prosperity (a message that he spelled out in detail in his controversial book *Ireland in the New Century*), the Recess Committee suggested that the restrictions imposed on the Irish economy in the past had damaged 'the temper and habits of the people in respect of industry, the lack of enterprise and perseverence [*sic*], and the thriftless ways which seem to have characterised them throughout the greater part of this century'.[46] For this reason the state should try 'to create a condition of things in which private enterprise shall be able freely to do its work; it should also try to promote a more enterprising attitude among the Irish population'. The distinction between the state's efforts to promote what would now be described as an enterprise culture, and the belief that the state should play a more direct role in economic development, was not fully understood by many who read the report of the Recess Committee, yet it goes to the heart of some of the difficulties that would later arise between the Department and the people.

In other respects the report appeared to support those who wished to reverse many of the economic trends of the nineteenth century. The Recess Committee came down in favour of promoting greater diversity in agriculture, referring to sugar-beet, tobacco, flax, afforestation and the merits of exporting dead meat instead of live cattle, although this recommendation brought a protest from William Field, the nationalist MP, who was president of the Cattle Traders' Association. The report echoed Sir Robert Kane's book, *The Industrial Resources of Ireland*, when it suggested that peat and water power offered profitable alternatives to coal. It also raised the possibility of re-establishing industries that had flourished in the past but were now in decline, such as glass and paper manufacture. Despite appointing a special Ulster consultative council, the report says almost nothing about Belfast and its successful industries. There is no mention of Guinness' brewery. As such it was more a nationalist than a unionist document.

When the Recess Committee reported in August 1896, legislation was being prepared to establish an agricultural board for Ireland, although its role would have been limited and there was no provision for technical instruction or industry.[47] This bill was withdrawn because Irish unionist MPs threatened to oppose it, and the support of Irish nationalists was also in doubt. Most unionist MPs were landlords and they were aggrieved that agricultural rates relief had not been extended to Ireland; nationalists were unhappy about the proposed financial arrangements for the board of agriculture.[48] The Conservative government had decided to introduce agricultural rates relief simultaneously with the reform of local government.[49] The Local Government Act of 1898 replaced unelected grand juries with elected county and urban district councils; the Act establishing a Department of Agriculture and Technical Instruction was passed in 1899.

THE DEPARTMENT OF AGRICULTURE AND TECHNICAL INSTRUCTION
(THE DATI)

The decision not to proceed with the 1896 bill was beneficial, because the 1899 Act established a department, not a board, and a department had greater financial autonomy and wider powers.

There were two aspects to the work of the DATI. In the first place it assumed responsibility for a wide range of tasks relating to agriculture, science and education that were scattered throughout other branches of the Irish administration. These included monitoring animal disease; regulating markets, fairs and fisheries; collecting agricultural statistics; and running the National Library, the National Museum, the Botanic Gardens, the Geological Survey and the Metropolitan School of Art. The cost of these transferred services and the salaries and expenses of the DATI's staff were funded by an annual estimate, which was the normal method of financing government services.

The DATI was also given wide powers to introduce measures to assist agriculture, technical instruction and rural industry, and these would be financed from a capital sum of approximately £200,000 and an annual endowment of £166,000. All expenditure from the capital fund or the annual endowment had to be approved by the Board of Agriculture and the Board of Technical Instruction, which were also established under the legislation. The 1899 Act required that a sum of £55,000 be set aside each year for technical instruction, and a further £10,000 for the development of sea fisheries, but the DATI was free to determine how the remainder of the money should be spent. Although all expenditure was subject to audit, projects funded from the endowment fund did not have to secure Treasury approval. This was extremely advantageous to the DATI, because the Treasury had opposed the establishment of a board or a department of agriculture in 1897 and again in 1899,[50] and it would appear that the work of the CDB was continually hampered by the Treasury.[51]

After 1909 the DATI received additional money from the Development Commission, a discretionary fund under the control of the Irish Chief Secretary that was used to assist various development programmes. The money was used to finance schemes for horse-breeding, forestry, fisheries and agricultural research.[52]

The Vice-President
As Sir Horace Plunkett had been the moving force behind the establishment

of the DATI, it was appropriate that he should become its executive head with the title of vice-president. The Recess Committee had recommended that the president of the new department should be an MP, who would report to Parliament independently of the Chief Secretary. However, the 1899 Act named the Chief Secretary as president of the DATI, although it anticipated that the vice-president, who would be the effective head, would be an MP. Gerald Balfour, who was the Chief Secretary at the time, claimed that he came under considerable pressure, presumably from Plunkett, although he does not say this, to separate the DATI from the Irish administration by making the vice-president independent of both the Chief Secretary and the Lord Lieutenant, but he was not prepared to agree to this.[53] Nevertheless, the understanding that the vice-president would be an MP appeared to offer the DATI a degree of autonomy.[54] Plunkett was appointed as vice-president of the DATI in November 1899, six months before it came into existence. At the time, he was the unionist MP for Dublin South, and a member of the government party. By April 1900, however, he had lost his seat in a general election.[55] Despite several attempts to find another Irish parliamentary seat, he never returned to Westminster.

Because Plunkett was not an MP, the Chief Secretary spoke for the DATI in Parliament, and Plunkett spent more time in Dublin on departmental business than would have been possible if he had remained an MP. Balfour told the 1906 inquiry into the DATI, that the vice-president was in the same relationship to the Chief Secretary as the Chief Secretary was to the Lord Lieutenant.[56] This was not a very accurate description, since the Chief Secretary was a member of the Cabinet and the Lord Lieutenant was generally not; in such cases, regardless of protocol, the Chief Secretary was the more powerful figure. Plunkett managed to surmount his rather anomalous status by force of personality. He was a close friend of Gerald Balfour's wife, Betty, and he used her as an influential conduit to the Chief Secretary. Relations with the Chief Secretary's office became more difficult when George Wyndham succeeded Balfour in 1900. Plunkett and Wyndham were not on friendly terms, and Wyndham wanted to incorporate the DATI into the regular Castle administration. Plunkett only survived as vice-president because there was no obvious candidate for the position.

When Plunkett was vice-president, the Chief Secretary was not closely involved in the administration of the DATI. In 1906 Plunkett told the inquiry into the DATI that the Chief Secretary was not normally supplied with copies of the minutes of meetings of the Board of Agriculture; neither were important papers submitted to him for approval. According to Sir

Kenelm Digby, who chaired the 1906 inquiry, this implied that the Chief Secretary was responsible to Parliament for the actions of the vice-president 'which he has no power of controlling'.[57]

Plunkett wrote *Ireland in the New Century*,[58] setting out his belief in the importance of co-operation and voluntary effort, to counteract Wyndham's views in favour of stronger state control and greater centralisation.[59] In addition to giving the early history of the co-operative movement and the DATI, the book contains a forthright critique of nationalist and unionist politics and some sharp comments on what Plunkett saw as the defects in the Irish character. He was even more outspoken about the influence of the Catholic Church on Irish society. According to Trevor West, 'for a member of the ascendancy (however lukewarm his own religious affiliation) to cast aspersions on Irish catholicism was, at all times, a delicate task; for one in the exposed position of a minister without a seat in parliament it was an unforgiveable sin'. *Ireland in the New Century* provoked heated exchanges between unionist and nationalist politicians during a debate on the estimates for the DATI in 1904.[60] The Irish nationalist MP John Dillon had long been a critic of Plunkett and the DATI. Dillon was exercised by Plunkett's statements that the DATI would kill the demand for Home Rule, and by Plunkett's encouraging the co-operatives to supply fertiliser and other farm materials in competition with local traders. Many members of the Irish Parliamentary Party agreed with Dillon. The publication of *Ireland in the New Century* fuelled their enmity.

When the Liberals came into office following the 1906 general election, Plunkett tendered his resignation. However, the Irish Chief Secretary, Sir James Bryce, asked him to remain in office until a committee of inquiry into the DATI had reported on its workings and its relations with other branches of the Irish administration. Bryce was a supporter of Plunkett and the inquiry appears to have been a device to fend off nationalist demands for Plunkett's removal.[61] Plunkett agreed to remain in a non-political capacity.[62] In December 1906, however, Augustine Birrell, who was much less sympathetic to Plunkett, succeeded Bryce as Chief Secretary, and in the spring of 1907 the Irish Parliamentary Party tabled a motion demanding Plunkett's resignation. Although several speakers on all sides of the House paid tribute to Plunkett, the motion was carried and Plunkett resigned.[63] He was succeeded by T. W. Russell, a liberal unionist and MP for East Tyrone. Russell was a successful hotelier of Scottish birth, an Ulster agrarian radical, and a vigorous supporter of Irish, and especially Ulster, protestants.[64] He had served as Parliamentary Secretary to the Local

Government Board during the late 1890s, but Ulster landlords had demanded that he be dismissed from office, and Lord Salisbury did not reappoint him after the 1900 general election.[65] Russell responded by organising a series of mass meetings throughout Ulster to campaign for compulsory purchase of landlord estates. In 1902 Redmond instructed nationalist voters in East Down to support him.[66]

The Council of Agriculture

The 1899 Act established a Council of Agriculture comprising 102 members, equalling the number of Irish MPs at Westminster. Sixty-eight were elected or selected by the county councils, four from counties Cork and Tipperary and two from each remaining county. The chairmen of county councils commonly served on the council, and the elected members were overwhelmingly nationalist. In theory, the thirty-two nominated members were chosen on the basis of one per county, although this was not rigidly observed. The president and vice-president of the DATI were members *ex-officio*. The council was required to meet once a year, its main function being to elect eight members to the Board of Agriculture (two for each province), and four members to the Board of Technical Instruction; otherwise the council was a purely consultative body. The first meeting of the council took place on 29 May 1900 at the Royal University Building in Earlsfort Terrace, Dublin.

T. P. Gill, the first secretary of the DATI, described the DATI as 'one of the governing authorities of the nation, a Department of State, representative of the Crown, of Parliament, and of the local authorities of the country, which has been constructed by the will of the Irish people of all parties and [is] the first representative institution of the kind in their possession'.[67] While Gill, a former nationalist MP, may have been justifying his decision to join the DATI, by suggesting that it furthered the cause of self-government, he was also reflecting the expectations of many nationalists that the elected representatives of the Irish people on the Council of Agriculture would exercise real control over policy and expenditure in the DATI. The first annual report of the DATI similarly stated that the DATI was to be 'representative at once of the Crown, the recently created local government bodies of the country, and those classes of people with whom its work is chiefly concerned'.

Although the Council of Agriculture was described as the 'farmer's parliament', few council members were engaged in farming. Of the eighty members of the 1900 council whose occupations have been identified by

Liam Kennedy, thirty-five, the largest single bloc, were landowners with valuations in excess of £100, who could be described as landed gentry. Most of these men were nominee members. They included Lord Monteagle, who was active in the co-operative movement; Lord Mayo; Lord Clonbrock; and Sir Josselyn Gore-Booth (brother of Countess Markievicz). There were ten farmers with holdings under £100 in valuation; eleven traders; six clergymen; three industrialists; several professional men; one creamery manager; one auctioneer; one land agent; and one newspaper proprietor. The small number of farmers reflected the fact that farmers were under-represented on the county councils, which had selected two-thirds of the members.[68] Only ten of the thirty-two nominees were not members or subscribers to the IAOS, although few of these were farmers. The composition of the council did not change significantly in later years. Eighty-four members of the first council served on the second council convened in 1903.

The council, which met twice a year, had very limited powers. R. A. Anderson of the IAOS, who served as a nominee during the early years, claimed that it was only a 'rubber-stamping body', and the meetings followed 'an orderly formality'. All resolutions originating from the DATI were passed as originally drafted. This compliance did not end when Plunkett stepped down.[69] Another council member, William McDonald, the chairman of Cork County Council, claimed that 'there was very little done at these meetings beyond hearing the Vice-President's address, which could not be criticised or discussed, and the election of provincial committees', who elected the members of the board.[70] Plunkett attempted to confine council discussions to matters of general, rather than local interest. He ruled out any discussions over appointments, as did his successor, T. W. Russell. At the second meeting of the council in 1901 Plunkett blocked a discussion of the livestock schemes operated by the county committees of agriculture. When Russell first addressed the council as vice-president in November 1907, council member Colonel Everard commented that his predecessor, Plunkett, had ruled 'to exclude any subject from discussion that might give rise to heated controversy'.[71]

Nevertheless, some members succeeded in airing specific grievances. One member repeatedly criticised the livestock schemes operated by the Limerick County Committee of Agriculture. Others were successful in having motions passed demanding the establishment of an agricultural school in County Kerry and improvements to a pier in County Clare. Council members heard the conflicting views of milling and fishery interests over water rights. In May 1907 the Cork port of Baltimore sent a deputation to Dublin, accompanied by a brass band, to lobby the council in favour of introducing a brand-name for Irish fish. Although some resolutions from the floor related to matters that were beyond the DATI's control, such as demands that more money be provided for arterial drainage, and motions urging the establishment of a vice-regal commission to inquire into the railway and canal systems, most of the resolutions concerned agriculture. The council showed a particular interest in horse-breeding, especially the fortunes of the Irish draught horse. While few members of the council were farmers, the majority displayed a practical knowledge and a concern for Irish agriculture.

Lobbying by the Council of Agriculture resulted in the establishment of a vice-regal commission to investigate the Irish railways. The council pressed the DATI to introduce measures to prevent the adulteration of butter, the eradication of noxious weeds, the prevention of livestock diseases such as scour, the eradication of sheep scab and the testing of all premium bulls for tuberculosis, all matters that were within the remit of the DATI, and on several occasions it responded to their demands.

The Board of Agriculture

The Recess Committee had recommended that executive power should rest with a board, whose members would be nominated. The 1899 Act established two partly-elected boards, one for agriculture and one for technical instruction, but neither board had any executive functions. They could veto decisions taken by officials, but they could not initiate policy, and their precise powers were not specified in the legislation.

Although all expenditure relating to agriculture had to be approved by the Board of Agriculture, this rapidly became a formality. At the first two meetings the board voted the DATI a sum of money, which it could spend as it saw fit, reporting back to the board on how the money had been spent. At the third meeting, in September 1900, Plunkett suggested that this practice should be continued 'so long as the present excellent relations between the Department and the Board, enabling the former to anticipate the wishes of the latter, subsisted'. According to the minutes of its meeting, the board, 'seeing that the plan facilitated administration', agreed,[72] and at the next meeting it voted the DATI a credit of £2,000, double the previous amount.

At the January 1901 board meeting it became apparent that the DATI had already decided to participate in the Glasgow International

Exhibition and had entered into financial commitments without the board's sanction. At the same meeting the board discussed whether it should consider schemes initiated by county committees of agriculture before the DATI's grants were determined. Plunkett suggested that, 'owing to the administrative difficulties of getting the Schemes into working order', it might be better, for the present, to authorise the DATI to determine the individual grants. The board could review the schemes in retrospect. After a lengthy discussion the board agreed to accept Plunkett's proposal for the current year,[73] but this practice appears to have continued in later years.

These procedures meant that it proved extremely difficult for the board to exercise control over expenditure, and there are several instances where expenditure on a project was vastly in excess of the sum originally approved. (It seems improbable that such practices would have been tolerated in any other government department at this time.) The DATI originally allocated £5,000 for the Cork Industrial Exhibition, but in October 1901 it sought approval to spend a further £10,000 'to ensure the success of their exhibit'. The board duly approved, although Plunkett asked that the amount should not be disclosed. In June 1902 the board was asked to approve a further £5,000 for the exhibition.[74] In 1906, however, the board restricted the DATI's expenditure on the Dublin International Exhibition.[75] By then a Liberal government was in office; Plunkett's days as vice-president were numbered; and the board had begun to assert its authority. During its first three years the board only rejected one proposal brought forward by Plunkett – the amount of financial assistance to be given to the North-East Agricultural Association – and it revoked this decision at a later meeting when Plunkett submitted a modified proposal.[76]

Some schemes were modified in response to board suggestions. At the first meeting on 14 June 1900, Count Moore urged the DATI to inquire into the present conditions for the transit of butter, and the DATI carried out an investigation into the transportation of all perishable goods.[77] In May 1906, at the first meeting of a new board (which included two new members, Reverend Dr James Daly, representing Connacht, and Patrick F. Mulally, representing Munster), there was a long discussion about the functions and powers of the board and its relation to the DATI. The minutes of the meeting noted that 'members were anxious that the controls exercised by the board should be maintained or even enhanced'. R. Downes, the chairman of Westmeath County Council, noted that although the board often made suggestions regarding the implementation of schemes, 'they were not legally entitled to make these suggestions'. This discussion was prompted by the decision to establish a committee of inquiry into the DATI. In a statement that could be interpreted as an attempt to influence the evidence that board members might present, Plunkett noted that:

> Not only could the Board block the Department's proposals, but they were in a very strong position if they desired to substitute proposals of their own. They had, in fact, very real powers of initiation. As regards administration, including patronage, he thought it would be extremely unwise for the Board to seek further powers in matters of this kind.

Downes replied that while the board and the DATI enjoyed harmonious relations, this might not be so in the future, and in this case it was 'most desirable that the position of the Board should be clearly defined'. He also suggested that the edited board minutes should be published. Plunkett agreed to this in principle, which was something of a *volte face*, given that he did not submit copies to the Chief Secretary. While board members acknowledged that the board enjoyed good relations with the DATI, and that officials gave 'fair' consideration to any proposals originating with the board, there is little doubt that they craved greater authority.[78]

All minuted requests for a modification or a review of existing policy are couched in such deferential terms that they convey the impression that members were pleading for privileges rather than exercising their statutory rights. This may reflect the force of Plunkett's personality. Robert Downes told the 1906 inquiry into the DATI, 'I have never met a man who could get on with a mixed body as well as he [Plunkett] can'. He feared that the board and the DATI might come into conflict if 'a man of a different calibre' became head of the DATI; 'at present there are certain courtesy privileges exercised by the Agricultural Board which may be refused at any time by the Vice-President'. Downes wanted these privileges transformed into rights.[79] When Russell became vice-president, the annual estimates were presented to the board in a more systematic manner than before, and the minutes convey an impression that the board was subject to less direction by the vice-president and senior officials.

Some nationalists serving on the board or the council were frustrated at their lack of influence. Robert Downes wanted the DATI to be controlled by a 'general Council for the whole of Ireland', which would be elected by the people – obviously some form of Home Rule parliament.[80] Many nationalists demanded the elimination of nominee members on the board and the council, arguing that they should be wholly-elected bodies. T. P. Gill was in favour of retaining nominee places, provided that the nominations were made by individuals or executives who were representative of the country. According to Gill, 'Because there is a feeling in the country that the Government is not responsible to the people that feeling manifests itself in the desire to extend the control of any species of democratic body over administration without regard to the special character or function of that body'.[81] Although Hugh de Fellenburg Montgomery, a Tyrone landlord and a unionist, who was a member of the Board of Agriculture,[82] denied there were divisions within the board between elected and nominee members, this was not necessarily true of the larger, less powerful council. As will be shown below, on the issue of the DATI's support for the IAOS, nominated members were strongly in favour of the grant, whereas elected members were divided.[83]

According to Andrew Gailey, Plunkett was staunchly opposed to the extension of democratic principles in Ireland; 'he had been pushed much further than he had intended to go' by including a democratic element in the legislation in order to secure cross-party support from Irish MPs. He remained firmly convinced of the need for 'a strong central executive'.[84] T. P. Gill told the 1906 inquiry into the DATI that he (and he claimed that his views were shared by the DATI) thought so highly 'of the character and capacity' of the men who had been elected to the council and boards, that he considered them 'fit to be trusted with any powers'. He described the experience of working with them as 'a revelation of the capacity of our people for exercising the responsibilities of self-government'.[85] This is an extremely revealing, even a patronising, remark by a former Irish Parliamentary Party MP.

The Officials
Plunkett was responsible for appointing all the senior staff of the DATI. The Board of Agriculture had no power over appointments, although some members wished to have the power of veto.[86] At a board meeting on 22 May 1906, Dr Healy, archbishop of Tuam, suggested that if the vice-president was not responsible to Parliament (was not an MP), there might be no check on his using the powers of appointment in a manner that amounted to patronage.[87] Many nationalists were of the opinion that several senior appointments in the DATI carried 'the taint of the Castle'. The under-representation of catholics in senior government jobs in Ireland was a highly contentious matter at this time,[88] and nationalist MPs tabled several

questions in Westminster seeking information about the religion, age, nationality and place of education of the DATI's salaried officials. Plunkett rejected one such request, but Wyndham agreed to provide information on salaries, education and previous occupation, but not on religion or nationality. When MPs requested further information in 1905, some officials in the DATI allegedly destroyed the circular.[89]

Ironically, the most controversial appointment was that of T. P. Gill as secretary of the DATI. Gill, a nationalist and a catholic, was reputedly a supporter of the Boers, who were then at war with Britain. Unionist opposition to Gill's appointment was a major factor in the decision to run a rival candidate against Plunkett in the 1900 general election, which cost him his seat. In 1906 Gill told the inquiry into the DATI that he had come under considerable pressure to take the job as secretary because the DATI needed to work through popularly-elected local bodies, and it was important that one of the two senior positions be held by somebody belonging to a popular party.[90] The rival candidate, R. A. Anderson of the IAOS, was alleged to have been passed over for this reason. Yet, as we have seen, Gill was the author of the report of the Recess Committee, which suggests that he already had the stronger claim to the appointment.

If Gill's appointment offended unionists, nationalists resented many of Plunkett's other choices. When the DATI was founded, Plunkett claimed that only one man in Ireland, Professor Thomas Carroll, the director of the Albert Agricultural College, had sufficient experience to be placed in charge of agricultural education, and he was nearing retirement.[91] He 'had to choose between men who knew Ireland and did not know their job, and men who knew their job and did not know Ireland, and we came to the conclusion that we might teach men their Ireland, but we could not teach them their jobs, so we had to get in aliens to start with.'[92]

James Campbell, a Scot, who was professor of agricultural science at Leeds University and director of agriculture for York County Council, became assistant secretary in charge of agriculture. The first assistant secretary for technical education was Captain T. B. Shaw from the London Board of Education and the Science and Art Department of South Kensington. The first superintendent of statistics was an Irishman, W. P. Coyne, professor of political economy at University College, Dublin. Unionists also objected to his appointment because he was a catholic.[93] When Coyne died in 1906, he was succeeded by W. G. S. Adams, who had lectured in economics at the universities of Chicago and Manchester. Adams resigned in 1910 when he was appointed as Drummond Professor of Political Economy at

Oxford.[94] W. Spotswood Green, head of fisheries, and R. Cantrell, the chief clerk, transferred from existing government departments. A former teacher of domestic economy became an inspectress of domestic economy; the superintendent of cheese-making was a former farmer who made cheese; Mary Nagle, a former teacher at the Cork School of Art, was appointed instructress in drawing to lace workers; T. W. Rolleston, author and journalist, and the managing director of the Irish Industries Association, became organiser of lectures.[95] An expert in tobacco was recruited from Kentucky; an expert in early potatoes from Scotland; a fruit preserver from the south of England; and the poultry-crammer (the term used by the DATI) came from Surrey.[96] Reverend S. L. Orr, a Presbyterian clergyman, was appointed as a bee-keeping instructor in County Monaghan. Lucy Douglas, formerly head gardener to H. S. Guinness Senior, of Gresham, Stillorgan, Dublin, became an itinerant instructor in horitculture in County Louth.[97] None of these jobs were filled by competitive examination, which was by no means unusual at the time.

AGRICULTURAL EDUCATION IN IRELAND BEFORE THE DATI

The high proportion of outsiders appointed to senior positions reflects the backward state of agricultural education in Ireland. Before the Famine the Commissioners for National Education had established model agricultural schools to train teachers or instructors in farming; the Albert Agricultural College at Glasnevin in Dublin was one of these schools. It was intended to provide experience in practical agriculture for trainee-teachers at the colleges in Marlborough Street and Kildare Place. Some national schools taught agriculture as part of the curriculum; there were 137 small farms attached to national schools in 1874;[98] and by 1900, 150 national schools had farms or gardens attached.[99]

When Queen's College, Cork, opened in 1845, five out of the original 115 students were studying agriculture, but in 1858 the Commissioners who examined the progress of the Queen's Colleges recommended the abolition of the chair in agriculture, and the agricultural department ceased to exist in 1868 with the death of the professor. According to Professor John A. Murphy, the course on offer was 'theoretical and dilettantish, and at best availed of by small numbers of prospective estate managers';[100] the Albert Agricultural College at Glasnevin attracted a similar type of student during the later years of the nineteenth century.[101] Sir Robert Kane, the first president of Queen's College, Cork, wished to establish a model farm on land adjoining the college. In 1853 this opened as the Munster Institute. Although the project was abandoned shortly afterwards, it was revived in 1880 when a committee organised by Queen's College, Cork, established the first modern dairy school in the United Kingdom. Queen's College, Belfast, also had a chair of agriculture, although there do not appear to have been any students. Although the Queen's Colleges did very little to further agricultural education, Curran suggests that the structure of the Cork course, which combined academic subjects with attendance as an extern pupil at a model farm, influenced later developments in higher education in agriculture.

The other formative influences were the RDS and the Museum of Irish Industry. During the 1790s the RDS had established the Botanic Gardens at Glasnevin in Dublin; it had also appointed a professor of chemistry and soil science and a professor of botany, and in 1802 a lecturer in veterinary science, which led to the establishment of a veterinary college at Ballsbridge in Dublin. In 1854 the RDS transferred most of its educational staff to the Museum of Irish Industry, which was financed under the British Science and Art Department.[102] In 1866 the Museum of Irish Industry was renamed the Royal College of Science, but it continued to operate in cramped premises on St Stephen's Green in Dublin. The Recess Committee recommended that a new college premises should be erected, close to the Science and Art Museum in Kildare Street in Dublin, and the establishment of the DATI gave new life to the Royal College of Science, because of the increased demand for qualified agricultural scientists. A faculty of agriculture was established at the college, with the Albert Agricultural College as a preparatory school for students sitting degree courses in agriculture. Additional staff were appointed to the Botanic Gardens to provide education in horticulture.

Work commenced on a new College of Science building in Upper Merrion Street in Dublin 1907 (the present Government Buildings), and the college was opened in July 1911. Work then began on two office buildings on either side of the college, one for the DATI, the other for the Irish Local Government Board,[103] a physical arrangement that emphasised the close links between the DATI and the College of Science.

The County Committees of Agriculture

The 1899 Act was designed to ensure that the DATI had a strong local dimension. The Recess Committee had suggested that this could be done through the co-operatives, but the 1899 Act gave this role to the new local authorities established under the Local Government Act of 1898. Each new county council was required to establish a county committee of agriculture and technical instruction, consisting of councillors and their nominees. No scheme would be implemented in a county without the approval and co-operation of the county committee, and the DATI was precluded from providing money for any county scheme unless it received matching funding from local taxes.[104] Each county was required to strike an agricultural rate of ½d in the pound and a similar rate for technical instruction.

The county committees of agriculture were one of the most innovative aspects of the DATI. The Irish administration was highly centralised, with policing and national education organised at national level, and boards of guardians and county and urban councils spending most of their time enforcing national regulations, such as public health acts, or drawing up housing and sanitary schemes in compliance with regulations set in either Dublin or Westminster. They were given little scope to devise local solutions to local problems. By comparison, the county committees of agriculture were given enormous freedom: they could select which aspects of farming needed the greatest attention in their county, and they could draw up their own programmes, although these would have to be approved by the DATI. In 1906 Plunkett told the inquiry into the DATI that 'the Department, as he [Gerald Balfour] fashioned it, affords in my opinion that most striking example of devolution of central government in these islands'.[105]

The first annual report of the DATI laid down two principles of administration:

(1) Administration of this kind must fail in its best results unless it seeks to evoke and fortify the self-reliance, enterprise, and sense of responsibility of the people. Both economic and social laws dictate this principle.
(2) In encouraging local initiative and responsibility the danger, on the other side, of an indiscriminate multiplication of unrelated local schemes must be guarded against by a due conservation of the principle of central direction. It is the duty of the Department to keep in mind

26

the national as well as the local point of view, and to bring to bear on schemes and problems that power of co-ordination and that expert aid which the resources of a Central Authority, acting and thinking with and for the whole country, can command.[106]

There is some evidence that the second principle dominated at the expense of the first, and this was strongly resented by the county committees of agriculture. Most members of county committees who gave evidence to the 1906 inquiry into the DATI, emphasised their wish for greater autonomy, whereas Plunkett defended the merits of central control. He told the inquiry that 'the most popular schemes with local authorities are probably in the Department's opinion, the least sound'.[107] The DATI generally sought the views of local agricultural experts before it introduced improvement schemes; committees of experts advised on horse-breeding, livestock, flax cultivation, tobacco and forestry. Before a new scheme was introduced, the DATI summoned the secretaries of the county committees to a conference,[108] to explain the scheme and to arrange meetings between the local committees and the DATI's inspectors to work out local details. T. P. Gill claimed that, 'even apart from the functions of the Council and the Boards, there is not a Department in the world which consults with and takes into account the opinion of the people concerned in its work and the circumstances of the country to the extent that is done by this Department.'[109]

Thirty-one of the thirty-three counties (Tipperary was divided into two counties for local government purposes) raised an agricultural rate during the year 1900/01. Mayo and Cork refused to do so for political reasons, although they relented in the following year.[110] At the beginning, no limits were imposed on the amount of money that a county could receive. The DATI was eager to promote its work, and if a particular scheme was approved by a committee of experts and by the Board of Agriculture, the DATI provided funds on condition that the county committee also made a contribution. Initially, the DATI paid half the costs of all schemes, except in poorer counties where it met five-ninths of the costs. By 1906, for every pound provided by a county, the DATI contributed £1.40 in poorer counties and £1.25 elsewhere. An examination of total expenditure in each county (that is, the agricultural rate and the departmental grant) indicates that in 1903/4 and again in 1912/13, expenditure per capita was greatest in Leinster, with counties Meath, Westmeath, Kildare, Queen's, King's and Carlow at the top of the table. The insistence on a contribution from the rates may have deterred less prosperous counties from providing a greater range of agricultural services.

By 1907 rising expenditure meant that counties could no longer be given a blank cheque.[111] Plunkett recommended that the Board of Agriculture should allocate specific amounts for central expenditure and for county schemes, and then determine how the money should be divided between counties. He suggested that a formula should be devised based on population, valuation and livestock numbers. The board deferred a decision.[112] When James Campbell, assistant secretary for Agriculture, presented the board with a proposal in May 1908 that would have given preference to populous and poorer counties, the representatives from Leinster protested. The board adjourned its decision for one year, and asked Campbell to fine-tune his scheme.[113] The matter disappeared from the agenda for two years.[114] It was resolved in June 1910, when the board decided that the cost of instructors' salaries should be allocated to central expenditure and thereby excluded from the calculations. Under the revised scheme, twenty-three counties would receive higher grants, and ten would suffer marginal reductions, although the latter were all among the counties with the highest expenditure to date. Counties Cork, Limerick and Kerry would benefit most under the proposed changes. The board modified Campbell's scheme slightly by drawing on unspent surplus funds to ensure that no county would lose money; it also added a proviso that any counties that failed to raise the required sum in rates would suffer a pro rata cut in their grant. The new scheme would apply for five years; the board agreed that these changes would not be announced,[115] which suggests a wish to avoid controversy.

In the first twenty years of the DATI's existence, 39 per cent of premia for bulls went to Ulster, 28 per cent to Leinster, 17 per cent to Munster and 16 per cent to Connacht. By 1903, however, the congested districts were already well supplied with bulls of a good standard, thanks to the schemes that had been promoted by the CDB.[116] The DATI went to considerable lengths to ensure that the county committees of agriculture spread resources equitably within each county. There were allegations that the poorer areas suffered because they were under-represented on the county committees.[117]

To begin with, the county committees of agriculture tended to be large and unwieldy bodies. In 1905 the Board of Agriculture rejected the proposed composition of the Leitrim County Committee of Agriculture, because it had over seventy members.[118] Campbell claimed that when he first joined the DATI he spent most of his time meeting county committees

28

of agriculture and explaining the workings of the 1899 Act. Each county committee had to submit an annual report to the DATI that included an assessment of the schemes it had operated during the previous year and suggestions for improvements. In 1906 Campbell told the inquiry into the DATI that county committees invited senior officers of the DATI to attend their meetings, adding that 'we are in very close personal relations with these men; they are all known personally to us'.[119] However, Sir Nicholas Gosselin, a member of the Monaghan County Committee of Agriculture and Technical Instruction, claimed that the people of County Monaghan believed that the DATI was 'rather autocratic in their dealing with them'.[120] Gosselin was scarcely motivated by nationalist sentiment. According to Patrick McQuaid, a member of the Cavan County Committee of Agriculture, 'We were only just there to pass what they [the Department] handed to us, and if we did not do that we might stop at home'.[121]

Most disagreements between the DATI and the county committees related either to expenditure or to appointments. One representative from County Limerick complained that 'they are always threatening us with the Auditor'.[122] Every county scheme had to be approved by the Board of Agriculture; in practice the sanction was given by senior officials. Once approved, it could not be altered. Several elected members of the Board of Agriculture suggested that the county committees should be permitted to vary the details of particular schemes.[123] Some county committees were disgruntled at the DATI's refusal to give them discretion as to how much they could spend on local agricultural shows.[124]

Plunkett described the agricultural instructor as 'the guide, philosopher and friend of the existing farmers'.[125] In October 1900 County Tyrone became the first county to appoint an itinerant instructor in agriculture and a poultry instructress. Down followed in December, and Antrim in January 1901. It is no coincidence that Ulster counties were the first to appoint instructors. County committees of agriculture were often forced to choose between appointing Scotsmen and Englishmen (mostly Scots) or waiting until the first agricultural science students graduated from the College of Science in Dublin. Campbell claimed that he had often encouraged counties to postpone appointing an instructor until they could hire a qualified Irishman.[126] In 1900, nine young men with a practical knowledge of agriculture enrolled in the College of Science; by 1906, twenty-one had graduated and there were a further thirty-five students, all funded by scholarships from the DATI. At this time there seem to have been more scholarships than qualified applicants.[127] By 1906, a total of 102 instructors (agricultural, poultry and horticultural) had been appointed, ninety-six of them Irish.[128] This had increased to 147 by 1911: forty in agriculture, thirty-nine in horticulture and bee-keeping, thirty-five in poultry-keeping and thirty-three for butter-making.

Many disputes between county committees of agriculture and the DATI arose because some county committees wanted to appoint natives of their county as instructors, irrespective of competence. At the beginning, because of the shortage of qualified instructors, the DATI did not object to the appointment of instructors who were natives of a county, provided that they were qualified for the post. After some years, however, it sought to end this practice. It was concerned that instructors who were natives of a county might spend too much time on the family farm. The possibility that he or she would be a friend or relation of some members of the county committee of agriculture was another cause for concern.[129] Campbell suggested that a prophet was unlikely to be honoured in his own country: if farmers knew an instructor they were less likely to follow his advice.[130] Itinerant instructors, moreover, were expected to live up to their title by constantly moving around their district. (No similar restrictions applied to county surveyors, county secretaries and teachers of technical subjects. Only an instructor employed by the CDB was prevented from working in his native district; he could be employed in another part of the county.)[131]

The ban on employing natives of counties caused considerable resentment. When the DATI refused to sanction the appointment of a native of County Limerick as a poultry instructress, the county committee refused to make any appointment.[132] As one Limerick curate remarked bitterly, 'A Limerick woman may not be a poultry instructress in Limerick'. By 1908 Limerick, Dublin and Queen's County were the only counties without poultry instructresses. A similar set-to developed with the Mayo County Committee of Agriculture, when the DATI refused to sanction the committee's choice of instructor in agriculture because he was not up to standard. The county committee wished to appoint a local man, despite his lack of training; having appointed him, it demanded that he be awarded a scholarship to the College of Science.[133] In 1906 Mayo was still without an agricultural instructor, while instructors had been appointed in twenty-two counties. One member of the Mayo County Committee supported the rejected candidate because 'the same qualifications in an instructor and instructress don't suit all Ireland'.[134]

Although disputes over appointments peaked in the early years, they did not disappear altogether. In 1908/9 the DATI vetoed the appointment

of secretaries to the county committees in Tipperary North and Leitrim, and the appointment of several instructors. T. W. Russell, the vice-president of the DATI, informed the Board of Agriculture that in all these cases the DATI had exercised its veto only after careful consideration.[135] Donegal was another county that came into conflict with the DATI on this matter, and as a consequence few of the DATI's schemes had been introduced in the county by 1906. In the same year the secretary of the Mayo County Committee of Agriculture stated emphatically that 'Agriculture and Technical Instruction in Mayo is, and certainly has been, a failure'.[136]

County committees of agriculture interpreted the rejection of local candidates as an indication that officials in Dublin were unwilling to take account of local circumstances. A witness from County Mayo to the 1906 inquiry into the DATI argued that the county was 'somewhat peculiar'; a scheme suitable in one district would be useless in another.[137] According to the chairman of Limerick County Council:

> I and some other members of the Commitee submitted to officials of the Department a scheme of practical instruction by demonstration, and were told that the Department could not entertain it. We considered that the best way to educate the rural population in improved methods of agriculture would be by means of experimental farms in the county where everything relating to agriculture would be demonstrated. The feeding and treatment of cattle, horses, sheep, pigs, and poultry, the rearing of young calves (which is one of the most important considerations for County Limerick farmers in view of the fatal diseases so singularly prevalent in this county), the experiments in seeds and manures, and everything connected with agriculture and products. Instead, we were sent down Scotch experts with lectures and pamphlets galore, and were inundated with leaflets about the ravages of the gadfly and daddy-long-legs, all of which the poor ignorant farmers laughed at and gave no attention to. ...
>
> Unfortunately the officials who have always been chosen by Government to deal with the land in Ireland are either ignorant or prejudiced and the greatest blunder of all is to bring over Scotchmen to teach us. Why we have never known a Scotsman to succeed in this country as an agriculturist ... the farmers who framed the Livestock Scheme for this county have, in my humble judgment, more brains, intelligence, and practical knowledge than the whole retinue of theorists together.[138]

Mayo County Committee of Agriculture reported that:

> ... the working of or progress of Department's schemes of agriculture in this county is unsatisfactory. Various reasons may be given for their failure, such as their adoption of a system of red tape, want of sympathy with the people, ignorance of the farmers' wants, and interference of local influences. We have also noted that the Department seemed not to take into their confidence the local committees, who after all, ought to be the best judges of what were most suitable for the requirements of their county. Their selection of inspectors and instructors, who were neither of nor with the people, was not fortunate, for the latter gave lectures on subjects of which they had only a theoretical knowledge. The struggling peasants could not be impressed with palliatives that rather protracted rather than cured the evils sought to be remedied. The people saw that their chief industry – tillage and the cultivation of green crops – was not considered by the Department. The committee were of opinion that the primary duty of an agricultural board was to supply qualified instructors to improve the much-neglected industry of agriculture. Resolution after resolution was drawn up by the committee, but they were not able to rouse the Department to a sense of their responsibility and duty.[139]

Mayo and Limerick were both in dispute with the DATI over appointments, so their evidence may have been partisan. Nevertheless, these quotations raise several important issues, such as the difficulty of providing instruction in agriculture to men and women who had limited education; the relative importance of practical demonstrations and more theoretical instruction; and the need to adapt national programmes to local conditions.

Limerick County Committee of Agriculture and the DATI disagreed over the most suitable strain of premium bull. The county committee wanted 'the best milking strain', but the DATI rejected many of the bulls favoured in the county. Limerick was probably correct. Although the DATI's scheme for cattle breeding stock had the stated aim of 'the improvement of dairy and store cattle in Ireland', the emphasis was on store cattle. Most bulls were selected from beef breeds such as Shorthorn, Aberdeen Angus and Hereford; Shorthorn bulls accounted for over 70 per cent of all premia up to 1915. At the time, there were allegations that the yields of Irish dairy cattle were declining, and although John O'Donovan claims that the records of the non-pedigree dairy herd at the Albert Agricultural College do not

confirm this, he acknowledged that the DATI should have paid greater attention to the needs of the dairy industry, particularly in Limerick, the county with the highest average milk yields. A DATI report, *The Decline of Dairying in Ireland,* published in 1920, confirmed that the beef-producing qualities of Irish cattle had been improved at the expense of milk yields.[140] The low level of expenditure in Limerick and Cork may reflect a bias against dairy farming in the DATI's schemes, perhaps because dairying was regarded as a matter for the IAOS.

The relative merit of practical and theoretical knowledge was another contentious issue. The DATI set out to educate farmers by organising classes and by producing leaflets on relevant topics. During 1901/2 the seven qualified instructors in Ireland each gave an average of 100 lectures; a further 850 lectures were devoted to poultry-keeping. In counties without a resident instructor, the DATI organised pioneer lectures (the title presumably reflects the fact that they were the first efforts by the DATI) on topics such as veterinary hygiene. Instructors organised winter schools during the slack season in the agricultural calendar, and the DATI flooded the countryside with leaflets – over 1½ million were distributed in 1905.[141] There were some complaints that lectures were too technical and that the leaflets were not relevant. Reverend John Doherty, a curate in Carndonagh, County Donegal, remarked that public lectures on phosphates and nitrates were 'above the people's heads'.[142] Sixty years later the debate on theoretical versus practical instruction was still not resolved. The Limerick Rural Survey, conducted in the early 1960s, found that, 'The majority of farmers interviewed thought that those sons who remained on the farm needed no formal agricultural training; they could learn farming in a practical way by working on the farm'.[143]

There was also a strong political dimension to the criticism voiced by the Mayo and Limerick county committees. Mayo condemned the DATI for neglecting tillage and green crops. Initially, the DATI concentrated on livestock schemes and on wiping out animal disease, because, according to Campbell, assistant secretary for Agriculture, 'tillage is a lost art in some districts'.[144] While the decision to concentrate on the most important sector in Irish agriculture was a pragmatic one, it could also be construed as indicating that the DATI favoured the status quo. One Mayo priest noted that, 'No Department at the present time in Ireland is of any practical utility that does not turn itself to the re-peopling of the country'.[145] Although he was referring to the programme for technical instruction, his comment could equally have applied to agriculture.

33

During its early years the DATI appears to have been most welcome in Ulster; certainly the representatives of county committees in Antrim and Derry spoke very favourably about the DATI. This may simply reflect the fact that landlords had retained much greater control over county councils and county committees of agriculture, and that the old deference was not yet dead. William Bulfin, a writer who was sympathetic to Sinn Féin, criticised the DATI along lines similar to those of Limerick and Mayo county committees:

> … a Department of Agriculture at present working under the auspices of Dublin Castle, which looks at Irish rural problems from an English point of view. This Department theorises a good deal, and, I believe, is to some extent troubled by the 'writing itch'. There seems to be something about it in the nature of the shearing of the goat – great cry and little wool. It would be quite useless, however, to expect any wonder working from such a source. Indeed it would be quite useless to hope that Ireland will ever be well governed in the interests of England, because the interests of the two nations are inimical. The English Department of Agriculture in Ireland does a good deal of pottering and sermonising, and goes through many elaborate experiments to try and overcome the difficulties of fusing oil and water. And periodically it publishes something or says something lamenting that Irish interests are the oil, and sympathising with itself for having failed to reverse the laws of nature. It sends out a lecturer to speak academically about cattle breeding when it should have practical experiments going on before the eyes of the people. It sends out gifted talkers to say learned things about manure, when it should have a model farm in every county to teach in practice what it preaches in theory. 'You would get a far more profitable return from your land' said one of these lecturers some time ago to an audience in one of the midland rural districts, 'if you would revolutionise your system of manufacturing; and I hope you will follow my advice'. Whereupon a hard-headed farmer rose and made the following speech: 'I'll tell you what, sir: talk is cheap. Will you take ten or twenty acres of land in this parish for a few years, and pay a pound an acre for it, and show us that you can make it pay by your plan for manuring, and all that?' The lecturer changed the conversation.[146]

Again, we see the juxtaposition of theoretical and practical knowledge and the argument that demonstration farms were a more effective means of instruction. However, the CDB had found it extremely difficult to secure demonstration plots,[147] and any attempt to acquire entire farms would have prompted allegations of land-grabbing and demands that the land be given to deserving landless men. When the DATI established provincial 'agricultural stations' in Ballyhaise, Athenry and Clonakilty to educate local farmers and their sons in conditions appropriate to the particular region, it was forced to retain the labourers who had formerly been employed on these estates in order to defuse local tensions, and this made it extremely difficult to introduce modern practices. Campbell, assistant secretary for Agriculture, suggested that once the DATI acquired a demonstration farm, the workers would immediately demand a doubling in their rate of pay.[148] In 1907 smallholders living in the vicinity of the agricultural station at Athenry demanded that the station should be closed and the land divided between them. When this demand was rejected, the labourers employed by the DATI went on strike, and a building on the station was destroyed by fire.[149]

Bulfin's comments echoed a widespread belief that the DATI was only tinkering with marginal aspects of Irish agriculture, while ignoring the fundamental problem – the distribution of land. When Mayo County Committee of Agriculture proposed tilling some of the vacant land in the county, the DATI informed the committee that it had no power to do so, and that it was unable to provide money for arterial drainage, despite resolutions from the Board of Agriculture to this effect. A witness from County Monaghan complained that 'drainage is at present no man's child'.[150] When the DATI was compared with the CDB, which had a much wider remit to deal with all aspects of economic activity, including land resettlement, its policies appeared limited.

Industrial Development and Technical Instruction

The limits on the DATI's powers were more apparent when it came to assisting industry and technical instruction. It was forbidden to establish apprenticeships, which were probably the most practical form of technical instruction at the time. Under the 1899 Act the DATI could undertake 'inquiries, experiments and research' in relation to agriculture and other rural industries, including cottage industries, and in relation to 'the cultivation and preparation of flax, inland fisheries, and any industries immediately connected with and subservient to any of the said matters and any instruction relating thereto'. However, there was widespread criticism when it awarded scholarships to workers in a new woollen mills at Kilkenny, which enabled the workers to receive training at mills in Kilmacthomas and Galway. The decision to provide a loan of £1,000 to assist in establishing a fruit-processing plant near Drogheda, and the DATI's role in establishing an experimental vegetable drying plant at Portadown (two initiatives that were designed to provide outlets for fruit and vegetable producers), prompted complaints to the Board of Trade from the English Confectioners' Association, and the DATI was forced to sell the factories.[151] In 1907 a minority report by W. L. Micks, the secretary of the CDB, to the inquiry into the DATI recommended the establishment of a separate industrial development department with power to provide assistance for industry throughout Ireland on a similar scale to that provided by the CDB.

THE DATI AND THE CONGESTED DISTRICTS BOARD

Relations between the DATI and the CDB were not harmonious during the early years. Plunkett made no secret of his desire to absorb the CDB into the DATI. He claimed that there were congested areas in all parts of Ireland and that the problem should be tackled by a body that covered the whole country, such as the DATI.[152] Gerald Balfour informed Plunkett that while he was committed to merging the DATI and the CDB in the long term, nationalists would not accept the erosion of 'political and clerical influences' within the CDB.[153]

The CDB survived because it was popular with nationalists. Although it could be described as a conventional 'Castle board', run by nominees, it was widely regarded as more in tune with the wishes of the people than the more democratic DATI. Admittedly, the CDB included Dr O'Donnell, bishop of Raphoe, and later the Reverend Denis O'Hara, parish priest of Kiltimagh, but the Board of Agriculture included Dr Kelly, bishop of Cloyne, and nationalist county councillors. Father O'Hara claimed that officials from the DATI were looked on as being of the Castle, although 'the taint of the Castle' did not extend to county committees of agriculture.[154]

In counties Donegal, Sligo, Leitrim, Mayo, Roscommon, Galway, Kerry and Cork, the boundaries of the CDB cut across county lines. Landholders in these counties who lived in the congested districts were provided with agricultural services that were wholly funded by Dublin Castle, whereas those living outside the scheduled areas had to pay an agricultural rate that covered part of the cost of agricultural schemes. Moreover, the CDB provided a wider range of schemes for its landholders.

In 1903 a clause in the Wyndham Act transferred responsibility for agricultural advisory services in the areas covered by the CDB to the DATI, freeing the CDB to concentrate on resettlement and land redistribution. By 1906 the CDB was demanding that the DATI provide further assistance for farming in the congested districts, although it refused to provide more than £2,000 per annum,[155] which was much less than what it had previously spent. One member of the CDB, the Mayo priest Fr O'Hara, claimed that the DATI had abandoned some of the agricultural schemes formerly provided by the CDB, and accused it of failing to supply sufficient machines for spraying potatoes.[156] Campbell, the assistant secretary for Agriculture, claimed that when Wyndham transferred responsibility for agricultural schemes to the DATI, he had announced that the congested districts would have to forego their right to preferential treatment for agricultural development until the primary task of land purchase had been carried out.[157]

Plunkett persuaded the Board of Agriculture to provide additional money from the DATI's funds towards the cost of agricultural services in the congested districts, although the Board of Agriculture believed that the money should come from the Chief Secretary.[158] This dispute was not resolved until 1909, when the Birrell Act (which extended the 1903 Wyndham land act) gave the DATI an additional £19,000 to meet the cost of agricultural services in the congested districts.[159]

When the potato crop failed in the congested districts in 1904, the DATI agreed to provide £10,000 towards the cost of providing seed potatoes on condition that it was permitted to select the potatoes, although official responsibility for providing assistance rested with the Local Government Board.[160] When the potato crop failed once more in 1906, the Local Government Board demanded that the DATI provide subsidised seed potatoes. On this occasion the Board of Agriculture passed a unanimous resolution refusing to take responsibility for relieving exceptional distress in the west because this was not the DATI's responsibility.[161]

The 1906/7 Inquiry into the DATI

In March 1906 the newly-elected Liberal government established a committee to inquire into whether the provisions of the 1899 Act and the methods by which the DATI had operated 'have been shown by experience to be well suited to the conditions of Ireland'. The committee of inquiry was asked to report on whether any changes were desirable in the provisions and methods, and to report on the relations between the DATI and the Council of Agriculture, the Boards of Agriculture and Technical Instruction, local statutory bodies and other government departments. It was also asked to comment on the DATI's funding and how it was used.[162] The committee was chaired by Kenelm Digby, a landlord with extensive estates in King's County and England. The committee reported in May 1907, shortly after Plunkett had resigned as vice-president.

The committee recommended that the detailed direction of the DATI should be in the hands of a vice-president, who should be neither an MP nor a permanent civil servant, but employed on a five-year contract with provision for reappointment. The vice-president should be independent of party politics. It also recommended that the board and the council should continue to include nominee members.

Carla Keating and Trevor West both state that the report of the inquiry vindicated Plunkett and the DATI from all allegations that had been made against them.[163] The report, which was signed by the chairman and three of the four other members, vindicated retrospectively the position that had resulted when Plunkett lost his parliamentary seat, although it is debatable whether Plunkett could be regarded as wholly independent of party politics.

The recommendations of the inquiry were not implemented. Plunkett was succeeded by T. W. Russell, who was MP for East Tyrone, which was consistent with the arrangement that was originally intended under the 1899 Act. Eunan O'Halpin noted that Russell's appointment took the DATI out of the political firing line, which was something that Plunkett had always wanted.[164] W. L. Micks, the secretary of the CDB, dissented from the majority view of the committee of inquiry that the DATI was suited to the conditions of Ireland.[165] Micks suggested that the DATI should be restricted to providing education in agriculture and technical instruction and that a new development board should be established with an annual budget of £1 million. The development board would have similar powers to the CDB; it would be a purely Irish department separate both from the British government and from Westminster, and answerable only to five commissioners, four elected by Irish MPs and a fifth nominated by the Irish government (that is, the Lord Lieutenant and the Chief Secretary). Such radical proposals had little chance of success.

The DATI and the IAOS

The relationship between the DATI and the co-operative movement is one of the most controversial aspects of the DATI's early years. It was a major factor in the hostility shown by Dillon and many supporters of the Irish Parliamentary Party towards Plunkett, but the issue persisted after Plunkett's resignation.

Plunkett regarded the DATI as an extension of the work of agricultural improvement that began with the co-operative movement. This is evident from a statement in the first annual report of the DATI:

> It is a chief aim of the Department to stimulate rather than to weaken the spirit of industrial self-help, and its action will be governed by this idea. Its endeavours will be mainly confined to removing the obstacles which at present hinder in Ireland the due exercise of initiative in industrial matters, and to creating a state of things in which private enterprise can act with confidence and freedom.

Plunkett wished to encourage self-help, including co-operation, as opposed to fostering widespread dependence on state money and state intervention. He believed that the DATI should follow the example of Denmark, where the Department of Agriculture worked closely with the co-operative movement. In Plunkett's opinion state aid would be more effective if channelled through farming organisations such as co-operatives. At the 1899 annual general meeting of the IAOS, the last before the establishment of the DATI, he noted that the IAOS:

> ... has already been giving a considerable amount of technical instruction ... the cost of which, if of proved utility, ought to be borne by the state, and not come out of funds subscribed for purely organising purposes. The I.A.O.S. will be able to say to the Department, 'We have a staff of experts giving instruction in agriculture, dairying, poultry breeding and egg packing, and so forth. We can prove that these men are duly qualified, and that their services are constantly in requisition, and that, owing to the spirit which pervades the societies among which they are engaged, the practical results attained, and the number of persons benefited, could not possibly be exceeded by any other means with similar expenditure. Either do the work for us, if you think you can do it cheaper or better, or let us do it for you at your expense.' Now

if the Department attaches any value to the practically universal experience of countries where similar Departments have succeeded in the work which now has to be done in Ireland, it will in such matters as these, while of course deciding each case on its merits, avail itself of the machinery which the people have themselves provided.[166]

When the bill establishing the DATI was going through Parliament, John Dillon, an inveterate opponent of the co-operative movement, moved an amendment that would prevent the new department from providing financial assistance to the IAOS. Although the amendment was not carried,[167] Dillon subsequently claimed that Balfour had given a promise that no public money would be channelled to the IAOS or similar organisations, although Balfour denied this.[168]

When James Campbell took up the position of assistant secretary for Agriculture, he had apparently been led to expect that Ireland had a strong co-operative movement, which could provide a mechanism for implementing the DATI's programmes.[169] However, co-operative societies were distributed throughout Ireland rather unevenly,[170] and it seems unlikely that they would ever have been in a position to provide a comprehensive service to farmers unless this was rectified. Shortly after the DATI's foundation it began to pay an annual sum to the IAOS to cover the salary and costs of its instructors – a move that had been anticipated in Plunkett's speech to the IAOS. At this time, according to T. P. Gill, secretary of the DATI, the county advisory system did not exist. Nevertheless, when the counties began to appoint instructors (whose salaries were paid, half by the DATI and half through the agricultural rate), the DATI continued to meet the entire cost of salaries and expenses for the IAOS instructors, at an annual cost of £16,915 by 1905. Although the DATI paid this amount to the IAOS, it never featured in IAOS accounts. In time, as Gill acknowledged, there were growing tensions between the two rival groups of instructors.[171]

Once the DATI came into existence, with the promise of government assistance for agriculture, the IAOS found that members and benefactors were no longer willing to provide it with money. By 1904 the organisation was in financial difficulties, and a joint committee drawn from the DATI and the IAOS met to discuss what should be done. The relationship between the DATI and the IAOS was discussed at considerable length at a meeting of the Board of Agriculture in January 1905. Although several members expressed the view that the DATI should take over the work being carried out by the IAOS, Gill and Plunkett countered that the IAOS could act as a useful 'buffer state' for the DATI. This meeting ended inconclusively.

In February 1906 the Board of Agriculture agreed that the DATI would provide the IAOS with money to cover the cost of its regional organisers. In return, two representatives of the DATI would join the board of the IAOS.[172] The DATI's support for the IAOS dominated meetings of the Board of Agriculture during 1905 and 1906, with Plunkett urging a rather sceptical board to provide additional funding. On 20 March 1906 he informed the board that if it agreed to support the IAOS, he would ask the Council of Agriculture to confirm this decision at its next meeting.[173] When the board met on 20 July 1906, Dr Healy suggested that the DATI should take over all the duties of the IAOS. Gill appears to have been convinced by Healy's argument, because he outlined the case for doing this in a memorandum to Plunkett some days later. In November 1906 Plunkett asked the Council of Agriculture to vote on the merits of subsidising the IAOS, and it voted in favour by a margin of fifty-two to twenty-five. The nominee members were overwhelmingly in favour; the elected members were evenly split[174] (the nominees had a much better attendance than the elected members).

By November 1906 a Liberal government was in office and Plunkett's time as vice-president appeared to be drawing to a close. The Council of Agriculture vote was a daring attempt to secure funds for the IAOS before he left office. This was the only occasion when Plunkett sought a mandate from the council for his actions. In February 1907, bolstered by the council's endorsement, Plunkett recommended to the Board of Agriculture that the DATI should contribute £5 for every £1 that the IAOS attracted from other sources, subject to a maximum of £3,000. If the IAOS managed to earn the £3,000 subsidy, the DATI would provide further assistance, to the tune of £3 for every additional £1 raised by the IAOS subject to a limit of £1,200, and £2 for every £1 raised by the IAOS above this limit. At this time the DATI gave the committees of agriculture in the poorer counties £1.40 for every £1 that they raised in local taxes, and in the remaining counties £1.25 for every £1 raised. The terms on offer to the IAOS were much more generous. During 1906/7 the DATI's grant to the IAOS had amounted to £3,700. The Board of Agriculture agreed to Plunkett's scheme on the understanding that if the cost exceeded £3,700, the matter would be referred back to the board.

When T. W. Russell succeeded Plunkett as vice-president of the DATI in May 1907, he recommended that the DATI should phase out the subsidy to the IAOS over three years, ending in December 1910.[175] The IAOS responded by demanding that the DATI relax its control over how this money was spent. In his opening address to the Council of Agriculture on 19 November 1907, Russell described the existing agreement between the DATI and the IAOS as 'the most unbusinesslike arrangement I have ever heard of'. He also accused the IAOS of setting out to create shopkeepers.[176] Plunkett had resumed the presidency of the IAOS and he used his presidential address in December 1907 to launch an attack on gombeen men and their political supporters. Hugh Law, a nationalist MP for Donegal, who was a subscriber to the IAOS, condemned Plunkett's 'treacherous assault upon the honour of the National Party', and pointed out the potential damage to the co-operative movement if it became identified with the programme of a political party which was 'the enemy of National aspiration'.[177]

The controversy over Plunkett's speech grew when the *Freeman's Journal* published a letter on 24 January 1908 from T. W. Rolleston to an acquaintance in St Louis in the United States, in which Rolleston had enclosed a copy of Plunkett's presidential address. Rolleston was a journalist and a supporter of Sinn Féin, who had formerly worked as a paid organiser for the DATI.[178] He claimed that Plunkett had suggested that he send copies of Plunkett's address to 'any friends in America or elsewhere who were interested in his policy for Ireland and who are not likely to get more reliable information about that policy than they could obtain from the organisations which have never ceased for fifteen years to attack and to traduce it'.[179] According to Rolleston, Plunkett's address marked 'an attempt to organise the Irish farmers to shake off the grip of the small country publican and gombeen men, who has [*sic*] hitherto controlled the Parliamentary representation of the country'. Rolleston claimed that, 'No sort of attack on Home Rule or upon Home Rulers as such is dreamt of. It is only insisted that Irish farmers shall not choose people who will use their power, as Dillon and the rest of the Parliamentarians have been doing to crush the farmers' movement for the better organisation of his business'. However, by explicitly linking gombeen men and the Irish Parliamentary Party, and by referring to Dillon by name, Rolleston transformed Plunkett's speech into a direct attack on the Parliamentary Party. On 27 January 1908 Dr Kelly, bishop of Cloyne, who was a member of the Board of Agriculture, wrote to Russell informing him that he had come to the conclusion that 'the alliance between the Department and the IAOS must be severed'. Kelly cited 'the restiveness of the Society under the Department's supervision of its own funds, the recent publication of Mr. Rolleston's letter, and other expressions of opinion at the meetings of the Society and in the Press, and the inexplicable desire of members of the Society to come into conflict with political organizations in Ireland.'

When Rolleston's letter was published in the *Freeman's Journal*, Russell wrote to Plunkett asking for his observations but Plunkett made no attempt to dissociate himself from Rolleston's remarks. When Russell brought the matter before the Board of Agriculture on 28 January 1909, he noted that if the IAOS remained committed to a policy of shaking off the grip of the gombeen men, the DATI could not continue the existing arrangement. Russell noted that, 'The Department must work with all parties in Ireland'; it could not be connected with an organisation 'which was at war with one of them'. The board confirmed a subsidy of £3,000 to the IAOS for 1908, provided that the money was used only for purposes already approved, and that the DATI audited the relevant accounts every month. This would be the final grant to the IAOS. This motion was supported by all members of the board who were present, including three who were members of the IAOS. They believed that the presence of DATI members on the board of the IAOS, and the DATI's insistence on supervising how their grant was spent, resulted in an unworkable arrangement.

In November 1911 Russell informed the Council of Agriculture that the grant to the IAOS had been withdrawn because the public mind had become impressed with the idea that the IAOS was associated with hostility to the Irish Nationalist Party. More importantly, 'certain trading interests in this country naturally objected to state aid being accorded to the formation of societies that were intended to enter into competition with them in the exercise of their legitimate trading operations'. 'Influential deputations' had pressed this point.[180]

The matter continued to fester. When the IAOS applied to the Development Commission for a grant of £6,000 in 1911,[181] Russell contended that the DATI should be responsible for developing co-operation, and he launched a bitter attack on Plunkett and the IAOS, rehearsing the events of 1907/8 at considerable length. By 1911 relations had deteriorated further because the IAOS was objecting to key clauses in the DATI's Dairying Industry Bill, which was designed to ensure the quality of Irish butter exports. Russell suggested that the DATI should become involved in promoting 'non-controversial co-operation', which he defined as co-operative schemes that were not in direct competition with ordinary traders, such as fruit-growing, potato-growing, flax schemes and agricultural credit. The Council of Agriculture supported Russell's proposal that any money awarded by the Development Commission to promote co-operation should be channelled through the DATI. This was the practice in England, where the Board of Agriculture had established a committee consisting of representatives of the Agricultural Organisation Society, the county councils, railways companies and the Board of Agriculture.[182]

Yet, when the DATI presented their Board of Agriculture with a scheme for the promotion of co-operation, the board refused to discuss the matter. Some members were opposed in principle to the DATI's becoming involved in co-operative projects, and others wished to avoid fomenting differences among board members.[183] Nevertheless, the DATI submitted a draft scheme to the Development Commissioners for the organisation of co-operative associations for fruit-growing, early potatoes, flax, cow-testing, bee-keeping and lime-burning. Although the Development Commissioners expressed scepticism about the co-operative character of these proposals, they awarded a grant for the establishment of cow-testing associations. It was quite common for the Development Commission to select some schemes and to reject others. The Commission also awarded a grant to the IAOS, although it appointed several members of the Council of Agriculture to a committee that would oversee its expenditure. The council responded by passing a motion condemning the Development Commission for usurping the functions of the council, and censuring council members who had agreed to serve on the monitoring committee. The DATI then withdrew its application to the Development Commission.[184] Between 1912 and 1922 the Development Commission replaced the DATI as a major source of funds for the IAOS, providing it with an annual grant of £5,500.[185]

The growing antagonism between the DATI and the IAOS and the withdrawal of DATI subsidies are often regarded as a triumph of evil over good, with the Irish Parliamentary Party and its allies, the gombeen men, triumphing over the noble and disinterested people who wished to improve the lot of Irish farmers. This is too simplistic. Despite trumpeting the merits of self-help, the co-operative movement relied heavily on the DATI's money. All county schemes were required to be partly funded from local taxes; they were subject to detailed scrutiny; and county committees of agriculture were subject to sanctions if they attempted to modify the proposal they had submitted to the DATI, even to a minor degree. However, until December 1905 there appears to have been minimal accountability for the money given to the IAOS: the DATI exercised no control over how the money was spent, and the IAOS adopted an arrogant attitude towards public accountability.

When the DATI was established, it set out to work with two distinct types of local organisation – the co-operatives and the county committees of agriculture. Local organisation was not sufficiently strong in rural Ireland to support two potentially competing bodies. Although farmers may have been under-represented on county councils and county committees of agriculture, the members of these organisations were elected, and it would be naive to assume that Irish voters were all in such thrall to extortionate traders that they willingly voted them into office.[186] Russell emphasised that the DATI was responsible to Parliament, whereas the IAOS was an 'irresponsible body'; he defied anybody to get 'A better Cabinet for Ireland or one more representative of the best thought in the country, than the Board of Agriculture'.[187] Comparisons are often drawn between the Danish and the Irish co-operative movements, a comparison that is not in Ireland's favour. Plunkett and his peers invested co-operation with an almost religious fervour and a decided political gloss. In Denmark, farming support for the co-operative movement was determined by strictly economic consider-ations.[188]

In his assessment of Plunkett's role as an agricultural reformer, Cyril Ehrlich concluded that 'the decade of incipient nationhood is not time for economic reformers'.[189] This suggests that the entire effort of the DATI before 1922 was wasted, which is surely too sweeping a claim. It also appears to endorse the traditional nationalist argument that self-government must precede economic reform. By the closing decade of the nineteenth century, although there was no immediate prospect of Home Rule, there was an unstoppable momentum in favour of greater democracy. Outside Ulster the revolution in local government created a new generation of nationalist politicians. In 1902 the DATI had justified its prominent role in the Cork Exhibition, with the hope that:

> Irish people generally will realise that there is room for expert skill and directing intelligence in the development of our agriculture, fisheries, and industries, and that there is hope before the work if these qualities be applied. They will moreover, have gathered from many things in the section that a national spirit and character can be given to the effort and to the work produced, and that, as with industrial movements everywhere, the movement in Ireland can be all the more effective if it is backed by a patriotic impulse, and by the desire to realise through its means a part of our national individuality.

Having fuelled these expectations it might have been better to concentrate on working through representative bodies such as the committees of agriculture, since these committees were another manifestation of the same patriotic impulse. If the county committees included dedicated co-operators, so much the better. Equally it would be incorrect to assume that all elected representatives were opposed to the IAOS; indeed, the evidence from both the board and the council of Agriculture suggests that members were reluctant to speak out against co-operation.

THE DATI AND IRISH AGRICULTURE, 1900–14

The outbreak of World War I in 1914 transformed Irish agriculture, so 1914 is an appropriate point for taking stock of the DATI's achievements. According to Turner's estimates, the value of agricultural output rose by 36 per cent between 1900 and 1914, from £37 million to £50.4 million. The value of tillage output reached a post-Famine low in 1897, but between 1900 and 1914 it rose by 35 per cent, which was almost identical to the 36 per cent increase in livestock output. By 1914 the value of agricultural output was at a post-Famine high and volume of agricultural output in 1914 was higher than at any time since the 1850s, apart from exceptional years such as 1868, 1875/6 and 1911. Output per agricultural worker rose from £46.3 in 1901 to £59.7 by 1911; output per head of estimated Irish farm population rose from £14.5 to £19.1. The gap between British and Irish agricultural workers also narrowed.[190] Turner concluded there was 'a period of *pronounced* growth after the 1890s' until the outbreak of World War I.[191]

It would be too simplistic to suggest that the rise in agricultural output was entirely due to the establishment of the DATI. By 1900 the long-term decline in agricultural prices that had begun in the late 1870s was at an end, and farmers responded positively to this. Land ownership was also undergoing a revolution. Although Raymond Crotty and Barbara Solow have suggested that tenant right and peasant proprietorship retarded Irish agriculture, this interpretation is not generally accepted. Ó Gráda's calculations show that productivity increased at a more or less constant rate between 1854 and 1908.[192] Turner claims that there was a relationship between higher productivity 'and the strong moves towards peasant independence, when a great share of income returned to labour which formerly may have gone to the landlord. This provided farmers with an incentive to perform even better than before'.[193] This suggests that the ending of landlord control may well have improved Irish agriculture. Equally, it is important not to present the performance of Irish agriculture between 1900 and 1914 in an unduly optimistic light: productivity growth was lower than anywhere in Europe except Britain; use of fertiliser remained too low.

Was the DATI simply lucky that its first years coincided with a modest improvement in the performance of Irish agriculture? Was it an improvement due to peasant proprietorship, or to the beneficial effects of higher prices, and can we pinpoint any areas where the DATI made a difference? Poultry was one sector that progressed thanks to the DATI. This was very much in line with the optimistic expectations that the DATI outlined in its annual report for 1901/2. The value of eggs exported to Britain rose by £1 million between 1904 and 1911; by then Ireland was the largest supplier of eggs and poultry to Britain.[194] On the eve of World War I poultry accounted for 9 per cent of agricultural output, compared with 5–6 per cent in the 1880s and 1890s. Up to 90 per cent of eggs produced in Ireland were exported.[195] All counties except Antrim, which operated a different scheme, set up hatcheries to supply farmers with eggs that were produced by new, high-quality breeds free of disease. Instructresses, who were trained in the Munster Institute, which was under the DATI's authority, advised the farm women who usually took charge of poultry. The DATI also worked to ensure that eggs shipped from Ireland were fresh and clean when they reached the market. Negotiations with shipping and railways companies to improve the transit of perishable agricultural produce brought definite improvements. In 1907 the DATI hired an instructor in the packing and grading of eggs and poultry and made his services available to shippers.

Nevertheless, quality remained a problem, partly because clean, fresh eggs did not necessarily fetch a better price. In 1911 the DATI warned those involved in marketing and selling eggs to test them for freshness, because egg producers and higglers continued to hold eggs in the expectation that prices would rise. Joanna Bourke claims that the DATI tried unsuccessfully to raise the status of poultry-keeping by persuading men to become involved; poultry remained an important activity for farm women but one that had to be combined with domestic duties. This may have limited the potential for expansion.[196]

The DATI provided loans to creameries for the purchase of pasteurising plants; it attempted to raise production standards by organising classes in dairy technology and creamery management, and by instituting regular inspections of creameries. The Butter and Margarine Act of 1906 provided for the registration of butter factories and all premises where butter was blended; it also specified the maximum amount of moisture permitted, and introduced controls over the labelling of margarine as butter and the adulteration of butter.

In 1905 the DATI appointed Lord Ikerrin to watch over the interests of Irish agricultural produce in Britain. Shortly after his appointment he took a case against a Manchester egg merchant who was selling eggs in cartons that were marked 'Pat Murphy, Castle Murphy'. Although the cartons were illustrated with an Irishman dancing and twirling a stick, the eggs did not originate in Ireland. By 1908 three additional officers had been appointed in Britain to investigate frauds relating to Irish agricultural produce, mainly the mis-labelling of produce from elsewhere as Irish. The DATI's authority to police the quality of Irish agricultural produce was strengthened by the Merchandise Marks Amendment Act of 1909, which gave it power to initiate prosecutions in Ireland. However, the market for Irish butter continued to be damaged by fragmented marketing, with individual creameries, butter 'factories', blenders and farmers all exporting butter of widely-varying quality. In 1910 a departmental committee on the butter industry recommended additional legislation, including a definition of 'creamery butter'.[197] Yet, when the DATI drafted a bill to this effect in 1913, it was opposed by the IAOS. Its hostility appears to have been prompted by antipathy towards the DATI.

Irish butter consumption rose during the early years of the twentieth century because families ate more bread and less maize meal and oatmeal as they became more prosperous. The number of milch cows remained static, as did average milk yields, so higher domestic consumption meant falling exports and rising imports of butter. By 1909 butter exports were almost entirely confined to the west of England. On the eve of World War I only 39 per cent of Irish butter was produced in creameries; 16 per cent was blended in butter factories; and the remainder was produced on the farm. One reason for the persistence of home dairying was the belief that calves did not thrive on skim milk returned from the creamery.[198] There was much talk about winter dairying, but apparently little success.

Given the importance that Plunkett attached to the dairying sector, and the close links in the early years between the DATI and the co-operative movement, which consisted almost exclusively of creameries, the failure to achieve any significant increase in the output or exports of dairy products is noteworthy. The DATI appears to have been more concerned with the manufacture and marketing of dairy produce than with the raw material – milk. It is highly probable that the dairy industry may have been a casualty of the division of labour and the disagreements between the DATI and the IAOS. The DATI's concentration on beef cattle may also have been a contributing factor.

The DATI investigated the possibility of establishing a dead meat trade with London, and its London office worked to promote sales of Irish fruit and early potatoes. It also assisted in the marketing of non-food products, such as tweed. Its record on dead meat seems mixed. Although exports of beef and mutton rose from 6,000 cwt in 1904 to over 320,000 by 1912, this was counter-balanced by a fall in bacon exports, which again may have been due to higher consumption at home. Imports of bacon were also rising. Nevertheless, the total value of dead meat exported was over £5 million in 1912.

The DATI's strategy for the Irish horse industry gave rise to controversy. In 1909 the Council of Agriculture approved a proposal from Campbell, assistant secretary for Agriculture, that only horses registered by the DATI should be used as sires, and in 1912 it approved the DATI's plans to introduce legislation to this effect.[199] However, the Board of Agriculture and the council remained divided on the relative merits of Clydesdales and Shire horses,[200] and the Horse Breeding Act, which required that all breeding stallions should be licensed by the DATI, was not enacted until 1918.[201]

Other important services introduced during the early years included a seed-testing station, opened in December 1900, which tested seed for purity, percentage of germination, and germinating energy. An inquiry carried out in April 1900 established that most farmers knew nothing about the quality of seed that they purchased. An initial staff of three in 1900 had grown to twenty-three by 1918. At the beginning, all samples tested were submitted voluntarily by farmers or seedmen, but the Weeds and Agricultural Seeds (Ireland) Act of 1909 gave the DATI the right to enter premises and take seed for testing and also the right to know the source of seeds supplied. At the beginning the DATI warned traders who supplied inferior seed, that if they failed to raise their standards, it would make these warnings public. The Act appears to have been effective in raising the quality of seed: in 1912, 69 per cent of the samples of grass seed tested was judged to be unsatisfactory, but by 1920 this had fallen to 1 per cent. Further legislation in 1920 made it an offence to sell or expose for sale seeds containing more than a specified quantity of seed from injurious weeds.[202]

Efforts to combat crop and animal disease also proved quite effective. When blight appeared in 1907, the DATI approved the granting of loans for the purchase of horse sprayers. In 1908 an order was made restricting the importation of hay and straw from countries where foot and mouth disease existed. A pilot scheme to establish veterinary dispensaries was introduced in County Wexford in 1908; in 1909 it was extended to twelve localities in the congested districts. During 1912 a serious outbreak of foot and mouth disease in parts of Leinster and County Fermanagh led to a reduction in cattle exports. This prompted the DATI to carry out a review of veterinary services, and it recommended that the DATI should take control of the Royal Veterinary College. (This matter was not resolved until the 1920s.) When an outbreak of foot and mouth disease was reported in 1912, the English Board of Agriculture introduced regulations requiring Irish cattle to be held at the port of arrival for at least twelve hours. Hugh Barrie, a unionist MP for County Derry, who succeeded Russell as vice-president of the DATI in 1919, proposed a motion condemning the action of the English Board of Agriculture – evidence that unionists and nationalists were in agreement on many agricultural matters.[203]

The report of the Recess Committee had recommended the creation of a bureau for agricultural and industrial statistics. Although an annual census of livestock numbers and crop acreages had been carried out by the RIC on behalf of the office of the Registrar-General since 1847, and additional statistics were collected by the Agricultural Department of the Land Commission (to enable it to determine judicial rents) and by the veterinary department of the Privy Council, the Recess Committee noted that no statistics existed for exports or the value of agricultural output. The statistics branch of the DATI was given responsibility for all official statistics other than the census of population, vital statistics and data on emigration.

The last official statistics on Irish trade with Britain related to 1825;[204] the DATI resumed this series. Although the first official trade statistics were issued in 1906, the series remained defective, because shippers were not obliged to provide detailed descriptions of the goods they were carrying. The first data on agricultural output was compiled for the year 1908, as part of the Board of Trade Census of Production. After 1922 the staff of the DATI statistical branch formed the nucleus of the statistical service of the Irish Free State.[205] Despite their shortcomings, the trade statistics compiled by the DATI proved a powerful weapon for the Irish Industrial Movement, which frequently cited data on imports and exports in support of its case – yet another instance where the DATI was used to enhance nationalist arguments.[206]

The DATI's international dimension was important at a time when Ireland was not an independent country. From the beginning, officials were exchanging information with ministries of agriculture throughout Europe and the Empire – the first Irish ministry to do this. From a position where professional training in agriculture, horticulture and poultry-keeping was almost unknown, the DATI had been responsible for building up the work of the College of Science, not simply in agricultural science, but in applied sciences such as engineering, and it played an important role in raising the number of Irish people with qualifications in science. If Irish nationalists complained in 1900 that so many of the top jobs in the DATI were filled by Scots, this was largely because no Irishmen were qualified; the position had improved substantially by the time of Independence.

Given the political and social changes that were under way in Ireland at the beginning of the twentieth century, the controversies and the divided views surrounding the early years of the DATI were probably inevitable. Yet, as the next chapter will reveal, by 1920, and probably earlier the DATI had ceased to be regarded as an instrument of British administration in Ireland. It was accepted as an organisation that met the needs of the Irish people. By 1914 the administrative and financial framework was in place that would serve the needs of an independent Ireland.

CHAPTER TWO

THE YEARS OF CHANGE, 1914–1922

The outbreak of World War I in 1914 marked the end of an era in European political and economic history. During the 1920s and the 1930s many people looked back to the years before 1914 as a golden age characterised by full employment, stable prices and more certain markets. However, such recollections were probably too positive and too uncritical. Ireland was faced with the prospect of major political changes even before the outbreak of war. Home Rule was due to come into effect in 1914, although there was some doubt whether this would be an all-Ireland administration, or one that excluded part of Ulster.

Between 1914 and 1922 Ireland underwent a political revolution that ended with the creation of two separate states, and a civil war in the Irish Free State. This revolution coincided with a period of considerable uncertainty for Irish farming. World War I had brought a sharp rise in agricultural prices, compulsory tillage and the introduction of statutory wages for agricultural labourers. By 1920 farmers had to adjust to falling prices and dislocated markets. The DATI had to contend with both the political and the economic revolutions and the existence of an alternative Dáil Éireann Ministry of Agriculture.

IRISH AGRICULTURE DURING WORLD WAR I

It is only in recent years that historians have come to recognise the importance of agriculture and food supplies in the story of World War I.[1] The outbreak of war disrupted international trade and there was a sharp fall in the amount of food imported into Europe from overseas. The first concern of belligerent governments was to see that their armies were fed, even if this reduced the amount of food available for the civilian population.[2]

In 1914 agriculture not only fed the troops, but also transported them: most military transport was provided by horses, and oats were the equivalent of oil in today's world.

When the war began the DATI cautioned farmers against selling off their breeding stock; it also urged them to reserve more seed than usual so that they would be in a position to plant extra crops. On 19 August 1914 agricultural instructors were summoned to a special meeting in Dublin to discuss what steps should be taken to increase the supply of food. They were encouraged to plant as many demonstration plots as possible with winter cereals and with catch crops that could be used to feed livestock during the spring. Instructors were also asked to do everything in their power to persuade farmers to till more land. The Council of Agriculture held a special meeting on 20 August, which passed a resolution approving these measures. It also urged farmers, labourers and everybody with suitable land to grow additional winter vegetables. The DATI distributed special leaflets. Some publicised the need for more tillage, while others provided technical advice on growing winter cereals and other crops. Most county committees of agriculture allocated extra funds to promote tillage, which often covered the appointment of special tillage demonstrators. Technical instruction committees organised classes in first-aid and nursing.

The Departmental Committee on Food Production
The key decisions on wartime agricultural policy were determined in Whitehall and Westminster, not in Dublin, and they were taken with British interests in mind. In September 1914 the British Prime Minister, Asquith, ruled out offering financial inducements to encourage farmers to grow more cereals, and agricultural labourers were permitted to enlist in the armed forces although this resulted in a shortage of labour.

When a coalition government was established in May 1915, the new president of the Board of Agriculture and Fisheries appointed a committee to draw up a food production programme for England and Wales. Another committee was established for Scotland.[3] In Ireland T. W. Russell appointed a Departmental Committee on Food Production, to determine what measures were needed to maintain, and if possible increase, the output of food, on the assumption that the war would be prolonged beyond the harvest in 1916. The committee included representatives of the DATI, the board and council of Agriculture, and Horace Plunkett in his capacity as president of the IAOS. The committee reported that priority should be given to four issues:

- increasing the acreage under tillage in order to provide more food for humans and for livestock;
- maintaining and improving the stock of breeding animals;
- making it easier for farmers to obtain agricultural implements and artificial manures;
- maintaining the Irish fishing industry.

The least controversial recommendations related to livestock. All parties recommended that the DATI should use the powers conferred by the Maintenance of Livestock Act of 1915 banning the slaughter or export of in-calf heifers and cows, pregnant sows and lambs, in order to prevent a serious depletion of livestock numbers. This was done. The committee was divided on the best means of increasing the acreage under tillage, and how to provide farmers with equipment and fertiliser. The majority report suggested that the most effective means would be to offer guaranteed minimum prices for wheat and oats for one year, although it acknowledged that this decision rested with the government at Westminster. Guaranteeing prices for more than one year 'would be to exceed what could be described as a war measure and would lead to sharp debate', although five members of the committee suggested that prices should be guaranteed for three years.[4] The majority report also recommended that the county committees of agriculture should introduce a loan scheme to enable smallholders to buy implements needed for tillage, and a ban on exports of artificial manures from the United Kingdom. These recommendations reflected the views of the county committees of agriculture, who believed that farmers needed incentives to take the risk involved in extra tillage.

Horace Plunkett had presented a motion to the committee, proposing that the IAOS and the DATI should establish a joint committee to co-ordinate efforts to raise food production. When this motion was defeated by eleven votes to four, Plunkett submitted a minority report to redress the absence of any reference to co-operation in the majority report. Plunkett believed that an educational campaign conducted by the co-operative movement offered the most effective means of encouraging tillage, although he does not appear to have entirely rejected the idea of guaranteed prices. Implements, fertiliser and seed would also be provided by co-operatives. This minority report rehearsed Plunkett's familiar complaints against 'well-organised and politically powerful vested interests' and the 'bitter opposition' that the co-operative movement had to surmount.[5] Referring to the Dairying Industry Bill, T. W. Russell countered that on the last occasion when he had established an advisory committee that included representatives of the IAOS, he had lost his Bill.[6] The divisions of opinion between Plunkett's minority report and the majority report, and between Plunkett and Russell, may be seen as the final episode in the long-running disagreement over the relationship between the co-operative movement and the DATI.

The divisions within the Irish committee were mirrored in the Scottish and English committees. This lack of unanimity on the appropriate policy, together with an apparent improvement in food supplies, persuaded Whitehall to rely on persuasion and publicity rather than on price subsidies for the 1915/16 season.[7] The DATI was forced to do likewise. Russell toured the country addressing meetings; 50,000 posters were printed and three million leaflets were distributed by the RIC and the national schools.

The higher grain acreage led to demands that county committees of agriculture should purchase threshing machines; the DATI did not approve. Applications for subsidies towards the cost of renovating disused mills received a more favourable response. The additional acreage under crops and the shortage of shipping space led to an acute shortage of fertiliser. Supplies of potash were completely cut off, although there was some improvement in 1917. In some instances, the DATI imported raw materials for the manufacture of fertiliser and arranged for these to be processed in Ireland.[8] Horses were also in demand to pull ploughs and reapers, at a time when the British army needed as many horses as it could get. The DATI feared that the quality of Irish horses would deteriorate as breeding animals were exported. The War Office suggested that horses, which were no longer fit for duty, could be sent to Ireland, but the DATI rejected this proposal because it feared they might introduce disease.

Compulsory Tillage
By June 1915 the acreage under tillage was 83,000 acres higher than in 1914, an increase of approximately 6 per cent. However, poor weather meant that the increase in output was disappointing. In 1916 the acreage tilled actually fell, and there was a poor crop of potatoes. Publicity and persuasion had not proved effective. There had also been poor harvests in Canada, Australia and Argentina. By the winter of 1916, with German submarines inflicting severe damage on food imports and no end to the war in sight, the British government invoked the Defence of the Realm Act to introduce compulsory tillage.

Under orders passed in December 1916 and January 1917, every occupier holding ten or more acres of arable land was required to till one-tenth of this land, in addition to the acreage tilled in 1916, although nobody was required to till more than 50 per cent of a holding. Grassland used to feed dairy cattle that supplied milk to towns was exempt, as was some of the land occupied by stud farms. Other Defence of the Realm orders required landholders to maintain all drains and streams on their land in order to prevent damage by flooding. Although these orders covered all arable land throughout the United Kingdom, during 1917 they were only applied in Ireland. Compulsory tillage was not introduced in England, Wales and Scotland until 1918 and the requirements in England were whittled down considerably, allegedly because of a shortage of agricultural labour.[9]

The DATI organised conferences with the county committees of agriculture and the agricultural and horticultural instructors, and sanctioned the appointment of temporary officers to enforce the tillage orders. Lack of agricultural implements was not accepted as a valid reason for evading the orders, as the DATI was taking steps to make additional implements available and to provide smallholders with loans for the purchase of seed and manure. In March 1917 the DATI established a motor tractor section. At the time there were only seventy tractors in Ireland; within six months this had increased to 300, and to 640 by September 1918. The DATI organised imports of tractors, supplies of spare parts, and ploughs suitable for use with tractors. Two-week training courses for tractor drivers were held at the Albert Agricultural College in Glasnevin. The Munster Institute introduced a special course for women who were interested in helping the war effort by becoming agricultural workers. Farmers who received a new tractor had to give an undertaking to hire it out when not in use; tractors owned by the DATI were also available for hire. The war resulted in a greater interest in machinery, although few farmers could afford to purchase tractors and milking machines. In 1918 and 1919 the Council of Agriculture called on the DATI to investigate which types of tractor were best suited to Irish conditions, to organise exhibitions of farm machinery and to encourage the use of milking machines.

An additional order passed in February 1917 gave the DATI authority to arrange for land to be cultivated if the occupier did not appear to be complying with the compulsory tillage order; the RIC was requested to report such cases to the DATI. In the first instance, defaulters were visited by a departmental inspector who tried to persuade them to obey the order; if they still failed to comply, the DATI could enter the land and it did so in 242 cases in 1917. Some of this land was rented out as conacre (land not occupied by long-term tenants); at Ballybunion, County Kerry, the local authority took over land and let it out in allotments. In 210 cases, the DATI decided that it was too late in the season to cultivate the land; this may have been a diplomatic decision.

According to the annual report of the DATI for 1917/18, the Corn Production Act of 1917 'marked a new departure in the agricultural policy of the United Kingdom', because it aimed not only at securing an increase in supplies of food for the duration of the war, but also 'to effect in the interests of national security, such permanent improvement in the agricultural industry as would secure to those engaged in it a fair return in future years for their labour of capital'. The Act set guaranteed prices for wheat and oats, and exports of these crops were controlled by licence. In 1917 landholders were required to increase their cultivated areas by 10 per cent over the 1916 levels, and in 1918 a further 5 per cent was required over the 1916 level. When the German offensive in early 1918 posed a further threat to food supplies, a supplementary order was issued, requiring another 5 per cent of land on farms greater than 200 acres to be cultivated. The Act also gave the DATI authority to intervene where land was not being cultivated according to the rules of good husbandry. If the DATI took possession of a farm, officials were empowered to stock and cultivate the land and to use the farm buildings to house humans, animals and equipment.[10] When the Board of Agriculture discussed the Corn Bill (as it then was) on 30 March 1917, T. W. Russell urged that it should indicate what it believed to be the appropriate acreage of cultivated land in Ireland in the future. However, there is no evidence that this was done.[11]

The DATI appears to have enforced compulsory tillage orders more actively during 1918 than in the previous year, entering holdings in twenty-four counties. In many cases this action was sufficient to encourage compliance by delinquent landholders and their neighbours. One defaulter, who was obviously a large landholder, hired twenty plough teams in order to comply with the Act. There was also a big push on drainage during 1918.

The most radical consequence of the Corn Production Act of 1917 was the establishment of the Agricultural Wages Board, comprising six representatives of employers, six representatives of workers, and four nominees.[12] The 1915 Departmental Committee on Food Production had expressed some concern as to whether there was sufficient labour in Ireland to cope with a substantial increase in tillage, and the DATI's annual report for 1915 noted that the best labour had left the country, and that farmers were complaining about labour shortages. At that time the DATI was opposed to the imposition of statutory minimum wages for agricultural labourers.[13]

In November 1917 the Agricultural Wages Board issued a schedule of minimum wage rates for adult males, which took account of regional differences. Additional orders set minimum rates for men under twenty-one years of age. The board also issued a table estimating the monetary value that an employer could assign to benefits in kind. By the autumn of 1918 the board had instituted legal proceedings against 226 employers for failing to pay minimum wages. Although the DATI set the regulations that governed the procedures of the Agricultural Wages Board, relations between the DATI and the board soon deteriorated. The board sought to assert its independence by refusing to provide Russell with copies of its minutes, and the Board of Agriculture was unhappy at the value that the Agricultural Wages Board had placed on the perquisites provided to farm labourers.

The Corn Production Act and the compulsory tillage orders resulted in a substantial increase in the acreage under cultivation. In 1917 the output of corn in Ireland was 545,000 tons higher than the average annual output between 1904 and 1913. An additional one million tons of potatoes were produced, and in 1918 the potato crop was 27 per cent above the pre-war average. In 1918 the output of grain was 62 per cent higher than the pre-war average: the wheat crop was four times the pre-war average and there was also a substantially higher acreage under oats, although the acreage under barley fell because of restrictions on the production of Guinness.

This additional food was produced at relatively little cost to the state. Middleton has calculated that the increase in food production throughout the United Kingdom cost the taxpayer over £9 million; but he estimated the cost of the food campaign in Ireland between 1917 and 1920 at approximately £625,000, much less than in England and Wales because the DATI took charge. The largest single expense, £275,000, was fertiliser. The extra food produced in Ireland in 1918 is estimated to have saved United Kingdom taxpayers over £1.2 million. The substantial rise in crop acreage in Ireland was possible because there were large tracts of temporary grassland that could be ploughed, giving high yields for a few years. Moreover, Ireland, unlike England and Scotland, did not experience a serious shortage of labour, because there was no conscription.[14]

The transformation of Irish agriculture, however, was not without cost. Barley acreage fell and the high prices for grain and wartime shipping difficulties led to a severe shortage of animal feedstuffs, which persisted well into 1919. By January 1918 the DATI was concerned at the fall in livestock numbers.[15] Nevertheless, the substantial expansion in crops during 1917 and 1918 rekindled interest in reviving tillage in Ireland.

Overall Agricultural Output
In March 1915 the Board of Agriculture had warned farmers that they should not become complacent because of wartime prosperity. It had pointed out that the Napoleonic wars were followed by a slump in agricultural prices, and recalled the agricultural depression of the late 1870s and the 1880s. In an exercise in economic forecasting that proved only too accurate, the board stated that 'the present high prices will, by an inevitable law, be followed at the close of the War by a period of low prices, depression, and perhaps, distress'. Farmers were advised to clear old debts, accumulate savings for the rainy days ahead, and refrain from additional borrowings, unless the money was intended to increase output; 'even from the low standpoint of the pecuniary advantage of Irish agriculture, the shorter the war the better, for the longer the war continues the longer and more acute will be the subsequent depression'.[16]

Did Irish farmers remember this warning in the early 1920s? They certainly paid little heed during the war, because borrowings increased as farmers competed to buy additional land. Record wartime prices also brought a more complacent attitude towards quality. Britain could no longer import eggs from the Continent and the DATI's annual reports from 1914 to 1918 contained warnings to egg exporters that they were losing a golden opportunity to gain a stronger position in the British market because of their careless approach to quality and freshness. The war created problems in packing and transporting eggs – there was a shortage of timber for packing boxes; new restrictions were introduced relating to unaccompanied packages on railways; and shipping services were less reliable.

The dairy industry was another casualty of the war. By 1918 butter exports were at little more than half the 1914 level, although exports of cheese showed a substantial increase. Butter exports fell because Irish producers regarded the maximum price set by the British food control regulations as too low. Although the maximum price order was lifted in Ireland in April 1918 following agitation, butter exports remained subject to control. Another factor in the decline in butter exports was wartime prosperity in Ireland, which meant that people, especially farming families, were using more butter. The brunt of the fall in butter exports was borne by the creameries. Some switched to producing cheese because it offered a better price, and exports rose from less than 10,000 tons in 1914, to 136,000 tons in 1918, and almost 286,000 tons in 1919. Unfortunately, the cheddar and caerphilly cheese produced was of low quality, and the market collapsed as soon as alternatives became available.[17]

The DATI and World War I

War brought budgetary stringency, although the problems were less acute for the DATI than for the CDB and the Land Commission, which were forced to abandon land purchase schemes owing to a lack of money. In 1915 the DATI cut the sum provided for county agricultural schemes from £50,000 to £40,000, and in 1916 courses for dairymaids were abandoned owing to lack of funds. Staff numbers were reduced by terminating contracts and not replacing men who enlisted in the armed forces. The annual report for 1914/15 recorded that out of a total staff of approximately 430, 130 officers had joined the forces, and ten had died in action. In all, 145 officers of the DATI served during World War I; twenty-four were either killed in action or died of wounds and disease; a further thirty-seven were wounded, and forty received distinctions.

In November 1915 the Lord Lieutenant addressed the Council of Agriculture as part of the recruiting drive. Not coincidentally, in the same month the Agricultural Instructors' Association demanded that the DATI grant them war service badges. These badges identified wearers as officials who could not be spared from their work to join the forces. Instructors were aggrieved because customs and excise officers had been given war service badges, and they believed themselves to be 'at least as well entitled to them'. The association claimed that several instructors had been prevented from joining the forces by their county committees of agriculture, and others would have enlisted 'were it not for the fact that they feel they are performing a valuable service to the nation, being important factors in the present Food Production'. The instructors were denied their badges because the Treasury cancelled the facility.[18] In June 1916 instructors requested the DATI to provide them with travel permits, which would allow them to move freely through the country and to obtain petrol more easily. But the Petrol Control Committee was unsympathetic to the DATI's request for a special petrol allowance for instructors. The Treasury refused to pay a war bonus to instructors similar to that paid to civil servants, although it gave the DATI permission to pay one from the endowment fund, backdated to January 1917.

In 1916 the Treasury suggested that the DATI should consider hiring women as clerks, to replace the men who had enlisted. The DATI already employed fourteen female typists, but no female clerks. Meyrick, a staff clerk and a future secretary of the Department, wondered whether there would be any objection to having the women work in the same room as the men; if this were not feasible, it would be necessary to evict a man from his office. By October boy clerks were again available, much to the DATI's relief: because they could be placed in any office, they could be assigned to any type of work.[19] The pressures of war duties meant that less urgent tasks were postponed; for example, the 1917 agricultural statistics were not completed until 1921.

From War to Revolution: Political and Social Unrest

By 1920 agricultural prices were approximately three times the 1913 figure. War brought unprecedented government regulation – compulsory tillage orders, guaranteed prices for grain, maximum prices for fertiliser, minimum wage orders, and perhaps most important, the temporary suspension of land purchase and redistribution. Although farmers benefited from higher prices, labourers and smallholders felt frustrated at being denied their share of wartime prosperity. Emigration also came to a halt because it was extremely difficult to travel to the United States, and Irishmen in England were liable to conscription. The enforced presence of these young men in the Irish countryside added to the volatile atmosphere that followed in the aftermath of the 1916 Rising and the threat that conscription would be extended to Ireland.

When war broke out in 1914 most people expected that it would have ended by Christmas. By 1917, with no such prospect in sight, there was evidence of growing unrest in rural Ireland. Until the establishment of the Agricultural Wages Board in 1917, the rise in agricultural wages lagged behind the rise in food prices, despite frequent complaints of a shortage of agricultural labour. During the spring of 1917 labourers went on strike in counties Clare, Cork, Kildare, Louth, Limerick, Meath and Wexford. Moribund rural land and labour unions were revived and new organisations emerged, demanding minimum wages for farm labourers, the redistribution of land to smallholders and the provision of allotments.[20] Men were entering grazing land, driving the cattle away, and ploughing or digging the land for tillage[21] – using compulsory tillage orders as justification for their actions. In other instances, demonstrators disrupted auctions for conacre land.

Although such actions were prompted by economic factors, they were also fuelled by the growth of militant nationalism. When the Council of Agriculture held its bi-annual meeting on 25 May 1916, less than a month after the executions of the leaders of the Easter Rising, a resolution condemning the widespread arrests (but not the executions) that followed the Rising was ruled out of order. T. W. Russell, the vice-president of the DATI, emphasised the 'non-agrarian' nature of the Rising,[22] but by the following year there was a much closer relationship between agrarian unrest and militant nationalism. Sinn Féin and the labour movement exploited the discontent resulting from higher food prices, claiming that Ireland was threatened with an artificial famine as a result of meeting the demands of the British food controller. Sinn Féin clubs in the west of Ireland divided untenanted land and grazing land and organised cattle drives. As a protest against the export of livestock, Diarmaid Lynch, Sinn Féin's food controller, organised a well-publicised seizure of pigs on their way to the docks; they were slaughtered and sold for local consumption.[23]

While many larger farmers prospered thanks to the high prices being paid for agricultural produce, they often resented the compulsory tillage orders and the minimum wage orders imposed by the Agricultural Wages Board. Compulsory tillage left graziers short of hay, and their cattle were sometimes undernourished as a consequence. Large farmers and current and former landlords were the targets of cattle driving and land seizures. In 1917 the Irish Farmers' Union (IFU) was founded to contest government regulations. Numerous local farmers' associations, which appear to have been dominated by larger farmers, also came into existence.[24] By 1920 the IFU had an estimated 60,000 members, with full-time agents in each county.[25]

When the war ended in November 1918, the DATI lifted the requirement that farmers with 200 acres or more should till an additional 5 per cent of their land on top of the normal requirement, but the other tillage orders remained in place. However, in 1919 it was more difficult to secure compliance with the tillage orders; the war had ended and several years of compulsory tillage were beginning to take their toll. During the 1919/20 season the DATI served seventy-four draft certificates of default on farmers who had failed to comply with compulsory tillage orders. Protests against compulsory tillage tended to come from larger farmers, who were rarely if ever supporters of Sinn Féin. Many would have been unionist sympathisers, yet ironically they were being alienated from the British administration at a time when their support was crucial. David Fitzpatrick suggests that the 'resultant antagonism between the promise of prosperity and the reality of agricultural disruption was a major factor in the fragmentation of the Protestant community in the revolutionary years'.[26]

For many farmers the question of compulsory tillage was inextricably linked with agricultural wages. On 13 November 1918, two days after the Armistice, the Council of Agriculture debated a motion calling for labourers' wages to be linked to maximum grain prices. The motion was withdrawn when another speaker warned of the danger of doing anything that might worsen relations between labourers and employers.[27] In the spring of 1919 the Irish Transport and General Workers' Union (ITGWU) launched a campaign to achieve higher agricultural wages; in the process it succeeded in bringing labourers out on strike in counties Meath and Kildare,[28] and there were threats of a nation-wide strike if Kildare farmers persisted in their plan to lock out all agricultural labourers unless they returned to work.[29] Many labourers rejected the wage rates laid down by the Agricultural Wages Board.

On 14 March 1919 senior officials of the DATI met a deputation of farmers who were demanding an end to compulsory tillage; the deputation included two representatives of the North Kildare Farmers' Federation, the Clare landlord and maverick unionist Colonel O'Callaghan Westropp, and farmers from Meath, Cork and Wexford. Devere, a large farmer from North Kildare, commented that the tillage order was 'the one great weapon' that labourers could employ against farmers. During the previous summer he had been unable to harvest thousands of acres of corn when his labourers went on strike; he objected to the fact that farmers were compelled to till their land, while labourers were free to strike and 'to demand whatever wages they liked'. When Gill reminded the deputation that Irish farmers were receiving higher guaranteed grain prices than farmers in Britain, O'Callaghan Westropp countered that guaranteed prices were worthless unless farmers had a guaranteed market, guaranteed labour and a guaranteed season to harvest their crops. Gill warned the deputation not to base their campaign for a relaxation of the tillage order on the present labour troubles. 'If it were announced that the Tillage Regulations were relaxed because of the pressure brought by the labourers on the farmers, it would mean an instant revolt and the trouble would become far worse'.[30] The strike in Meath and Kildare continued into the summer months, and retaliatory boycotts initiated by the labour movement resulted in fairs and markets being abandoned and widespread destruction of crops.[31]

The DATI was in favour of abolishing the compulsory tillage order, while retaining other measures to encourage tillage, such as a guaranteed price for oats (there is much less mention of a guaranteed price for wheat), and measures to ensure adequate supplies of potash at a reasonable price. An internal memorandum, dated 10 March 1919, shortly before the DATI met the above-mentioned deputation, noted that if the compulsory tillage order were lifted and the guaranteed price for cereals retained, farmers might be prepared to meet the labourers' demand for a moderate increase in wages. The DATI pressed the British Ministry of Food to give a commitment to buy the 1918 crop of oats at the prices announced shortly before the end of the war. On 11 March 1919 the British Ministry of Food conceded that, while the case for decontrolling the price of oats in Britain was 'irresistible', in Ireland, 'the conditions are rather different', and it agreed to honour its undertaking to buy 10,000 tons of oats a month in Ireland at the previously-announced price until July 1919. It also agreed to restrict exports of British oats and oatmeal into Ireland.[32]

When the Council of Agriculture met in May 1919 Campbell, the assistant secretary for Agriculture, persuaded it to withdraw a motion calling for an end to compulsory tillage, because the requirements under the order were in the process of being eased. The council was also persuaded to withdraw a motion condemning the DATI for failing to invite farming representatives to a meeting it had organised between labour representatives and traders, in an effort to end a labour embargo on the export of food.[33] Although the DATI avoided a major clash with the Council of Agriculture on this occasion, these resolutions are indicative of the tensions that existed between farmers and the DATI.

In April 1919 labourers in Derry and east Donegal, an area with good tillage land, went on strike in support of a demand to be paid more than the statutory minimum wage. Although a matter for the Ministry of Labour, Gordon Campbell, head of the Irish section of the Ministry of Labour (and a future secretary of the Department of Industry and Commerce), asked the DATI to arbitrate. Campbell suggested that the two departments should consider establishing conciliation boards, where farmers and representatives of agricultural labourers could bargain over wages and conditions, and they held some inconclusive discussions on this matter. The DATI was reluctant to become involved unless it had the support of both farmers and labourers.[34]

In November 1919 the Board of Agriculture expressed support for continuing the compulsory tillage orders, if only to provide jobs for labourers. It hoped this would reduce labour unrest.[35] This decision is surprising, in that it reversed the board's previous attitude, and in the past, few members of either the board or the council of Agriculture had expressed any interest in rural labourers. Compulsory tillage still applied for the 1920 season, but early in 1921 the DATI eventually revoked it. It had become apparent that Irish farmers would no longer benefit from the guaranteed prices paid under the Agriculture Act of 1920, following the enactment of the Government of Ireland Act in the same year (establishing parliaments in Dublin and Belfast). The Agricultural Wages Board was abolished in October 1921.

THE DÁIL ÉIREANN MINISTRY OF AGRICULTURE

From 1919 there were two authorities administering agriculture in Ireland – the DATI, accountable to the British Parliament, and the Ministry of Agriculture, accountable to Dáil Éireann. Agriculture was not a priority for Dáil Éireann when it first met in January 1919. The original Cabinet, or Dáil Ministry (a term used at the time to describe the collective decisions of Dáil Ministers), of five – a president, and ministers of finance, foreign affairs, home affairs and defence – left economic and social matters to one side. When de Valera extended the Cabinet to include ministers of labour and industries, agriculture was again excluded. However, on 2 April 1919 Dáil Éireann confirmed the appointment of Robert Barton as Director of Agriculture, a position outside Cabinet.[36]

Barton was a former officer in the British army, who had served in the 1916 Rising on the British side. A County Wicklow landowner with a family home at Glendalough, he had also been chairman of a co-operative bank.[37] Barton served as Director of Agriculture until he was arrested in January 1920. On 27 February 1920 the Cabinet decided that Art O'Connor should be invited to act as substitute Director. O'Connor, a member of a well-known farming family in County Kildare, held a degree in engineering from Trinity College, Dublin (TCD) and was TD for North Kildare. When Barton was released after the truce in mid-1921, he was appointed Minister for Economic Affairs with a seat in the Cabinet, and O'Connor became Minister for Agriculture, reporting to Barton.[38] The choice of Barton and O'Connor as directors of agriculture may well have been designed to assuage the fears of larger farmers, since both men came from families with substantial landholdings.

The National Land Bank

The matters of most immediate concern to Dáil deputies were land redistribution and providing employment for agricultural labourers. On 4 April 1919, two days after Barton's appointment, Liam de Róiste, TD for Cork City, asked whether the government intended to give directions requiring an increase in tillage. Griffith replied that the Director of Agriculture would submit a report to the next session of the Dáil. On the same day Alex McCabe and Countess Markiewicz tabled a motion pledging Dáil Éireann to a fair and full distribution of vacant lands and ranches to farmers with uneconomic holdings and to landless men. This motion also declared that any purchase of land by a private individual since Easter Monday 1916 should be deemed illegal, as should any future purchases of non-residential land in the congested districts, or land that was required for resettlement. Although the resolution was withdrawn without a vote, the matter was referred to a sub-committee of Dáil Éireann – the Land Committee – which would assist Barton in drafting a land policy.[39]

On 27 May 1919 Barton sent de Valera a copy of a letter headed 'The Ministry of Lands' and addressed to 'those interested in securing the transfer of the Cloncurry Cattle Ranches to Irish Peasant Farmers'. Beginning with the well-known quotation of James Fintan Lalor, 'that the entire ownership of Ireland, moral and material, up to the Sun, and down to the centre, is vested of right in the People of Ireland', the letter noted that 'we [?] who had taken the Oath of Allegiance to the Irish Republic have my entire sympathy in their attempt to secure the use of the Ranch lands in their District'. The letter stated that land used solely for cattle ranching was a national menace. It would appear that Barton sent this letter to 'the Cloncurry people' without seeking Cabinet approval.

Barton asked de Valera whether the policy outlined in the letter met with his approval, drawing attention to the fact that the letter applied only to conacre land, and that it sanctioned the use of force, which would take 'the usual form of cattle driving and intimidation of graziers'. De Valera informed Barton that it would be 'obviously altogether irregular' to send such a letter in his official capacity and to commit the Cabinet to a policy it had not debated: 'the schemes of individual ministers must be forwarded to the Cabinet as a whole for sanction'. He asked Barton to withdraw the letter if at all possible, but as a concessionary gesture promised the Cabinet would discuss it as a recommended policy. Barton responded with a humble apology.[40]

Any endorsement by Dáil Éireann of a policy along the lines of that outlined in Barton's letter would have been interpreted as sanctioning land seizures, and it seems doubtful that the limits specified by Barton – that only conacre land would be seized and force would be limited to cattle driving and boycotting graziers – would have been observed. The Cabinet asked Barton to outline a general policy for dealing with cases like the Cloncurry case, 'so that they might be dealt with on their merits as this type of work is exactly what is required to solidify our position in the country'. It recommended that he summon a meeting of the Land Committee, which had been appointed at the April session of Dáil Éireann. Diarmaid Ó hEigeartaigh, Secretary to the Ministry (Cabinet), suggested that Barton should have travelled to the Cloncurry estate and 'dealt with the case on the spot'; alternatively, Art O'Connor should investigate and report back to the Land Committee. In the event, Arthur Griffith despatched O'Connor to the Cloncurry estate without notifying Barton; Ó hEigeartaigh claimed that O'Connor just happened to visit Griffith's office on the day following the Cabinet meeting.

The Land Committee held its first meeting on 13 June 1919 at 12 Ranelagh Road, the home of Seán T. O'Kelly. It decided that the Ministry of Agriculture should discourage the sale of tenant right[41] by landlords of untenanted land. However, if the landlord proposed to divide the land into holdings of not more than 25–35 acres and to make provision for common grazing of cows belonging to labourers and smallholders, the Ministry would not interfere. If it was proposed to divide the land into large farms, the Dáil government would 'lend such assistance as it deems fit and in such manner as it deems wise to prevent the transference of the Tenant Right to fresh ownership'.[42]

When the Dáil reconvened on 17 June, Barton was unable to attend and Griffith read his report.[43] On the following day W. T. Cosgrave, speaking apparently on behalf of the absent Barton, noted that the only proposal so far relating to the Cloncurry estate was that the Director of Agriculture should interview Lord Cloncurry. Other speakers revisited issues that had been discussed at the April session, such as the need for increased tillage, and the fact that 'it was essential for the Dáil to take up a definite stand with a view to securing the land for the people'. The Dáil approved a motion that, 'The provision of land for the agricultural population now deprived is decreed and a Loan Fund under the authority of Dáil may be established to aid this purpose'.[44]

After this session the Dáil Land Committee appears to have been superseded by a Committee on Agriculture (later known as the Committee of the Agricultural and Land Mortgage Bank), which held its first meeting on 30 July 1919. Most of this meeting was devoted to discussing land acquisition. The committee noted that there was an urgent need to devise a land scheme that would meet the requirements of a growing population and prevent emigration. Barton favoured a scheme of co-operative land ownership, referring to the co-operative land scheme at Ralahine in the 1830s. Other committee members emphasised that most people would reject as unacceptable anything other than individual ownership. As a compromise, the committee made provision for both co-operative and individual ownership.

When the Committee on Agriculture met again on 18 August, Barton outlined proposals for co-operative land societies and a land mortgage bank. The co-operative land societies would admit all classes of the rural community who were likely to be forced into emigration by want of land, such as small farmers on uneconomic holdings, resident sons and daughters of farmers, agricultural labourers, and others in the rural community with a knowledge of farming but whose trade or occupation did not provide them with sufficient means of support. A land mortgage credit bank would only be used to finance land purchase for the categories mentioned above; it would not provide funds for a scheme of land purchase similar to that provided for under the Wyndham Land Act of 1903.[45]

On 20 August Barton reported to Dáil Éireann that the committee had recommended the formation of a state-financed national co-operative mortgage bank, Banc na Talmhan, with an initial capital of £200,000. The bank would lend money directly to purchasers, or preferably through local co-operative land societies. Smallholders and landless men wishing to acquire land would first have to establish a co-operative society, with a minimum of six members, which would have to be registered under approved rules, with duly appointed committees and trustees. Land would be leased from the co-operative society; the occupiers would never become outright owners. If one member defaulted on repayments, all would be liable. Each society would determine whether to divide the land into individual holdings or retain part or all as commonage.[46] This was an attempt to implement the philosophy of landownership favoured by Michael Davitt and James Connolly; perhaps even to recreate property relationships found under Brehon law.[47] Individual purchasers were required to find a deposit equal to 25 per cent of the cost of the land, a decision which meant that it would be almost impossible for genuine smallholders or landless men to obtain a mortgage from the bank (after 1885 all the British land acts provided 100 per cent mortgages), but no deposit was required for sales to co-operative societies.[48] Barton circulated all deputies with a copy of the scheme, with a request that they contact him with any suggestions for modifications. Most criticisms related to the power to provide loans for individual purchasers; Barton claimed that this clause had been included for the purpose of drawing criticism.[49]

In October 1919 the Committee of the Agricultural and Land Mortgage Bank issued a memorandum 'for use of Teachtaí only', explaining the Dáil Land Act. This opened with a promise that 'The Land Act will repopulate Irish Rural areas with Irish people. ...The Land Mortgage Bank will find the money'. The most significant change from the original proposal was the decision that co-operative societies that proposed dividing all or some of the land among individual members would be required to find a deposit of 25 per cent, whereas those that held it in common would be granted 100 per cent mortgages. According to this document, the establishment of the Land Bank meant that all land for sale in Ireland 'will be brought within the reach of men who will use it'; this would increase the value of the land and the national wealth and ensure a rising population. Poor people would be in a position to compete for land with rich ranchers, confident of victory because they would be supported by public opinion.[50] On 27 October the Dáil voted a sum of £1,000 to meet the initial expenses of the new bank; one Mayo deputy immediately asked whether the £1,000 would be available to men in his constituency, who were anxious to buy land.[51] Others pressed the claims of their constituents, but Griffith pointed out that no loans would be provided until the bank had accumulated at least £50,000.

In December 1919 the National Land Bank began to process applications for loans. The initial capital of £200,000 would be provided by Dáil Éireann (from the Dáil Loan), and it was hoped that additional money would be raised by deposits from the public. Four of the eight directors would be appointed by Dáil Éireann; the bank's president would be a member of the Cabinet (Michael Collins, the Minister for Finance); and Lionel Smith-Gordon, a former employee of the IAOS, was appointed as managing director.[52]

By April 1920 the National Land Bank was open for ordinary business. During an outbreak of land agitation during the spring of 1920 the directors of the bank issued a statement declaring that 'the influence of the Land Bank has been most vigorouly directed against any form of violence, and that in no case where money had been advanced has any such violence taken place'. On 29 June 1920 the Dáil approved a request from Michael Collins that £25,000 be made available to enable the bank to open six branch offices.[53] An undated report noted that during its first year the bank had provided £200,000 to finance the purchase of 10,000 acres. At the beginning, in order to popularise the scheme, loans were granted without taking local deposits into account. In future, funds would be provided proportionate to local support for the bank.[54]

In January 1921 Art O'Connor, the acting Director of Agriculture, complained that public representatives had not supported the National Land Bank as much as they should. 'Districts which received large advances knew where the Bank was situated when loans were required, but forgot its existence when deposits were to be made'. He claimed that there had been 'huge increases' in the deposits of the joint stock banks, which was tantamount to 'financing the enemy in his attacks', because these banks invested heavily in British government securities.[55] By June 1921 the National Land Bank had loaned over £316,000 to thirty-five co-operative land societies with a combined membership of 800, enabling them to purchase 15,750 acres. Most of these societies were in the midlands.[56] While impressive, this made little impression on the numbers of smallholders and landless men, and the amount of land purchased through the National Land Bank during these years was much less than the land bought by commercial farmers with loans from joint-stock banks.

The Dáil Éireann Land Courts

The Dáil Éireann Land Courts were another element in the Dáil's effort to contain land agitation and to prevent it from distracting attention from the campaign for independence. While the National Land Bank was the brainchild of Robert Barton, his successor, Art O'Connor, was a key figure in the establishment of the Land Courts.

O'Connor was involved in efforts to quell land unrest before his appointment as acting Director of Agriculture. As we have already seen, Griffith had despatched him to the Cloncurry estate in May 1919, and in February 1920, shortly before he became acting Director, Griffith sent him to County Kerry to deal with a particularly violent outbreak of agrarian violence.[57] In a report on the Kerry disturbances, dated 21 Febuary 1920, O'Connor concluded that shootings and burnings would cease when the root causes were removed; land, not wages, was the root of the evil. He recommended convening a conference of farmers and workers under the authority of the Dáil Ministry of Labour. O'Connor continued to undertake similar missions after his appointment as acting Director.[58] In May Griffith sent him to Connacht, where a group of landowners, who had been victims of cattle-driving and land-grabbing, had asked Dáil Éireann to intervene. He was accompanied by Kevin O'Sheil, a young barrister, who was involved in Sinn Féin.

In June 1919 Dáil Éireann had authorised the establishment of arbitration courts to reconcile the conflicting interests of those battling for possession of land. Arbitration courts were established in west Clare and in some other regions of the west, although only on a limited scale. Conor Maguire, a Mayo solicitor, asked O'Connor to convene an emergency land commission to arbitrate on disputes in his area, with O'Connor and O'Sheil acting as commissioners. This session in Ballinrobe on 17 May 1920 is believed to have been the first sitting of the Dáil Land Courts. The commissioners decided in favour of the landholders – two farmers with large families, whose joint farm consisted of just over 100 acres.[59] The attention of the claimants was diverted to a nearby undivided ranch of 700 acres in the hands of the CDB.[60]

O'Connor returned to Dublin and O'Sheil continued to adjudicate on disputes in Roscommon and other western counties.[61] O'Connor reported back to the Dáil Cabinet, and on its instructions he convened a special conference of constituency representatives, commandants of the Irish Volunteers, and TDs from Connacht, to examine the land problem in the west. On 29 June he told the Dáil that the problem must not be tackled 'in a half-hearted dilettante manner': a land commission should be established to adjudicate on land ownership and control, and should operate in conjunction with the National Land Bank. Both organisations would report to the Ministry of Agriculture.[62] O'Connor demanded that the land commission should be given a specific mandate to tackle land disturbances, although he was concerned that some local commandants would continue to tolerate land-grabbing.[63] He told the Dáil that the land question should not distract attention from the struggle for independence: Irish energies should be directed towards 'clearing out – not the occupier of this or that piece of land – but the foreign invader of our country'.[64]

The Dáil approved the establishment of a land commission on 6 August,[65] probably retrospectively, since some form of land commission or land courts had been operating for several months. Kevin O'Sheil described the decree that established the Land Settlement Commission as 'one of the longest and most elaborate decrees passed by the first Dáil'. It followed the lines of the British legislation that had established the Land

Commission, and O'Sheil regarded it as 'much too complicated for the times and conditions it was destined to meet'.[66] The commission was granted jurisdiction over all matters relating to land: it could recommend that the National Land Bank or a joint-stock bank should grant loans to persons that it deemed suitable to lease or buy untenanted land; it could determine whether any block of land was suitable for acquisition; and it had power to acquire land.[67] O'Sheil was soon joined by Conor Maguire, who had been present at the first provisional meeting of the Land Settlement Commission.[68] They negotiated land purchase agreements between farmers and landlords, and arbitrated on disputes between rival family members and between landless men and occupying tenants. Most of their time was spent reacting to disputes. O'Connor noted that land disputes were like a fever that broke out every year on 1 May; the 1920 outbreak was more violent than in previous years.[69]

The Dáil was determined to bring this fever under control. A decree from the Ministry of Home Affairs dated 29 June 1920 announced that no claims to farms or holdings that were being worked by the occupier as agricultural residential holdings would be considered, unless the claimant was granted a written licence by the Ministry of Home Affairs. In August 1921 O'Connor reminded the Dáil that the Land Settlement Commission had been forced to take on the task of arbitrating on land, because of the 'attempted land revolution of last year'.[70] By then the problem was on the wane; in May 1921 he had reported that land settlement courts were continuously in session in counties Mayo, Roscommon, Sligo, Leitrim and Carlow, although there was little land agitation.[71]

O'Connor was concerned that the wave of land transfers would tie the hands of future governments. 'Lords of the Soil are trading upon sentiment and the land hunger of the people. They fear a change. They are delighted to get an opportunity to clear out the country with their pockets well lined with Irish money'.[72] He would have preferred that the Land Settlement Commission give occupiers security of tenure under a state guarantee, but this was unlikely to meet the aspirations of the majority of Irish households to own some land.

Forestry
Re-afforestation was another favourite project for many Irish nationalists, conscious of the depletion of Irish woodlands since the late middle ages. In 1904 the DATI had established a school for practical foresters in the former Parnell estate at Avondale in County Wicklow, and in 1912 a

professor of forestry was appointed at the College of Science. During World War I large numbers of mature trees were felled when timber imports were curtailed. In 1919 the British government handed responsibility for forestry matters throughout the United Kingdom to a newly-established Forestry Commission. This decision meant that Irish forestry policy would be controlled from London. The removal of forestry from the DATI was rather surprising, particularly as Ireland was about to achieve self-government, but it gave Dáil Éireann an opportunity to develop a forestry programme that would not be in competition with the DATI.

Barton seems to have been especially enthusiastic about forestry, perhaps because of his Wicklow background. He established a separate forestry committee, and W. I. Cole was appointed inspector of forestry. Between 31 July and 1 November 1919 the forestry committee met five times to organise Arbour Day, held on 1 November 1919. Enormous numbers of evergreen and deciduous trees – horse chestnut, beech, elm, sycamore, willow, Norway spruce, larch and Scotch pine – were despatched to local railway stations for planting by schools, clergy and other interested parties.[73] In June 1920 Cole estimated that between 250,000 and 300,000 trees had been planted.[74] Each farmer was encouraged to plant sixteen trees, one for each of the men executed in 1916.[75]

O'Connor adopted a more cautious approach, concentrating on the conservation of timber stocks rather than engaging in mass planting. He told the Dáil that, 'To attempt reafforestation in a state of war is as fruitless as setting a tent in the teeth of a gale'.[76] He showed no enthusiasm for a second Arbour Day, and, while wishing to protect mature woodland, emphasised that it was not automatically a crime to cut mature trees. O'Connor believed that establishing a school of forestry training should be the first priority, but the Dáil failed to allocate money for this purpose.[77]

Staffing the Dáil Ministry of Agriculture

All the ministries of Dáil Éireann were tiny operations, working out of obscure offices in Dublin's city centre. The Ministry of Agriculture had its offices in a couple of rooms over a tailor's shop in North Earl Street. Kevin O'Sheil described these offices as 'in the centre of the city war zone, with frequent raids and arrests'. In November 1921 it moved to two floors over Bewley's tearooms in Westmoreland Street, a much more peaceful part of the city,[78] where a room was also provided for the Ministry of Fisheries. According to Leon Ó Broin (a future secretary of the Department of Posts and Telegraphs), who joined the Ministry of Agriculture in November 1921,

Art O'Connor, 'the chubby, good-looking and good-humoured TD', who was the Director, dealt personally with the strictly agricultural correspondence, with the surreptitious assistance of Dan Twomey, who was an inspector in the DATI, and a future secretary of the Department of Agriculture under the Irish Free State. Ó Broin claimed that there was 'precious little correspondence of that character'.

The first member of the Ministry's staff was appointed in June 1920 – typist Kathleen Devany. Gearóid McGann was appointed secretary in August, and on 20 October 1920 O'Connor notified Collins, the Minister for Finance, that Seosamh Ó Broin had been appointed as registrar of the Land Settlement Commission. Seosamh Ó Broin and McGann were placed on an identical salary of £320–£330 per annum. When Seosamh Ó Broin was interned in Ballykinlar, his place was taken by Leo Quinn, but it is not clear how long he remained with the Ministry.

On 29 August the Accountant General notified Art O'Connor that Henry O'Connor had joined the Ministry's staff. Leon Ó Broin has described Henry O'Connor as 'a tall young Protestant barrister, who wore spats and smoked cigars'. He was responsible for registering the agreements that had been worked out by the Dáil Land Settlement Commissioners. Leon Ó Broin mentioned that the commission was given part-time assistance by Martin Heavey of the Valuation Commission, although Heavey had apparently stepped down from this position by 30 June 1921.[79] O'Sheil and Maguire were described as circuit court judges. They had been assigned, at their own request, to the Land Settlement Commission, but they also sat on occasions in other courts.[80] A return of officers attached to the Aireacht Talamhuidheachta, or the Agricultural Department, signed by Patrick Hogan in February 1922, states that Maguire had been appointed 'about 1 October 1920'.[81]

The Ministry had few staff other than those who were engaged in the Land Settlement Commission. By August 1921 Gearóid McGann was described as assistant secretary to the Ministry. McGann later transferred to work with de Valera, and Leon Ó Broin took over most of his duties, with the rank of clerk, and was also involved in the activities of the Land Settlement Commission. In his memoirs Ó Broin describes a trip to Galway where he acted as registrar for the land commissioner Alec (Conor A.) Maguire. The remainder of the staff consisted of two secretaries (one was Eibhlín de Barra, a sister of Kevin Barry); a messenger; and an agricultural inspector, John Gould. The modest sum assigned to the Ministry of Agriculture in the Estimates of Dáil Éireann for the calendar year 1921,

£8,840,[82] taken with the small number of staff, confirms that the Ministry concentrated on land rather than agricultural matters.

THE DATI DURING THE ANGLO-IRISH WAR

The general election in November 1918, which led to the establishment of Dáil Éireann, saw the return of a coalition government in Britain, dominated by Conservative and unionist MPs, under the premiership of Lloyd George. Hugh Barrie, an Ulster unionist MP for North Londonderry, was appointed vice-president of the DATI.

Barrie was a successful grain merchant, who had led the Ulster unionist delegation at the Irish Convention (which the British government had summoned in 1917 in an unsuccessful attempt to solve the Irish question), and had earned the respect of Lloyd George.[83] A former member of the Council of Agriculture, Barrie had denounced Russell's attitude towards the IAOS.[84] (Russell died in 1920, and in the vote of sympathy passed by the Council of Agriculture in May 1920, one speaker described him as 'A Scotchman by birth, an Irishman by adoption ... [who] became more Irish than most Irishmen'.) Barrie kept a low profile. He was absent from the twice-yearly meeting of the Council of Agriculture in November 1919, when T. P. Gill took his place. His absence may well have been deliberate given the tense political situation.

In May 1919 T. P. Gill informed the Council of Agriculture that he planned to resign as he had reached the age of sixty. He relented, however, when the Council asked him to remain until a new administration had been established, and he remained a member of the DATI for several years after the founding of the Irish Free State. As a former nationalist MP, Gill was much more sympathetic to Irish nationalism than most other senior officials of the Dublin Castle administration, who tended to be either English or Scottish by birth or from Anglo-Irish families.[85] This may explain why the DATI weathered the years of the Anglo-Irish war comparatively successfully. The final report of the DATI, for 1930/1, remarked that it had originally been constituted so 'that the interest and responsibility of the people themselves ... should be engaged in its work'. For this reason, 'the "Department" enjoyed a very large measure of popularity, so that even in the disturbed years immediately preceding the establishment of Saorstát Éireann, its work went on uninterruptedly throughout the country'.[86]

A comparison between the experience of the DATI and the Local

Government Board, another government agency that operated throughout provincial Ireland, highlights the nature of the DATI's success. Most county councils severed all contact with the Local Government Board after the local elections in June 1920, but the county committees of agriculture, whose members were appointed by the same county councils, remained in regular contact with the DATI. Although the importance of agriculture was undoubtedly one factor, the behaviour of the DATI was also important. Whereas the Local Government Board had adopted an antagonistic attitude towards Sinn Féin-controlled local authorities, setting out to deprive them of income and attempting to re-establish the board's authority as an expression of British rule in Ireland, the DATI adopted a much more conciliatory approach.

Creameries and Fairs

The DATI may also have benefited from the perception that it did not approve of the ban imposed by the British authorities on markets and fairs, and the destruction of creameries by Crown forces. It became quite common for the British authorities to ban markets and fairs in areas where there was widespread cattle-driving or armed demonstrations. The first bans were imposed early in 1918 and the bans continued to be imposed from then until the truce in July 1921, much to the distress of farmers and the annoyance of local traders. Initially the bans were introduced in an attempt to curb public demonstrations, but they were subsequently used as a form of reprisal in areas where republican forces were active.

The DATI was concerned at the impact of the bans on the livestock trade. On 15 November 1919 Gill forwarded a request to the Under-Secretary from the residents of Roscrea asking permission to hold a fair, with a note stating that the DATI supported their request. When a fair was held without incident on 29 November, he supported the town's demand to resume regular fairs. It would appear that Gill intervened on Roscrea's behalf without the knowledge of Barrie, the vice-president.[87]

In November 1919 a group of County Clare farmers, who were members of the Anglo-Irish landlord class, including Lord Inchiquin, Sir Michael O'Loghlen, G. de L. Willis and the ubiquitous O'Callaghan Westropp, demanded the immediate lifting of the ban on markets and fairs in County Clare. They informed the DATI that, although they were most unwilling to attack the government's policy in public, they were close to doing so. The DATI drafted a reply to this letter, expressing the hope that the prohibition on fairs could be lifted, 'because the restrictions constitute a very serious interference with the agricultural trade of the communities concerned and hit hardest the decent, industrious section of the people', but the letter was not sent. A note on the file informs the secretary, Gill, that 'the Vice-President regrets he cannot see his way to approve this minute. He is afraid it would be rather strong for him to make representations which, in effect, amount to a criticism of the measures being taken to preserve life and property in certain disturbed parts of the country'. Barrie advised Gill that 'all that can be done' was to forward such resolutions to the Chief Secretary without comment. The Clare landowners were dissatisfied at the response to their protest and went public, as they had threatened. The story surfaced in the London *Times* in December 1919, under the headline 'Irish Official Blunder; Influential Protest'.[88]

Creameries were destroyed as a reprisal for IRA activity in a locality. Most attacks took place during the summer of 1920. On 28 August the DATI asked agricultural instructors to notify them of all attacks on creameries in their districts. On 30 August Thomas Scott, instructor in agriculture in County Limerick, reported that creameries at Knocklong, Rear Cross, Hospital, Upperchurch, Newport and Killonan had been attacked in recent weeks. On 2 September another Limerick instructor, M. Ward, informed the DATI that the creameries at Newcastle West and Shanagolden had been destroyed; the fire at Shanagolden destroyed three months' stock of cheese. By 2 September it was reported that nineteen creameries or separating stations in counties Tipperary, Limerick and Clare had been wholly or partly destroyed. The cost of the damage varied, from £493 at Kilcommon and £720 at Hospital to over £1,000 at Dombanna and £10,000 at Garryspillane. Damage to five creameries belonging to the Condensed Milk Company was estimated at over £24,000.

Horace Plunkett sent a strong protest to the government, and the Chief Secretary, Sir Hamar Greenwood, promised that efforts would be made to track down the culprits. Yet, in October, Greenwood defended the creamery burnings in the House of Commons, suggesting that the Crown forces had acted in self-defence. General Macready, commander of the British army in Ireland, claimed that the troops who destroyed Newport creamery had been provoked by an attack carried out by rebels hiding in the creamery. Plunkett gave evidence at Nenagh Quarter Sessions on behalf of Newport Co-operative Society, when it attempted to recover £12,349 in damages from the Crown. He claimed that the general credit of the co-operative movement had been severely damaged. Co-operatives would be forced to insure their property against risks that they had never anticipated.

Plunkett regarded Newport as a test case, and hoped the government would respond generously; the creamery was awarded a decree of £12,349 against the Crown. Yet, within days, the British forces had destroyed Kildimo creamery, County Clare, and several creameries in north Kerry. Although most of the destruction took place in the leading dairying counties of Limerick, Tipperary, Clare, north Kerry and Cork, which were also the most active areas in the Anglo-Irish war, the Crown forces also destroyed creameries in Donegal and Sligo. Sir Hamar Greenwood claimed that the manager of one of the Sligo creameries was known to be 'one of the extreme Sinn Féiners'. In November 1921 R. A. Anderson, the secretary of the IAOS, claimed that each creamery that was destroyed put 800 farmers out of business, and in December *The Irish Homestead* estimated that the cost of the damage inflicted on forty-two creameries amounted to £215,000, and the list was not yet closed. Tuaree creamery, Glin, County Limerick, was the target in January 1921, and a further ten creameries were attacked in the following weeks, the majority in Limerick and north Kerry. Although the burning of creameries had ceased by the summer of 1921, creameries continued to be closed by military order. In June 1921 M. Commons, an instructor, informed the DATI that nine creameries had been closed in Limerick and North Tipperary.[89]

Creamery burnings placed the DATI in a difficult position. In November 1920 the Chief Secretary's office asked the DATI to compile details of the creameries that had been attacked, and they complied, while emphasising that their's was not an official record. In January 1921, following an office conference, it was decided that instructors should continue to keep the DATI informed about attacks on creameries. They were also asked to give whatever assistance they could in repairing or reconstructing damaged creameries. However, Poole Wilson, an inspector of dairying, warned that instructors 'should be most careful not to convey any impression that they were acting as valuers of damage done and the cost of replacement'. It was eventually decided that instructors could prepare a plan and specifications for rebuilding a creamery. If these documents were used as a basis for claiming compensation, the DATI could not be held responsible. When Cope, of the Chief Secretary's office, contacted the DATI in April 1921, with a request that it supply details of the number of creameries in Ireland, the number destroyed or damaged and the number rebuilt, the DATI referred him to the IAOS.[90]

Many of the damaged creameries were still out of commission early in 1922. According to James Douglas, a Dublin businessman, who was a director of the Irish White Cross Association (an organisation that provided relief for victims of the Anglo-Irish war), no efforts had been made to reconstruct several of the damaged premises; other creameries that had reopened were struggling owing to lack of capital or machinery. Farmers in mountainous areas of North Tipperary were forced to transport milk for up to ten miles, owing to the destruction of the Newport creamery. Many had reverted to making butter at home, although Douglas feared that they would not find a market for this butter.[91]

The DATI and the County Committees of Agriculture

In the past many county committees of agriculture had expressed resentment at undue central control. The rise of a more militant nationalism gave new life to this point of view, as did resentment at compulsory tillage and other wartime restrictions. In August 1918, some months before the general election, an official in County Limerick reported to Gill that the attitude of many members of the county committee of agriculture at a recent meeting was 'unsympathetic and hostile to the Department'.[92] In February 1919 Cork County Council voted not to strike an agricultural rate, 'as a protest against the treatment of this county by the Government' and as a protest at the recent appointment of Ulster unionist MP, Hugh Barrie, as vice-president of the DATI. A. O'Sullivan, an instructor in Mallow, claimed that the protest had been orchestrated 'by persons who had always been antagonistic to the Department', and this is confirmed by the tone of the debate at the county council. J. O'Mahony, who seconded the motion, argued that, 'Too long they had shown themselves abject slaves of Russell and those others who had been appointed by the Government to those Departments, and who had characterised their administration by sheer extravagance'.[93] Allegations of extravagance were a common feature of Sinn Féin rhetoric. They offered a neat way of reconciling demands for lower taxes and claims for additional services.

Cork County Council was informed that their failure to strike an agricultural rate meant that the DATI could not legally contribute to any agricultural scheme in the county. (One of the requirements in the Local Government Act of 1899 was that all schemes must include a contribution from the local authority.) On 10 March E. Corcoran, of the Cork County Committee of Agriculture, wrote to F. J. Meyrick, a staff clerk who became secretary of the Department in 1923, expressing the hope that the Cork decision would be reversed. He claimed that most councillors had not been aware of the consequences of refusing to strike a rate. On 13 March the county council voted by thirty-four votes to two to strike a rate of 1s 2d in the pound for agricultural services.[94]

Threats by Cork and other county councils not to strike an agricultural rate gave rise to particular anxiety among the instructors, because the withdrawal of funds by the DATI threatened their security of employment. In March 1919 their association demanded an urgent meeting with the vice-president, Hugh Barrie, to press their demand for some guarantee of security of employment. Although the meeting was prompted by the action in Cork, this was a long-standing grievance. The first record of representations to the DATI on this matter is in 1905. Instructors were appointed from year to year, because all county schemes depended on the annual agricultural rate, but they were generally reappointed without difficulty and the DATI did not believe that this arrangement jeopardised their job security.[95] By 1919, however, their position was more vulnerable, owing to the founding of Dáil Éireann, and the DATI became more sympathetic to their demands. Representatives of the instructors' association pressed their case in a meeting with Barrie and senior officials of the DATI.

> We want to be allowed to carry on our respective duties without being interfered with by Local Authorities, by the Department, or by any other bodies, provided always we give satisfactory service. We want to be regarded – as practically all other public servants are regarded – as holding permanent positions. We want to be relieved of all those embarrassing incidents which threaten our means of livelihood, take all the heart out of us for work and render our outlook on the future miserable and uncertain. What can be expected from any public servant who is in yearly dread of being deprived of his post through no fault of his own, through no defects in the Scheme but simply through the whims of some public representative.[96]

They outlined many instances where county councils had suspended the rate in aid of agriculture for political reasons, such as a soldier in uniform attending a class in a Cork technical school. Officials were forced 'to resort to the degrading and disgusting practice of canvassing the Members [of the county committees]' in order to have the rate restored. They urged that local authorities should be deprived of the right not to strike such a rate. If there was any uncertainty over striking a rate in 1919, they feared that farmers would be reluctant to commit themselves to schemes such as the purchase of a premium bull, because they could not be sure of receiving a subsidy. Frizell, secretary of the Wexford County Committee of Agriculture, expressed fears that within a year 'there may be a different class of councillor on the local bodies' than in the past. The agricultural rate should be made compulsory before this happened.

Gill told the deputation that the DATI was pressing the Treasury for the introduction of a superannuation scheme, but that, although he was sympathetic to instructors' demands, setting a permanent rate was not 'practical politics'. Barrie informed the deputation that imposing a compulsory rate would be 'most undemocratic', although obviously desirable; he would support the idea 'if public opinion could be educated up to that point'. Any attempt to introduce a compulsory rate in 1919 would have doomed the DATI's chances of remaining on good terms with nationalist local authorities, and made matters worse for the instructors.

Sinn Féin captured control of twenty-eight of the thirty-three county councils in the local elections held in June 1920. Barrie had anticipated such a result; in autumn 1919 he had expressed the wish that the local elections might be postponed for some months in the hope that sanity might prevail (there is no evidence that the British authorities contemplated doing this).[97] Having captured the county councils, Sinn Féin was now in a position to determine the composition of the county committees of agriculture. The local elections in the summer of 1920 marked the beginning of a policy of non-co-operation with the Local Government Board, which was signalled by various acts of defiance such as dismissing the treasurer to the county council (a local bank that had been formally appointed by the Lord Lieutenant), instructing rate collectors to lodge money in secret accounts and not in the official account, and refusing to have their accounts audited by the Local Government Board auditor.[98]

When county councils broke off contact with the Local Government Board on the instruction of Dáil Éireann, the question of severing connections with the DATI was also raised. County committees of agriculture were required to submit their accounts for audit by an officer appointed by the DATI. At some unspecified date before mid-September 1920, Art O'Connor presented a memorandum to the Dáil Ministry of Agriculture urging county committees to make a 'clean break' (the term used to refer to the formal breach between the local authorities and the Local Government Board) with the DATI. He presented five reasons in support of this recommendation: some can be described as political, or quasi-political; the remainder were based on a fundamental criticism of the *modus operandi* of the DATI.

O'Connor acknowledged that the DATI was doing its utmost to continue to work with the county committees, but he was suspicious of its motives. He suggested that the DATI had set out to subvert the county committees of agriculture by adopting a friendly attitude even towards hostile committees, offering them additional funds and relaxing traditional red tape. Although officials in the DATI probably wished to remain on good terms with the county committees, O'Connor believed that the Treasury would withdraw all grants to rebel local authorities. The break between the county councils and the Local Government Board had made it 'intolerable' for county committees of agriculture to do business with an 'English Department'.

O'Connor rehearsed many of the traditional criticisms that nationalists had levelled against the DATI. He claimed that under the present legislation neither the council or board of Agriculture nor the county committees had any real authority over the financing or administration of agricultural schemes or local appointments. According to O'Connor, 'its [the DATI's] passing would occasion few regrets'. In spite of the 'huge sums' that it disposed of, the DATI 'has never really caught the grip of the Irish Agriculturist … it has never been clear of the suspicion of putting English interests first when a clash came'. County committees could provide services that were at least as effective as those currently provided by the DATI, with only a marginal increase in the agricultural rate. The only argument in favour of retaining links with the DATI was the fear that the 'English' Board of Agriculture would ban imports of Irish cattle if they were not inspected by recognised officials.

O'Connor went through the 1920/1 estimates for the DATI, distinguishing the few services that he regarded as effective. The items that he classified as ineffective included all salaries, wages and travel expenses; grants in aid of agricultural education; schemes to eradicate tuberculosis in cattle; the £3,270 allocated for experiments in tobacco; the Agricultural Wages Board; fishery development; most of the money spent in connection with food production; and expenditure relating to the resettlement of ex-soldiers on the land. The list of effective services was considerably shorter: less than half the sum allocated for agricultural statistics; one-third of the expenditure on food production; land purchase in connection with afforestation; animal disease; milk production; and miscellaneous developments.

The broad outlines of an alternative agricultural service can be construed from this document. County committees and their staff would be retained, but the committees would apparently be free from central supervision. The cost of agricultural services would be met from the rates, 'if not through State Grants'. Agricultural education would be concentrated in primary schools. Afforestation would be given high priority. Although tuberculosis in cattle was an extremely serious matter, 'it might be allowed to stand for a year or so'. Animal inspection was an essential service, as were measures to protect and enforce Irish trade marks on dairy and poultry exports. Instruction in agriculture would be given 'on a centrally-situated farm run on farming and business lines'; 'the day of itinerant instruction seems over'. Instructors would be redeployed to collect agricultural statistics (a task formerly carried out by the RIC), 'with great profit to the State and little loss to the Farmers'. Dáil Éireann (or perhaps the county committees) would continue to provide financial assistance towards local agricultural shows, since the money 'is always pretty well spent' and the shows were extremely popular. It would be unwise to withdraw support, especially as 'The English Department played on this string this year very extensively to try to recapture some of its lost prestige'.

O'Connor's report had three major weaknesses: the assumption that county committees of agriculture would be able or willing to provide a full range of agricultural services with little or no supervision; the belief that many existing schemes could be abandoned without opposition; and the question of funding. O'Connor skated lightly over this last subject. He began by assuming that the cost of agricultural services could be reduced from over £650,000 to £115,000, a sum that could be raised by a rate of 2d in the pound, or four times the current agricultural rate. This was unrealistic, since most local authorities were finding it extremely difficult to collect the existing rate demands. On this point O'Connor conceded that if the counties could not meet the full cost, 'it could easily be adjusted as to what proportion the Committee would send to the Central Executive Government for Common National Estimates'.[99] Again, this begs the question, where would Dáil Éireann find the money.

On 17 September 1920 O'Connor informed Dáil Éireann that although he had recommended 'the clean cut with the British Department of Agriculture', he was unwilling to see the county committees of agriculture lapse, because they had fostered an export trade worth £64 million in 1919.[100] The Dáil's attitude towards the DATI and the radical impulse in favour of a clean break was tempered by such considerations, as was the attitude of the Cabinet. In October 1920 Diarmaid Ó hEigeartaigh, the secretary to the Ministry (Cabinet), and a former private secretary to T. P. Gill,[101] informed O'Connor, who was not a member of the Cabinet, that at its next meeting the Cabinet would discuss whether the county committees should submit their books for audit 'by Departments of the enemy Government'.[102] At this time the Cabinet was attempting to enforce a policy of complete non-cooperation between the local authorities and the Local Government Board, and it was extremely unforgiving towards any councils that did not comply.[103] Nevertheless, no decision was made about auditing the books of the county committees of agriculture. On 15 November Art O'Connor and W. T. Cosgrave, the Minister for Local Government, were asked to draft a scheme that would enable the Dáil to provide for the county committees of agriculture for the next six months. On 29 November Ó hEigeartaigh informed Joseph McDonagh, TD, that the Cabinet had considered the matter 'at several meetings recently. ... the general feeling is that they should not be allowed to do so [submit their accounts for audit by auditors appointed by the British authorities] provided that the essential services administered by these Committees can be kept going in the absence of the Departmental Grant'. In the opinion of the Dáil Ministry of Agriculture, a lot of the DATI's expenditure was wasted, although this criticism was mainly directed at technical education committees. It also acknowledged that some essential services should be maintained, specifically the Diseases of Animals Acts.[104] (It is rather ironic, therefore, that one of the first economies introduced by local authorities was an end to sheep-dipping.)

On 20 November the Cabinet received a report from Cosgrave and O'Connor, recommending that the county committees of agriculture should continue to work with the DATI. The decision was based entirely on financial considerations. The annual cost of essential agricultural and technical instruction schemes was estimated at £273,000. 'We have no hestitation in saying that local Authorities could not provide this sum or half of same and we could not recommend that provision be made in the next years (sic) estimate for the cost of these services'. This report was much less sanguine as to the competence and commitment of the county committees; it suggested that some form of central direction was essential. At present the Dáil Ministry of Agriculture was unable to put an alternative agricultural scheme into effect. 'Enemy interference would destroy its organisation in the Country and its collapse would seriously affect our prestige'. They 'regretfully recommend[ed] carrying on as heretofore'. While there should be no break with the DATI, supporters of Dáil Éireann should attempt to gain control of the board and council of Agriculture, when the existing council stepped down in March 1921, and they should use these agencies to modify agricultural policies.

By November 1920, when this report was drafted, county councils were finding it increasingly difficult to sustain the policy of non-co-operation with the Local Government Board, and local services were on the point of collapse owing to lack of money. Several county councils had begun to retreat from the position of total intransigence, at least to the extent of reappointing their official treasurers. In the light of the difficulties councils were experiencing, it would have been foolhardy to aggravate the financial crisis by breaking with the DATI, especially as the DATI's officials were adopting a conciliatory approach. On 11 December it was decided that composite committees (of agriculture and technical instuction) might submit their books for audit. Meanwhile, a sub-committee would investigate the feasibility of county councils meeting the cost of agricultural services. In January 1921 O'Connor admitted to Dáil Éireann that he was relieved that the Cabinet had not followed his advice to break with the DATI. In a veiled threat to any militant county committee, he emphasised that refusing an audit, 'which had no sinister motive behind it', could not be justified, given that it would entail a loss of grants amounting to four or five times the sum provided by the local rate in aid of agricultural services.[105]

The DATI went to considerable efforts not to create problems for the county committees. The report of the DATI for 1920/1 refers to 'King's County (Offaly)' and 'Queen's County (Laois)', an acknowledgement that both counties had changed their names when the Sinn Féin-controlled councils met in the summer of 1920.[106] Moreover, in contrast to the Local Government Board, the DATI made no objections when Leitrim County Committee of Agriculture dismissed the Northern Bank as its treasurer in compliance with the Belfast boycott,[107] and it abandoned the requirement that instructors had to be re-appointed annually by the county committees.[108] County committees of agriculture had viewed this as another example of vexatious departmental control. In March 1920 Roscommon County Committee of Agriculture passed a motion stating that 'we intend the appointment of our Instructors as permanent and request the Department not to ask us in future to go through what we regard as the empty formality of making an annual re-appointment'. This decision may have been influenced by the possibility that some instructors might be removed from office as a result of the revolution in Irish local politics: any instructor who lost his job would find it difficult to obtain compensation for loss of office if he or she was subject to annual re-appointment, and their right to a pension under the Local Government Act of 1919 would also be in jeopardy.[109] When Kerry County Committee of Agriculture passed a resolution in May

1921, asking whether it was necessary to reappoint instructors every year, the DATI replied that it did not consider it was.[110]

The conciliatory attitude adopted by the DATI paid dividends. In January 1921 O'Connor informed the Dáil that most county committees of agriculture were functioning as usual. Although one or two had threatened not to strike a rate in aid of agriculture, all councils struck their usual rate for 1919/20 and 1920/1, and they remained in regular communication with the DATI. This was true even of the counties most active in the Anglo-Irish war.[111] The Sinn Féin takeover of local government does not appear to have brought any dramatic changes in this respect.

In November 1920, when the Anglo-Irish war had escalated, Kerry County Committee of Agriculture submitted its plans for the coming year to the DATI. It proposed to spend less on the cottage and farm prize scheme and on nominations for brood mares, and more on poultry and administration. Other county committees of agriculture behaved in a similar manner. A reader, unaware of the conditions in Ireland at the time, would conclude from the general tone of the correspondence between the county committees and the DATI that conditions throughout the country were quite normal.[112] During 1921/2 all county committees administered approved schemes for improving cattle and swine breeds; twelve counties provided prizes for cottages and small farms (much the same number as in previous years); and twenty operated horse-breeding schemes.[113]

Other aspects of the work of the DATI continued as before. Throughout 1919 and 1920 the DATI devoted considerable time to investigating allegations by Irish suppliers that they were being treated unfairly by salesmen at London's Smithfield market. Officials organised a meeting between Irish consignors of eggs and dead meat and representatives of the London Central Markets committee, to discuss what could be done to improve the handling of Irish produce. They attempted, without much success, to enlist the assistance of the British Ministry of Agriculture,[114] and they continued the thankless effort of developing an export market for Irish cheese.[115] In 1921 the DATI announced a new grant scheme to encourage research in agricultural science.

The Agricultural Policy of the Dáil Ministry of Agriculture

One explanation for the apparently untroubled relations between the Dáil Ministry of Agriculture and the DATI is that they were not in direct competition. The Dáil Ministry concentrated on land settlement, arbitration and forestry. According to Leon Ó Broin, the Dáil Ministry received very little correspondence of a strictly agricultural nature,[116] and what there was was of a very varied nature.

One man in Kanturk requested information about new methods of producing dried milk (he had read something in the newspaper); a correspondent from Borrisoleigh protested that he was 'not getting fair play' from his local creamery. Thomas Gleeson from Cratloe in Clare asked whether the Ministry printed 'any of the leaflets like the English [sic] Department of Agriculture'. Somebody involved in the egg trade in Portadown presented the Ministry with a detailed analysis of the religious and political affiliations of the DATI poultry section, complaining that the DATI preferred to hire Methodists and Freemasons. A correspondent in Newry suspected that the DATI's recent diagnosis of black scab on potatoes in his area, which led to exports being suspended, was politically motivated. The Knights of Columbanus in Lurgan wished to develop a trade for local farm produce at the Dublin market, 'to make them independent of the bigots'. A man requesting information about sowing winter barley was informed that the Ministry could provide no recommendations. A farmer in Banteer in County Cork sent Art O'Connor a copy of his farm accounts for 1920. Most correspondence consisted of resolutions from farming and labouring organisations concerning the price of butter or the need for more tillage.[117]

Sinn Féin believed that provisioning the home market should take priority over exports, and that the export of live cattle should be discouraged in order to develop an export trade in dressed meat. In October 1919, after the arrest of Ernest Blythe, the Director of Trade and Commerce, Barton and the Agriculture Committee assumed responsibility for promoting the dead meat trade. There were plans to establish a co-operative meat-processing factory in Waterford, similar to a plant that had opened in Wexford in 1912. A leaflet produced to drum up support for this venture mentioned that it was essential that meat-processing plants should be run on a co-operative basis; otherwise, the industry would be controlled by large meat trusts, as had happened in the United States. Work on the Waterford plant was postponed because of fears that it would be destroyed by the British authorities.[118]

In 1918 the acreage under crops and horticulture was greater than at any time since the 1870s, but by 1919 it had declined by almost one-seventh, leaving many rural labourers unemployed. Sinn Féin had long believed that tillage farming was good and cattle farming bad, so it is not surprising that in the summer of 1919 deputies demanded that the Director of Agriculture make some statement on this matter. They also asked that efforts be made to prevent Irish agricultural labourers from migrating to seasonal jobs in Britain.[119] In July 1919 the Agriculture Committee urged Barton to warn the public about the danger of food shortages. At its September meeting the committee discussed the possibility of establishing national granaries and facilities for drying grain.[120] There is no evidence of any serious shortage of grain; the campaign may well have been prompted more by security considerations. There was a further decline in tillage during 1920, and in October 1920 David Kent, TD, proposed to introduce a Corn Production Bill, making it compulsory for all landholders to put under cultivation as much of the land 'as will ensure a sufficient supply of food for the people of this country'. He proposed that those with less than fifty acres should cultivate 10 per cent; between 50 and 100 acres, 15 per cent; and larger holdings, 20 per cent. Financial penalties should be imposed on those who failed to meet these requirements. In his report of August 1921 O'Connor noted laconically that Kent's 'unfortunate arrest by the enemy prevented the many interesting points in his Bill from being discussed'.[121]

The first official communication from the Dáil Ministry of Agriculture to the county committees of agriculture was issued in November 1920. It began by saying that, while there was no cause for alarm about food supplies, the county committees should take contingency steps in case of a failure of the potato crop. The county committees were urged to encourage farmers to devote 'a small percentage' of land to wheat 'as a National Duty if other considerations fail to impress him'. A list of detailed instructions followed: potatoes should be lifted and stored as soon as possible; potatoes fit for human consumption should not be fed to pigs; meal, swedes and palm nut cake should be used as pig-feed; seed potatoes should be secured as soon as possible; instructors should advise farmers on the most suitable varieties of wheat. All farmers were expected to grow wheat. Indifferent farmers – a term that would appear to refer to farmers who were indifferent to their national duty to grow wheat – would not be permitted to shelve their responsibilities by arguing that their land was not suitable; 'each type of land has its affinity in wheat which a little intelligent inquiry can discover'. Farmers should be reassured that any difficulties in milling their crops would be surmounted.[122]

This circular may be regarded as an attempt to defuse pressure for the introduction of compulsory tillage. In August 1921 O'Connor told the Dáil that during 1920, at a time when he believed 'we were in for a very prolonged war', he had drafted a bill providing for increased production of corn, which included an element of compulsion, but he was arrested 'before the Session came on'. No trace of this bill survives, and his claim seems improbable, because in a report outlining the work of the Dáil Ministry of Agriculture up to December 1920, O'Connor expressed his opposition to compulsion, 'as the majority of our people have a loathing for compulsion and compulsion creates a necessity for control which would be very difficult to exercise in the present circumstances'. He asked for suggestions as to how to achieve an expansion in tillage: some scheme was needed 'to rid us of the spectre of Unemployment'.[123] In March 1921 O'Connor reported that unemployment had become more acute in recent months; he was putting forward proposals, which he hoped would yield results.[124] The nature of these proposals remains unknown. In August he noted that tillage was 'giving us a great deal of uneasiness lately'; wheat seemed to be 'going out of cultivation'; potatoes and oats were scarce. In a few years, 'this country will be nothing else but a wilderness on which cattle will be browsing'. This assessment was based on the response to a circular that the Dáil Ministry had issued to every agricultural instructor in Ireland in July 1921. The overwhelming majority of instructors responded, including instructors with addresses in counties Antrim, Tyrone and Fermanagh, although one respondent from County Antrim did not give his name. The report submitted by an instructor in Listowel, County Kerry, described how agriculture had been disrupted by both economic factors and the state of the country:

> The area under crops generally is considerably reduced. This is due partly to the disturbed state of the county and also to the fact that a good deal of the land broken up under the tillage order has again been laid out to grass. The prospects of cheaper imported food stuffs and the continued high prices for artificial manures has also something to do with it. The labour difficulty also was another factor. Many of those who in the ordinary course would be working steadily on their farms could not do so while many again would not work near to or along certain roads. I am informed also by merchants that the amounts of artificial manures bought this year is considerably less than usual. This indicates a smaller tillage area, but it may also to some extent be due to the cost and the difficulty of getting them owing to the many stoppages of railway services.[125]

Falling agricultural prices and the reduction in tillage resulted in higher unemployment and pressure from farmers for a reduction in agricultural wages, while labourers' representatives demanded that the Dáil provide either land or work.[126] Unemployed farm workers were reported to be flocking to the towns, although no work was available. In August 1921 O'Connor told the Dáil that 'the attitude of big farmers to the little farmers, and of farm-workers to all farmers is frequently one which requires the most careful and delicate handling from those in control of affairs'. He suggested that the best solution was to give them access to land, so that they could support themselves and avoid becoming 'a burden on the community and a menace to the well-being of the State'. He would prefer that the access to land was resolved on a voluntary rather than a compulsory basis. This threat may have been an attempt to persuade farmers to hire more labourers: he mentioned that a bill to increase the cultivated acreage was being prepared, and in the meantime he appealed to farmers 'not to wait for compulsion, but to produce as much food as they can to enable us to win the war'.[127] O'Connor also invoked patriotism, noting that 'at no period in our history did Patriotism demand more insistently that tillage be kept up than now'; it was essential to ensure that Ireland would be in a position to withstand a blockade by Britain. If patriotism failed, he would endorse the use of 'moral suasion' in the form of boycotting and an embargo on bringing cattle to market.[128] During the autumn of 1921 he attempted to convene a meeting between farmer and labourer representatives, in the hope of establishing a conciliation committee 'to arrive at an understanding between Farmers and Workers so that Tillage may continue and Unemployment be avoided'.[129]

In November 1921 the IFU asked O'Connor to arrange a meeting with de Valera; it wanted to inform him of the indignities that had been heaped on farmers by 'certain men'. There is no indication that this meeting took place, although on 8 December 1921 the executive of the IFU and the ITGWU met to discuss how agriculture could be assisted to survive 'the present critical time by reconcilement of the various costs and incidentally to keep down Unemployment'.[130] This was two days after the Treaty had been signed, and it would appear that the efforts at conciliation evaporated in the political uncertainty that followed. In November 1921 the Cabinet proposed the establishment of a food committee to be controlled by the Minister for Economic Affairs, Robert Barton. Barton noted that no terms of reference were suggested; in his opinion 'any attempt to interfere with the normal conflict of economic forces by governmental control of the prices of food commodities would be a very dangerous policy to adopt at the present time'. A later memorandum suggested that the food committee would have a purely advisory role: it would assemble information on the state of food supplies, both domestic and imported, and it would devise a scheme of local administrative committees in the event of a disruption in central communications owing to the resumption of the Anglo-Irish war.[131]

The Dáil and the Council of Agriculture

The Dáil Ministry of Agriculture was slow to determine what attitude to adopt towards the Council of Agriculture and the Board of Agriculture. As these bodies were partly elected, it should have been possible for Sinn Féin to capture control after the 1920 local elections. When Cosgrave and O'Connor recommended against breaking with the DATI in November 1920, they suggested that Dáil supporters should follow this strategy. In March 1921 Cosgrave informed the Dáil that he had taken steps to see that the county councils elected the best representatives to the Council of Agriculture, in the hope that they might gain control. If this was achieved, 'some very interesting things were bound to happen'. He gave a commitment that a definite policy for republican representatives would be formulated before the next meeting of the council in May 1921.[132]

By this point the Government of Ireland Act of 1920 was being implemented. The Act left open the possibility that agriculture would be handled by an all-Ireland organisation. The report of the Dáil Ministry of Agriculture dated May 1921 stated that 'it seems fairly certain' that the DATI would continue to function as a reserved service, that is, on an all-Ireland basis. It speculated that this would be done in order to prevent the emergence of an agricultural party in the Parliament of Northern Ireland, 'with its attendant troubles, but principally to keep a link with the rest of Ireland which is predominantly agricultural'. The Ministry believed that there was a distinct possibility that the Council of Agriculture would come under republican control, although it feared that the British authorities would vary the composition of the council (which was two-thirds elected and one-third nominated) in order to make it safe.[133] Given the uncertainty, O'Connor suggested that it was difficult to know what policy to pursue.

The minutes of the Council of Agriculture on 15 March 1921 suggest that many of those in attendance regarded it as the final gathering, and there was a nostalgic tone to the occasion, despite the fact that for a majority of its members this was their first meeting. New names included Professor Alfred O'Rahilly, of University College, Cork (UCC); P. J. Ruttledge of

Ballina (a future Fianna Fáil Minister); and J. J. Clancy of Sligo. Twelve of the eighteen nominees from Ulster councils, on the other hand, were unchanged. The meeting ended with an emotional speech by T. P. Gill and the following resolution.

> That this Board, representative of all parts of Ireland, desire to place on record the fact that for twenty-one years they have worked together in unbroken harmony, in discharging the responsible duties entrusted to them, and they venture to express the hope that under some arrangement or other, this useful and gratifying co-operation will not be wholly dispensed with in the future.[134]

The council and board of Agriculture went out of office on 31 March 1921. A new council should have been summoned in May, but this did not happen, presumably because of the uncertain political conditions. On 29 July 1921 the General Council of County Councils met to elect new members of the Council of Agriculture, and on 12 August Art O'Connor presided over a meeting of the council, which was attended by delegates of all county committees in the future Irish Free State and by two delegates from County Fermanagh, but none from the other counties of Northern Ireland.

O'Connor's address emphasised the continuity with earlier meetings of the Council of Agriculture. He announced that he would not follow 'the usual custom of making a long statement'. He referred to the first meeting of the council in 1900, and noted that the failure to convene a new council and a new board meant that the DATI's endowment fund was being handled by a body that was 'not representative of Ireland. ... you have been left like Mahomet's Coffin as far as agricultural control is concerned'. The agenda listed nine items for discussion, including food supplies, relations between farmers and workers, the marketing of agricultural produce, improving livestock, and agricultural education. However, the fragmentary minutes that survive refer only to constitutional matters and food supplies, and it is unclear whether the other items were discussed. Most of the time was spent discussing the attitude to be adopted towards the DATI. Dr Walsh, archbishop of Dublin, representing the Dublin County Committee of Agriculture, recommended that they should adopt 'a dignified attitude'. There was a lengthy discussion as to whether this council meeting had the legal authority to elect members of the Board of Agriculture. Many speakers expressed the view that unless the Council of Agriculture represented all Ireland it would be useless. Porter, a delegate from Fermanagh, noted that although he and his partner differed on politics, 'we do not allow politics to enter into agricultural matters'.[135]

The meeting failed to decide on a strategy if the DATI convened a meeting of either the council or the board. Gill summoned a meeting of the council for 8 November 1921, to be held in the usual venue, Leinster House. On 20 October O'Connor sent a circular to all Dáil Ministers reminding them of the functions of the council and the board of Agriculture, and noting that 'it is necessary to discover why it is now being convened and whether we should prohibit the Republican representatives of the County Councils from attending'. The fact that several members of the Cabinet were in London, negotiating the Anglo-Irish Treaty, appears to have added to the confusion. On 26 October Diarmaid Ó hEigeartaigh informed O'Connor that provided there were no objections from London, it had been decided that republican representatives should not attend the council meeting, 'as the Minister [O'Connor] reported the extreme improbability of securing control'. A note to this effect was given to de Valera, but O'Connor asked de Valera to reconsider this decision. T. P. Gill had contacted him, urging that republicans should attend: boycotting the council would mark a change in the Dáil's policy towards the DATI. Hitherto, the British authorities had made an exception of the DATI, 'chiefly because of the fact that the constitution of this Department is largely representative', and Gill suggested that it might be unwise to damage 'a body representing the whole of Ireland which is attended by the members from all the Ulster counties', and which conducted its meetings 'usually in a very harmonious manner'. Gill suggested that the meeting of the Council of Agriculture could become 'a great anti-Partition Demonstration', and it would appear that he gave O'Connor a commitment that republicans would secure seven of the twelve places on the board. If republicans boycotted the council meeting, the board would be improperly constituted, and as the board had to approve all expenditure, the DATI's monies would be forfeit.

Although the Cabinet reconsidered its decision in the light of the letters from Gill and O'Connor, it held to the view that republicans should boycott the Council of Agriculture. However, the letter drafted by Ó hEigeartaigh suggests that Cosgrave at least was in two minds on the matter, because it records his opinion that any financial loss caused by the withdrawal of the DATI's grants, 'would be so considerable as to cause unnecessary hardship'. Cosgrave only supported the decision to boycott the council because he believed that the republican representatives would not be of sufficient calibre to secure control.

A copy of the Cabinet's decision, dated 1 November 1921, was sent to the Irish delegates in London. On the same day, before they could possibly have been aware of Gill's letter or the recent Cabinet decision, Eamonn Price informed Ó hEigeartaigh that the Ministers in London were of the opinion that the Minister for Agriculture was best able to decide on the matter; if he was of the opinion that republican representatives should attend, 'the Ministers here feel that unless the question is regarded as one affecting a vital principle, the improbability that control of the Boards be secured need not be looked upon as an insurmountable reason for abstention'. On 3 November Price wrote to O'Connor and informed him that de Valera 'considers that the views of the Ministers in London are in favour of Republican abstention from the Council. He considers that the last paragraph in the letter [the paragraph leaving open the possibility of participation] should be discounted'.[136]

This would appear to indicate that de Valera was opposed to participating in the Council of Agriculture; he may have regarded attendance as unwise at such a sensitive moment in Anglo-Irish negotiations. This disagreement on whether or not to attend the Council of Agriculture anticipates the split over the Treaty, with the London delegates in favour of compromise and de Valera and the other Cabinet members in Dublin, other than Cosgrave, adopting a more militant position. Having failed to secure the attendance of Sinn Féin members, the DATI postponed the council meeting until a later date.[137] No further meeting took place.

THE GOVERNMENT OF IRELAND ACT, 1920

Although the introduction of Home Rule was postponed for the duration of World War I, during 1914 and 1915 discussions were held between senior members of the Irish Party and the Chief Secretary's office in Dublin Castle over the future shape of a Home Rule administration. Initially, the Irish Party wished to establish a combined department of agriculture and industries along the lines of the proposed department in the report of the Recess Committee. It later agreed to a separate ministry of industry, to reassure Ulster interests, who claimed that otherwise industry would take second place to agriculture. It then proposed a joint ministry of lands and agriculture, uniting the DATI and the responsibility for land purchase and distribution then being exercised by the CDB and the Land Settlement Commission.[138] These plans are of merely historical interest, although they may have influenced the structure of the department that was established by the Irish Free State. The Irish Convention, established in 1917 and chaired by Horace Plunkett, had even less influence on the shape of the new department: it only passed one resolution relating to agriculture, a motion urging the immediate introduction of a further scheme for land purchase.[139]

In the event, the Government of Ireland Act, passed in December 1920, provided for the establishment of separate administrations in Belfast and in Dublin, and a Council of Ireland with equal representation from north and south. In the original proposals for what may be regarded as the fourth Home Rule Bill, Walter Long, the Irish Chief Secretary, intended that responsibility for agriculture would not be devolved to the two governments, because he believed that it was more appropriate that it should be handled on an all-Ireland basis. The Council of Ireland would advise the United Kingdom authorities on agricultural matters for one year. After that date the DATI would be either partitioned or transferred to the Council of Ireland, if the governments in Dublin and Belfast were in agreement.[140] As we have already seen the Dáil Ministry of Agriculture believed, as late as March 1921, that this policy would prevail.

Although the plan not to partition agricultural services was abandoned, it indicates a realisation that both parts of Ireland had common interests concerning agriculture. Agriculture was eventually included among the services to be transferred to the new governments in Dublin and Belfast, but responsibility for fisheries and the administration of the Diseases of Animals Acts were reserved for the Council of Ireland, following an amendment in the House of Lords that went against the wishes of the government.[141]

Senior officials in the DATI received a circular from John Anderson, of the Treasury office in Dublin Castle, dated 29 March 1921, informing them that no date had yet been agreed for the transfer of services to the two new administrations. Although the estimates had provided the DATI with the necessary money for a full year (as if no change were taking place), officials were informed that 'it is obvious that the result will be an underspending'. In order to ensure that this was so, Gill sent a circular to the heads of the various offices under his control, such as the director of the National Museum and the registrar of the Royal College of Science, asking them to submit quarterly returns of expenditure, broken down under all subheads, for the years 1918–20; explanations would be sought if the rate of expenditure during the early quarters was exceptionally high. Inspectors were instructed to observe the 'strictest economy' in relation to travel and subsistence expenses.[142]

The transfer of staff was an extremely sensitive matter. By September 1921 six officials in the DATI were on temporary loan to the Northern Ireland government, to assist in setting up the new Ministry of Agriculture. There were lengthy negotiations to determine who would bear the cost of their salaries and their subsistence during this interim period; those on temporary transfer became extremely angry when their subsistence allowances were abruptly terminated by a Treasury circular issued on 14 November. On 24 October 1921 Sir John Anderson had issued two contradictory letters to the DATI. One set out the formal regulations: all officers whose work was exclusively based in one jurisdiction would be assigned to that jurisdiction; and others, whose current work covered both jurisdictions, would be assigned to one government or the other, and their salaries would be paid from a suspense account, until the Civil Service Committee had made its final decision, and the Treasury would then claim the cost of their salaries from their new employer. Another letter, with the same date, reminded the DATI that as the transferred officers would have no right of appeal to the Civil Service Committee, it should consider whether those employed solely within the area of either government 'are suitable for, and desire, transfer to the service of that Government'. Anderson warned that 'every care should be taken that, subject to the exigencies of the public service, no officer is now appointed to the performance of duties which will eventually involve automatic transfer under this section contrary to his wishes or those of the Government to whose area he is appointed'.

On 19 November 1921 Campbell, assistant secretary for Agriculture, asked all officials of the DATI, including the local instructors, to indicate, by the first Friday in December, their attitude to permanent or temporary transfer to Northern Ireland. One official, Ring, asked whether his position would be improved if he transferred to Northern Ireland; Campbell's reply was non-committal. Fortunately for the DATI, most officers expressed a wish to remain where they were. Six instructors, three resident in Donegal and Sligo, expressed a willingness to relocate to Northern Ireland, and five were willing to go anywhere (in many, if not all, cases these were temporary staff who were keen to obtain a permanent or quasi-permanent position).[143] Given that instructors were employed by county committees of agriculture, their transfer from one jurisdiction to another would have presented considerable difficulties.

Of the six officials who went to Belfast on temporary loan – Coyle,

Gordon, Finlay, Sloan, Devlin, and Miss O'Neill – at least four, Coyle, Gordon, Sloan and Miss O'Neill, joined the Northern Ireland Ministry of Agriculture. (The fate of the other two is unclear.) This suggests that they had been deliberately selected for temporary assignment, because they had expressed a wish to transfer to Northern Ireland. James Coyle, the senior staff clerk at the DATI, was the most senior official to move to Northern Ireland. A catholic educated at Belvedere College, Trinity College, Dublin, and the King's Inns, he had served in the office of the Collector-General of Rates, before joining the DATI in 1900 as deputy chief clerk. From 1919 to 1921 he was chairman of the Agricultural Wages Board. He was an assistant secretary in the Northern Ireland Ministry of Agriculture from 1922 to 1930.[144] J. S. Gordon, the deputy assistant secretary and chief inspector in the Agricultural Branch, was the most senior official in the Agricultural Branch. S. Sloan and W. T. Finlay were second-division clerks. Others who moved to the Northern Ireland Ministry were J. Getty, an inspector who became chief inspector in Northern Ireland; Harry Cuthbertson, a livestock inspector; and J. G. Rhynehart, a flax expert.[145]

When we examine the history of the DATI and the Dáil Ministry of Agriculture and how they both operated in the area of the Irish Free State between 1919 and 1922, it is immediately obvious why Patrick Hogan was given the title of Minister for Lands and Agriculture in 1922. Whether Hogan was aware of this or not, the title reflected the dual origins of his Department – the concentration on land reform by the Dáil Ministry, and the work of the DATI on more stricly agricultural matters. The priority that Dáil Éireann gave to land ownership and resettlement reflects the nineteenth-century nationalist belief that the best way to bring about improvements in Irish agriculture was to reform land ownership and distribution. By comparison, the DATI concentrated on raising productivity, and improving the quality of output without altering the existing pattern of land settlement. There is a tendency to regard the Dáil Ministry of Agriculture as a socially-conservative body but its emphasis on land redistribution and on co-operative ownership was in the radical nationalist tradition of Davitt, Connolly and Fintan Lalor. By setting up the National Land Bank as a quasi co-operative bank and in the unfulfilled plans for a co-operative meat-processing plant, the Dáil Ministry also reflected Plunkett's tradition of the state and the co-operatives working together. This linkage anticipates the policies pursued between 1922 and 1932.

The Dáil Ministry see-sawed between pragmatism and radicalism. The decision not to break with the DATI was due to the realisation that the break with the Local Government Board had proved very costly, and that a similar break with the DATI would also be expensive, and was unnecessary.

As for the DATI proper, its ability to remain on good terms with the county committees of agriculture is yet another indication that the DATI was no mere Castle board. Indeed, the destruction of the creameries meant that the DATI could probably be listed among the victims of the British armed forces. During these difficult years the DATI went to considerable lengths not to precipitate a breach with the county committees. T. P. Gill undoubtedly played a key role in these conciliatory efforts, as is evident from his communications with O'Connor in the autumn of 1921. These conciliatory efforts were probably worthwhile. No other institution established by Westminster was able to display as much continuity after Independence as the DATI. The Department's name remained unaltered until 1930, and the numbering of its annual reports continued on after Independence as if nothing had changed.

One of the most interesting, and hitherto-unnoticed, aspects of these years was the role of the Council of Agriculture. It was an all-Ireland organisation, two-thirds of whose members were elected by the local authorities. The sentiments expressed at the council meeting in March 1921, and the meeting that was summoned by O'Connor in August 1921, indicate a widespread realisation that agriculture was a matter on which all Ireland could agree.

CHAPTER THREE

'ONE MORE COW, ONE MORE SOW, AND ONE MORE ACRE UNDER THE PLOUGH', 1922–1932

The Irish Free State was an overwhelmingly agricultural country. Farming employed just over half of the workforce, and many of the most important manufacturing industries and wholesale and retail businesses depended on agriculture. In 1924, 86 per cent of total exports consisted of agricultural produce – food and drink. Partition accentuated the dominance of agriculture, because many of the largest manufacturing industries were located in north-east Ulster.

The creation of the Irish Free State presented fewer difficulties for the DATI than for most other agencies that survived from the era of British rule in Ireland. No organisation came through the Anglo-Irish war and the civil war unscathed, but whereas the new government was forced to construct a police system from scratch, and to carry out major reforms of health and welfare services, the changes within the DATI were much more modest. All the key features were retained: the inspectors, county committees of agriculture, the rate-in-aid of agriculture, and the local advisers, although the council and the board of Agriculture were not reconvened.

AGRICULTURAL ADMINISTRATION IN THE IRISH FREE STATE

Although Art O'Connor had outlined an alternative strategy for a department of agriculture, replacing itinerant instructors with model farms in each county and giving county committees of agriculture much greater control over agricultural schemes,[1] there is no evidence that this was given serious consideration. If councils had been prepared to meet a higher proportion of the cost of agricultural services, the county committees of agriculture might have been given more leeway. However, there was little prospect of this happening at a time when it proved difficult to collect the existing rates demands, and farmers were campaigning for the derating of agricultural land. In practice, the new government preferred greater central-isation, in the belief that it was more efficient and more honest, and probably because of fears that the Irregulars (the losing side in the civil war) would use local government as a platform for anti-government activity.

In 1917 the DATI had moved into the south block of the new Public Offices in Upper Merrion Street, Dublin. The offices had been erected after the demolition of several Georgian houses previously occupied by the DATI, and during their construction the DATI occupied adjoining houses in Upper Merrion Street and additional premises in nearby Baggot Street. Forming part of the present Government Buildings, the DATI's offices adjoined the College of Science, which was controlled by the DATI. The north block of the new Public Offices, which had been earmarked for the Local Government Board, became the headquarters of the provisional government and the Department of Finance.

The office complex had been designed by the London architect Sir Aston Webb and the Dublin architect Thomas Manly Deane. The façade of the College of Science included a seated figure of Science and full-length figures of the Irish scientists Rowan Hamilton and Robert Boyle by the Dublin sculptor Oliver Sheppard. The parapet over the DATI carried two sculpted female figures and a small child by another Dublin sculptor, Albert Power. The figures represented abundance in agriculture and instruction.[2]

In October 1922 the provisional government took temporary possession of the College of Science, and the departments of Agriculture and Finance were at the heart of the new Irish administration.[3] By comparison, the Department of Industry and Commerce was in cramped offices beside Dublin Castle and the Department of Local Government camped in various temporary premises pending the reconstruction of the Custom House.

Patrick Hogan was appointed Minister for Agriculture in the provisional government on 20 January 1922, and his appointment was confirmed by Dáil Éireann on 28 February 1922.[4] His appointment has been described as 'the most startling ... of the January ministries'.[5] Hogan was born in Kilrick, County Galway, the son of a prominent farmer, who was also a senior inspector with the Land Commission. As a young man, he allegedly read many of the leaflets issued by the DATI. He qualified as a solicitor and practised in south Galway, but retained a strong interest in farming. In

October–November 1920 he asked the Dáil Land Courts to hold a sitting in Loughrea. Although not a supporter of Sinn Féin, Hogan realised this was the only way to control land agitation, which was particularly troublesome in south Galway. This action led to his arrest and internment in Ballykinlar camp,[6] where he made the acquaintance of Joe McGrath, a Sinn Féin TD who became acting Minister for Labour in the Dáil Éireann government following the arrest of Constance Markiewicz, the previous Minister for Labour in the provisional government. Hogan was not known to either Collins or Griffith and it was on McGrath's recommendation that he was appointed a minister.

Although he was a Dáil deputy, Hogan was an extern minister. This mechanism enabled governments to appoint ministers who were not necessarily members of Dáil Éireann or of a political party. Extern ministers could not be members of the Executive Council, and Tom Johnson, the leader of the Labour Party, complained that the 1923 Ministers and Secretaries Bill relegated ministers who were not members of the Executive Council 'into a position of subordination'.[7] This anomaly was corrected in June 1927, when the Cabinet was expanded to include all ministers.[8] Despite this apparent handicap, Hogan was one of the strongest ministers during the years 1922–32. He always emphasised the agricultural aspects of his portfolio, although he was to give his name to the last major land act, in 1923. He believed that the prosperity of Irish agriculture depended above all on the British market: the Department of Agriculture should concentrate on controlling costs and improving quality; tariff protection was not a realistic option; neither was compulsory tillage.

Hogan was more in sympathy with the larger commercial farmers, who produced the bulk of agricultural exports, than with small farmers. Joseph Lee, repeating (without acknowledgement) the gibes of Dáil deputies, claimed that Hogan saw the 200-hundred-acre man as the ordinary farmer.[9] 'Two hundred acres' may be an exaggeration, but the general point is correct – Hogan favoured larger holdings. In 1928 Hogan told the Dáil that the Agricultural Credit Corporation (ACC) was not intended to help the 'downs and outs', but those with security. In 75 per cent of cases where farmers were down and out, Hogan was of the opinion that it was their own fault.[10]

Hogan succeeded in getting his message across because he closely followed the path the DATI had mapped out before 1922, indeed before 1914. Very few measures were introduced during the 1920s that could not have been implemented by the DATI before Independence, although in contrast to Westminster, which passed only one piece of legislation initiated by the DATI between 1900 and 1922, Dáil Éireann and the Irish government gave priority to legislation relating to agriculture. Like Plunkett, Hogan believed strongly in co-operation rather than in direct state aid, and during his time as Minister, the Department provided substantial funding for the co-operative movement. Hogan wished to help the farmer to help himself, an objective that was almost identical with the one set out by Plunkett in the first annual report of the DATI.

The Department of Agriculture

If any government department epitomises Ronan Fanning's claim that there was considerable continuity in Irish administration before and after Independence,[11] it is the Department of Agriculture. Although the Ministers and Secretaries Act of 1924 changed the minister's title to the Minister for Lands and Agriculture, the Department continued to be known as the Department of Agriculture and Technical Instruction. Although the Ministers and Secretaries Act stated that the minister was a 'corporation sole', in other words the department was the minister, the Department of Agriculture appears to have retained a more independent existence, although it would difficult to point to any practical consequences resulting from this. This administrative anomaly ended with the Agricultural Act of 1931, which gave the Department a legal basis identical to other departments, and changed its name to the Department of Agriculture. The Minister and Dáil deputies all regarded the 1931 Act as purely procedural, and the Department's annual reports during the 1920s suggest continuity, not change. The report covering the years 1923–6 was titled *The 24th General Report of the Department of Agriculture and Technical Instruction*, and the report for 1930/1 carried the title *The 29th and Final General Report of the Department of Agriculture and Technical Instruction for Ireland*.

The report of the Department for 1921/2, published in 1924, signalled the transition to an independent Irish state by opening with an introduction in Irish, although this was not repeated in the next report. The report for 1921/2 also carried the name of a new secretary, P. S. Ó Meiric (F. J. Meyrick). Educated at Blackrock College in Dublin, Meyrick had joined the civil service in 1893, when he was appointed to the RIC office. He was awarded an MA in Mental and Moral Philosophy and an exhibition by the Royal University in 1898. In June 1905 he joined the DATI as a second-division clerk, and in 1919 was promoted to the rank of senior staff clerk.[12] He became secretary of the Department of Agriculture on 20 January 1923.

Meyrick was an active member of the Society of St Vincent de Paul and the Leo Guild, a group that studied catholic social teaching.[13] He also belonged to the sodality organised by the Society of Jesus in Gardiner Street, and the Irish Lourdes Association.[14] He remained secretary to the Department until January 1934, when he was appointed as technical adviser to the Minister.[15]

The establishment of a full range of Irish government departments relieved the DATI of many of its non-agricultural functions. The Department of Industry and Commerce became responsible for trade statistics and the transit of livestock and goods. In January 1923 the Ministry of Fisheries was established, and under the Ministers and Secretaries Act of 1924 it became the Department of Fisheries and Rural Industries, with responsibility for the industries which had previously been assisted by the DATI and the CDB. The Ministers and Secretaries Act also transferred technical education, and cultural and educational institutions such as the National Museum, the National Library, the National Gallery, the Geological Survey and the Metropolitan School of Art, to the new Department of Education, although the order implementing these transfers was not approved until December 1927.[16]

The only aspect of these changes that gave rise to debate in Dáil Éireann was the establishment of the Department of Fisheries and Rural Industries, most deputies believing that fisheries should be under the Department of Agriculture.[17] The changes, however, were consistent with the views of Patrick Hogan. In November 1922 he had told the Dáil that, 'The Department of Agriculture should confine itself to agriculture'; there was a need for 'some division between the educational functions of the Department of Agriculture and what I call its proper functions'. Hogan also believed that in the past, fisheries had received insufficient attention because it was 'lumped in with agriculture'.[18]

In the reshuffling of functions, the Department acquired one new responsibility. The Forestry Act of 1919 had established a Forestry Commission that would operate throughout the United Kingdom (a strange decision on the apparent eve of Home Rule), and officials in the DATI's forestry division had been transferred to the new organisation. In 1923 responsibility for forestry reverted to the Department of Agriculture.

Under the Ministers and Secretaries (Amendment) Act of 1928 the Minister for Lands and Agriculture became the Minister for Agriculture, and responsibility for Lands passed to a newly-created Minister for Lands and Fisheries, a change that took account of the report of the Commission on the Gaeltacht.[19] This chopping and changing was an attempt to reconcile the demands for a regional policy and a programme of land reform, with measures to develop agriculture, fisheries and rural industries. The relative merits and disadvantages of concentrating on regional development rather than on a specific sector, such as agriculture, and the complex relationship between land reform and agricultural development, remained difficult issues long after 1922. However, the decision to offload responsibility for economic development in the Gaeltacht or former congested districts to another department of state was consistent with Hogan's belief that agriculture was primarily a business, rather than a means of relieving poverty and emigration.

In 1923 the Department assumed responsibility for awarding premia for livestock, which had previously been carried out by the county committees of agriculture, but this decision was reversed some years later. Surviving files suggest that all schemes organised by the county committees, be it a ploughing match or awards for cottage gardens, were subject to detailed scrutiny by the Department. The Department scrutinised the minutes of meetings of the county committees of agriculture, whereas the Department of Local Government and Public Health had abandoned this long-standing procedure.

This tendency towards tighter administrative control led to the endowment fund of the DATI being wound up on 31 March 1925. At the time, the fund provided the Department of Agriculture in Dublin with an annual sum of £144,700, and the Northern Ireland Ministry of Agriculture received £45,300. When the sums earmarked for technical education and sea fisheries were excluded, the Department was left with £92,050 per annum. The Department could spend these monies as it wished, without having to seek sanction from the Department of Finance, although expenditure had to be approved by the (defunct) Board of Agriculture. According to the report of the DATI for the years 1923–6, the financial freedom provided by the endowment fund had been 'of considerable advantage at a time when the public administration of Ireland was subject to the control of the British Treasury'. Now that Ireland was self-governing, 'the same conditions no longer applied'. From April 1925 the Department of Agriculture was funded like other government departments, by annual votes of the Oireachtas, and all expenditure was sanctioned by the Department of Finance.

Hogan was philosophical about the loss of the endowment fund. He claimed that whenever the Department applied for money for some new venture, it had to show the Minister for Finance that there was no money remaining in the endowment fund. This meant that in practice the endowment fund was 'really on the Vote, and was as much under the control of the Minister for Finance as if it was voted by the Dail'.[20] Some of the ensuing anomalies, such as the pensions for officers of the Department, whose salaries had traditionally been paid out of the endowment fund, were not tidied up until 1931.[21] In 1925 the Executive Council also terminated the annual payment of £19,000, which the Department had received since 1909 for providing special agricultural services in the congested districts, a decision also justified by the need to secure greater control by Finance.[22]

The new state disapproved of the plethora of 'Castle boards', which had become a feature of the Irish administration by the beginning of the twentieth century. The new government preferred an administrative system organised around ministers and departments, with a department of finance exercising overall control over expenditure.[23] The CDB was a casualty of this belief, so were the Council of Agriculture and the Board of Agriculture. Although the council and the board were not abolished until 1931, they had not been convened since 1920. In 1931 Hogan dismissed the council as 'a debating chamber' whose sole function was to elect the board.[24] The Department continued the tradition of appointing committees to advise on policy in relation to specific sectors, such as eggs or livestock, but, unlike the Board of Agriculture, these committees lacked statutory authority and meetings took place at irregular intervals.

The Agricultural Act of 1931 strengthened the statutory position of the county committees of agriculture by insisting that local agricultural schemes be administered through the county committees. Up till then it was possible for a county council to dispense with the county committee of agriculture. The 1931 Act made the committees smaller: every electoral area was required to return either three or four members. This meant that the largest county committee would not exceed thirty-two members. Hogan claimed that despite a large membership in the past, it was often difficult to achieve a quorum at meetings of county committees, unless appointments were being made.[25] Hogan had a very low opinion of the county committees: in a letter to Horace Plunkett in 1927 he noted that, 'they are wrongly constituted; they are nominated by the County Councils. The County Councils, so far as they are composed of farmers at all are composed of the bad farmers; the good farmer has not time to go on the County Council and in any event has no inclination to enter local politics. The County Councils of course nominate, with rare exceptions, people like themselves.'[26] Plunkett would probably have agreed.

Agricultural Advisers

In the early 1920s there were two distinct sets of agricultural instructors: those employed by the county committees of agriculture, and those employed directly by the Department. The latter were responsible for creamery management, cow-testing, marketing agricultural produce, flax cultivation, and instruction in the former congested districts.

The traditional methods of instruction, such as winter classes, remained important, but some new schemes were introduced. The Commission on the Gaeltacht emphasised that it was important to provide agricultural education through Irish, if new methods of farming were to be transmitted to landholders in Irish-speaking districts. It took some time for the Department to meet this need, but in 1930 it appointed twenty Irish-speaking assistant agricultural overseers, who had undergone a special training course at the agricultural station in Athenry.

The opening of the state radio network, 2RN, in January 1926 offered a new medium of instruction. The first director, Seamus Clandillon, was keen to introduce talks on agricultural topics and to produce market prices, although the Department was initially less enthusiastic. However, it agreed to sponsor a series of talks on gardening by G. O. Sherrard of the Albert Agricultural College. By the following May the station was also providing weekly information on market prices, a service that was much in demand from farmers, and Miss Hennerty, the Department's superintending poultry inspector, began a series of broadcasts on poultry-keeping some months later. The Department was represented on the Broadcasting Advisory Board, established by the Minister for Posts and Telegraphs. Given the limited number of radio sets in Ireland (in 1930 only one household in thirty in County Waterford had a radio), and the perennial problem of charging batteries, one wonders how many farmers actually heard these broadcasts.[27]

From 1927 instructors appointed by the county committees of agriculture were recruited and recommended for appointment by the Local Appointments Commission (previously the Department was the recommending body). The absence of promotional opportunities was a long-standing grievance. In 1924 the report of the Commission on Agriculture had recommended that the secretaries (or chief executives) of the county committees of agriculture should be replaced by graduates in agricultural science who would be known as chief agricultural officers. (The last secretary to a county committee of agriculture retired in the 1950s.[28]) The Agricultural Act of 1931 made important improvements in the service conditions for those officers in the Department who had originally been paid from the endowment fund, and consequently did not have pension rights, but further anomalies relating to pension rights remained.[29]

Agricultural Education

Hogan firmly believed that 'the future of agriculture in Ireland is the future of agricultural education', although he regarded university education and research as more important than agricultural education in primary schools. This was completely at variance with the views expressed by the first Dáil, although it was probably consistent with the views of the DATI. Hogan wished to create an institution that would carry out scientific, agricultural and industrial research, in keeping with the recommendation of the Commission on Agriculture.

The 1923 Ministers and Secretaries Bill proposed transferring responsibility for all educational matters to the Minister for Education. Several deputies criticised this decision; one suggested that if the Minister for Agriculture lost control of the College of Science, he would find it extremely difficult to develop a programme of agricultural research.[30] However, Hugh Kennedy, the Attorney General, substituting for Hogan in the Dáil, claimed that this was evidence of the government's wish to exclude 'anything in the nature of intellectualism from the pursuit of agriculture'; the government rejected an amendment that would have left the College of Science under the Department of Agriculture's control, although it accepted a vague, compromise amendment which provided that the Department might promote agriculture by means of educational grants.[31]

Under the Ministers and Secretaries Act of 1924 the Department of Agriculture remained responsible for the Botanic Gardens and the Veterinary College in Dublin, and for farm institutes owned or controlled by the government, including the Albert Agricultural College in Glasnevin, Dublin. When Meyrick contacted the secretary of the Executive Council, seeking to have a large section of the College of Science buildings restored to the College (they had been taken over by the provisional government in 1922), the matter was referred to the Department of Education. In May 1924 the Department of Education recommended that the College of Science be merged with University College, Dublin (UCD). Legislation providing for the transfer of the College of Science, and the Albert Agricultural College, to UCD was delayed by a dispute between Hogan and the Department of Finance as to which minister would be responsible for giving money to UCD for the purchase of land and repair of accommodation.[32] This suggests that the Department of Agriculture was keen to retain a role in agricultural education. Under the University Education Act of 1926, the College of Science and the Albert Agricultural College were both transferred to UCD, and a faculty of dairy science was established at University College, Cork (UCC). In 1929 the Department of Agriculture persuaded the Executive Council to increase the capital grant for the construction of the faculty of dairy science at UCC.[33]

According to Hoctor, the establishment of faculties of agriculture and dairy science at UCD and UCC 'left a void in the Department'.[34] In the years following World War I the Department had recruited a small team of agricultural research workers, but most of these left to take up positions in the new faculties.[35] The question of reuniting agricultural education, research and the advisory service in one institution was to resurface after World War II during discussions over the establishment of an agricultural institute.

Veterinary Training
The founding of the Irish Free State presented problems for veterinary education. The Royal College of Veterinary Surgeons (RCVS) in London had been responsible for the registration of veterinary practitioners in Ireland, but their jurisdiction ended with Independence. Irish students continued to sit the examinations of the RCVS, but Irish veterinary surgeons were no longer permitted to practise in Britain or in Northern Ireland, and the RCVS was unable to prosecute unqualified practitioners in the Irish Free State.

Although the Department of Agriculture had controlled the Royal College of Veterinary Surgeons of Ireland since 1915, it was not in favour of establishing an independent Irish register, preferring the RCVS to continue to be responsible for registration, provided that Irish veterinary surgeons were adequately represented on its council. Meyrick believed that a separate Irish register would damage the standing of the Dublin veterinary college, because it would not be recognised internationally, and this would present problems in enforcing the Diseases of Animals Acts. He also feared that many aspiring veterinarians would opt to study in Britain. In December 1926 the Executive Council received a petition signed by 294 of the 320 veterinary surgeons in the Irish Free State, requesting that the government enact legislation restoring the previous arrangement with the RCVS.

The Cabinet deferred a decision, although it agreed that no change would be introduced without adequate notice. In a change from his previous stance, Meyrick suggested that Irish students should sit the examination of the RCVS, but that a separate register and veterinary council would be established in the Irish Free State. This may have been an attempt to accede to the wishes of some ministers for a greater degree of separation between the British and Irish veterinary professions. If so it was not successful. In March 1927 McDunphy, in the Office of the President, reported that the Executive Council was not convinced that such a 'quasi-dependent connection with the RCVS' was necessary. Meyrick countered that such an arrangement should be seen not as 'quasi-dependency but mutual recognition'. In December 1928 the Chief State Solicitor informed the Department that the veterinary college was no longer an affiliated college of the RCVS; therefore, the RCVS did not have authority to set examinations for the Dublin college, and under current legislation it did not have the authority to delegate the powers to hold examinations there. That put paid to the solution favoured by the Department: that the Dublin College would be a qualified college of the RCVS.

The Department now opted for legislation along the lines of the Dentists Act, which provided for the establishment of a dental board and a register. The veterinary college would be transferred to UCD; the National University of Ireland (NUI) would organise examinations and award diplomas; an Irish veterinary council would have authority to determine the appropriate qualifications for registration; and Irish-qualified veterinarians would be included in the General Register of Veterinary Surgeons of Great Britain. When Hogan and McGilligan, minister for External Affairs and for Industry and Commerce, tried to reach an agreement with the RCVS, the Royal College was prepared to concede the authority to regulate and discipline the profession within Ireland to an Irish veterinary council; however, it insisted that the examinations must be conducted by the RCVS, in order to ensure uniform qualifications. It agreed to allocate four places on the council of the RCVS to representatives of the Irish Free State, and to ensure that Irish professors would serve on the boards when examinations were conducted in the Irish Free State. This ultimately formed the basis of an agreement.[36]

Relations with Northern Ireland

During the early months of 1922 Hogan exploited the Department of Agriculture's status as an all-Ireland department, in an effort to retain a toehold in Northern Ireland. On 1 February 1922 the provisional government decided not to accede to a request from Edward Archdale, the Northern Ireland Minister for Agriculture, for an interview with officials of the provisional government to discuss matters relating to the transfer of services to Belfast. Hogan was particularly exercised by the decision of the British government in April 1922 to hand over the administration of the Diseases of Animals Acts to the Northern Ireland government, apparently in contravention of the Anglo-Irish Treaty. The Treaty provided that the executive functions of the Council of Ireland, which included responsibility for fisheries and the Diseases of Animals Acts, would pass to the provisional government; there was no provision for the government of Northern Ireland to assume responsibilities that had been assigned to the Council of Ireland. Hogan argued that the provisional government should exercise these powers in Northern Ireland as agents of the British authorities, pending the establishment of the Council of Ireland. In his opinion, the Department of Agriculture had been founded as an all-Ireland body and should continue as such.[37]

Hogan claimed that the Northern Ireland government lacked the trained staff to operate a veterinary department, and it would find it difficult to establish one, 'especially if they are forbidden access to office records or if they are unable to obtain the services of a member of the existing staff of the veterinary department'. An undated memorandum on the administration of the Diseases of Animals Acts noted the importance of consultation and joint action by both governments. If the provisional government decided, as a matter of policy, not to co-operate with the government of Northern Ireland, the memorandum noted that such a decision would inflict much greater losses on Northern Ireland than on the Irish Free State. Because Irish cattle, including cattle originating in Northern Ireland, would not be admitted to Britain without an export certificate issued by a recognised veterinary inspector, a policy of 'complete isolation' would mean an end to cattle shipments from ports in Northern Ireland and massive damage to the cattle industry in the province. The Donegal cattle trade would also suffer, because most Donegal cattle were shipped through the port of Derry.[38]

On 8 May 1922 Hogan instructed all veterinary officers in Northern Ireland not to provide the government of Northern Ireland with any information unless he instructed them to do so. He also appointed several veterinary inspectors in Northern Ireland on the authority of the provisional government, including a Mr McCluskey, who was assigned to the port of Derry. McCluskey was supported by local cattle exporters, who refused to recognise the rival inspector appointed by the government of Northern Ireland. Britain responded by asserting its right to appoint the Northern

Ireland government as its agent in enforcing the Diseases of Animals Acts. As a consequence, by July 1922 authorities at the English port of Heysham were refusing to accept cattle whose certificates were signed by McCluskey. Hogan claimed that this breached an agreement that, pending settlement of the dispute, signatures of inspectors approved by either government would be accepted. Michael Collins wrote to Winston Churchill protesting that the British actions showed:

> … little, if any, grasp of the foundation of the Treaty, or sympathy with the hope of the signatories that there may emerge from it our ideal of a United Ireland. They seem to be engaged rather in completing the bad work of severing from us our North Eastern Counties partly accomplished by your Act of 1920.

> Any extension of the powers of that Government [Northern Ireland] is a blow to the cause of re-uniting the country and clear violation of the spirit of the Treaty. To confer on that Government powers which are by agreement reserved to be conferred on an all-Ireland authority must make the creation of such authority well nigh impossible because the difficulty of taking back powers once given would probably be insuperable.[39]

Although Churchill replied that the Northern Ireland government was merely acting as the agent of the British government until a decision was made whether or not to establish the Council of Ireland, Britain agreed to assume direct responsibility for the Diseases of Animals Acts within Northern Ireland.[40]

Hogan may have had some legal standing for his actions in relation to the Diseases of Animals Acts, but the policy of non-cooperation extended to matters where there was no legal basis. The Department of Agriculture was unwilling to transfer files covering a long list of topics, including agricultural schools, crop disease, flax, egg marketing, food and drugs legislation, and the establishment files of the transferred staff.[41] In November 1922 Hogan told the Dáil that he planned to make some arrangement with the Northern Ireland Ministry of Agriculture regarding the collection of statistics in their area.[42] This suggests that Hogan wished to continue the collection of agricultural statistics on an all-Ireland basis. The policy of non-cooperation with the Northern Ireland Ministry appears to have been only short-term. Donal Creedon claims that there was always a close relationship between the two departments of agriculture, especially on matters such as disease control.

THE LAND ACT, 1923

By 1922 more than 70 per cent of agricultural land was owned by the occupying farmers; the remaining 30 per cent consisted of 'the hard knots that it had been impossible to disentangle under the system of voluntary purchase'.[43] Pressure for land reform did not disappear with the establishment of the Irish Free State. On the contrary, the agricultural recession and the winding up of the Agricultural Wages Board meant that rural labourers were more likely to see the acquisition of land as the only reliable means of raising their standard of living. In February 1922 the North Meath Comhairle Ceanntar of Sinn Féin passed a resolution demanding the reintroduction of compulsory tillage, 'to tide us over the few months between this date and when land purchase began in earnest'.[44]

Although the Land Settlement Commission inspected 5,000 acres between 14 January and 14 April 1922,[45] the provisional government adopted a more conservative attitude towards land resettlement than the first and second Dála. When the Evicted Tenants' Association demanded a system to arbitrate between its members and landlords, or 'land-grabbers', Hogan announced that he had no objection to arbitration, provided there was no question of duress. He added that, 'it is not at all certain that all cases [where evicted tenants regained land] had been free from duress', prompting a protest from the Evicted Tenants' Association.[46] In April the Department responded to demands by evicted tenants for reinstatement by referring to a decree issued by Dáil Éireann on 29 June 1920, which debarred the Department of Agriculture from such action, except by written licence of the Minister of Home Affairs.

The attitude of the provisional government seems to have prompted smallholders to act of their own accord. A woman wrote to the Department of Agriculture from Dromod, County Leitrim, describing how she and her neighbours, all holding less than ten acres of land, had attempted without success to buy part of the untenanted grazing land belonging to the Harlech Gore estate. When the estate's solicitor rejected their offer, each took 'a portion of land'.[47]

In the Dáil, demand for land reform became identified with opposition to the Treaty. On 10 May 1922 one anti-Treaty deputy, Dáithí Ceannt, asserted that membership of the farmers' unions and landlords' unions included hundreds of men who employed only a man and a dog and they all supported the Treaty.[48] Hogan complained in August 1922 that 'all constructive work in the Department was being hampered by the action of an armed minority'. The land settlement courts had ceased to function and at least two land inspectors had joined the army (of the Irish Free State).[49] The winding-up of the Dáil courts in July 1922 had brought the legality of the Land Settlement Commission into question.[50] On 26 August 1922 the provisional government, which was coping with the sudden deaths of Griffith and Collins, as well as the civil war, decided not to proceed with any scheme of land purchase until the Constitution had come into effect. (The provisional government had no power to legislate.) Hogan informed the Dáil of this decision on 12 September, in reply to a question from Darrell Figgis. Figgis and other deputies continued to press the provisional government for a statement on its policy on breaking up ranches and land settlement in general.

The British government also regarded land settlement as a matter of urgency. On 9 December 1922, when the Irish Free State was not yet one week old, the Secretary of State for the Colonies, the Duke of Devonshire, sent a special despatch to the government of the Irish Free State, via the Governor-General, Tim Healy, listing a number of matters that needed to be discussed, 'with a view to an immediate and final settlement'. Top of the list were the financial arrangements for completing land purchase.[51] In February 1923 Patrick Hogan, W. T. Cosgrave and Hugh Kennedy, the Irish Law Officer, travelled to London to discuss the matter. The Irish government agreed to collect and pay the land annuities outstanding from previous land acts. It is also probable that the outline of a land purchase act was discussed. Land purchase would be financed by issuing Irish government stock at $4\frac{1}{2}$ per cent, and the capital and interest on the stock would be guaranteed by the British government, 'in the same way as it might guarantee a Colonial or Dominion Government loan'. In return for guaranteeing the stock, the terms of the land act would be 'subject to the concurrence of the British Government'. The details of this agreement were not committed to paper, because it was highly sensitive. Ronan Fanning believes that the Executive Council agreed to the broad terms of the 1923 Land Bill at its next meeting on 13 February, although the minute is cryptic in the extreme.[52]

On 17 December 1922, eight days after the special despatch from the Duke of Devonshire, Hogan gave a commitment to the Executive Council that he would organise a conference of landlords and tenants to discuss a land bill. This attempt to replicate the Dunraven Conference, which had produced the Wyndham Land Act of 1903, was delayed by the disturbed state of the country. In April 1923 Hogan informed Cosgrave that it would be impossible to enact anything approaching an equitable land bill, because of the widespread agrarian violence, the house-burnings and the threatened shootings. He believed that these incidents were being carried out for agrarian rather than political motives. 'At the best of times three or four tenants who are prepared to commit criminal injuries can hold up a sale.' He estimated that there were up to $1\frac{1}{2}$ million landless men prepared to enforce their claims 'with the gun and the torch', but only 30,000 vacant holdings. On the basis of these figures, any land bill 'must give a first claim to all the available land to the occupying tenants, herds, genuine cases of evicted tenants, and to the tenants who need additional land in order to make their holding economic, and it is only when these are satisfied, that a very limited number of sons of tenants, viz: landless men, can be dealt with'. It would be impossible to get such a bill through Dáil Éireann, 'unless there is a drastic change in the present state of affairs within a very short time'. This 'drastic change' should be achieved by employing the special infantry forces to stamp out unrest. If this did not happen, 'the present dishonouring class war' would continue; the houses of 'every large farmer and land owner' would be burned; and agrarian outrages would rage for several years.[53] The special infantry forces consisted of contingents of soldiers who were used by the government during the civil war to deal with civil order offences.

Cosgrave seems to have been less exercised by the threat of agrarian unrest than Hogan. He urged Hogan to open negotiations immediately with the landlords, because if talks were postponed until order was restored the landlords would make 'exorbitant' demands.[54] The landlords wanted a settlement along the lines proposed at the 1918 Irish Convention, which had formed the basis of the aborted 1920 Irish land bill. This provided for the automatic acquisition by the Land Commission of all land that was to be transferred to occupiers within three years, and guarantees that the current landowners would be permitted to retain ownership of their demesnes and home farms; that no legislation jeopardising that position could be enacted within twenty years; and that vendors would receive 5 per cent stock at face value, as well as a guaranteed cash bonus.[55] Hogan informed Cosgrave that the tenants' representatives, Gorey, Baxter and Noonan, had warned the landlords that circumstances had changed.

Landlords now constituted an unpopular minority; the people were determined to 'have the land cheaply, and that if the present Government did not meet the wishes of the people in this respect they would put in a government the next time who would'. Rent arrears were a major cause of dispute: the tenants wanted large write-offs, while landlords were pressing for full payment. Hogan told the spokesmen for the tenants that the government believed that 'fair play and justice all round did not change with majorities'. If the tenants were not prepared to make some concessions, he would present his own bill, 'embodying what I considered to be fair terms'.[56]

The 1923 Land Bill probably fulfilled Hogan's wish to secure 'fair terms'. This was achieved by suppressing land disturbances and by exploiting the potential divisions between tenant farmers, labourers and smallholders. In February 1923 Hogan ordered a series of ordnance survey maps covering the most disturbed parts of Ireland – counties Galway, Roscommon, Sligo, Leitrim, north Kerry, north Tipperary, Clare and Carlow – so that he could identify the location of all land disturbances. With the end to the civil war in sight, the special infantry forces and the land settlement inspectors were redeployed to prevent land seizures, the burning of houses, hay and other crops, and other instances of aggression. By April Hogan reported that there was very little land trouble in Sligo and Leitrim, and the special unit was concentrating on seizing poteen and preventing the illegal cutting of timber. He described the latest talks with the tenants' representatives as 'not unsatisfactory'. The farmers' representatives in Dáil Éireann 'are afraid if they accept the help of the Bolshevists in regard to the reduction of rent, the Bolshevists would begin to look for something more, namely a reduction in the size of the holdings' and 'the landlords now understand what they are up against'. Reasonable landlords were prepared to take whatever they could get 'now, provided it is anything approaching fair play'.[57]

When Hogan informed a reconvened conference of landlord and tenant representatives that the government was prepared to offer landlords Irish stock at 4½ per cent, with capital and interest guaranteed by the British government, the tenants became suspicious (quite correctly) that the Irish government had been forced to make certain promises to Britain. Hogan did not inform them that the guarantee was dependent on the tenants' accepting the terms, because he feared that this would be interpreted as confirmation that the terms of the Land Bill had been drawn up in Britain. He urged that the Land Bill should be introduced as rapidly as possible, because landlords were about to begin issuing writs to recover rent arrears, and he wanted to deal with arrears as part of the Bill. He feared the consequences if the Bill was defeated in Dáil Éireann.[58]

The Executive Council was aware that the government of Northern Ireland was also introducing a land bill, and it wondered whether it should wait until that bill was out of the way (the Northern Ireland Land Purchase Act was not enacted until 1925).[59] On 26 June 1923 the Duke of Devonshire, Secretary of State for the Colonies, reminded the Governor-General, Tim Healy, that under the agreement between Britain and Ireland, reached on 12 February 1923, the Irish government had assumed responsibility for collecting land annuities and remitting the money to Britain. Britain was concerned that the proposed Land Bill might undermine this agreement. On 17 July Healy informed the Duke of Devonshire that the bill had been modified to take account of these concerns.[60]

The 1923 Land Act provided that all land to be transferred, whether tenanted or untenanted, was to be vested in the Land Commission. Purchase prices were calculated on the basis of the judicial rents, subject to a reduction of 30 or 35 per cent, and repayments would be spread over $66\frac{1}{2}$ years. Landlords would be paid fifteen years' rental as the purchase price. The money would come from the amount loaned to the purchasing tenants; in addition, landlords would be paid a 10 per cent bonus. They had the option of buying back their demesnes on the same terms as tenant farmers. Rent arrears for the period before 1920 were forgiven, and a 25 per cent remission was given on later arrears. Tenants were required to pay rent to the Land Commission until the sale had been completed.[61]

Apart from providing for compulsory purchase (which had previously only applied within the congested districts), the Land Act of 1923 was a conservative measure. Like the earlier land acts, it confirmed the existing pattern of land settlement. Most land was bought by occupying tenants; landlords were compensated for the loss of property. Where untenanted land was available, it was given to occupiers of uneconomic holdings, migrants, evicted tenants, and labourers who had lost their jobs as a result of land purchase. On this occasion, the relief of congestion was not given precedence. In Dáil Éireann, the Act was criticised for being unduly favourable to 'the minority'. Several deputies argued that fifteen years' rental was too high a price to pay, that the treatment of arrears was ungenerous, and that there was no provision for dividing ranches among landless men.[62]

The 1923 Land Act ended the utopian, and largely unsuccessful, experiments in co-operative land ownership that had been undertaken by Dáil

Éireann. Arrears to the Land Bank were paid off, and land in the possession of co-operative schemes was vested in the Land Commission. By the late 1920s the Land Commission had taken over 237 estates from these local groups. The state ended up having to meet almost 40 per cent of the purchase price in such cases.[63] Once the 1923 Act was agreed, the government moved swiftly to enforce the payment of land annuities and to suppress any further seizures of land. In August 1923 four cows, four calves, and one horse and cart were seized from smallholders in Ballycastle and Glenamoy, County Mayo, for debts averaging £4 to £5. One inspector noted that, 'at times it was necessary to fire a few rounds over the heads of people who were inclined to put up a fight and in one instance attempted to seize stock'.[64]

The successful enactment of the 1923 Land Act at a time of political and social unrest testifies to Hogan's strength as a minister. Without this Act, it would have been extremely difficult to advance other aspects of agricultural policy, because larger farmers would have been deterred from investing by the threat of future land redistribution, while smaller farmers would have been tempted to dream of a utopian solution to their difficulties as an alternative to producing fresh eggs and clean milk.

While the 1923 Land Act is generally regarded as the last major piece of land legislation, it did not mark the end of land disputes. Subdivision and subletting proved to be rife on many of the estates vested in the Land Commission under the 1923 Act, and the government was forced to deal with this problem in the Land Act of 1927.[65] Land agitation, however, spluttered out. Labourers, smallholders and landless men lost heart, not least because of poverty and unemployment. With the government signalling that it would not engage in radical redistribution of land and no immediate prospect of a change of government, many landless men and smallholders emigrated to Britain or the United States. In June 1925 Hogan told deputies who had criticised the Department of Agriculture for its failure to deal with the problems of landless men that, 'unless you drain the sea', there was simply not enough land to give viable holdings to all the congests and landless men. In his opinion, the 'real agricultural problem' was how to provide for 'the second, third and fourth son of the ordinary farmer'. He did not offer any solution to this problem.[66]

Hogan's estimate in April 1923 that there were only 30,000 vacant holdings available for resettling landless men proved accurate. Between 1922 and 1932 the Land Commission distributed 450,000 acres to 24,000 families,[67] a far cry from the estimated 1½ million landless men. Between

1923 and 1933 more than 110,000 holdings changed ownership under the land acts.[68]

The Commission on Agriculture, 1922–3

The early 1920s were a difficult time for Irish agriculture. The final stages of the Anglo-Irish war had seen the end of the agricultural boom that had started during World War I, and prices continued to fall during the early years of the Irish Free State. The report of the DATI for 1922/3 noted that this was 'a year of anxiety and struggle. The post-war depression, which manifested itself so acutely in the year 1922 continued to weigh on Irish agriculture, though towards the end of the period the situation improved and the prospect brightened'.[69] The acreage of tilled land fell sharply from its wartime peak, bringing unemployment among agricultural labourers and less work for small farmers and their relations. Land redistribution was seen as one panacea by the rural poor; others believed the solution lay in making Irish agriculture less dependent on exporting livestock, dairy and poultry produce to Britain; and yet others eschewed the demands for a radical change in agricultural policy, urging continuity with the past.

In June 1919 Dáil Éireann established a Commission of Inquiry into the Resources and Industries of Ireland, with a brief to report on the present condition of natural resources and manufacturing and productive industries in Ireland and how they could best be developed and encouraged.[70] Arthur Griffith invited sixty people to serve on the commission; forty-nine accepted. Eight were members of Dáil Éireann; the remainder comprised business-men, academics, and the labour and trade union leaders Tom Johnson and William O'Brien. A Dublin businessman, John O'Neill, was appointed as chairman; when he resigned in September 1920, Colonel Maurice Moore became chairman. Darrell Figgis acted as secretary. Despite its wide terms of reference, the commission divided into two sub-committees, one devoted to fuel and power, the other to food and agriculture; the food and agriculture sub-committee was chaired by Tom Johnson, the leader of the Labour Party. Other manufacturing industries were not considered.

In March 1920 the food and agriculture sub-committee produced an interim report on milk production; a report on stock-breeding for pure-bred dairy cattle was published in April 1921; and a report on milk products was published on 30 March 1922. The most surprising feature of these reports is the absence of any wishful thinking about the future of Irish agriculture and their practical content.

The first report, on dairying, highlighted the problem of low milk yields; the need to establish cow-testing associations, in order to determine which animals should be eliminated and which should be kept in a herd; the importance of selecting appropriate bulls; and the merits of autumn calving. It recommended that creameries should organise cow-testing stations; if there was no local creamery, the testing-station should be based on a parish or chapel area. Cow-testing associations should come together to form a national dairy council. The report on stock-breeding questioned the heavy reliance in the past on Shorthorn cattle as the basis of the dairy herd. It suggested that other breeds, such as Friesians, should be promoted, and recommended establishing stud farms with animals proved to have high milk yields. The report on milk products stated bluntly that, 'the dairy industry has failed to satisfy the human needs of the home population'. Moreover, the export market was 'in grave peril'. It criticised the dairy sector for its poor performance during World War I and noted that Irish dairy exports were facing increased competition from countries such as Denmark, which had been excluded from the British market during World War I. Almost one-half of the industry could be described as 'not organised in a dairy sense at all', with butter being manufactured at home, and the remainder was divided between co-operative and proprietory creameries. However, when it came to marketing butter, the co-operative creameries did not co-operate.

The sub-committee recommended establishing a national brand that would apply to all products of the Irish dairy industry, irrespective of where they were manufactured. This would be administered by the industry 'organised as a whole, and represented in a National Dairy Council', which would be given statutory responsibility for the brand. The national dairy council would represent all sections of the industry and other interested parties such as medical officers of health, with the Minister for Agriculture as president. The effective business of the dairy council would be conducted by a twelve-man committee – nine elected by the council itself, and three members appointed from Dáil Éireann to represent the public interest. Proposals for legislation would originate with the dairy council, and the Dáil would give the council responsibility for enforcement. The other noteworthy feature of the sub-committee's reports is their preference for the dairy sector to be self-regulating.

This model of a national council and a smaller controlling body is reminiscent of the council and the board of the DATI. Tom Johnson, chairman of the sub-committee on food and agriculture, probably devised this scheme. In November 1922 he told the Dáil that:

> ... in regard to the habit that has developed in agricultural Ireland and in industrial Ireland and in official Ireland, to denounce at all times the Department of Agriculture, as one who has followed its working a good deal in the last 15 or 18 years, I am not at all convinced that there is justice in that general denunciation. I believe that it has in the main, done its work well; and I think that, while in many cases the policy adopted has been inadvisable, it has been done with the assent and consent of the agriculturists, and has proved itself beneficial to the country as a whole.[71]

There is no indication that any of the reports of the sub-committee on food and agriculture had any immediate impact. By March 1922, when the report on milk products was completed, the security of the state was the overriding concern.

On 25 September 1922, while civil war was still raging, the provisional government approved the appointment of a Commission on Agriculture, which revisited some of the topics that had been investigated by the Commission on Resources and Industries. This latter commission was appointed in response to a resolution moved in Dáil Éireann by Thomas Nagle, TD, urging the government to initiate a programme of compulsory tillage.[72] Many sections of the rural community associated compulsory tillage with prosperity and plentiful employment: it appeared to offer a happy alternative to the falling prices and unemployment of 1922. With the announcement that Canadian store cattle would be admitted to the British market from April 1923, cattle exports also appeared to be threatened. Since Irish cattle were regarded as 'foreign' cattle, they would be held for six days at the port of entry, under measures designed to prevent the spread of cattle disease.[73] Irish livestock farmers and exporters had long feared competition from Canadian cattle; the subject had been raised on numerous occasions by members of the Council of Agriculture and by nationalist MPs at Westminster between 1900 and 1914.

For the hard-pressed provisional government, the Commission on Agriculture was a means of buying time. It was asked to investigate the causes of the present depression in agriculture and 'to recommend such remedies as will secure for Agriculture and for Industries subsidiary to it, an assured basis for future prosperity'. Items on the commission's agenda included the role of conacre and ranching in Irish agriculture, and the provision of alternative employment in rural areas; the impact of current prices and costs of production on tillage and on employment on the land; the marketing and transit of Irish agricultural produce; agricultural education; agricultural credit; and the impact on the Irish cattle trade of the opening of 'the English market' to imports of Canadian cattle. Many of these items would have been familiar to Horace Plunkett or to older members of the Department of Agriculture.

Initially the commission was to be chaired by James McNeill, a future governor-general. He was replaced by J. P. Drew, professor of agriculture at the College of Science, who had been appointed as an ordinary member of the commission.[74] The other original members were Sir John Keane (a southern unionist TD); R. A. Butler and M. Doyle, representing the Farmers' Party; T. Johnson and E. Mansfield of the Irish Labour Party and Trade Union Congress (TUC); and Sean Hales, a pro-Treaty TD, who was murdered by the anti-Treaty forces in December 1922. When McNeill and Mansfield resigned, they were replaced by C. M. Byrne, representing the government party, and M. Duffy for the Irish Labour Party and TUC. Two economists, George O'Brien of UCD and Joseph Johnston of Trinity College, Dublin (TCD), were added in January 1923.[75]

Five interim reports – on tobacco growing, butter, the marketing and transit of eggs, licensing of bulls, and agricultural credit – and the majority final report provided Hogan with a blue-print for agricultural policy for the remainder of the decade.[76] The reports recommended continuing the policies that the DATI had pursued in the past, although the commission's strong support for the co-operative movement (in the interim report on agricultural credit they described themselves 'as propagandists of the co-operative doctrine') was more consistent with the ethos of the DATI under Plunkett than under Russell. This continuity in policy is probably not surprising, since most of the staff of the DATI gave evidence to the commission. One member of the commission, George O'Brien, noted that the DATI staff:

> ... taught me a good deal about the problems of Irish agriculture. ... To have the policy of the Department explained and defended by its principal officers was equal to attending a first class course of lectures on agricultural economics. ... The foundations were laid in my mind of the general principles of agricultural policy in which I have continued to believe in spite of all the agricultural protectionism that has been so

loudly preached. These were the principles which formed the basis of Hogan's policy.

The commission argued that the depression affecting Irish agriculture was due to international factors. Since 1914 the prices paid to farmers had risen by only 40 per cent, whereas the cost of living had increased by 80 per cent, labour costs by 70 to 80 per cent, and local authority rates by 150 to 200 per cent.[77] The commission rejected suggestions that farmers should be encouraged to grow cereals as a cash crop, since they could be bought for less than the cost of production. There was, however, a case for growing cereals as food for livestock, as a component in successful farm practice, and as a means for retaining a pool of permanent agricultural labourers.[78] State assistance should be limited to promoting better practice in the production and marketing of farm produce, and to supporting agricultural education.[79]

The recommendations in respect of dairy produce closely followed those of the Commission on Resources and Industries – a national dairy council, a national brand, and measures to improve quality. This matter was becoming urgent in the light of a decision by the British Ministry of Agriculture that all imported food should indicate the country of origin (a quasi-protectionist measure).[80] The commission was opposed to any measures that would raise the cost of production, such as protective tariffs; it recommended that steps should be taken to reduce local rates, a major tax on farmers, by transferring the cost of some services to the exchequer.[81]

On issues such as ranching, conacre and land redistribution, the commission's approach was consistent with the philosophy behind the Land Act of 1923. 'As a general principle, it cannot be disputed that the larger the number of people living in comfort and decency on and from the land, the better for the country. Small holdings certainly connote a large rural population.' It was essential to ensure that smallholdings did not bring destitution, so 'any closer settlement policy must, therefore, be handled with great care, or it may produce calamitous results.' Land should not be allocated to persons with no previous agricultural experience, or to persons who happened to live nearby; 'settlers must be drawn from men and from families in whom the habits of industry and hard work attaching to tillage farming have been strongly implanted.' Any proposal to settle families on grassland or ranching land 'should have due regard to the market which these lands at present afford for the finishing of stock reared on poorer land and on smaller farms'.[82]

With the exception of the recommendations that it made concerning the marketing of agricultural produce, the commission suggested few changes from the policies followed by the DATI before 1920. In a variant of the well-established infant industries argument, however, it acknowledged that there was a case to be made for the state assisting experimental ventures such as tobacco-growing, sugar-beet, the production of industrial alcohol from potatoes, and reclaiming boglands. It disagreed with witnesses who claimed that there was no prospect of developing a dressed meat trade, although it suggested that the initiative should rest with individuals or co-operatives, not with the state.[83] TCD economist Joseph Johnston suggested that there was a good theoretical case for imposing an export tax on live cattle, although this should only be done with the support of cattle producers.[84] The commission offered a new lease of life to the co-operative movement. It recommended a return to the earlier practice of paying an annual government grant to the IAOS, although it acknowledged that the society had to become more efficient, that it should recruit new members for its board, and that the state grant should be conditional on the IAOS accepting four government nominees as full voting members of the board.[85]

A minority report, signed by Labour representatives Tom Johnson and Michael Duffy, adopted a more radical approach. They recommended setting a limit on the amount of land held by a single owner; the abolition of conacre (the majority report argued that it enabled widows and minors to retain legal control of land); and the introduction of fiscal measures to encourage wheat-growing and a dressed meat trade. Priority should be given to raising domestic food consumption (the same question was raised in the reports of the Commission on Resources and Industries), and they recommended that:

> ... the policy of the Ministry of Agriculture should be diverted in this direction away from the conception that the Irish farmer exists solely to supply the British consumer all he can produce of beef, pork, butter and eggs at an internationally competitive price, and to buy from the British producer all he wants in the way of manufactured foods, and from the American, Australian or European exporter an illimitable variety of expensive, tasty (and often unwholesome) food products.[86]

This divergence of views between the majority and minority reports anticipated a succession of later divisions on agricultural policy. The merits of promoting wheat-growing and discouraging the export of live cattle were debated again, with similarly divided views, in the report of the Tariff

Commission on flour, and by the all-party Dáil Economic Committee established in 1928.[87] Several proposals in the 1923 minority report anticipated measures that were introduced by the Fianna Fáil government after 1932, including the requirement that millers include a proportion of home-grown wheat in their flour and that imports of flour should be restricted. In 1924, however, Fianna Fáil did not exist; Irish republicans were boycotting Dáil Éireann; and such views attracted little support in Dáil Éireann. However, some deputies complained about the large amounts of malt being imported by Guinness brewery, and there was considerable support for measures to encourage home-grown tobacco.

Hogan agreed with the majority report of the Commission on Agriculture that dairying was the foundation of Irish agriculture, although he pointed out that dairy farmers also produced bacon and beef. He favoured a more intensive form of dairying and livestock farming than was generally practised. He wished to encourage 'winter farming' – feeding dairy and store cattle throughout the winter with cereals, silage (with which the Department was experimenting), and fodder crops. When deputies demanded that he find an alternative market for barley to Guinness brewery (which was offering low prices), Hogan suggested that farmers should feed the barley to cattle.[88]

AGRICULTURAL POLICIES, 1924–32

In January 1924, in a memorandum to the Executive Council, Hogan emphasised that 'national development in Ireland, for our generation at least, is synonymous with agricultural development and that, therefore, we must enunciate as soon as possible a policy for the development of agriculture which will get the sympathy and support of the intelligent go-ahead farmers of the country.' The government 'must have, as a Government an agricultural policy'; indeed, the matter could not be left to any one minister, 'even though he be an External Minister'.[89] This document should be interpreted in the light of three other factors – the publication of the majority report of the Commission on Agriculture; the publication in November 1923 of the report of the Fiscal Inquiry Committee, which came down firmly against tariff protection and in favour of an economic policy based on exporting agriculture and a limited number of large industries;[90] and the depressed state of agriculture.

According to the report of the Department of Agriculture for the year ending 30 September 1923, 'the post-war depression, which manifested itself so acutely in the year 1922 continued to weigh on Irish agriculture, though towards the end of the period the situation improved and the prospect brightened'. Appalling summer weather resulted in a shortage of hay and turf, a poor grain harvest, and outbreaks of liverfluke. In the following year farmers were forced to sell large numbers of cattle and pigs at very low prices because they were unable to feed them.[91] By 1924 Irish-American papers were reporting that the west of Ireland was threatened with more severe famine than at any time since 1847. Although these reports were exaggerated, many farming families were in considerable difficulty. The 1924/5 season brought even worse weather conditions, more disease and greater misery. O'Connor and Guiomard have estimated that for 1924/5 the volume of net and gross output was 12.5–13 per cent below the 1912/13 figure; the volume of crops declined by 16.3 per cent, and the volume of livestock by 9.3 per cent. Cattle numbers fell as livestock died when wet weather led to outbreaks of liverfluke and other parasitic diseases. Oats and potato yields were also badly affected.[92]

While the 1924/5 season was undoubtedly the worst year in this particular crisis, the Department was already coming under pressure to do something for farmers by the end of 1923. In January 1924 Hogan asked the Executive Council to give urgent consideration to providing some form of assistance for agriculture. He suggested that the Land Act of 1923 should be implemented as rapidly as possible; a sum of £100,000 should be given to the Land Commission for relief works in the congested districts (this would employ 4,000 labourers for six months); small farmers should be provided with loans to enable them to build new houses; and the government should provide start-up loans for new industries. Rates relief on agricultural land and some scheme of agricultural credit should also be considered, particularly some means of providing credit for farmers who might otherwise not survive.

Hogan also used this emergency to put pressure on the government to announce a long-term policy for agriculture. He set out priorities under four headings:

- establishing standards and a national brand for butter, bacon and egg exports;
- developing a livestock policy that would produce milch cows and pigs of a quality equal to or better than the best Danish animals, while giving 'fair play' to the beef trade;

- improving the facilities for agricultural education; and
- reorganising the Department of Agriculture so as to make it an efficient instrument to administer these programmes. (Hogan did not indicate what he had in mind under this final heading.)

There was also an urgent need to reduce the cost of production for farmers, by cutting rates and wages. Hogan was particularly critical of the high wages paid to local authority labourers, which pushed up agricultural wages. He was also concerned that, since 1914, the cost of freight, fertiliser and necessities such as food and clothing had risen substantially more than farm prices. (He also noted that agricultural wages had risen by only 70–80 per cent since before the war, while the wages of industrial workers had risen by 185–300 per cent. He did not draw the possible inference that agricultural wages were too low.) Hogan claimed that the government must assist farmers by bringing about a reduction in the cost of living.[93] Achievement of this programme would depend on overall government policy, and partly on the Department of Agriculture and the co-operative movement.

Co-operatives: a new lease of life?
The 1920s brought renewed interest in the role of the co-operative movement as a key agent in the programme of agricultural development. Because of the severe financial difficulties caused by the civil war and the high cost of security, the government was forced adopt a very restrictive attitude towards public expenditure. It preferred to assist economic development indirectly. This was the model adopted in the case of sugar-beet, and the Industrial Trust Company, which was a disastrous attempt to set up a venture capital company to assist manufacturing industries.[94] The co-operative movement was seen as a valuable agent in this policy. In addition, co-operation was regarded as a form of organisation that suited Ireland's needs, not least because Aodh de Blacam, James Connolly and others had suggested that under brehon law property had been held on a co-operative basis.[95] Co-operation offered a middle way between capitalism and socialism, and for that reason it was attractive both to labour leaders and to advocates of catholic social teaching. The Commission on Resources and Industries and the Commission on Agriculture had both advocated a major role for co-operatives in developing agriculture.

In 1922 the provisional government agreed to continue an annual grant of £5,000 to the IAOS, which had previously been provided by the (now defunct) Development Commission. A memorandum submitted by the

IAOS in support of its application listed Ernest Blythe, soon to become Minister for Finance, as one of its members. In 1923 the Cabinet approved an overdraft of £20,000 from the National Land Bank for the Irish Agricultural Wholesale Society, the organisation that supplied fertiliser, seed and agricultural supplies to the co-operative societies (in 1926 the National Land Bank was forced to write off £13,000 of this sum).[96] During these years Hogan was in regular correspondence with Horace Plunkett. Although Plunkett was resident in England, he kept in touch with the negotiations that were taking place between the Department of Agriculture and the IAOS. In the autumn of 1925 he was pressing Hogan, McGilligan, Minister for Industry and Commerce, and O'Higgins, Minister for Home Affairs, for a formal statement of the government's agricultural policy, which for Plunkett appeared to involve a commitment on the future role of the IAOS.[97] In January 1926 the Cabinet agreed to provide the IAOS with an annual grant of £8,000 for the next five years.[98]

Hogan planned to hand over responsibility for agricultural credit and the dairy sector to a reformed co-operative movement. In January 1927 he told the Executive Council that once the proposed Co-Operative Organisation Bill, designed to improve the capital structure of co-operative societies and to give the IAOS much stronger control over the co-operatives, and the Agricultural Credit Bill became law, 'all future agricultural development and Credit must be provided for under the provisions of these Acts, and all direct Government aid, such as that now proposed, must come to an end'.[99] While the Agricultural Credit Bill was enacted, the Co-Operative Organisation Bill never materialised.

But before direct government aid ended, Hogan was determined that the dairy industry should be restructured. Dairying was at the heart of his blue-print for mixed farming. In June 1924 he told Dáil Éireann that, 'Dairying is the foundation of Irish agriculture. Any weakness in dairying is immediately reflected in every aspect of agriculture, and if by any mischance the dairy farmer should go out of business the wheels of industry would immediately stop short.'[100] There were an estimated 400 co-operative creameries and 180 proprietory creameries in the Irish Free State, although according to Hogan the organisation of the co-operative creameries was 'to a large extent unsound'. Most co-operatives were controlled 'by a small and enthusiastic minority', who exercised 'a disproportionate and detrimental influence on where the creamery is sited'. Many societies were not true co-operatives, since most of their capital came from bank borrowings, not from shareholders. There was little co-operation between the co-operative creameries, and not all were affiliated to the IAOS.[101] Ireland was the only country in Europe where co-operatives competed to buy milk and to sell dairy produce. English multiple grocers exploited these divisions to drive down the price of butter, and creamery managers were unable to insist on higher quality because, when suppliers were reprimanded, they simply moved to another creamery. Rival creameries were often established as a consequence of local disputes, or because competing banks were willing to provide capital. The majority of creameries were under-capitalised and operating below capacity.

The Department of Agriculture intended to give the co-operative movement responsibility for the dairy sector. For this reason it was decided not to establish a national dairy council. Hogan rejected two attempts by Dáil deputies to insert a clause establishing a national dairy council in the Dairy Produce Bill of 1924.[102] As a first step in strengthening the co-operative principle, the Department proposed to introduce legislation requiring that only shareholding farmers could supply milk to co-operative creameries; co-operatives would be required to have a specified minimum proportion of their capital in the form of paid-up shares, and be affiliated to the IAOS. Yet, in 1927 Hogan acknowledged that these provisions could not be enforced, because in more than three-quarters of the dairy areas, co-operative and proprietary creameries were competing for suppliers. Any insistence that suppliers should be shareholders would drive the 'loose suppliers' away to the proprietary creameries, resulting in the collapse of fifty or more of the best co-operative societies. This would 'raise a fierce storm from the very best farmers in the country'.[103]

The Dairy Disposal Company
In 1926 the collapse of a large proprietory creamery company, the Condensed Milk Company of Ireland, presented the Department of Agriculture with the opportunity to reduce the power of proprietory creameries and to rationalise the industry. The Condensed Milk Company controlled 114 of the 205 proprietory creameries then in operation, as well as ten large condensing plants, making it the second biggest player after the co-operatives. In 1923 the Condensed Milk Company took over and modernised the processing plants that had formerly belonged to Cleeves, a County Limerick company best remembered because some of its workers organised a 'soviet' in 1920. In 1925 the Condensed Milk Company took control of the Newmarket Dairy Company in County Clare. The major shareholder in the Condensed Milk Company was a large firm

of British wholesale grocers, Lovell and Christmas. Andrew O'Shaughnessy, TD, owned another block of shares.

When Cleeves had gone into liquidation, it had owed a considerable sum of money to farmers who had supplied milk, and they were naturally reluctant to supply the Condensed Milk Company because they had not been paid. In order to regain suppliers, the Condensed Milk Company was forced to bid against co-operative creameries in counties Tipperary, Limerick and Cork. This milk war threatened to bankrupt several of these creameries and they applied to the IAOS for assistance. Andrew O'Shaughnessy informed Hogan that the Condensed Milk Company had sufficient resources to crush the co-operative movement in Ireland; they were only deterred from doing so because 'there are a few advanced co-ops that could hold out long enough to make life difficult, and the government would be forced to intervene'.[104]

In November 1926 the Condensed Milk Company offered to sell its operation to the IAOS. This may well have been an indirect approach to the government, since the company must have been aware that the IAOS lacked the necessary capital. According to Hogan, the Executive Council realised that 'this decision involved the Government in a most unusual role, and could only be justified as an essential part of a general policy for the reorganisation of the whole dairying industry'.[105] It was in light of this realisation that Hogan informed the Executive Council that he was 'forced to the conclusion, therefore, that we have no alternative except to consider the proposals for sale made by the Condensed Milk Company'. He expressed the opinion that the purchase should go ahead as soon as possible, adding that 'the transaction is an extremely serious one – both from the point of view of its actual cost and its implications'. Once it became known that the government intended to buy out the Condensed Milk Company, Hogan anticipated that the remaining sixty-eight proprietory creameries would also be offered for sale, and the government would be forced to buy these as well. According to Hogan, sixty-seven of the 114 creameries owned by the Condensed Milk Company and forty of the other sixty-eight proprietory creameries were redundant, because there was a co-operative creamery nearby.

Hogan emphasised that he did not want to see the government saddled with egg-grading stations or bacon-curing plants. The government's takeover of creameries was justified by 'special circumstances'. Dairying was 'the keystone of agriculture in this country, and must be put on a proper footing to clear the way for the Co-operative Organisation Act and the

Agricultural Credit Corporation Act.' He emphasised that the government had subsidised several manufacturing industries by introducing tariffs, and that these subsidies had been awarded at the expense of agriculture; agriculture deserved equal treatment. In Hogan's opinion, the takeover of the Condensed Milk Company would remove the long-standing problem of competition between the co-operative and proprietory businesses, which only existed 'in an acute form' in the dairy industry.

The Department took advantage of visits by its inspectors to the plants owned by the Condensed Milk Company to estimate the value of the premises on offer. They valued the creameries at £180,000 and the condensed milk plants at £120,000. The company was demanding £350,000. Hogan recommended that the negotiations should be conducted by the IAOS, provided that the team was competent, with the government providing the money. The Cabinet gave approval in principle to the purchase of the Condensed Milk Company, subject to its agreeing on the purchase price. On 1 March 1927 the Cabinet approved a price of £365,000, provided that the Department of Finance was satisfied with the details. For this money the government acquired 113 creameries, ten condensing stations, grain mills, egg-collecting stations, dwelling houses, shops, a fleet of motor vehicles, and other miscellaneous property.

The objective was to dispose of most of the creameries as soon as possible. If a creamery was regarded as viable, the Department would determine its value, with a view to selling it to suppliers who would form a co-operative. If the co-operative failed to raise sufficient capital from shareholders, the Minister for Finance would make up the short-fall in the form of a loan to the society. If a proprietory creamery was being closed down and its milk supply transferred to an adjoining co-operative creamery, the milk supply would be valued in shares, which would be offered to members of the co-operative, with the Minister for Finance making up any short-fall.[106] As the planned Co-Operative Organisation Bill was still under negotiation, the Department introduced what became the Creamery Act of 1928. This enabled co-operative societies to issue share capital in order to buy the former proprietory creameries. A section of the Act gave the Department the authority to prevent the establishment of new creameries, where this would damage an existing creamery.[107] The report of the DATI for 1927/8 reported that twenty-nine of the creameries had been sold, fifty had been closed, and the remaining thirty-five had been organised into groups of five with a view to sale.

By May 1928 the remaining thirty proprietory creamery owners operated forty central and fifty-four auxiliary creameries. Most of these creameries were located in counties Cork and Kerry, and Meyrick suggested that the Department of Agriculture should buy these at an estimated cost of £209,000. Disposing of them would entail a loss to the exchequer of approximately £87,000. He was less concerned about taking over proprietory creameries in other parts of Ireland, since they were not in direct competition with co-operatives. Meyrick also emphasised that some co-operative creameries should be closed and others should become auxiliary creameries. He hoped that the mergers and closures could be effected by voluntary agreement. If the overwhelming majority agreed, the state could use compulsion in the remaining cases. The Executive Council approved these proposals in May 1928, and by June 1929 the Department had purchased an additional thirty-six creameries.

The government had anticipated that the Dairy Disposal Company, a government company, would act as temporary owner of the acquired creameries, pending their transfer to co-operative ownership. But farmers were reluctant to provide share capital for co-operative creameries. Hogan had also anticipated that the Agricultural Credit Corporation (ACC) would provide capital for co-operative societies, including the co-operatives that would supplant the Dairy Disposal Company. The failure to develop a satisfactory relationship between the ACC and the co-operative sector put paid to these plans. Instead of disposing of creameries, the Dairy Disposal Company acquired yet more creameries in order to create more efficient units of production or to wean farmers away from home butter-making.

In April 1931 Meyrick wrote to J. J. McElligott, secretary of the Department of Finance, concerning the West Clare Co-Operative Creameries Limited. The company had been established in 1930 to build a central creamery at Kilrush and auxiliary creameries serving a large section of west Clare. Of the 6,000 £1 shares issued, only 600 had been paid for, and the society had accumulated large losses. Five co-operatives had failed in the area in recent years, including a home butter-making factory, which packed and marketed home-produced butter. Butter merchants were undercutting the creamery by offering better prices to suppliers. Meyrick informed McElligott that in the Minister's opinion, if creameries were to develop in County Clare, the best course was for the government to take responsibility for building, equipping and running them until they were on a firm basis. When this had been achieved, it should be possible to transfer ownership to local farmers on terms that would enable the government to recoup most of the cost. West Clare was not exceptional. Hogan believed that the government should also take responsibility for establishing creameries and seeing them through their teething troubles in other areas, because no private operators were in a position to undertake the task and the co-operatives were unable to raise the necessary capital.

McElligott's reply was predictable. The Department of Finance viewed 'with apprehension the enlargement of your Department's activities'. He was aware that the Department of Agriculture planned to reorganise creamery services in counties Sligo and Leitrim on similar lines to those proposed in west Clare. The proposal involved 'undue risks' and it represented 'experiments in State Socialism which should not be undertaken without the fullest consideration'. If the Department of Agriculture took on the task of establishing and equipping new creameries, in Mc Elligott's opinion, no further co-operative creameries would be established. The matter was referred to the Executive Council. In a supporting memorandum, the Department of Agriculture denied any intention of promoting state socialism. It contended that the reorganisation had helped the dairy industry to weather the difficult market conditions of recent years. If a proper creamery network was established in west Clare, farmers would receive up to one-third more for their milk. Dairying was losing ground in the north-west: if the industry was not reorganised, it would disappear entirely in that area, and yet, reorganisation was a difficult task since the average farmer supplied much smaller quantities of milk than in southern counties, and consequently a creamery needed many more suppliers in order to survive.

Hogan asked the Executive Council to hold a preliminary discussion on the proposals to take over the Kilrush creamery at its meeting of 19 May 1931. The West Clare Co-Operative Creameries had gone into liquidation on 12 May. On 22 May the Department of Agriculture submitted additional reports on the South Leitrim Co-Operative Creameries at Mohill, which was also about to go into liquidation, and a report on creameries in Sligo, where there was less of an emergency. On 2 June the Executive Council approved the Department of Agriculture's scheme to take over the West Clare Co-Operative Creameries and agreed to move a supplementary estimate of £48,100 for the purpose. The South Leitrim Co-Operative Creameries was taken over by another local creamery.[108]

The Department of Agriculture was still involved in reorganising creameries after 1932: in 1933 it was weighing the relative merits of establishing auxiliary creameries linked to main creameries, or building one large central creamery with milk collection depots.[109] It was also trying to resolve the question of redundancy payments for managers and other employees who were made redundant when creameries were closed.[110] And far from disappearing, the Dairy Disposal Company remained in existence until 1975.[111]

Agricultural Credit
The Dairy Disposal Company remained in existence because of the failure to transform the creameries into co-operatives. Farmers proved either unwilling to become shareholders or were unable to do so because of lack of capital. This is hardly surprising given that the 1920s were marked by low prices and several years of appalling weather. Hogan had always believed that a proper scheme of agricultural credit was essential if creameries were to be established on a sound co-operative basis. Farmers had long complained that they were unable to obtain credit on suitable terms and conditions, and there are innumerable descriptions of the alleged shortcomings of the commercial banking system, which forced them to have recourse to money-lenders or gombeen men. Whether, in fact, Irish agriculture was seriously handicapped at this time by a lack of capital remains to be proved.

From its foundation the Department of Agriculture had believed that access to credit was one of the keys to improving Irish agriculture. T. P. Gill claimed that it was useless to instruct farmers about the importance of using manure or investing in better strains of livestock if they were unable to buy these items.[112] The Department's programme to improve the quality of livestock was handicapped because farmers often sold the progeny of premium bulls as heifers, in order to realise an immediate gain, rather than keeping them for breeding.[113]

Plunkett had intended that the co-operatives should play a major role in providing agricultural credit. In April 1901 the Board of Agriculture voted £1,000 for the promotion of agricultural credit associations and a further £10,000 as initial capital for these societies.[114] The DATI continued to provide assistance to the co-operative credit societies until 1909. By then, however, Plunkett was no longer vice-president of the DATI and co-operative societies were out of favour. In 1914 the Departmental Committee on Agricultural Credit in Ireland reported that co-operative credit was in a very unsatisfactory condition owing to a combination of factors, including incompetence, dishonesty and over-reliance on the state. It recommended that the DATI establish an agricultural credit section, which would inspect existing credit societies and arrange for others to be established. New societies should be limited liability companies, not co-operatives, and the committee recommended against establishing a central agricultural mortgage bank to provide long-term capital.[115] This report was regarded as extremely hostile to the co-operative movement. L. Smith-Gordon and C. O'Brien, two men who were active in the IAOS, claimed that it displayed an 'extraordinary amount of ignorance on the whole subject'.[116] No action was taken on foot of this report because of the outbreak of World War I.

The standing of co-operative credit undoubtedly rose under Dáil Éireann. Robert Barton enlisted the assistance of Smith-Gordon in setting up the National Land Bank, which was to be run on co-operative principles with state assistance. The 1923 Commission on Agriculture reversed the key recommendations of the 1914 departmental committee, recommending that the IAOS, rather than the Department of Agriculture, should be responsible for overseeing agricultural credit societies and for promoting the creation of others. The state would provide a legislative framework and provide grants for education in co-operative credit. On the provision of long-term credit, the commission again reversed the decision taken in 1914, recommending the establishment of a land mortgage bank, with capital of approximately £1 million to be provided by the commercial banks. This would be 'a legal and accounting entity with no physical existence'. Applicants would apply to their local bank manager, loans would be approved and guaranteed by the state, and the state would be responsible for recovering interest from defaulters.[117]

Agricultural credit was high on the Department of Agriculture's agenda during the 1920s. The appalling weather conditions in 1923 and 1924 forced farmers to sell off their stock prematurely because of a shortage of fodder, and the outbreak of liverfluke further depleted livestock numbers. By 1925 the Department believed that farmers needed assistance in re-stocking their holdings. Using administrative powers dating from before 1922, it provided a sum of £100,000 to the agricultural societies to provide credit. The IAOS agreed to promote the establishment of new co-operative agricultural credit societies in areas where they did not exist, and as an incentive the Department promised to advance £1 for every £1 raised locally; this was later increased to £2 for every £1 raised locally. Despite many statements welcoming this new scheme, the take-up was extremely low. By 31 March 1926 only £28,373, little more than one-quarter of the money, had been allocated to these co-operative agricultural credit societies; by 1930 the sum advanced stood at £87,495. Arrears on these loans rose sharply when prices fell after 1930.[118]

The decision to advance £100,000 to co-operative agricultural credit societies was an emergency measure. Hogan wished to postpone the creation of a permanent agricultural credit agency until prices and economic conditions had settled down. He was also convinced that it was essential to reform the dairy industry before introducing the Agricultural Credit Corporation Bill.[119] The Agricultural Credit Act of 1927 followed the lines recommended by an interim report of the 1926 Banking Commission. Although the ACC would have authority to lend money to individual farmers, it would also strengthen the lending efforts of the co-operative societies by providing them with rediscount facilities. The legislation also took account of the recommendations of a report on agricultural credit that had been drawn up by the British Ministry of Agriculture, which formed the basis for the British Agricultural Credits Act of 1928.[120]

When the Agricultural Credit Bill was published, one member of the Irish Banks Standing Committee described the proposals as 'grossly unfair to Banks, other lenders and other persons' and the secretary of the Irish Banks Standing Committee recommended that the bill should be opposed in Dáil Éireann. The committee feared that the ACC would be in competition with the commercial banks and it was determined to protect the banks' interests. In particular, it wanted a commitment that debts to the commercial banks should take priority over debts to the ACC in the case of individual borrowers.[121] Three-fifths of the £500,000 capital for the ACC was provided by the state; most of the remainder was subscribed by the commercial banks.

The Minister for Finance appointed three of the seven board members of the ACC, including the chairman; the remaining four were elected by the shareholders, although it was agreed that three of these would be nominated by the Irish Banks Standing Committee.[122] McElligott, secretary of the Department of Finance, discussed the names of ministerial nominees with Patrick Hogan, and two of the three nominees were probably suggested by the Department of Agriculture – Patrick F. Walshe, a principal officer in the Department of Agriculture, and Senator Michael O'Hanlon, former secretary of the IFU.[123]

In April 1929 Patrick F. Walshe, secretary of the ACC, sent Hogan a draft bill that would enable the ACC to advance loans on the security of unregistered land. Many farmers did not have registered title to their land and remedying this was 'long, difficult and offputting'; yet, without a registered title, farmers were often unable to raise a mortgage. This bill became law in July 1929.[124]

The Agricultural Credit Act of 1929 was also an attempt to strengthen the links between the ACC and the co-operatives by extending the power of the co-operative societies to make loans to members from funds provided by the ACC, and by enabling them to act as guarantors for loans taken out by their members from the ACC. (The report of the DATI for 1927/8 had expressed fears that the co-operative credit societies would not survive when government grants were discontinued.) However, this plan for the ACC to work in conjunction with the co-operative societies did not materialise. The government did not compel the co-operative societies to deposit their surplus funds with the ACC, because, as the Commission on Banking, Currency and Credit (established in 1934) noted, the deposits held by the co-operatives were insignificant. At the same time, the societies protested at the high rate of interest charged by the ACC, and that, in contrast to the commercial banks, they were not represented on its board.

When agricultural prices began to fall in 1930, the co-operative societies found it increasingly difficult to secure the repayment of outstanding loans, and many of the societies that had been established during the 1920s collapsed. By the mid-1930s four of the eight loans that the ACC had made to co-operative credit societies were in default, and three of the societies were in liquidation. Only 1 per cent of the ACC's business took the form of loans to individual members through co-operative societies. By 1936 a majority of those borrowers, 159 out of 257, were in arrears. This scheme proved unpopular because prospective borrowers were required to disclose financial details to their co-operative society. According to the *Report of the Commission on Banking, Currency and Credit*, defective administration seemed to be 'inherent in any method of co-operative credit organisation in this country and [were] not remediable in a satisfactory manner by State action', a statement that suggests that the Banking Commission saw no future for co-operative credit.[125]

An unpublished report by the Department of Agriculture some years later repeated a number of familiar points: the societies had failed to raise sufficient capital; their unlimited liability deterred investors; they were unduly reliant on state funds. It also suggested that the IAOS was rather lax in monitoring and assisting the credit societies, because the government grant to the IAOS was based on its income from member societies, and the largest contributions came from co-operative creameries.[126] Because the co-operatives and the general public failed to deposit sufficient money with the ACC, it evolved into a state corporation almost by accident.[127] In 1944 the *Report of the Commission on Vocational Organisation* noted that, 'It [ACC] is a limited liability company, not a department or office of State, and is supposed to be independent of Government and political influence'.[128] The strong influence exerted by the commercial banks and the weakness of the co-operative societies limited its role. In 1928 the ACC gave a private undertaking to the Irish Banks Standing Committee that it would notify the banks in all cases where it intended to make a loan to one of their customers,[129] and the interest rate charged on ACC loans was broadly in line with the rates charged by the commercial banks.

Nevertheless, the apparent scarcity of agricultural credit during the 1920s may not have been entirely a bad thing. In 1926 Hogan spoke about the potential for disaster in providing unwise credit, adding that 'during the last three or four years I have regarded every day that passed without giving these credits as a day gained';[130] something similar could be said about the early 1930s.

Both the ACC and the Dairy Disposal Company are instances of state companies emerging by default. The government had set out to develop a co-operative agricultural credit agency and to create a strong co-operative creamery sector. Hogan's expectation that by reorganising the creameries, creating an agricultural credit corporation with strong links to co-operative credit societies, and enacting a co-operative organisation bill, he would reduce the need for state intervention in agriculture, was not fulfilled.

The proposed Co-operative Organisation Bill never saw the light of day because the Department of Agriculture and the IAOS were unable to agree on the terms of possible legislation. By 1933 the IAOS was almost wholly dependent on state grants, and the Department was planning to assume responsibility for controlling and reorganising the co-operatives. In July 1933 one official wrote that, 'The IAOS as you and I have known it for over thirty years has now almost run its course'; he went on to refer to 'the eve of the IAOS' dissolution'.[131] On 28 September 1933 James Ryan, Minister for Agriculture in the Fianna Fáil government, noted in a letter to Seán MacEntee, Minister for Finance, that the IAOS would end with the Co-operative Organisation Bill.[132] In October 1933 the Department of Agriculture submitted a bill to the Executive Council, emphasising that the Minister regarded it as an urgent item and hoped it would be introduced in Dáil Éireann by January 1934.[133] However, the bill never reached the Dáil. When de Valera inquired in November 1957, why the bill had not gone ahead, the Department informed him that it had worked 'intermittently' on it between 1933 and 1949: in 1949 the then Minister for Agriculture, James Dillon, had asked the IAOS to outline what form of legislation they considered necessary; the Department was still awaiting a reply.[134]

Marketing and Quality Control

During the 1920s marketing and quality control were top of the list of measures to raise agricultural income in countries that decided not to opt for agricultural protection or for other forms of direct subsidy. In New Zealand, legislation passed in 1921 and 1922 gave monopoly control over the export of meat and dairy produce to a meat producers' board and a dairy producers' board.[135] The Northern Ireland Ministry of Agriculture wasted little time in drafting the Livestock Breeding Act of 1922, which required the licensing of all breeding bulls, and the Marketing of Eggs Act of 1924.[136] In Britain, the 1924 Report of the Linlithgow Commission on the Distribution and Production of Agricultural Produce presented a series of recommendations for the improved marketing of British agricultural produce,[137] including the proper grading of eggs and the introduction of a national mark. These measures were implemented by the Agriculture Produce Grading and Marketing Act of 1928 and the Agricultural Marketing Act of 1931.[138]

In Dublin, the Department of Agriculture had been trying for many years to exercise better control over the quality of exported produce. In 1912 a bill that would have banned the export of sub-standard produce collapsed as a result of opposition from the IAOS.[139] The Agriculture Produce (Ireland) Bill of 1920 marked a second attempt to control the quality of produce exported, but the bill never became law because of the passing of the Government of Ireland Act in 1920. The 1924 Dairy Produce Act was a more detailed version of the 1920 bill. The 1924 Act was regarded as the first step towards implementing a national brand for all dairy exports. It planned to begin by grading and inspecting all butter consigned for export; a national brand would not be launched until satisfactory standards had been attained. The legislation also gave the government authority to require all butter exporters to be registered, and the power to carry out inspections of all premises used for packing or blending butter and other dairy produce. Premises that failed to meet acceptable standards could be deregistered within two weeks. Registered premises were required to record details of all consignments of dairy produce.[140]

The Agricultural Produce (Eggs) Act of 1924 prohibited the export of dirty eggs and required that all exporters should be licensed; and premises where eggs were packed for export were to be subject to inspection. A consultative committee of people involved in producing eggs was established to advise the Department.[141] When the legislation was being prepared, the Department suggested that all Irish eggs exported to Britain should be stamped with a harp, but this proposal was abandoned, because it was decided not to introduce a national brand until standards were assured.[142] Additional legislation passed in 1930 closed some loopholes in the 1924 Act and gave the Gardaí power to enter premises that were trading illegally in eggs, and to seize the stock.[143] The Agricultural Produce (Potato) Act of 1931 introduced regulations covering the export of potatoes.[144] The Livestock Breeding Act of 1925 set out to raise the quality of Irish cattle, by preventing the use of unsuitable bulls. A guide to this Act, issued by the Department of Agriculture, stated that 'while the standard will not be unduly high when the Act is first put into operation it is intended to aim at a progressively higher standard in the future'. In 1922 only one in forty bulls in Ireland was registered; by 1928 this had risen to one in nine.[145] This was quite impressive, because the Department also raised the qualifying standard for bulls during these years. By the 1940s, however, this Act was widely criticised for allegedly favouring beef breeds at the expense of dairy stock.

In 1923 the Irish government was informed that in future Irish meat would be classified as foreign meat in Britain and would therefore be subject to inspection. Although Britain subsequently agreed not to enforce these regulations, in 1928 the Dominions Secretary informed the Department of External Affairs that Britain wished to introduce a system of inspection, because several cargoes of diseased meat from Ireland had been seized at British ports. The Scottish Board of Health complained that many carcases imported from Ireland were either dirty or diseased; a substantial proportion were affected with tuberculosis. Similar complaints came from the health authorities in Manchester and Cardiff.

In January 1929 Joseph Walshe, the secretary of the Department of External Affairs, asked the secretary of the Executive Council to arrange a discussion on what steps should be taken to preserve the reputation of Irish beef on the British market.[146] The complaints were arising at a time when exports of carcase beef and veal were increasing: in 1926 they had amounted to 6,519 cwt; in 1927 this had trebled to 20,593 cwt; and in 1928 exports of beef and veal had risen by a further 340 per cent.[147] On 31 January 1929, two weeks after Walshe's request, Patrick McGilligan, the Minister for External Affairs, informed the Secretary of State for the Dominions that legislation was being prepared to provide for the inspection of all meat for export; in the meantime the Department of Agriculture would discourage the export of unsound meat. Yet, on 20 March, the British authorities condemned thirty-one out of ninety-six quarters in a cargo of meat that had been shipped from Rosslare. The Agricultural Produce (Fresh Meats) Act, which provided for the inspection of exported meat, eventually came into force in September 1930. By then, exports of fresh meat had been falling for over a year.[148]

Bovine tuberculosis also threatened Irish cattle exports. The Diseases of Animals Act of 1927 gave the British authorities power to slaughter any diseased cattle arriving at British ports. Irate Irish farmers demanded compensation. The Department of Agriculture proposed introducing an inspection scheme, which would be funded by a levy on all cattle exports, so that conscientious farmers would be forced to pay for the shortcomings of less scrupulous farmers; however, this legislation was not enacted, and the matter was handled by livestock shippers instead.

While the Acts introduced by the Cumann na nGaedheal government undoubtedly helped to improve the quality of Irish agricultural exports, the Department of Agriculture had much less power to restrict the export of sub-standard produce and to prevent damaging competition among Irish exporters than the governments in New Zealand or Northern Ireland. Although both the Commission on Resources and Industries and the Commission on Agriculture had recommended establishing a national brand for dairy exports, this did not happen. In 1928 the IAOS formed Irish Associated Creameries Limited to market dairy produce, and participating creameries agreed to deliver their entire output to the company for three years. However, up to 20 per cent of creameries, including some of the largest suppliers, refused to become members, and some member creameries failed to abide by the agreement. During 1928/9 Irish Associated Creameries handled approximately half the total output of Irish creameries, but with the onset of the agricultural recession in 1929, buyers were well placed to exploit the divisions in the Irish creamery sector and the company ceased trading in 1930.

When Irish Associated Creameries closed, the Department of Agriculture established a tribunal, chaired by John Dulanty, the Irish trade commissioner in London, to inquire into the marketing of Irish butter. It was asked to advise on the most effective marketing method to increase the demand and price for Irish butter in export markets, and to advise on the effect of combined marketing on demand and price.[149] The tribunal interviewed 139 witnesses, representing a total of seventy-nine creameries. In December 1930 it issued an interim report recommending the establishment of a society, with members drawn from every co-operative creamery. The new society would assist creameries in marketing their butter by putting them in contact with new business, pooling supplies where no single creamery could fill an order, improving services such as transport, and issuing directives on the appropriate range of prices (in order to prevent the dumping of butter).[150] In February 1931 the co-operative creameries voted to reject this proposal by a small margin, and the tribunal ceased its work. No final report was issued.[151] The seasonal fluctuations in Irish butter output were a further handicap in marketing Irish butter in Britain: between May and November, 92 per cent of Irish butter was exported, while in winter Ireland imported butter.[152]

The value and the volume of Irish agricultural exports may well have been damaged by the failure to establish stronger national marketing boards. Yet the New Zealand experience suggests the lack of strong central support may not necessarily have been the cause. During the 1920s the New Zealand government did everything Hogan could have wished for: it created strong export marketing boards, and local finance boards to lend money to co-operative credit associations that provided farmers with credit to buy livestock or fertiliser; there was also a long-term mortgage fund that provided farmers with long-term capital. Yet the country's share of the British market for meat and dairy produce remained stable, and one researcher has concluded that marketing boards and concessional finance were not successful measures for maximising net farm income during the 1920s.[153] Ireland's share of the United Kingdom market for butter, eggs and cattle was also stable between 1924 and 1928.[154]

Sugar-Beet

Sugar-beet was the only crop to receive price support during the 1920s (although a limited tax concession was granted on home-grown tobacco). This support for sugar-beet could be justified because the crop was experimental. It is rather surprising that the Commission on Resources and Industries did not investigate the possibility of growing sugar-beet in Ireland, since the matter had been raised on a number of occasions before 1920, and there had been a substantial rise in the acreage of sugar-beet grown in Europe during World War I, when supplies of cane sugar from overseas were disrupted.

In 1924 Britain decided to encourage the growing of sugar-beet by offering prospective manufacturers a subsidy consisting of a remission of excise duty (sugar was a major source of tax revenue) and a tariff on imports of cane sugar.[155] Later in the same year the Irish government appointed an interdepartmental committee consisting of Joseph Hinchcliffe, representing the Department of Agriculture, R. C. Ferguson, assistant secretary of Industry and Commerce, and J. L. Lynd of the Department of Finance, to investigate the merits of an Irish sugar-beet industry. By then the government had already received a number of applications from continental producers wishing to set up factories in Ireland. One came from a Dutch businessman, Van Rossum, who described the establishment of sugar-beet processing in Ireland as ' "prairie" pioneer work'. He claimed that the Irish government would need to offer much more generous terms than those on offer in Britain.

Although such an argument would obviously have been in Van Rossum's interest, a preliminary report from the inter-departmental committee concurred. There was no data available as to the yield and quality of sugar-beet that might be grown in Ireland, but there were indicators that the production costs would be high. An efficient sugar-beet plant required a minimum of 10,000 acres, and the committee believed that 5,000 acres was the maximum that could be grown in Ireland; during the early years most of the permanent employees would be foreign and would demand higher wages; an Irish plant would require better equipment than in Britain, because Ireland had few facilities for carrying out repairs; a promoter would find it extremely difficult to raise the necessary capital. The report also noted that in most European countries sugar-beet processing had only developed with state assistance. Despite these disadvantages, the committee acknowledged that sugar-beet would be an attractive cash crop; it would help to promote tillage, and a sugar factory would provide at least 500 seasonal jobs between October and January, a slack time in the farming calendar.

Van Rossum demanded a subsidy of 25s 8d per cwt on beet, more than 60 per cent higher than in Britain. This would cost approximately £150,000 per annum and the committee suggested that a decision should be deferred, in the hope that others would come forward with competitive bids. After further consideration and a journey to the Continent to meet proprietors of sugar-beet processing plants, the government was left with two serious contenders: Van Rossum, and a Belgian sugar producer, M. Lippens. In February 1925 Hinchcliffe and Ferguson were authorised to conclude a deal with Lippens. His offer was favoured because it offered a higher price to the farmer, and the scale of the proposed factory (and consequently the cost to the exchequer) was lower – a plant processing 40,000 to 50,000 tons of sugar-beet, as opposed to 100,000 tons in the case of Van Rossum. Lippens was also demanding a smaller guaranteed acreage of sugar-beet – 2,500 acres as opposed to 5,000.[156]

By 1925 trial sugar-beet plots were being grown in Leinster and east Munster. The Department supplied Lippens with data giving the yields in the various areas, but left him a free hand in selecting Carlow as the location for his factory. At a late stage in negotiations, the government received a third proposal, from the Czech firm of Skoda and a Dutch businessman de Berker. De Berker visited north Cork, an area that had strong hopes of becoming the site of the first sugar-beet processing plant, where he encouraged the formation of the Irish Beet Growers' Association. Despite De Berker's strong backing from the North Cork Industrial Development Association and several Cork TDs, the government continued to support Lippens.

The Carlow plant received its first consignment of sugar-beet on 6 November 1926. Cosgrave and Hogan paid an official visit to the plant on 17 January 1927. During its first year the factory processed over 85,000 tons of beet, which yielded almost 12,000 tons of sugar. By 1930/1 it was producing over 23,000 tons of sugar, approximately one-quarter of Irish consumption. The original agreement specified the exact subsidy to be paid to the promoters for the first seven years; the subsidy would be reduced substantially in the fourth year. When this duly happened in 1929/30, the company cut the price it paid to beet growers from between 56 and 58 shillings per cwt to 51 shillings. When the subsidy was again reduced in 1931/2, the price to growers fell to 42s 10d. These cuts were strongly resented by the Irish Beet Growers' Association; the 1931/2 price resulted in a strike by growers, which forced Lippens to raise the price to 46s 6d.[157] By 1931 sugar-beet producers were in a comparatively privileged position, even with the reduction in price, as they had a secure market at a time when there was increased competition and falling prices for all agricultural produce.

Between 1926 and 1932 the direct and indirect cost (in taxes foregone) of the subsidies awarded to the sugar-beet industry amounted to almost £3.5 million. Lippens returned annual profits in excess of £200,000 for 1927/8 and 1928/9, on a capital investment of £400,000. Fianna Fáil argued that the company was making excessive profits, and that the subsidy was unduly generous. However, Hogan pointed out that only foreign companies had the necessary expertise, and it had been extremely difficult to persuade anybody to invest in Ireland given the troubled conditions of the early 1920s.

We had to go outside the country. Look at the proposition from the angle of a Belgian, a Dutchman or an Englishman investing £400,000 worth of capital in this country at a time when we had hardly repaired the bridges. They were broken at the time. We had hardly repaired or replaced houses that were destroyed. The smell of petrol had hardly left the country. That was put up to us, time and time again, by every single one of them, and we had to go out of our way, in spite of all that evidence that was under their noses, to assure all these firms which we were anxious should come into this country and compete for the industry, that the state of affairs was not going to recur.[158]

Once the Carlow plant was in operation the government came under pressure from Clonmel and from north Cork to establish another sugar-beet factory. The standard reply emphasised that the Carlow plant was an experiment, which was still being monitored; that the government had played no part in selecting the location; that if other factories were established, Cork, Clonmel and every other town would be considered; and that 'financial considerations preclude[d] the extension of the beet sugar industry in this country with assistance from the government'.[159] Hogan does not seem to have favoured expanding sugar-beet; the large subsidy would have been anathema to his laissez-faire philosophy. In 1933, when he was out of office, he told the Dáil that 'any extension of beet growing for the manufacture of sugar is unsound and uneconomic'; it required a subsidy of £28 to £30 per acre.[160]

Agriculture and the Irish Economy

Hogan consistently argued that as agriculture was the largest employer and the source of the overwhelming majority of Irish exports, economic policy must ensure that Irish farmers remained competitive with farmers in Denmark, Britain and elsewhere. He was opposed to higher welfare payments, because they would result in increased taxation and they might deter rural labourers from taking jobs in farming. He was also determined to bring about a reduction in agricultural wages. This reduction was best achieved by controlling the wages of local authority labourers, because in rural Ireland agricultural labourers often worked for part of the year as local authority labourers, and by ensuring that other rural workers, such as the labourers employed on the Shannon Scheme, did not achieve significant wage increases.[161] For the same reason, it was important to ensure that the state was not unduly generous in providing relief works or unemployment benefits. Agricultural rates were also within government control, and Hogan tried on many occasions to secure a reduction in agriculture's share of the rates bill. County committees of agriculture and county councils also regularly passed resolutions demanding either full or partial relief on agricultural land. Hogan's case was strengthened by the fact that the British government progressively derated agricultural land and this concession extended to Northern Ireland.

In February 1924, and again in the following month, Hogan presented the Executive Council with two long memoranda detailing the burden that agricultural rates placed on farmers, at a time when bad weather meant that agriculture was in crisis. As an emergency measure, he suggested that the government should reduce the current year's rates demands on farmers from approximately £2.8 million to £200,000, by doubling the grant in relief of agricultural rates and permitting local authorities to meet the balance by borrowing. The government eventually agreed that councils could remit agricultural rates by up to two-thirds, and borrow the money to make up the difference. In 1925 it doubled the agricultural rates grant and this concession was continued in subsequent years.

Notwithstanding, Irish farmers received much less generous rates relief than farmers in Britain and Northern Ireland, who were relieved of approximately 75 per cent of their rates bill in 1923. In 1928 agricultural land in the United Kingdom was derated. Such a concession was not feasible in Ireland because agricultural land accounted for 72 per cent of county valuations. An interdepartmental committee, which examined the matter, concluded that derating would raise living standards for farmers without stimulating any increase in agricultural output. In 1931 a commission of inquiry into derating endorsed this conclusion, although all farming representatives on the commission dissented. In 1931, in response to pressure from farming interests, the government increased its annual grant for agricultural rates relief from £600,000 (the figure set in 1925) to £750,000.[162]

Although the Department of Agriculture wished to reduce the overall level of taxation on agriculture, it was not prepared to cut the local contribution towards the cost of agricultural services. Indeed, the Agricultural Act of 1931 made it obligatory for county councils to raise a rate of 2d in the pound, which would be devoted exclusively to agricultural services; councils were permitted to raise an additional 1d in the pound if they so wished. The contribution to the cost of agricultural services had been declining for some years, with most counties providing only the minimum statutory rate of ½d in the pound.

Public expenditure was tightly controlled during the 1920s; the government adopted a frugal attitude towards welfare entitlements, relief work, housing, roads and other areas of public investment. This was in accord with Hogan's convictions, and with the views of larger farmers, although smaller farmers, their sons, and farm labourers, who depended on relief works for part-time employment, would probably have favoured more generous public spending.

Free Trade or Protection: the Agricultural Interest

The most important strategic question in Irish economic policy during the 1920s, and a contentious issue, was whether or not to embark on a programme of tariff protection.[163] Although the Fiscal Inquiry Committee, which reported in 1923, had come down firmly in favour of free trade, with Professor George O'Brien, who was a friend of Hogan's, speaking on behalf of agricultural interests on the committee,[164] this did not end the debate. It was widely believed that the report of the Fiscal Inquiry Committee gave scant attention to the views of the majority of Irish manufacturers, and the government was under pressure to make some concessions on tariff protection.

On 21 January 1924 Joseph McGrath, the Minister for Industry and Commerce, promised Dáil Éireann that the government would introduce limited protection on items where it would not injure agriculture. Two days later Hogan told the Dáil that farmers should be compensated for any increase in the cost of living resulting from tariff protection.[165] The government's attitude towards tariff protection was strongly influenced by the decision of the British Prime Minister, Stanley Baldwin, to call a general election in Britain in December 1923 in order to seek a mandate from the electorate for the introduction of tariff protection. If Baldwin had been returned to office, the Irish government might well have introduced tariffs in the knowledge that Britain would be doing likewise. But Baldwin lost the election and Britain's first Labour government, which was committed to free trade, took office on 22 January, the day between McGrath's and Hogan's statements in Dáil Éireann.

The momentum towards tariff protection suffered another setback when McGrath resigned from the government in March 1924 over army demobilisation. He was succeeded as Minister for Industry and Commerce by Patrick McGilligan, who had been a classmate of Hogan's at UCD. McGilligan's papers contain numerous memoranda from Hogan on the importance of agriculture, the need to control costs, and arguments against the imposition of tariff protection, which indicate that Hogan made a considerable effort to keep McGilligan in the free-trade camp. Hogan was probably aware that Gordon Campbell, secretary of the Department of Industry and Commerce, and other senior officials favoured selective protection. Campbell was lukewarm, at best, about Hogan's argument that a prosperous agriculture, based on exports, would provide a spring-board for Irish economic development. In January 1927 Campbell presented McGilligan with a scathing criticism of Hogan's policy of 'mixed farming':

> ... a form which supports a low proportion of persons, which produces a relatively small volume of wealth and which is very sensitive to conditions in other countries on which it is necessarily dependent. It may be an inevitable concomitant of land division at its present stage. But it will not increase the population nor produce the maximum wealth possible nor be stable unless conditions in Britain are stable.[166]

There is no evidence of disagreement between Hogan and McGilligan, and Hogan appears to have exercised a veto over the protectionist policies of the Department of Industry and Commerce. Hogan's position was considerably strengthened by the fact that his views on protection also coincided with those of the Minister for Finance and senior officials in the Department of Finance.

From April 1925 until December 1926 all applications for tariffs were considered by an interdepartmental conference that included a representative from the Department of Agriculture. The Department lodged formal objections against applications for tariffs on rosary beads, briar pipes, down quilts, woollens and various other items, claiming that they would lead to 'some increase in the cost of living without any compensating benefit to farmers'. Only applications for tariffs on mineral oils, brushes, and corsets escaped its censure. Its most vocal objection related to a proposed tariff on farm machinery, sought by the Wexford manufacturer Pierce.[167]

Although farmers were opposed to tariffs on manufactured goods, they were more divided on the question of protecting agricultural produce. Livestock farmers saw no benefits in protection, but the position of grain-growers was rather different. By 1924/5 the acreage under tillage was

147

substantially lower than in 1914, owing to the combined effect of low prices and appalling weather. In August 1925 a conference organised by the Kildare County Committee of Agriculture and the Grain Growers' Association demanded the introduction of tariffs on wheat, oats and barley. It also urged county committees of agriculture to carry out experimental trials to encourage farmers to grow more wheat, and called for a subsidy or tax concessions on every acre of ploughed land. It also argued that if land was being acquired for redistribution, owners who tilled 25 per cent of their holdings, or more, should be exempt. When a deputation from the conference demanded a meeting with Hogan, it was informed that he was out of town.

In October 1925, as a concession to the grain-growing lobby, the Department announced that it would arrange trials to investigate the possibility of extending the acreage under wheat.[168] These experiments began during the 1926/7 season. In its annual report for 1926/7, the Department noted that the stabilisation of wheat prices on the international market 'makes the cultivation of the crop in this country a proposition well worth considering'. The first series of trials was halted in 1928, but a further 209 demonstration plots were organised in twenty-one counties during 1929.

Trial plots failed to placate the grain-growing lobby. In the autumn of 1925 Laois County Committee of Agriculture passed a motion demanding a tariff on barley. Barley-growers had been campaigning for some years for restrictions on imports of malting barley. Hogan persisted in refusing to meet a delegation from the Grain Growers' Association. However, J. J. Walsh, the Post-Master General and chairman of Cumann na nGaedheal, proved more sympathetic to their case.[169] Walsh may have influenced the government's attitude, because in January 1926 Earnest Blythe, Minister for Finance, announced that he was considering extending tariff protection to agriculture. This provoked a resolution from the annual meeting of the IFU, reminding the government that it had no mandate for such action.[170] The Irish Flour Millers' Association, on the other hand, submitted an eight-page report to Hogan in support of its demand for a tariff on imported flour.

The Department of Agriculture debated whether a tariff on imported flour would encourage farmers to grow more wheat. According to a report that appeared in *Milling*, the trade magazine of the British flour-milling industry, the Department had concluded that farmers would grow more wheat, if the impression was created that the tariff would bring a substantial increase in the price of flour. On this basis, according to the report, it recommended that tariffs should be imposed on imports of wheat and flour from 1 March 1926. However, this proposal does not seem to have reached the Executive Council. Takei notes that opinions within the Department of Agriculture were divided.[171] An interdepartmental conference, which included representatives from the Department of Agriculture, examined the merits of protecting oats, barley and wheat, and concluded that oatmeal was the only item where a tariff might be of some benefit to agriculture, and even there the benefit would be slight.[172] Nevertheless, a tariff on oatmeal was introduced in the 1926 budget. Ernest Blythe, the Minister for Finance, informed the Dáil that the tariff would create 300 additional jobs in milling and provide farmers with a market for an additional 20,000 tons of oats.[173]

December 1926 saw the end of contentious decisions on protection, with the matter being placed in the hands of a statutory three-man tariff commission, under the authority of the Department of Finance. One of the three members was J. H. Hinchcliffe, a senior official in the Department of Agriculture. During the summer of 1926, when the Department of Finance was refining its proposals for legislation establishing the tariff commission, Meyrick contacted Joseph Brennan, secretary of the Department of Finance, to demand that the Minister for Agriculture should be in a position to initiate tariff applications. Meyrick also suggested that the bill establishing the tariff commission should include provision for assisting the development of industries by other fiscal means, such as export bounties and waiving of excise duties, and that these provisions should apply to agriculture as well as industry. Finance rejected these proposals, claiming that they would enlarge the functions of the tariff commission unduly.[174] All applications for tariffs had to come from the responsible industry. However, the Department of Agriculture's proposals suggest that Hogan was prepared to consider a range of fiscal measures to assist either agriculture or manufacturing industry, provided they did not damage agricultural interests.

The Tariff Commission adopted a leisurely approach, often taking several years to reach a decision. The delay in processing applications indicates a distinct lack of enthusiasm for protectionist measures. Some applications were not pursued, including those for tariffs on cooked foods, animal feed, maize and agricultural produce. This list indicates that there was a growing agricultural presence in the protectionist camp by this time. The commission recommended granting tariffs on rosary beads, margarine, down quilts and some grades of woollen cloth, but it rejected applications for tariffs on motor bodies, fish barrels, paper products and flour.[175]

Although all these reports were unanimous, the report rejecting an application for a tariff on flour included an addendum by Professor Whelehan,
the nominee of the Department of Industry and Commerce. Whelehan
favoured paying a bounty on Irish-grown wheat in order to ensure that
some flour was produced from native wheat. Hinchcliffe, however, did not
support Whelehan's addendum. Whelehan's proposal was similar to one
from the Irish Farmers' Protectionist Union, an organisation representing
approximately 200 farmers in mixed tillage areas such as Kildare, Laois,
Louth, north Tipperary, Kilkenny, Wexford, Offaly and east Cork.[176]
However, their case and the arguments of J. J. Bergin, the chairman of the
Grain Growers' Association, were outweighed by the opposition of the IFU,
the largest farming organisation at the time.

The publication of the Tariff Commission's report on flour in 1928
sparked yet another series of resolutions demanding government aid for
grain growers. In response, the government asked the ministers for
Agriculture, Industry and Commerce, and Finance to consider Whelehan's
proposal, noting that 'it may be anticipated that Deputy de Valera will return
to the question again and will establish what progress had been made'.[177]
There is no evidence that the three ministers ever reported on this matter
or that they even met to discuss it. (The minutes of the Executive Council
during these years reveal numerous instances of ministerial inaction on
contentious matters.)

In the autumn of 1928 the Irish Grain Growers' Association demanded
an inquiry into the merits of requiring that a designated proportion of
Irish-grown grain should be included in all animal feedstuffs sold in Ireland.
Although the proposal was not within the terms of reference of the Tariff
Commission, the government asked that it report on the matter. Hogan
seems to have been in favour of this inquiry and he sought to have Mr
O'Donovan, an official in his Department (presumably C. O'Donovan, an
inspector), appointed as secretary. However, support for holding the inquiry
does not necessarily imply that Hogan was in favour of the proposal. Around
this time the Department of Agriculture was arguing that imposing a duty
on imported barley would only give rise to embarrassment, unless a general
policy of protecting agriculture were adopted.[178] Conceding a tariff on
barley, but not on wheat, would have been seen as favouring a relatively
small group of farmers, and the Fianna Fáil opposition would undoubtedly
have accused the government of abandoning its free-trade policy. Reports
that the government was setting up another inquiry prompted a new wave
of resolutions, such as one from Wicklow County Council that it could 'see

no harm' in giving a trial to the scheme requiring the inclusion of Irish-grown grain in animal feed.[179] As it happened, the Tariff Commission did not report until July 1931, when predictably enough, it rejected the application.

When W. T. Cosgrave was forced to establish an all-party committee of Dáil Éireann in December 1928 to consider what steps might be taken to reduce unemployment, Fianna Fáil used the opportunity to reopen the question of encouraging the cultivation of wheat. This topic split the committee and led to its premature demise. A majority report, signed by government supporters, recommended that there should be no subsidy for domestic wheat-growing; the minority report adopted the contrary position.[180] The Department had no formal role in the committee's deliberations, although J. J. Hassett, the superintendent of the Athenry agricultural station, and J. R. O'Donnell, an agricultural inspector, and five agricultural instructors, gave evidence to the committee.[181]

By 1930 the protectionist lobby in Irish agriculture was becoming more vocal because of the international recession and the fall in agricultural prices. It was widely claimed that agricultural produce was being dumped on the Irish market, although according to Louden Ryan, a comparison of imports for the first five months of 1929 and of 1930 provides no supporting evidence. Ryan is correct in suggesting that there was no substantial increase in imports, although the imports of bacon, which had declined from 1924 to 1928, had begun to rise and prices were falling.[182] Given the inelastic demand for agricultural produce, a comparatively small rise in imports was sufficient to trigger a substantial fall in prices, and this was the main cause of grievance among Irish farmers. At the time it was widely believed that dumping was taking place.

A conference organised by the Irish Grain Growers' Association in October 1930, which attracted a wide attendance of county councillors and TDs, passed resolutions demanding a complete ban on imports of oats, and the establishment of a tribunal to investigate to what extent foreign barley and malt were essential to the successful operations of the Irish brewing industry, with the intention of banning or limiting imports. The conference also demanded that duties should be imposed on imports of bacon and that there should be a complete ban on bacon imports within eighteen months. Other resolutions demanded bans on the importation of butter, cream, condensed milk and eggs. These resolutions were forwarded to the government in a letter signed by TDs and senators representing Cumann na nGaedheal, Labour and Fianna Fáil.[183]

Hogan responded by proposing that the Executive Council should replace the existing part-time Tariff Commission with a permanent tariff commission with full-time officials. Initially it was agreed that John Leydon, an official in the Department of Finance, would be the new chairman, with W. McAuliffe, representing Agriculture, and W. B. Maguire, representing Industry and Commerce. The Executive Council later decided to postpone a final decision on the proposed new tariff commission until the views of Patrick McGilligan and Desmond FitzGerald, two government ministers who were in London, could be sought. In the event, the new Tariff Commission was chaired by Henry O'Friel, secretary of the Department of Justice; Agriculture was represented by Daniel Twomey, a future secretary; John Leydon of the Department of Finance became an ordinary member; and Industry and Commerce had no representative.

The reform of the Tariff Commission brought speedier reports and a greater willingness to grant protection, which can be regarded as a response both to the international recession and to the demands expressed at the Kildare Conference in October 1930. The reports on butter, oats, bacon, linen piece-goods and some types of leather all recommended the introduction of tariffs. In the case of butter, the government did not wait for the Tariff Commission to report: it introduced an emergency tariff in November 1930, two days after the application for a tariff was lodged, and several months before the commission reported.

When the commission recommended reducing the minimum price at which woollen cloth could be imported free of duty, to compensate for the falling price of cloth, the Cabinet originally approved the recommendation, only to rescind the decision at its next meeting. Hogan was absent at the first Cabinet meeting but present at the second, and it seems likely he was responsible for the change of mind.[184] This would suggest that, while Hogan was prepared to contemplate some limited protection for agricultural produce by 1930, he remained hostile to any extension of tariffs on consumer goods if they threatened to raise the cost of living for farmers. As for tariffs on agricultural produce, there was a substantial difference between protecting items such as butter and bacon, where Ireland was a major producer and a substantial exporter, and introducing protection or subsidies for wheat. Bacon imports consisted of cheaper and lower-grade American bacon; butter was imported to make up for seasonal shortages. There was a case for protecting Irish producers from the threat of dumping during a major agricultural depression.

Achievements of the 1920s

The story of the Department of Agriculture from 1922 to 1932 has always been closely identified with the Minister, Patrick Hogan. Many scholars who have examined the Department's performance during these years have given a very favourable verdict, although probably none as favourable as the account given by George O'Brien, in an obituary on Hogan, who was killed in a car accident in 1936.

> If Hogan's policy be regarded in relation to the situation in the Free State for the first ten years after the treaty, it can be defended on the following grounds. In the first place, it utilized to the maximum the physical and geographical resources of the country; secondly, it developed those branches of production which are particularly suitable for the average Irish farm; thirdly, it did not involve any breach of continuity in the tradition of Irish farming or in the constructive programme of the Deparment of Agriculture; fourthly, it promised to provide abundant rural employment as the agricultural statistics prove that mixed farming with dairying as its principal feature gives more employment per acre than almost any other type of agricultural activity; fifthly, food production would be stimulated and the population of the Free State could never be reduced to famine in war-time. The alternative objectives of agricultural policy, namely employment and food production, would thus be incidentally secured. The final justification of the policy is that it ensured that any public money spent on agriculture would be employed productively by being devoted to the building up of the efficiency of the industry rather than to deflecting production from one line to another.[185]

Assessments of Hogan's contributions to Irish agriculture have benefited from his early death, and from the fact that the 1930s were an especially difficult time for Irish agriculture. The 1920s have been regarded in a much more favourable light than they appeared at the time. It has frequently been noted that the volume of Irish exports in 1929, consisting over-whelmingly of agricultural produce and food and drink, was not exceeded until 1960. However, the focus on exports (and a substantial share of food and drink exports are attributable to Guinness) distorts the record. A recent assessment of trends in agricultural output suggests that the performance was much less successful.

Notwithstanding the slogan of the time – 'one more cow, one more sow, one more acre under the plough' – no increase took place in the number of cows, other cattle or pigs, while the area under crops fell by nearly one-fifth between 1922 and 1932. The volume of gross agricultural output in 1924/5 was 13 per cent below the level of 1912/13 and although it had recovered by over 10 per cent in 1929/30, it was still 4 per cent below the pre-war level. Livestock and livestock produce had increased their dominance still further, while crops and turf accounted for only 16 per cent of the value of gross output in 1929/30 as against 22½ per cent in 1912/13. The value of net output – the closest proxy for farm incomes at this time – was 5 per cent less in 1929/30 than in 1924/25.[186]

And 1924/5 was a crisis year!

Should the fact that agricultural output in 1929/30 was below the pre-war level, be blamed on agricultural policies? The markets and price trends for agricultural produce were highly unfavourable during the 1920s. The agricultural price index (1911–13 =100) peaked at 288 in 1920, fell to 160 in 1922, and to 110 by 1931.[187] These years also saw a deterioration in agricultural prices relative to other prices, as the Commission on Agriculture and Hogan both pointed out. Britain, Ireland's main export market, was a more competitive market than in 1914, and the British economy was also in a depressed state. There is little doubt that market conditions provide the major explanation for the poor performance of Irish agriculture during these years.

In turn, the difficult market conditions and the over-supply of produce, such as butter, meant that Irish producers were tempted to compete against each other. The collapse of Irish Associated Creameries was one result. The Department of Agriculture appears to have been reluctant to take a lead in this situation. Louis Smith contrasted the hesitant attitude of the Department towards controlling the marketing of agricultural produce, with the much more interventionist approach adopted by the Northern Ireland Ministry of Agriculture. The legislation passed in Northern Ireland ensured that marketing arrangements were compulsory, and that they were under state control. All traders and exporters were brought within the Acts, and penalties were imposed for non-compliance. Although the marketing boards established by the Ministry of Agriculture in Northern Ireland included representatives of producers and middlemen, they were firmly under government control. Smith concluded that the combination of compulsion and government control was essential to their success. Ironically, when the legislation was going through the Parliament of Northern Ireland, government speakers referred at some length to the findings of the Commission on Agriculture established by the Irish Free State to support their case for strong marketing boards.[188] Although the New Zealand experience indicates that strong marketing organisations did not offer a panacea for the market difficulties of the 1920s, the failure to establish a dairy marketing organisation indicates the destructive power of vested interests in the industry, and the Department's inability to overcome them.

This sense of the Department's impotence may be seen, for example, in its lack of success in monitoring Irish cheese production and exports. The amount of cheese produced in Ireland rose sharply during World War I, but the quality was so poor that officials feared it might damage Ireland's reputation as a food producer. The Department's London office tried to relay information to Dublin about market opportunities in Britain, but its efforts were severely handicapped because Irish cheese producers remained secretive about their sales and the types of cheese they were producing. Consequently, most of the reports from London consisted of rumours: that some creameries had dismantled their cheese plants; that the men involved in cheese production were 'lukewarm' at the moment; or a report in December 1924 that Irish creameries were offering substantial amounts of cheese for sale at present. At the beginning of 1925, when the Department of Agriculture tried to discover which creameries were planning to produce cheese in the coming year, and an approximate estimate of their weekly output, several of the Department's inspectors noted that they were not very confident as to the accuracy of their information.[189] This was hardly the ideal way to promote dairy exports. The Department had no legal authority to require producers to provide information on output or sales, and Irish producers appear to have been intent on guarding their independence, even from the Department of Agriculture.

Under Hogan, the Department continued to assume that the co-operative movement would play a major role in reforming agriculture, and this was especially so in the case of dairying, yet the co-operatives were either incapable or unwilling to undertake the task. In the area of agricultural credit, the government appears to have been equally reluctant to intervene in the market. Three of the seven directors of the ACC were nominated by the Irish Banks Standing Committee, and the ACC did not compete on interest rates with the commercial banks.

Both these examples of agricultural policy suggest that the Cumann na nGaedheal government was reluctant to impose its authority in economic matters. There are a number of explanations for this. The original philosophy of the Department of Agriculture, as spelled out by Horace Plunkett, involved working through the co-operatives, and the practice during the 1920s continued in this tradition. The legacy of the civil war influenced every aspect of political life: during the civil war and for many years after, the government was forced to operate with a very firm hand in matters relating to national security, and there may well have been some reluctance to extend this strong-handed approach into economic matters. Despite winning the civil war, the Cumann na nGaedheal government remained extremely vulnerable, and as a result often found it necessary to avoid alienating powerful elements within the state, such as the commercial banks.[190] The need to exercise a tight budgetary regime, because of the cost of the civil war and the fear of becoming unduly dependent on the Irish banks, meant that the state only became a shareholder in the ACC and a long-term owner of creameries via the Dairy Disposal Company by default.

Hogan, in particular, believed that the years of the Anglo-Irish war had created unrealistic expectations, which had to be quashed. It was rather difficult to persuade farmers to give attention to dairy hygiene and clean eggs, when a social revolution appeared to be at hand. During the debate on the estimates for the Department in 1926 Hogan remarked that:

> During that period [the civil war] there was a deliberate attempt made to mobilise all the historical weakness of the rural community. The doctrine 'Ireland is yours for the taking - take it' was explained expounded and understood to mean 'If you are in debt, if you want money for pleasure or any other purpose, take the neighbour's land; take his money out of the bank; seize his cattle, and above all pay no rents, rates or taxes'.[191]

Hogan reacted to this mentality by insisting on self-help, farmers' taking responsibility for their own economic welfare and the survival of the fittest. He regarded farming as a business; there is no evidence that he viewed life on the land in a sentimental fashion. Yet, while farming was undoubtedly a business for those with thirty acres or more of reasonable land, matters were very different for the large numbers of smallholders, who relied on emigrants' remittances, migratory labour, and relief work schemes for their survival. Moreover, the message of self-help does not take account of the fact that farmers' livelihoods depend on factors outside their control, including the weather, trends in agricultural prices and market conditions.

Criticism of agricultural policy between 1922 and 1932, both inside and outside the Dáil, concentrated on issues such as the government's reluctance to impose protection or to expand the production of sugar-beet, and its failure to provide land for landless men and de-rate agricultural land. There was little interest in the quality of agricultural produce or the failure to introduce a national brand for agricultural exports.

One institution that played a surprisingly minor role in the history of the Department of Agriculture during the 1920s was the Department of Finance. Since the publication of Ronan Fanning's *History of the Department of Finance,* the overriding power of Finance and the belief that it thwarted various economic initiatives has almost become a cliché in the history of twentieth-century Ireland. Yet there is no evidence to suggest that the Department of Agriculture was deprived of the money it needed during these years. Money was immediately forthcoming to buy out the Condensed Milk Company; sugar-beet was granted substantial subsidies and tax concessions; and although McElligott condemned the Department's plan to buy out more proprietory creameries in 1931 as 'experiments in State Socialism', the government approved a supplementary estimate. Agriculture seems to have had few difficulties with Finance during these years because Hogan's economic philosophy was close to the Finance position. Both departments believed that Ireland was essentially an agricultural country; that the well-being of the Irish economy was dependent on agriculture, and in turn the best prospects for agriculture lay in increased exports to Britain. By 1931, however, these assumptions were being challenged by the collapse of agricultural prices and by Britain's decision to abandon free trade in favour of protecting its agriculture.

CHAPTER FOUR

'THE PLOUGH MEANS STABILITY, BUT THE BULLOCK IS STILL A GAMBLE',[1] 1932–1939

The 1930s were crisis years for agriculture throughout the world. Falling prices created large stocks of unsaleable produce, which in turn led to rural poverty and forced sales of agricultural land in many countries. In Ireland cattle prices fell by up to 50 per cent and on occasion farmers found it impossible to dispose of livestock at any price. Livestock were seized and subjected to forced sales in order to meet debts to private creditors and arrears of rates.[2] Such incidents conjured up memories of earlier land agitation and the files of the Department of Agriculture contain letters from aggrieved farmers demanding compensation for the decline in the value of their stock, and requests for loans to tide them over their difficulties. One widow with three young sons, who was living on a farm of twenty acres, requested help in clearing her debts to the bank; she claimed she was unable to sell either her cattle or her pigs.[3]

Although Irish farmers were not immune to the impact of the crisis in international agriculture, they fared much better than they had during the last great agricultural depression of the 1870s and 1880s. In that previous era the majority of Irish farmers had been tenant farmers, and falling prices had brought the threat of eviction; in the 1930s few Irish farmers were forced to surrender their farms. The report of the Banking Commission noted that agricultural indebtedness was much less of a problem in Ireland than elsewhere, because farmers collectively were net creditors of the banks.[4] Nevertheless, the 1930s saw a rise in the level of unpaid debt. In May 1932 the ACC cleared over 89 per cent of the sum owed; by November 1932 this had fallen to 82 per cent, and by November 1936 only 71 per cent of the sum due for collection was realised.[5] Three-quarters of co-operative agricultural credit societies were in arrears on their repayments to the

158

Department of Agriculture by 1934.[6] Arrears of rates on agricultural land increased, although the problem was more acute in Leinster and east Munster than in the poorer counties of the west of Ireland.[7]

Irish agriculture relied heavily on exports, with Britain being the major market. In 1931 Britain decided to reintroduce protection for its farmers, reversing the policy that had existed since the repeal of the Corn Laws in 1846. Between 1929 and 1931 Irish exports, which consisted almost entirely of agricultural produce, fell by 10 per cent in volume, from £47 million to £36 million in value,[8] and the decline seemed likely to continue. At the 1932 Imperial Conference in Ottawa, Britain began to negotiate new arrangements for importing agricultural produce, giving preference to Empire countries. In theory, this should have given Ireland favoured access to the British market. However, as Britain was encouraging its own farmers to produce more food, Irish exporters would face increasing competition from British farmers and from other Empire producers such as New Zealand and Australia, who were also experiencing the effects of economic depression.

In 1932 the Irish Free State embarked on a radical change in economic policy. Fianna Fáil came into power with a commitment to self-sufficiency both in agricultural and industrial produce. Tariffs and quotas were introduced on a wide range of manufactured goods, including farm machinery and basic equipment such as spades. Heavy duties were imposed on imported butter and bacon, and on less important items such as rhubarb and rhubarb stools, rose stocks, trees, shrubs and bushes, honey and fresh and dried vegetables. Farmers were encouraged to reduce their reliance on raising cattle for the British market and to concentrate instead on the domestic market. In the future it was hoped that most Irish sugar would be produced from Irish sugar-beet; that up to 50 per cent of Irish flour would be derived from Irish wheat; and that pigs and poultry would be fattened on home-grown barley and oats instead of imported maize.

The 1930s brought a fundamental change in the market for Irish agricultural produce. For almost a century, except during World War I, Irish farmers had operated in a free trade economy, buying raw materials and animal feeds on the world market, and competing against all comers both at home and abroad. From the 1930s the market for agricultural produce was regulated by price controls and other mechanisms. This altered the role of the Department of Agriculture, and the relationship between farmers and the state. Until the 1930s the Department had concentrated its efforts on providing advice and education and on improving the quality and the marketing of Irish produce. After 1932 the emphasis switched to price stabilisation, bounties and compensation payments, subsidies to domestic producers, and measures designed to achieve the government's self-sufficiency programme. The prices that farmers received for their produce were often determined by the Department, or by the government. The Department influenced the location of flour and provender mills, determined the quota of native grain that flourmillers were required to use in a particular year, and set the price that creameries received for their butter. Although the Department continued its traditional activities, such as supplying premium bulls to improve the quality of livestock, and trials to select the varieties of seed that were most appropriate to the Irish soil, efforts to promote better farming often took second place to the task of regulating the market for agricultural produce. Price subsidies for agricultural produce became an important category in government spending, accounting for 41.6 per cent of the rise in government spending between 1932 and 1938.[9] Expenditure under the estimate for the Department of Agriculture quadrupled between 1931/2 and 1932/3, the first year of the Fianna Fáil government.

TABLE 1: Estimates of Expenditure for the Department of Agriculture, 1931–9

	Gross (£)	Appropriations in Aid (£)	Net (£)
1931–2	670,898	227,615	443,283
1932–3	2,531,986	£617,495	1,914,490
1933–4	3,640,362	1,239,048	2,401,314
1934–5	5,290,447	1,641,942	3,648,504
1935–6	4,596,957	1,539,119	3,047,837
1936–7	4,089,426	1,622,459	2,466,966
1937–8	3,898,629	1,158,805	2,739,823
1938–9	2,579,840	1,093,106	1,486,773

Source: Annual Reports of the Minister for Agriculture.

The Minister for Industry and Commerce, Seán Lemass, was the key economic minister in the Fianna Fáil governments of 1932–9. He had a status akin to that of the previous Minister for Agriculture, Patrick Hogan, under Cumann na nGaedheal. James Ryan, the new Minister for Agriculture, adopted a centre position within Cabinet, between Lemass' militant protectionism and the more conservative views of the Minister for Finance,

Seán MacEntee. Ryan, the son of a Wexford farmer, had won a county council scholarship enabling him to study medicine at UCD. He took charge of a medical unit in the General Post Office in Dublin in 1916 and was interned at Frongoch, qualifying as a doctor shortly after his release. In the 1918 general election he won a seat for Sinn Féin in South Wexford. During the Anglo-Irish war he was brigade commandant in south Wexford and chairman of Wexford County Council. A founder-member of Fianna Fáil, he became the party's first spokesman on agriculture. According to Liam Skinner, Ryan was 'the painstaking plodder rather than the dazzlingly brilliant man, but he can be depended upon to stay the course'. Farming was his only hobby.[10] Meyrick retired as secretary of the Department in 1934, although he appears to have been retained in a consultancy capacity. His successor, Daniel Twomey, had been an inspector in the Department of Agriculture. A native of Macroom, Twomey had graduated in agricultural science in 1908. He is the only secretary of the Department to have worked as an agricultural adviser.

Fianna Fáil's programme of self-sufficiency presented certain difficulties for the Department of Agriculture. Between 1922 and 1932 agriculture had been regarded as the dominant sector in the Irish economy, and this meant that decisions on taxation or government spending were often made on the basis of their impact on agriculture. After 1932 the interests of manufacturing industry assumed greater importance, and these did not necessarily coincide with the needs of agriculture. While the Department of Industry and Commerce embraced protectionism with enthusiasm, there is no evidence of a similar fervour in the Department of Agriculture. Most manufacturers, with the exception of a handful of large firms such as Guinness, Ford and Jacobs, gained under the programme of economic protection. In agriculture, there were often as many, if not more, losers than gainers.

There was also a shift in political power from the larger, commercial farmers to the smaller farmers, who were more likely to support Fianna Fáil. The early 1930s brought a resurgence of the strain in nationalist economics that regarded tillage as good and cattle farming as bad, because tillage seemed to offer more employment and a better future for small farmers. Indeed, at the extreme, the economic ideals of the 1930s envisaged a return to a less commercial, more peasant-based form of agriculture, the reverse of what the Department had been trying to achieve since its foundation. In 1935 the Department welcomed evidence that many farmers were having their wheat milled for their own use and expressed the hope 'that the time is not far distant when wholesome bread, baked at home from home-grown wheat, will form the staple food of our rural population'.[11] It also suggested that in Denmark the Depression had prompted a reaction against 'over-capitalised' agriculture, resulting in an expanding 'peasant movement'.[12]

Despite such rhetoric, the Department went to considerable lengths to ensure that the traditional livestock base of Irish agriculture did not suffer irretrievable damage from misguided efforts to reverse long-term patterns in agricultural output. It successfully countered proposals from Lemass that large numbers of farmers and agricultural workers be removed from agriculture and placed on public works or turned into dole recipients. Although the collapse in livestock prices suggested that there was a strong economic argument for reducing the number of cattle, on several occasions James Ryan succeeded in blocking proposals to this effect. The Department of Agriculture believed that farmers should be supported through the crisis by price subsidies, not by relief work or the dole.

AGRICULTURE AND THE ECONOMIC WAR

In 1932, shortly after coming into office, the Fianna Fáil government decided to suspend the payment of land annuities owed to Britain under the Land Purchase Acts.[13] In retaliation, Britain imposed ad valorem duties of 20 per cent (later increased to 40 per cent) on the most important imports from Ireland, including live animals, butter, cream, eggs, bacon, pork, poultry, game and other meat. This dispute, which became known as the Economic War, has commonly been blamed for all the problems that Irish farming experienced during the 1930s. However, when the dispute broke out in the summer of 1932, the volume and the value of Irish agricultural exports had already fallen substantially, and Britain had already imposed duties on many Irish exports under the Import Duties Act of 1932. The duties were to come into effect after the Imperial Conference in Ottawa during the summer of 1932. Ryan, Lemass and Seán T. O'Kelly, the Minister for Local Government and Public Health, attended the conference, where Britain set out to create a new Empire trading-zone.[14]

Britain would undoubtedly have imposed some restrictions on imports of Irish cattle during the early 1930s, even if both governments had remained on friendlier terms. Between 1931 and 1933 prices for livestock and livestock products in Britain fell to levels last seen before World War I.

Irish agriculture had been lulled into a false sense of complacency because the fall in cattle prices had only become pronounced towards the end of 1931, much later than the fall in prices for other products.[15] Most Irish stores were bought by arable farmers, who fattened the animals on turnips and other root crops grown as part of a tillage rotation. The crisis in British tillage farming meant that farmers there could no longer afford to buy stores. During the autumn of 1932, when the number of Irish cattle entering the British market had already dropped sharply owing to the Economic War, British cattle prices continued to plummet, with the result that the market almost ceased to function, and some cattle could not be sold at any price.[16]

As Walter Layton, the editor of *The Economist*, noted in November 1932, the British tariff war against Ireland had been launched either to foment a coup against Fianna Fáil, or 'more probably, in order to satisfy the insistent clamour of English agriculture'.[17] In 1947, reviewing the recent history of Anglo-Irish trade, the Department of Agriculture noted that:

> While the measures taken by the British to improve the position of the cattle industry in the 1930s must be regarded as part of their set agricultural policy it is of course possible that the unfavourable treatment accorded to Irish cattle under these measures was to some extent facilitated by the existence of the Economic War, the measures were not however a result of the Economic War.[18]

During the remainder of the 1930s Britain took steps to reduce imports of agricultural produce that could be produced by British farmers. In 1933 the Dominions were forced to accept a voluntary restriction on exports of meat to Britain, and Canada had to agree to a 'voluntary' reduction in shipments of live cattle.[19] Other agricultural economies such as Denmark and the Netherlands also experienced a decline in the volume and value of their exports to Britain. Denmark protected its market share by granting Britain concessions in respect of exports of coal, iron, steel and other manufactured goods to Denmark.[20] Ireland, however, offered no such concessions and suffered a greater fall in the volume and value of its agricultural exports to Britain than other economies. In 1931 Ireland supplied 4.5 per cent of British food imports, but by 1937 this had declined to 2.1 per cent. By 1936, when the impact of the Economic War had eased considerably owing to the coal-cattle pact, Irish cattle in Britain were fetching only 53 per cent of the 1926 price; the comparable figure for British cattle was 73 per cent.[21]

Between 1932 and 1938 the annual debate on the estimates of the

Department of Agriculture was dominated by the Economic War, with opposition deputies blaming all difficulties on the dispute with Britain. During the estimates debate for 1932/3, Ryan emphasised that he had supported the government's decision to renege on the land annuities that led to the Economic War. He claimed that 'a great deal of the advice on the agricultural policy that has been adopted by the Executive Council has been taken from me, possibly most of it. In any case, nothing has been adopted by the Executive Council with which I have not agreed and I am prepared to take responsibility for it'.[22] In May 1934 he suggested that for most farmers the reduction in land annuities more than compensated for the loss in income from lower cattle prices.[23] In 1937 he presented data on world agricultural prices, or the prices obtaining on the British market for British cattle and Australian butter, in an effort to prove that Irish farmers were not alone in experiencing a sharp fall in agricultural prices. He claimed that the only two commodities where Irish farmers received less than the world price were cattle and sheep, although he failed to mention that cattle was one of the key sectors in Irish farming.[24]

By the autumn of 1932 the implications of the collapse of the export market for Irish agricultural produce were becoming apparent. During the summer the government had introduced a scheme of export bounties to offset the cost of the British duties. Although these were costing an estimated £3 million per annum, livestock prices continued to fall. On 1 November 1932, in a memorandum marked 'confidential', Seán Lemass urged the Executive Council to establish a three-person board, under the control of the Minister for Industry and Commerce, with responsibility for regulating international trade. The board would become the sole exporter of agricultural produce and would pay farmers a fixed price, making good any loss on export sales from its own resources. Existing bounties on agricultural exports would end. Although agricultural produce accounted for almost all Irish merchandise exports, Lemass assigned the Department of Agriculture a very marginal role in the proposed trade board; the Minister for Industry and Commerce would consult the Minister for Agriculture 'where agricultural interests are involved'. Lemass assumed that the board would remain in existence, irrespective of the outcome of the trade dispute with Britain.[25] On 7 November he suggested that Ireland should negotiate bilateral trade treaties with various countries, in order to reduce its dependence on the British market. He also urged the establishment of an agricultural marketing organisation to advise exporters on foreign markets and to be responsible for marketing Irish agricultural produce.[26]

Lemass also presented de Valera with a number of more radical proposals. He began by referring to the sharp fall that had taken place in the prices paid for agricultural exports, emphasising that 'the situation has nothing to do with the British tariffs. It would exist if these tariffs had never been imposed or were removed tomorrow'. In his opinion the collapse in livestock prices had destroyed any realistic prospects of developing tillage, since the tillage programme (other than wheat and sugar-beet) relied on substituting home-grown grain for imported feedstuffs, yet Irish feeding barley and oats were more expensive than imported grain. Consequently, self-sufficiency would inflict further damage on the Irish livestock industry. Although wheat was not dependent on a healthy livestock trade, Lemass claimed that it would be necessary to offer a subsidy amounting to £4 per acre, which was greater than the wages paid and profits earned per acre. He concluded that 'wheat growing cannot be considered, under present conditions anything more than a national luxury and it is questionable if we can afford it'.

The recent fall in agricultural prices meant that many farmers, who would previously have been classified as economic, were now uneconomic and it was necessary to provide them with an alternative or supplementary livelihood. Lemass recommended reducing agricultural output to the quantity that was necessary to meet the needs of the Irish people, together with whatever could be exported at a profit, or even at a loss, in order to pay for essential imports. Farmers and farm workers not needed to produce essential food should be taken off the land and employed on public works. A scheme should be implemented to ensure that people could buy all the farm produce they needed at prices that would cover the cost of production, while leaving the remaining farmers with a reasonable profit. Export bounties on agricultural produce should cease, with the money being used to subsidise food prices. Untenanted land should be divided into five-acre plots and given to labourers.

It is unclear whether Lemass intended these 'revolutionary' proposals to be implemented; they may well have been drawn up in order to scare the Cabinet into abandoning the Economic War. Lemass claimed that he could not see 'any alternative to such a national re-organisation', other than abandoning the Economic War, 'until we are in a better position to fight it' and attempting to negotiate a secure market in Britain for Irish agricultural exports. On this, at least, it seems probable that the Department of Agriculture would have agreed.

The Department of Agriculture does not seem to have responded directly to Lemass' revolutionary proposals, perhaps because it was evident they were unlikely to be implemented. The proposals were roundly condemned by J. J. McElligott, the secretary of the Department of Finance, who remarked that although the export of agricultural produce would mean a loss to the state if subsidies were paid, and a loss on paper if they were not paid, it was unquestionably better 'for the fullest advantage to be taken of our natural agricultural resources than that people should be maintained in idleness and lands and farms allowed to become derelict'. Any increase in agricultural production would 'bring its own advantages in more normal times', whereas the damage resulting from a reduction in agricultural output would not be remedied for a generation.[27]

The Department of Agriculture concentrated its fire on Lemass' proposal to establish a board for international trade. In a memorandum to Cabinet on 19 November, Ryan set out the present position on the marketing of agricultural produce, 'having as little resort as possible to figures and unnecessary detail'. He presented a reasonably optimistic picture of the prospects for butter, noting that the Department had been more successful in securing alternative markets for butter than for other produce. With sufficient effort he was confident it would be possible to market all the butter available for export on the Continent, although he made no reference to price. The Department had requested creameries to send all available supplies of butter to the Dairy Disposal Company so that it could fulfil large orders in Belgium and France. The prospect of finding alternative export markets for pigs and bacon was much less promising; two-thirds of output were sold in Ireland, the remainder exported. There was an urgent need to regulate the pigs and bacon industry in order to reduce the wide fluctuations in supplies (the notorious 'hog-cycle'[28]) and to stabilise prices to producers. A scheme for rationalising bacon factories, which had been drawn up by the Limerick bacon producer Stephen O'Mara, was under consideration, but this would not solve the problem of finding an alternative to the British market. The market for eggs in continental Europe appeared more promising, although many large exporters were reluctant to lose contact with the British market for the sake of a temporary advantage. There was no obvious alternative market for poultry.

Cattle remained the main problem. During the final quarter of 1931, 242,000 cattle were exported to Britain – 136,000 stores and 106,000 fat cattle. In a normal year, total cattle imports by Germany, Italy, France and Belgium amounted to only 30 per cent of the Irish cattle surplus. Nevertheless, Ryan believed that there would be immense benefit in selling even a proportion of exportable cattle on the Continent, since it would create a scarcity of live cattle on the British market (a rather optimistic assumption). The difficulty in finding new markets for cattle was compounded by the fact that countries such as the Argentine, which had also lost sales in Britain, were seeking markets in Europe. Ryan noted that some continental traders had a 'shrewd suspicion' that Irish cattle exporters were only interested in the European market because of the trading difficulties with Britain and would return to the British market when these difficulties had ended. Ryan also had concerns about the feasibility of diverting Irish agricultural exports to continental markets. With the exception of dairy produce, which could be handled by the Dairy Disposal Company, all exports were controlled by private traders. Lemass wished to see the proposed board of international trade become the sole exporter of agricultural produce; Ryan believed it would be best not to interfere with private traders, although some form of state trading board would be necessary if Ireland negotiated bilateral trading agreements that included quotas for agricultural produce.[29] J. J. McElligott believed that the job could be adequately handled by existing government departments.[30]

By September 1932, several weeks before Lemass proposed establishing the board of international trade, a Markets Advisory Committee was operating in the Department of Agriculture, although with a role limited to investigating alternative markets for agricultural produce and advising on export subsidies.[31] When the Executive Council asked the secretaries of Agriculture, Industry and Commerce, and External Affairs, to report on the best means of co-ordinating the work of the three departments in relation to external trade, they suggested that the duties of the Markets Advisory Committee should be extended to include all products, and that its membership should include representatives from Finance and Industry and Commerce. The committee would report jointly to the ministers for Agriculture and Industry and Commerce. They also suggested, although without obvious enthusiasm, that the committee might be retained when normal times returned, but with a more limited role, 'unless the present emergency leads to a serious and permanent change in the course of our foreign trade'.

The Executive Council approved these recommendations on 22 May 1933. There seems to have been some delay, however, in implementing the decision. In June 1933 J. V. Fahy, of External Affairs, drafted 'hurried notes' on the subject. He pointed out that no government department was responsible for procuring alternative markets for Irish exports: although agriculture accounted for the overwhelming percentage of exports, the Department of Agriculture did not determine economic policy; the Department of Industry and Commerce controlled all imports, but it was not responsible for agricultural products, and knew little about the export market for agricultural produce. In addition, Industry and Commerce had failed to consider the prospects of finding markets in Europe for agricultural produce when it imposed import duties on manufactured goods. External Affairs had been forced 'to try to centralise the information and views available (incidentally keeping the others informed) with a view to hammering out a common line on each question'. Fahy believed that a new organisation should be given overall responsibility for imports and exports.

On 4 September an interdepartmental conference was held to discuss Fahy's memorandum. The meeting noted that the Markets Advisory Committee had carried out considerable research on potential markets. This was essential 'since traders in agricultural produce in the Saorstát were not prepared to explore for themselves the prospects of foreign markets'. The conference reached the conclusion that, 'European markets do not under existing conditions, hold out prospects of absorbing any large proportion of Saorstát products and livestock'. Exports to continental countries would only become profitable if it proved possible to secure the removal of quotas, duties and other trade restrictions. If this was to be attempted, tariffs and quotas would have to be revised with a view to negotiating bilateral agreements.

Although the question of establishing a body responsible for imports and exports was on the agenda for the Executive Council, it was withdrawn at Fahy's request. A note on the file stated that de Valera, Ryan and Lemass had reached agreement on what should be done. On 9 October 1933 the Executive Council approved the decision to transfer the work previously carried out by the Markets Advisory Committee in the Department of Agriculture to a new trade section in the Department of External Affairs.[32] This decision took account of the reservations that the Department of Finance had voiced about the establishment of a separate powerful trade board outside the departmental structure; it may also be regarded as a compromise between the competing interests of the departments of Agriculture and Industry and Commerce.

The Department of External Affairs carried out the functions to the best of its ability. Officials in Berlin, Brussels and other European capitals advised the Department of Agriculture regularly about market prospects.[33]

168

The Irish High Commission in London provided the Department of Agriculture with information on cattle sales, market conditions and the technical problems relating to export licences in the major cattle ports of Liverpool, Glasgow and Birkenhead. The High Commission was also in regular contact with cattle importers, in an effort to maintain a minimum price per cwt for Irish cattle and to reduce the profit margin taken by dealers.[34]

There was a real danger that in the depressed market conditions of the 1930s Irish exporters would be tempted to dump produce on foreign markets. In order to prevent this happening, the Agricultural Products (Regulation of Export) Act of 1933 gave the Minister for Agriculture the authority to regulate and control the export of any agricultural product that was covered by the British emergency duties. In 1935 the Cabinet extended these powers to cover exports to other countries. This was done to enable the government to negotiate bilateral trade agreements.[35] In 1935 agreements were negotiated with Germany and Belgium, providing for the export of Irish cattle, butter and eggs in return for Ireland's agreeing to import coal. Some efforts to secure alternative markets can only be regarded as foolhardy, or desperate, such as the attempt to strike a deal with Poland, which was a major agricultural exporter.[36]

In 1935 the government set up yet another committee, headed by Seán O'Grady, parliamentary secretary to the Minister for Agriculture, to advise on potential markets for Irish agricultural produce. However, the harsh realities were that most countries were committed to protecting their own farm produce; there was a surplus of foodstuffs on the world markets; and Britain remained the most promising customer for Irish agricultural exports. Indeed, the main benefit from the trade agreement with Germany was to prompt Britain into agreeing the 1935 and 1936 coal-cattle pacts.[37]

The Cattle Trade

Livestock farming occupied a curious position during the 1930s. In 1929/30 five-sixths of livestock output was exported, almost entirely to Britain. Cattle producers bore the brunt of the Economic War; most of the emergency levy that Britain imposed on Irish agricultural produce was paid on cattle exports. Yet the Irish themselves had an ambivalent attitude towards the crisis in the cattle industry. On the one hand the government paid a subsidy to offset the cost of British import duties, and on the other hand, many government supporters welcomed the dethroning of livestock farming from its dominant position in Irish agriculture. Others hoped that the dispute would provide an opportunity to develop a trade in meat or fat cattle at the expense of stores. On 4 August 1932 Matt O'Reilly, TD for Meath, told the acting Minister for Agriculture, Frank Aiken (Ryan was attending the Ottawa trade talks), that the Economic War could be a blessing in disguise because it would encourage farmers to fatten their cattle properly.[38]

When the Economic War broke out in August 1932 the government asked the Department of Agriculture to devise a scheme of export subsidies. The Department suggested that a subsidy should apply only to fat cattle. To qualify, cattle should have four broad teeth, indicating that they were over two years old. However, many of these cattle were not properly finished, and veterinary inspectors were unwilling to distinguish between fat and store cattle. Eventually it was decided to pay a 12.5 per cent subsidy on both store and fat cattle. This was approved by the Executive Council on 30 September 1932. When the government decided to halve land annuity payments in December 1932, Ryan suggested that the export bounty should be reduced for all cattle other than those that were stall-fed. However, the Department's Markets Advisory Committee claimed that if Ireland stopped supplying stores to Britain, English and Scottish farmers would fill the gap, and the market for Irish cattle in Britain would suffer. On the committee's advice Ryan urged the Executive Council to continue to pay a subsidy on all classes of cattle.[39]

Despite wishing to encourage an export trade in beef, the Department of Agriculture was reluctant to introduce a subsidy on beef exports. P. O'Connor, a principal officer, noted that Irish cattle were not finished to a standard where they could compete with Scottish beef – 'the very most we could hope for our beef is that it would be classed second best'. A bounty would only revive 'the detestable old cow beef trade which got us into such bad odour in Great Britain'; this would conflict with the Department's policy of exporting only the best produce. His opinions were shared by others, including J. C. Landy of Irish Co-operative Meat Limited in Waterford. Meat from Irish cattle slaughtered in Britain was sold as British beef and commanded the highest price; Irish cattle slaughtered in Ireland would be labelled as Irish beef; and in 1931, 40 per cent of cattle slaughtered in Britain originated in Ireland.[40] Nevertheless, Ryan introduced a bounty on beef exports in May 1933; the deciding factor seems to have been jobs in beef-processing plants.[41]

When British cattle prices continued to fall throughout 1933, despite the penal duties on imports from Ireland, Britain imposed import quotas on Irish cattle. The quota for fat cattle was set at 50 per cent of the 1933 level; imports of store cattle and dairy cows were frozen at the 1933 numbers; and beef imports were prohibited. These measures had the effect of reducing the 1933 volume of cattle imports from Ireland by 12.5 per cent. Britain claimed that these additional restrictions were necessary to protect British farmers; there was no mention of the Economic War.[42] The livestock quotas were announced in the House of Commons on 20 December 1933, less than two weeks before they were due to come into effect.[43]

From January 1934 Irish cattle exports required a licence. Britain supplied the Irish government with licences every month, varying the numbers to suit its needs. In January 1934 over 30,000 store cattle licences were issued, 160 per cent of the number exported in January 1933. In April the quotas was set at 28,000, or 65 per cent of the number shipped in April 1933. The Department of Agriculture allocated licences between shippers, mainly on the basis of their previous shipments to Britain, although some licences were held in reserve for dealers based along the western seaboard, and for feeders who urgently needed to dispose of fat cattle. The quotas created acute problems for the fat cattle trade. In March 1934 there was only one licence available for every seven cattle that were ready for marketing; in April the figure was one in ten. All the licences were allocated to feeders rather than to dealers.[44] In 1935 the Department gave the county committees of agriculture responsibility for allocating licences for fat cattle, to ensure they were distributed among feeders as widely as possible. Ryan refused to divulge to Dáil Éireann the names of those awarded licences.[45] The decision to transfer responsibility to the county committees of agriculture received general approval from Fianna Fáil deputies.[46]

Livestock numbers rose during 1933 because farmers held on to stock in the hope that prices would improve, but prices continued to fall. In December 1933 Ryan presented a memorandum to the Executive Council, spelling out the change in relative living standards. Agricultural prices were at 80 per cent of the 1911–13 level, whereas the cost of food, clothing, fuel and light was considerably higher. Ryan contrasted the substantial state assistance that was provided to industrialists with the less generous treatment of farmers, and insisted that the specific circumstances of farming were not given sufficient weight in the formulation of economic policy. The only direct savings passed on to farmers since the government had come into office were a reduction in land annuities and an increase in agricultural rates relief. Tariff protection was fixed at a level that enabled employers to pay trade union wages to their workers, while giving 'a handsome return on capital', whereas the prices set for wheat, beet and other commodities assumed that farmers would earn a weekly wage of 24s. (This was approximately half the weekly wage of a male operative in a shoe factory.) Ryan claimed there was an assumption that agricultural labourers would be paid only when they were actually required for work, and they would not be employed on wet days or during slack seasons. Ryan acknowledged that the prices paid to farmers for cattle, sheep and horses could not improve appreciably unless the sum provided in the estimates for export bounties was quadrupled, but he also acknowledged that this would be 'an utter impossibility'. Nevertheless, he argued that the Executive Council had been foolish to fix such low prices for wheat and sugar-beet. In his opinion the government could justifiably make consumers pay considerably more for bread, sugar and butter, and in future they should fix prices 'at a level that will enable farmers and their workers to live in comfort, being good customers for native manufactured goods'.[47]

Ryan was making his case at a time when the cost of agricultural subsidies was rising. Britain's decision to impose quotas on Irish cattle imports prompted the government to re-think its overall policy. Export subsidies on cattle would end, and farmers would be assisted by increasing the agricultural grant (de-rating agricultural land), and by improving the domestic market for cattle.[48] On 2 January 1934 the Cabinet requested the Minister for Agriculture to devise a scheme to boost home consumption of beef.[49] At the next Cabinet meeting the Minister for Local Government and Public Health was instructed to submit proposals for the distribution of vouchers for free meat to all persons in receipt of home assistance. The Department of Agriculture suggested that all recipients of social welfare payments should qualify for free beef. It estimated that providing $1\frac{1}{2}$ lb of meat every week to welfare recipients and their dependants would cost approximately £500,000 per annum; this figure was later revised to £728,000. Although the government was keen to act, it could not agree on how the scheme should be financed. An interdepartmental committee suggested that the cost should be met by local authorities. The Department of Agriculture suggested cutting unemployment assistance, but Finance suggested that it would prove 'politically impossible' to reduce the rate of unemployment assistance in order to pay for free beef, because beef was not a necessity. In July 1934 the Cabinet decided that free beef should be provided for all recipients of unemployment assistance and home assistance until the end of 1936. The exchequer would bear the full cost for an 'experimental period'.

The free beef scheme was linked to measures to establish a minimum price for cattle and sheep. Under the Slaughter of Sheep and Cattle Act of 1934 the Minister for Agriculture set a minimum price per cwt for bullocks and heifers and for sheep. All victuallers and slaughter-houses had to be registered; farmers were prohibited from slaughtering livestock and selling meat; and a levy was imposed on each animal slaughtered. The Department of Agriculture reimbursed butchers for the value of meat supplied to social welfare recipients. The minimum price orders were lifted in the spring of 1935, on the advice of the Consultative Council on Livestock set up to monitor the scheme, but were reimposed some months later at the same council's request.[50]

The free beef scheme was extremely popular. Men who received unemployment assistance refused to take jobs on relief works because they would forfeit their entitlement to free beef.[51] In January 1935 Ryan claimed that Irish households were eating twice as much beef and almost twice as much mutton as in 1931.[52] Daniel Twomey, secretary to the Department of Agriculture, told the Banking Commission, 'There are very large numbers of people in this country who were formerly on the bread and tea line and who are now eating meat at least once a day'.[53] The high cost remained a problem. When the 1935/6 estimates were being drafted, the Department of Agriculture asked for a sum of £640,000 to cover the cost of the beef scheme, but Cabinet cut this to £325,000 and it decided that recipients should pay 2d per lb, which was half the wholesale price. Cattle prices were recovering by the beginning of 1936, and the Department of Agriculture informed the secretary of the Executive Council that 'from the purely agricultural point of view it would not be a matter of prime importance that the supply of beef to recipients [the free or subsidised beef to social welfare recipients] should be continued'. By then, 109,000 people were receiving subsidised beef. In December 1936 responsibility for the beef scheme was transferred from the Department of Agriculture to the Department of Local Government and Public Health.[54]

In January 1934, when the crisis in the livestock industry was most acute, the Department began to explore the possibility of buying elderly and diseased animals, and cows with poor milk yields, for conversion to meat meal. There was a problem in disposing of old cattle because the market for meat meal was depressed, and the sole Irish processor had no spare capacity.[55] Newspapers carried reports of dead livestock lying in fields and cattle being killed in public places.[56] By May 1934 the Department was negotiating with the Fianna Fáil TD Robert Briscoe, a cattle exporter Con

173

Crowley, and a German businessman, about a proposal to erect a meat meal factory at Roscrea to process up to 1,000 animals every week. The state would provide 75 per cent of the cost of the plant, up to £16,000; in return it would receive preference shares.[57] The Roscrea plant processed old cows. Notices were placed in local newspapers, and farmers wishing to dispose of animals contacted the local Garda barracks. Officials of the Department of Agriculture paid farmers £2 10s for each animal and arranged for the animals to be transported to Roscrea at the Department's expense. In 1936, 45,000 animals were bought under this scheme. Another plant was opened in Waterford in 1936 to process younger cattle from mountain areas in Waterford, Kerry and Cork, where the market had collapsed. The Department had approached J. C. Landy, the manager of Irish Co-operative Meat Limited in Waterford, and the company had agreed to provide premises and working capital in return for a ten-year monopoly on sales of canned meat and meat extract in Ireland. The plant would purchase cattle from the Department at 10s a cwt; the Department would pay farmers 16s per cwt and would also pay the cost of transport. At an annual throughput of 10,000 cattle, the scheme would cost an estimated £21,000 each year.[58] Rural households disliked tinned meat, and the Department estimated that 10,000 cattle was the maximum number that could be canned, although it was interested in exploring the possibility of providing tinned beef as part of the free beef scheme.[59]

By 1935 the beef scheme was removing up to 1,000 cattle a week from the market.[60] The Roscrea plant disposed of older animals that had no market value. The Waterford plant and the subsidised beef scheme together accounted for a maximum of 60,000 animals per annum. The coal-cattle pact agreed between Britain and Ireland in December 1934, whereby Britain agreed to take 33.3 per cent more Irish cattle of all classes from 1 February 1935 in return for Ireland agreeing to buy more British coal,[61] provided a much greater boost to livestock farmers than the free beef scheme and the measures to dispose of older cattle combined. The British Ministry of Agriculture also proved to be a rather unlikely benefactor to Irish livestock farmers. In 1934 it introduced a price subsidy on fat cattle that was designed to encourage UK farmers to increase output. Irish cattle fattened in the UK for at least three months before slaughter qualified for this subsidy.[62] In 1935 over 671,000 cattle were exported to Britain, compared with 511,000 in 1934; and the value of cattle exports rose from £4.25 million to £5.36 million.

DAIRYING

Although livestock numbers fell in 1934 and again in 1935, the 1935 total was only marginally below the 1931 figure, and the number of cows had increased by 110,000 or 9 per cent. Cattle numbers remained high because dairying was relatively prosperous and calves were an inevitable by-product of milk.

Until the 1930s the price of butter in Ireland was determined by market forces and a substantial quantity of imported butter was consumed during the winter months. Butter exports were badly affected by Britain's decision to introduce protection in the autumn of 1931. By the following spring the price offered for Irish butter in Britain was so low that exports were no longer profitable. Shortly after it came into government, Fianna Fáil imposed a levy on all butter produced by Irish creameries and factories, using the money to subsidise exports. When Britain imposed additional duties on Irish butter in July 1932, because of the Economic War, the government reduced the levy on domestic butter from 3d to 2d per pound, and an exchequer subsidy was introduced to compensate exporters for the additional duties. Under the new scheme, creameries would be paid 117s per cwt for butter, irrespective of whether it was exported or sold on the home market.

The domestic market offered some scope for expansion. Imports of condensed milk, cream, cheese and almost all manufactured dairy produce other than dried milk were banned.[63] The Dairy Disposal Company bought stocks of butter, storing it for sale during the winter and spring.[64] By 1935 Ireland was producing 30,000 cwt of cheese, more than ten times the 1932 figure.[65] By the following year Ireland was self-sufficient in cheese, and exports were running at 9,000 cwt per annum.[66] In 1932, in an effort to increase the amount of milk consumed in Ireland, the Department drew up proposals for a milk depot in Dublin to supply cheaper milk to poorer areas of the city.[67] A campaign to encourage people to drink more milk was launched in 1933. The government met two-thirds of the cost, with the other third coming from the Irish Dairy Shorthorn Breeders' Association.[68] Irish per capita consumption of milk and butter was already extremely high by international standards: in 1926 it was the equivalent of 129 gallons, compared with 65 gallons in Britain and 50 in Denmark.[69] Nevertheless, the quantity of milk used for personal consumption rose from 82 million gallons in 1929/30 to 88 million gallons in 1934/5 and 92 million gallons by 1938/9.[70]

By the mid-1930s powdered milk was the only dairy product that had not yet been subjected to protection. The Department was reluctant to impose a tariff on baby food. As the Minister explained:

The troubles are more psychological than economic. I would not like to take the responsibility of compelling mothers to use an Irish product in this case for their children because they may possibly afterward say that if they had been permitted to import the old food, whatever it may have been their child's life would have been saved.[71]

In 1938 he announced that Dungarvan Co-operative Creameries would manufacture Cow and Gate, a well-known British formula, under licence for the Irish market, with the Department providing an estimated subsidy of £2,500 per annum. The planned output was 1,000 cwt.[72]

Despite these measures there remained a surplus of dairy produce, mostly butter, that had to be exported. By 1934/5 export subsidies for dairy produce were costing the exchequer more than £2 million a year.[73] The Markets Advisory Committee of the Department of Agriculture claimed that the subsidy was of considerable benefit.[74] Irish farmers received 10–15 per cent above the world price for their milk, compared with cattle and sheep prices, which were 40–50 per cent below the world price.[75] In February 1935, shortly before the Dairy Produce (Price Stabilisation) Acts of 1932 and 1933, which fixed the price of butter, were due to expire, the Department of Finance suggested that the export subsidy should be limited to £500,000 during the coming year, and that it should then cease. Finance argued that it was fundamentally unsound to offer a guaranteed price in an industry where the surplus had to be exported at a loss. It recalled that under the original 1932 Act, exports of dairy produce were subsidised by consumers, not by the exchequer. The Department of Agriculture claimed that ending the exchequer subsidy for dairy produce carried the risk of 'wrecking the dairying industry of this country – a responsibility which the Department is not prepared to assume'. The Department of Agriculture prevailed: the Dairy Produce Act of 1935 continued the existing system.[76]

This proved to be only the first in a succession of skirmishes as the Department of Finance attempted to contain the cost of agricultural subsidies by reducing the number of calves and cows, and restricting the output of livestock and dairy produce, while the Department of Agriculture insisted that farmers should be free to operate without licences or other restraints. When the matter was discussed at Cabinet during the summer of 1935,

Ryan again asked who had gained from the policy of self-sufficiency, and who had paid the cost. He pointed out that the new manufacturing industries were heavily dependent on imports of raw materials and semi-processed goods, an import bill that was mainly paid by exports of agricultural produce. In a memorandum dated 28 July, and carrying the label 'Confidential. For Ministers Only', he protested that,

> It appears illogical and unfair to ask the agricultural community to go on exporting, admittedly at a loss, in order to enable our manufacturers to import raw materials which they will use, admittedly to their own profit. We have unblushingly admitted that our manufacturers cannot carry on at world prices. We are asking our farmers in most cases to take less than world prices ... .
>
> It is neither reasonable nor just to expect farmers to go on producing at a loss in order to maintain the balance of trade for the benefit of the whole nation.

Ryan claimed that 'the only class which have [*sic*] suffered a severe loss in income and, consequently, a lowering of the standard of living, is the agricultural community'. Farm labourers were under-paid, and were unable to improve their position, owing to the surplus of rural labour. The circumstances of farmers and farm labourers compared unfavourably with those of industrial workers, who were protected by trade unions, by the Factory Acts, and by the 1935 Conditions of Employment Bill, which became law in 1936.[77] When employees at two large Dublin milk distributors, Hughes and Craigie, secured an increase in wages, Craigie reduced the price paid to suppliers to compensate for the increased cost. Ryan claimed that the Depression had had no significant impact on the living conditions of professional people, and the unemployed, old and disabled had seen their circumstances improve. He contended that farmers should receive 'a fair price' for their produce.

This could be achieved by one of two means. Production could be restricted to the amount necessary for home consumption and prices fixed 'at the proper level'. Alternatively, export prices could be set 'at the proper level' and trade allowed to continue as at present, with the gap between the price paid in Ireland and the world price being bridged by an export subsidy, or all agricultural exports could be channelled through a state board, with the exchequer bridging the gap between domestic and export prices. He believed that it would prove impracticable to restrict agricultural output, because it would be impossible to limit the numbers of sheep, poultry and eggs. The solution lay in establishing one or more state export boards. As to the 'proper level' for agricultural prices, Ryan seems to have been thinking in terms of the prices paid in 1929, before the onset of the Depression. The cost could be offset by 'a small all-round tariff on imports'. If farmers were assured of higher prices, it would be possible to introduce some mechanism for regulating (raising) agricultural wages, for which Fianna Fáil and Labour deputies had been pressing for some time.[78] If agricultural prices were set at the 'proper level', he conceded it would be necessary to place a ceiling on agricultural output. This could be done quite easily in the case of pigs and cattle; it might be desirable to reduce pig and cattle numbers by 5 per cent every year, until they reached 80 per cent of the existing numbers.[79]

On 27 August 1935 the Cabinet requested Ryan to prepare plans for the reorganisation of the cattle industry along the lines of his memorandum. However, the preliminary proposals, which he submitted in November, suggested that he was having second thoughts. If the government embarked on 'a drastic scheme of control of production', Ryan claimed there would be a risk of 'serious disturbance' in the agricultural economy. This report can be read as a determined attempt to protect Irish farming against radical change, and to promote a rethinking of the rather simplistic pro-tillage, anti-livestock agricultural policy, which had been prominent for some years. It suggested that an increased acreage under tillage was 'in no way incompatible with the continued production of dairy produce and cattle raising on a scale equal to, or even greater than, production in recent years'. Efforts to limit the numbers of dairy cattle and dry stock would probably turn out to be 'a most serious obstacle to an expansion in corn-growing and may in fact bring a reduction in the area of cropped land'.[80] Ryan believed it highly unlikely the government would have considered reducing cattle numbers, if it had not been engaged in a trade dispute with Britain.

Ryan conceded that some curbs on livestock numbers were necessary, given the rising cost of export subsidies. This could be achieved by placing a limit on the number of calves being raised, perhaps by licensing, although such a proposal would have 'serious political repercussions' and would be difficult to implement. In February 1936 the Department of Agriculture recommended that 100,000 old cows should be killed every year, and that 100,000 calves should be slaughtered, with the government paying a bounty on calf-skins. As it would take some time to organise a scheme for culling cows, the Department suggested that 200,000 calves should be slaughtered during the coming season. Rather surprisingly, it adopted a very conservative stance on the eradication of tubercular cattle. Although officials believed that up to one-third of all milch cows, 440,000 animals, would react to the tuberculin test, only 24,000 suffered from open tuberculosis. They recommended that these 24,000 animals should be slaughtered immediately, but it would be impossible 'on economic grounds' to eliminate the remaining 416,000 reactor cattle. They proposed establishing 'accredited herds', where all animals would be certified as free of tuberculosis.[81]

The Department's planned programme of calf slaughtering was never put into effect. By February 1936 the pressure to reduce cattle numbers was receding with the renewal of the coal-cattle pact. Britain reduced the import duty on Irish cattle on 18 February, enabling the government to end export subsidies.[82] The cost peaked at £529,772 in 1934/5; in 1935/6 it fell to £296,808; and by 1936/7 it was a mere £1,918. The cost of dairy subsidies fell by 40 per cent to £1.2 million for 1935/6, as the gap between world prices and Irish prices narrowed considerably.[83] These fortuitous changes meant that Irish livestock escaped a radical slaughter programme, similar to those carried out in other countries during the 1930s. Denmark had begun slaughtering dairy cattle in the summer of 1932.

Small Farmers in Western Areas
Any extensive slaughter scheme would have presented serious political problems, even for a Fianna Fáil government. Despite the common assumption at the time that livestock farming was the preserve of large farmers, cattle were the main source of cash income for many farmers subsisting on upland and marginal land in western areas, where climate and soil conditions ruled out all crops except potatoes and oats. In 1934 Patrick J. Rogers, TD for Leitrim–Sligo, asked Ryan to comment on 'the suffering of small farmers in the Ox Mountains, who as a result of Government policy have to pay heavy duties on their sheep and young cattle'. Land on the Ox Mountains was so poor that cattle matured slowly and they could not be sold in the depressed circumstances. Farmers were reported to be slaughtering cattle and sheep, and selling meat door-to-door.[84] In mountainous areas of County Kerry the Department of Agriculture encouraged farmers to switch from dry cattle to dairying to compensate for the collapse of the livestock trade. However, the poor quality of land

and the low stocking rates meant that auxiliary creameries could not operate profitably, so the Department established travelling creameries organised by the Dairy Disposal Company.[85]

In 1937 the Fianna Fáil Cumann at Inchigeela in West Cork responded to a request from de Valera for suggestions as to what should be done to improve the circumstances of small farmers living in mountainous areas. The Fianna Fáil parliamentary party had established a sub-committee to investigate the problem in 1935.[86] The Cumann recommended that the government pay a subsidy of 4d per gallon on the first 3,000 gallons of milk supplied to a creamery from all farms in the congested districts. It also wanted grants to enable them to construct cowsheds. The Inchigeela Cumann noted that dairying would enable households to survive on 'uneconomic holdings', since 'it would be economically impossible for persons to raise cattle for the purpose of disposing of the surplus to make a livelihood as was done heretofore'. A report on conditions among small farmers in West Cork noted that farmers in the Bantry area had traditionally grazed Kerry cows and mountain sheep. The growing of potatoes and a few vegetables for the house were the only tillage practised in that area. In 1937 Prendergast, an inspector in the Department of Agriculture, reported that farmers in the Bantry area had been living off their capital for several years, with the result that cattle and sheep had practically disappeared. The most effective means of improving the economic circumstances of these farmers would be to provide loans that would enable them to restock their land. Although Prendergast emphasised that Bantry was exceptional, in that the land was suitable only for rough grazing, Bantry and Inchigeela were by no means the only areas where small farmers had depended on livestock for their livelihood. The various schemes that had been introduced to promote tillage brought no benefit to these farmers; rather they were forced to pay higher prices for sugar, bread, animal feed and butter.[87]

Promoting dairying in mountain areas made good economic sense. Dairying offered a more intensive form of livestock farming than store or fat cattle. The Department of Agriculture wished to encourage dairying, and with this in mind the guaranteed price paid for butter and the export subsidy were set at relatively generous levels.[88] The Department of Finance complained on numerous occasions that dairying was one of the most profitable farming enterprises because the subsidies were too high.[89] The Department of Agriculture believed that the long-term market for butter exports was promising. Imports of butter into Britain rose 20 per cent (by volume) between 1931 and 1935, the largest percentage increase recorded for any agricultural produce,[90] and butter consumption was rising. Twomey told the Banking Commission that he did not anticipate any decline in the quantity of livestock produce for export, although there would be fewer heavy beef cattle 'because they are not wanted', and greater quantities of other produce[91] such as butter. In 1935 the Dairy Produce Consultation Committee established a sub-committee to discuss the marketing of Irish creamery butter in Britain. This resulted in the creation of a butter marketing committee, which attempted to bring creameries into contact with suitable importers, and to negotiate contracts for future deliveries that would guarantee quantity and price.[92]

Nevertheless, the 1930s revealed some serious problems in the dairy sector. The number of milch cows peaked at 1,349,000 in 1936, but milk yields declined. Raymond Crotty suggested that this may have been due to the higher price of animal feed or the poor quality of heifers.[93] Animals that would otherwise have been sold as stores may have been retained as dairy stock. The Department continued to subsidise cow-testing associations, which monitored milk yields of individual cattle, but apparently with little success.

Pigs and Bacon

The number of pigs fell by almost one-quarter between 1931 and 1933, from 1,227,000 to 931,000. In 1931 Ireland exported 220,000 cwt of bacon and ham at an average value of £3.3 per cwt. In the same year imports amounted to 156,000 cwt and were valued at £3.1 per cwt.[94] Imports were prohibited in 1932 and the consumption of home-produced bacon rose by 65 per cent between 1932 and 1935. Irish bacon was more expensive than imported bacon, however, and overall, consumption fell by 14 per cent between 1929 and 1935.[95] Some families may have switched from bacon to cheap or free beef.

A plan to rationalise the bacon-curing industry was under consideration in the Department of Agriculture by 1932, and this began to take effect in 1935 when the Pigs and Bacon Act established two marketing boards – the Bacon Marketing Board and the Pigs Marketing Board. The boards were responsible for grading pigs, with a preference for low-fat animals. They fixed the prices paid by curers and allocated British export quotas to the factories.[96] These procedures were essential because Britain had begun allocating national quotas for imports of bacon and pig meat in September 1933.[97]

By 1936 the Department of Agriculture was claiming that Irish bacon could command prices in Britain equal to that got for the best English bacon. However, this favourable position was threatened by over-capacity among Irish bacon-curers and some co-operative societies were planning to move into the pork trade.[98] To prevent this, the 1935 Act was amended to limit the amount of bacon produced by smaller plants. The Department tried to persuade pig exporters to keep records of each animal, in the hope that this would assist in tracking disease.[99] In 1937 the marketing boards were authorised to set export quotas for all foreign markets, thus removing the threat that Irish bacon excluded from Britain would be dumped in other markets.[100] In 1939 the two boards merged to form the Pigs and Bacon Board, which became known as the Pigs and Bacon Commission.[101] Raymond Crotty was highly critical of government restrictions on the establishment of new bacon-curing plants, and he has suggested that it enabled bacon-curers to earn monopoly profits. Yet, a profitable export market for bacon could only be achieved by controlling quality and preventing over-capacity.[102] The establishment of a marketing agency for pigs contrasts with the weaker arrangements for marketing dairy produce, and the absence of any agency responsible for livestock and beef exports.

PROMOTING TILLAGE

The acreage under grain and root crops fell by over 40 per cent between the Famine and the outbreak of World War I. One of the central tenets of Sinn Féin's economic policy had been that Ireland should substitute tillage for raising cattle. It believed that tillage would provide more employment, and promote self-sufficiency. Wheat was regarded as the most important item, and the idea of Irish bread, made from Irish wheat and ground in an Irish-owned mill, became a potent symbol of self-sufficiency. The blue-print for Fianna Fáil's wheat programme first appeared in a report of the 1928 Economic Commission, an all-party committee consisting of members of the Oireachtas and some outsiders. The commission divided along party lines on the merits of protecting wheat and flour. A minority report written by the Fianna Fáil members suggested that 50 per cent of the country's flour could be produced from home-grown wheat within ten years, if millers were required to use a pre-determined percentage of home-grown wheat at a subsidised price.[103]

In 1932, shortly after he became Minister, Ryan asked officials in the Department of Agriculture to review this report. The officials, who formed a committee known as the Committee on Agricultural Production,[104] began by noting they had not been asked to determine whether it was desirable for Ireland to grow more wheat, and they had not considered this matter.[105] On this basis they endorsed the recommendations in the 1928 report. The committee subsequently issued a second report, examining how farmers might be encouraged to increase the acreage under crops. Again the committee emphasised it was trying to give effect to government policy, a coded indication perhaps that it had some doubts as to its merits. It strongly advised against resorting to compulsory tillage, and was sceptical about the benefits of offering a subsidy to farmers to grow oats, barley or root crops, although it believed a subsidy would be effective in the case of wheat. Most oats was used to feed animals on the farm; a higher price would merely divert this grain on to the market. The market for barley was limited to supplying the needs of maltsters; there was no scope for increasing sales by offering a higher price. Most root crops were used on the farm as animal fodder; offering a subsidy per acre tilled would be both inequitable and difficult to administer. The committee suggested that the most effective means of increasing the acreage of crops other than wheat (and presumably sugar-beet, which was also a cash crop) would be to restrict imports of animal feed, because this would provide farmers with an incentive to substitute home-grown roots and grain. The committee recommended that all compounders of animal feed should be required to use a designated percentage of Irish grain, a variant of the scheme they had already recommended for wheat. Imports of maize meal, the most common grain then used as animal feed (and sometimes as human food), would be banned. The committee also recommended that export bounties should be paid on bacon, eggs (but not poultry), and butter to offset the higher cost of animal feed.

Ryan submitted the committee's interim report on wheat-growing to the Cabinet in June 1932. Several weeks earlier the Department of Industry and Commerce had presented its plan to protect flour-milling, including proposals that did not require millers to use Irish-grown wheat.[106] At a marathon Cabinet meeting on 1–2 July 1932, the government agreed to enact legislation promoting native wheat, although some details had yet to be worked out.[107] Agriculture's recommendations relating to animal feed were accepted by Cabinet in late August, and the draft Agricultural Produce (Wheat) Bill, originally intended to apply only to wheat, became the Agricultural Produce (Cereals) Bill.[108] By October, the departments of Agriculture and Industry and Commerce had agreed that Industry and Commerce would be responsible for administration and legislation concerning flour-mills, and Agriculture would be responsible for the measures relating to wheat and other cereals.[109] The Cereals Bill was before the Seanad in January 1933 when de Valera called a surprise election and it lapsed as a result. When the new Dáil met, a motion was introduced resuming the passage of the bill, and it became law on 3 May 1933.[110]

There was some urgency about this legislation because farmers had been encouraged to plant wheat during the winter and spring of 1932/3. In January 1933 the Department of Agriculture presented Cabinet with details of an advertising campaign that would run in thirty-five provincial papers, including the *Derry Journal*, which was widely read in County Donegal. Ryan believed newspaper advertising was the cheapest and most effective means of reaching farmers. The campaign planned for 1933 appealed more to patriotism than to profit: farmers were told that Ireland should be independent of foreign wheat. The advertisements were scheduled to run for six weeks from 16 January, but they did not appear because the Cabinet had not given its approval before the general election was called.[111] Nevertheless, the acreage under wheat more than doubled in 1933. In order to qualify for a wheat bounty, farmers had to register as wheat-growers by 31 July; many failed to comply, so the Department arranged for legislation to be introduced extending the registration date.[112] The Department also took account of the practical difficulties of reviving wheat-growing. In 1932/3 it appointed tillage instructors in counties Limerick, Westmeath and Leitrim. In the annual report for 1934/5 it was noted that 'the attitude of farmers in many parts of the country towards the idea [of growing wheat] was not merely apathetic, but prejudiced, owing to the false notion that had somehow grown up that the climate and soil of this country were inimical to successful wheat production'. However, 1933 and 1934 were blessed with ideal weather.

In the autumn of 1933 the quota of Irish-grown wheat to be used by flour-millers for the coming year was set at 4 per cent. This was later reduced to 3.5 per cent, but in practice only 1.59 per cent of the wheat used was grown in Ireland. When the acreage under wheat rose substantially in the following year, the quota was increased to 10.75 per cent, but again the amount used was less than half this figure. Under the Cereals Act of 1933 millers were obliged to secure sufficient home-grown wheat to meet the quota, but many growers complained that they were unable to dispose of their wheat. Most farmers wanted to sell their crops in the weeks immediately after the harvest because they needed the cash and they had no suitable place to store them. The millers explained that they were unable to meet the official quota for native wheat because the high moisture content meant that it had to be kiln-dried before it was milled and few mills had kilns. The millers were also short of storage space.

The Department of Industry and Commerce, responsible for ensuring that millers complied with the Act, appears to have adopted a lenient attitude. The Department of Agriculture, on the other hand, decided to confront these problems. In December 1934 it proposed to the Executive Council that the Minister for Agriculture should be given 'complete control over the purchase, storage and drying of home grown wheat', and that responsibility for determining the quota for native wheat should be transferred from Industry and Commerce to Agriculture. It also recommended that the Minister for Agriculture should be given power to require each mill to dry and store a specified quantity of wheat, although millers could sub-contract this task with the Minister's approval. Alternatively, the Minister for Agriculture could take responsibility for purchasing, drying and storing all native wheat and for supplying the mills. The Department and the Cabinet preferred the first option, which was regarded as less expensive. Loans would be provided to finance the cost of providing storage and drying facilities. Agriculture recommended that the Minister for Agriculture should have the authority to buy or sell home-grown and imported wheat and that in future the cost of the bounty on native wheat should be met by the consumer, not by the exchequer.[113] The Department also wished to fix the price of wheat two years in advance, in order to give farmers some security when they were planning crop rotations. The Cabinet accepted most of these proposals, although it refused to give the Minister for Agriculture power to buy and sell home-grown and imported wheat, and insisted that the Minister for Industry and Commerce should be consulted on many of these measures.[114] These provisions were implemented in 1935.

The 1935 Act brought a sharp rise in the percentage of flour produced from native wheat, from 5 per cent in 1934 to 15.6 per cent in 1935, and 26 per cent by 1938, and the gap between Irish wheat prices and world prices widened sharply from 1935. From the perspective of wheat growers and the Department of Agriculture the Act was a success, although the retail price of bread and flour rose sharply as a consequence. And yet, Ireland

TABLE 2: Annual Average Price of Irish, British and other Wheat
per Cwt, 1933–9[115]

	Irish (d)	British (d)	Imported to Britain (d)
1933	80	64	70
1934	82	56	65
1935	111	55	73
1936	130	69	81
1937	142	106	116
1938	142	99	112
1939	141	55	66

was still far from achieving its target of producing 50 per cent of its flour
from native grain. In 1939, the best pre-war year, millers used 3.6 million
cwt of home-grown wheat as opposed to 6.8 million cwt of imported wheat.
The quantity of wheat grown per capita in the mid-1930s was higher than
in 1851, when Ireland was self-sufficient in wheat.[116] But by the 1930s bread
had replaced potatoes as the staple food and this made it more difficult to
achieve self-sufficiency.

By 1939 the acreage under wheat was 255,000 acres, twelve times the
amount grown in 1932. In 1935 the yield was 21.9 cwt per acre on 163,000
acres, which was above the average yields for 1931 and 1932. The 255,000
acres planted in 1939 produced an average of 19.9 cwt. In 1938 a special
departmental committee, established to report on increased agricultural
production in times of emergency, noted that the acreage under wheat
appeared to have stabilised at 225,000–250,000 acres. In its opinion a higher
acreage would only be achieved if farmers were offered higher guaranteed
prices.[117] By 1936 the Department was concentrating its efforts on encouraging farmers to plant more spring wheat. In the past spring wheat had proved
to be an unreliable crop because the seed varieties sold as spring wheat
often failed to ripen. In January 1937 the Department suggested planting
trial plots at Ballinacurra in County Cork with Red Marvel, which was
regarded as the most suitable variety of spring wheat. This was intended to
demonstrate the success of this strain, while producing sufficient pedigree
seed to extend the acreage. The Department of Finance almost prevented
the scheme going ahead because it delayed sanction for the expenditure
of £400 – £50 for seed and £350 for administration – until late February.
Finance argued that the participating farmers should pay for the seed.
The trial plots were not particularly successful. In 1937 yields were low

owing to bad weather and the 1938 crop was infected with loose smut. The scheme was suspended in 1939.[118]

Efforts to increase the acreage of oats and barley proved much less successful. Throughout the 1930s the acreage of oats remained below the 1929 figure. Ireland traditionally exported a modest quantity of oats to Britain but this market disappeared after 1931, and the decline in the use of horses for transport reduced the main cash market in Ireland. There was a modest rise in the cultivation of barley until 1934, but by 1938 this had fallen back to the 1929 level. Many farmers who had formerly grown oats and barley switched to wheat. The Department was already aware in 1932 that there would be problems substituting native for imported maize. Although maize was primarily used as animal feed, it remained an important source of human food in the west of Ireland. The Department set one stone as the maximum size of bags of pure maize meal that could be retailed, fearing that if maize were retailed in larger sacks, it would be used as animal food.

Most of the Seanad debate on the 1933 Cereals Bill was devoted to the impact of the new legislation on families who consumed maize meal as part of their regular diet. As The McGillycuddy of the Reeks noted, 'individuals who will be forced to spend more on maize meal will receive none of the benefits of the bill as they will not be growing oats or barley'. Ryan responded, 'Nobody can complain from the national, economic or public health point of view if we can drive the people of Kerry and Donegal to the consumption of oatmeal instead of maize meal'.[119] However, the debate prompted the Department to issue questionnaires to advisers in counties Donegal, Mayo, Roscommon, Sligo, Leitrim, Clare, Galway, Cork and Kerry, asking about the use of maize as human food. The responses revealed widely differing patterns, even within counties. The largest quantities of maize were consumed in Donegal, up to two stone per family every week. Many families in the west of Ireland traditionally bought maize in five-stone bags. However, most reports suggested that these households had not been seriously affected by the Cereals Act of 1933.[120] Some millers exploited the fact that maize was used for human food to sell pure maize meal for animal feed. The Cereals Act of 1936 attempted to stop this practice by licensing producers and setting quotas for pure maize meal.[121]

Although the Department had hoped to compensate exporters for the increased cost of feeding animals on home-produced grains, by paying additional export subsidies on butter, bacon and eggs, these subsidies never materialised. Demand for animal feed fell because of the depressed market for agricultural produce. The 1933 Cereals Act required compounders of animal feed to use a specified proportion of Irish-grown grain, but farmers found it impossible to dispose of the 1933 oats crop: millers and compounders had imported and stored large quantities of maize (no apparent problem with storage facilities here) in advance of the Act, despite a ban on the import of maize except under licence.[122] Officials in the Department of Agriculture claimed that by working their mills night and day in the days immediately before the controls were imposed, the millers had accumulated enough pure maize meal to glut the market for several months. The Department struggled to find a market for Irish oats. Although it had the authority to increase the quota of Irish oats to be incorporated into animal feed, if the meal was to be edible it was necessary to remove the husks, and this was an expensive option. In the opinion of the Department of Agriculture it would be simpler to require flour-millers to blend some oats into flour. It acknowledged that this would be unpopular with the public, because Irish people 'have become accustomed to the use of a flour in which wholesomeness has been sacrificed to appearance', but it suggested that the Economic War made it more likely that this proposal would be acceptable. As flour-millers were not even meeting the quota for use of home-grown wheat at the time, this was a rather unrealistic proposition. Ultimately it was decided that merchants should buy the oats, with the government guaranteeing them against loss.[123] During 1933 and 1934 farmers obtained between 23s 6d and 25s a barrel for wheat, but only 6s 6d or 7s a barrel for oats and 12s or 13s a barrel for barley.[124] Ryan blamed the low prices on panic among farmers, prompted by scare headlines in the *Irish Independent* and *The Irish Times*.[125] The price of oats fell once more in 1935 owing to a shortage of milling capacity, and again the Department had to persuade merchants to buy the crop at fixed prices, with a promise that the government would relieve them of surplus grain. The Agricultural Produce (Cereals) Act of 1936 regularised these emergency measures by giving the Minister for Agriculture the authority to purchase oats and barley at a fair price and ensure that compounders of animal feed used the required proportion of Irish grain.

Many farmers firmly believed that the meal mixtures were more expensive and inferior in quality to the pure maize meal they had previously used. The Ballingeary Cumann of Fianna Fáil claimed that Sceim Meascán na Mine (the maize mixture scheme) had increased the cost of animal feed to the point where it was no longer profitable for small farmers to raise pigs and poultry as a commercial venture. Mr Ó Suibhne, a national teacher in Ballingeary, told Prendergast, a Department inspector, that local farmers complained that the meal mixture 'fails to give as good results' as Indian meal. Prendergast informed him that the mixture only contained 25 per cent of home-grown grain. He also suggested that pigs could be successfully raised on potatoes, barley and milk.[126] Although potatoes had been the traditional feedstuff for pigs since before the Famine, the acreage under potatoes fell during the 1930s, which suggests that farmers did not substitute potatoes for maize. The cultivation of turnips, another root crop used as animal fodder, also declined; the acreage under mangels rose, although by less than the decline in turnips.[127]

Farmers' protests at the additional cost of animal feed were understandable, since it was estimated to account for 75 to 80 per cent of the cost of farm materials. In 1934/5 the volume of farm materials used was 15 per cent lower than in 1912/13.[128] Although the additional cost of the meal mixture was a factor in reducing the use of animal feed, the depressed market for pigs and eggs was probably more important. When the Economic War ended in 1938, the Department proposed that all restrictions on the import and milling of maize should be lifted, and it wished to end the requirement to mix a percentage of home-grown meal into maize meal.[129] However, the regulations were not modified until 26 July 1939, and when Britain declared war on Germany one month later, new restrictions were introduced.

The campaign to increase the acreage under grain had mixed success. The substantial rise in the acreage under wheat was largely achieved at the expense of a fall in the acreage under oats and barley. Farmers in Leinster and Munster benefited most from guaranteed wheat prices; farmers in Connacht, west Munster and Ulster were probably net losers. The Department went to considerable efforts to encourage farmers in the west and north-west to grow wheat where soil and climate permitted, and with this in mind, it commissioned a report on County Leitrim. The lack of milling facilities was identified as one deterrent, and the condition of the active mills in the county was described as 'generally poor' or 'shockingly poor'. Many were owned by farmers and small businessmen, who lacked the capital to put them into order. In 1934 loans were made available for the repair and modernisation of existing mills, and preference was given to applications from the traditional congested districts and north-west Cavan and north Longford. By 1936 the Department concluded that the provision of loans to repair and modernise mills in western and northern counties had been a failure.[130]

Other crops such as sugar-beet brought disproportionate benefits to farmers in Leinster and east Munster, many of them farming larger holdings. By 1937 the acreage had increased to 62,000 compared with 14,000 in 1930/1, and imports of sugar had declined to one-quarter of the pre-1932 volume. Most of the momentum for expanding the Irish sugar industry came from the Department of Industry and Commerce, although the Department of Agriculture was represented on the interdepartmental committee that considered how this should be achieved. In May 1933 Lemass reported to Cabinet that the interdepartmental committee had recommended that a limited company should be established to construct four factories, each with an estimated capacity to process 20,000 tons of sugar-beet. The company would acquire the existing factory at Carlow on terms to be arranged. The capital would come partly from public subscriptions, with the balance provided by the state. The committee rejected the suggestion that the new factories should be co-operatives, because 'efficient conditions of the industry would be almost impossible'. It also determined that the climate was suitable for growing sugar-beet in all areas except the north, although the Carlow area was probably the most suitable. Farmers who supplied the Carlow plant were already heavily engaged in tillage; consequently they had the necessary skill, labour, equipment and machinery to grow beet. Sugar-beet was a labour intensive enterprise, requiring 250 man-hours per acre, three times the labour requirements of barley and oats. Only potatoes, at 319 hours, required more man-hours. Yet, based on the experience of the Carlow plant, the committee concluded that expanding sugar-beet would not provide any additional jobs in farming, although existing workers would be more fully employed. The Department of Agriculture said little about the proposal, although on 10 July, after the Cabinet had given its approval, Ryan submitted a memorandum expressing doubts that the public could be persuaded to invest in the new company unless the state guaranteed the principal or the interest. As this would be the first manufacturing company to be launched by the Irish government, success was essential. Despite Ryan's reservations, the Cabinet decided to confine the government guarantee to debenture stock. Ryan, Lemass, de Valera and MacEntee were involved in the decision to select Mallow, Thurles and Tuam as the sites for the new factories.[131]

Responsibility for the industry and for setting the price for sugar-beet rested with the state-owned company Cómhlucht Siúicre Éireann Teoranta and it reported to the Minister for Finance. When negotiations between the company and the Irish Beet Growers' Association over the price of beet for the coming season broke down in November 1938, the growers expressed a wish that the Minister for Agriculture should become involved in conciliation efforts. Agriculture was undoubtedly more sympathetic to the growers' demands than the Department of Finance. In January 1939 Ryan noted in a memorandum to government, 'We are at present in this country in danger of a change-over in Agriculture from mixed farming to the production of meat. If a number of farmers depart from beet growing this year, a much higher price for beet will be required to get them back than would be necessary now to keep them in production'. The Department of Finance conceded that the Department of Agriculture should be represented on a board of inquiry to determine the price of beet for the coming season and it retained this role in future years.[132]

The Department of Agriculture played only a minor role in the decision to establish industrial alcohol plants, although they were set up to encourage tillage in areas where it was not possible to grow sugar-beet. In 1933 R. C. Ferguson of the Department of Industry and Commerce noted that 'while the tillage of beet is practically impossible in Donegal, Connemara and certain other parts of the country, potatoes could be raised'. Potatoes were a labour-intensive crop offering a high return per acre. Ferguson suggested that they could be used to manufacture industrial alcohol, which would be mixed with petrol. The Department of Agriculture was very much in favour of the idea because there was a large surplus of potatoes on the market owing to the loss of export sales to Britain. It was hoped that the plants would buy up to 400,000 tons of potatoes, or one-seventh of the annual crop, at a price of 30s a ton. Ferguson suggested that other countries had introduced similar schemes 'for the purpose of keeping agriculture alive during a period when, owing to the general fall in agricultural prices, the farming community found itself in many countries unable to exist'.[133] Lemass kept the project very much under the control of Industry and Commerce. There is no evidence that his officials sought information from the Department of Agriculture about the supplies of potatoes in the vicinity of the locations that were under consideration. Twomey demanded an assurance on behalf of the Minister of Agriculture that agricultural interests would be adequately represented on the advisory board responsible for establishing the new industry. He warned that farmers might be unwilling to sell their crop to the industrial alcohol company at prices that the company might regard as economic in years when potatoes were fetching a high price on the retail market. Twomey also asked what role was envisaged for potato merchants in procuring supplies.[134]

Distilleries were erected at Cooley in County Louth, Carrickmacross in County Monaghan, Convoy in County Donegal and Labbadish in County Mayo. From the beginning all the plants suffered an acute shortage of potatoes.[135] In 1937 Cooley, the plant with the best supplies (the area had a long tradition of growing potatoes), could only acquire 7,000 tons, which was sufficient for 175 days; after that it had to rely on imported molasses.[136] The acreage under potatoes fell during the 1930s, despite the drive for additional tillage; the decline was common to all parts of Ireland.

Tobacco was another tillage crop that promised to raise the incomes of small farmers living on poorer quality land. During Plunkett's years as vice-president, the DATI had recruited G. N. Keller, a tobacco expert from Kentucky, to promote the crop. Several former landlords, including the Earl of Dunraven and Sir Nugent Everard, became fervent supporters of the crop. Most of the 1923 Seanad debate on the estimate for the Department of Agriculture was devoted to the prospects for Irish tobacco, and the government introduced excise relief for Irish tobacco in the 1924 budget. In 1926 a special committee concluded that 'tobacco of a fairly good quality can be grown in Ireland, suitable for blending with certain types of American tobacco in roll and plug'. Irish tobacco could also be used as shag tobacco and in the manufacture of cheap cheroots. Tobacco was a labour-intensive crop that was suitable for small farms; it also enriched the soil, making it very suitable for inclusion in crop rotation. The committee argued that 'some temporary sacrifice of State revenue would be justified in order to keep alive an industry which might in the future be particularly useful in promoting tillage and increasing employment'. It recommended a further reduction in the excise duty on home-grown tobacco. The Department of Finance did not agree. In its opinion manufacturers were reluctant to use Irish tobacco because smokers had acquired a taste for American blends.[137]

During the 1920s the number of growers and the amount of tobacco qualifying for excise remission had been tightly controlled. In 1933 these restrictions were lifted and all farmers were permitted to grow tobacco free of duty. Although this led to a sharp rise in acreage, manufacturers continued to shun the Irish leaf. Unable to dispose of their crop, many small farmers decided to extend the concept of self-sufficiency by curing and smoking their own leaf. The exchequer lost an estimated £250,000 in excise duties as a result. In February 1934 the Department of Agriculture noted that 'cases have been mentioned of farmers and the family who have been in the habit of spending sums varying from 4/- to 12/- per week on tobacco having ended this expenditure altogether from the date on which the 1933 crop of tobacco became fit for use'. The Department conceded that it was necessary to prevent the unrestricted growing of tobacco. It wanted to encourage a gradual increase in the use of Irish tobacco, so that smokers would become accustomed to the change in taste. It calculated that the provisions in the Tobacco Bill of 1934 would make it possible for growers to realise almost £15 an acre.[138] (In 1932 the Department had estimated that sugar-beet gave a return of almost £9 an acre; potatoes, over £5; wheat, £2 4s; oats, £1 14s; and barley, a mere 14s.)[139] Because tobacco thrived on poorer soil it suggested that licences should be restricted to certain areas and to small farmers.[140] Ryan argued that:

> ... the small farmer is practically precluded from the advantage of our wheat scheme both by the quality of his soil and the economy of his farm. He is also excluded from our Beet Scheme in many cases owing to his geographical position or for the same reasons as apply to wheat growing. It would appear to be due to him that at least this remunerative crop might be reserved for him alone.

Drying and trading in tobacco leaf could be restricted to the co-operative societies.[141] None of the above proposals were implemented; indeed they were not even brought to Cabinet. Ryan was undoubtedly aware that they would be opposed by the Department of Industry and Commerce. In 1934, 1,500 growers cultivated a total of 1,050 acres of tobacco; in 1935, 1,120 growers cultivated 820 acres.

The Tobacco Act of 1934 followed similar lines to the Cereals Act of 1933. The excise duty on native tobacco was substantially lower than that on imported leaf. Manufacturers were required to buy a quantity of Irish tobacco proportionate to their overall output, at a similar price to that for imported tobacco. The government could require manufacturers to incorporate a proportion of home-grown tobacco in their blends, but this was not enforced.[142] Although the two largest manufacturers, Carrolls and Players, duly bought the quantity of Irish tobacco required under the 1934 Act, they refused to use it in their products because they claimed Irish tobacco was only suitable for pipe tobacco or the manufacture of inferior cigarettes. In 1938 they applied for a licence to export the unused tobacco. The Department of Industry and Commerce was in favour of granting an export licence, but the Department of Agriculture retorted that the requirements of the 1934 Act 'have been evaded or, to an extent, made inoperative'. It believed it would not be practicable to continue encouraging the cultivation of Irish tobacco in the coming season unless the legislation was strengthened, and the Minister for Agriculture was made responsible for its administration. If the Cabinet did not agree to these demands, Ryan threatened not to issue any licences. MacEntee and Lemass both disagreed. Maurice Moynihan, secretary to the government, minuted that C. Sheehan, private secretary to the Minister for Agriculture, was of the opinion that there was no likelihood of an agreement being reached before the meeting of the government. An angry Ryan claimed that there was no point in officials of the Department of Agriculture meeting officials from Industry and Commerce:

> I have sent you some correspondence with regard to beet growing. In this case it appears to me that I am debarred by Cabinet procedure from raising the matter in a regular way. The Minister for Finance is the responsible Minister in that case and I am quite sure he will never bring the question up because he is not concerned with the state of chaos which is developing.[143]

Ryan's frustration is understandable. The Department could encourage farmers to grow tobacco, sugar-beet and wheat, but with the exception of wheat, it could not ensure that manufacturers complied with the legislation guaranteeing a market for these crops. Its frustration was probably accentuated because it had made serious efforts to improve the quality of Irish tobacco. The 1,500 growers who cultivated 1,050 acres of tobacco in 1934 were reduced to 730 growers and 580 acres by 1936, owing to the 'voluntary' withdrawal of growers who failed to reach the meet strict grading standards.[144] In 1935 the Department had rejected applications for licences from growers who had produced inferior tobacco in two consecutive years.[145] The failure to provide co-operative curing facilities meant that growers had to provide them from their own resources, and small farmers lacked the capital to do this.

By 1940 the Department was of the opinion that the higher profits from growing wheat or sugar-beet threatened an end to tobacco growing, unless the excise duty on Irish-grown tobacco was reduced still further. The Department of Finance responded that 'the time has come when the question of abandoning the scheme should be considered. ... all experience has shown that the crop is an unwanted product which has no place and it is not likely ever to have a place in the agricultural economy of the country.

... there is no more case for continuing to encourage the cultivation of this crop than there would be for encouraging as a matter of industrial policy the production of a commodity for which there was positive antipathy.'[146] It is impossible to determine whether there was any real prospect of developing a market for home-grown tobacco. Irish tobacco had a much stronger flavour than American tobacco, but this was equally true of tobaccos grown in France, Italy and the Balkans, yet these countries developed strong domestic markets, because tobacco was manufactured by government-controlled monopolies. This was not feasible in Ireland because of the presence of several large commercial manufacturers, who had fostered a market for cigarettes made from milder tobaccos.[147]

In the case of tobacco, as of wheat, oats and sugar-beet, there were obvious conflicts between the objectives of the Department of Agriculture and other government departments, in particular the departments of Finance and Industry and Commerce. These also surfaced when Industry and Commerce sought to establish an Irish plant to manufacture nitrogenous fertiliser. Agriculture was concerned that this would force farmers to pay much higher prices. Despite the drive for tillage, the amount of fertiliser used declined between 1932 and 1935, presumably because of the depressed state of agriculture. During the 1930s the large ICI (Imperial Chemicals Industries) plant at Billingham in the UK was running well below full capacity,[148] and Irish farmers benefited from low fertiliser prices, because there was no competing Irish producer. When Industry and Commerce brought proposals to the Executive Council in 1935 for a deal with the Swiss firm, Hydro-Nitro, Agriculture demanded assurances that the prices charged would not 'at any time, exceed the price at which similar manures could be imported duty free', and that the estimates for the cost of the plant should be referred to an independent expert. The Executive Council approved the proposal to establish a nitrogen plant, subject to a satisfactory scheme, 'particularly as regards the price of the product'. An inter-departmental committee that examined the proposal asked ICI to tender for a similar plant. When the ICI estimate came to £1,170,000, compared with the figure of £300,000 submitted by Hydro-Nitro, Agriculture and Finance concluded that the Swiss scheme had been 'heavily under-estimated'. The question of establishing a nitrogen plant was unresolved when war broke out in 1939.[149] Agriculture was equally unenthusiastic about efforts by Industry and Commerce to expand the production of agricultural machinery, since the Department feared that farmers would end up paying higher prices.

The Anglo-Irish Trade Agreement, 1938

The trade agreement negotiated with Britain in the spring of 1938 ended the Economic War. This brought a decided improvement in the market for agricultural exports, but there was no return to the conditions that had existed in 1931. Britain removed the special duties introduced in the summer of 1932 on livestock, meat, poultry, butter, eggs and cream, and Ireland was belatedly admitted to the terms of the 1932 Ottawa Agreements Act. The Ottawa Agreement only guaranteed duty-free entry for eggs, poultry, cheese, butter and other milk products until August 1940. The preference that exports from Ireland and other Commonwealth countries enjoyed against non-Commonwealth countries would expire at that time. Ireland could export livestock, bacon and pork products to Britain free of duty,[150] but so could Denmark and any other country, and Irish producers also had to compete against farmers in Britain and Northern Ireland, who benefited from price guarantees for bacon.

The interests of agriculture were foremost in the minds of the Irish delegation at the 1938 trade talks, although it was also anxious to ensure that the new protected industries would not be damaged. When negotiations opened in January, de Valera expressed a wish to see Irish agriculture develop, so that the supply of food could be greatly increased in the event of a crisis. De Valera anticipated that Ireland would play a major role in feeding Britain in the event of war.

When the detailed trade talks began, the Irish delegation[151] sought unrestricted access to the British market for all agricultural produce, but the British Ministry of Agriculture was determined to retain some control over imports from Ireland. Britain claimed that there would be alarm in Northern Ireland if the Irish Free State secured the right to export as much agricultural produce as it wished. The British authorities were particularly concerned at the prospect of unrestricted exports of butter and other products that qualified for export bounties. The British Ministry of Agriculture feared that increased imports of eggs and poultry from Ireland would jeopardise their new scheme to develop the British poultry industry.[152] If prices fell as a consequence of increased imports from Ireland, the Ministry anticipated that British farmers would demand higher subsidies in compensation.[153]

Ryan tried to reassure the British negotiators by emphasising that the volume of Irish agricultural output had been constant for many years and there was little danger of Irish produce flooding the British market. He remarked that Ireland would probably retain the export bounty for butter.[154]

In February he informed the British ministers that it would be politically impossible for him to return to Dublin with an agreement that granted free entry for Irish cattle, but not for eggs and poultry. He was obviously concerned that the agreement might be seen to favour cattle farmers at the expense of small-farm enterprises.[155]

The 1938 trade agreement was a compromise. Ireland gave an undertaking to consult Britain from time to time about the volume of eggs and poultry exports. If they failed to reach 'a satisfactory arrangement', and if imports continued to rise and endanger the stability of the British poultry market, Britain would be entitled to impose quotas or import duties. In 1937 Twomey had told the Banking Commission that there was a growing market for poultry and eggs in Britain, so this section of the agreement was regarded as extremely important.[156] With respect to imports of agricultural produce in general, the 1938 agreement included an undertaking that the British government would not seek to regulate the quantity of Irish agricultural produce imported into Britain unless it appeared to the British government that the 'orderly marketing of such goods could not otherwise be secured'. The wording of this clause indicates that the balance of advantage rested with Britain; the key consideration was the stability of the British market, not market stability for Irish farmers. Nevertheless, agriculture gained most from the 1938 agreement. Any potential losses would fall on the manufacturing sector.[157]

The greatest benefits went to the livestock trade. During 1938 cattle exports to Britain were valued at £8,400,000, and exports to Northern Ireland were worth a further £828,000. Comparable figures for 1937 were £6,660,000 and £519,000 respectively. In 1939 cattle exports to Britain were worth over £10 million. Although this was less than the 1931 figure, it was more than double the value of cattle exports in 1934, and in 1934/5 livestock exports had had to be subsidised by the exchequer at a cost of more than £500,000. Britain was primarily interested in importing stores; the British Livestock Act of 1934 introduced a subsidy on all cattle fattened in Britain as part of the policy of encouraging British agriculture, and this subsidy was extended to Irish cattle fattened in Britain for a minimum of three months before slaughter.[158] This subsidy remained a key feature of Anglo-Irish trade in later decades, and it exerted a long-term influence on the Irish livestock industry. Export bounties on all products other than dairy products and eggs were removed following the 1938 trade agreement. The cost of export bounties fell from more than £2 million in 1937/8 to £750,000 in 1938/9.

TABLE 3: Value of Exports to Britain, 1937 and 1939

	1937 (£)	1939 (£)
Live Animals	9,803,607	14,200,000
Butter	1,311,713	1,386,750
Cheese	49,085	55,297
Eggs	667,880	1,112,997
Condensed Milk	140,178	243,900
Milk Powder	17,871	28,066
Cream	134,617	137,228
Live Poultry and Game	105,193	157,751

Source: Trade Statistics, *Statistical Bulletin*, 1938 and 1939.

The signing of the 1938 trade agreement provided the government with an opportunity to review the state of Irish agriculture and to plan for future developments. On 1 November 1938 the Cabinet decided to establish a commission of inquiry into agriculture. This decision was prompted by a private members' motion tabled by opposition deputies Thomas Burke and Patrick Cogan, calling for the provision of long-term loans to farmers and a moratorium on farmers' debts. An amendment tabled by James Dillon called for the establishment of a commission of inquiry into the agricultural industry, which would examine proposals for increasing the value and volume of agricultural production. The Department of Agriculture suggested that the commission should be 'purely technical in its aspects and composed only of agricultural experts. The problem is to increase the volume, value, and profitability (consistent with retaining, at least, the present agricultural population). The problem is technical and not economic. A Commission composed of bankers, business men, labour members, will be of little use', although it did not rule out the appointment of foreign experts. Nevertheless, a list of possible members submitted by the Department of Agriculture suggested that the commission should be chaired by economist Professor Timothy Smiddy from University College, Cork, and should also include Liam Ó Buachalla, professor of economics at University College, Galway. The list named representatives of labour, financial and business interests; of tillage farmers, small farmers, dairy and livestock farmers, poultry and women's interests; three TDs and one senator. No foreign experts were mentioned.

The final list included more senators and TDs, but the sole woman, who was to have represented women's interests and poultry, was dropped. The wide-ranging terms of reference required the commission 'to consider and make recommendations as to the measures which it might be practicable in the national interest to take for the purpose of promoting and maintaining increased agricultural production'. Smiddy drew up a list of subjects on which the commission would welcome submissions. This included all the major agricultural sectors; the factors influencing costs; organising the buying of raw materials; the marketing of agricultural produce; agricultural credit; education and research; forestry; and the flight of the rural population from the land.[159] Two interim reports, on silage and on the pig and bacon industries, were published in 1940. At that point the commission was suspended, because it was decided that the rapidly changing circumstances in a time of war meant its recommendations would be out of date before they could be implemented.

Agricultural Labourers

Given that Fianna Fáil took power in 1932 with the support of the Labour Party, it is perhaps surprising that nothing was done to improve the wages or working conditions of agricultural labourers until 1936. The Agricultural Wages Board, established during World War I, had lapsed in 1921, and during the 1920s and the early 1930s the wages and working conditions of agricultural labourers were not regulated. While this was consistent with the economic philosophy of Patrick Hogan, it was not in keeping with Fianna Fáil's more egalitarian ethos or with its efforts to improve wages and working conditions of workers in manufacturing industry.

In December 1933 the Department of Agriculture calculated that farm labourers were receiving 23s 6d for a sixty-hour week, compared with 33s in 1920. The Department expressed fears that the wages of some agricultural labourers would fall to pre-war levels. In 1913 a farm labourer had earned the equivalent of 30 gallons of milk; a tradesman had earned three times that amount. By 1933 a farm labourer was earning the equivalent of 45 gallons of milk (at current prices), whereas a tradesman was earning the equivalent of 300 gallons, almost seven times the agricultural wage.[160] Although unemployment assistance and a substantially expanded programme of relief works[161] helped to supplement the wages of agricultural labourers, unemployment assistance was withdrawn in rural areas during the busy times in the agricultural calendar. Ryan's 1935 memorandum to the Executive Council indicates that while he was concerned at the low level of agricultural wages, he was unwilling to introduce minimum wage rates until farmers were receiving higher prices.

The Agricultural Wages Act of 1936 re-established an agricultural wages board similar to that which had operated between 1917 and 1921. The country was divided into five regions, each with a local committee responsible for determining the regional wage rate. Many of the employer representatives on the committees were nominees of the county committees of agriculture; others were chosen by the Irish Beet Growers' Association. Several county committees refused to nominate worker representatives, so Ryan wrote to all TDs, except those representing Dublin and Cork cities and the universities, asking them to submit names. Rural branches of the Labour party also forwarded names.

Many farmers resented the re-establishment of the Agricultural Wages Board. The committee of the Annacotty Co-Operative Creamery in east Limerick passed a motion expressing its disapproval, and calling on the Minister for Agriculture to reconsider the matter.[162] Carlow County Committee of Agriculture passed a motion 'demanding such prices for Agricultural Produce that will admit of the payment of Agricultural Workers of a living wage'. The Cavan and Monaghan Farmers' Co-Operative Society pressed for the minimum prices of all agricultural produce to be doubled, so that farmers could afford to pay the statutory agricultural wages. The strongest protests came from dairy farmers, because, as the Limerick County Committee of Agriculture noted, 'cows cannot be milked 14 times in 54 hours [the statutory working week] to get the best results'. Fourteen county committees of agriculture passed resolutions critical of the Act; the majority wished to have wages determined by efficiency, not on the basis of age.[163]

The choice of representatives for the workers' panel also prompted complaints. The Department asked agricultural instructors to report whether those selected from their area were suitable. Only half the thirty-four worker representatives passed this assessment: some were farmers; most of the remainder were found not to be agricultural workers, but a 'motley crew' including barmen, postmen and road workers.[164]

Wages of agricultural labourers did not rise significantly until the 1938 Anglo-Irish Trade Agreement; in 1937 the index stood at 83.9, in 1938 it rose to 103.8. The establishment of an agricultural wages board seems to have accelerated the decline in the agricultural labour force. The number of assisting relatives was also declining, although at a slower rate. There was a slight rise in the number of permanent agricultural workers aged between 14 and 18 years, which may indicate that some farmers replaced adult workers with teenagers.

Northern Ireland

The 1930s brought a widening gap between the two Irish economies, north and south. Sales of bacon and pork from the Irish Free State to Northern Ireland almost disappeared and the plethora of protective measures presented major difficulties for farmers and agricultural processing plants in the border region. In addition to being required to pay import duties, farmers were only permitted to bring goods across the border at approved points where there was a customs post. This often involved journeys of twenty miles (a forty-five mile journey was reported) instead of a journey of one or two miles using an unapproved road. An owner of a corn mill beside the border in County Louth claimed that he would be forced to close his business because the new regulations made it impossible for his regular customers from Northern Ireland to bring their grain to his mill and then bring it home for their own use. The Department was unable to offer any assistance.[165]

When the Irish government imposed an import duty on milk, it created havoc for creameries in border regions. Farmers from Northern Ireland, who supplied milk to Pettigo creamery in County Donegal, were faced with import duties of 3d a gallon. Farmers from the Irish Free State who supplied milk to creameries in Northern Ireland were liable for import duties if they brought skimmed milk home from the creamery. Clones Co-operative Creamery could no longer take milk from its separating station at Roslea, in County Fermanagh; Killeshandra Creamery lost sixty suppliers living in Northern Ireland; up to a dozen other creameries in the Irish Free State were similarly affected. Most aggrieved parties believed that the Department of Agriculture 'had made this awful mess'.

The Department succeeded in persuading the Revenue Commissioners to issue licences to existing suppliers from Northern Ireland, exempting them from import duties. No licences were issued to new suppliers, because of fears that farmers in Northern Ireland would divert milk to the Irish Free State to take advantage of higher prices. The Revenue Commissioners also insisted on setting a quota for each farmer from Northern Ireland. At the beginning farmers from Northern Ireland who supplied a creamery in the Irish Free State were required to clear their milk with a customs official on every occasion; the fact that customs posts did not open until 9 am was an added complication. The IAOS estimated that up to 70 per cent of northern suppliers would be lost. The manager of Tyholland and Middletown creamery reported that milk was going sour because of delays at customs posts. By the autumn of 1932 the customs authorities agreed to permit milk suppliers to use a limited number of unapproved roads between the hours of 8 am and 11 am. By 1934 there were complaints that supplies of milk from Northern Ireland were increasing, which meant that 'we are paying the British Government 30/- per cwt. plus about 1d per gallon to the Northern Ireland suppliers for the privilege of manufacturing their butter'. An official in the Department of Agriculture explained that these supplies were helping to keep some creameries working.[166] Fears of excess supplies from Northern Ireland disappeared shortly after this time, when Britain altered the basis of its price support for dairy produce.

The Irish Free State had traditionally exported substantial quantities of live pigs to Northern Ireland for processing, but this ended when Britain imposed a quota on imports of pork and bacon products from the Irish Free State. Pig dealers who traditionally supplied curers in Northern Ireland had to obtain a licence, which was regarded as part of the Irish quota for bacon exports to the UK. By August 1933 officials in the Department were trying to devise a scheme to ensure that the same pigs were not counted twice, once on behalf of a Northern Ireland curer, once on behalf of an exporter or agent.[167]

Smuggling emerged as a new and rewarding activity for farmers on both sides of the border. Ryan cited instances of produce being smuggled from Northern Ireland, in support of his claim that farmers in the Irish Free State were receiving favourable prices. Animal feed was a popular item for smugglers. In 1936 opposition deputy James Dillon claimed that he was paying 8s per cwt for maize meal mixture, whereas farmers in Britain could buy equivalent feed for 5s.[168] There was one unusual instance of co-operation in 1935, when the governments of the Irish Free State, Northern Ireland and Britain agreed to introduce simultaneous measures to wipe out warble fly.[169]

Farmers in Northern Ireland benefited considerably from the changes in British agricultural policy after 1931 and from the exclusion of Irish produce from the British market. In 1926 tillage was more important in Northern Ireland than in the Irish Free State; by 1938 this had been reversed.

Table 4: Sectoral Shares of Agricultural Output, North and South, 1926 and 1938[170]

	North (%) 1926	North (%) 1938	South (%) 1926	South (%) 1938
Tillage	21.6	12.0	14.6	19.0
Milk	19.4	17.3	24.1	24.0
Cattle	23.2	14.9	24.3	22.4
Sheep	4.3	3.5	5.0	6.6
Pigs	9.3	29.9	16.0	13.5
Poultry	22.3	22.4	15.9	14.6

Achievements of the 1930s

Popular memories of the 1930s recall cattle being seized from farmers who defaulted on their rates and calves being slaughtered and a crisis in Irish agriculture. Some vestiges of these stories crop up in the files of the Department of Agriculture, such as the widow living on twenty acres who was unable to sell her stock, or the small farmers in the Ox Mountains who slaughtered their cattle and sold the meat door-to-door. However, the human consequences of the agricultural depression were more likely to be witnessed by other government departments. The Board of Works and the Department of Local Government organised relief works, in which the county committees of agriculture were also involved. The Department of Local Government had to dispose of cattle seized in lieu of rates (one Waterford rate collector complained that farmers willingly gave him cattle which he could not dispose of), and it was forced to dissolve local authorities that accumulated high rates arrears.[171]

Most farmers blamed the depressed state of agriculture on the Economic War. The remedy was seen as either a change of government or a change in Fianna Fáil policy. Opposition and frustration over the Economic War were expressed through political rather than farming organisations. According to Mike Cronin, the Economic War was a major factor behind the rise of the Blueshirts.[172] The strongest farming organis-ation at the time, the Irish Beet Growers' Association, was a major beneficiary of the policy of self-sufficiency.[173] Although many disgruntled farmers blamed de Valera's government for their problems, their anger does not appear to have been directed specifically at the Department of Agriculture. In 1934 some Fianna Fáil TDs alleged that Department officials had spoken in critical terms about government policy. Ryan gave a commitment that if deputies supplied him with sworn affidavits to this effect, he would dismiss any official instantly, but there is no indication that the evidence was forthcoming.[174] Nevertheless, the allegations suggest that the Department was not universally regarded as supporting the change in agricultural policy. Although the Department determined the price of wheat and butter, it was not yet seen as exercising a major influence on farm incomes.

The responsibilities of the Department of Agriculture expanded considerably after 1932. Officials had to deal with applications for licences to import parrot food, prize drakes, puppy food, macaroni and many other exotic items.[175] It had to determine the proportion of Irish wheat to be used by flour-millers; set the price of butter and the level of export subsidy; keep a close eye on Irish poultry exports to Britain and the possible threat of British restrictions. From 1935 the Department had the authority to buy and store oats. The Department's Export Advisory Committee purchased and exported cattle to continental Europe.[176] Compound animal feed could only be manufactured under licence from the Department; it analysed the compound to ensure that it contained the stipulated proportion of home-grown grain.

These measures played a major role in determining the prosperity of Irish agriculture and the relative profitability of different enterprises. In 1939 the Department estimated that the guaranteed prices for butter had resulted in a net gain to Irish creameries of £4,647,000 between April 1932 and December 1938. But the extra tasks placed heavy demands on staff. In 1935 the Department estimated that implementing the Dairy Produce Price Stabilisation Act would require sixteen extra staff of various grades.[177]

The impact of the new agricultural policies on the Department can be seen by comparing its staffing and administrative structure in 1926 and 1936. In 1926 the Department consisted of nine divisions: Education and Production; Legal and Control; Accounts; Intelligence and General; Forestry; Establishment; Agricultural Inspectors; Veterinary Inspectors; and Technical and Advisory. There were 97 inspectors and 224 staff. By 1936 the Department's staff had more than doubled, to 650 (excluding Fisheries). There were four divisions in addition to Accounts, the Inspectorates and Technical. The descriptions of the work carried out by these divisions illustrate the range of responsibilities handled by the Department. Division

One was responsible for the Dairy Produce and Eggs Acts; Marketing; Export Bounties on Dairy Produce; Eggs and Poultry; Cereals and Tobacco Acts; the Potato Act; and Weeds and Seeds Acts. Division Two dealt with the County Committees of Agriculture; Loans for the Purchase of Livestock and Implements; Improvements of Dairy Cattle; Agricultural Education; the Gaeltacht and Congested Districts Agricultural Schemes; Diseases of Animals Acts; the Livestock Breeding Act; Horse Breeding Act; Agricultural Produce (Fresh Meat Act); Pigs and Bacon Act, and Bacon Export Quota; and Export Bounties on Livestock Products. In addition to Establishment, Division Three was responsible for Import Duties; Transit; Agricultural Credit Societies; Allotments (a scheme to provide allotments for town-dwellers seems to have taken a lot of the Department's time, judging by the large number of files that survive); Agricultural Exports (Foreign Trade Agreements); Intelligence and General. Division Four, which employed over 150 staff, was concerned with the Slaughter of Sheep and Cattle Act and the Elimination of Old and Diseased Cows.

During the 1930s the Department presented an annual report to the Department of the President, setting out what had been done to give effect to the policy of self-sufficiency. In addition to the major policies examined above, this involved conducting trials to establish the most suitable varieties of seed; schemes for the propagation of pedigree stocks of oats, so that Ireland would no longer be depending on imported seed oats; and ensuring self-sufficiency in seed potatoes. As part of the campaign to promote tillage, a subsidy was introduced to persuade farmers to use more lime.[178] A subsidy for phosphate fertiliser was introduced in 1938.[179]

Ryan made several radio broadcasts to announce new developments, such as the establishment of marketing boards for pigs and bacon, and the measures to encourage farmers to grow tobacco. In an effort to give farming programmes a wider appeal, a special panel of farmers was selected to give radio talks. The Department rejected a suggestion that it should finance an advertising film to promote wheat: the Agricultural Director, J. M. Adams, told Twomey that he questioned whether more than 5 per cent of the Irish cinema audience 'could be influenced in any way by wheat propaganda'. Twomey was equally unenthusiastic: 'the operations in connection with the seeding and harvesting of wheat are not spectacular and do not lend themselves to attractive presentation on film'.[180] Although the Department's stand at the Spring Show publicised new breeds of chicken, such as Les Marans and Houdans, the industrial stands were attracting more attention. In 1934 one official noted, 'It should be realized that opportunities to provide fresh items of interest each year are urgently needed'.[181]

Many of the new schemes were operated by the county committees of agriculture. Their expenditure increased from £142,000 in 1931/2 to almost £190,000 by 1938/9, although this was a drop in the ocean compared to the cost of export subsidies. The county committees were also involved in the programme of unemployment relief works, administering grants for schemes to extend or rebuild creameries and to provide shelter belts.[182] County committees of agriculture continued to run egg-laying competitions and to provide subsidies for agricultural shows and grants for bee-keeping, but there was a growing emphasis on providing loans for agricultural implements and measures to promote new enterprises such as onion-growing. In 1938 schemes were introduced for the purchase and erection of poultry houses and poultry-keeping equipment. County committees were also allocated grants for the purchase of rotary blowers to pump poison gas into rabbit burrows in order to reduce the rabbit pest. Fianna Fáil TDs received numerous complaints from farming constituents about the rabbit pest.[183] Exports of rabbits to England qualified for Department subsidies. Cavan, Donegal and Leitrim county committees of agriculture introduced bounties to encourage farmers to exterminate foxes; others soon followed suit. However, in 1935 the Department terminated the employment of the musk-rat trapper, who had been employed to patrol the banks of the river Shannon and its tributaries from Banagher in County Offaly to Limerick City, because it was believed the animal (which had escaped from fur farms) had been wiped out.

The range of new activities carried out by the Department contrasts with the lack of change in the volume and composition of agricultural output. Despite the disruption to trade and the commitment to self-sufficiency, the dominant trends in post-Famine agriculture were not reversed. Changes in agricultural output were of a marginal nature, even at the height of the Economic War. In 1937 the Report of the Banking Commission noted that the total acreage under crops was less than in 1911, although the acreage under grain was marginally higher. By 1939 the total acreage under tillage was 2 per cent higher than in 1930; the number of milch cows had risen by 3 per cent; the number of other cattle had fallen by 1 per cent. Irish agriculture was still dominated by livestock. Indeed, livestock and livestock products accounted for an even greater share of agricultural exports by the late thirties than ten years previously. In 1938/9 the output of cattle, at 937,000, was 9,000 greater than in 1929/30, although the estimated value was £11.9 million compared with £14.9 million in the earlier year.[184]

The expansion in tillage was concentrated in Leinster and Munter, while the acreage tilled in Connacht and Ulster declined. Of the additional 226,000 acres of wheat, 214,000 were planted in Leinster and Munster; and of the additional 29,000 acres under sugar-beet, 22,000 were planted in Leinster and Munster, with most of the remainder grown in County Galway near the Tuam factory. County Donegal produced a surprisingly high acreage under peas and beans; otherwise these crops were mainly found in counties Dublin and Kildare, close to the processing factories. Dublin, Kildare and Wexford accounted for almost half the acreage of fruit, although counties Monaghan and Cavan, which were adjacent to the traditional fruit-growing area in Armagh, were also important. By 1939 the Department was expressing confidence that tomatoes, grown in glasshouses, would offer a promising new enterprise along the western seaboard.[185]

Fianna Fáil devoted greater attention to the needs of small farmers than the previous government. Ryan's reluctance to accept any restrictions on poultry and egg exports to Britain reflected this concern, as did the efforts to earmark tobacco as a crop for small farmers and to use industrial alcohol plants to provide a market for potatoes in areas that did not benefit from sugar-beet. Yet the introduction of unemployment assistance in 1933 did more to protect the living standards of small farmers and assisting relatives than any of the elaborate forms of price support. Although the number of males engaged in farm work showed a slight increase between 1932 and 1934, from 558,920 to 579,409, this probably reflected the collapse of emigration, and perhaps the impact of the 1933 scheme that enabled farmers to offset rates against the cost of employing a full-time male agricultural worker. In 1934 almost 67,000 farms claimed rates relief under this heading for 126,000 workers. By 1938 the number of males engaged in agriculture had declined to 537,222. Raymond Crotty noted that there was no relationship between the increase in tillage and changes in the agricultural workforce (encouraging tillage was supposed to create jobs in agriculture, or at least prevent a decline). The number of agricultural workers in Munster and Leinster fell significantly despite an increase in the amount of tillage, while the rate of decline in the number of agricultural workers was much less in Connacht where the acreage under tillage fell.[186] This would not have surprised the Department of Agriculture. In 1932 it had predicted that a dramatic rise in the acreage under sugar-beet would not create any additional jobs in farming. Indeed, the Department, unlike many naïve commentators at the time, was consistently sceptical about the possibility of increased employment in agriculture. In 1938, when drawing up possible terms of reference for the Commission on Agriculture, it referred to maintaining the present agricultural population.

Land redistribution and land resettlement were the responsibility of the Land Commission. Although the Minister for Agriculture always served on the Cabinet sub-committees that considered each Land Bill, the Department of Agriculture does not seem to have expressed any views on the legislation.[187] However, the Department was involved in administering grants for land reclamation, which were designed to make small farms more self-sufficient by increasing the amount of land available for growing animal feed. The field drainage scheme was first introduced in 1931 in the former Congested District areas.[188] In 1933/4 lime subsidies were introduced in the same counties. These schemes were extended to north-west Cavan in 1934/5, and in 1936/7 parts of Limerick Longford, Monaghan, Tipperary and Waterford became eligible. By 1939, 27,700 acres had been reclaimed, and a further 11,500 acres were being reclaimed during 1939 under the eye of fifty-four supervisors. Prendergast, an inspector, noted that in West Cork the reclamation, lime and seed schemes 'are serving a most useful National purpose'. He suggested that the amount of money provided for land reclamation should be increased.[189] The liming and reclamation projects of the 1930s were the forerunners of much more elaborate schemes after World War II.

The Department of Agriculture's views on agricultural policy are probably best summarised in the evidence that Daniel Twomey, the secretary of the Department, gave to the Banking Commission in 1937. Twomey expressed the view that farming in the Irish Free State would continue to be dominated by livestock, although the emphasis would switch from cattle to dairy produce, eggs, poultry and bacon and pork.[190] This was remarkably similar to the pattern of Northern Ireland farming at this time; it also anticipated the direction that Irish agriculture tried to pursue after World War II. This product mix was better suited to farmers in Northern Ireland than their counterparts in the Irish Free State, who were at a considerable disadvantage, owing to the higher cost of animal feed and less favourable access to the UK market, even after 1938. The extent of this disadvantage emerges from Cormac Ó Gráda's estimate of the value of the output of farms in the Irish Free State on the basis of the prices available in Northern Ireland. In 1935/6, total output was valued at £42.6 million in 26-county prices, but at £48.4 million in 6-county prices; prices in Northern Ireland were almost 14 per cent higher than in the Irish Free State. Crop prices in Northern Ireland were somewhat lower, but prices for livestock products were substantially higher. By 1938/9 output per worker in agriculture in the Irish Free State was £89, compared with £92 in 1925/6; in Northern Ireland output per worker rose from £75 to £87 in the same period.[191] These calculations suggest that in the 1930s farmers in the Irish Free State were paying a high price for Irish independence and this continued to be so after 1939.

Twomey believed that Irish agriculture should continue to be based around livestock and to rely heavily on the British market. More interestingly, he suggested that this was not necessarily incompatible with the goal of self-sufficiency. He told the Banking Commission that complete self-sufficiency in cereals and root crops would only require the breaking up or tilling of 1.5 million acres of grassland, approximately 15 per cent of the acreage then under grass and hay. In the course of questioning Twomey on this point, Per Jacobsson, the distinguished Swedish economist, remarked that the Department's policy entailed using subsidies 'to move the margin' rather than a complete upheaval in the composition of Irish agricultural output. Twomey's response was quoted in the Commission's Report:

> We do not expect as a result of the present policy, there will probably be what you would term a profound change of economy. There will be adjustments. If we continue at the present rate, we will in time extend the acreage under wheat from the present 165,000 acres to 650,000. Although that is very important in itself, one cannot say that it is going to bring about a profound change in our agricultural economy.[192]

There would be an opportunity to see whether or not this judgement proved correct when the outbreak of war in 1939 transformed self-sufficiency from an ideal into a matter of national survival.

CHAPTER FIVE

THE EMERGENCY, 1939–1945

While World War I is generally remembered as a properous time for Irish farmers, their recollections of World War II are rather mixed. James Meenan commented, 'The picture of a neutral Ireland waxing prosperous on wartime prices is therefore grossly misleading'.[1] Raymond Crotty gave the war years scant attention, because in his opinion 'they left no permanent imprint on Irish agriculture'.[2] Farmers fared reasonably well by comparison with other sections of Irish society. In 1945 net agricultural output, which is a close approximation to income from farming, was 16.8 per cent higher than in 1938/9, and although some of this rise was due to a substantially higher output of turf,[3] most of it was due to the expansion in tillage. This improvement reversed the deterioration in the living standards of farmers during the 1920s and the 1930s. In 1943 Seán Lemass noted that 'during almost the whole of the inter-war period the economic balance between agriculture and other activities was not equitable, and [that] farmers had to bear the brunt of the economic war. In fact, the difference in economic trends since the beginning of the war, in their net effect, have not been altogether unfavourable, in so far as they have been relatively to the advantage of agriculturists.'[4] Although the British market offered no wartime bonanza, Ireland's enforced self-sufficiency gave farmers the security of a guaranteed price and a guaranteed market for most commodities.

The years from 1939 until 1945 saw the emergence of more assertive and better-organised farming lobbies. The Department had to cope with a growing number of deputations, delegations and resolutions. However, the apparent prosperity of farming and demands for further price increases occasionally served to polarise the interests of farmers and the non-agricultural population. Before 1939 the government does not appear to have been unduly concerned if households had to pay more for bread and sugar as the price of self-sufficiency. During the Emergency, however, the Cabinet was much more conscious of the impact of higher farm prices on consumers. Politicians and civil servants began to make critical comments about the farming community; and there were occasional allegations that farmers were furthering their own interests at national expense.

The Emergency changed self-sufficiency from a nationalist dream to a question of survival. From 1939 until 1947 access to imported goods was severely limited by a shortage of shipping space and the inability to obtain goods from other countries. Shortages of fertiliser, farm machinery and animal feed brought a decline in pig numbers, depleted soil fertility and caused long delays in completing the harvest. The damage to soil fertility reduced productivity for several years after the war ended, and by the latter years of the war Irish agriculture was no longer capable of meeting home demand for butter and bacon.

Most of the Department's time was taken up with managing compulsory tillage, attempting to ensure that there would be sufficient labourers for the harvest, negotiating export arrangements with Britain, and making the case for higher farm prices in opposition to the departments of Finance, Industry and Commerce, and Supplies. By 1944 the Department employed up to 200 tillage inspectors (many of them former inspectors with the Land Commission), in order to ensure that farmers complied with the spirit and not just the letter of the tillage orders.[5] The Department was also responsible for enforcing restrictions on the export of agricultural produce; allocating pigs between the various bacon plants; doling out supplies of fertiliser to farmers and allotment holders; and allocating paraffin to power tractors, kerosene to light dairies and coal for threshing machines.

The Emergency got its name from the 1939 Emergency Powers Act, which enabled the government to make an emergency order covering almost any matter, without going through the time-consuming process of enacting legislation in the Oireachtas. During 1942 and 1943, for example, emergency powers orders were introduced to ensure the equitable distribution of fertiliser among farmers; regulate the quality of animal feed on the market; police the sale of seed potatoes; control the purchase and distribution of grain; ban the sale of barley as animal feed; and control the export of agricultural produce.

Propaganda was another important aspect of the Department's work. Radio broadcasts, ministerial speeches and newspaper advertisements emphasised that neutrality and the survival of the nation were dependent on the ability of farmers to provide sufficient food. The advertising campaign was managed by the Wilson Hartnell agency.[6] Posters at railway stations, creameries and schools urged farmers to till more land; radio broadcasts carried stirring titles such as 'More and More Wheat'. The text of a broadcast by the Minister for Agriculture, James Ryan, on 27 October 1941, dealing with fertiliser and food production, was sent to the bishops and clergy of all denominations and to school principals. A short film on food production was commissioned in 1941. Late autumn and winter, when farmers planned the crops for the coming year, saw a spate of publicity about the importance of growing wheat. Ryan toured the country speaking to county committees of agriculture. These campaigns were an annual event until the autumn of 1945, when the Department decided to cut back on the annual publicity drive because the situation appeared less urgent. In 1945 it abandoned films and radio talks because they had never been satisfactory.[7]

Many wartime speeches made direct or indirect reference to the Great Famine. In January 1942, in a letter sent to all clergy, Daniel Twomey, secretary of the Department of Agriculture, remarked, 'It would be tragic if, in view of the natural resources available, we failed to provide the means of feeding the people, and as a consequence had to face a repetition of the hardships endured during the forties of the last century'. The text of a radio broadcast in November 1942 stressed that the task of growing sufficient crops to feed the population should not be beyond the resources of Irish farmers; Irish farmers had fed the population a century ago – why not now? Another broadcast referred to the importance of tillage in time of war and noted that the first ploughing competitions were held during the Napoleonic War. In April 1944 de Valera commented that although conditions were serious, he did not expect them to deteriorate to the level of Bengal, China, 'or in Ireland a century ago'.

National solidarity was a recurring theme. Farmers were reminded that the poor would suffer hardship if they were remiss in their duty. In April 1944 de Valera told a meeting in Killarney, at which the bishop of Kerry presided, that 'in times like these the nation must stand together. If hardship occurs in one place, it will have its reaction in other places'; he urged farmers to think of those who lived in towns and cities, who were entirely dependent on farmers for their food.[8] This message was not lost on one agricultural contractor from Macroom in County Cork, who wrote to the Department in 1942 appealing against seven summonses for violations of the Road Traffic Acts owing to the condition of his tractor:

Ministers for Agriculture

Horace Plunkett 1900-1907

Robert C. Barton 1919-1920

Art O'Connor 1920-1922

Patrick Hogan 1922-1932

Dr. Seamus Ó Riain 1932-1947

Patrick Smith 1947-1948/1957-1964

Thomas Walsh 1951-1954

James M. Dillon 1948-1951/
1954-1957

Frank Aiken 1957

Sean Moylan 1957

Charles J. Haughey 1964-1966

Neil T. Blaney 1966-1970

James Gibbons 1970-1973/
1977-1979

Mark Clinton 1973-1977   Ray McSharry 1979-1981

Alan Dukes 1981-1982   Brian Lenihan 1982

Austin Deasy 1982-1987

Michael O'Kennedy 1987-1991

Michael Woods 1991-1992

Ivan Yates 1994-1997

Joe Walsh 1992-1994/1997-2002

... in the present crisis of the food problem when from every platform, alter [*sic*] and pulpit, the heads of the people both Government and clergy are doing their best to try to get the people especialy [*sic*] the farmers, to produce as much food as possible to keep the people of the citys [*sic*] and towns from starvation which they are surely facing in this present situation.

He also referred to 'the poor people who are depending on the likes of me and the farmers to keep the hunger from their door'.[9] Yet the new-found economic strength of the farming community was something of a two-edged sword. In July 1940, shortly after the fall of Dunkirk, at a time when there was a real possibility of a German victory, Erskine Childers, Fianna Fáil TD for Longford–Athlone, noted that if England (*sic*) were defeated, 'An authoritarian campaign of agricultural instruction and propaganda, the shocking of the farmers into a true state of their position, and an almost military mobilisation of industrial effort will be required if we are to survive'. He complained that farmers were more interested in securing higher prices than in increasing agricultural output.[10] In January 1941 John Leydon, secretary of the Department of Supplies, emphasised the point:

> ... farmers should be made to realise that it was their duty to undertake the maximum production possible and not to be content with the minimum standards of tillage laid down by the Order. The land is the country's principal asset, and the great majority of farmers had received State assistance in acquiring their holdings. It should not, therefore, be too much to ask them in a time of crisis to consider first the country's needs without regard to the question of securing enhanced prices for their crops, and everyone should be made to feel that the farmer who fails to produce the maximum possible amount from his farm is a public enemy.[11]

Preparations for War

War had appeared imminent on several occasions before September 1939. At the time of the Munich crisis in September 1938 John Leydon, secretary of the Department of Industry and Commerce, told the Irish Flour Millers' Association that the government wished the millers to hold one year's reserve of wheat; arrangements would be made to compensate them, either through an increase in the price of flour, or by a direct government loan or subsidy.[12] In December 1938 an interdepartmental committee reported to the Cabinet on measures to be taken in time of war. The Department of Agriculture would be responsible for ensuring that farmers produced more food, and for regulating exports of surplus agricultural produce and the importation and distribution of agricultural requisites. The committee appears to have assumed that imported wheat would continue to be available, since it set a target of producing 50 per cent of flour from native wheat. It was also of the opinion that the numbers of sheep and pigs could be readily increased. In April 1939 it concluded that little could be achieved for the coming season 'other than to perfect plans for increased acreages of tillage crops in 1940' and to accumulate extra stocks of imported agricultural supplies and ensure that the 1939 harvest was put to the best possible use. An official in the Department of Agriculture was appointed to liaise with the Supplies section of the Department of Industry and Commerce to determine priority imports of farm machinery, feeding stuff, spraying materials and other essential items.[13] According to the annual report for the Department of Agriculture for 1939/40, it worked closely with Industry and Commerce to build up strategic supplies in the months immediately before the outbreak of war. However, this seems an exaggerated claim, because when war broke out fertiliser stocks were at an extremely low level, and there was only three to four weeks' supply of maize in stock, although the acreage of oats and barley was known to be 78,000 acres below the 1938 figure.[14] Stocks of imported wheat were above average.

On 25 September, shortly after the outbreak of war, economist Professor Timothy Smiddy, chairman of the commission of inquiry into agriculture set up following the 1938 Anglo-Irish Trade Agreement, warned de Valera that shortages of fertiliser and animal feed would present major difficulties. In 1938 imports of maize were valued at £2.25 million. Maize had been unobtainable during World War I and it would probably be necessary again to substitute home-grown feed. Farmers should be encouraged to use farmyard manure to make up for the anticipated shortage of fertiliser. But in order to produce more farmyard manure it would be necessary to increase the numbers of stall-fed cattle and the number of pigs being fattened, and this would be difficult given the shortage of animal feed. A lack of manure would also frustrate efforts to grow more wheat and sugar-beet. If the acreage under sugar-beet was increased, it would be necessary to hire additional labourers and they would probably demand higher wages, if 'compulsory methods' were not employed, because farm labourers disliked the hard effort involved in pulling beet.[15]

Despite Smiddy's warnings, there was a lack of urgency about supplies during the early months of the so-called 'phoney war', when there was no significant loss of ships at sea. This lack of urgency also prevailed in Britain. Throughout the 1930s there was considerable over-capacity in shipping, and officials in Ireland and Britain assumed that there would be ample shipping space available to carry additional supplies following the outbreak of war. A world surplus of grain and fuel supplies contributed to this complacency. Yet the panic that followed the outbreak of war led to an acute shortage of shipping, and this made it impossible to import extra wheat and fertiliser during the autumn and winter of 1939.[16]

AGRICULTURAL TRADE WITH BRITAIN

James Meenan claimed that, 'During the six years that followed [the outbreak of war] agricultural policy depended on events that were far beyond the power of any Irish government to control: it could not be framed by deliberate choice'.[17] Britain was probably the most important identifiable influence on agricultural policy, since it provided the only market for Irish exports during the war. Imports of wheat, animal feed, farm machinery and fertiliser were generally shipped through Britain, where these items were very much in demand.[18] Although in theory the 1938 trade agreement remained in operation, the outbreak of war transformed the market relationship.

On 25 August, shortly before Britain declared war on Germany, the Irish Cabinet minutes note that, 'It was decided provisionally that the Department of Agriculture should, through the department of External Affairs, organise discussions with representatives of the British Government on the export of livestock'.[19] The Irish government was aware that the Ministry of Food would control all imports of food into Britain during the war, and it was essential to examine the implications of this new arrangement for Irish agriculture. On 25 September Smiddy told de Valera that, 'In the last war the prosperity of Irish agriculture was due entirely to the great rise in prices, but agriculturists would be unwise to rely on a similar phenomenon on this occasion'. He did not anticipate a significant rise in the export prices during the war because Irish agriculture would not have any outlet except the Ministry of Food.[20] Smiddy was correct in this assessment. Britain introduced rationing of butter and bacon in January 1940; meat was rationed from March 1940.[21] This reduced the demand for imports and enabled the Ministry of Food to control the prices of imported produce.

In March 1940 officials from the departments of Agriculture and Supplies met British officials to discuss Anglo-Irish trade. Britain was reluctant to provide Ireland with raw materials that would not be used to produce items that Britain needed. Although Britain was keen to substitute Irish and British produce for imports from overseas, it gave priority to increasing the output of British farms. Daniel Twomey, secretary of the Department of Agriculture, had some difficulty in establishing which items of food Britain wished to import from Ireland. He claimed that it was probable that Britain would not require large quantities of Irish butter and bacon:

> The position appears to be that in order to decide what lines our agricultural production can most profitably follow, an understanding with the British Government is essential both as regards the quantities of our various products they are prepared to take and the prices they are prepared to pay. Such an understanding entails also an understanding about the quantities of various feeding stuffs, fertilisers, etc., we are to import, and the shipping facilities to carry them. This indicates the necessity for a comprehensive agreement, which, as it will involve major issues of policy, seems to require the intervention of Ministers.

On 21 March 1940 de Valera raised at Cabinet the question of opening trade negotiations with Britain. A minute, apparently written by Kathleen O'Connell, de Valera's personal secretary, noted that 'I was instructed that no note of the discussion was to be recorded in the minutes. No memorandum was before the Government'. The minute continued: 'I am informed by the Taoiseach that he has since decided that a despatch should be sent to the British Government suggesting the opening of negotiations'. This despatch, which was drafted by Twomey, Leydon (secretary of the Department of Supplies) and Joseph Walshe (secretary of the Department of External Affairs), read as follows:

> In the course of recent discussions between officials of the two Governments, concerning our mutual trade position, it became apparent that something more than [provisional] arrangements of an administrative character were [might be][22] required to meet the needs of the war situation. It appears to the Irish Government that it would

be advisable, as a matter of long term policy, to determine the extent and nature of agricultural production in this country in relation to the requirements of the home and the British markets. The relation of production to the prices obtainable and to the supply of raw materials essential therefore would also have to be determined. These and other related issues seem to the Irish Government to warrant the holding of a conference between Ministers of the two Governments. The discussion at the conference would reveal whether or not a general agreement were necessary.

This despatch suggests that the government was willing to co-operate with Britain on food supplies; de Valera had already indicated this during the 1938 trade talks. On 28 March the Cabinet decided to ask Dulanty, the Irish Minister in London, to report on his negotiations with British Ministers. Officials in Dublin were asked to report on their discussions with the British Minister in Dublin, Sir John Maffey. Ryan and Lemass would prepare memoranda. If it was decided to embark on trade negotiations, Lemass and Ryan would go to London for discussions 'of general exploratory character'. A decision as to whether de Valera would travel to London would be taken later. Walshe reported that Dulanty believed that ministerial talks should only take place if it appeared probable that Ireland would obtain definite concessions such as a higher export price for butter, but Dulanty was not optimistic. Despite this discouraging message, the Cabinet decided that Dulanty should speak to British officials along the lines of the draft despatch. On 19 April it agreed that Lemass and Ryan should travel to London for trade talks, and a press statement to this effect was drafted, but not issued. Rumours of the trip must have circulated, however, because on 25 April Fine Gael's Richard Mulcahy tabled a question in Dáil Éireann asking how often and when Irish ministers had conducted trade negotiations with British ministers since April 1938. De Valera replied that no negotiations had taken place.

A memorandum from the Department of Agriculture to Cabinet in April 1940 concluded that wartime circumstances did not require 'a radical alteration' in 'the existing agricultural economy'. Irish agriculture would be in a fairly satisfactory position if sufficient supplies of raw materials, fertiliser and animal feed could be secured to maintain output at the current level. The Department urged that in the coming trade talks,

... the utmost effort should be made to get the British to agree to take our surplus production to the extent of at least its present volume. This necessarily means that the British would take supplies of fat cattle, butter and eggs which hitherto were exported to Germany. The prospect of finding alternative markets for live stock or commodities such as meat, butter or eggs under the present conditions is negligible.

The Department was keen to secure an increase in the price paid for Irish fat cattle, by persuading Britain either to extend the subsidy on domestic fat cattle to Irish fat cattle or to contribute to the cost of transport. In the case of store cattle, lambs and fat sheep, the Department wanted an assurance that the trade would not be interrupted or restricted. It was also keen to secure a higher quota for bacon, or alternatively, greater flexibility in filling the existing quota, which was set at 40,000 cwt per month. It also wished to ease the difficulties being experienced by the fresh meat trade. The Department claimed that the British Ministry of Food delayed imports of fresh meat because it preferred to import live cattle; imports of canned meat were only permitted under licence. The terms offered for Irish butter were described as poor and to date no agreement had been reached with the Ministry of Food for exports of other dairy produce. In the case of eggs and live poultry, the Department wanted reassurance that Britain would not impose any restrictions.[23]

The terms of reference given to Lemass and Ryan prior to the trade talks noted that they should discuss and come to agreement as to the disposal of Irish agricultural produce on the British market, the supply of raw materials and essential commodities, the provision of foreign exchange, bulk purchasing and freight. The minute stated that, 'It is understood that no agreement will be entered into in respect of any matter comprised in the scope of the negotiations which will have the effect of prejudicing the position of this country as a neutral in the present European War or could reasonably be regarded by any of the belligerants [sic] as affording ground for an attack on this country'.[24] Ryan and Lemass were accompanied by the secretaries to the departments of Agriculture, External Affairs and Supplies, and by the Director of Agriculture, J. M. Adams. Talks took place between 1 and 4 May and were then adjourned. They were due to resume on 9 May, the date of the critical Westminster debate that led to the resignation of Neville Chamberlain as prime minster, but they were postponed indefinitely.[25] Churchill became prime minister on 10 May, the day that Belgium and the Netherlands fell to the Germans. With a German victory seemingly inevitable, Britain put pressure on de Valera to abandon neutrality in return for a promise to end partition.[26]

Trade talks between British and Irish officials resumed in late August. On 23 August representatives from the Board of Trade and the Dominions Office informed Dulanty that they were unable to present him with a draft agreement, because the British Ministry of Food and Ministry of Agriculture could not agree on cattle prices. Although this statement was correct,[27] there were more important obstacles to achieving a trade agreement. Britain wished to use Irish ports and territorial waters to transfer cargo from large vessels to small coasters in order to relieve congestion at British ports, and it wanted to make this a condition of any trade agreement. Sir William Brown, acting secretary of the Ministry of Supplies, informed Dulanty that if Ireland did not make a concession on trans-shipment there would be no agreement. He emphasised that Britain had no intention of publishing the section of any agreement that related to trans-shipment. Dulanty replied that this 'made the proposal less acceptable – if that were possible'.

The draft trade agreement presented by Britain in September 1940 would have given Irish agricultural produce an assured market until 31 August 1941; it offered Ireland guaranteed supplies of essential imports, access to British shipping space, foreign exchange and the prospect of a substantial number of jobs in ship repair. In return, Britain demanded trans-shipment facilities. J. J. McElligott, secretary of the Department of Finance, described the schedule of prices for agricultural exports as 'unsatisfactory', and F. H. Boland of External Affairs, in a minute to Kathleen O'Connell, warned that conditions in Britain could develop to the point – the Battle of Britain was then under way – where any agreement might become 'wholly or largely inoperative'. In that case Ireland would have suffered all the disadvantages without reaping the benefits. Boland was also of the opinion that there would be no trade agreement unless Ireland gave Britain facilities for trans-shipment. Consequently, there was little to be gained from negotiating the other details and leaving trans-shipment until the end. On 24 September the Cabinet decided that the draft agreement was unacceptable. While trans-shipment was the sticking point, the Cabinet decided that the Irish reply would also include 'other obser-vations'.

On 18 October, more than three weeks later, Walshe, secretary of the Department of External Affairs, sent de Valera a résumé of a suggested reply to the British proposals. He recommended that the Irish authorities should emphasise that the prices Britain was paying for Irish agricultural

219

produce were depressing output, given the increased cost of production. Unless Britain offered higher prices, there was a danger that Irish farmers would return to subsistence agriculture. A number of detailed comments relating to agriculture followed. It was suggested that a proposed subsidy of £500,000 offered by Britain should be spread across different products and not restricted to fat cattle; the prices offered by Britain for dairy produce and fat cattle should be increased; the market for sheep should be restored to the position that existed prior to 15 July 1940; prices for pigs and eggs should correspond to the prices paid to British producers; the price paid for flax should be identical to the price in Northern Ireland; the quota for Irish bacon should be increased to 600,000 cwt (from 500,000) at a price of 133s 6d per cwt; prices for dressed meat should correspond to dead-weight prices agreed for live cattle; there should be a quota of 30,000 cwts for exports of lard; and the Ministry of Food should accept up to 10,000 tons of surplus Irish seed and ware potatoes. The list was so extensive as to be unrealistic. The memorandum contained equally detailed demands relating to shipping, insurance and supplies. Trans-shipment was left to the very end. Britain's request for facilities was rejected because it 'would constitute a threat to Ireland's neutrality and gravely endanger the lives and prosperity of Irish citizens'.[28]

Relations between Britain and Ireland deteriorated during the autumn of 1940, when Ireland rejected Britain's request for trans-shipment facilities. In December 1940 the colonial secretary, Viscount Cranbourne, suggested that Britain should adopt a policy of 'silent sanctions' towards Ireland in order to keep 'her lean' and to make the Irish public aware that they depended on Britain for their survival.[29] In January 1941 Britain cut back considerably on the supplies of goods that it allocated to Ireland and on Irish access to space on British ships. While this resulted in acute shortages of imported goods, it transformed the Irish balance of trade from a chronic deficit to a substantial surplus. This was entirely contrary to expectations. In September 1939 Smiddy had predicted that during the war the cost of imports would rise much more rapidly than the price obtained for exports, and that Ireland would have to export substantially greater quantities of agricultural produce to meet its import bills.[30] In February 1941, however, J. J. McElligott, the secretary of the Department of Finance, informed Twomey that,

We have already enough assets and investments in Britain to meet our various requirements and it is unnecessary to increase them at the rate of £16 million a year if that £16 million or a part of it could be otherwise more profitably invested at home. There is the additional argument that in the event of a depreciation of the pound sterling and a fall in the value of British securities we may suffer substantial losses in our assets and securities held in Britain.

Any scheme whereby some of our exports could be retained more profitably at home without undue hardship to the producers of such exports should be favourably considered.

McElligott recommended that exports of dairy produce should be restricted and that the national dairy herd should be culled, removing weak and sickly animals.[31] Irish butter exports had been heavily subsidised since 1932, and the subsidies continued after the outbreak of war because the price that Britain offered – 126s per cwt in the spring of 1940 – was substantially below the domestic price of 152s.[32] Stopping butter exports to Britain would mean a substantial saving to the exchequer. McElligott suggested that it would be preferable for 'some of our surplus cattle to be more profitably used for our own purposes rather than have them translated into sterling assets and bank balances which might fall considerably in value owing to the war'. While he acknowledged that there was a 'real' conflict of interest on this issue, he claimed that financial considerations should prevail over agricultural.[33]

In July 1941 the Cabinet established an interdepartmental committee chaired by Joseph Walshe, the secretary of External Affairs, to co-ordinate the views of government departments on negotiations with Britain over trade and related matters. The other departments represented were Agriculture, Industry and Commerce, Supplies, and Defence. Towards the end of 1941 it appears that Britain and Ireland discussed the possibility of a barter arrangement, similar to the coal-cattle pacts of the 1930s, but no agreement materialised. A hand-written note by Walshe, in February 1942, apparently to Maurice Moynihan, the secretary to the government, stated that, 'A difference between the Departments of Agriculture and Supplies in their approach to the subject makes it difficult or impossible to secure proper co-ordination by a committee of Heads of Departments'. Walshe had already spoken about this matter to de Valera in his capacity as Minister for External Affairs. De Valera asked John Leydon, secretary of the Department of Supplies, and Twomey for their observations. Having spoken to Twomey, de Valera decided that each department should prepare material as though negotiation for a comprehensive agreement on trade and supplies were about to commence. Both departments seem to have dug in their heels, because these reports never materialised despite repeated requests. A hand-written note dated 2 April 1943 states tersely that, 'No report was received. It was decided to take no further action in this Department [presumably External Affairs]'.[34]

While the Cabinet took no formal decision on reducing dairy exports to Britain, it was slow to concede higher guaranteed prices for milk and butter. In consequence, the output of butter declined to the point where it barely met domestic needs, and dairy exports ceased in the summer of 1942. Exports of pork and bacon came to a halt in 1941, mainly owing to the shortage of animal feed. Exports of eggs continued because they were profitable, although this resulted in seasonal shortages in Ireland. The Department of Agriculture resisted pressure from the Department of Supplies for restrictions to be imposed.[35] From 1941 exports of eggs, poultry and rabbits were handled by a company called Eggsports, which was set up with the Department's encouragement. The directors were chosen from the Consultative Council for Eggs and Poultry.[36]

Flax exports increased despite the fact that, according to Ryan, officials in the Department of Finance 'appear to disagree with the entire flax-growing policy'. The acreage under flax rose from little more than 1,000 acres during the 1930s, to 15,500 in 1941 and 25,000 in 1942. The flax trade was profitable: the British Ministry of Supplies agreed to buy the entire Irish output at a favourable price and the crop brought some prosperity to the border counties of Monaghan and Cavan.[37] Flax was also grown in other areas, including West Cork.

The lucrative export trade in rabbits led to a significant fall in the number of complaints to the Department about rabbits eating farmers' crops.

FOOT AND MOUTH

The livestock trade only came under threat during 1941, when the market was disrupted by an outbreak of foot and mouth disease. The first case was reported in County Donegal, near the border with Derry, on 20 January. Another outbreak was reported in County Laois four days later. By late February it had spread to Dublin city, Wicklow, Meath and Kildare. The disease seemed to be waning by late March, but a fresh outbreak was reported in County Kilkenny on 6 April. In May cases were notified in Tipperary, Limerick, Kerry and Meath. On 21 June the first case was reported in County Carlow, which was the last county to be hit by the disease; the last case was reported in Carlow on 22 September. In all, there were 556 cases reported, affecting almost 6,000 cattle and several hundred pigs and sheep. A total of 27,942 cattle, 10,187 sheep, and 3,310 pigs and 608 goats were slaughtered. The outbreak in Dublin was particularly serious since it proved very difficult to isolate cattle in the city and the nearby countryside. The Department blamed the extensive spread of the disease on the 'lamentable indifference' of the public. People continued to visit infected premises and milk from infected herds was sent to creameries. Some farmers who concealed cases were prosecuted.[38] Ryan made a statement in the Dáil to counter rumours that the disease was being spread by the Department's inspectors, and that veterinary surgeons were deliberately spreading the disease to extend their employment.[39]

Britain banned livestock imports from Ireland from January to October 1941. Some restrictions would have been imposed during 1941 regardless, because an acute shortage of animal feed in Britain made it necessary to reduce livestock numbers. In February 1941 a livestock policy conference in Britain recommended that imports of beef cattle from the Irish Free State should be reduced. Another report demanded a reduction of 20 per cent in the number of beef cattle, although the British Ministry of Agriculture prevented this being implemented.[40] The 1941 outbreak cost the Department of Agriculture approximately £480,000 in compensation to farmers for animals that were compulsorily slaughtered.[41] When farmers were unable to dispose of cattle, the Department arranged for them to be purchased and slaughtered by the Dublin Emergency Meat Supply Committee and by meat-processing plants and co-operatives in Waterford and Roscrea.[42] Temporary slaughter houses were registered to cope with demand. Although western counties remained free of the disease, farmers were unable to dispose of their cattle because of restrictions on the movement of livestock within Ireland. The Department tried without success to arrange for livestock from western farms to be shipped to Britain from Northern Ireland or ports such as Sligo, Galway or Ballina.[43]

When the outbreak ended, Britain admitted Irish fat cattle but continued to exclude stores for some time.[44] Fat cattle were slaughtered on arrival at British ports, and this posed no disease risk. Stores, on the other hand, were despatched throughout Britain, and therefore posed a much greater risk of spreading disease. It seems probable, however, that the decision to exclude stores was not based solely on disease considerations but may have been prompted by Britain's food policy at the time.

Throughout World War II livestock remained the most profitable agricultural export in every year except 1941, although the shortage of feed-stuff in Britain meant that prices for fat cattle and dairy cattle rose more than the price for stores. The average price for fat cattle doubled from £13 18s in 1939 to £27 16s in 1943; prices for milch and springers rose from £18 to £32 14s; the average price paid for store cattle rose from £17 4s to £27 16s.[45] In 1945 live animals accounted for almost half the total value of exports and this was so throughout the war, except during 1941. By 1943 exports of fresh and canned meat were absorbing an estimated 100,000 cattle. The Department hoped that this market would expand after the war.

COMPULSORY TILLAGE

Self-sufficiency became the overriding consideration during the Emergency, particularly after 1941. Although the Department of Agriculture continued to emphasise the importance of maintaining exports, this took second place to the need to ensure a sufficient supply of bread and flour. The volume index for the gross output of crops and turf rose from 100 in 1938 to 139.5 by 1945; the volume index for livestock fell from 100 to 87.1.

Wheat was essential for national survival. When older farmers recall the Emergency years they are likely to mention compulsory tillage and tillage inspectors. Non-farmers remember the bread, which was dark brown and widely regarded as of inferior quality. People who lived near the border with Northern Ireland often crossed over to buy white bread. Compulsory tillage and dark brown bread were two elements of the same objective: to feed the population. In 1939, the best pre-war year, native wheat provided approximately one-third of the country's needs. By 1945 the wheat acreage had reached 662,498 acres, more than two and a half times the 1939 figure, although the additional acreage brought lower average yields.

On 26 August 1939, when war seemed imminent, the Executive Council asked the Minister for Agriculture to produce a memorandum on compulsory tillage. This document, dated 31 August 1939, noted that a substantial increase in the acreage tilled would be needed if Ireland was to provide even half its flour requirement from native wheat. This could only be achieved through compulsion, because the Department anticipated that

TABLE 5: Irish Cereal Output, 1939–45

	Wheat (Acres)	Wheat (000 Cwt)	Wheat (Yield per Acre) (Cwt)
1939	255,280	5,106	20.0
1940	305,243	6,257	20.5
1941	463,206	8,708	18.8
1942	574,739	10,230	17.8
1943	509,245	8,708	17.1
1944	642,487	10,922	17.0
1945	662,498	11,461	17.3

	Oats (Acres)	Oats (000 Cwt)	Barley (Acres)	Barley (000 Cwt)
1938	570,414	11,181	117,843	2,204
1939	536,749	10,793	73,784	1,476
1940	680,920	14,488	132,272	2,778
1941	782,201	13,689	163,342	2,858
1942	877,766	15,361	186,242	3,445
1943	936,253	15,916	208,947	3,761
1944	945,236	15,596	167,622	3,051
1945	834,206	11,461	170,339	2,998

TABLE 6: Grain Milling Industry – Materials Used, 1938–44[46]

	Wheat (000 Cwt)			Maize (000 Cwt)	Barley (000 Cwt)	Oats (000 Cwt)
	Home	Imports	Total			
1938	2,564	6,935	9,199	6,374	366	1,078
1939	3,650	6,800	10,450	7,441	308	866
1940	3,462	6,566	10,128	5,594	209	780
1941	4,361	3,066	7,427	857	261	1,005
1942	4,384	2,597	6,981	3	25	558
1943	5,226	2,718	7,944	–	154	788
1944	5,207	3,939	9,146	–	595	897

wartime price trends would encourage farmers to 'lean towards livestock rather than tillage'. The Department recommended that a guaranteed price for wheat should be announced when the compulsory tillage order was introduced. On 12 September 1939 the Cabinet decided to adopt a compulsory tillage order but deferred an announcement, presumably to give the Department an opportunity to work out the details. When de Valera met a deputation of farmers, representing the Irish Beet Growers' Association, the National Ploughing Association and the Irish Farmers' Federation,[47] at the Department of Agriculture on 15 September 1939 (Ryan was indisposed), to impress on them the need to increase tillage, he referred to compulsory tillage only as a possibility.[48]

The Department of Agriculture suggested that 12.5 per cent of all arable land on holdings greater than ten acres should be devoted to tillage. While farmers would be free to plant whatever crop they wished, they should be encouraged to grow wheat. For that reason wheat should be the only crop with a guaranteed price. Agriculture proposed offering a guaranteed price of 37s 6d a barrel, which was almost 30 per cent higher than the 1939 figure of 29s 6d.[49] The Department urged the Cabinet to announce the price of wheat as soon as possible, because the time for planting winter wheat, which was a more reliable crop than spring wheat, was approaching. Despite this advice, the government postponed a decision, apparently because it was concerned about the impact of a higher wheat price on the price of bread and flour. Initially the government contemplated setting a guaranteed price of 33s 6d because the Department of Supplies was confident there would be ample supplies of imported wheat. However, in mid-October the government agreed to make a compulsory tillage order and to offer farmers 35s a barrel.[50]

For the 1940/1 season the compulsory tillage order was extended to 20 per cent of arable land, with the objective of supplying 50 per cent of flour from native wheat.[51] In the autumn of 1941, when the prospects of further grain imports seemed particularly bleak, the quota was raised to 25 per cent, and an order was passed preventing owners of conacre land from stipulating that wheat must not be planted. In 1942/3 the order was extended to all holdings greater than five acres, and the Department was given power to specify which section of a holding should be tilled. This measure was introduced to prevent farmers from reserving their best land for pasture. In 1943/4 the order applied to three-eighths of all arable land and landholders were required to sow a specific proportion of this land with wheat: the amount varied by county to take account of climate and soil.

The first major threat to wheat supplies came at Christmas 1940 when Britain cut Ireland's access to shipping space. The Cabinet raised the guaranteed price of wheat to 40s and the Minister for Supplies was instructed to undertake a campaign to increase the supply of food, with a particular emphasis on wheat. Lemass immediately sent a letter to all TDs asking for their co-operation in a 'grow more wheat campaign'. Shortly after this letter was issued, there was a meeting between Twomey and de Valera, where Twomey emphasised 'the undesirability of two Departments engaging in the same kind of work and the danger of an adverse effect on our farmers'. De Valera claimed that the government had decided that Supplies should undertake publicity of a general nature, drawing the public's attention to the seriousness of the situation, encouraging conservation of existing stocks and creating an 'active public opinion generally in regard to the importance of home production'. All Ministers were expected to do the same. He asked Twomey to define the basis for a division of labour between Agriculture and Supplies, but there is no indication that this happened. On 13 January, two days after this meeting, Ryan requested a meeting with de Valera to sort out the matter as agreed at the last Cabinet meeting, although it is unclear whether this meeting took place.

This stand-off between Lemass and Ryan is symptomatic of wider disagreements between Agriculture and Supplies over the price of food and the allocation of supplies. In December 1939 the Cabinet appointed a committee drawn from the departments of Agriculture, Industry and Commerce, and Supplies and the Price Commission to advise the Minister for Supplies on flour prices. Despite repeated reminders, this committee never reported. On 30 January 1941, more than a year after the committee had been constituted, Padraig O'Slattery, private secretary to the Minister for Supplies, reported that Agriculture and Industry and Commerce had such divergent views on flour prices that the committee believed that there was 'no likelihood of agreement being reached on a report which would be helpful or informative to the Government, there is nothing to be gained by a continuance of the Committee's deliberations'. On 25 March the Cabinet gave its approval for the committee to be wound up.[52]

As concern over wheat stocks mounted during the winter of 1940, farmers pressed for higher prices. In January 1941 Patrick Belton, a Fine Gael TD, demanded the recall of Dáil Éireann to discuss the crisis. Farming organisations were demanding 50s a barrel. Belton and Cogan, an independent TD from Wicklow, who later joined Clann na Talmhan, sought to have the compulsory tillage order annulled, although their main objective was to secure a higher price, not an end to compulsory tillage. On 23 January the National Farmers' Conference, an organisation that was closely allied with Belton, passed a motion demanding an immediate meeting with de Valera. De Valera refused their request and informed them that this was the domain of the Minister for Agriculture. Elizabeth Bobbett, the secretary of the National Farmers' Conference, replied that compulsory tillage was a matter of national policy.[53] De Valera made a radio broadcast on 29 January, where he spoke about the urgent need to increase the area under wheat from 300,000 to 650,000 acres.[54] In March the Department estimated that only 400,000 acres had been planted (the actual acreage was 463,000), but it anticipated a substantial rise in the acreage under oats, barley and potatoes. On 21 March Seán Moylan, parliamentary secretary to the Minister for Defence, sent de Valera a memorandum suggesting that the government should pay farmers for all the food that they produced, and that payments should be made on a phased basis: 20 per cent on proof of preparation of land, 20 per cent when crops were sown, and so on. This scheme would be supervised by the Gardaí and tillage inspectors, in co-operation with parish councils.[55] Moylan argued that,

> There is very little use telling such people that if they produce the food they are sure to find a market for it. There is very little of the speculative tradition in ordinary farmers. They are, instead, apt to be over cautious. They are not endowed with the particular type of foresight that would enable them to see that increased voluntary food production in their part is a good business proposition. And even if they had all these qualities they have not the capital resources that would enable them to produce the food. I speak from very intimate knowledge of the farmers' position throughout the country and I would impress on you that the only real method of securing food production to the limits of our need is by an extension of the system of payments by which beet production was secured, to the other crops needed.[56]

Moylan's memorandum suggests that every member of the government believed that they had a free hand to put forward policies on compulsory tillage. Hugo Flinn, parliamentary secretary to the Minister for Finance, suggested that the state should assume power to enter land to enforce compulsory tillage. He also urged that the Department of Agriculture should express 'a definite and quantitative opinion' on whether it would be possible to achieve any 'very considerable increase in tillage'.[57] Flinn was reflecting the strong feelings within the Fianna Fáil parliamentary party in favour of much more stringent measures to enforce compulsory tillage. Ryan repeatedly tried to persuade deputies that a strong-arm approach would be counter-productive.[58] The Cabinet endorsed Flinn's proposal for compulsory entry onto private lands at its next meeting, although it emphasised that this would only be done where the order was not being observed. It also noted that the primary objective was 'increased production of food, not the giving of employment'. This frenzied atmosphere threatened to revive practices such as cattle-driving and the enforced digging and ploughing of land, which had been common during the later years of World War I.

Following the Cabinet decision, Flinn informed de Valera that County Limerick had been selected as the place to carry out an 'advance experiment to test reactions and develop necessary administrative machinery in emergency cultivation measures'. Tractors and ploughs were being mobilised. The role of the Department of Agriculture was limited to supplying seed and technical advice.[59] There is no evidence that the government went ahead with Flinn's experiment.

Flinn also suggested that it was essential to ensure that grain distribution was advantageous to the community. He proposed that sales should be subject to licence, with a limit on the amount that a farmer could retain for personal use. This could be done either by a department of state, or by an independent board. Although officials from the departments of Agriculture and Supplies discussed this proposal on several occasions, they were unable to reach agreement. On 30 April 1941 the Department of Supplies recommended to Cabinet that the Irish Flour Millers' Association be granted a monopoly on the purchase of native wheat, and that a separate organisation be established to buy and distribute oats. The Department of Agriculture was reluctant to disrupt the existing system for purchasing grain because grain merchants filled an important function in providing farmers with credit. The Cabinet was obviously sympathetic to this point of view, because it decided that Agriculture should be given responsibility for collecting, storing and disposing of the 1941 crop. Merchants would buy and sell grain as before, but would have to register with the Department. Agriculture proposed that grain would be allocated on the basis of the following priorities: food, seed, then feed-stuffs. The government also announced guaranteed prices for barley and oats.[60]

Wheat yields fell in 1941 because wheat was now being planted on less suitable land, and soil fertility was deteriorating owing to a shortage of fertiliser and the continued cropping of the same fields. Bread rationing was avoided by raising the extraction rate – the percentage of the wheat that was used to manufacture of flour – from 75 per cent in September 1940 (the pre-war figure was 70 per cent) to 80 per cent in early January 1941, 90 per cent on 25 January and 95 per cent on 18 March.[61] This resulted in an extremely coarse flour, which was unpopular with Irish consumers who had long been accustomed to using fine white flour. The Department of Agriculture cited the falling yields as justification for raising the guaranteed price of wheat to 45s a barrel. However, the Department of Finance was sceptical of Agriculture's claim that soil fertility was being depleted and that farmers were being forced to plant wheat on less fertile land. Taking Agriculture's estimate that wheat could be grown on two-thirds of the 11.5 million acres of arable land, Finance concluded that the same land should only be planted with wheat at thirteen-year intervals.

The 1942 wheat price was set at 41s, one shilling higher than in 1941. This provoked widespread protests within the Fianna Fáil parliamentary party. Martin Corry, TD for East Cork, who was a member of the Irish Beet Growers' Association, demanded a bounty of £4 per acre on wheat. Corry contended that the prices announced for 1942 would encourage farmers to grow oats or barley instead of wheat. Ryan used these complaints and the extremely vocal views expressed at meetings of the Fianna Fáil parliamentary party[62] to persuade the Cabinet to increase the guaranteed price to 45s a barrel. Ryan then made a ministerial broadcast urging farmers to grow more wheat, and Twomey sent a letter to all clergy requesting their assistance. When de Valera addressed the General Council of County Councils in January 1942 he reminded farmers of their responsibilities towards other sections of the community. He also warned that the Minister for Agriculture would be forced to take strong action if farmers failed to comply with the need to till.[63] This speech was followed by a second letter to all clergy. Twomey informed them that:

> It would be tragic if, in view of the natural resources available, we failed to provide the means of feeding the people, and as a consequence had to face a repetition of the hardships endured during the forties of the last century. Yet the plain fact is that unless the growing of wheat is greatly increased, the country will be afflicted with the calamity of prolonged shortage of bread.

The decision to send this second letter, less than three months after the first, indicates growing concern over wheat supplies. By January 1942 ministers were warning that it might prove necessary to ration flour. On 28 January the Department of Agriculture informed the Cabinet that unless the price of wheat was raised to 50s a barrel, the country's needs would not be met. On 4 February deputies Belton and Cogan tabled a censure motion in Dáil Éireann over the government's tillage campaign. The motion, which suggested that the 1942 wheat crop would be smaller than that in 1941, used the word famine on two occasions. By early February deliveries of flour to bakeries and shops were restricted to 80 per cent of normal supplies, and on 16 February millers were instructed to extract 100 per cent flour from wheat, the highest figure yet. It was also announced that a scheme for bread rationing had been drawn up.[64] On 17 February the Cabinet raised the price of wheat to 50s.

The quantity of wheat planted in 1942 proved to be substantially higher than in previous years. For 1943 the Department of Agriculture suggested that it was unnecessary to raise the tillage quota; indeed, it claimed this would be counter-productive as it would damage the soil and reduce yields. It would be more effective to enforce the existing orders with greater rigour.[65] The Department appears to have been unduly complacent, because the 1943 wheat acreage was almost 66,000 below 1942, although a higher acreage was planted with oats and barley. In September 1943 the Department of Supplies noted that the native wheat crop plus expected imports would be insufficient to meet the country's needs, and recommended that a compulsory order be introduced requiring flour-millers to include 7 per cent barley (at 70 per cent extraction rate) in the manufacture of flour; Supplies also recommended suspending exports of beer. The Cabinet agreed to require millers to add barley to flour and to reduce exports of beer by 50 per cent.[66]

By this time medical experts had become concerned that flour extracted from wheat at a rate of 100 per cent contained a high level of phytic acid, which reduced the body's ability to absorb calcium. Dublin hospitals were reporting an increased incidence of rickets among children; there were complaints of a rise in the number of digestive ailments; and it was suspected that calcium deficiency made people more susceptible to tuberculosis.[67] In September 1943 the Department of Local Government and Public Health submitted a report from the Medical Research Council arguing against the introduction of bread rationing and against 100 per cent extraction. It recommended that calcium should be added to bread, which was then the practice in Britain. These warnings came to Cabinet when the 1943 harvest was becoming available, and at a time when there was no immediate threat of shortages. Despite the advice of the Department of Agriculture, the Cabinet reduced the wheat extraction rate to 85 per cent and the proportion of barley included in flour was increased to 10 per cent.

For 1944 the Department of Agriculture suggested that every farm should be required to plant a specified proportion of tilled land with wheat in order to reach a target acreage of 700,000. To sweeten the pill it recommended raising the price by five shillings a barrel, to 55s, and providing fertiliser credits. The Department of Finance supported compulsion, but was opposed to the higher price:

> Unlike other sections of the community farmers have, as the following figures indicate, profited substantially as a result of the emergency. There is therefore all the less justification, even when additional obligations are being imposed on them, for holding out further financial inducements. As regards the suggestion of resentment by reason of the introduction of compulsion, the Minister thinks that farmers, whose incomes have undoubtedly increased substantially since the commencement of the emergency, have as a whole had infinitely less cause for complaint than persons in industrial employment whose remuneration has been severely restricted by the operation of the Wages Control Orders.

Finance claimed that confidential data supplied by the Irish Banks Standing Committee showed that between 1931 and 1941 farmers' deposits in commercial banks had risen by £2.1 million; in 1942 they had increased by a further £4.8 million. Higher wheat prices would give farmers additional purchasing powers, which 'in present circumstances have obvious dangers in its reaction on the price of commodities, with particular reference to black market activities'. Although the Department of Supplies was of a similar mind, the Cabinet agreed to offer 55s for the coming season, but increased the tillage quota to 37.5 per cent. Ryan announced the higher quota in a speech at Tullamore on 16 November. The Department issued a booklet *Why Compulsory Tillage?*, which was to be read in class by pupils in sixth and higher classes in all national schools outside the county boroughs of Dublin, Cork, Waterford and Limerick. Pupils were encouraged to discuss it with their parents and other adults. The highest wheat acreage was recorded in 1945 – 662,000 acres, 2.6 times the 1939 acreage and yielding 2.4 times as much wheat as the 1939 harvest.

In January 1940 T. O'Connell, the chief inspector at the Department of Agriculture, listed the tillage crops in order of priority as wheat, sugar-beet, potatoes, oats, barley and roots. While the first year of the Emergency saw a substantial rise in the acreage under wheat, the amount of oats and barley planted fell by 80,000 acres. With the exception of a small amount used to manufacture oatmeal, most oats was used as animal feed. Barley was used for malting and as animal feed. Malting barley was an essential ingredient in the manufacture of beer and whiskey and there was a strong demand in Britain for Guinness throughout the war. In September 1939, shortly after war broke out, Guinness raised the price it offered for malting barley.[68]

By January 1940 there was an acute scarcity of barley for livestock feed. Although imported feed-stuffs were available, Lemass noted that it was no longer profitable to contemplate importing large quantities, given the poor prices on offer in Britain for Irish pigs and poultry.[69] By December 1940 the Cabinet was considering offering guaranteed prices for oats and barley,[70] but this was not done for several months. Nevertheless, in 1941 the acreage planted with oats and barley increased by 14 and 29 per cent respectively. In August the Minister for Agriculture established a Cereals Distribution Committee to advise him on how best to collect and distribute oats and barley from the 1941 harvest. The committee would act as the Minister's agent, instructing grain dealers on how to allocate supplies of oats and barley. Very little of the oats crop actually reached the market. Farmers seem to have planted extra oats as a substitute for imported feed and they preferred to keep the crop for their own use, although oatmeal was in demand as a substitute for scarce flour.[71] By December 1941 the Department was suggesting that authorised purchasers should be permitted to offer higher prices in order to encourage farmers to sell, but the Department of Finance preferred to deal with this problem by taking 'drastic action against black market transactions'. Some oats was apparently being bought by unauthorised dealers at higher prices than those set by the Department of Agriculture.[72]

When the country was threatened with an acute shortage of wheat in January 1942, the government suspended the malting of barley for brewing and distilling and an emergency powers order was introduced banning the sale of oats and barley as animal feed. The restriction on malting barley was lifted some months later when wheat supplies improved, but the prohibition on selling oats or barley as animal feed continued.[73] Guaranteed prices for oats and barley were announced in advance of the 1942/3 season and the acreage under oats and barley rose by 60,000 acres and 25,000 acres respectively, almost matching the fall of 83,000 acres planted with wheat and potatoes. This suggests that the guaranteed price, especially for oats, was unduly favourable. Alternatively, farmers may have welcomed the Minister for Agriculture's decision to abandon efforts to control the buying and distribution of oats.[74]

From 1942 the Department of Agriculture eased its controls over oats and barley. Exports of pigs and pigmeat had ceased, and pig numbers had fallen to the point where supplies of animal feed were no longer regarded as an urgent matter. In January 1944 the Department recommended ending the price guarantee for oats, as there was no shortage of oats. However, it wished to raise the guaranteed price for barley because farmers were feeding barley to poultry and livestock rather than bringing it to market, and there was a shortage of malting barley. The Department offered reassurances that a higher guaranteed price would not result in a higher price for beer.[75] The fact that barley was being used in the manufacture of flour was an added argument in favour of offering a guaranteed price.[76]

During the Emergency the Department tried to encourage farmers to make silage, which was the subject of a timely interim report by the Commission on Agriculture in 1940. It concluded that 'good silage can be made from semi-mature grass without the addition of either acid or molasses [which were probably in short supply] provided careful attention is given to the details of filling and packing'. Despite this optimistic assessment, the authors of the report 'cannot visualise the adoption of the process in its present stage of development to any appreciable extent in this country'.[77] Nevertheless, the Department persevered, setting up demonstration plots and introducing a special scheme of loans towards the cost of constructing silos.[78]

By the late 1930s Ireland was producing approximately three-quarters of its sugar requirements, compared with one-third of the annual demand for wheat. In 1939 the Department estimated that 65,000 acres of sugar-beet would be necessary to achieve self-sufficiency.[79] This figure was substantially exceeded in 1941, 1943, 1944 and 1945, although the 1940 and 1942 figures were well below this target. The output of sugar-beet fluctuated during the Emergency, from a low of 399,000 tons in 1942 to a high of 732,000 tons in the following year. There was less difficulty in adjusting sugar-beet to wartime conditions than was the case with other crops. From 1926 onwards sugar-beet had been grown under contract to the factories, and by 1939 growers were thoroughly familiar with the demands of the crop. Growers were offered a guaranteed price at the beginning of every season provided their crop met the required standard for sugar content. The only significant change as a result of the Emergency was that the price of beet was determined by the Cabinet, rather than by negotiations between the Irish Beet Growers' Association and the sugar company. The price offered for wheat was a factor in determining the price for sugar-beet. In November 1945, some months after the war ended, the government reverted to pre-war practices when it minuted that, 'subject only to the Government's functions in regard to the price of sugar and the duty thereon, the full responsibility for the economic operation of the sugar industry and for negotiations and discussions with the beet growers rests on Cómhlucht Siúicre Éireann Teoranta, and the Chairman of the Company should be so informed by the Minister for Finance'.[80]

Compulsory tillage orders were enforced by inspection. Penalties were enforced on farmers who failed to fulfil the orders. By 1943 the Department employed fifty tillage inspectors assisted by sixty-three tillage supervisors. Yet in October of that year the Department admitted that only 36,000 holdings had been inspected since 1940. Approximately 300,000 holdings in excess of five acres were liable to compulsory tillage orders. By 1943 a shortage of car and bicycle tyres was restricting inspectors' mobility. When the Cabinet decided that the 1944 tillage orders would require farmers to plant a specific proportion of tilled land with wheat, the Department insisted that the number of inspectors should be increased to sixty, and the number of supervisors to 200.[81] During the 1941 season 100 holdings were occupied and there were 140 prosecutions under the complsory tillage orders; 116 holdings were entered in 1942. Non-compliance was greatest in traditional grazing counties. In 1940, 415 landholders in County Meath, 35 per cent of those inspected, failed to comply fully with the order; the comparable figures in County Westmeath were 291, or 41 per cent of inspected holdings. By 1941, only nine holdings in Meath and two in Westmeath were entered and tilled by the Department because of non-compliance. However, in 1941 inspections were seriously disrupted by the outbreak of foot and mouth disease.

Some farmers contested compulsory tillage orders. Of the 140 prosecutions undertaken in respect of the 1940 orders, 124 convictions were obtained; seven were quashed on appeal, and three cases were dismissed.[82] In the spring of 1941 the Department of Agriculture came under pressure to introduce a schedule of minimum fines for breaches of the compulsory tillage orders, because several ministers were of the opinion that some judges were unduly lenient. Agriculture informed the Department of the Taoiseach that it was opposed to legislation of this type, since no such provision applied to any other emergency orders. It also believed that setting a minimum penalty would encourage a rash of appeals. It was confident that district justices had realised the gravity of the situation and would act accordingly.[83] The Cabinet asked Ryan to reconsider this decision on several occasions, but he refused. However, in January 1942, when a decision by the Galway circuit court appeared to open the possibility that landholders, whose land was entered by tillage inspectors, could take action against the Minister, the government introduced another emergency powers order to prevent this happening.

When a number of farmers in Tipperary appealed against fines for failing to meet tillage requirements in 1942, the Attorney General expressed the opinion that the judge would rule in their favour. He advised the Cabinet to avoid this happening by making an emergency order, enabling a judge of the circuit court to refer cases about which he was unsure to a higher court; this was duly done in Emergency Powers No 185.[84] Although Ryan informed Dáil Éireann that, 'I prefer, as I am sure many Deputies prefer, price inducements to compulsion',[85] by 1943 he was pressing for the Department to be given power to retain any profits earned from letting land that had been seized from non-compliant landowners. A new order enabled the Minister to reclaim all expenses in connection with entering the holding, but any remaining profits would be given to the occupier.[86] In the autumn of 1943, when the Department decided that every farmer would be required to devote a certain percentage of their land to wheat, there was considerable pressure from opposition deputies for the Department to establish an appeal tribunal. Ryan argued that it would be impracticable, because many farmers would probably appeal and by the time the appeals were decided it might be too late to plant crops.[87]

The substantial increase in the amount of grain to be harvested put considerable strain on threshing machines. Farmers had to wait for much longer than in the past to have their grain threshed, and there were complaints of over-charging. Shortages of fuel and breakdowns in machinery were additional problems. When a deputation of TDs met Ryan and de Valera in August 1941 to protest at the failure to allocate any coal for threshing machines, they were told that threshing would have to depend on turf and timber.[88] In September 1942 the Department of Agriculture applied for an emergency order enabling it to set maximum charges for the use of threshing machines for the coming season. Owners would be permitted to increase charges by 10 per cent over the previous year to cover additional costs. This order was extended in later years.[89]

Horses were essential both for ploughing and harvesting, and for transporting agricultural produce to markets and fairs. The export of horses that were suitable for farm work was banned; only old, useless and thoroughbred animals could be exported.

Shortages of cereal seed were also a problem because traditionally most seed had been imported. By January 1940 the Department of Agriculture had sufficient stocks of seed for winter wheat, but there was a shortage of spring wheat seed. Seed oats was also in short supply; the Department's chief inspector, T. J. O'Connell, hoped that farmers had reserved some of their own.[90] In August 1941 the Department negotiated with the Irish Seed and Nursery Trades Association to hold a reserve of 100,000 barrels of seed wheat suitable for spring sowing,[91] and in June 1942 a special premium was offered to farmers who supplied seed wheat.[92]

Import duties were lifted from agricultural machinery, machinery parts, horse shoes and other materials in 1941,[93] but this was of little practical benefit since imports were not available. There were shortages of horse shoes, which were traditionally imported from Sweden; turnip seed, which normally came from Britain; spare parts for farm machinery and creamery equipment; and tyres for tractors and bicycles. The Department urged blacksmiths to construct spare parts for threshing machines. Special restrictions on the use of binder twine were introduced in December 1942;[94] in later years the Department bartered Irish flax in return for binder twine from Britain. By 1943 there was an acute shortage of horse shoes and a special collection of scrap metal was organised with a view to manufacturing them at the Irish Steel Plant in Hawlbowline, although it emerged that the furnaces were not suitable.

One insight into the practical difficulties resulting from the shortage of materials comes from a letter to the Department from an agricultural contractor with an address in the Macroom area of West Cork. In 1941 and 1942, when threshing and ploughing were completed around Macroom, he travelled to Cappoquin in County Waterford, an area where tillage equipment was scarce and the agricultural season was later than in West Cork. In March 1942 he attracted the attention of an over-zealous Garda sergeant at Watergrasshill, who issued him with seven summonses for breaching road traffic regulations. The offences included not having proper tyres, not having a red rear light, and not having a white light on the number plate or the front of his tractor. His letter explained that it was impossible to find any rubber tyres for tractors, and he had tried to get red glass for his rear light, but there was no red glass to be had and he had even painted half the glass with red paint. The white light was missing from the front of the tractor because at the time he was using it to light a primus stove, 'matches being so very scarce'. If the summonses were enforced, he would be forced to lay up his tractor and machinery until special fittings became available – when the war ended.[95]

FERTILISER

When war broke out fertiliser was in short supply because a subsidy scheme introduced during the 1938/9 season had increased demand by 25 per cent, and this had exhausted all reserve stocks. Britain had introduced a similar scheme in 1937, to improve soil fertility in the expectation of war,[96] but there is no indication that this had been a consideration in Ireland. The Department of Agriculture had planned to continue the fertiliser subsidies during the 1939/40 season. When war broke out, however, supplies of phosphates from the Mediterranean came to an end, and the Department was forced to cut back on the scheme.

By January 1940 the Agricultural Production Consultative Council reported that the price of fertiliser had risen so sharply that the benefit of the subsidy had been eroded. Nevertheless, most demands for fertiliser were satisfied during the first year of the war, although the Department was forced to restrict the quantity available during the final months of 1939, to conserve fertiliser for tillage crops during the spring.[97] During the summer of 1940 the Department decided that all the limited stocks of fertiliser on hand should be reserved for tillage and it issued a notice to farmers to this effect.[98] By November 1940 there were still reasonable supplies of superphosphates and compound manures, and ample stocks of sulphate of ammonia, but there was a shortage of potash. The Department was confident, however, that there was no marked potash deficiency and there was no reason to fear a decline in production because of 'this temporary shortage'.

The shortage of fertiliser became much more acute in 1941. In October Ryan made a radio broadcast encouraging farmers to make greater use of natural manures. Farmers living close to the sea were urged to use seaweed.[99] By 1942 there was only one grade of compound fertiliser available. Called emergency compound fertiliser, it was distributed only by licensed distributors to farmers who had bought artificial fertiliser from the same distributor during the previous year.[100] Phosphate deposits in County Clare and pyrites at Avoca, County Wicklow, were quarried, and imports of phosphates from Spain and Florida, carried by the state-owned Irish Shipping Ltd, provided some relief. When supplies of raw materials became available they were doled out among licensed manufacturers, and regulations for distributing the fertiliser were determined by the Department. The prolonged shortage of fertiliser damaged soil quality. In 1944 the Wicklow Farmers' Party alleged that cattle were dying owing to a deficiency of calcium and magnesium. The state-owned company Mianraí Teo proposed establishing a company to organise the production of ground limestone. The Department of Industry and Commerce wished to delay a decision pending a comprehensive geological survey, but the Department of Agriculture wanted immediate action. The introduction of a comprehensive ground limestone scheme was delayed until after the war.[101]

AGRICULTURAL LABOUR

Emigration to Britain rose sharply during the late 1930s, and by 1939 it was claimed that there was a shortage of seasonal workers for heavier tasks such as harvesting sugar-beet. There were also suggestions that unemployment assistance was discouraging rural labourers from seeking employment. When T. W. Smiddy assessed the impact of the war on the Irish economy in September 1939, he noted that a sufficient supply of labour would be essential if the volume of agricultural output was to rise. There was 'an immense reserve of labour in receipt of unemployment assistance'. The question was how to direct them to farm work. Smiddy advised against offering higher agricultural wages, because this would increase the cost of production. He favoured a combination of propaganda and 'some form of gentle compulsion', including an end to unemployment assistance in rural areas.[102] This had already been suggested by J. J. McElligott, secretary of the Department of Finance, at an interdepartmental committee to consider responses to the Emergency. McElligott argued that if this were not done, there would be a shortage of labour for wartime tillage.[103] However, the Cabinet insisted that special consideration should be given to the 'Black Area' – the counties along the western seaboard, where it was not anticipated that farm workers would benefit from the expansion in tillage.

In February 1940 Ryan informed Hugo Flinn that many western farmers had experienced a fall in their standard of living in recent months. Ryan noted that 'there would appear to be little prospect they are now benefiting or will benefit in future to any appreciable extent from war conditions'. Western smallholders earned their cash income from store cattle, eggs and pigs. Although store prices had risen, this was of little assistance, because their livestock tended to be in need of supplementary feed, which was costing 20 per cent more than in the past. Although the price of eggs had increased by 25 per cent, the price of feed-stuff was 30 per cent higher. A similar argument applied to pigs.[104]

Emigration and turf provided a life-line for the west of Ireland during the Emergency. By the beginning of 1940 agents representing British construction firms were hiring large numbers of men in western towns. This put pressure on local wages and there was the added danger that rural Ireland would be left without sufficient workers to save the turf and the harvest. Turf-cutting employed up to 49,000 labourers during the spring and summer months throughout the Emergency.[105] Farmers and turf schemes often competed for the same labourers. There was little evidence of labour shortages during 1940, but by the spring of 1941 newspapers and Dáil deputies were suggesting that the army should be deployed for agricultural work.[106]

In May 1941 Twomey wrote to all agricultural instructors, asking whether the turf campaign had led to a shortage of agricultural labour in their area. The overwhelming majority reported no difficulty. Twomey believed that the position was satisfactory and that a crisis would be averted because many of the jobs on turf schemes would finish in late June, just before haymaking. Nevertheless, claims persisted that turf was creaming off agricultural workers. Hugo Flinn, in his capacity as Turf Controller, gave a commitment to prevent any overlap between the peak demand for turf labourers and agricultural workers. He told the Dáil that he would suspend all turf schemes if necessary, although he does not appear to have done this, and throughout July the Department of Agriculture received numerous reports of shortages of haymakers. On 23 July Ryan asked Flinn to give him an assurance that all turf work would cease. Flinn sent Ryan statistics showing that there were over 31,000 men working on the bogs on 19 July, and asking Ryan what action should be taken. Ryan demanded that the county surveyors, who were responsible for overseeing turf schemes, be instructed to suspend turf-cutting in sixteen counties. The suspensions should begin in the most southern counties and extend northwards as the harvest commenced. However, E. MacLaughlin, of the Office of Public Works, claimed that many turf workers in the west of Ireland were unlikely to find jobs in agriculture, and consequently there would be a loss of turf without any corresponding benefit to agriculture. Teddy Courtney of the Department of Local Government contacted all county surveyors, asking them to determine how far turf and farming were competing for labourers, and the implications of stopping work on the bogs. By the second week of August it was agreed that turf work would be suspended where local agricultural advisers reported a labour shortage. The majority of advisers reported that there was no shortage. In north Kildare, one of the few exceptions, the county surveyor and the advisers resolved the problem by staggering turf-cutting until the peak of farming work was over.[107]

It is difficult to determine if there was a serious shortage of agricultural labour during 1941. In any event the Cabinet decided to impose restrictions on emigration to Britain. From October 1941 emigration was prohibited for persons under twenty-two years of age, and for anybody for whom work was available in Ireland, although areas with a tradition of seasonal migration were exempt. Similar restrictions were extended to emigration to Northern Ireland in May 1942.[108] This meant that unemployed urban workers were free to emigrate, but men living in rural areas, outside the congested districts, were not.[109]

Bad weather in the spring of 1942 meant that the turf harvest was late, and the peak demand for labour would coincide with a busy period on farms. As an interdepartmental committee debated how to tackle this problem, the Department of Industry and Commerce sent a memorandum to Cabinet suggesting that no person who had previous experience of working in agriculture or in turf should be permitted to emigrate. On 19 May the government decided that travel permits would not be issued to men with agricultural experience who were resident in tillage districts, and that the ban would last until 30 September 1942. When this order lapsed Industry and Commerce demanded that the embargo be extended until further notice, and Agriculture requested that it should apply to men who had worked in farming but were living in urban areas, and to the congested districts. Industry and Commerce opposed this proposal,[110] but to placate Agriculture proposed establishing a reserve register of men available to work in food or fuel production. They would be paid a weekly retainer of 5s, in addition to unemployment assistance while out of work. The Cabinet approved the idea and it was implemented by emergency order. However, few men signed up to the reserve register, because to do so automatically disqualified them from emigrating. A further disincentive was the requirement to take work anywhere in the state. At its peak, in March 1943, the register contained only 3,287 names.[111]

Although emigration from rural areas other than the western seaboard remained subject to restrictions for the remainder of the war, the Department continued to receive complaints about labour shortages. Turf schemes competed with agriculture, particularly in midland areas. In the summer of 1942 agricultural workers and turf workers both received 33s a week, which was similar to the wages paid to county council road workers. A forty-eight hour week on the bogs was deemed equivalent to fifty-four hours in agriculture, taking into account the time spent travelling to and from work, although turf workers were eligible for national insurance stamps, whereas agricultural workers were not. Following a series of strikes by turf workers during the summer of 1942, Hugo Flinn, the Turf Controller, raised the 1943 wages for turf workers to 38s, two shillings more than the agricultural wage, and turf workers continued to receive two shillings more than agricultural workers until 1946.[112] In 1943 the Irish Trade Union Congress (TUC) called for a national minimum wage for all agricultural workers, 'such wage to be sufficient to enable the agricultural workers to bring up his [sic] family in decency and "frugal" comfort.' The TUC also demanded a harvest bonus of £2 per labourer.[113] Many labourers apparently preferred jobs in turf. In February 1944 a farmer from Ballincollig, County Cork, informed Ryan that two of his three labourers had left to work on a turf scheme in Kildare, although he had offered them four shillings a week more than the minimum wage stipulated by the Agricultural Wages Board. They claimed that they could earn more money – turf workers were often on piece-rates[114] – and they would have more free time. The third labourer left shortly afterwards despite an offer of six shillings more than the statutory wage.[115]

Many farmers demanded that the Department supply them with labour. Several eccentric letters protested that all the labourers had absconded to trap rabbits. There was a lucrative business exporting rabbits to England. One farmer in north Cork demanded that the Department 'suspend this trapping business altogether until next November'. In January 1943 J. J. Bergin of the Irish Beet Growers' Association claimed that farm workers in Kildare were taking jobs in the asbestos plant in Athy, where they were depriving urban workers of employment. Although this claim cannot be dismissed, it would have been highly unusual, because many factories were either closed or on short time owing to shortages of raw materials. In February 1943 the Wexford County Committee of Agriculture passed a motion demanding that the government ban all agricultural workers from cutting turf. The Cork Farmers' Association wanted soldiers and turf workers to be made available for farm work. In May 1943 Westmeath County Committee of Agriculture asked that a special register of harvest labourers should be established; it claimed that grain had been lost during the previous year because of a lack of labour. In August P. Conroy, an instructor in Westmeath, reported that farmers had complained that they were losing workers to a wood-charcoal-burning plant at Multyfarnham; they wanted the plant to suspend operations for several weeks. Twomey replied that this was impossible as there was an urgent need for charcoal.[116] Castlemahon Co-operative Creamery in Limerick passed a resolution in January 1943 expressing alarm at the daily exodus of agricultural labourers to England and to midland bogs, which was making it impossible to maintain the normal output of milk or tillage. Some months later Harry Spain, an instructor in County Limerick, reported that the labour shortage in the county was getting worse. Many labourers were leaving without giving notice, and some dairy farmers had been forced to sell their cows.

The Department of Agriculture referred all these complaints to the Department of Industry and Commerce. Industry and Commerce reported that in most cases, according to the unemployment register, there was no shortage of agricultural workers in the area. When farmers supplied names of agricultural labourers who were intending to emigrate, Agriculture intervened to ensure they were denied travel permits. In June 1943 it informed a Westmeath farmer that two brothers who were agricultural labourers had been denied travel permits following his complaint. When one of these men subsequently emigrated to England, the farmer wrote a letter of complaint.

For many farmers the defence forces were the obvious source of harvest labour and the Department of Defence received numerous requests from farmers asking for a relative, neighbour or former agricultural labourer to be given temporary release. Individual soldiers were often granted temporary release for a period of up to two months; some former agricultural labourers refused such offers. In May 1943 Dr Henry Kennedy, secretary of the IAOS, warned the Agricultural Production Consultative Council that the labour supply was so low that it would be disastrous if agricultural work were hampered by bad weather. He suggested that the army, 'the only big reservoir of labour now available in the country', should be deployed. Although others agreed, Ryan was not in favour of using soldiers en masse, because many were from the city. Nevertheless, he asked Oscar Traynor, the Minister for Defence, to permit the use of local army units to assist farmers in cases of acute need.[117] Traynor did not reply until 24 July, one month after Ryan's letter, when he rejected the proposal.

Traynor emphasised that troops were already heavily engaged in saving turf, and that their primary duty was national defence.

Nevertheless, when Twomey contacted the Department of Defence during the 1943 harvest, to ask whether the off-duty hours of soldiers stationed in counties Meath, Westmeath and Kildare could be extended, to enable them to help with the harvest, the Department of Defence readily agreed. Soldiers in Kildare were released at 1 pm each day and equipped with bicycles. The commanding officer in Mullingar released twenty soldiers for harvest work. Farmers in Meath suggested that soldiers from Gorman-ston Camp could pitch tents on Fairyhouse race-course while they helped with the harvest, but the Department of Defence suggested that this was not a good idea, because fifty soldiers would be unlikely to get much work done if they remained as a group. It would be preferable to release them in groups of two to eight. Yet when soldiers arrived in Ratoath to help with the harvest, in response to a request from a tillage inspector, farmers refused their assistance.[118]

It is impossible to establish the precise extent of labour shortages. Of the 525 vacancies notified to the Department of Industry and Commerce in July and August 1943, 460 were filled and fifty-four requests were cancelled. In September/October only seven of the 429 notified vacancies were not filled. In June 1943, however, Nagle, a future secretary of the Department of Agriculture, noted that most of the 27,000 men on the unemployment register in the spring of 1943 with experience of agricultural work, lived in the congested districts, and they were not prepared to travel long distances.[119] Farmers, who had been accustomed to a choice of labour, found it difficult to adjust to a tighter labour market. An article in the *Irish Press* in October 1943 suggested that the shortage of labour was due to poor working conditions. Labourers left agricultural jobs if they could find more regular employment. 'Unless the farmer – and all interested in the land – concentrate on finding a steadier employment and a better wage for the farm labourer, they will not show honesty in deploring the flight from the land or the labour shortage at harvest time'.[120]

In January 1944 the Department of Agriculture issued a questionnaire to all tillage inspectors, seeking information about prospective labour shortages. Michael Barry, a future secretary of the Department of Agri-culture, summarised the replies as follows: 'prima facie there is no shortage of agricultural labour in the country', according to statistics from labour exchanges. However, the tillage inspectors claimed that farmers tended to regard all men hired from the labour exchanges as 'no good' and consequently they were unwilling to hire men from the unemployment register. There was a shortage of accommodation for labourers hired from a distance, and farmers had to be persuaded to hire men for at least six months. Barry suggested that men on the unemployment register should be interviewed to establish whether or not they were suitable for agricultural work. Officials in the Department of Agriculture were divided on the question of recruiting agricultural workers through the labour exchanges. Some wished to push farmers in that direction; others, notably Nagle, disagreed. Austin noted that during the previous autumn, although the Mullingar labour exchange indicated that there were many experienced agricultural labourers for hire, it proved necessary to bring in the army, because in the opinion of the local farmers only a fraction of the unemployed were capable of agricultural work. Austin suggested that more drastic measures were needed to tackle the shortage of agricultural labour, such as a complete ban on emigration. All intending emigrants were required to obtain a Garda signature, stating that they had not been employed in agriculture or in turf. Austin regarded the Gardaí as 'the weak link in the present chain of Emigration regulations'. He suggested that the Department of Justice should circularise all Gardaí, pointing out that genuine agricultural workers were being permitted to emigrate, and announcing that disciplinary action might be taken against Gardaí who signed their release forms.

The spring of 1944 saw renewed calls for the army to be made available; it was also suggested that urban workers give a hand. Cork County Farmers' Association warned Ryan that unless its members were assured of adequate harvest labour they would only sow 'as much as we are satisfied we can reasonably save'. By March the Turf Development Board was seeking an additional 700 workers, although it reassured a sceptical Nagle that these would be recruited from the unemployment register. Much to the Department of Agriculture's relief, in May 1944 the Department of Industry and Commerce extended the restrictions on emigration to those living in towns with a population of less than 5,000. Although the Cabinet approved this measure, Industry and Commerce soon changed its mind, and demanded that it be repealed because it was causing hardship for unemployed construction and industrial workers.[121] Agriculture opposed any relaxation of the controls on emigration, even after V-E Day, but the Cabinet eased the regulations in the autumn of 1945.

There is little doubt that all agricultural workers had to work much harder during the Emergency to cope with the demands imposed by the rise in tillage. According to the annual Census of Agricultural Workers, the number engaged in agriculture rose until 1941, and then fell; by 1945 it was below the 1939 level. Claims for agricultural rates remission in respect of employees or assisting relatives increased from 57,706 in 1939/40 to 63,216 by 1945/6. Farmers made claims in respect of 49,152 male assisting relatives in 1939/40, and 49,156 in 1945/6; the number peaked at 50,626 in 1942/3.[122] There was a slight rise in the number of permanent agricultural labourers in 1943 and 1944, which may suggest that farmers were trying to hold on to workers by offering them greater security. However, the recurring complaints from farmers about the poor calibre of farm labourers suggests that farmers found it difficult to adjust to the tighter labour market that existed during the war years.

The improved employment opportunities during the Emergency resulted in a changing attitude towards jobs in farming. Men employed on turf were eligible for unemployment insurance, whereas agricultural labourers were not. In 1945 Louth County Committee of Agriculture reported that road workers who voluntarily broke their employment to work with a farmer automatically lost their entitlement to one week's holidays with pay (this only applied to permanent road workers).[123] There are countless statements indicating that agricultural labourers wanted greater security and more regular spells of employment. During 1945 the Department of Agriculture operated a scheme where men on the unemployment register were assessed for their suitability as harvest workers. A total of 530 men were employed under the Harvest Labour Scheme and the vast majority were reported as satisfactory, although the number is so small that it is difficult to draw any conclusion as to the overall quality of workers on the unemployment register. Most farmers refused to join the Harvest Labour Scheme because they claimed that the wages set for harvest workers were too high; others subsequently complained that the workers were unsatisfactory.[124] During the Emergency there was a sharp fall in the number of prosecutions under the Agricultural Wages Act. Many inspectors were transferred to compulsory tillage. Farmers who failed to comply with the conditions of the Agricultural Wages Act would have found it impossible to hire workers.

TABLE 7: Males Engaged in Farm Work, 1939–46[125]

Age Category of Worker	14-18 Family	14-18 Other Perm	14-18 Temp	Over 18 Family	Over 18 Other Perm	Over 18 Temp	Total
1939	30,610	4,634	3,116	364,317	76,567	51,655	530,899
1940	31,543	4,285	2,790	373,493	77,434	54,292	543,837
1941	31,050	3,947	3,046	377,287	80,271	60,000	555,601
1942	27,477	4,016	2,527	370,316	81,019	55,826	541,181
1943	25,925	4,135	2,898	364,121	82,321	56,983	536,383
1944	24,971	4,334	2,361	359,218	83,240	52,023	526,147
1945	23,981	4,126	2,391	356,110	84,460	50,912	521,980
1946	24,727	3,720	2,259	355,588	85,300	48,040	519,634

Milk and Butter

Ireland had a long tradition of exporting dairy produce, bacon and eggs, so at first sight it might seem improbable that there should be domestic shortages of these commodities during the war. Yet there had been seasonal shortages of food in Ireland during the later years of World War I, and Ireland imported significant quantities of bacon and butter until the early 1930s. Output of creamery butter fell from 766,460 cwt in 1938 to 579,534 cwt in 1944; it declined in every year except 1941, when there was a marginal increase. The output of bacon, ham and gammons fell from 1,080,944 cwt in 1938 to 272,942 cwt by 1944; the sharpest fall occurred in 1942 owing to the loss of imported feed-stuffs.[126]

The dairy sector was not in a very healthy condition when war broke out. Milk yields per cow had fallen during the 1930s, and the 1938 Anglo-Irish Trade Agreement brought little benefit to dairy exports. The government was forced to retain export bounties on dairy produce because of acute competition in the British market, whereas they were abolished on all other products. On a more positive note the Department of Agriculture was satisfied with the structure of the creamery sector; the industry had been thoroughly reorganised in the late 1920s and early 1930s. In the spring of 1939, before war broke out, Ryan rejected a request from the Limerick County Committee of Agriculture for a meeting to discuss the dairy industry. The Department reminded the county committee about the large sums provided to the dairy sector through direct and indirect subsidies. Milk yields fell during 1939 because of a poor hay crop, and throughout the following winter the Department was bombarded with resolutions from the Irish Creamery Managers' Association and the committees of co-operative creameries, demanding an increase in the price of butter. Cork County Committee of Agriculture passed a motion stating that it would be 'a grave national disaster' if the dairy industry sank.[127] The flow of resolutions continued during the summer of 1940.

The government adopted a tough line on the price of butter, because any increase would require a larger subsidy to bridge the gap between the domestic price and the price in Britain. A higher price would also encourage an increase in output, which would have to be exported with a subsidy. When Ryan met deputations from the industry during 1940, he emphasised that the government had failed to secure a higher price from the British Ministry of Food. On 17 October 1940 *The Irish Times*, the *Irish Independent* and the *Irish Press* reported correctly that the Cabinet was to discuss the dairy industry.[128] A memorandum from the Department of Agriculture, dated 16 October, noted that if the price of milk was not increased, dairying would decline, with 'catastrophic consequences for the country's agricultural output'. Deputations representing dairy farmers had claimed that it was no longer economical to produce milk, and farmers were being forced to sell their cows. The Department asked the government to provide an additional £200,000, of which £180,000 would be spent on creamery butter, bringing the wholesale price to 155s per cwt, which was equivalent to 6d a gallon for milk. Although the Department did not regard this as an economic price, it suggested that 'it will go some way towards maintaining confidence in the industry'. The cost of the subsidy could be met by raising the retail price of butter from 1s 7d to 1s 10d per pound. It predicted that this would lead to a fall in butter consumption, not a bad thing as there was a danger of a butter shortage during the winter.

Yet raising the price of butter would jeopardise the government's prices and wages policy. At the time, the Minister for Industry and Commerce was proposing to introduce a standstill order covering wages, distributed profits, and the prices of essential commodities. The Department of Finance claimed that raising the price of butter would be 'a manifest departure from the Government's declared policy of preventing price increases in order to avoid inflation' and it would embarrass ministers who had rejected demands for wage and salary increases. It suggested that it would be more rational to restrict butter exports. The Cabinet played for time: the ministers for Agriculture and Finance were instructed to discuss alternative proposals for fixing the price of creamery butter in order to give milk suppliers 6d a gallon; the price agreed should make no allowance for increased wages to creamery workers or higher profit margins to wholesalers or retailers, which would have knock-on effects on other sectors of the economy.[129]

The price of 6d a gallon was substantially less than the farmers' demand. By November 1940 seventeen county committees of agriculture had passed motions demanding a subsidy that would enable creameries to pay suppliers 8d a gallon in summer and 10d in winter. Agriculture dismissed these resolutions as 'to some extent merely playing to the gallery'.[130] Agriculture and Finance determined that a wholesale price of 158s would give farmers 6d a gallon. This would cost the exchequer an estimated £928,000, if the retail price was not increased; if the retail price were increased, as Agriculture had suggested, the cost to the exchequer would be £328,000. Both departments agreed that it would be necessary to introduce butter rationing if the retail price was not increased, but the Cabinet agreed to pay farmers 6d a gallon, and to freeze the price of butter until the following March.

The Department of Agriculture revived the campaign for higher milk prices in June 1941. It had received yet more resolutions from co-operatives and county committees of agriculture. By 1941 the attitude of other government departments was heavily coloured by the indications that many farmers were prospering at a time when other sections of the population were experiencing a fall in their standard of living. Although Industry and Commerce acknowledged that the price paid to milk producers had only increased by 15 per cent in the previous two years, much less than the average of 45 per cent for agricultural produce in general, it also pointed out that net output in agriculture was 'massively up'. Income should be redistributed to dairy farmers from more profitable branches of farming, such as wheat and sugar-beet. Industry and Commerce also suggested that the decline in milk output was not an unmixed evil, since it reduced the cost of export subsidies, and asked whether it would be 'quite impracticable to divert any substantial part of dairy farming temporarily into more profitable branches of agriculture?'

The Cabinet discussed the price of milk on 22 July 1941, but the matter was then withdrawn with a view to further examination by the departments of Agriculture and Finance. In November Ryan requested to have the item restored to the Cabinet agenda because Finance and Agriculture had failed to reach agreement. A Cabinet discussion on 2 December also ended without agreement. A note from Smiddy to de Valera (Smiddy advised de Valera on a wide range of economic issues) suggests that Smiddy had been juggling around with exchequer grants and milk prices in an effort to resolve the impasse.

In April 1942 the Department of Agriculture reported that the output of creamery butter in 1941/2 was the same as in 1940/1, despite more suitable weather. The Minister was 'growing seriously apprehensive that the stability of the industry [had been] undermined': farmers were threatening to withhold milk from creameries; there had been a shortage of milk in the Dublin area during January and February. Yet the fact that Agriculture only recommended raising the price of milk from 6d to 7d a gallon – it had recommended 8d a gallon in the previous year – suggests that it was conscious of the forces marshalled against it. The arguments were much as before. Finance suggested that as dairy produce could not be exported at a profit, output should be held to a level that would provide only a sufficient surplus to afford 'a reasonable safeguard against scarcity'.

Dairy farmers should be content with a lower subsidy, and should try instead to improve milk and butterfat yields, 'both notoriously poor'.[131] The Cabinet finally conceded a price of 7d a gallon; the retail price of butter was increased to 1s 9d a pound, and the exchequer would meet the balance of the additional cost.

The Cabinet probably conceded an increase in the price of milk because it was proving difficult to ensure adequate supplies of milk and butter in the cities and the larger towns. Many farmers who had previously supplied liquid milk had switched to tillage. In 1941 an emergency powers order was introduced permitting the local authorities in Dundalk and Drogheda to sell milk.[132] In April 1942 newspapers reported that no butter had been available in Dublin during the previous week. According to *The Irish Times*, Ryan acknowledged that wholesalers had ignored a request from the Department of Agriculture to stockpile 100,000 cwt of butter to meet demand during the winter and spring, and the Department did not take any steps requiring them to do so.[133] Although Ryan used the Dairy Produce (Amendment) Act of 1941 to stop the export of butter during the summer of 1942, in order to build up reserves, the risk of butter shortages continued. The Department recommended that the price of milk should be raised to 9d a gallon, to discourage farmers from making their own butter instead of sending milk to the creameries. It also suggested that the retail price should be raised to 2s per pound.[134] Butter consumption was rising because margarine was no longer available, owing to a shortage of raw materials. In 1942 only 5,358 cwt of vegetable fats were available to manufacturers, compared with 85,193 cwt in 1940.[135] Louie Bennett of the Irish Women Workers' Union favoured paying farmers a higher price for milk in order to ensure adequate supplies of butter; she also supported calls for the introduction of rationing. On 4 September 1942 the Cabinet agreed to raise the price of milk and the retail price of butter to 9d per gallon and 2s per pound respectively, with a ceiling on the butter subsidy for the coming year of £700,000. Although rationing was introduced in Dublin on 16 September, supplies remained uncertain. The Department of Supplies wanted to license all butter traders and to subject the sale and distribution of butter to government controls, but Agriculture suggested that shortages could be overcome through voluntary agreement with the creameries. The Cabinet decided that in future all sales of butter by creameries should be controlled by the Department of Agriculture, 'in accordance with the requirements of the Minister for Supplies'.[136]

By this stage in the war the government was concerned to balance the interests of consumers and farmers. When the Department of Agriculture launched its annual campaign for high milk prices in the late spring of 1943, Lemass suggested that the issue should not be seen in terms of the conflicting interests of agriculture and commerce, 'because, in his view, such an antithesis is meaningless. The interests of non-agriculturists and of agriculturists are always complementary and never more vitally so than at the moment'.[137] If higher agricultural prices were conceded, he claimed, there was a danger of 'gallopping inflation', which might well be followed by the devaluation of the Irish pound. If this happened farmers would be the major losers because they held the largest share of bank deposits. Lemass noted that in recent years higher milk prices had failed to stem a fall in butter output; any threatened shortage could be averted by banning the export of milch cows. This would leave farmers with two alternatives: producing milk or slaughtering their cows.

Because of the divisions within the Cabinet, the matter was referred to an interdepartmental committee, which submitted two reports. The minority report, signed by representatives from the departments of Agriculture and of Local Government and Public Health, recommended an increase in the price of milk; the majority report, signed by representatives from the departments of Supplies, Finance and Industry and Commerce, disagreed. The majority report suggested that the decline in output was due to shortages of animal feed, not to the low price paid for milk. It claimed that dairy farmers were attempting to secure a constant income, despite falling output; if they succeeded they would have no incentive to produce more milk. The Cabinet eventually decided to raise the price of milk in December and to offer a higher price for milk delivered to creameries between December and March, in order to encourage winter production. Butter prices would rise from 2s to 2s 4d from December,[138] and the butter ration could be cut from eight ounces a week to six.

Pigs and Bacon

When World War II broke out, the Department of Agriculture was considering plans to rationalise the pig-processing industry. The industry had been badly hit during the 1930s by restrictions on imported feed and a declining market in Britain. It began to recover following the signing of the 1938 trade agreement and the expectation that maize would again be freely available. By 1940 the number of pigs was the highest it had been for almost a decade. By the summer of 1941, however, pig numbers had fallen by one-quarter and they continued to plummet: in 1943 they were only 37 per cent of the 1940 numbers. This resulted in severe over-capacity in bacon-curing plants, and a threatened shortage of bacon for Irish customers.

The Department of Agriculture responded with a series of emergency orders eliminating all competition in the industry. In September 1941 the Pigs and Bacon Commission was authorised to fix quotas for bacon-curing plants in order to ensure that the stock of pigs was shared equitably between them. This removed any incentive for curers to offer producers more than the prices set by the commission. Another emergency powers order in the spring of 1942 authorised the commission to require curers to sell a specific quantity of bacon; this order was designed to thwart efforts by curers to force an increase in bacon prices. In the autumn of 1942 the commission imposed controls over the numbers of pigs bought by individual dealers and the price they could pay, in response to allegations that butchers were getting an unfair share of the available pigs.[139] These regulations failed to halt the collapse in pig numbers; indeed, they may well have precipitated it, since farmers were not compensated for the additional cost of feeding their stock. Price controls may also have stimulated a revival of home-slaughtering and curing. In December 1942 four additional emergency powers orders enabled the commission to prohibit anybody who was not a licensed bacon-curer from curing bacon for reward.

These orders seem to have been regarded as a short-term response to the shortage of pigs, because an interdepartmental committee was established to recommend long-term measures.[140] In August 1942 it recommended establishing a central authority with overall control over the industry. Shortly after the committee had reported, J. M. Adams, the Director of Agriculture, sent some comments on the matter to Leydon in the Department of Supplies. According to Adams, while the Emergency had obviously aggravated the problems of the pig and bacon industry, these problems were of a long-standing and deep-rooted nature. There was an urgent need to reorganise the processing industry, but if the task were left to the industry it would be better left undone. He suggested that a pigs and bacon board should follow the precedent of the Dairy Disposal Board in purchasing and closing down curing plants that were surplus to the industry's needs, by compulsion if necessary. Owners of processing plants and redundant workers would be compensated. The Department of Finance feared that such measures would prompt demands for compensation from the thousands of industrial workers and the owners of plants that had closed owing to shortages of supplies. J. J. McElligott, secretary of the Department of Finance, did not believe that the industry could be reorganised effectively 'without a material increase in the number of pigs'; it would be difficult to determine which factories should be closed while pig production was at such a low point. He suggested that any reforms should be agreed by the bacon-curers, not imposed by government.

The Department of Supplies favoured yet another approach. It wanted to encourage greater efficiency by restoring competition and recommended that the practice of allocating pigs to individual factories and guaranteeing prices should end. While it favoured retaining a minimum price for pigs, curers would be free to offer higher prices. Supplies believed that this would encourage farmers to increase the number of pigs. Although the Department of Agriculture was in favour of greater flexibility in the price of pigs, it opposed every other aspect of this report. Agriculture wanted the industry to remain under the control of the Pigs and Bacon Commission, as Adams had proposed. On 30 October 1942 the Department of Supplies withdrew its memorandum until further notice.

In April 1943 the two departments again locked horns over restructuring the bacon industry. Agriculture now claimed that there was no need for a major reorganisation: the measures already introduced were working, and there was no reason to assume that producers were dissatisfied with existing arrangements for buying and selling pigs. Agriculture had also changed its mind over minimum prices. It contended that allowing curers to compete on prices would disrupt the orderly conditions now obtaining in the industry and that some plants might be forced to close. In its opinion it would be preferable to raise the guaranteed price for pigs; while this would mean a higher retail price for bacon, the cost would be outweighed by the benefit of higher pig numbers. According to the Department of Supplies this memorandum indicated that the Minister for Agriculture had been lobbied by the Irish Bacon Curers' Association, which was determined to secure an increase in bacon prices. Supplies asserted that their proposals would result in increased production without higher bacon prices.[141] When Agriculture submitted another memorandum to the Executive Council, reiterating the case for offering a higher guaranteed price for pigs, de Valera refused to permit it to be discussed at Cabinet, because Agriculture had failed to comply with Cabinet procedure.[142] Agriculture seems to have regarded this as tantamount to a rejection of its request, since it did not raise the matter again for several months.

In September Agriculture presented a new report to Cabinet, giving an even gloomier account of the industry. The continued decline in pig numbers meant that it was becoming increasingly difficult to secure an equitable distribution of bacon, and a black market was emerging for pigs. Many pigs were being sold at well above guaranteed prices. Some bacon-curers were working part-time; others had closed entirely; some plants had been taken over by other producers. The Pigs and Bacon Commission recommended that either the proposals of the 1942 interdepartmental committee should be implemented, or the fixing of prices and quotas should be abandoned, 'leaving the industry to adjust itself to existing circumstances'. Agriculture was opposed to both of these options. It recommended replacing fixed prices for pigs with minimum prices, while retaining production quotas for individual curers; otherwise, in the Department's opinion, it would be impossible to ensure an equitable distribution of pigs between curers and pork dealers. On 17 September 1943 the Cabinet agreed to raise the minimum price for pigs to 125s per cwt, and to remove the production and sales quotas on curers.[143] These recommendations were very much in line with the plan presented by the Department of Supplies.

Pig numbers fell to their lowest point in 1944, but began to recover in the following year. In June 1944, approximately nine months after the removal of the quotas and price controls, the Department of Agriculture suggested that the market for pigs and bacon should be divided into a number of regional zones and that farmers should be required to sell within one or more zones in order to economise on transport. Although a draft emergency powers order to this effect was drawn up, it was withdrawn in November 1944 and replaced by tighter regulatory controls; these went a considerable way towards reversing the greater competition that had been permitted in 1943. Several prosecutions under the emergency powers orders had failed in recent months because there was no legal definition for bacon; other loopholes had also emerged.[144] Despite the enormous drop in pig numbers, the structure of the bacon-curing industry showed little change. In 1944 there were thirty-seven establishments, two fewer than in 1938, although gross output had fallen to less than £4 million compared with £6.652 million in 1938.

Despite the increased dependence on home-produced wool, the number of sheep also declined as land was used to plant crops. The shortage of bacon meant that there was a growing demand for lamb and mutton, and prices rose. However, as in previous decades, sheep seem to have attracted relatively little attention, either in the Department or at Cabinet.

EGGS AND POULTRY

Poultry numbers fell from 19.5 million in 1939 to a wartime low of just over 17 million in 1943, recovering to 18.3 million by 1944. Poultry fared better than pigs because the strong demand for eggs in Britain made it more difficult to control prices in Ireland, and it was easier to find enough food for hens. The normal winter shortage of eggs was exacerbated by a strong demand in both Britain and Ireland. Eggs had assumed a greater importance in the Irish diet because of shortages of other produce. Once again, the objectives of the Department of Supplies and the Department of Agriculture came into conflict.

In October 1943 the Department of Supplies demanded the imposition of maximum retail and wholesale prices for eggs and restrictions on exports when eggs were scarce. Agriculture countered that the most effective means of preventing a seasonal shortage was to keep production running at a high level during the spring and summer. A good export trade encouraged an increase in output. The Department of Agriculture anticipated a promising export market for eggs when the war ended, and it was essential to maintain production so that Ireland could take advantage of this. Fixing a low price for eggs would encourage producers to sell directly to customers and this would create even greater shortages in Dublin. Nevertheless, the Cabinet decided that the price of eggs should be controlled, and Agriculture and Supplies were asked to devise measures to ensure that priority would be given to the home market.

In November 1943 the Department of Supplies attempted to block an agreement between Eggsports, the company with a monopoly over egg and poultry exports, and the British Ministry of Food, because 'the whole agreement is ... against the interests of the home consumer'. The Department of Agriculture reiterated that unless producers got an adequate price, fewer eggs would be offered for sale. If this happened, Supplies suggested that producers would kill their birds but they could be forestalled by imposing restrictions on poultry exports. Supplies wanted to restrict poultry exports, because it claimed that at the time 'only the best-off sections of the community can afford such food at all'. Although the Cabinet approved the export deal with Britain,[145] Supplies imposed a standstill order, fixing the price of eggs on the home market at the summer price, which took no account of seasonal scarcities.

The 1943 export agreement proved attractive to producers, and poultry numbers rose by almost one million in the following months. In July 1944

Agriculture wanted to offer producers a higher export price for eggs, but if the standstill order remained unchanged, this would lead to shortages on the Irish market, because producers would divert eggs to the export market. The Department contended that egg producers had been encouraged to hatch more chickens early in the year on the understanding that the price of eggs would rise. On this occasion the Cabinet agreed to a price increase.

When the Department of Agriculture sought permission to renew the contract with the British Ministry of Food in the autumn of 1944, the Department of Supplies again demanded that ample stocks of eggs should be held back for the Irish market. The Cabinet approved the export deal on condition that the Minister for Agriculture undertook to take all possible steps to prevent a shortage of eggs in Ireland.[146]

AGRICULTURE DURING THE EMERGENCY

Ireland survived the Emergency without any serious food shortages, thanks to the substantial increase in tillage and greater overall reliance on home-produced food. Unlike Britain, where wartime food supplies were regarded as a strategic issue, Irish food policy was much more *ad hoc*. For example, the Department of Supplies was in favour of setting maximum prices for eggs, but it wanted to remove the maximum prices for pigs and allow competition within the industry. The Department of Agriculture championed the interests of farmers, although it was much more successful in the case of wheat than of dairy produce. Farm households became more self-sufficient. In 1938/9 an estimated 33 per cent of gross output was consumed on the farm; by 1941/2 this had increased to over 38 per cent; by 1942/3 it was in excess of 42 per cent. Although the rise in self-sufficiency was mainly due to the lack of imported feed and commercial fertilisers, the Department of Agriculture feared that farmers would revert to making their own butter and curing their own bacon unless they were offered higher prices.

The agricultural sector's share of national income rose from 28 per cent in 1938 to 37 per cent by 1944/5.[147] Although farmers fared better than other sections of the community, prosperity was selective. For dairy farmers, and the small farmers who depended on milk, pigs and poultry for their cash income, poultry was the only commodity that was consistently profitable. In 1940/1 Professor Michael Murphy of the Department of Dairy

Science at UCC estimated that dairy farmers in West Cork needed a price of 8.64d per gallon for milk, if they were to cover operating costs, pay assisting relatives the statutory agricultural wage, and earn a return of 4 per cent on capital. At the time farmers received 6d a gallon.[148]

Generally, however, throughout the Emergency it was believed that farmers were prospering, and this prompted a more critical attitude towards farming and state subsidies. When the Department of Agriculture recommended that Muintir na Tíre should receive an annual grant from the Department, de Valera suggested that this 'would constitute nothing short of a disservice to the Association, because it would deprive it of the spirit of self-reliance and self-help so sorely needed in this country as a whole and among the farmers in particular'.[149] In January 1944 the Department of Finance noted that:

> It is quite apparent that though the farming community have done great service to the nation as a whole they have rendered this service only at a price, and in extorting this price they have failed to grasp that to the extent to which it is not being paid by the consumer, it is being borne by the taxpayers as a whole. This lack of realisation on their part must be attributed mainly to the fact that farmers are not seriously affected by direct taxation and are, therefore, not deterred in their quest for higher prices by the disagreeable reactions of these prices on themselves personally.[150]

Finance estimated that between 1938 and 1944 the share of national income going to the agricultural community had risen from 26 to 35 per cent, whereas the share accruing in salaries and wages to the non-agricultural community had fallen from 44 to 35 per cent. In 1944 Finance suggested that the exchequer should recoup part of the cost of agricultural subsidies by imposing a levy of £2 a head on exported cattle.[151] It also recommended a reduction in rates relief on agricultural land. The Cabinet dismissed these proposals, perhaps because, as Lemass noted, agricultural interests were 'powerfully entrenched'.[152]

Feeding the Irish population imposed considerable wear and tear on Irish farming. Soil fertility was depleted; milk yields fell. In 1941 the Department of Agriculture was forced to abandon the Commission on Agriculture. Although the Department began to plan post-war agricultural policy in 1942, no major improvements were possible before the late 1940s. The Emergency extended the range of government controls over the agricultural sector. Farmers were increasingly aware that their standard of living depended on the prices and regulations that were determined by the government and they responded by lobbying ministers and TDs and by demanding that farming representatives should be involved in making decisions on agricultural policy.

In September 1939, shortly after the outbreak of war, the National Farmers' Federation[153] criticised the government for failing to consult them 'on agricultural matters to alleviate their present distress'. Ryan appointed a Consultative Council for Agricultural Production to advise him on the best means of dealing with the problems created by the war. The council's thirty-one members included representatives of the county committees of agriculture, who were selected to represent each province; representatives of farming organisations and other agricultural interests, such as the National Executive of the Irish Livestock Trade; and individuals with special expertise or knowledge.[154] This was the first representative, or quasi-representative, council for agriculture to be summoned in Ireland since 1921, although consultative councils representing specific industries, such as dairying and livestock, had been in existence since the early 1930s.

The Consultative Council for Agricultural Production met on eight occasions between September 1939 and August 1941. The Agricultural Produce (Eggs) Consultative Council was the only other consultative council to meet on more than one occasion in the three years before August 1941.[155] Twomey was asked by the Commission on Vocational Organisation whether the Consultative Council for Agricultural Production was an effective method of consultation, given that it lacked any independent powers of research, and the Minister for Agriculture set the agenda and determined when and if the council met. Twomey responded that the Oireachtas was the most appropriate forum for discussing agricultural policy, although 'at a time like the present', when agricultural policy was undergoing 'frequent and fundamental changes', he acknowledged that some form of vocational council representing agricultural interests would be desirable.[156] In October 1943 Ryan paid tribute in Dáil Éireann to the role of the consultative council in assisting the tillage drive, and expressed the intention of reconstituting it as an *ex officio* and permanent institution.[157] However, it is difficult to point to any instance where the consultative council influenced wartime policy on agriculture; its views were not cited on Department or Cabinet files.

The Department of Agriculture suffered in the general backlash against government that characterised neutral Ireland during World War II. The Emergency made farmers more resentful of the government than before, and this was undoubtedly a factor in the emergence of Clann na Talmhan, a small farmers' party founded in 1939. By 1941 the party claimed a membership of 40,000, with the overwhelming majority of members living west of the Shannon. The party won six seats in the 1943 general election.[158] In addition to the predictable animus against tillage inspectors, there was a growing tendency to criticise the advice proffered by experts, whether they were senior officials in the Department or university professors. In 1942 for example, the Fianna Fáil TD Martin Corry, a prominent member of the Irish Beet Growers' Association, told the Cork County Committee of Agriculture that farmers 'had some rather bitter experience of interference in agriculture by professors'.[159]

In 1942 several county committees of agriculture passed resolutions demanding that more farmers should be appointed to the committee that was examining post-war policy.[160] The Irish Farmers' Federation submitted a long report to the Catholic hierarchy that included a demand for the establishment of an agricultural council, consisting of 'practical and experienced farmers nominated by the Association', to devise a long-term policy for agriculture. The federation was insistent that 'practical farmers rather than Department Officials' should lay down regulations governing agriculture and that they should have 'freedom to promote our interest in the Press and criticise regulations which we regard as unfair and unjust'.[161] The increase in wartime emigration to Britain, which saw men willingly abandoning jobs in agriculture, was a foretaste of the social problems that would face rural Ireland and the Department after the war. Farmers, their sons and farm labourers increasingly hankered after the trappings of modern life, such as a regular cash income and regular leisure time.

Raymond Crotty claimed that the war years left no permanent imprint on Irish agriculture.[162] I would dispute this. The depleted soil and run-down machinery may have been the most obvious legacy, but others may have had greater long-term significance. Agricultural prices rose much less during World War II than during World War I because the British Ministry of Food proved extremely skillful at managing the market and UK farmers increased their output. This proved to be the forerunner of Britain's post-war agricultural policy, which provided limited opportunities for an expansion in Irish agriculture. The Emergency involved the Department further in subsidising agricultural prices. Consequently farmers increasingly looked to the government and especially to the Department to meet their demands for higher prices and an improved standard of living, at a time when other sections of the population believed that their needs should take precedence because they had suffered a greater fall in living standards during the war years.

CHAPTER SIX

THE DEPARTMENT OF AGRICULTURE IN THE POST-WAR YEARS, 1945–1958

The years between the end of World War II and the onset of the first oil crisis in 1973 have come to be known as the 'Golden Age of Economic Growth'. Gross domestic product rose at an average annual rate of 4.7 per cent in the developed economies of western Europe.[1] The concept of economic growth was new, as was the ability to measure changes in national income; both were the outcome of developments in economic theory and new statistical skills. Achieving higher economic growth became a major objective, and with this in mind most European governments drew up plans to increase investment.

From 1932 until the end of World War II the Department of Agriculture had had to devote most of its energy to the immediate problems posed by agricultural depression and wartime neutrality. During the final years of the war, however, it began to set out a long-term development plan for Irish agriculture. Although this plan was modified and updated on many occasions, between 1945 and Ireland's accession to the EEC in 1973, the same objectives remained paramount:

- improving the quality and productivity of Irish agriculture by using science and technology;
- placing a special emphasis on grassland output;
- improving the terms on which Irish agricultural produce was sold in the UK market, and, if possible, securing a link between the prices paid to UK farmers and the prices of Irish produce in the UK market.

This chapter begins by looking at the years immediately after the end of World War II. This is followed by a brief summary of political change and the policies pursued by the various governments between 1948 and 1957, which provide a back-drop to a more detailed discussion of the various programmes to improve Irish agriculture after 1948, and the market conditions for Irish agricultural produce.

THE IMMEDIATE POST-WAR YEARS

The end of World War II did not bring an immediate return to normality. When the war ended in Europe in May 1945, supplies of wheat became more plentiful, as did supplies of agricultural materials and spare parts, but this was something of a false dawn.[2] Most countries gave priority to meeting their own needs, and they were unwilling to release farm machinery or fertiliser for export, although some tractors were acquired from Canada and the United States during 1946.[3] In 1947 the acute shortage of fuel in Britain and the sterling crisis[4] created additional headaches for Irish importers. Supply problems did not end until 1948. Many of the emergency orders introduced between 1939 and 1945 remained in place. For example, a 1943 order restricting the industrial use of potatoes was not lifted until 1954, and the controls exercised over the pig and bacon industry by emergency orders were not replaced by legislation until 1956. The Department's report for 1954/5 was the first since 1939/40 not to include a section headed 'Emergency Measures'.

After the D-Day landing in June 1944, Irish newspapers began to carry reports of starvation in various parts of Europe. These stories were used to persuade farmers not to relax their tillage efforts. In April 1945 the government established a European Relief Scheme, and additional aid was channelled through the International Red Cross. On 28 May 1945 the Department of External Affairs presented the Department of Agriculture with a copy of a statement issued by Britain, Canada and the United States, warning of a world food shortage.[5] During the following month the *Irish Press* reported that representatives of the Belgian government had arrived in Ireland to purchase cows and horses, and for the remainder of the year there were reports of ships leaving Ireland with food for continental Europe. Ireland sent cattle, horses, bacon, butter, dried and condensed milk, cheese and baby food. The European Relief Scheme continued until 1948. In 1949 the Department of Agriculture provided over 1,000 tons of canned stewed meat to distressed Jews; one-third of the consignment was in the form of kosher meat.

In the spring of 1946 the Department launched a campaign designed to encourage farmers to produce more food. De Valera made a broadcast titled 'The World Food Shortage – Our Own Position'. Farmers were asked to plant more wheat and de Valera also announced that the extraction rate for flour, which had been reduced to 80 per cent in October 1945, was being raised to 85 per cent, so that Irish people would not be competing with the starving people of Europe for American wheat. The extraction rate rose to 90 per cent in April 1946.[6] Although the 1945/6 wheat acreage was the highest since 1847, the appalling weather conditions in the summer and autumn of 1946 made it difficult to harvest the crop. By September the Labour party was demanding the recall of Dáil Éireann and there were calls for the suspension of all GAA matches. TDs from every party asked the government to compensate farmers for their losses.[7] When de Valera broadcast an appeal on 8 September for a 'united national effort to save the harvest', he emphasised the importance of making Ireland independent of foreign food. In his speech he referred to food shortages in Europe and Asia, the possibility of mass deaths by starvation, and made a brief reference to the Great Famine of the 1840s.

Gardaí and troops were put on special harvest duties and civil servants were released for harvest work. The emergency was co-ordinated by the Department of Agriculture. When the work was completed, the Minister, James Ryan, reported that, 'Not alone did they [the civil servants] prove earnest and capable workers in the fields but their help in planning the despatch and distribution of other volunteers was most useful'. Some officials worked until 11 pm and throughout the weekend, organising rosters of workers. Ryan claimed that the fieldwork of civil servants 'earned the praise of farmers wherever they went', so that farmers were asking to be assigned civil servants. The satisfactory reports applied to men and women alike. While the harvest was eventually saved, the sharp drop in yields led to a severe shortage of fodder during the winter. One farmer in Lixnaw, County Kerry, reported that he had lost thirty winds (large cocks of hay) because of flooding; his potatoes were rotten and black; and he would be forced to sell his cows because he could not feed them.[8] The Department of Agriculture recommended that Ireland should cooperate with the proposal from the Emergency Conference on European Cereals for the co-ordinated purchase of cereals from the Argentine. This decision forced the government to introduce bread rationing, which had been avoided during the war,[9] because otherwise Ireland would not be allocated wheat by the International Emergency Food Council.[10]

The wet summer and autumn of 1946 were followed by the worst winter of the century. There were heavy falls of snow in January 1947 that did not thaw until March, and work in the fields was delayed by several weeks. On 19 March Patrick Smith, who had succeeded Ryan as Minister for Agriculture, informed the Dáil that more than 2 million acres would need to be ploughed if the tillage acreage of the previous year was to be reached.[11] Many livestock died because of a shortage of fodder. In June 1947 Father Gaynor, the parish priest of Kilmihill, County Clare, who was a long-standing correspondent of de Valera's, wrote to him 'in memory of old times and in good-will towards the Irish Government'. Father Gaynor claimed that both the cattle and the young farmers of west Clare were dying, owing to the hard conditions under which they lived, and he suggested that the government provide grants to compensate farmers for lost output. He reminded de Valera that Clann na Talmhan (a party, whose policies were designed to attract small and medium farmers) had promised help. If de Valera refused this request, Father Gaynor warned that Fianna Fáil might lose votes. An official of the Department of Agriculture was despatched to meet Father Gaynor, with instructions to reassure him that farmers in his area would receive a sympathetic hearing.[12]

In 1947 the Department introduced a special scheme of temporary loans through the ACC to enable farmers to replace stock lost during the previous winter. Although the loans were free of interest and repayments were postponed for eighteen months,[13] only 4,281 farmers took advantage of this scheme. By January 1948 cattle numbers had fallen so far that the Minister for Agriculture refused to permit the slaughter of calves for export as veal.[14] In July 1948 James Dillon, introducing the estimate for the Department of Agriculture, told the Dáil that 'the livestock population of this country has fallen to the lowest levels that have ever been known in our recorded history'.[15] A shortage of milk during 1947 meant that the weekly butter ration was reduced from six ounces to four, and then to two ounces, and the use of cream except for making butter was banned. When the shortage eased during 1948, the butter ration was increased to six ounces.

PLANNING FOR POST-WAR AGRICULTURE: THE COMMITTEE ON POST-EMERGENCY AGRICULTURAL POLICY

The appalling weather conditions during 1946 and 1947, the scarcity of materials, and a shortage of convertible currency owing to the sterling crisis, delayed the start of a planned programme of investment in agriculture. In April 1942 the secretary to the government, Maurice Moynihan, contacted Ryan's private secretary, with the suggestion that he should establish a committee to examine the problems that would arise in relation to agriculture following the end of the Emergency. This was part of a wider government programme of post-war planning.[16] When de Valera asked for a progress report in July, Ryan reported that he had appointed a planning committee with wide terms of reference. The committee was chaired by Professor Timothy Smiddy of UCC, and included J. P. Drew and E. J. Sheehy from UCD, C. Boyle from UCC, Joseph Johnston from TCD, Henry Kennedy of the IAOS, and Robert Barton, the former Director (Minister) of Agriculture under Dáil Éireann. The Department was represented by the chief inspector, T. J. O'Connell. When O'Connell became Director of Agriculture, J. Mahony, who had succeeded him as chief inspector, replaced him on the committee.

By October Smiddy had drawn up a list of priority subjects for investigation by the committee:

- the restoration of soil fertility after wartime damage;
- ensuring long-term fertility by a programme of ploughing, re-seeding, better conservation of farm-yard manure and increased use of fertiliser;
- measures to provide sufficient winter and spring fodder for livestock, which would improve the quality of cattle and raise milk output, while enabling farmers to keep calves for a longer period;
- better instruction and research on veterinary problems, such as contagious abortion;
- a new strategy for pig and poultry production by small farmers, who traditionally relied on imported feed;
- restructuring the bacon industry;
- the marketing and distribution of creamery butter.

In March 1943 the Cabinet Committee on Economic Planning recommended that post-war agricultural policy should be considered in conjunction with the policy on land purchase and distribution.[17] This would have marked a major change in approach because up to then there is no indication that the work of the Land Commission and the Department of Agriculture had been co-ordinated. In December 1943 Smiddy presented the government with a further list of topics that merited investigation:

- government policy on land utilisation;
- livestock disease and veterinary services;
- agricultural education and research;
- agricultural credit;
- marketing, taxation, administrative and consultative bodies,
- agricultural labour and wages;
- land division;
- social amenities in rural Ireland.[18]

When the Cabinet Committee on Economic Planning discussed the role of agriculture in post-war economic development in September 1944, it emphasised three matters, which were to be of central importance to government policy for many years:

- the need to achieve greater efficiency in production;
- the importance of the export market in maintaining and improving living standards, because higher agricultural exports were essential if Ireland was to be in a position to pay for imports of consumer goods and industrial raw materials;
- the importance from the national and social point of view of maintaining as many families as practicable on the land in economic security.

A memorandum on agricultural policy, which appears to be a summary of Ryan's statement to the Cabinet committee, concentrated on somewhat different priorities. This began by noting that agricultural policy should ensure that the main food requirements of the population could be provided from domestic sources; that those engaged in agriculture should be in a position to earn a reasonable living; and that a proper balance should be maintained between tillage and livestock farming. It suggested that the prospects for agricultural exports after the war were uncertain. Britain had already entered into agreements to buy large quantities of dairy produce and bacon from New Zealand and Canada respectively, at prices that would not be economic for Irish producers. However, the market for cattle and poultry exports seemed more promising. This document suggested it was essential to maintain a quota of tillage, although this should be done through guaranteed prices rather than by compulsion.[19]

In December 1944 Smiddy presented the Cabinet with an early draft of the introduction to the final report of the Committee on Post-Emergency Agricultural Policy. The publication of interim reports on the cattle and dairy industries and on poultry production had already been approved.[20]

Irish agriculture had been stagnant since the mid-1920s. Output had failed to respond to changes in price, legislation or advances in education. It was essential to increase the value of agricultural exports in order to pay for the raw materials and capital goods that industry would require, but this would only be possible if farming became more efficient. The government could assist this process by controlling farmers' costs. Smiddy suggested that taxation should be reduced and that tariffs should be set at a moderate level. He was advocating a variant of Patrick Hogan's policy for agriculture, which gave primacy to the export sector, whereas Ryan had emphasised the importance of self-sufficiency. If the stagnant condition of Irish agriculture was to end, Smiddy suggested that 'radical methods' might be necessary, including the removal of bad farmers.[21]

Seán Lemass, the Minister for Industry and Commerce, was thinking along similar lines. In November 1944 he asked what concessions would be necessary in order to secure a guaranteed market for Irish agricultural exports to Britain. Lemass assumed that the *quid pro quo* would be the removal of protection for Irish industry. While this would reduce farmers' costs, he was not convinced that it would result in higher agricultural output or greater profits. In his opinion the most effective way to raise agricultural output was to offer farmers a guaranteed market for their produce. Better marketing arrangements would ensure that farmers reaped higher profits from lower costs. He suggested that consideration should be given to subsidising agricultural exports outside the sterling area, and exports of butter and bacon to Britain, in order to ensure their re-entry into the British market. However, Lemass believed that an increase in agricultural output would do little to prevent that rise in unemployment that was expected to follow the ending of World War II.

In January 1945, in the course of a forty-five page report on the 1944 British White Paper on Full Employment, Lemass suggested that the experience of the war years had shown that the supply of Irish agricultural produce was relatively inelastic. Higher prices did not necessarily lead to increased output; indeed, falling prices sometimes resulted in a higher output as small farmers tried to maintain their incomes. If the government wished to ensure a rise in agricultural output, it would be necessary to reorganise the system of landholding. He queried Fianna Fáil's goal of settling the maximum numbers on the land:

By one method or another, it is necessary to ensure that the Nation's resources of agricultural land are fully utilised. The rights of owners should not include the right to allow land to go derelict or be utilised below its reasonable productive capacity. Only a limited number of families can be settled on the land on economic holdings, and policy must be directed to ensuring that ownership will be confined to persons willing and capable of working them adequately.

Lemass suggested that farmers should be encouraged to become more efficient by increasing mechanisation and making greater use of co-operation. He noted that the lowest production costs were found on large farms. It would be desirable to offer farmers stable prices for their produce, but this could only be done if the government was prepared to become involved in wholesaling agricultural produce, either directly or indirectly. However, he was opposed to offering a guaranteed price for wheat after the war, and he queried the merits of guaranteeing producer prices for butter and bacon, if this meant that consumers would have to pay higher prices. Lemass favoured establishing state trading organisations to promote agricultural exports, but he warned that exports would have to be of a high quality.[22]

Ryan refused to countenance any suggestion that bad farmers should be removed. Where a farm was neglected, he claimed that it was often because the owner was incapacitated, and the neglect would be rectified in the next generation. In his opinion, 'It would be unthinkable to disturb the family in such cases no matter how much below the desired standard the farm might presently be'. Ryan also disputed Lemass' views on the relationship between price and output. He suggested that mixed farming was most likely to provide employment throughout the year: dairying gave steady employment; tillage, especially on large holdings, gave less employment than was generally assumed; grazing offered the least employment for a given size of farm. A typical farm in a rich grazing area would provide greater output and employment if part of the land were under cultivation, but Ryan believed that this could only be achieved through compulsion.[23] Although Ryan and Lemass were not in agreement over a development strategy for Irish agriculture, it is evident that neither had fully worked out their views on this matter. At one point Ryan favoured compulsory tillage; in another document he was against the idea. Lemass appeared to be in favour of offering farmers stable prices for their produce, yet he was opposed to guaranteed prices for wheat and dairy produce.

The final reports of the Committee of Inquiry into Post-Emergency Agriculture, one majority and two minority reports, reflected divisions of opinion on issues such as tillage, self-sufficiency and the importance of export markets. Both the majority report, signed by Smiddy, Drew, Boyle, Johnston and Barton, and one of the minority reports, signed only by Henry Kennedy, were a reprise of Hogan's agricultural policy. They regarded agriculture as the basis of the national economy and claimed that a more prosperous agriculture would result in an expansion in manufacturing and service industries. To achieve this it was essential to raise agricultural output and exports, which would require greater efficiency. Both reports recommended more intensive grassland production, using ley farming (growing clovers), to improve soil fertility and raise grassland output. This in turn would provide more food for livestock. As part of the process of ensuring soil fertility, they also recommended more intensive cultivation of potatoes and other root crops, but a reduction in the acreage under cereals. According to the majority report, potatoes and root crops were 'but the precursors of grass crops and a means to the production of more remunerative grass of better and more enduring quality'. Kennedy suggested that cabbage, kale and silage should be fed to livestock, which would be kept in the farmyard during the winter. The majority report recommended that cereal growers should be offered guaranteed prices until supplies of imported grain were assured; at that stage price guarantees should be withdrawn for all grain other than wheat; and the guaranteed price for wheat should disappear when 'international political and economic stability is assured'. The report noted that it might be judged desirable, for strategic reasons, to continue to offer a guaranteed price for a limited quantity of wheat. Guaranteed prices should be retained for sugar-beet, to ensure that the existing factories remained in operation, but once the Emergency had ended, unrestricted imports of maize and other livestock feed should be permitted. The price of butter should be guaranteed for five years. By then, the majority report anticipated, the industry would be more efficient, and the subsidy could be phased out.

In contrast, the second minority report, signed by J. Mahony of the Department of Agriculture and Professor E. J. Sheehy of UCD, was committed to self-sufficiency.[24] It suggested that agricultural policy should aspire to meeting the maximum needs of the home market, 'and at the same time to avail to the greatest possible extent of the foreign market in so far as that market offers a profitable return'. Farmers should be required to cultivate at least 15 per cent of their land, with the objective of growing at least 400,000 acres of wheat and 60,000 acres of sugar-beet. Imports of all fruits and vegetables that could be grown in Ireland should be prohibited.

The sale of margarine should be either prohibited or taxed. Guaranteed prices should be offered on a wide range of produce including milk, wheat and sugar-beet. Every acre of arable land should be subject to an intensive rotation of tillage, cropping, manuring and re-seeding with grasses and clovers. Imports of maize should be taxed and the volume regulated in line with trends in the exports of pigmeat and poultry; similar controls should apply to oil cake and other concentrated animal feed.[25] A series of articles by Edmund Sweetman in the *Irish Independent* in February 1946, shortly after the publication of these reports, noted that the majority report could have been written by Patrick Hogan; it had 'an air of unrestrained optimism'. He described the minority report signed by Mahony and Sheehy as 'a brilliant piece of special pleading', which made the case that the primary function of the farmer was to feed the people. According to Sweetman the difference between the two reports was between 'free and natural development against caution, rigidity, and actual Government control'.[26]

Ryan outlined his views on post-war agricultural policy in a speech to representatives of fourteen county committees of agriculture in February 1946. He gave a commitment to end compulsory tillage as soon as this became practicable. Guaranteed prices for wheat and sugar-beet would be continued in order to encourage farmers to grow a substantial acreage of these crops. Imported animal feed would be made available at favourable prices in order to reduce the cost of producing pigs, although farmers would also be encouraged to feed more potatoes to their stock. Ryan raised the possibility of establishing a single export agency for eggs and poultry, another for dairy produce, and a third for pigmeat.[27]

While this speech seems to suggest that Ryan had accepted the broad thrust of the majority report of the Committee on Post-Emergency Agricultural Policy, three white papers issued by the Department suggest a more complex picture. The white paper on dairying, published in January 1946, gave a commitment to maintain a guaranteed market for dairy produce for the next five years, in line with the majority report.[28] The white paper on pigs and bacon closely followed the reform proposals that the Department had drawn up during the Emergency. The Pigs and Bacon Commission would be replaced by a new board with the power to acquire all processing plants, including those in co-operative ownership, by compulsion if necessary. The board would act as monopoly purchaser of pigs; it would regulate marketing and exports; it would improve the management of existing plants; it would allocate supplies of imported maize, and it might also be given responsibility for the purchase of other forms of animal feed and the preparation of pig rations. Capital for the acquisition of pig factories, in order to reduce over-capacity, would be provided by the Minister for Finance. When the industry had been thoroughly restructured, it would be transferred to co-operative ownership.[29]

When the white paper was published, the Department organised a conference, which was attended by farming interests, representatives of the pig industry and trade unionists. Ryan suggested that board members should be elected by curers, producers and other interest groups,[30] but in September 1947 the Department announced that these plans had been abandoned, allegedly because of a shortage of imported pig feed. In reality the change of policy reflected the views of Patrick Smith, who became Minister for Agriculture in 1947, in succession to Ryan. Smith urged the removal of all controls over the pig industry and the abolition of the Pigs and Bacon Commission. Although the government rejected these proposals, it agreed to abandon the planned restructuring of the pigs and bacon industry.[31]

The third white paper, setting out policy on crops, pastures, fertilisers and feeding stuffs,[32] was the most intriguing. As already noted, Ryan had given a commitment in February 1946 to end compulsory tillage when the Emergency ended. He had also expressed the hope that imports of animal feed would become available shortly.[33] These commitments were consistent with the majority report of the Committee on Post-Emergency Agriculture. Yet the draft white paper, submitted to Cabinet in April 1946, was much closer to the views expressed in the report by Sheehy and Mahony. It stated that 'the balance of advantage' lay in retaining compulsory tillage 'as a permanent feature of the country's agricultural policy', although the quota should be reduced when conditions warranted. Compulsory tillage was being retained because the experience of the past six years had shown that some occupiers would only engage in tillage 'when obliged to do so by law'. Compulsion had brought back into production land that had been regarded as useless, and the Emergency had persuaded many farmers of the benefits of tillage. The white paper gave a commitment to provide some form of price support for feeding barley and wheat, but not for oats. Imports of maize would be controlled by a central agency, which would buy surplus quantities of barley; imports of oil seed and other protein feeds would not be restricted unless they were jeopardising home production. The Cabinet postponed a decision on this report on three consecutive occasions – on 25, 26 and 30 April 1946. On 3 May it approved the proposals, subject to minor modifications, including the fact that the white paper should not specify the quota for compulsory tillage or a target acreage for wheat.[34]

All three white papers raised the problem of who should be responsible for setting prices for agricultural produce in a protected market. In July 1946 J. Mahony, the chief inspector at the Department of Agriculture, who was the chairman of the Agricultural Advisory Commission, submitted a report to the secretary of the Department, Sean Ó Broin, on the merits of establishing an agricultural prices commission. Mahony noted that if the state were directly responsible for fixing prices, it would be subject to lobbying and agitation by producers, with the result that 'the question of agricultural prices may be removed from the plane of high policy and objective consideration'. He believed that there would be problems in transferring responsibility to an independent body or a vocational organisation. In his opinion the best course would be to establish a permanent price tribunal or commission, whose duties would be determined by the Minister for Agriculture. He emphasised that unless the commission operated within definite terms of reference drawn up by the Minister, it would serve no useful purpose. The tribunal should be fully informed about all relevant aspects of government policy and the final decision on prices would rest with the government. When the Department of Agriculture sought Cabinet approval for this proposal, the Department of Industry and Commerce objected to a tribunal controlled by the Minister for Agriculture having any say over wholesale and retail prices.

Nevertheless, the Cabinet gave the Department of Agriculture the green light to draft a bill setting up an agricultural prices tribunal. The Minister for Agriculture would have authority to set prices by statutory order following a report from the tribunal. All reports would be presented to the Oireachtas. The Department of Industry and Commerce continued to object to the tribunal having any role in fixing retail prices for meat and milk. Agriculture noted that Industry and Commerce was intent on acquiring similar powers through the Industrial Efficiency Bill.[35] In February 1947 the new Minister for Agriculture, Patrick Smith, gave a commitment in Dáil Éireann to establish a tribunal to investigate the cost of production of farm produce in order to ensure that farmers obtained an economic price.[36] By then a draft bill was in existence, but its character had altered, so that instead of setting prices, the Agricultural Costs Commission, which was the term used in the bill, would merely investigate costs. The bill was subjected to further redrafting following a second reading in the Dáil. On

24 May it was withdrawn from the Cabinet agenda at Smith's request. In October 1947 Smith informed TDs, who had tabled questions on the matter, that he had decided not to proceed with the establishment of an agricultural costs commission; instead he would establish a costing section within the Department of Agriculture.[37]

The three white papers published in 1946 and 1947 indicate a substantial degree of continuity between agricultural policy during the Emergency and the immediate post-war years. This is not surprising: the transition to a peacetime economy was slower than anticipated. International trade remained subject to restrictions. The introduction of bread rationing and the continuation of butter rationing justified the decision to retain compulsory tillage and a guaranteed price for dairy produce. The white papers took little account of the recommendations in the majority report on post-emergency agricultural policy, which emphasised the importance of exports, livestock and grassland enterprises, and the need for increased investment. By 1948, however, Irish agricultural policy began to come more into line with the views expressed in that report. Two factors accounted for this change. In 1947 the US government launched its European Recovery Programme (ERP), popularly known as the Marshall Plan. This emphasised the need for Europe to move towards free trade and closer integration of the European economies.[38] Secondly, the general election in February 1948 saw the return of a coalition or inter-party government that was supported by all parties in Dáil Éireann other than Fianna Fáil, and by a large bloc of independent TDs.

IRISH ELECTORAL POLITICS, 1948–57, AND CHANGES AT THE DEPARTMENT OF AGRICULTURE

The 1948 general election marked the beginning of almost a decade of volatile politics. The general elections in 1948, 1951, 1954 and 1957 all resulted in changes of government. Between 1922 and 1945 Ireland had had only two ministers for Agriculture: Patrick Hogan, who served from 1922 until 1932, and Jim Ryan, whose fifteen-year term as Minister for Agriculture ended in 1947, when he became the first Minister for Social Welfare. Between 1947 and 1957 no Minister for Agriculture served for more than three consecutive years. Ryan was succeeded by Cavan TD Patrick Smith. He was a farmer, a veteran of the War of Independence and a founding member of Fianna Fáil, who had served as chairman of Cavan

County Council from 1936 until 1941. From 1943 until 1947 he was parliamentary secretary to the Minister for Finance, with responsibility for the Office of Public Works. In 1948 James Dillon became Minister for Agriculture in the first inter-party government. At the time he was an independent TD, having resigned from Fine Gael in February 1942 because he disagreed with the party's support for wartime neutrality. The son of the Irish Party MP and Land League founder, John Dillon, he favoured a florid parliamentary style, which was in marked contrast to the delivery of Jim Ryan. Patrick Smith, Dillon's predecessor as Minister for Agriculture, took to peppering his speeches from the opposition benches with quotations drawn from earlier Dillon speeches, and this meant that the debate on the estimate for Agriculture became much longer than in the past.

When Fianna Fáil returned to office in 1951, de Valera appointed Thomas Walsh, TD for Carlow-Kilkenny, as Minister for Agriculture. Walsh, who was first elected to the Dáil in 1948, farmed 224 acres near Goresbridge, County Kilkenny. He was the first Minister for Agriculture to have attended an agricultural college: he had studied at the Salesian Agricultural College at Palleskenry and at Mount Bellew Agricultural College. Walsh was a former member of Kilkenny County Committee of Agriculture and Kilkenny County Council, and an active member of the Irish Beet Growers' Association and the GAA.[39] He died in 1956 at the age of fifty-five following a heart attack.[40] Dillon was reappointed as Minister for Agriculture in the second inter-party government from 1954 to 1957. After the 1957 general election, Frank Aiken, the Minister for External Affairs, was acting Minister, until the appointment of Seán Moylan. Moylan, another veteran of the War of Independence, had served for many years as TD for North Cork. Having failed to be elected to Dáil Éireann in 1957, he became a senator, which explains the delay in his appointment as Minister. The only senator to date to have served as Minister for Agriculture, he was Minister for Lands from 1943 to 1948 and Minister for Education from 1951 to 1954. During the Emergency he expressed firm opinions on government policy towards agriculture and he did likewise when he served as Minister for Education from 1951 to 1954. Moylan had little time to make his mark on the Department of Agriculture, since he died in November 1957, six months after taking office. Aiken again served as acting Minister, until the appointment of Paddy Smith, who held the post until he resigned from office in 1964.

Seán Ó Broin became secretary of the Department of Agriculture in 1947, in succession to Daniel Twomey, who had retired at the age of sixty because of ill health. When Ó Broin, a native of County Clare, joined the civil service in 1910, he was assigned to the Local Government Board. He moved to the DATI at the beginning of World War I, where he served as assistant secretary to the Council of Agriculture and the boards of Agriculture and Technical Instruction and as private secretary to T. P. Gill, the secretary of the DATI. When the Irish Free State was established, he spent two years on the staff of Dáil Éireann, moving to the Department of Finance in 1925. He rejoined the Department of Agriculture in 1934. During the Emergency he was responsible for compulsory tillage. Ó Broin retired in 1955 after forty-five years' service.

On 29 July 1955 the Cabinet decided that John Dempsey should be 'retained in employment so as to fill the office of Secretary of the Department of Agriculture for three years, despite being beyond retirement age during this period'.[41] A graduate of the College of Science, he had joined the staff of the DATI in 1916 as housemaster of Athenry Agricultural School. In 1919 he became housemaster at the Albert College in Glasnevin and a member of the teaching staff. He was appointed as a junior inspector in the Department in 1925, chief agricultural inspector in 1947, and assistant secretary of the Department in 1948.[42]

Agricultural Policies in the 1950s

The alternating Fianna Fáil and coalition governments between 1948 and 1957 meant that each election was followed by changes in policy towards agriculture, although the differences between the parties were much less pronounced than during the 1920s and the 1930s. There were many reasons why Fianna Fáil lost the 1948 general election. One was the resentment in certain sections of the farming population at the Department of Agriculture's enforcement of compulsory tillage and the continuation of these regulations after the war had ended.

In July 1948 Dillon announced that compulsory tillage would end in the following season. This was entirely in keeping with his economic philosophy – during his years on the opposition benches he had been extremely critical of what he regarded as undue intervention in economic matters by Fianna Fáil. Patrick Smith claimed that the decision was promoted by 'a studied attempt to reverse Fianna Fáil policy in regard to tillage'.[43] In November 1948 Dr T. F. O'Higgins, who was acting Minister for Agriculture in Dillon's absence, noted, 'If the present Minister for

Agriculture did nothing else for agriculture he did this: he made the farmers of this country free men, the owners of their own land and free to work it their own way'.[44] Although Dillon did not rejoin Fine Gael until 1952, he presented himself as an heir to Patrick Hogan. In June 1950 he informed the Dáil that he had 'sought to crystallise the agricultural policy of this Government in the aphorism: "One more cow, one more sow, one more acre under the plough".'[45]

When Fianna Fáil returned to office in 1951 it made a determined effort to reverse the decline in tillage, placing a special emphasis on wheat. A memorandum to government from the Department of Agriculture, shortly after the new government was appointed, stated that 'it is Government policy to encourage maximum tillage. The real danger is, however, that in view of the high prices now obtaining for cattle and other livestock, farmers may reduce their tillage area still further reducing employment on the land. If farmers reduce their tillage area it would be extremely difficult to increase tillage at a later date without resort to compulsion'.[46] During the depressed economic circumstances of 1957 several members of Fianna Fáil wrote to de Valera, suggesting that a new drive for agricultural self-sufficiency offered a solution to the unemployment crisis,[47] but by then enthusiasm for self-sufficiency had waned, at least among the party leaders.

While Dillon showed much greater enthusiasm for free trade than the Fianna Fáil ministers for Agriculture, his actions were tempered by the views of Cabinet colleagues and by political considerations. In 1955, in a speech to the United Nations Food and Agricultural Organisation, Dillon suggested that the solution to the problem of agricultural surpluses could be found in the removal of trade barriers and the creation of a common-wealth of free movement. He also deprecated the practice of supporting the prices of crops that were unsaleable. When Tom Walsh, the former Fianna Fáil Minister for Agriculture, asked the Taoiseach, John A. Costello, whether Dillon's speech was in accordance with the government's attitude towards tillage and the growing of wheat, Costello replied that the sentiments 'embody personal and stimulating opinions of the Minister'. Costello referred Walsh to other statements that confirmed the government's commitment to giving farmers a fair profit and an ample margin above the world price for wheat.[48] In contrast to Fianna Fáil ministers, Dillon was opposed to offering subsidies or price guarantees on agricultural produce, although his reservations were based on pragmatic grounds. In 1949 he told Dáil Éireann that Ireland lacked the industrial wealth to subsidise agriculture. In Ireland agricultural subsidies were ultimately paid for by the farming population itself.

Yet in many respects the agricultural policies of Fianna Fáil and those of the inter-party government were quite similar. Clann na Talmhan, a party that drew its main support from western farmers, was a member of the first inter-party government. James Dillon was TD for County Monaghan (a county of small farms), and the proprietor of a retail and wholesale business in Ballaghdereen on the Roscommon/Mayo border, so he could not be accused of not understanding the interests of small farmers. Dillon believed that intensive livestock produce such as pigs and poultry offered a lifeline for small farms. If Dillon placed greater emphasis on exports than Smith or Ryan, this was at least partly because international trade had become easier by 1948, and he was highly optimistic about the prospects for agricultural exports under the 1948 Anglo-Irish Trade Agreement. Similarly, while it might appear that Fianna Fáil had turned the clock back in 1951, when it urged farmers to grow more wheat, the tillage campaign was a logical response to the Korean War, which was widely seen as the beginning of a third world war. Moreover, the devaluation of sterling in 1949 had made Irish-grown wheat a much more economical proposition, and increasing the output of native wheat would reduce the balance of payments deficit.

After 1948 Irish agricultural policy no longer divided along the great fault-line of protection and free trade. The objective of increased exports co-existed with a policy of protection for sugar-beet, wheat, feeding barley and horticultural produce. The major share of agricultural exports consisted of cattle and beef and their cost of production was not increased by the protection given to wheat or sugar-beet, although the protected market for feeding barley raised the cost of producing bacon, eggs and poultry. Although Fianna Fáil continued to encourage tillage throughout the 1950s, this was increasingly seen as a means of producing better grass and increasing the productivity of livestock farming, not primarily as a means of achieving self-sufficiency.[49] The old gibes against bullocks and graziers became less common, at least in mainstream politics, although they surfaced occasionally in fringe political groups. In 1952 Dillon asked his colleagues on all sides of the House to rejoice 'that so large an area of agricultural policy in this country appears to have been withdrawn from the arena of political controversy'.[50] Schemes such as the Land Rehabilitation Project and the eradication of bovine TB that were initiated under one administration were continued by its successor. The differences between Fianna

Fáil and the inter-party governments over the parish plan were very much
an exception.

From the end of the war until the 1960s all Irish governments acknowledged that the key to economic prosperity was an expansion in agricultural
output and agricultural exports. This was the message of the majority report
of the committee on post-Emergency agriculture in 1944/5; it was reiterated
in *Ireland's Long-Term Recovery Programme*, a government white paper,
published in January 1949 as a requirement for Irish participation in the
Marshall Plan. This white paper set out a four-year plan to increase
agricultural output by 50 per cent.[51] The ambitious target reflected the
expectations that the 1948 Anglo-Irish Trade Agreement would encourage
an expansion in Irish agriculture, while funds provided by ERP would ensure
that investment in agriculture was not handicapped by a shortage of foreign
exchange or a lack of capital. There were two dimensions to this objective:
investment in agriculture, and developing the market for Irish agricultural
produce both at home and abroad. The remainder of this chapter examines
the Department's major post-war investment programmes and the market
for Irish agricultural produce.

Land Improvement

I saw hundreds of fields which are growing just as little as it is physically
possible for the land to grow under an Irish sky. This statement is not
intended as a criticism of the competence of the farmers, or of the
policy of any government, but it is a commentary on the circumstances
which have combined to bring about such a state – more than thirty
years of political and economic instability, some sixteen years of
hopelessly inadequate fertiliser supply, with the nine years just past
during which the compulsory tillage was superimposed upon a
desperate famine for fertiliser. It is a miracle that some of the land is
able to grow grass at all.[52]

This description comes from a 1949 report by G. A. Holmes, the New
Zealand government's agricultural attaché in London. Holmes gave a talk
at the RDS annual Bull Show in 1948, and as a result James Dillon, the
Minister for Agriculture, invited him to prepare a report on Irish grasslands.[53] Holmes noted that 'there is no area of comparable size in the
northern hemisphere which has such marvellous potentialities for pasture
production as Éire undoubtedly has'. He recommended an extensive

programme of land improvement that included the establishment of a national drainage board; a national soil survey; a soil research institute; a grassland research institute; a well-planned scheme to provide farmers with lime; improved fencing and measures to provide water in fields; a commission to examine the Irish fertiliser industry; and a scheme to provide farmers with cheap, perhaps free, fertiliser. The government should assist farmers to acquire fertiliser spreaders and farm machinery to carry out a programme of ploughing and reseeding. Farmers should be encouraged to make silage and to make weed control a priority. The objective on every farm should be to sow at least one field every year with new pasture. Many of these recommendations had been anticipated by the majority report of the committee on post-emergency agriculture. However, Holmes' report came at an opportune moment. Compulsory tillage had ended. Fertiliser and pipes for field drains were becoming available, and Ireland's participation in the ERP meant that there would be sufficient dollars to purchase the necessary fertiliser and machinery to put such a plan into effect. The emphasis on grassland was linked to the anticipation that the 1948 Anglo-Irish Trade Agreement would bring a substantially increased output in the Irish livestock sector.

The Marshall Plan was of immense importance to Irish agriculture. It provided a modest grant and a much larger loan in the form of dollars that could be used to purchase essential imports. In turn the currency that Irish importers exchanged for dollars created funds – the Loan Counterpart Fund and the Grant Counterpart Fund – that were available to the Irish government for investment. All decisions on the allocation of money from the Grant Counterpart Fund had to be approved by the US authorities, but the Irish government was free to determine how the Loan Counterpart Fund should be used.[54] The US authorities were determined to use the Marshall Plan as a means of transforming the economies of the participating countries. A related objective was to reduce European dependence on imports from the US. They believed that Ireland's contribution to economic recovery in Europe should be to produce more food for export, particularly to Britain. This would reduce British and European dependence on food imports from the dollar area and encourage the expansion of the Irish economy. A position paper on Ireland, written by the Economic Co-operation Administration (ECA), stated:

> Agriculture is Ireland's basic industry and it is in the agricultural sphere that the country can make the most effective contribution to the success

of the European Recovery Programme. By increasing the production, and, thereby, the exports of the foods of high protein value on which she has traditionally concentrated and which she is particularly suited to produce – meat, eggs and dairy produce – Ireland can play an important part in meeting an urgent demand and reducing the dependence of Participating Countries (especially Great Britain) on dollar sources of supply.[55]

The Department of Agriculture's share of government spending rose from 2 per cent in 1943–5 to 16 per cent in 1950–2.[56] The importance that the ECA assigned to Irish agriculture is indicated by the selection of the senior ECA officials in Dublin. Joseph Carrigan, the first head of the office, was a former dean of agriculture at the University of Vermont, where he had been involved in organising the agricultural extension (advisory) programme for the state of Vermont. In September 1950 Carrigan was succeeded by Paul Miller, who had served as director of agricultural extension services in the University of Minnesota since 1938. Miller was a member of the US Soil Conservation Commission and an agricultural consultant to the Organisation for European Economic Co-Operation (OEEC).[57] Carrigan and Miller were both conscious of the importance of agricultural education and of the merits of working with rural organisations. The ECA provided money and training for the rural farm education organisations Macra na Feirme and the Irish Countrywomen's Association. From 1948 teams of Irish experts, many of them from the Department of Agriculture, travelled to the United States to study topics such as animal genetics, infertility and sterility in cattle, artificial insemination in cattle, pig and poultry diseases and soil science.[58] Carrigan played a key role in persuading James Dillon of the importance of establishing an agricultural institute, and when the institute opened in 1958 the Grant Counterpart Fund provided $1 million as an endowment fund.

In May 1948 the Minister for External Affairs, Seán MacBride, who was responsible for overseeing Ireland's Marshall Aid programme, recommended that £2 million per annum of loan counterpart funds should be used to finance a land reclamation programme, with an additional £4 million being allocated for a fertiliser scheme. Because livestock numbers had been seriously depleted as a result of bad weather during 1946 and 1947, MacBride also recommended allocating £3 million in the coming year to enable farmers to restock their herds. James Dillon's list of priorities for the Loan Counterpart Fund included land reclamation, fertiliser and lime schemes, grants towards the improvement of farm buildings, a scheme to improve livestock breeding stock, agricultural education, and providing pig and poultry farmers with subsidised maize.[59] Not all of these materialised, but the extensive list, and the substantial sums of money involved, are an indication of the manner in which the ECA Loan Counterpart Fund transformed the possibilities for investment in agriculture.

The land reclamation plan was a priority for the Loan Counterpart Fund because it attracted the support of all the parties in the first inter-party government. Before entering government they listed ten major objectives, including a commitment to increase agricultural and industrial output, and the launching of a national drainage plan.[60] Although the DATI did not carry out any schemes to promote land drainage or land improvement during its early years, because these were matters for the Land Commission, the Commissioners of Public Works and the CDB, in 1932 the Department of Agriculture introduced a scheme to provide needy smallholders in the congested districts and other disadvantaged areas with grants amounting to one-quarter of the cost of reclaiming waste land. By 1940 over 47,000 acres had been reclaimed at a cost of £213,000, or £4 10s an acre. In the autumn of 1940 it was superseded by a more extensive Farm Improvement Scheme, which provided grants towards the cost of draining and reclaiming land, constructing fences and improving farm roads and farmyards on all farms with a valuation of £200 or less. By 1949 over 132,000 acres had been reclaimed under this programme at an average cost to the exchequer of less than £5 per acre and a total cost of almost £2.5 million.[61]

On 16 February 1949 the Minister for External Affairs and leader of Clann na Poblachta, Seán MacBride, proposed the establishment of a land development authority with responsibility for forestry, land reclamation and improvements in soil fertility, together with responsibility for agricultural research and education and state companies relating to agriculture, such as the ACC and the Irish Sugar Company. The authority would be authorised to borrow up to £50 million by issuing land bonds. A land authority had been one of the major planks in his party's election manifesto. The proposal was similar to the recommendations in the third minority report to the 1938 Commission on Banking, Currency and Credit, by Peadar O'Loghlen and Mrs Berthon Waters.[62] MacBride's proposal would have deprived the Department of Agriculture of responsibility for some crucial aspects of agricultural policy. In the event the Cabinet postponed a discussion of this proposal and within days the Department had submitted an alternative proposal to reclaim or drain a total of 4 million acres over a ten to twelve year period, to be administered by the Department. Two million tons of limestone and large quantities of phosphate fertiliser would be needed to bring the newly-drained land into condition. The annual cost was estimated at £4.9 million.

The Cabinet gave approval in principle to the Department of Agriculture's proposal on 22 February 1949, and it was announced in Dáil Éireann on 3 March by the Minister for Industry and Commerce, Dan Morrissey. The fact that the announcement was made by Morrissey, who had no direct role in the matter, suggests that the government had not yet decided how the scheme should be administered. On 19 March Maurice Moynihan, secretary to the government, issued a minute to the private secretaries of all ministers, informing them that the memorandum submitted by External Affairs on 16 February (proposing the establishment of a land development authority) had been withdrawn, although MacBride's private secretary denied that this was so. When Clann na Poblachta TD Con Lehane tabled a parliamentary question on 29 March, asking whether a board would be appointed to run the land reclamation scheme, Dillon informed him that the scheme would be organised by the Department of Agriculture.[63] Dillon wanted to establish a land reclamation fund, using money from the Loan Counterpart Fund, which would not be subject to detailed scrutiny by the Department of Finance. He argued that the DATI endowment fund provided an administrative precedent, but the Department of Finance rejected the proposal because it would undermine its authority.[64]

By June 1949 the text of a bill introducing the land rehabilitation scheme had been approved. In the course of a radio broadcast announcing the scheme, Dillon urged farmers to show

> … the same faith in ourselves and in our future as a nation, as that which lit up the darkness of 1879 for Michael Davitt and his men, time will vindicate us as it did them and our grandchildren will be as proud to boast of their grandfathers' part in the land project of 1949 as we are to boast of our people's past in the Land League of 1879.[65]

The official launch took place at the Imperial Hotel (formerly Daly's Hotel) in Castlebar, where the Land League had been founded in 1879, on 16 August, the anniversary of the founding of the Land League. Dillon unveiled a commemorative plaque linking the two events. The Department arranged to reprint and distribute copies of a special twelve-page supplement in *The Farmers' Weekly*, with the title 'Emerald Into Gold: The Land Rehabilitation Project 1950' to promote the scheme.

The land project covered an extensive range of improvements including field drainage, land reclamation, improving and constructing watercourses, removing unnecessary fences, repairing and constructing fences, improving hill grazing, and draining and reclaiming estuarine marsh land and callows. A report by Moses Griffith of the University of Wales at Aberystwyth, on the most effective method for improving hill-grazing, recommended that trials should be carried out in each province over a four-year period, with the results being assessed and published. Dutch civil servants provided expert advice on the drainage of estuary land; the first site chosen was the land adjoining the 'back strand' in Tramore.[66] The Irish Sugar Company conducted experiments in growing crops on reclaimed bogland.

The legislation provided for two methods of carrying out land reclamation. Under section A, farmers could either carry out the work themselves, or hire a contractor, with part of the cost being met by a grant from the Department of Agriculture. Applicants under section B would have the work carried out by the Department on their behalf, and they would make a contribution towards the cost, either in cash or as an annuity charged to their land (those who had bought land under the 1903 or the 1923 Land Acts were still paying a land purchase annuity). Soil surveys were carried out on all participating farms and loans were provided to cover the cost of fertilising the rehabilitated land. Contractors were eligible for loans and grants to meet part of the cost of purchasing drainage and lime-spreading equipment.

Progress was slower than anticipated. According to an undated memorandum written about August 1951, expenditure during 1949/50 was £228,147, or less than half the projected figure of £520,000. In 1950/1 expenditure reached £566,600, against a projected figure of £3.1 million. By the summer of 1951 the Department was anxious that the targeted expenditure of £2.5 million for the current year would not be met. Shortages of excavators and drainage pipes presented a problem. Only a small quantity of clay pipes was manufactured in Ireland, so pipes had to be imported from Northern Ireland and the Continent. In some instances work had to be postponed until the arterial drainage schemes of the Office of Public Works or the minor drainage schemes carried out by local authorities on rivers and streams had been completed.[67]

By June 1953 a total of 102,000 farmers had applied for grants to reclaim 878,000 acres, and 72,000 applications relating to 336,000 acres had been approved. Only 15,280 farmers had applied to have the Department carry out work on their behalf.[68] Larger farmers accounted for a disproportionate number of applications. While the land reclamation scheme was obviously popular, fewer applicants applied for loans under the associated fertiliser credit scheme, because it required farmers to fertilise all the agricultural or potentially agricultural land on their farm.[69] The Department of Agriculture suggested that grants should be increased from two-thirds to three-quarters of the cost, subject to a maximum cost of £30 per acre, in the hope that this would persuade more small and medium farmers to apply. But the Department of Finance countered that, 'Farmers who demand larger grants are surely not worth helping as they will have no proper appreciation of the value of the reclaimed land and will not properly maintain the land after reclamation'. Finance also questioned the practice of spreading repayments for fertiliser loans over a period of sixty years; repayments were added to the cost of land annuities.

Reclamation schemes carried out directly by the Department appear to have been less satisfactory than schemes organised by individual farmers, perhaps because many of the Department's schemes were carried out on poor-quality land. Under one scheme in Roundstone in Connemara occupiers paid a maximum of £1 per acre and were provided with free fertiliser. By November 1952 the Department informed the government that it was seeking a legal method of ensuring that farmers whose land was reclaimed by the Department would maintain it in the improved condition; the Department of Finance suggested that this indicated that farmers did not appreciate work done on their behalf at little cost to themselves.

Although the land project was closely identified with James Dillon and the first inter-party government, it was continued by the Fianna Fáil government of 1951–4. Indeed, in 1952 it increased the provision in the annual estimate by £200,000, at a time when difficult budgetary conditions resulted in the abolition of food subsidies.[70] The ending of Marshall Aid in 1951 meant that the entire cost now had to be met by the exchequer, and the Department of Finance was becoming increasingly critical of the project. The Department of Agriculture fought vigorously to protect the scheme, although officials agreed that the work carried out directly by the Department should end. In November 1952 the Cabinet appointed an inter-departmental committee to review the project. The employment provided by the reclamation work had become an important consideration and it was decided to continue section B (work carried out by the Department on behalf of farmers) for this reason. However, in an effort to curb costs, the Cabinet decided that the maximum grant paid by the exchequer from May 1953 should be £30 an acre. Between April and September 1953 a total of 67,741 acres was reclaimed at a cost of £1.462 million, or £21 11s per acre, compared with 60,187 acres at a cost of £26 14s per acre for the previous year. This suggests that tighter cost controls had proved effective, although up to 50 per cent of applications were being rejected for reasons of cost.[71]

When the second inter-party government came into office in 1954, Dillon persuaded the Cabinet to raise the maximum grant per acre because 'an appreciable amount of land of good agricultural potential, particularly in the poorer part of the country, [is] being excluded from Land Project Operations'. The maximum permitted cost under section B was increased to £60 per acre, with a maximum state contribution of £39, at an estimated annual cost of £200,000. Although exchequer finances were under acute pressure during 1956, an additional sum of £150,000 was approved for the land project in November of that year.[72] By March 1957 a total of 617,000 acres had been reclaimed or improved at a cost of £17 million.

In 1958 T. K. Whitaker's *Economic Development* drew a contrast between reclamation carried out by farmers, where the average grant per acre was £10, and that carried out by the Department, where costs exceeded £40 an acre in more than 80 per cent of cases. He described the latter as an instance of 'misdirected State aid', which was 'fast becoming a social service' and he recommended that this section of the land project should be abandoned with the savings being used to subsidise the cost of phosphatic fertilisers. The announcement brought protests on behalf of the people of Connemara, and it was alleged that many 'married men in poor circumstances' would be unemployed as a consequence. Agricultural contractors were also aggrieved,[73] but farming organisations expressed no opposition.[74] Although the Department of Agriculture no longer carried out land reclamation work, farmers continued to avail of grants under the land rehabilitation project. By 1969, twenty years after the scheme began, 1.75 million acres had been reclaimed at a cost of £30 million.[75] In 1949 Dillon had estimated that 4 million acres could be reclaimed within ten to twelve years. The land project was eventually wound up in February 1974, when it was superseded by the Farm Modernisation Scheme; all eligible schemes had to be completed by 30 September 1976.[76]

Testing the quality of soil to identify mineral deficiencies was an integral part of the land rehabilitation project. During the 1940s research carried out by the Department of Agriculture into a physiological defect in cattle prevalent in counties Offaly and Kildare established that this was caused by a deficiency of phosphorous in their diet. Another research project revealed that sheep that grazed on excessively sandy soil failed to thrive because of cobalt deficiency.[77]

Britain began to carry out surveys of soil fertility during the 1930s, and in 1937 the British Ministry of Agriculture introduced a land fertility scheme that included the provision of subsidised lime and fertiliser to farmers.[78] Although a soil science department was established in the Faculty of Agriculture at UCD in 1930, it does not appear to have had a significant impact on Irish farming before World War II. In 1942 Patrick Gallagher, the head of this department, informed de Valera that the Department of Agriculture took little account of their work, and it had failed to consult him when devising a land improvement scheme. Gallagher urged de Valera to approve a general soil survey and the development of a soil advisory service in association with UCD. Tim O'Connell, the chief inspector at the Department of Agriculture, wished to establish soil laboratories at the Department's agricultural schools, where samples would be analysed by staff, who had undergone a short training course, but Gallagher claimed that more extensive training was necessary to evaluate the results of soil tests. This disagreement came to a head in December 1943 when O'Connell criticised the UCD soil science department, during an inaugural meeting of the UCD Agricultural Society, which was attended by de Valera.[79] Gallagher and four colleagues, Dr Tom Walsh, Bernard Crombie, Professor Michael Caffrey (a former official in the Department of Agriculture) and William Brickley, demanded a judicial inquiry to clear their reputations, but the matter was resolved by a skilfully-drafted letter to Gallagher from James Ryan.[80] In 1945 Tom Walsh was appointed as the Department's soils advisory officer.

The 1946 white paper on crops, pastures and fertilisers had given a commitment to establish a soil advisory service, and this opened at Johnstown Castle, County Wexford, in 1951 under Walsh's direction. Johnstown Castle had been given to the Irish state to be used as an agricultural college by Captain Lakin, who had inherited the estate from his brother, who was killed in action in 1943. The Department of Agriculture also established a horticultural school at Johnstown Castle, and in 1951 it began to conduct field trials on different varieties of grasses, roots and cereals on the estate. In 1952 Walsh became the head of a new technical group in the Department of Agriculture with responsibility for research and specialist advisory services on soils and grasslands.[81]

An analysis of samples tested by the soil advisory service in 1950 showed that over 90 per cent were very, or moderately, deficient in phosphorous, over 50 per cent were deficient in potassium, and less than 50 per cent were regarded as satisfactory for lime.[82] Although lime had been spread intensively on Irish land during the nineteenth century, it fell out of fashion at the beginning of the twentieth century. In 1934 the Department introduced a lime subsidy scheme, which distributed an average of 46,500 tons of burnt lime every year. By 1950 Irish farmers were spreading approximately 100,000 tons of lime per annum. In addition to the Department's burnt lime scheme, waste lime was supplied by the four sugar factories, where lime was used as part of the manufacturing process.[83] When the Department introduced a new ground limestone scheme in 1951, which included a substantial transport subsidy, the use of lime rose substantially, to 545,000 tons by 1952/3 and over one million tons in 1955/6. The Cabinet applied for assistance under the ERP Grant Counterpart Fund for this pro-gramme, and in 1954 the US authorities approved a grant of £1.75 million. Yet, in 1957, a research paper by Tom Walsh and his colleagues in the Department of Agriculture concluded that the amount of lime being applied annually was insufficient to replace losses as a result of drainage. The average level of lime in the soil was less than 10 per cent of the optimum level.

Walsh's paper also revealed that of 12,000 soil samples tested in January 1957, the level of phosphorous was very unsatisfactory or unsatisfactory in 85 per cent of samples, and 53 per cent showed unsatisfactory, or very unsatisfactory, levels of potassium. These figures indicate that there had been little improvement since 1950. This is not surprising since Irish farmers spread much less fertiliser than farmers elsewhere in western Europe. According to an OEEC study carried out in 1954/5, British farmers used seven times more nitrogen, two-and-a-half times more phosphate and three times more potash per acre than Irish farmers.[84] Despite the emphasis in the 1949 Holmes report on the importance of fertilising pasture, and repeated reminders by the Department to this effect, only 35 per cent of permanent pasture and little more than half of the 1956 hay crop received any fertiliser.[85] The OEEC study suggested that the low usage of fertiliser by Irish farmers was due to the high cost. Prices for a wide range of artificial fertilisers were substantially higher in Ireland than in Denmark or the Netherlands because of protective tariffs.[86]

The Department regularly expressed concern about the low usage of fertilisers. In 1953 it tried to persuade the Cabinet to introduce a scheme of interest-free fertiliser loans, financed by the National Development Fund. As this fund was designed to finance short-term employment schemes the proposal was rejected, but the government subsequently agreed to introduce a loan scheme to be operated by the ACC, with the government indemnifying the ACC against any losses on fertiliser loans. However, as the interest rate charged on the loans was 6 per cent, it did not prove very popular.[87] Despite the critical comments by the OEEC about the high price of fertiliser, the government approved a further increase in the price of superphosphates in 1955, on foot of a recommendation by the prices advisory body. In October 1956 the Taoiseach, John A. Costello, tried to satisfy the competing claims of farmers and manufacturers when he gave a commitment 'to arrange for the supply of superphosphates to farmers at world prices, while ensuring that the entire output of the Irish fertiliser industry will be taken up at prices that will enable them to continue operating at their full capacity'. In the same month the Cabinet suspended the customs duty on superphosphates despite opposition from the Department of Industry and Commerce. It also agreed to subsidise the price of fertiliser; manufacturers were placated by higher prices.

By 1957 the Department of Agriculture was operating five separate schemes to encourage the use of fertilisers: two loan schemes and three separate grants. Nevertheless, the incoming Minister for Agriculture, Seán Moylan, proposed to add a sixth scheme that would provide farmers with interest-free loans. The ACC, which was expected to operate the scheme, was not enthusiastic, and submitted a report by P. F. Quinlan, its agricultural adviser, to the Department of Finance, suggesting that spreading additional fertiliser on grassland was not the most effective means of raising agricultural output. Quinlan recommended that farmers should be encouraged to spread more lime, but not potash and superphosphates. He claimed that 'our farmers are still being asked to go into debt so that they may waste fertiliser in growing bigger and better weeds'.[88] This argument was thoroughly refuted in the paper that Tom Walsh and his colleagues in the Department's soils advisory service read to the Statistical and Social Inquiry Society of Ireland in April 1957.

When the Cabinet referred Moylan's proposal to provide farmers with interest-free loans for the purchase of fertiliser to an interdepartmental committee, its deliberations became entwined with Industry and Commerce's marathon campaign to erect an ammonium nitrate factory. Industry and Commerce wanted to divert money from the agricultural grant (the exchequer grant to reduce rates on agricultural land) to pay for this project. This was a rather outrageous suggestion, since a nitrogen plant would undoubtedly increase the cost of fertiliser, whereas the agricultural grant was designed to reduce farmers' costs. If government money were available, the Department of Agriculture suggested that it should be used to encourage farmers to spread more phosphates and potash on grassland. It gave a lower priority to increasing the use of nitrogen. The Department of Finance agreed. In a revealing comment in April 1958, that foreshadowed the publication of *Economic Development* some months later, the Department of Agriculture suggested that the World Bank should be consulted on the economics of an Irish ammonium nitrate plant, and that any decision must be taken in the context of an overall government policy on fertilisers. However, Industry and Commerce persisted in its campaign, and in August the *Irish Press* reported correctly that the government had decided to erect an ammonium nitrate factory at Blackwater Bog in County Offaly.[89] This plan was abandoned. The Department of Agriculture continued to campaign against the establishment of a nitrogen factory, because it feared that it would result in higher costs for farmers. When the state-owned company Nitrogen Éireann Teoranta opened a plant at Arklow in 1965, it had to operate without tariff protection.[90]

The land rehabilitiation project, soil testing and fertiliser schemes were among the major initiatives undertaken by the Department of Agriculture in the decade following the end of World War II. The major benefit from the land rehabilitation project came in the jobs that were provided while the work was being undertaken. In 1953 Fianna Fáil noted that the project provided employment for 12,500 people, although 10,000 of these were casual workers.[91] In June 1949 Thomas Derrig, Fianna Fáil spokesman for Lands, stated that he would have preferred to see a higher proportion of ERP money used to provide cheap fertiliser.[92] Derrig's judgement was sound. In 1957/8 the annual subsidy on superphosphates amounted to only £200,000 in a total package of state aids to agriculture of £18.2 million.[93] The combined cost of subsidies for lime and fertiliser was £866,000, roughly one-third the cost of the land project in that year. This was probably a misallocation of resources. A survey carried out by the Department of Finance in 1968 revealed that while field drainage was a worthwhile investment, half the farmers could have achieved the same rise in income by cheaper alternative investment, and more than one-third of the schemes did not cover their costs.[94] While land was being drained and improved at government expense, large areas were being neglected by elderly bachelor farmers and by owners who had emigrated and rented their land as conacre.[95] Irish fertiliser usage remained far below the European average, and that fertiliser was more likely to be used on tillage than on grassland. Although the high cost of fertiliser is one explanation for the low usage, another factor may have been the poor incentive to increase output, owing to market conditions.

THE EXPORT MARKET FOR IRISH AGRICULTURAL PRODUCE

The 1938 Anglo-Irish Trade Agreement appeared to mark the beginning of a new arrangement for Irish agriculture, combining a close trading relationship with Britain and the continuation of protected markets for wheat and sugar-beet. The outbreak of war in 1939 disrupted the 1938 agreement, but throughout the war the Department remained conscious of the long-term importance of the UK market. During the late 1940s Ireland negotiated several bilateral trade agreements with continental countries. Under an agreement with Spain in 1948 Ireland bought potash and Spain bought potatoes. France provided fertiliser in return for horses, cattle and seafood. An agreement with the Netherlands secured yet more fertiliser in return for 30,000 fat cattle. Similar agreements were negotiated during 1949/50 with Germany, Sweden, France, Spain and the Netherlands, involving an exchange of cattle for fertiliser.[96] Nevertheless, the Department regarded these as of minor importance compared with Anglo-Irish trade.

The 1938 trade agreement was scheduled for review in 1941, but this was postponed owing to the war. When British and Irish officials met for trade talks in the spring of 1946, John Leydon, the secretary of the Department of Industry and Commerce, informed British officials that most of the benefits that Irish agriculture had gained from the 1938 agreement had been eroded during the war.[97] These talks were held against the background of the International Trade Organisation talks at Geneva, which aimed at freeing up international trade, and Britain suggested that it would be advisable to postpone detailed negotiations until the Geneva talks had ended.[98]

It appears that the next round of trade talks was initiated by James Ryan.[99] In February 1947 H. Broadly of the British Ministry of Food wrote to Seán Ó Broin, the secretary of the Department of Agriculture, noting that 'your Minister' had recently spoken to the British Minister in Ireland, Lord Rugby (the former Sir John Maffey), of his 'desire to consider the future agricultural programme of Éire in the light of the long term needs of the UK market'. The Ministry of Food wished to send a team of agricultural economists to Ireland in order to assess the capacity of Irish farming to produce more food. The British authorities requested a statement of Ireland's post-war economic policy, including plans for developing agriculture and industry; estimates of future crop acreages, livestock numbers, agricultural output and exports. They asked if there was any evidence 'that the apparently somewhat leisurely acceptance of improvements in technique by the Irish farmer will now give place to more speedy technical development? Has the Éire government the intention of ensuring that agricultural development takes place?' Assuming remunerative markets, what classes of production would be expanded? What factors might limit this expansion? They requested an estimate of Ireland's future needs of fertiliser and agricultural machinery, whether Ireland would have sufficient foreign exchange to buy these items, and whether transportation and power supplies would be sufficient to support an expanding agricultural sector. Britain was also interested in establishing what impact Ireland's economic policy would have on Irish emigration to the UK. It also asked what export markets Ireland was interested in, other than the UK, and whether there were plans to develop industries related to agriculture, such as vegetable-processing. The list of detailed questions included the potential for increasing the output of grass and other home-grown animal feed; the possibility of reducing seasonal fluctuations in the marketing of livestock; future intentions as to the balance between store and fat cattle; whether Ireland was capable of increasing the volume of milk available for export; the prospects for reducing seasonality of milk production; and whether imports of feed for pigs and poultry would be restricted as a matter of policy.

Although Britain had some justification for asking questions about Ireland's future requirement of foreign exchange, fertiliser and machinery (because they would be bought with the Irish sterling balance, and most of the goods would be transported on British ships), the detailed list of questions suggests that Britain regarded Ireland as a subordinate regional economy. Two agricultural experts, Dr Raeburn and Mr Menzies-Kitchen, visited Ireland in the spring of 1947, and submitted a report to the British ministries of Food and Agriculture. They expressed concern at the fall in calf numbers because they feared this would result in lower livestock exports. They emphasised that farmers needed more feeding stuffs and suggested that British prices for Irish cattle should be increased in order to encourage a rise in calf numbers. Although they did not anticipate an immediate increase in the output of bacon, they recommended that Britain should indicate that it would buy any additional bacon that became available. They expected more eggs to be produced when cheaper animal feed became plentiful, but they saw little prospect of an increase in butter output, unless the Irish authorities improved the breeding strains, and encouraged farmers to spread more fertiliser to provide more winter food for cows. The Department of Agriculture, who received a sanitised version of their report, concluded that it dealt 'fairly and scientifically' with the present general agricultural situation. It hoped that the report would assist Ireland to secure more equitable terms from Britain for its agricultural produce.

In August 1947 a shortage of foreign exchange forced Britain to suspend the convertibility of sterling, which meant that Ireland was unable to buy farm machinery, fertiliser, or any other items from countries outside the sterling area, unless Britain agreed to provide foreign exchange. The sterling area conference, called to discuss this crisis, lasted from 19 September to 6 October. Ireland was determined to use its sterling holdings (which had risen substantially during the war) as a bargaining weapon to secure a new trade agreement. A memorandum prepared in advance of the conference noted that Ireland would not agree to restrict its expenditure of hard currency unless Britain conceded adequate trade arrangements. In addition, Ireland would have to be satisfied that the prices offered for agricultural produce were economic, that there would be no discrimination between the prices paid for British and Irish agricultural produce in Britain, and that Ireland would have access to adequate supplies of fertiliser, seed, machinery, industrial equipment, raw materials and coal.[100] This was something of a tall order given the run-down state of the British economy, and it is unclear what concessions the government was prepared to offer in return. Britain was concerned to conserve its dollar holdings. Importing food from Ireland, rather than from the dollar area, offered one means of doing this, and this was Britain's goal when British and Irish ministers met in November to review economic relations between the two countries.[101]

When British officials reviewed the outcome of these talks, they quoted a remark by Patrick Smith, the Irish Minister for Agriculture, that Ireland's natural advantage lay in supplying food. One British official added:

> … we should also want to secure that the highest possible proportion of Éire's exported supplies of agricultural produce should be assigned to the United Kingdom and that increased production is not absorbed by increased consumption in Europe and that there should be some

clear indication forthcoming of the additional quantities that will be exported to the United Kingdom. ... It might be necessary therefore, in order to assist a swing from industry to agriculture to offer prices and contracts for agricultural products which would make agriculture more attractive than industry and enable it to draw to itself labour and other resources which would otherwise tend to flow to industry.

Britain was determined to resist Ireland's demand for price parity with British farmers, because this would lead to demands for similar treatment from Denmark and the Dominions. British officials suggested that higher agricultural prices deterred Irish farmers from raising output, 'bearing in mind Éire's natural characteristics'. Another version of this argument crops up in another memorandum of May 1948:

> ... easier money would be more likely to result in small farmers eating more and doing less. The Irish are nearer to subsistence farming mentality than we are, and have yet to learn the attraction (or alleged attractions) of farming to make money for the purchase of buying things that the farm cannot produce. This needs a fairly lengthy process of education. The Irish farmers – or more particularly their wives – have to acquire a taste for things that money will buy . ... My short point is that higher prices will simply be a waste of our money.[102]

Britain was also determined to retain a dominant share of Irish agricultural output. During 1946 and 1947 Irish exports of cattle and canned meat to continental Europe rose sharply, at a time when Irish livestock output was depressed because of bad weather. Although the continental market had yielded higher prices for farmers, the Department of Agriculture was uncertain how long this trade would continue. In November 1947 the Irish authorities gave an undertaking that after 1 February 1948 the volume of Irish cattle exports to the Continent would be the subject of consultation between the Department of Agriculture and the British Ministry of Food. In return, Britain agreed to pay an additional 5d in the pound on fat cattle exported to Britain during the winter of 1947/8. When James Dillon became Minister for Agriculture in February 1948, he pressed Britain to abolish the price differential between Irish fat and store cattle on the British market (since 1934 Irish stores fattened in Britain for a minimum of three months had been eligible for the price guarantees given to British cattle, whereas Irish fat cattle were treated as foreign cattle), or alternatively for a continuation of the additional payment for fat cattle. Dillon informed Britain that if it made one of these concessions, it would be much easier politically for him to reduce exports of fat cattle to continental Europe. Britain agreed to extend the payment of 5d in the pound until the end of May, on the understanding that future arrangements would be discussed in the course of Anglo-Irish trade talks, and provided that Irish cattle exports to the Continent were limited to 40,000 for the current season.[103]

During the final week of May, the departments of Agriculture and Industry and Commerce presented the government with memoranda setting out their priorities in the forthcoming trade talks. Agriculture was determined to protect the right to export agricultural produce to Britain free of customs' duties, and to ensure a continuation of Ireland's right to preference over non-Commonwealth produce in the case of dutiable goods. The Department was also keen that Britain should confirm the undertaking given in 1938 not to impose import quotas on Irish agricultural produce without prior discussion. Agriculture noted that the benefits of customs-free entry for Irish produce had been considerably reduced since the beginning of the war, because the British Ministry of Food controlled all imports, and as a rule it paid lower prices for Irish produce than for comparable British produce. Agriculture wanted a written undertaking that there would be 'a reasonable relationship' between the prices paid for British and Irish produce, and a commitment by Britain to supply Ireland with fertiliser and other agricultural requisites. For the Department of Agriculture the most important issue was the abolition of the price differential between store and fat cattle on the UK market; if that were conceded, the Department would agree to restrict cattle exports to the Continent to 50,000 head per annum.[104]

Britain was keen to secure long-term contracts for the exclusive supply of cattle and pigs from Ireland (in other words, Ireland would only export cattle and pigs to the UK) at prices lower than those paid to British farmers, and no higher than those already agreed with Denmark and New Zealand. However, Britain was not prepared to divert supplies of animal feed to Ireland. British officials noted that Ireland could be provided with additional fertiliser only at the expense of UK agriculture. One noted that 'we should like Éire to revert to a source of food stuffs, particularly cattle products'.[105] Curbing Irish cattle exports to continental markets was a contentious matter. On 15 June Fianna Fáil TD Martin Corry, who was an inveterate parliamentary opponent of James Dillon, asked him whether it was 'considered Government policy to sell agricultural produce, including meat, to Britain at a lower price than to other countries'.[106] Dillon was known to favour closer trade links with Britain. According to Patrick Lynch, who was an official in the Department of the Taoiseach at this time, what Dillon wanted was essentially the integration of Irish and British agriculture, although, according to Lynch, he was prevented from achieving this by farming interests.[107] In his reply to Corry, Dillon began by stating that he would not agree to sell produce to Britain 'at an inequitable price' that could be sold elsewhere 'at scarcity prices', but he was not prepared in the name of the Irish government,

> To attempt to extract from an old and valued customer prices for her traditional purchases from this country, which were measured exclusively by comparison with prices offered from other sources where acute temporary shortages give rise to the offer of prices out of all relation to the fair value of what we want to sell.[108]

When trade talks began on 17 June, the Taoiseach, John A. Costello, emphasised that Ireland 'was prepared "to put all their eggs in the British basket", but they would "watch that basket carefully".' By the following day it was accepted in principle that Britain would enter into a four-year agreement guaranteeing to pay certain prices for Irish agricultural produce in return for an Irish guarantee to supply specified quantities. However, Ireland would have to meet its dollar requirements from its own earnings, together with the sums that were provided under Marshall Aid. This meant that imports of wheat, animal feed, fertiliser and tractors would have to be paid from these sources.

By 20 June the draft heads of an agricultural agreement, which differed little from the final text, had been agreed. In the case of cattle and meat, Britain was determined that Ireland would concentrate on supplying store cattle to British farmers. The agreement discriminated against exports of fat cattle, carcase beef and canned meat. The objective was to raise Irish exports of fat and store cattle to Britain to at least pre-war numbers; at least 75 per cent of the cattle should be stores, but this would be subject to review if increased supplies of Irish stores and fat cattle failed to materialise. Irish exports of fat cattle would be subject to the availability of facilities for handling and slaughtering at British ports. Exports of cattle to continental Europe would be limited to 50,000 during 1948, and at least 25 per cent of these would be second-class animals. In the remaining three years of the agreement, cattle exports to the Continent would not exceed 10 per cent of the total. Shipments of carcase meat to Britain would be limited to a maximum of 200 tons per week and 3,000–4,000 tons per annum. Britain agreed that 'no excessive differential' would be introduced between British and Irish fat cattle prices over the existing figure of 5s per cwt. It claimed that this price was equivalent to the price paid for Irish stores fattened in Britain, subject to an allowance for marketing costs. This was regarded as a significant concession on Britain's part. A price differential of $1\frac{1}{2}$d a pound between fat cattle and carcase meat would be maintained. Britain expressed a preference for importing better quality Irish beef, either alive or as carcase meat, but not canned meat. Britain expected to import approximately 7,000 tons of poultry from Ireland during 1948 and wanted to see this rise to 10,000 tons. As long as the Ministry of Food was responsible for imports, Irish poultry producers would obtain the same price as British suppliers. An agreement already existed for Ireland to supply Britain with eggs during the next three years at agreed prices; Britain would be happy to accept additional quantities and would also be happy to import pre-war quantities of bacon and butter and possibly more; the price would be determined in negotiation between officials.[109]

Seán Lemass described the agreement as 'a counterpart of the Treaty of 1921, a partial surrender of Irish economic freedom', although his censure was directed at Ireland's inability to convert its sterling holdings into dollars and the clauses relating to manufacturing industry, which do not concern us. The *Irish Press* claimed that 'to suit British policy' Ireland had surrendered the right to sell agricultural produce 'where we could and where the prices offered were most attractive'. It added that the agreement discouraged Ireland from developing a dressed meat trade and associated industries. Although this was obviously a partisan point of view, a more measured evaluation by *The Statist* noted that the agreement relied heavily on mutual trust between the two countries: Ireland would attempt to increase its agricultural output, but this depended on Britain supplying the necessary raw materials. (Britain had agreed to supply Ireland with 1.57 million tons of coal in 1949 and a larger quantity in 1950.) A more up-beat assessment by *The Irish Times* concluded that the Minister for Agriculture had secured everything that he set out to secure.[110] This was the line that the government adopted in Dáil Éireann. According to Costello,

It would be difficult to see what we could have obtained for our cattle industry, our agricultural industry in general, which we have not obtained. There is no limitation now upon our farmers. There is nothing to stop our farming industry, our agricultural industry, from prospering in a way it never prospered before.[111]

In a speech introducing the estimate for the Department of Agriculture in July 1948, Dillon expressed the opinion that Ireland was 'standing on the threshold of the greatest period of expansion in the agricultural industry of the country that we have ever known'. He believed that it should be possible within the next five years to increase the volume of agricultural output by 25 per cent and to double the volume of agricultural exports.[112] When a group of Irish civil servants[113] prepared economic forecasts for the years 1948–52 some months later, they estimated that agricultural exports would more than double and that there would be a substantial rise in output.[114]

Yet an economic attaché at the American legation in Dublin described the Irish gains as 'relatively modest',[115] and one British official minuted that 'the negotiations were concluded on the lines of the UK brief'.[116]

When the 1948 trade agreement was negotiated, it was already apparent that Britain planned to continue the agricultural policy that had evolved during the 1930s, which combined cheap prices for consumers and generous subsidies for its own farmers. The Agriculture Act of 1947 gave farmers in Britain and Northern Ireland guaranteed prices and assured markets for the principal agricultural products.[117] Food continued to be rationed and the Ministry of Food remained the monopoly importer, which meant that deals were negotiated between the Ministry and the Irish Department of Agriculture, or organisations operating with the Department's sanction. Consequently, there was no immediate pressure on Ireland to develop export marketing organisations or clearly defined brands. In the late 1940s it was widely assumed that food shortages would continue. Yet thanks to the policy of deficiency payments, the UK output of poultry, eggs, pigmeat and dairy produce rose steadily. As Britain became less reliant on imports, Ireland, Denmark, New Zealand and other exporting countries had to compete in a declining market, where the prices on offer were substantially below those paid to British and Northern Ireland farmers.

THE CATTLE AND BEEF TRADE

The Irish livestock sector was badly hit by the harsh winter conditions of 1947. Total exports of fat cattle and stores in 1949 were 446,000, compared with 754,000 on the eve of World War II. In 1950 output was 7 per cent below the 1938/9 volume.[118] At the time there was an acute shortage of cattle and beef in continental Europe, and Ireland had no difficulty in finding markets for the 10 per cent of cattle that it was permitted to export to third countries under the 1948 trade agreement. On 5 December 1949 Seán Ó Broin, the secretary of the Department of Agriculture, asked the Department of External Affairs to ascertain whether Italy, Israel and France intended to import the quantities of Irish cattle that they had been allocated; if they were no longer interested the cattle would be shipped to the Netherlands.

When the 1948 agreement was drafted Ireland exported negligible quantities of meat to countries other than Britain, and this trade was not mentioned in the agreement. By 1951/2, however, exports of canned and carcase meat to Europe and the United States amounted to almost 36,000 tons, double the figure for the previous year. Exports of frozen meat to the United States totalled 6,500 tons, valued at $6 million, which was almost three times the figure for the previous year. The trade grew as a consequence of the Korean War and the 1949 devaluation of the pound, which made Irish produce extremely competitive.[119] The United States bought either premium beef or low quality beef, which was used in the manufacture of canned soups. In November 1951 an interdepartmental committee that examined the potential export market for dressed meat in the dollar area – Ireland was making considerable efforts to increase its dollar exports at the time – predicted that annual exports could rise to 10,000 tons, with a value of $10 million. (Lamb exports were expected to reach $400,000 per annum if adequate facilities existed for processing and shipping.) The industry was self-financing and profitable. If beef exports to the USA reached 10,000 tons, however, it would be necessary to curtail exports of premium cattle to the UK. The committee recommended investigating the possibility of developing chilled rather than frozen exports, and that the industry should continue to operate on the basis of private enterprise, with liaison between exporting firms and the Department of Agriculture being maintained through the Fresh Meat Exporters' Society. It also recommended that the state-owned Irish Shipping Ltd should provide a trans-Atlantic service to the industry.[120]

In 1952 a report on Ireland's industrial potential by IBEC, a US firm of business consultants, claimed that,

> ... the essential fabric of Ireland's cattle policy has been based on a warp of pessimism crossed by a web of timidity, it could only be justified by pessimism, and we have heard a variety of such justifications by an appraisal of market outlook sufficiently dismal to warrant adherence to a pattern that had been proved devoid of dynamic growth, on the ground that meagre certainty is better than the most promising hazard.[121]

IBEC was extremely critical of the degree to which the 1948 Anglo-Irish Trade Agreement militated against the development of beef-processing. It argued that the terms of the agreement should be modified to allow Ireland to ship carcase meat to Britain, and that the commitment that stores should account for 75 per cent of live cattle exports should be ended. It noted that exports of carcase meat to countries other than Britain were subject to 'strict licence'. Before any dealer could fulfil a contract he had to apply to the Department of Agriculture for a licence.[122] The IBEC report said that it was generally understood within the livestock trade 'that this arrangement was maintained because Ireland had committed herself to hold combined cattle shipments in any form to areas other than the United Kingdom to 10 per cent of the live cattle sold to the United Kingdom'. A trader who obtained an export order, and then proceeded to arrange refrigerated shipping facilities, had no assurance that he would be granted a licence to fulfil the order; the 'generally more lucrative orders' were shared out among producers, as opposed to being filled by the producer who had obtained the order. When the IBEC team questioned the Department of Agriculture, it was told that the shortage of chilling plants and of refrigerated shipping made it difficult to develop a trade in meat to countries other than Britain. The report claimed that the beef-processing industry had the potential to generate substantial employment and to provide raw materials for other industries, and an expanded beef-processing industry would mean higher cattle prices for farmers. In support of this latter argument IBEC presented data showing that Irish cattle prices were much lower than prices in other markets that were equally close to large consumer markets, and the differential was much greater than the generally accepted differential of 5s per cwt between Irish and UK cattle prices.[123]

The report was commissioned by the Industrial Development Authority and the comments on the livestock trade formed a small part of a report highly critical of the Irish economy. Seán Lemass and Frank Aiken, the Minister for External Affairs, were in favour of publishing the report, but Walsh, the Minister for Agriculture, objected. He claimed that it was full of 'inaccuracies' and 'false assumptions'. J. C. Nagle, an assistant secretary in the Department of Agriculture, reported that Stacy May, the consultant who wrote the report, had 'rushed in here and addressed us as if he was prosecuting counsel'. The Cabinet approved publication but denied it the official recognition of a white paper.[124]

The Department of Agriculture adopted a cautious attitude towards the beef-processing industry. In May 1951 it expressed concern at the growing export trade in open-pack products during the summer months. In the past, meat-canning firms had ceased operations during the summer months under a gentleman's agreement, which facilitated the livestock trade, but this was no longer being observed. When a number of Dublin butchers approached the Department seeking facilities to export sausages and other produce to Britain (it is unclear whether these were made from beef or pork), they were informed that export licences would not be granted unless the produce were being prepared at privately-owned, registered fresh-meat export premises. In March 1952 the Department noted that plans for the construction of additional meat-processing plants would more than double the existing capacity of 100,000 tons. In the past the Department had granted registration to all premises that complied with the technical standards and regulations of the Agricultural Produce (Fresh Meats) Act, but if this practice continued, the Department feared it would result in over-capacity, with meat-processing over-concentrated in Dublin. The Department preferred the industry to be decentralised, which was consistent with government industrial policy at the time. Officials recommended that the Minister should make a speech drawing attention to these difficulties and suggesting that he would take them into consideration when granting future licences. Foreign capital investment would be discouraged.[125] When a British food producer approached the Department with plans to establish a plant to produce quick-frozen pre-cooked meals, officials expressed fears that he would come to dominate the market.[126] This was consistent with the official attitude towards foreign investment at the time.[127] Between 1947 and 1950 the Department only granted four licences annually for the export of meat, but the number increased to six in 1952, ten in 1953 and 25 in 1954.[128] This suggests that they may have taken some account of the criticism contained in the IBEC report.

The limitation on Irish livestock and beef exports to third countries dominated discussions on the revision of the 1948 trade agreement. Some sections of the agreement were due to expire in 1952. In August 1951 the Foreign Trade Committee, chaired by the Department of External Affairs, recommended that Ireland should insist on securing the maximum leeway under the terms of the 1948 agreement. When the committee met on 29 September 1951, the Department of Agriculture reported exports of cattle and meat to countries other than Britain would probably amount to 75,000 head of cattle or 15 per cent of total exports of livestock and beef in the current year. In addition to the growing market for beef in the United States, Ireland had secured a large contract to supply meat to US forces in Germany, and there was a steady demand from continental countries. In a draft memorandum to be submitted to Cabinet, the Department suggested that unless the government decided to restrict exports of live cattle and dressed beef to third countries, the Irish ambassador in London should inform the British authorities informally of the extent of these sales, while emphasising 'the dollar aspect of this trade' and 'the British failure to deliver the stipulated quantity of coal in 1951' under the terms of the 1948 agreement. Other members of the Foreign Trade Committee argued that nothing should be said unless Britain raised the matter. If Britain broached the subject, Ireland should insist that the agreement only applied to live cattle. But Nagle warned that if exports of cattle and beef to third countries exceeded 10 per cent of the total, the British Ministry of Food would not be slow to raise the matter. To exceed this limit without informing the Ministry,

> ... would endanger the cordial but delicate relations which existed between that Ministry and the Department of Agriculture and might lead to the position where the Ministry of Food would take the view that the Agreement was no longer of the same value to them as heretofore and would withdraw or refuse to continue the various uncovenanted benefits in the agriculture sphere that had developed since the agreement had been concluded.

Nagle suggested that Britain should be informed as a matter of courtesy; 'while there is no doubt as to the strict legal interpretation of the Agreement, it was true that in concluding the Agreement the British had in mind that they would have available to them 90 per cent of our total beef exports whether in cattle or other forms'. In his opinion there would be an element of danger in the Irish government's deciding not to restrict exports of beef to markets other than Britain. On 26 October 1951 the Cabinet decided that the Irish ambassador to Britain should inform the British authorities informally at an appropriate opportunity that Ireland's exports of dead meat were expanding, and that it was government policy to encourage this trade. If the trade developed as seemed possible, supplies of livestock to Britain might be reduced as a consequence. This information was being conveyed to Britain 'as a friendly gesture to help the British Government to plan their policy in regard to meat'. The ambassador was instructed not to refer to the 1948 agreement or the 10 per cent limit on cattle exports to third countries.[129]

In July 1952 the British Ministry of Food proposed that both countries should open informal discussions on re-negotiating the annex to the 1948 agreement, which had expired at the end of June. An undated memorandum from the Department of Agriculture noted that, 'There can be little doubt that one of the main objectives of the Ministry of Food in the proposed discussions would be to secure some agreed limitation on the exports of dressed beef to destinations other than Great Britain'. Agriculture was optimistic that it might be possible to establish the Irish dressed beef trade to Britain on a firmer basis, but other members of the Foreign Trade Committee were concerned that Britain would demand a limit on Irish exports of carcase beef to other countries.

When the talks opened on 25 August Britain immediately indicated that the demand that 90 per cent of Irish beef exports should be channelled to Britain 'was at the heart of the present arrangements', and this quota should apply to processed and to carcase meat. According to the record of the talks prepared by the Department of Agriculture, the Irish representatives stressed that they could give no commitment on this point; they also emphasised the importance of developing the meat-processing industry. During a later session the Irish officials reiterated that 'it would be a very difficult step to pull down the curtain on outside markets'; the proposal to restrict Irish beef exports to third countries could only be presented to the Irish government if Britain offered very definite concessions. Although the Irish officials pressed for a relaxation of the 10 per cent quota, Britain was only prepared to make concessions on exports of meat of low-grade cow and bull meat, and on sales to the US forces.

On 4 September Nagle sent Charlie Murray of the Department of the Taoiseach a copy of a draft annex arising from these talks. This reiterated the 1948 requirement that 75 per cent of Irish cattle exported to Britain should be stores. Britain noted that Ireland wished to develop a meat-processing industry, and it undertook to purchase as much carcase meat as Ireland produced, but no price was mentioned. Ireland agreed to restrict exports of live cattle and carcase meat to third countries to 10 per cent of total exports; 25 per cent of the cattle exported to countries other than Britain would be second-class cattle. No decision was reached on how a reduction in the price differential between cattle raised in Britain and those raised in Ireland would be achieved; if Britain failed to concede a reduction it would make a contribution to the cost of eradicating bovine tuberculosis. Britain agreed to take all Irish lambs and sheep, either live or in the form of meat, at prices equivalent to current prices and to take all exportable eggs, but no price was mentioned.

The first indication that these terms might not be acceptable to all members of the government came when the *Irish Press* reported a statement by Seán Lemass in Bonn that it was the government's aim to come to an agreement whereby Ireland was no longer required to send 90 per cent of its cattle and beef exports to Britain.[130] Lemass noted that the government wished to develop a meat-processing industry. His views were very much in line with the IBEC report, which was available to the government by this time, although it had not yet been published. Shortly after this Lemass informed the Cabinet that he did not approve of the draft annex, and Frank Aiken, Minister for External Affairs, supported his demand that it be amended. When the draft annex was discussed by the Foreign Trade Committee on 18 October 1952, the Department of Industry and Commerce protested that it would restrict the development of trade with countries other than Britain and discourage exports of carcase meat. Industry and Commerce suggested that British and Irish interests were not identical. Britain was aiming at securing the maximum supply of meat from Ireland at the lowest price, and wished to take most of its supplies in the form of stores; Ireland's interests lay in developing alternative markets, and in encouraging meat exports. Industry and Commerce claimed that exports of beef to third countries would not have developed in recent years had this new annex existed, and if it applied in the current year it would mean a reduction in exports equivalent to 22,000 head of cattle. Any restriction would reinforce Ireland's dependence on Britain, and consequently the potential market for Irish livestock would be determined by British requirements. By restricting the ability to earn foreign currencies, it would reinforce Irish dependence on the sterling area pool.[131]

Nagle countered that although the government had been aware that Britain would raise the question of restricting Irish meat exports to third countries, the negotiating team had not been given any direction on the subject. He added that 'a direction had not been sought since'. The Department of Agriculture had entered into the talks 'without express instructions, and of course, without the authority to enter into any commitments'. However, Murray, of the Department of Industry and Commerce, claimed that the Department of Agriculture 'could not but be aware of the attitude of Ministers concerned to the 10 per cent limitation on cattle exports'. Although it had been assumed that these informal talks would not involve any commitment,

> ... based on the record of the talks that was prepared by the Department of Agriculture, it appeared that they did result in commitments of a kind, viz. Firstly, on the first mention by the British of a limitation on meat exports, the reaction on the Irish side did not appear to have been strong enough; secondly, the Department of Agriculture representatives had undertaken to recommend the proposed settlement.

Nagle countered that members of the committee were well aware that it might prove necessary to concede Britain's demand to extend the 10 per cent restriction to cattle as well as meat. The Department's objective was to discover the highest price that Britain would offer in return for this concession. He claimed that Agriculture had succeeded in getting Britain to agree tentatively to 'very valuable concessions in return for the proposed limitation'. He suggested that the 10 per cent figure 'seemed to be an obsession on all sides. The British were perhaps committed to it as much for appearance's sake and in order to preserve their position vis-à-vis other food-supplying countries as for any intrinsic value it might have for them'.

The departments of Agriculture and Industry and Commerce also disagreed about the potential export market for Irish meat. Agriculture claimed that exports of high-quality frozen meat to the US had practically ceased, and it would be difficult to develop an export trade to the US in chilled meat because of a shortage of suitable shipping. It also believed that the volume of beef and livestock exports to non-British markets during 1951/2 was exceptional. In its view the value of the concessions that Britain had offered clearly outweighed 'the largely theoretical restriction which would represent the status quo'. It was also confident that the concessions would encourage an expansion in the beef-processing industry. Industry and Commerce feared that Britain would use any new agreement to discriminate in favour of live cattle and against exports of meat.[132] F. H. Boland, the Irish ambassador in London, cautioned that unless Ireland could achieve a special arrangement with Britain, the live cattle trade would undermine efforts to develop an export trade in meat. 'So we are left with the position that the market which on demand, currency, import policy and other grounds seems to offer the most stable prospects, is virtually closed against our dead meat industry by the price factor'. According to Boland, 'that the concessions we are asked to make are disadvantageous from our point of view goes without saying'. In his opinion the real issue was whether they were too heavy a price to pay for the guarantee of stability for Ireland's meat trade. Boland mentioned that Australia had insisted on the right to sell a large quantity of butter in markets other than Britain, only to see the other markets collapse.[133]

Lemass continued his public campaign against any restrictions on Irish livestock and meat exports. Speaking in Athlone he noted that,

> Our main prospect of developing manufacturing processes which could be maintained from raw materials depended on agriculture. ... Heretofore Irish agricultural production had in the main been directed to the supply of products, for export in the lowest form, involving the least possible degree of processing in this country. The long-term aim of policy must be to change all that.[134]

Dillon told his constituents in County Monaghan that Lemass 'has pushed the Minister for Agriculture to one side'. He claimed that Lemass was negotiating a reduction in the price that Britain paid for Irish livestock in return for a subsidy on exports of carcase meat. If Lemass prevailed, Dillon warned that the price of cattle would fall by £5 to £6 a head. Walsh was forced to refute these allegations on several occasions.[135]

When the Cabinet discussed the proposed annex to the 1948 trade agreement on 23 January 1953, it asked the Foreign Trade Committee to draft a note for the British authorities, and this formed the basis of the instructions that the Cabinet gave the Irish ambassador in London on 3 March. The principal objectives of the government were to avoid any restriction on exports of cattle and meat, including the elimination of the existing 10 per cent limit on cattle, and to secure the abolition of price differentials between British and Irish agricultural produce. Boland was instructed to refer to recent policy statements by British ministers, which envisaged fundamental changes in Britain's trade in food and agricultural produce, as justification for further trade discussions. (Boland had recently reported that the British Ministry of Food was determined to de-control the market in beef and cattle as soon as possible.) The British authorities should be informed that the best means of guaranteeing a high Irish output of livestock and meat was to give farmers an assurance that they would receive adequate prices, and the dressed meat trade to countries other than Britain would provide such an assurance. If Britain offered a competitive price for Irish livestock, exporters would send their cattle to Britain. The Cabinet agreed that Boland should not submit any counter-proposals to those raised in August, and he was not to refer to any British contribution towards the cost of eradicating bovine TB in Ireland, or the need for special arrangements to offset the extra cost of marketing dressed meat in Britain.[136] The Department of Agriculture offered somewhat different advice. It recommended that Boland should indicate that 'other proposals in the draft Annex of August 1952 are in general regarded as a not unsatisfactory basis for further discussion', specially the proposals concerning carcase meat.[137]

When Boland informed the British authorities of the Irish change of mind, they replied that it would be necessary to reconsider the concessions that they had offered. Talks reopened in April 1953. Dr Hill, the parliamentary secretary to the British Ministry of Food, who led the British delegation, argued that in view of Britain's policy towards their own producers and trade arrangements with Commonwealth meat-producing countries, a percentage or a fixed quota on Irish exports to third countries was a *sine qua non*; it was also the *quid pro quo* for Britain's agreeing to link Irish livestock and meat prices to those paid to British producers. When the talks ended in deadlock, Britain suggested that existing arrangements should be extended for twelve months, by which time Britain's agricultural policy would be clearer. Although the Irish embassy favoured this arrangement, the Cabinet instructed the ambassador to continue the talks. On 10 April the embassy reported that Britain was demanding a commitment by Ireland to supply 675,000 head of cattle annually, dead or alive. The British would not discuss prices unless there was a possibility of agreement on a numerical limit on Irish cattle and beef exports to third countries. Britain again intimated that it would prefer to postpone talks for a further twelve months. On 11 April the Cabinet decided to accept a quota on Irish livestock exports to third countries, provided that the remaining terms agreed in August 1952 were honoured.

On 1 May Maurice Moynihan, the secretary to the government,

mandated the Department of Agriculture to reach agreement on the basis of the revised annex that it had presented to government on 20 November 1952. This involved Ireland agreeing to restrict exports of livestock and beef to markets other than Britain to 10 per cent of the total. In return Britain would reduce the price differential between British and Irish cattle to 4s 6d per live cwt, compared with the present 5s, and would pay up to £150,000 per annum to compensate the Irish authorities for the additional sum needed to make exports of carcase beef competitive with fat-stock exports. The agreement would operate for three years, with a review after $2\frac{1}{2}$ years. Ireland would be given prior notice of any decision to decontrol a particular product. An accompanying confidential letter stated that the 10 per cent quota would be calculated on the basis of livestock and meat exports during the previous year. Certain exports of beef to the US would be excluded from the calculation.[138] When the Minister for Agriculture, Tom Walsh, informed the Dáil that an agreement had been reached, he emphasised that the restrictions on livestock exports did not apply to cows and bulls or their meat, and he suggested that these categories constituted the most promising market for sales in continental Europe. The *Irish Press* announced that the agreement promised better export prices and an assured market for the dressed meat trade.[139]

Britain published a white paper some months later announcing its intention to de-control the market for livestock, meat, milk and milk products, although farmers in Britain and Northern Ireland were assured that prices for cattle and beef would continue to be guaranteed. Irish officials pressed for guarantees to be extended to Irish produce but the talks adjourned without agreement. When they resumed in late December the British officials announced that while they were obliged to give certain guarantees to British producers under the Agriculture Act of 1947, there was no obligation to extend these to Irish producers. On Cabinet instructions, Walsh sent a note to the British government, suggesting that a continuation of some variant on the existing price arrangements would be beneficial to both economies. The Cabinet decided that Walsh and Lemass should seek a meeting with British ministers. Talks opened in London on 4 March 1954. On 9 March the Department of Agriculture reported that it was unclear how Britain would organise the end of rationing and price controls. Britain gave an undertaking not to introduce quotas on Irish agricultural produce, but refused to extend price guarantees to Irish fat cattle or beef. Further talks brought minor concessions over store sheep and a reduction of the period that Irish stores had to spend in Britain before qualifying for price guarantees, from three to two months.[140] Irish store cattle fattened in Britain would receive a guaranteed payment, but it would be less than the payment on cattle that originated in Britain.[141] In 1955 these arrangements were extended for a further three years, although the qualifying period before Irish cattle could benefit from UK price guarantees was again extended to three months in 1956.[142]

The lifting of controls on the British food market brought little benefit to the Irish livestock and meat trade. When imports were controlled by the Ministry of Food, as was the case until 1954, they were less subject to price fluctuations. During 1955 and 1956 average prices for fat and store cattle were lower than in any year since 1952. In 1956, although the volume of cattle exported to Britain rose by 9 per cent, compared with 1955, the value increased by less than one per cent. Stores accounted for more than three-quarters of live cattle shipped to Britain in every year except 1956, when they fell to 72 per cent.[143] In December 1957 Nagle noted that,

> With the termination of bulk purchase we fell back drastically from this position [where the prices paid for Irish produce were linked to the prices paid to British producers] and matters were made worse by the fact that at this stage the effect of British domestic policy began to be felt. We did not expect to be able to dictate to Britain about her agricultural policy but the solid fact was that it had serious results for us and among other things affected our ability to purchase industrial goods from abroad.

Nagle believed that the balance of the 1948 agreement had now 'tilted towards London'.[144] It might be argued that this had always been the case. Irish meat exports to the UK increased from 1952 until 1954, but they fell sharply with the ending of bulk purchase arrangements. In 1956 Britain bought less fresh, chilled and frozen beef and veal from Ireland than in 1952, and sales declined further in 1957. By 1958 there were 56 licensed beef and mutton exporters, but seven exporters accounted for over 90 per cent of the trade. The decline in meat exports to the UK resulted in considerable over-capacity in the industry, and several meat-canning plants had ceased production.[145]

The development of an export trade for beef and fat cattle was handicapped by the strong market for Irish stores in Britain and by the fact that they were eligible for British price guarantees, whereas fat cattle and beef had no such advantage. This resulted in a shortage of fat cattle for

TABLE 8: Meat Exports, 1952–8[146]

		Fresh/Chilled and Frozen			Tinned
Year	UK	USA (000 cwt)	Other	Total Value (£000)	Value (£000)
1952	286	122	94	5,091	3,927
1953	445	47	35	5,157	2,509
1954	740	22	103	9,490	2,444
1955	244	19	74	3,753	3,092
1956	146	26	144	3,545	2,674
1957	50	75	357	5,952	2,172
1958	57	274	193	7,263	2,208

TABLE 9: Exports of Fat Cattle and Store Cattle, 1952–8

	Fat			Stores	
Year	UK (thousand head)	Eur (thousand head)	Value (£000)	UK (thousand head)	Value (£000)
1952	81	33	6,972	354	17,000
1953	31	28	3,106	397	21,543
1954	109	15	7,632	485	25,843
1955	128	9	9,260	471	26,424
1956	112	68	10,963	488	25,095
1957	48	29	4,779	746	40,616
1958	37	15	3,546	595	34,607

processing and export. Although store sheep also qualified for UK price guarantees, exports of lambs and sheep for slaughter and exports of mutton and lamb were not distorted to the same extent. By 1958 exports of mutton and lamb were valued at £1.8 million, compared with £1.2 million for exports of sheep and lambs.

The trade negotiations relating to cattle and beef indicate that the Department of Agriculture was unwilling to do anything that might jeopardise the British market, or the possibility of securing a link between Irish and British prices. However, Nagle's comment in 1956 that the 1948 agreement had 'tilted towards London' suggests a belated awareness that

Britain had manipulated the Irish livestock market to serve its own interests. In 1922 the economist Joseph Johnston had proposed a levy on livestock exports to encourage the meat-processing trade, and the Department of Finance made a similar recommendation in 1944. In 1952 Johnston, now a senator representing Dublin University, suggested that all cattle exported should be subject to a levy of £5 or £10 a head, to encourage the development of a dead-meat trade. However, the Minister for Finance, Seán MacEntee, dismissed the proposal as 'foolhardiness', and de Valera denied that a levy was under consideration. Any attempt to impose a levy on livestock exports would have led to protests from farmers and livestock exporters, and it would have presented the opposition with an attractive political issue. In 1954 Oliver Flanagan, the parliamentary secretary to the Minster for Agriculture in the second inter-party government, claimed that Fianna Fáil had planned to impose such a levy when it was in government from 1951 to 1954. Tom Walsh, the former Minister for Agriculture, challenged Flanagan to provide evidence that this was so. James Dillon, the Minister for Agriculture, sided with Flanagan in this exchange. Flanagan continued to repeat this allegation in speeches widely reported by provincial newspapers, but in November 1954 officials in the Department of the Taoiseach confirmed to John A. Costello that no such proposal had been brought to Cabinet since 1944. Although Costello informed the Dáil of this, Dillon and Flanagan continued to repeat the allegations.[147]

DAIRYING

Dairy farming was regarded as the cornerstone of Irish agriculture, since it underpinned the livestock sector, with the skim milk that was a by-product of butter manufacture being used to feed calves and pigs. It was a more intensive enterprise than drystock farming; it provided a better conversion rate for food; and it was seen as offering a good living and adequate employment on small farms.[148] Although butter was one of Ireland's traditional exports, the market collapsed during the 1930s and it failed to revive following the end of the Economic War, and the decline had continued during the Emergency. However, Irish butter consumption had increased and the Department was conscious that Irish creameries could not meet demand if rationing ended. Although the Department had been advocating winter dairying since the days of Horace Plunkett, the output of milk and butter remained very seasonal.

In an attempt to reverse the decline in milk output, in 1946 the government announced that milk prices would be guaranteed for the next five years. This does not seem to have had any immediate impact, since the output of milk and the number of cows continued to decline, although this was probably due to the appalling weather conditions and to the loss in soil fertility. With milk prices now determined by the government, dairy farmers were becoming an increasingly vocal lobby. In January 1947 M. Gleeson, the chief agricultural officer in County Limerick, forwarded a resolution from the county committee of agriculture calling for a 50 per cent increase in the price of milk if dairy farming was to be preserved 'from extinction'. The Department recommended that the price paid to producers should be increased by over 40 per cent during the peak milk-producing months and it suggested that this could be financed by raising the price of butter and of liquid milk. The government agreed to raise the price of winter milk by one-third, and milk produced during peak months by one-quarter, with the cost being shared by the exchequer and the consumer. The Cabinet conceded this price increase because of a threatened shortage of butter. On 30 June 1947 the Department of Industry and Commerce, which was opposed to the increase, noted that current butter production was not sufficient to supply the 6-ounce weekly butter ration, and it recommended that exports of dairy produce be curtailed. However, the Department of Agriculture was unwilling to sacrifice promising export markets and suggested that butter should be imported to meet any shortfall; the Cabinet agreed to this.[149] The 1947 price increase appears to have been effective, because there was a rise in the number of milch cows and heifers in calf. By 31 March 1948 butter stocks were satisfactory and Agriculture recommended an end to restrictions on the export of cream.

During James Dillon's first term as Minister for Agriculture, Emergency controls on dairying, such as the restrictions on the sale and distribution of farmers' butter, were removed. But Dillon consistently opposed demands for higher milk prices, despite persistent lobbying by farmers. In 1949 he told Dáil Éireann that the main obstacle to greater prosperity was the low yield from dairy cattle, not the price of milk. His refusal to raise milk prices seems to have been justified, because by 1949 supplies of butter had risen to the point where there was a surplus available for export and the Cabinet approved the export of 500 tons of butter to France; the French exporter had wanted 5,000 tons. Under the 1948 trade agreement Britain agreed to import up to 20,000 tons of Irish butter annually, at a similar price to Danish butter, but the price on offer from France was substantially higher.[150]

In 1949 the butter ration was increased to 8 ounces a week and rationing was only retained in order to prevent subsidised butter being smuggled to Northern Ireland. Many households no longer claimed their full ration. By this point the Department believed that long-term export prospects for butter were poor, and suggested that the producer price for milk should be reduced, although the new price should be guaranteed for five years. It also recommended an end to butter rationing, controls on the retail price of liquid milk and the retail subsidy on butter. While the retail price of butter would undoubtedly rise, these measures would save the exchequer £2 million per annum. The recommendations were opposed by the departments of Industry and Commerce and Social Welfare, because they would result in higher inflation, and demands for increased social welfare payments. Although the matter first came before the Cabinet in November 1949, the government repeatedly postponed making a decision. In February 1950 it referred the matter to the Cabinet committee examining the draft estimates for 1950.[151] The indecision reflected differences of opinion between ministers, and between the political parties that comprised the inter-party government. The extensive lobbying being carried on by the creameries and dairy farmers was also a factor. On 18 March 1950 Dillon and Costello promised a deputation of TDs and senators that the price of milk would not be reduced without first securing the agreement of the creameries. But two days later the *Irish Independent* outlined proposals by Dillon for a five-year plan for the dairy industry that included a phased reduction in milk prices, and a modest increase in the retail price of butter. Dillon emphasised that the existing level of subsidies could not be continued indefinitely; 'sooner or later output must be reduced or production must be made economic'. His proposal was obviously regarded as politically unacceptable. Although the Department of Finance supported the idea, it suggested that it would be difficult to implement, and the proposal disappeared from the Cabinet agenda.

By 1950 a new organisation, the Irish Creamery Milk Suppliers' Association (ICMSA), was challenging the traditional role of the IAOS as the representative voice of the dairy sector. On 27 November 1950 the secretary of the ICMSA, Liam Barry, demanded a meeting with Costello to discuss the price of milk in the coming year. Dillon replied, refusing to meet the ICMSA, because he was determined that all consultation would continue to take place through the IAOS.[152] On 2 March 1951 Barry wrote to each TD, asking them to support a resolution passed by the council of the ICMSA demanding an independent tribunal to determine the price of milk. He claimed that this would only give milk suppliers the same treatment as every other section of the community. The co-operatives joined in the campaign; TDs representing dairy farming areas came under particularly strong pressure. By then the Cabinet had agreed to concede an increase of 1d a gallon in the producer price of milk, although this had not yet been announced; this price would apply until March 1956.[153] The announcement of an additional penny a gallon for milk triggered the collapse of the inter-party government. Two TDs resigned from Clann na Talmhan, protesting that the price increase was not adequate, and independent TDs withdrew their support. Costello dissolved the Dáil on 8 May, knowing that the alternative was a defeat on the agricultural estimate.[154] Discontented dairy farmers featured prominently in the 1951 general election campaign. Dillon described the ICMSA as 'a Fianna Fáil Rump'.

When Fianna Fáil returned to government it increased the price of milk by another 1d a gallon.[155] This concession evoked little gratitude from the ICMSA, who continued to lobby for a higher price. In September 1951 the ICMSA published an open letter to the Minister, with the title *Why the Present Price of Milk is Insufficient*.[156] In a memorandum to government, the Department of Agriculture accused the ICMSA of 'endeavouring to usurp the functions of the Irish Agricultural Organisation Society' and of adopting 'a most dictatorial attitude on the question of milk prices with a view, it is believed to forcing the Government to increase existing prices'. Walsh recommended establishing a committee to investigate the cost of producing milk, under the chairmanship of Professor Michael Murphy of the Faculty of Dairy Science at UCC, who was 'a widely respected authority in this area'.[157] This proposal had the advantage of having originated with the ICMSA. Fianna Fáil was much more favourable to fixing prices for agricultural produce than Dillon had been.[158] Walsh suggested that representatives of consumers and producers should consult with Murphy from time to time. The list of representative organisations included the Dublin and Cork District milk boards, Muintir na Tíre and Macra na Feirme, but not the ICMSA. It appears that the decision to exclude the ICMSA was controversial, because on 20 December, the Department of Agriculture submitted a memorandum to Cabinet on this topic. It suggested that representatives of milk suppliers should be nominated at regional meetings organised by the IAOS. If some of these representatives happened to be members of the ICMSA, the Minister would have no problems with their appointment. However, he was unwilling to give official recognition to the ICMSA because he regarded its attitude as dictatorial, and he was uneasy about its encouragement of extreme measures. Nevertheless, Agriculture conceded that the government might consider it prudent to have the ICMSA represented on the consultative body.

On 4 January 1952 the government decided to establish a five-man tribunal that would work under the direction of Professor Murphy, although he would not be a member of the tribunal. There would be no consultative committee. Agriculture countered with a proposal that the inquiry team should consist of Professor Murphy; two officials from the Department; two representatives of milk suppliers; and one representative each from the Dublin and Cork District milk boards. Walsh insisted that the creameries and the milk boards should select their own representatives; otherwise he feared that farmers would be prejudiced against the inquiry. As a former member of the Irish Beet Growers' Association, Walsh would have been sensitive to the need for farming organisations to be represented. Walsh's views eventually prevailed.

When the government announced the establishment of the milk costings commission in February 1952, 174 branches of the ICMSA sent telegrams to de Valera demanding that the ICMSA be represented.[159] Because of lack of co-operation from farming organisations, the commission did not begin its work until the autumn of 1952. The need to collect data for an entire year meant that a report was not expected until 1954.[160]

When the appointment of a milk costings commission was first considered, dairy subsidies were costing the exchequer in excess of £2 million per annum, and this was set to rise. However, the economic crisis in the spring of 1952, which was caused by a sharp deterioration in the balance of payments owing to the Korean War and the ending of Marshall Aid, resulted in the exchequer subsidy on butter being withdrawn at a saving of £2.3 million.[161] In 1950 Ireland had exported over 61,000 cwt of butter, but in 1951 exports fell to 4,510 cwt, and the Department had to import over 100,000 cwt of butter from Denmark and New Zealand.[162] When the butter subsidy was removed the retail price rose from 3s to 3s 10d per pound, without a significant fall in consumption.[163] Butter consumption in 1952 was 73 per cent greater than in 1938[164] and imports totalled 110,000 cwt or 15 per cent of domestic output. Irish families complained that Danish butter tasted sour.[165] Most of the imported butter was sold in Dublin and Bray.

In January 1953 the Department had to buy 1,000 tons of New Zealand butter from the British Ministry of Food. The cost of imported butter in 1953 amounted to £1.8 million and imports of dried and powdered milk cost an additional £859,000. Dairy exports were valued at £2.1 million, which meant that Ireland was a net importer of dairy produce at a cost of £559,000. Ireland could have been self-sufficient if milk had been used to manufacture butter rather than chocolate crumb and condensed milk for export, or if restrictions had been placed on the use of butter by manufacturers of cakes and confectionery. In October 1952 Fry Cadbury sought an additional 350,000 gallons of milk for the manufacture of chocolate crumb. If this request was granted, the Department of Agriculture believed it would lead to similar demands from other manufacturers. However, the Cabinet decided not to restrict the use of milk and butter for manufacturing.

With a shortage of butter in prospect during the winter of 1952, the Department of Agriculture suggested that milk producers should be offered a price increase. The numbers of calves and milch cows had fallen during the past two years, and the Department claimed that higher milk prices were essential if livestock and meat exports were to continue at current levels. Low milk prices also perpetuated low milk yields, because farmers had no incentive to feed cows adequately during the winter. Winter feeding would encourage more tillage.[166] In mid-January 1953 Liam Barry of the ICMSA reminded de Valera and the Minister for Agriculture, that the Tánaiste, Seán Lemass, had promised an announcement about the price of milk would be made in early January. As this promise had not been honoured, the ICMSA was withdrawing milk supplies. Farmers supplying liquid milk to Dublin also declared a strike.

The strike began on 21 January 1953 and continued until mid-February. The government refused to concede higher milk prices while it continued. Walsh insisted that prices should be based on the findings of the milk costings commission. He also noted that there would be serious problems if higher prices resulted in a substantial milk surplus. The future market in Britain for chocolate crumb and other milk products was uncertain because British milk output was rising sharply, while consumption had reached a plateau. The Department of Agriculture anticipated that Britain would have a milk surplus within a short time. Although the price of butter was considerably higher in France and Germany, Irish butter was excluded by trade restrictions. Walsh noted that 'from an economic point of view the problems of the dairying industry cannot, in the long run, be solved merely by continual increases in price'. It was essential to raise yields by a combination of 'better feeding and better breeding'. Some form of price control should continue; if the market was fully de-controlled and imports were permitted, the price of butter would fall to the British level.[167] When the strike ended the Department of Agriculture recommended that the price of butter should be increased, which would enable creameries to pay a higher price for milk. A draft press notice suggested that the government was considering a plebiscite of milk producers on the merits of de-controlling milk and butter prices, but this did not happen and the price controls remained in place.

The decision to end the exchequer subsidy on dairy produce in the 1952 budget became a major issue in the 1954 general election. John A. Costello promised that the coalition government would reduce the cost of living if elected.[168] On 14 June, shortly after the formation of the second inter-party government, the Cabinet reintroduced a butter subsidy. The proposal originated from the Department of Agriculture; it was a response to the growing butter surplus. Between September 1954 and January 1955, 60,000 cwt of butter were exported at a cost of over £222,000 in subsidies. The surplus was rising because the market for chocolate crumb was declining. In 1957 Fianna Fáil terminated the exchequer subsidies on butter and bread, saving the exchequer £9 million, and removed controls on wholesale butter prices.[169] As a consequence the retail price rose by 15 per cent and consumption fell by 28 per cent, at a time when milk output was rising. At the beginning of 1957 export subsidies for butter were costing approximately £400,000 per annum; with the decline in domestic consumption this was expected to rise to almost £3 million.[170] It appeared that the government was left with two unpalatable and expensive options: subsidising butter consumption at home, or subsidising exports.

The report of the milk costings commission was not completed until 1958. Professor Murphy resigned in March 1953, allegedly because of ill-health; his role as technical expert was assumed by J. L. Brophy, an inspector in the Department of Agriculture. We can only speculate as to the causes of the further delays, but disagreements between farmers and other members of the commission seem the most likely explanation. In 1956 one member of the commission, Liam Barry of the ICMSA, condemned the report as 'fantastic and a departmental fabrication'. He alleged that it was a 'purely departmentally prepared document'; the Department of Agriculture had made up its mind not to reveal the true findings of the investigation. On 13 October 1956 The Irish Farmers' Journal reported that the report had been strongly criticised by the assistant director of the CSO, M. D. McCarthy, for failing to adhere to the terms of reference. Four days after this statement appeared, the director of the CSO, Roy Geary, informed Maurice Moynihan that McCarthy would resign from the commission if the confidentiality of meetings was not maintained. In December 1957

Smiddy tendered his resignation, having submitted a report, which was dated August 1956.

Although the report of the milk costings commission was never published, some of the data trickled into the newspapers. The statistics collected during the 1952/3 season revealed that the cost of producing a gallon of milk ranged from 4½d to 2s 9¾d for milk delivered to creameries and from 1s 4¼d to 2s 8¾d a gallon for milk for liquid consumption.[171] By 1957 these statistics were of merely historic interest. Moreover, the wide variation in the cost of production made it impossible to agree on an average figure that could be used as the basis for determining milk prices.[172] Irish milk yields remained low by international standards; indeed, the 1951 average of 408 gallons per milch cow was below the 1926/7 figure of 416. This compared with average yields in excess of 800 gallons in the Netherlands and 740 gallons in Denmark.

LIVESTOCK BREEDING POLICIES AND VETERINARY HEALTH

By 1958 the number of cattle had increased to almost 4.5 million, which was the highest figure recorded in the history of the state. Most of the increase occurred in the category 'other cattle', which meant beef cattle; the number of milch cows, 1.26 million, was almost identical to the 1914 figure. The greatest advance in breeding policy and practice was the introduction of artificial insemination (AI).

The first AI station opened at Ballyclough Co-operative in Mallow, County Cork, in 1946, and according to Patrick Smith, the Department of Agriculture 'had their own doubts and misgivings' about this development.[173] In 1946 a committee in the Department had recommended that AI should be regulated in the interests of the livestock industry to prevent indiscriminate exploitation of breeding.[174] An Act passed in 1947, which came into effect in February 1948, gave the minister power to license and inspect insemination stations and to control import and export of semen by licence. A second AI station opened at Mitchelstown Creamery in 1948. In 1950 the Department established a national headquarters for AI at Grange, County Meath, and by 1956 there were nine stations scattered throughout the country. The licensing system introduced by the Department meant that small stations did not proliferate in Ireland, as happened in the Netherlands.[175]

One of the most hotly-debated topics concerning livestock breeding was the dominance of the dairy Shorthorn, or the dual-purpose cow. The ICMSA blamed low milk yields on the Department's livestock breeding policy, which aimed at producing animals suitable for both dairy farming and beef. In a memorandum presented to de Valera in 1953, the ICMSA quoted a statement by Professor J. J. Lyons that the demands of the livestock trade were dominant, and the breeding needs of dairying had suffered as a consequence. The ICMSA noted that in 1947 the Minister for Agriculture, Patrick Smith, had stated that there was no such thing as a dual-purpose cow, but the current Minister, Walsh, did not agree.[176] In 1952 the IBEC report condemned the policy of the dual-purpose cow as fatal for dairy production. Both Walsh and Dillon defended the policy of relying on dairy Shorthorns as the dominant breed. Dillon referred disparagingly to dairy breeds such as Friesian and Guernsey cattle as 'the Pekinese'; he claimed that, unlike the Shorthorns, they were too delicate to withstand the rigours of life on an Irish farm.[177]

In November 1952, shortly after the publication of the IBEC report, the Cabinet requested the Department of Agriculture to draft proposals for the establishment of a committee to examine current livestock policy. In February 1953 the Minister for Education, Seán Moylan, presented the Cabinet with a memorandum on agricultural policy, which opened with a statement that, 'For some considerable time past dairying has been decadent, while for some decades the entire agricultural industry has been static'. Moylan claimed that the dairy industry was 'of the utmost importance': a unit of food used to produce milk gave a much higher return than the same unit used to produce beef. He recommended that the dairy industry should be developed so that it could compete on the export market, although that would involve 'reforms of quite a revolutionary nature'. He believed that the breeding policy pursued in the past had been fatal. When farmers discovered that their milk yields were declining, they lost faith in the advice they were being given, and Moylan believed that this accounted for the lack of interest in cow testing. In 1950 there were 193 cow-testing associations, with 4,776 members, and almost 60,000 cows were tested, which was approximately 5 per cent of the national herd. By 1957 the number of cow-testing associations had fallen to 144 and fewer than 45,000 cows were tested. Moylan presented a detailed memorandum on the merits of dairy breeds such as Jersey and Friesian cattle, together with projections for future growth in the number of cows. He recommended that measures should be introduced to improve winter feeding for cows and better housing for animals, and that farmers should be encouraged to develop suckling herds.[178]

There is no indication that Walsh responded to this report. However, at a meeting of the Dairy Consultative Council in February 1953, one member, Owen Binchy, asked, 'are we acting foolishly in clinging blindly to our so called dual purpose cow?' He noted that Patrick Smith was the only Minister for Agriculture who had not supported this policy, despite the fact that every other dairying country had 'long ago abandoned the idea of getting milk and beef under the same hide'. Binchy pointed out that milk yields were not taken into account in deciding which bulls should be licensed, though a recommendation that this should be done had been made in an interim report of the Committee on Post-Emergency Agricultural Policy in 1944. Walsh defended the dual-purpose cow at this meeting. He noted that the Livestock Consultative Council, which appears to have been dominated by beef interests, favoured dairy Shorthorns, but de Valera, who also attended the meeting, was much more open to the merits of Friesian and Jersey cattle.[179] When the Department had not yet responded to the Cabinet's request of November 1952 to submit proposals for the establishment of a committee to review breeding policy, Maurice Moynihan issued a reminder. Walsh's private secretary replied that when the Minister discussed the matter with the Livestock Consultative Council, he discovered that they were 'far from unanimous in their views', and he wanted to meet the council again before acting. Given Walsh's views on the matter, this may well have been a delaying tactic, and he failed to report back to Cabinet before the end of the Fianna Fáil government's term of office.[180]

In August 1954 Moynihan again asked the Department of Agriculture to present Cabinet with proposals for a review of livestock breeding policy. By then James Dillon was the Minister for Agriculture and he also favoured the dairy Shorthorn. On this occasion, Seán Ó Broin reported that further meetings with the Livestock Consultative Council, which he described as a 'very representative statutory body', had revealed a marked difference of opinion between those who wanted to concentrate on improving the quality of Shorthorns (the dual-purpose animal) and those who wished to promote dairy breeds. Breeding policy in respect of cattle, sheep and pigs had been 'exhaustively discussed at very representative meetings attended by all the interests concerned,' and the Minister could see no point in setting up another committee because the same divisions of opinion would re-emerge. He added that 'the Minister considers that the livestock policy he is pursuing is best suited to the country's needs'.[181]

The existing breeding policy was continued until the end of the 1950s, with minor modifications. In 1951 the Department's AI stations only supplied semen from Shorthorns and Kerry cattle. By 1956 Friesian, Aberdeen Angus and Hereford semen was provided at all stations except Clarecastle, County Mayo, giving farmers a much greater choice. Dairy Shorthorns were imported from England in an attempt to improve the milking capacity,[182] but veterinary regulations made it impossible to import animals from continental Europe. Milk yield rose substantially during the 1950s, from an average of 408 gallons in 1951 to 497 gallons by 1957, which was marginally higher than the average of 493 gallons recorded in 1966.[183]

During the second inter-party government Dillon set farmers the target of raising the cow and heifer population to 2 million, an objective that depended on increasing the carrying capacity of grassland.[184] In 1959 the report on livestock and meat by the Advisory Committee on the Marketing of Agricultural Produce concluded that 'the output of cattle is basically dependent on the number of milch cows'. The committee expressed the hope that at some future date new breeding techniques would enable a given cow to produce a greater number of calves. For the present, however, a higher output of cattle could only be achieved by increasing the number of milch cows. This would result in an increased output of milk, which would mean more dairy produce exported at a loss. While the decision to persist with the 'dual-purpose cow' was obviously open to criticism, because it did not maximise milk yields, the market prospects for dairy produce were so unfavourable that giving preference to beef-breeding quality may have been the correct decision. However, high-yielding dairy herds would have reduced the cost of producing milk, and this might have made it possible to export dairy produce without subsidies. The Department was frequently condemned for failing to consult agricultural interests. Yet the Livestock Consultative Council was reluctant to consider any major changes in breeding policy; no doubt because many of the members were specialists in existing breeds. In 1960 the committee expressed strong opposition to plans to import Charollais cattle, presumably for similar reasons.[185]

Some advances were made in veterinary health in the years immediately after the war, although the main thrust of the Department's campaign for the eradication of bovine tuberculosis did not take place until the end of the 1950s. In 1949, in agreement with the Veterinary Medical Association of Ireland, a scheme was introduced to have cows and heifers vaccinated against contagious abortion. In 1953 Erskine Childers, the Minister for Lands, claimed that 'if drastic veterinary measures were taken, the total cost of which would be by comparison quite negligible, an additional 250,000 calves could reach maturity'.[186] The Department estimated that diseases were causing annual losses running into millions of pounds. White scour was a major killer of calves. Up to 100,000 calves were lost every year owing to infertility, abortion and stillbirths; infectious disease was a major cause of infertility. There was an urgent need to encourage farmers to vaccinate their herds against contagious abortion, but the Department claimed that 'really satisfactory progress cannot be generally made until the veterinary staff of the Department of Agriculture is strengthened'.[187] This did not happen because of opposition from veterinarians in private practice.

By the mid-1950s antibiotics were beginning to play an important role in animal health, but many farmers continued to buy useless remedies. Although the report on veterinary services compiled by the Committee on Post-Emergency Agricultural Policy recommended that all manufacturers, importers and vendors of animal remedies should be licensed, and that the Minister should have power to control the advertising of animal remedies and to require manufacturers to list the ingredients, these recommendations were not implemented until 1954.[188]

Little progress was made in eradicating liverfluke and warble fly until the 1960s. Up to 80 per cent of fat cattle exported to Germany in the mid-1950s had diseased livers owing to fluke infestation, which was estimated to cost the livestock industry £1.5 million every year. Warble flies could result in cattle losing up to $\frac{1}{2}$ cwt in weight and a loss of two gallons of milk per week in the case of cows; they also caused considerable damage to hides. The failure to de-horn cattle resulted in livestock being injured and damaged, particularly when they were being transported. Although the Department tried to educate farmers about the benefits of preventing disease, the majority remained indifferent to the message, perhaps because they could see no personal benefit, or because of lack of education.

EGGS AND POULTRY

When the 1948 Anglo-Irish Trade Agreement was signed there were expectations of a substantial increase in exports of eggs and bacon, but this did not materialise. Ireland exported eggs to Britain throughout the war, often in the teeth of opposition from the Department of Supplies, because the Department of Agriculture had anticipated that there would be an expanding market when the war ended. An interim report from the Committee on Post-Emergency Agricultural Policy noted that a substantially higher output of eggs would be needed to supply the Irish market and the almost unlimited demand that was anticipated in Britain after the war. It recommended that the Department encourage the establishment of hatcheries to distribute day-old chicks, and that additional places should be provided to educate women in poultry-keeping at the Munster Institute and other agricultural schools and colleges. During the late 1940s the Department made significant efforts to improve the quality of poultry by introducing new strains and stamping out disease. The Poultry Hatcheries Act of 1947 required that all hatcheries should be licensed.

Under an agreement reached in November 1947 the British Ministry of Food had agreed to pay an additional 5s per great hundred (120) eggs, or 20 per cent more than the former price. The Department of Agriculture hoped that this would encourage an expansion in output. In January 1948, before Fianna Fáil left office, plans were in place to establish 100 commercial hatcheries, with ten farms supplying eggs to every hatchery. Sales of day-old chicks would be subsidised and grants would be provided for the purchase of heaters and other equipment. It was estimated that this three-year development plan would cost £1.35 million.[189] The first inter-party government implemented it, adding special incentives for poultry-keeping in Gaeltacht areas.

The post-war egg and poultry trade became strongly identified with James Dillon. When he arrived in London for trade talks in June 1948 he informed reporters that, 'We will drown you in eggs within the next two years'.[190] On Christmas Eve 1949 *The Irish Times* reported that in the Gaiety pantomime, Jimmy O'Dea appeared as 'one of our national assets – the hen that produces Mr Dillon's export eggs'. The Irish-language pantomime at the Abbey Theatre depicted Dillon as a hen-like creature, who cackled and flapped his wings.[191]

But when Dillon visited London in February 1949, in an unsuccessful attempt to negotiate a long-term agreement giving Irish egg producers access to British guaranteed prices, the British authorities complained that Irish supplies were highly cyclical; they were especially interested in getting eggs during the winter. John Strachey, the Minister for Food, also expressed the hope that the Department of Agriculture would not concentrate unduly on eggs; Britain was more interested in procuring bacon. The price offered to British egg producers was so attractive that the output had risen considerably, and British farmers preferred to produce eggs and poultry rather than pigs.

The 1949 talks resulted in a reduction in the export price paid for eggs by one-sixth, but the price was guaranteed until 31 January 1951.[192] Poultry numbers rose sharply in 1949 and again in 1950. In 1950, the peak year, exports of eggs were valued at £5 million. By 1951 poultry numbers had fallen by 16 per cent and egg exports by 50 per cent, because British prices were no longer attractive. Under the 1949 agreement the price paid for eggs fell by a further 10 per cent from 31 January 1951, but in May 1951, faced with falling supplies from Ireland, the British Ministry of Food restored the price to its previous level and gave a commitment to increase prices in September 1952. The Department of Agriculture replied that the cost of producing eggs had risen and the prices on offer were too low, but the Ministry of Food claimed that it could buy large quantities of eggs from Denmark, Holland and Australia at lower prices.

Although the market for eggs was decontrolled in March 1953, the Ministry of Food remained the sole importer. Ireland reluctantly agreed to sell its eggs through NEDAL, the distribution agency of the Ministry of Food. Consequently, all exports continued to be channelled through Eggsports, the agency that had been established during the war. By the summer of 1953 British egg prices were below the prices that Eggsports paid producers, which meant that exports were being subsidised. Walsh argued that Irish exporters should negotiate their own deals in Britain, and it was decided that Eggsports should be wound up. Representatives of the industry attempted without success to establish a company to market egg and poultry exports on a voluntary basis.[193]

In Britain the production of eggs and poultry was transformed during the early 1950s from small-scale farmyard enterprises into large intensive units. Economies of scale brought a sharp fall in prices. By the mid-1950s Britain was self-sufficient in eggs, and a limited export trade had developed. In Ireland eggs continued to be produced by farmers' wives in free-range conditions, but at the time there was no strong consumer preference in Britain for free-range eggs. The output of eggs continued to fall from 1950. By 1957 it was 20 per cent lower than in 1938/9, and the quantity exported was less than one-tenth of the 1938/9 level. The domestic market accounted for 97 per cent of total output. Egg production remained highly seasonal; 80 per cent were produced between February and July, and this added to the difficulties in establishing an export trade.[194] Exports of poultry were negligible.

PIGS AND PIGMEAT

By the end of the war the number of pigs had fallen to 40 per cent of the pre-war figure and the 1939 level was not regained until 1954, and then only briefly. The 1931 figure was not exceeded until 1961. During the 1948 trade talks Britain indicated that it was willing to import at least the 1939 volume of bacon from Ireland and perhaps more. On the strength of this commitment and the prospect of improved supplies of animal feed, pig numbers rose from 457,000 in 1948 to 675,000 in 1949. Exports of bacon to Britain resumed in 1949 but Irish producers did not regard the prices offered by the Ministry of Food as profitable, although they were similar to those offered for Danish bacon. As a consequence pig numbers fell and exports ceased in the middle of 1950.

In March 1951 Britain agreed to supply Ireland with 100,000 tons of coal in return for eggs and pigmeat, but the agreement was not concluded.[195] However, the 1951 negotiations resulted in a new export market for live pigs at prices closely linked to the prices paid to producers in Britain and Northern Ireland. In a variant of the 1948 agreement on livestock, Ireland agreed to give Britain 90 per cent of total exports of pigs and pigmeat. Again, the price that Britain offered for live pigs was substantially more attractive than the price for pigmeat and bacon. The Department of Agriculture claimed that 'this arrangement offered a hope of getting an average price which would be economic for Irish pig producers'. In order to ensure that producers would get the same price, irrespective of whether pigs were exported live or as bacon, the Department wanted to impose a levy on every pig exported live, but the Cabinet disagreed. It decided that all exports of bacon and live pigs would be handled by the Pigs and Bacon Commission, which would average out the price.

By 1952/3 pig numbers had risen to the point where there was a substantial export to Britain. In 1954 the general principles behind the 1951 agreement were extended until 1956.[196] The trade in pork was decontrolled in 1954, and that in bacon in 1956. In January 1956 the Department of Agriculture indicated that Britain was not prepared to extend the 1954 agreement, but was prepared to purchase pigs and bacon from Ireland on similar terms to those already agreed with Denmark. Alternatively, Irish pigs and bacon could be sold on the open market, the option favoured by the Department, and this is what transpired.

Although James Dillon had removed the wartime controls over the allocation and price of pigs in 1949, price-fixing was reintroduced, so that in 1956 the Pigs and Bacon Commission fixed the price for every grade of pig. The Department of Agriculture argued that this practice should continue, even though Irish pigs and bacon exports would now be sold on the open market, as otherwise pig numbers would decline. The Cabinet approved this recommendation, and determined that the cost would be met partly by a levy on producers and curers, and partly by the exchequer.[197] For the financial year 1957/8 the export subsidy cost almost £1.3 million, or 30 per cent of the value of exports of bacon, ham and pork.[198]

Throughout the 1950s the volume of bacon and ham exported remained far below the 1938 figure of 555,000 cwt. In 1957, a record year, perhaps because the price was heavily subsidised, exports were fractionally below 300,000 cwt. Most bacon consumed in Britain was imported, but in 1957/8 Ireland supplied only 6.5 per cent of imports, or 4 per cent of the UK market. Despite the export subsidy, the home market was more profitable because imports were prohibited and prices were consequently higher. Because pig numbers fluctuated widely, the amount available for export ranged from 55,000 cwt in 1954 to 300,000 cwt in 1957. Exports were regarded as a residual item after home demand had been satisfied.[199] This made it impossible to establish long-term contracts and Raymond Crotty notes that as a consequence Irish bacon was sold at a discount of 20s to 30s per cwt compared to other bacon of comparable quality.[200] The fact that pig numbers did not regain the 1931 level until 1961 meant that the over-capacity in processing, which was a cause of concern during the 1930s, persisted. Restrictions on imports of animal feed, designed to protect tillage farming, meant that the cost of feeding pigs was higher than in Denmark or the UK.

TILLAGE

One of the more intriguing features of Irish agriculture during the 1950s was the continuing high acreage that was tilled. This is especially notable given the sharp fall in the agricultural labour force. In 1944 the acreage under crops, fruit and horticulture was the highest since the early 1870s. Although the end of compulsory tillage brought a predictable decline, in 1957 it was higher than at the beginning of the century, and the acreage under wheat and barley was higher than in the 1930s. Tillage remained an attractive option, particularly on the larger fertile holdings in the midlands and the south, because the increased use of fertiliser and modern weed-killer and the Department's work on propagating wheat resulted in higher yields. In 1956 and 1957 the average wheat yield was in excess of 25 cwt, whereas the highest yield during the Emergency was 20½ cwt. Tractors, combine-harvesters and other modern equipment made it possible to cultivate large acreages without a correspondingly large labour-force. Guaranteed prices were an important incentive.

As we have already seen, the Committee on Post-Emergency Agricultural Policy was divided on the future role of tillage, and a similar division can be detected between the views of Fianna Fáil and the inter-party government. James Dillon believed that growing wheat on Irish land, when imports were available, was 'a cod and a waste of land'. He urged farmers to grow oats and barley instead, and in March 1948 advertisements appeared in the newspapers urging farmers to do so. The inter-party government preferred to ensure a strategic supply of wheat by investing in storage capacity.[201] Dillon was opposed to subsidies and price-fixing, but was forced to modify this stance. In the autumn of 1948, with a glut of oats on the market, the Cabinet agreed that Grain Importers Limited (the company established to handle wartime imports) would buy oats from farmers at a fixed price.[202] When Dillon announced an end to compulsory tillage in June 1948, he also gave a commitment to continue a guaranteed price for wheat for five years.[203] In March 1949 regulations were put in place for the pricing, marketing and distribution of wheat and the Department of Agriculture became responsible for procuring wheat from abroad in place of the Department of Industry and Commerce, although the responsibility reverted to Industry and Commerce when Fianna Fáil returned to office.[204] The 1949 devaluation of sterling made home-grown grain a much more attractive proposition, and by 1950 Dillon was urging farmers to grow a higher proportion of their feed grain. As an encouragement he offered guaranteed prices and the promise of storage and drying facilities in every county.[205] This scheme was implemented by Fianna Fáil in 1951, when it provided loans for millers and the Merchants Warehousing Company to erect storage silos at Dublin port and in provincial centres.[206]

When Fianna Fáil returned to government in 1951 it renewed the tillage drive, with a special emphasis on wheat.[207] In January 1952 de Valera urged the chief agricultural officers of the county committees of agriculture and the agricultural instructors to persuade farmers to plant more crops. He emphasised that Ireland should become more self-sufficient, given the precarious state of world food supplies. Seán Ó Broin, the secretary of the Department of Agriculture, wrote to each chief agricultural officer and secretary of every county committee of agriculture impressing on them the key points in de Valera's speech.[208] In the first of a series of five radio broadcasts, designed to press home this message, de Valera noted that Ireland's wheat imports were currently guaranteed under the 1949 International Wheat Agreement. However, this agreement was due for revision in the coming year, and future supplies were not assured, because world demand for wheat had increased and production had fallen. Most wheat imports came from the dollar area, and with the ending of Marshall Aid and the lack of convertibility of sterling, dollars were difficult to obtain. De Valera suggested that they should be reserved for items that could not be produced in Ireland. An increased output of native wheat would also reduce the balance of payments deficit.[209] Walsh ended a talk to Longford County Committee of Agriculture on the same theme, quoting the county's most famous poet, Oliver Goldsmith:

But self-dependent power can time defy
as rocks the billows and the sky.[210]

The Department of Agriculture made vigorous attempts to persuade the Cabinet to approve a substantial increase in the price paid for home-grown wheat for 1952, but without success,[211] and the acreage under wheat fell. This persuaded the Cabinet to offer a higher price for the 1953 crop, as did the imminent expiry of the International Wheat Agreement, which meant that Ireland might be forced to pay the full market price for imported wheat, which was expected to be high.[212] When Walsh addressed a regional meeting of county committees of agriculture in Sligo in January 1953, he told his audience that good tillage and good grassland went hand in hand. Agricultural instructors were asked to hold a series of food-production meetings. When de Valera addressed the final regional conference in Dublin on 22 January he spoke about his 'keen disappointment' at the poor results of his 1952 appeal. January 1954 saw Walsh and de Valera addressing another round of regional conferences. The wheat acreage rose substantially in 1953 and again in 1954; the total acreage tilled also increased significantly in the latter year.

A report to Cabinet in January 1954 setting out the Department's policy on wheat, emphasised that it was in the best interests of the state that all flour should be produced from native wheat. The 1953 harvest would supply two-thirds of total demand; if the 1954 yield equalled the 1953 figures, the Department was optimistic that Ireland would be self-sufficient in wheat.

The Department of Industry and Commerce objected to Agriculture's goal of self-sufficiency, because Ireland was committed to purchasing wheat under the International Wheat Agreement. It suggested that the long-term goal should be to produce 50 per cent of flour from native wheat. The Cabinet compromised on a figure of two-thirds, which had been the outcome in 1953.[213]

During the 1954 election campaign Fianna Fáil claimed that Fine Gael was opposed to tillage; Seán Lemass told farmers that their tractors would rust if a coalition government were returned, but Dillon gave a commitment that, if elected, Fine Gael would honour the price of wheat agreed for the current year.[214] Nevertheless, the change of government brought a modification in policy. In August 1954 the Cabinet agreed to retain a guaranteed price and market for home-grown wheat for the next five years. Prices for the coming year would be announced in September or October. However, the prices announced in October 1954 were from 12 to 20 per cent lower than the previous year.[215] In March 1955 the Department of Agriculture informed the Cabinet that the high guaranteed price offered for wheat had distorted tillage patterns. It claimed that Fianna Fáil would also have been forced to reduce the price.[216] The reduction in wheat prices proved extremely unpopular and the government was subject to sustained lobbying by the National Farmers' Association and the Irish Beet Growers' Association. Several county committees of agriculture passed votes of protest. When Fianna Fáil returned to power in 1957 it partly reversed the policy of the inter-party government by declaring that the objective should be to produce 75 per cent of flour from native wheat. If output exceeded this amount, the surplus would be used for animal feed or exported.[217]

There was much wider agreement between Fianna Fáil and the inter-party governments over encouraging farmers to grow animal feed. Dillon made numerous speeches on this topic. In 1953 Walsh told the Dáil that 'there can be no permanent and profitable expansion of live-stock production in this country, and particularly the production of pigs and poultry, so long as we depend largely on the production of maize'. He emphasised the merits of growing feeding barley, potatoes, fodder beet and silage.[218] The original intention behind this policy was to encourage pig and poultry producers to grow barley for their own use, but a considerable trade in feeding barley developed between the barley-growing regions of the east and south-east and small farmers in the west and north, who specialised in pigs and poultry.[219] Grain Importers Limited purchased feeding barley and sold it on to farmers at a loss; it also subsidised maize imports in order to assist pig and poultry producers.[220] Nevertheless, the cost of animal feed remained higher than in the UK and other major producers of pigs and poultry.

WAS THERE AN ALTERNATIVE MARKET IN EUROPE?

Between 1951 and 1956 the real output price of Irish agricultural produce fell by 16 per cent,[221] and with the exception of milk, where the price was set by the government, the fall was not within the government's control, because prices were determined by the export market. By 1950/1 agricultural production in the OEEC had already exceeded the 1939 level. By the late 1950s it was 50 per cent higher than before the war, although the population had only risen by 20 per cent. Throughout the 1950s the prices of all the major agricultural commodities produced in Ireland, except beef, fell on world markets, and by the end of the decade every government in western Europe was providing price support for farm produce. Although the numbers engaged in agriculture fell sharply in every OEEC country, farm incomes rose at a slower rate than incomes in manufacturing industry or services.[222] These trends presented major problems for countries where agriculture was the mainstay of the economy. Ireland was not the only country whose economic performance suffered for this reason. The Danish economy grew very slowly, and Denmark experienced balance of payments problems for similar reasons.[223]

Britain was slow to relax food rationing when the war ended and the Ministry of Food continued to control all food imports well into the 1950s. In later years the Department of Agriculture expressed regret that this arrangement had ended. The continuation of bulk purchase agreements meant that there was no reason to devote resources to marketing. On the eve of World War II British agriculture supplied less than 40 per cent of the country's requirements of temperate foodstuffs (the items that Ireland exported); by the early 1960s Britain was 60 per cent self-sufficient in temperate foodstuffs, despite the fact that the UK population had increased by over 5 million.[224] The expansion in UK output put paid to Ireland's hopes of becoming a major supplier of eggs or bacon in post-war Britain. Britain exploited Ireland's dependence by insisting on securing a guaranteed proportion of Irish livestock exports, and by using its system of price guarantees to favour store cattle at the expense of fat cattle and beef. Nevertheless, the Department regarded Britain as the only reliable long-term market for Irish produce.

The Department's attitude may have been prompted by pessimism, or by a realistic appreciation of the difficulties that Irish agriculture would face in a European-wide free trade area. When Ireland took part in talks organised by the OEEC in 1950, on the liberalisation of trade throughout Europe, Nagle noted that 'the ultimate effect of a long-term European policy of liberalisation on our position in the British market must remain a paramount consideration for this country'. In his opinion moves to liberalise trade in agricultural produce would damage Ireland's position in the British market, because Irish produce would face greater competition from continental producers, without any corresponding increase in sales to continental Europe.[225] The Department also believed that the introduction of European-wide free trade in agricultural produce would threaten the survival of small family farms.

In March 1951 France invited all OEEC countries to attend a conference to discuss the possibility of creating a 'Green Pool' to promote trade in agricultural produce. Two months later the special committee for agriculture of the Council of Europe (of which Ireland was a member) recommended that a supra-national authority should regulate agricultural production and marketing in western Europe. In December 1951 the Council of Europe convened a conference of experts to prepare a draft treaty instituting a European agricultural authority. Ireland concluded that this proposal would be inimical to its interests. If Britain participated, Ireland would lose its preferential position in the British market; if Britain did not become involved, other European countries would bring pressure to bear on Britain to abandon the preferential treatment afforded to Irish produce. The Department was conscious that many European countries had more efficient agricultural sectors than Ireland, and that it would be difficult to compete in a European agricultural market. It also feared that freer trade in agricultural produce would result in 'upheavals in the social structure', in other words a sharp fall in the rural population and the disappearance of small family farms. As there was no obvious political advantage in joining such an authority, the Department of Agriculture recommended that Ireland should do nothing to encourage the development of an integrated market for agricultural products, or anything that would make it more difficult for others to resist the idea.[226]

Of the fifteen countries that attended the Paris meeting in March 1952, France, Netherlands, Austria, West Germany, Greece, Italy, Turkey and Luxembourg expressed their support for the plan. Denmark and Belgium were also in favour, although they were concerned at the creation of a supra-national authority. Sweden, Switzerland, Norway, Britain and Ireland questioned the principle behind the proposal. When France called a further meeting in March 1953, the Department of Agriculture reiterated its opposition. 'For us it may mean jeopardising lines of production on which our small-holding economy greatly depends.' Walsh, the Minister for Agriculture, suggested that the Irish delegation should indicate that the Irish government was 'unable to accept unreservedly the thesis of the economic entity of Western Europe particularly in the field of agriculture'. He believed that no supra-national authority could give farming communities 'the assurance and confidence' that they could hope to obtain from national governments.

Parallel with the French efforts to establish a Green Pool, the OEEC was pressing for a progressive freeing of trade in agricultural produce. In June 1953 the Department of Agriculture recommended that Ireland should not participate in talks on this proposal, despite the fact that attendance would enable them to monitor the attitude of the British government. The Cabinet accepted this advice.[227] When the steering board for trade at the OEEC questioned the Irish delegation in 1954 about its negative attitude towards trade liberalisation, it was informed that Irish farmers were rather conservative and much more interested in stable markets that in international integration. But despite the reservations expressed by the Department of Agriculture, in 1954 the second inter-party government agreed that Ireland should take part in these discussions, and James Dillon was elected a vice-chairman of the OEEC's ministerial committee for food and agriculture in March 1955, on a British proposal.[228]

As the OEEC pressed ahead with the establishment of a European free trade area, the Department of Agriculture held to its belief that this would present serious difficulties for Ireland. It claimed that Irish dairy producers would face competition on the home market, as would the horticultural sector. The only product that seemed secure from continental competition was livestock, because imports of cattle into Britain and Ireland were restricted by stringent veterinary regulations. The Department believed that any gains in continental markets would be more than offset by losses in the UK and this remained the Department's position throughout the abortive negotiations on a European free trade area from 1956 to 1958.

Britain was determined to exclude agricultural produce from the proposed European customs union, because it wished to maintain preferential access for Commonwealth producers. In 1956 the Department of Agriculture concluded that it would be in Ireland's interests if agriculture were excluded from the proposed customs union, because exports of Irish agricultural produce to Britain would rise on the strength of Britain's prosperity owing to increased exports of industrial goods to the Continent. The Department remarked that the OEEC talks had indicated that if agriculture were included in a free trade area, it should be done by creating a common market that would ensure that agricultural policies of member countries were brought into harmony, with due recognition of the special problems of European farmers.

In October 1956 the government asked a committee, consisting of the secretaries of the departments of Agriculture, External Affairs, Finance and Industry and Commerce, to examine the probable effects on Ireland of the establishment of a free trade area. In a report circulated in January 1957 the committee of secretaries concluded that Ireland had reason to be worried about such developments, and about the country's future economic and political prospects in general. The departments of Agriculture and Industry and Commerce agreed that there was little prospect of a substantial increase in exports to continental Europe if Ireland joined a free trade area. The report noted that 'the prospects of expansion of agricultural exports would continue to lie mainly in the British rather than in the continental markets'. Despite such pessimism, it recommended that Ireland should explore the possibility of joining the proposed free trade area, 'with adequate safeguards as a country in process of economic development', and the second inter-party government decided to adopt this line in the forthcoming talks. The government also agreed that no steps should be taken to explore alternatives, such as special bilateral arrangements with Britain, or membership of the six,[229] until the OEEC talks had progressed further. Irish officials kept a close eye on Britain's position. On 6 February T. K. Whitaker, secretary of the Department of Finance, sent Dempsey, secretary of the Department of Agriculture, a note that he had received from the British authorities, which confirmed that, while Britain supported the idea of a free trade area, it would only participate if trade in agricultural produce were excluded. Whitaker and Dempsey drafted a reply, stating that Ireland was also in favour of excluding trade in agricultural produce from the proposed free trade area.[230]

When the Council of Ministers of the OEEC met in February 1957 to discuss the proposed free trade area, the Irish general election campaign was in progress, and Ireland was represented by W. P. Fay, the Irish ambassador to France and permanent delegate at the OEEC. The meeting decided to open negotiations on establishing a European free trade area. It was agreed that special attention would be paid to trade in agricultural products and the needs of developing countries, a category that would include Ireland.[231] This decision prompted Britain to open trade talks with major Commonwealth suppliers. Nagle informed James Dillon that talks between Britain and New Zealand were scheduled for March.

> There is apparently to be a New Deal, in which the 'Common Market' aspects will be considered. Britain recently concluded a fresh agreement with Australia, but it seems that the entire network of Ottawa Agreements [the Commonwealth trade agreements that Britain negotiated during the 1930s] is to be replaced by a new regime.

Nagle suggested that Anglo-Irish trade talks would be a logical development.[232]

In March Dempsey and the secretaries of the departments of Industry and Commerce and the Taoiseach – J. C. B. McCarthy and Maurice Moynihan – travelled to London for a meeting with British officials to discuss 'the possible implications for Anglo-Irish trade of the Free Trade Area concept'. Lintott, the deputy-secretary at the Commonwealth Relations Office, told the Irish officials that Britain had not given much thought to this matter. If the free trade area enabled Ireland to increase exports of agricultural produce to continental Europe, he asked whether this would compensate Ireland for a decline in industrial exports. A minute of the talks, prepared by Charlie Murray of the Department of the Taoiseach, noted that 'The general impression created by the British was that they did not know precisely how trade in agriculture will be dealt with in the area'. He added that, 'It is significant that the British showed no desire to discuss in any detail the implications of the formation of the Area in so far as Anglo-Irish Trade Agreements are concerned. This cannot be attributed to the fact that they have overlooked – or intend to ignore – such implications.'[233]

Throughout the summer of 1957 officials in the departments of Agriculture and Industry and Commerce worked closely on a submission to Cabinet in advance of Anglo-Irish trade talks. This noted the Minister for Agriculture's view that 'while we must be agriculturally associated with the Free Trade Area if we are to keep and develop Continental markets, Britain will continue to be the greatest importer of foodstuffs in the world, and we must therefore strive at the same time to retain and improve our special position in that market'. The Department of Agriculture recommended that Ireland should endeavour to hold on to its existing bilateral preferential arrangements with Britain even if both parties joined the proposed free trade area.

On 1 November 1957 the Cabinet decided that Ireland should seek trade talks with Britain at ministerial level before the next meeting of OEEC ministers. The Irish delegation was instructed to ask Britain to confirm that imports of Irish agricultural produce would automatically benefit from the waiver on agricultural tariffs that Britain was demanding as a condition for joining the free trade area. The delegation suggested that Ireland should be compensated for the loss of preferences on industrial exports to Britain because of the free trade area, by being granted additional concessions for agricultural produce. Ireland requested Britain to remove the price differential between Irish and British fat cattle. It sought a continuation of existing preferences for agricultural produce, and a commitment that Britain would consult Ireland 'on agricultural production and marketing policies with a view to securing the balanced agricultural development of both countries'. It also requested that, in the negotiations over a free trade area, Britain would support the proposition 'that there should be a recognition of a special economic relationship between this country and Britain – particularly as far as trade in agricultural products is concerned'. Ireland wanted a commitment that the special arrangement would continue, and that the OEEC would agree that any bilateral arrangements between the two countries were not incompatible with the rules of the free trade area.[234]

The position that was outlined in this memorandum remained the official line on Anglo-Irish trade for many years to come. The talks in London on 12/13 November were led by Seán Lemass, the Minister for Industry and Commerce, and Frank Aiken, the Minister for External Affairs, who was acting Minister for Agriculture following the sudden death of Seán Moylan. Nagle reported that Reginald Maudling, the Paymaster-General, adopted a reasonably positive attitude towards the Irish demands, but the Minister for Agriculture, Heathcoat Amory, was not prepared to give an undertaking to include Ireland in any waiver on agricultural tariffs that Britain was negotiating for Commonwealth producers. When Lemass noted that 'the position would appear to be that we would lose our industrial preferences and had little prospect of making good the loss through increased trade in agriculture', J. C. B McCarthy, secretary of the Department of Industry and Commerce, noted that he was not contradicted by the British ministers. Sir David Eccles, president of the Board of Trade, noted that Ireland was a prospective member of the free trade area, unlike

Australia and New Zealand, and consequently it would be difficult to obtain a waiver for Anglo-Irish trade. By the end of the talks the Irish hopes of obtaining concessions on agricultural trade to compensate for the anticipated loss of industrial markets had disappeared, and the Irish delegation was concerned that the creation of the free trade area would result in the loss of Ireland's agricultural preferences.[235]

The OEEC's efforts to establish a free trade area foundered in November 1958. At that point western Europe divided into two trade blocs: the six countries that formed the European Economic Community (EEC), and the 'outer seven' members of the European Free Trade Area (EFTA).[236] While the EEC included agriculture in its trade policy, EFTA only covered manufactured goods. Ireland remained aloof from both blocs. The Department of Agriculture saw no advantage in joining EFTA, since Britain was the only EFTA member that offered a substantial market for Irish agricultural produce, and the Department of Industry and Commerce was reluctant to expose Irish manufacturers to competition.[237]

AGRICULTURE – A WAY OF LIFE OR A BUSINESS?

Between 1949 and 1958, 15 per cent of the public capital programme was devoted to agriculture, fishery and forestry development. This was the third largest item, after housing, which accounted for 35 per cent, and power (21 per cent).[238] Net agricultural output rose by 17.7 per cent between 1949/51 and 1959/61. Yet in 1958, which was admittedly a depressed year, the volume of agricultural output was only 2 per cent higher than in 1912.[239] Between 1949 and 1959 the number of men engaged in farming declined from almost 482,000 to 389,000 (there are no accurate figures for the number of women), and the rate of emigration returned to a level last experienced during the depressed 1880s. The post-war British economy was enjoying full employment and there were unlimited jobs available for Irish emigrants as building labourers or domestic workers. Farm labourers and farmers' sons opted for life in London or the English midlands in preference to remaining on the land, and their sisters took jobs as waitresses, servants or as student nurses. Most countries in western Europe experienced a similar decline in the numbers engaged in agriculture. In Ireland and in southern Europe, manufacturing industry failed to provide alternative jobs, and workers had to emigrate to the industrial cities in Britain, Germany and other northern European countries.

Despite the evidence that the share of employment and national income provided by agriculture was declining throughout Europe, in Ireland an expanding agriculture was still regarded as offering the solution to mass emigration, low living standards and the balance of payments deficit. In 1948 the inter-party government established a commission generally known as the Commission on Emigration.[240] The majority report, published in 1954, expressed the belief 'that the present agricultural population could produce very much more real wealth than at present', and that higher agricultural productivity offered the solution to population decline and emigration. It also expressed the belief that the increased purchasing power of the farming population 'should, at the very least, tend to prevent population on the land from declining further' and that in turn this would lead to additional employment in rural Ireland. A minority report, written by Dr Cornelius Lucey, the Roman Catholic bishop of Cork, was insistent that the government should set an objective of increasing the number of small farms. The majority report and Dr Lucey's minority report both believed that increased agricultural productivity would be achieved by an expansion in dairy farming and in pig and poultry farming.[241] Neither took account of the difficulties involved in finding a market for these items, or the fact that small farmers engaged in pig and poultry production were being undercut by large factory-farming units. The Department of Agriculture noted that:

> Running through the Report in regard to agriculture there is the admission that agriculture deserves a better deal and that its expansion and development are essential to provide the means to create directly or indirectly additional employment opportunities. Much of the comment on agriculture is, however, badly informed and is too closely related to theoretical employment prospects which have not been assessed in the light of the overall economic situation and the inter-relation of the different sectors of the economy. In this matter the Commission appear to have suffered from a lack of appreciation of (a) the internal changes which have taken place in the structure and conditions of agriculture over the past century, (b) the fact that within the present century there has been no long period of economic stability in agriculture, and (c) the extent to which agriculture is affected by the requirements and vagaries of export outlets. The Report contains nothing which is new in its comments or recommendations on the subject of agriculture.[242]

The statement suggests a certain weariness. During the 1950s there was no shortage of critical statements about the shortcomings of Irish agriculture, or agricultural policy; many have already been cited. In 1952 the IBEC report noted that, 'There has been no dearth of programs for promoting agricultural expansion and the fact that there has been so little effectiveness to date strongly suggests that their pattern should be searchingly examined and overhauled'. Some months later, in February 1953, Seán Moylan, the Minister for Education, circulated a memorandum on agricultural policy that began by stating that 'for some decades the entire agricultural industry has been static'. In a comment that anticipates some of the comments by T. K. Whitaker in *Economic Development* (1958), Moylan noted that one of the most difficult problems at present was 'the cynical attitude of the farmer, as expressed in a lack of confidence in farming as a means of producing an income adequate to maintain labour on the land.' Bringing about a change in mental outlook would require farmers to be shown new methods of farm management that would result in higher output and make farming an attractive occupation.[243] In August 1953, not to be outdone, Erskine Childers, the Minister for Lands, informed de Valera that 'no new policy for Agriculture is forthcoming. … The propaganda Department in the Department of Agriculture is out of date'.[244]

One of the favourite explanations for the poor performance of the Irish economy during the 1950s is the conservative attitude of the Department of Finance towards public expenditure.[245] In the case of agriculture, this is not an altogether convincing argument, since the land rehabilitation project, which was the most costly programme undertaken by the Department of Agriculture, was exempted from budgetary cuts in 1952 and again in 1956. Indeed, it is more plausible to argue that investment was misdirected. The land rehabilitation project soon came to be regarded as a job-creation scheme, and very little attention was paid to ensuring that the improved land was farmed productively. The money could have been used more productively to provide farmers with cheap fertiliser. The decision to retain the dairy Shorthorn as the main breeding stock was not prompted by lack of money, but by conservative attitudes on the part of ministers for Agriculture and the vested interests of livestock breeders.

Throughout the 1950s agriculture and food accounted for approximately 70 per cent of Irish merchandise exports, providing essential foreign exchange for the purchase of industrial raw materials and consumer goods. Although the continuation of bulk purchase by the British Ministry of Food postponed the need to develop modern marketing agencies in the UK, the origins of a modern meat-processing industry can be traced to the export trade to the United States in the early 1950s. Yet the competitiveness of Irish agriculture suffered as a result of the protection afforded to Irish manufacturers. Farmers paid higher prices for fertiliser, weed-killer, veterinary medicines and agricultural machinery. Pig and poultry producers paid higher prices for animal feed because of the protection given to barley-growers, while Irish consumers paid more for milk, butter, bacon and bread, because of protection. The National Farm Survey carried out in 1955, 1956 and 1957 revealed that the most profitable farms, when account was taken of size, were engaged in dairy farming, tillage, or a combination of the two.[246] Tillage and dairy farmers enjoyed the security of prices that were guaranteed by the government, whereas livestock, pig and poultry producers had to contend with volatile prices and uncertain export markets.

One theme that begins to feature during this period is the potential conflict between economic development and social objectives, such as preserving the family farm. In 1945 James Ryan, the Minister for Agriculture, noted that 'we are up against a sort of conflict as between the social and economic aim. The social aim is to put as many people as we can on the land, the economic aim is to give the farmer a better living. It is doubtful if we can get the two policies to coincide'.[247] When Ireland was invited to attend a meeting in Paris in 1952 to explore the prospect of establishing a European-wide market for farm produce, the Department declined the invitation. Seán Ó Broin, the secretary of the Department of Agriculture, noted that,

> There is in many countries a long tradition behind the form of agricultural production as at present practised. Besides being an industry agriculture must be regarded as a way of life. Any schemes involving large-scale alteration of the pattern of production might, in countries like Ireland, give rise to serious disturbances of the social and demographic structure. Because of these considerations the opinion of the Irish Government is that very great caution should be exercised in endeavouring to deal with agriculture on the basis of an integrated European market as the ultimate ideal.[248]

Yet the record level of emigration during the 1950s indicates that traditional rural life was disintegrating. The Commission on Emigration noted that the absence of electricity and running water in rural homes discouraged young women from marrying farmers. This point had already been noted.

The Committee on Post-Emergency Agricultural Policy recommended that further reports should be drawn up on the ways and means of equipping farm homesteads with labour-saving amenities, particularly with running water, and that plans and specifications be provided for more hygienic farm buildings, and with a view to economising on labour. Most rural homes had electricity by the mid-1950s, but progress in supplying running water in rural areas was slow.[249]

One positive response to this sense of crisis in rural life was the growth of Macra na Feirme, an organisation dedicated to promoting agricultural education and social amenities that would make rural life more attractive for the farming community. Macra na Feirme was founded in 1944; by 1951 it had almost 15,000 members in 400 clubs.[250] Although Macra na Feirme refused to take on the task of representing the economic interests of farmers, preferring to concentrate on educational and social matters, it played an important role in the formation of the ICMSA in 1951[251] and the National Farmers' Association in 1955. Irish farmers were adopting similar tactics to farmers elsewhere in Europe, where farm lobbies became a feature of post-war politics. This reflected a growing realisation that farm incomes were increasingly being determined by government.

Irish historians have tended to draw unfavourable contrasts between the ten to twelve years immediately after the end of World War II and the economic successes achieved during the 1960s. Yet the agricultural policies that were pursued under the various programmes for economic expansion were based on the recommendations of the Committee on Post-Emergency Agricultural Policy, and the schemes that were introduced in the years immediately after the end of the war. The years between 1945 and 1958 have probably been regarded in an unduly critical light. In the Department of Agriculture there was a shift from the introspective atmosphere of the 1930s and the war years. Many Irish agricultural scientists travelled to the United States under the ERP technical assistance programme, and the Department became involved in international organisations such as the OEEC and the United Nations Food and Agricultural Organisation (FAO). These contacts created a greater awareness of scientific and economic trends in other countries, which resulted in a more critical assessment of domestic policies.

The objectives of FAO included raising levels of nutrition and living standards in member countries; securing improvements in the efficiency of production and distribution of all food and agricultural products; bettering the condition of rural populations; and assisting economic expansion. Membership of the FAO was extremely important for Ireland, given that it was not admitted to the United Nations until 1956. When Ireland joined FAO in September 1946, James Ryan, the Minister for Agriculture, noted that membership would assist Irish agricultural exports and provide access to scientific knowledge.[252] In November 1948 James Dillon was elected as the third vice-chairman of the 57-nation FAO conference. Among the items on the agenda were the problem of food surpluses and the question of providing aid and technical assistance to underdeveloped countries.[253] The origins of Ireland's programme of technical assistance to less-developed countries can be found in its membership of FAO. In 1960 the FAO launched a 'Food for the Hungry' campaign, which led directly to Ireland's 'Freedom from Hunger' campaign and the establishment in 1965 of Gorta, a government agency to promote awareness of the FAO campaign and third-world hunger.[254] This was a forerunner of other Irish agencies that focused on providing relief and development aid to the Third World.

CHAPTER SEVEN

AGRICULTURE AND THE PROGRAMME FOR ECONOMIC EXPANSION, 1958–1963

The years between 1958 and 1963 brought a number of critical changes in Irish government. The *Programme for Economic Expansion*, published as a government white paper in November 1958, set the objective of raising economic growth by re-directing government investment from social investment, such as housing or hospitals, to more productive purposes. It suggested that economic growth offered the only means of reducing emigration and unemployment, and warned that the imminent free trade area in Europe presented an additional challenge to the small Irish economy.[1] The white paper was based on a report by T. K. Whitaker, secretary of the Department of Finance, called *Economic Development*, which was published one week after the publication of the *Programme for Economic Expansion*.[2]

In 1959 Éamon de Valera retired from active political life to become President of Ireland. He was succeeded as Taoiseach by Seán Lemass, who favoured a different style of government. Lemass had been a very active Minister of Industry and Commerce, with a penchant for extending his interests beyond the remit of that department. As his biographer John Horgan noted, 'the Department of the Taoiseach has not got a domain. It was the office of the chairman; it was a department that was only tangentially concerned with policy and devoted primarily to the machinery of government'.[3] Lemass' pro-active style triumphed over the conventions of the Department of the Taoiseach. During his years as Taoiseach Lemass relied heavily on a committee of secretaries of the departments of Agriculture, External Affairs, Finance and Industry and Commerce to formulate policy both on economic matters, such as EEC membership and foreign trade, and on other questions, including north-south relations. This committee, chaired by T. K. Whitaker, reported to a committee of ministers from the same departments, which was chaired by Lemass.[4] As a consequence, the Department of Agriculture was involved in key areas of government policy-making, while Lemass, his officials and the ministers and senior officials in the departments of Finance, External Affairs and Industry and Commerce also played a more active role in determining agricultural policy than in the past.

On 3 July 1959, ten days after he became Taoiseach, Lemass sent a letter to Juan Greene, the president of the National Farmers' Association (NFA), inviting him and other representatives of the NFA to meet him in order to discuss the present economic situation, the prospects for economic development and the best means of maximising agriculture's contribution to economic growth. Similar letters were despatched to the presidents of the Federation of Irish Industries, the Irish Congress of Trade Unions and the Association of Chambers of Commerce of Ireland. When Lemass and Smith met a delegation from the NFA on 27 July, Lemass told the delegates he was anxious to have regular consultations with the NFA on 'major aspects of economic policy'.[5]

The year 1958 brought a new era in the administrative history of the Department of Agriculture, with the appointment of John Charles Nagle as secretary – the first secretary of the Department who had not served with the DATI.[6] Nagle had graduated from UCC with a degree in commerce and economics and pursued post-graduate studies in economics at Cambridge University, before joining the Department of Finance in 1933 as an administrative officer.[7] When the British Ministry for Agriculture prepared personality profiles of Irish government ministers and senior officials in 1960, in advance of trade talks, it noted that, 'though at first sight a lugubrious-looking individual – responsibility for maintaining Irish agricultural exports in the face of European economic grouping from which the Republic is excluded is a daunting one, – his gloomy appearance conceals a sharp intellect and a considerable flair for patient and astute negotiation'.[8]

AGRICULTURE AND THE *PROGRAMME FOR ECONOMIC EXPANSION*

In the 1958 blue-print for Irish economic growth it was assumed that agriculture would be the most dynamic sector. *Economic Development* stated that 'in general it would seem that attention should be concentrated primarily on raising the efficiency and volume of production in agriculture and in industries based in agriculture'. Eight chapters deal exclusively with agriculture, and three of the remaining seven discuss agriculture at some length. Most of the key ideas in *Economic Development* were included in the *Programme for Economic Expansion*. The proposals concerning agriculture had emerged from meetings of an interdepartmental committee, consisting of a chairman, two members nominated by the Minister for Agriculture, and one member each nominated by the ministers for Finance and for Lands and Local Government. Appointed in April 1957, shortly after Fianna Fáil returned to office, the committee was asked to examine changes in the provision of agricultural credit in order to encourage an increase in agricultural output; how best to encourage farmers to improve soil fertility; and whether the agricultural grant (the rates remission on agricultural land) could be used in a more effective manner to encourage a rise in agricultural output.[9] The fact that the file on this committee's work carries the title Post-Emergency Agricultural Policy indicates that it was regarded as a continuation of earlier programmes.

Economic Development set an expansion in livestock as the key objective for Irish agriculture. The attraction of livestock was simple: 'unlike dairy or crop products, cattle are produced and exported without State protection or subsidy. The grasslands, if improved, could carry bigger numbers of cattle and sheep without a commensurate increase in costs'.[10] It suggested that there was considerable scope for producing more meat. According to figures published by the OEEC, output per acre of grassland could be doubled. This would involve a substantial increase in the use of lime and fertiliser, and it recommended the introduction of a fertiliser subsidy. This subsidy would enable farmers to provide more food for their livestock during the winter months instead of the present 'wasteful rhythm of summer abundance and winter privation that marks the life of cattle from birth to beef'.[11]

Within days of the publication of the *Programme for Economic Expansion*, the Department of Agriculture organised a conference, where the secretaries and chief agricultural officers of the county committees of agriculture were urged to give priority to the *Programme*'s aim of increasing productivity in grassland and livestock.[12] In December it introduced a subsidy of £4 per ton on phosphatic fertiliser, backdated to the previous September.[13] In May 1959 the Department reported that county committees of agriculture were being encouraged to carry out demonstrations of improved grassland and silage making.[14] Other priorities included the control and prevention of animal disease, especially bovine TB, and the selection of the most suitable livestock breeds and animals.[15] Many of these schemes were a development of work that was already under way. This was particularly true of the campaign to eradicate bovine TB and the efforts to raise grassland productivity. The recommendations concerning pigs and dairy farming also concentrated on improving breeding-stock and raising productivity. *Economic Development* included a lengthy section on agricultural education and the advisory service, which is discussed in chapter eight.

In June 1959 the Department outlined the heads of agricultural policy, which expanded on the recommendations in the *Programme for Economic Expansion*:

1. The basic aim is to increase output for export. Any increase in output would have to be exported, though crops such as wheat and beet that are only produced for the domestic market would continue to be supported.
2. The most suitable export products are livestock and livestock products.
3. Productivity must be increased if Ireland is to gain a greater share of export markets.
4. Trade relations are important in order to ensure that exports are remunerative.
5. An agricultural country cannot make price or export subsidies the foundation of agricultural expansion.
6. Increased productivity should follow from the very large expansion that has taken place in the advisory service.
7. Improvement in grassland is the most important objective in order to achieve a higher carrying capacity. Fertiliser subsidies should be geared towards this objective.
8. The elimination of bovine tuberculosis should be given priority because within six years only accredited cattle would be allowed into Britain from Ireland.

In a note that accompanied this list Michael Barry indicated that, 'In principle Government expenditure which increases productivity permanently is to be preferred to Government expenditure in the form of price subsidies'.[16]

This view prevailed during the years 1958–63. Thanks to the fertiliser subsidy introduced in 1958, the retail cost of fertilisers fell by one-third between 1957 and 1960, and prices remained stable until 1965.[17] By 1959/60 the annual cost of the subsidy was almost £2 million.[18] Between 1958 and

1961 the use of phosphate fertiliser rose by one-third.[19] A subsidy for potash was introduced in 1960, and was increased the following year. By 1963/4 fertiliser and lime subsidies cost almost £4.2 million, which was almost double the cost of the land project, yet farmers were spending 20 per cent more on fertiliser than in 1958.[20] The cost of animal feedstuffs also fell by 4–5 per cent.[21]

Other forms of government assistance were designed to reduce costs and to raise quality and efficiency. Twenty years' rates remission was granted on all new farm buildings in 1959.[22] A substantial increase in the value of grant assistance for the construction of modern piggeries was announced in February 1960, with a view to reducing mortality.[23] The 1960/1 budget provided funds for additional grants for the construction of new cow byres and the repair and improvement of existing farm buildings. By the end of the 1961/2 financial year, over 200,000 farmers had received grants under the farm building schemes totalling almost £6.25 million.[24] The agricultural grant, which offset part of the cost of rates on agricultural land, increased from £5.5 million in 1957/8 to £8.9 million in 1963/4.[25]

Irish farmers had traditionally been reluctant to borrow money to finance investment, perhaps because in the past debt often meant rent arrears, which were followed by evictions. Bank deposits by farmers generally exceeded borrowings. In 1959 Fred Gilmore, the deputy-governor of the US farm credit administration, delivered a report on farm credit in Ireland, which had been commissioned by the Department of Agriculture. The report recommended that farmers should be given more information about credit; that the commercial banks should develop a better knowledge and understanding of the needs of farmers and farming practices; and that legislation should be introduced to revitalise the ACC, which was under the control of the Department of Finance. The report also suggested that farmers seeking credit should present the bank or other credit agency with a plan and records showing their ability to repay the loan.[26] In the light of Gilmore's report the departments of Agriculture and Finance held talks with the ACC and the commercial banks to persuade them to provide farmers with better credit facilities,[27] and the advisory service encouraged farmers to become less averse to borrowing for investment.

LIVESTOCK AND BEEF

Measures to improve the livestock sector included the various fertiliser and grassland schemes mentioned above, plus a programme to raise the quality of Irish herds and the eradication of disease. On livestock breeding policy, *Economic Development* suggested that the choice should not be seen as one between either Shorthorns or purely dairy breeds; it quoted the advice given by Dr John Hammond of Cambridge that Ireland should introduce dual-purpose Friesians. The main advance in terms of breeding stock was the introduction in 1959 of progeny testing of both beef and dairy animals. The testing units were attached to AI stations.[28] One aim of the programme was to determine which AI dairy bulls produced 'thrifty high-class beef progeny' and this was done by regular weighing of animals to assess weight gain, and by weighing and grading the carcases of these animals after slaughter.[29] By the late 1950s AI was catering for almost 40 per cent of breeding stock, and this proportion steadily increased, until by 1964 a majority of cows were inseminated by the cattle breeding stations. The increasing use of AI made it much easier to transform the breeding structure of the Irish cattle population within a relatively short period of time, since 400 bulls accounted for the majority of calves.[30] The Department reformed the existing milk recording schemes, so that milk records were linked with progeny testing. The AI stations under the Department's control were gradually transferred to co-operative ownership.

Decisions on livestock management and breeds were increasingly based on the outcome of research work carried out by the Agricultural Institute. Until the 1960s the veterinary regulations meant that it was impossible to import livestock from outside the UK. Although the regulations served to keep Irish livestock free of disease, it seems probable that they were also used as a protectionist device to prevent the import of continental breeds. In 1961 Lemass was approached on behalf of a German livestock breeder who wished to import Friesian cattle into Ireland for breeding purposes. Lemass forwarded the correspondence to Smith, who replied that the Department of Agriculture was concerned about the danger that imported breeds might transmit foot and mouth disease. He claimed that any threat to the disease-free status of Irish livestock would damage a valuable trade in the United States. The Department refused to import of Friesian cattle from the Continent, although Smith claimed that its objections were motivated by 'practicality not principle'. It was promoting the Friesian breed by importing animals from the UK.[31] In 1962 fourteen Charollais cattle and two polled Hereford bulls imported from the USA became the first cattle to reach Ireland from a destination other than Britain for more than sixty years.[32] As the USA was free from foot and mouth disease, these animals did not present any difficulty. Around this time the possibility of establishing an Irish quarantine station arose. Officials hoped that in addition to acting as a quarantine station for livestock imported from continental Europe, the station might be used to quarantine livestock being exported from continental Europe to the USA, and this was discussed in talks with the US secretary for agriculture, Orville Freeman, but to no avail.[33] In 1964 a quarantine station opened at Spike Island in Cork harbour.[34] The first Charollais bulls were imported from France that year, and Friesian bulls and heifers and Texel sheep were imported from the Netherlands.[35]

From this point the Department became much more receptive to the introduction of different livestock breeds, and farmers responded accordingly. By 1965 Friesians accounted for 55 per cent of inseminations at AI stations, compared with 30 per cent in 1963. In 1962 the Vatican asked the Department to recommend a suitable Aberdeen Angus breeder; it was looking for a young Aberdeen Angus bull for the papal farm at Castelgandolfo. The Minister immediately offered to present a bull to the papal farm. Nagle wrote to the Vatican official, who had contacted the Department, to inform him of the government's gift. 'May I say how much I appreciate your consulting me on such an important matter as a Papal bull'.[36] For many years the Department had resisted demands to facilitate the import of Landrace pigs, on veterinary advice, and the early Landrace pigs were imported by individual farmers, generally from Northern Ireland.[37] By the early 1960s it had become the favoured breed among pig farmers. In 1958 the Department established a progeny testing station.[38] An accredited pig herd scheme began in 1960 with the object of assessing the overall performance of the breeding herds from which boars were selected.[39]

BOVINE TB AND ANIMAL HEALTH

The eradication of bovine tuberculosis (TB) was the most important scheme carried out by the Department of Agriculture during the Programme for Economic Expansion. It was also the most expensive. By the time the Department declared the eradication scheme completed in 1965, the net cost was estimated at almost £40 million. Twenty-four Department veterinary surgeons, 600 private vets and 210 Department officials had taken part.

Proposals for testing and eliminating tubercular cattle had been under examination since the 1930s, but the 1935 Act only provided for the slaughter of advanced cases; it did not attempt to stamp out the disease. The matter went into abeyance during the Emergency.[40] While the first inter-party government is remembered for Noel Browne's campaign to treat and prevent human TB, it did not regard bovine TB as a priority, although a pilot investigation was carried out into the incidence of bovine TB in Bansha, County Tipperary. The impetus for a national eradication programme came from Britain, where the government was committed to eradicating the disease by 1961. Irish cattle would be excluded from Britain after that date unless they were certified as free of TB.

An undated memorandum from the Department of Agriculture, probably written after Fianna Fáil's return to office in 1951, seeking £1 million in grant counterpart funds towards the cost of eradicating bovine TB, noted that the disease was rife in Ireland. Thirty per cent of the cattle and 44 per cent of the cows tested in Bansha tested positive for the disease, and a further 9 per cent of tests carried out on cattle and 14 per cent of tests on cows were inconclusive. The Department recommended introducing several pilot programmes, some in areas with a high incidence of bovine TB, others where the incidence was low. Farmers living outside these areas, who wished to develop a tubercule-free herd, could avail of free tuberculin testing, and they would be compensated for the loss of reactor cattle.[41] The cost of a comprehensive campaign was estimated to be at least £15 million.[42] In March 1952 the Department asked the Cabinet to approve a pilot voluntary testing programme in counties Limerick and Clare, two dairy counties with little inward movement of cattle. When the majority of herds in these counties had been tested, the Department planned to move to a compulsory scheme. In order to encourage farmers to participate in the pilot scheme, it recommended that livestock should also be tested and treated free of charge for mastitis, contagious abortion and other diseases. The Cabinet failed to decide on these proposals for several months, and during that time the departments of Agriculture and Finance fought a predictable battle over the respective costs and benefits of eradicating bovine TB. Eventually the Department of Agriculture agreed to scale down the pilot scheme to cover only County Clare, but pressed the Cabinet to provide creameries with grants towards the cost of pasteurising skim milk (to prevent the spread of TB), in anticipation of receiving ERP funds for this purpose. On 25 November 1952 the Cabinet approved the pilot TB eradication programme,[43] on the understanding that the money would be provided by the ERP. However, the US authorities did not approve ERP funding for the Clare scheme and the pasteurisation programme until 1955, because the Irish authorities had delayed sending detailed proposals to Washington.[44]

With no immediate prospect of receiving ERP funds, in the autumn of 1953 the Department of Agriculture suggested that a separate pilot programme should be introduced in County Limerick, which might be financed by the National Development Fund. Although the National Development Fund Committee approved the application in March 1954, de Valera refused sanction because he feared it might compromise the application for ERP funding. When he voiced these concerns to the US ambassador, he was reassured that this would not happen, and the Limerick pilot scheme was duly announced.[45] Fianna Fáil lost office some weeks later, following the 1954 general election, and the incoming minister, James Dillon, abandoned the Limerick pilot scheme in favour of programmes in counties Clare and Sligo and Bansha in County Tipperary, an area that included part of east Limerick. Dillon announced this change without first securing Cabinet approval.

The switch from Limerick to Sligo was prompted by representations from the Irish Veterinary Medical Association. It had opposed the choice of Limerick, allegedly because the incidence of TB in the county was so high that it feared farmers would be discouraged from participating. In its opinion a county with a low incidence of the disease, such as Donegal or Sligo, would be more appropriate. The veterinary association was also opposed to the Department's plan to provide participating farmers with free treatment for other animal diseases, regarding this as an invasion of private practice. Dillon conceded their demands, although officials in the Department of Agriculture warned that this had removed a major incentive for farmers to have their cattle tested. The Department and the veterinary association eventually reached agreement on fees for TB testing, which meant that farmers could have their animals tested by the veterinary surgeon of their choice.[46]

Farmers in the pilot eradication areas were also offered double the normal grants towards the construction of byres and farm buildings, if they had their animals tested. Modern farm buildings were regarded as an important means of improving veterinary health. Grants towards the cost of erecting farm buildings had been first provided by the CDB in the 1890s; the Department operated a grant scheme in western counties from the 1930s; the first nation-wide scheme of farm grants was introduced in 1949.[47] By 1958 grants towards farm buildings and water supplies were costing £720,000 per annum and expenditure rose sharply under the Programme for Economic Expansion.

A voluntary nation-wide programme of TB testing began in 1954. By then Irish newspapers and the farming press was publicising the threat to livestock exports if the disease were not eradicated. By April 1955 the owners of 480,000 cattle, 11 per cent of the national herd, had applied for testing, but only 195,212 animals had actually been tested; 17 per cent of the animals tested were infected. The lowest incidence was recorded in the north and west; the highest in the dairy counties of the south. When John A. Costello outlined the second inter-party government's policy on agriculture in 1956, he indicated that money would be found for the bovine TB eradication scheme, despite the pressure to economise on public spending, 'because as I have already said, the future of the cattle export trade depends on the early and successful completion of the scheme'. This commitment was honoured. The eradication scheme was exempted from the cuts in public spending during 1956.[48] In October of the same year Costello told a meeting of inter-party government TDs that money would be provided for a nation-wide intensive eradication programme. Shortly afterwards a nation-wide accredited herds scheme was introduced, which accredited any herd that was free of the disease on two successive tests. The livestock committee of the NFA had suggested this scheme. A pre-intensive scheme was introduced in counties Galway, Kerry, Donegal, Leitrim, Mayo and Roscommon, which offered farmers free testing and additional grants towards the cost of cattle byres.

Up to this point all testing had been voluntary. In January 1957 the Department of Agriculture urged the Cabinet to introduce compulsory testing, restrictions on the movement of livestock, and regulations covering markets and fairs. Fianna Fáil approved the introduction of legislation on these matters shortly after it returned to government, and the measures became law in July 1957.[49] Their speedy enactment was prompted by pressure from the UK. In June 1957 the British Minister for Agriculture, Heathcoat Amory, informed Seán Moylan, the Minister for Agriculture, that Britain would be an attested area (free of bovine TB) within four years and only attested cattle could be imported from that date. Large areas in Britain were already attested as free of the disease. Irish stores that passed a single TB test within fourteen days of shipping had to be isolated for sixty days in Britain, and were then required to pass another test before being admitted into an attested herd. When Moylan addressed the Dáil during the second reading of the Bovine TB Bill, he emphasised that the disease could only be eradicated with the co-operation of farmers. He expressed the hope that public opinion would encourage farmers to adopt a more positive attitude towards TB testing, but he warned that the testing programme might be delayed by a shortage of veterinary scientists.

Economic Development stated that eradicating bovine TB was 'perhaps the most immediate and most outstanding problem facing the cattle industry at the present time'. By 1958 only one-quarter of the cattle population and one-third of all herds had been tested. As ERP funding was about to expire, the existing exchequer bill of £1 million per annum would increase.[50] In June 1958 the Irish authorities informed Britain that 100,000 once-tested cattle would be exported during the current year; 200,000 in 1959 and 300,000 in 1960. By 1960 they hoped to export 100,000 fully-accredited animals (animals that had passed two tests).[51] British officials informed the Department of Agriculture that they were coming under pressure from British farming organisations to restrict livestock imports from Ireland after 1961 to fully-accredited animals. However, in March 1959 Britain agreed to admit once-tested cattle for up to five years. The decision was widely welcomed by farmers and by the livestock trade.

By the end of 1959 compulsory schemes were in operation in Connacht and Ulster, and in County Clare, but the eradication programme remained on a voluntary basis throughout the rest of Munster and all of Leinster. In the dairy counties of Limerick, Waterford and Tipperary, only half of all herds were participating in the scheme. Lack of finance was no longer a problem. In June 1959 the Department confirmed that all the money needed was being provided.[52] In order to encourage a better response from farmers it introduced a grant of £15 for every reactor sold to a participating canning plant, in addition to the price paid by the cannery. If the farmer obtained a clear test for his entire herd within three years, he would receive a bonus payment of £8 for each reactor cow that had been culled, or £4 for every cow in the herd when it was attested as free of TB.

Progress in eradicating the disease was hampered by a shortage of veterinary practitioners and supervisors, and by the difficulty in replacing reactor cows in southern counties. The Department of Agriculture reported that many farmers were indifferent or even opposed to the eradication campaign. Some dairy farmers refused to co-operate, as a tactic in their campaign for higher milk prices. Nevertheless, the Department claimed that 'nobody now seriously challenges the need to clear the country's herds', although many farmers were slow to take the necessary steps. While the eradication programme in the south would remain 'an uphill struggle', the Department was hopeful that the pace could be speeded up.[53] In an attempt to accelerate the eradication campaign in non-clearance areas, an export subsidy for reactor cattle was introduced in April 1960. By 1961 the compulsory clearance areas had been extended to include all of Leinster, except Kilkenny, and the remaining six counties (Kilkenny and Munster with the exception of County Clare) became clearance areas in 1962. Farmers in a clearance area could sell their reactor cattle to the Department at market value.[54]

By the beginning of 1962 Nagle informed Whitaker that owing to the rapid progress in eradicating bovine TB, the British and Irish authorities had agreed that the import of once-tested cattle into Britain should cease at the end of the year, three years earlier than previously agreed. The Irish authorities agreed to bring the date forward 'because there is a prestige and morale aspect involved'.[55] The Department of Agriculture was conscious that the delay in eradicating bovine TB had damaged the reputation of Irish livestock. In 1959 Paddy Smith warned Lemass that the British National Farmers' Union (NFU) was suggesting that British herds could be reinfected by Irish stores. John Salter Chalker of the NFU visited Ireland in 1959, as a guest of the NFA, to inspect the conditions under which Irish livestock were sold. During a meeting with the Department of Agriculture he expressed shock that livestock were still being sold at street fairs, although he was favourably impressed by the new livestock marts being developed. The NFA supported the development of cattle marts, many of them in co-operative ownership, but cattle dealers wanted to continue selling livestock at street fairs. Smith told Lemass that marts had an essential part to play in the eradication of bovine TB, because they were more hygienic and it was easier to check the condition of animals, but he was not prepared to insist that all sales should be conducted in marts.

The NFU alleged that some Irish exporters were shipping reactors to Britain, while claiming that they had passed a fourteen-day test. While the Department admitted that some irregularities had occurred it claimed that it had no evidence of serious abuse.[56] This may have been true in 1959, but by 1962 the Department was becoming concerned at the extent of fraud and abuse in the TB-testing programme. In June 1962 James Dillon, the leader of Fine Gael, informed Lemass privately that he had information that thousands of fourteen-day tested and even reactor cattle were being shipped to Britain as fully tested, because of lax, or corrupt, supervision at the ports. When Lemass asked the Department of Agriculture to comment on these allegations, he was informed that the Department had uncovered a number of malpractices relating to the TB eradication scheme. However, it proved extremely difficult to assemble sufficient evidence to sustain a successful court prosecution, because of lack of co-operation from members of the public. The Department also believed that the Department of Justice was reluctant to prosecute such cases, and Paddy Smith complained about this to the Minister for Justice, Charles Haughey.

> They [the public] are wondering why prosecutions haven't yet taken place in any of them. They think there is some sinister hand at work that is preventing such prosecutions taking place. I am not saying that there is anything in that, but I don't blame them for feeling like that, in view of the abnormally long delay in bringing of these cases forward.

In 1962, before Dillon contacted Lemass, the Department had detected a major fraud at the North Wall, the major embarkation port for Irish livestock exports to Britain. On 30 October 1962 Smith protested to the Attorney-General at the delay in bringing the case to court. 'I am convinced that the ventilation of this case is of the utmost importance to our cattle export trade and to the success of the Bovine Tuberculosis Eradication Scheme'. When the case opened, a major cattle exporter from County Roscommon, one of his employees and a ship inspector employed by the Department of Agriculture pleaded guilty. They were each sentenced to twelve months in prison, but the sentences were quashed on appeal and fines from £100 to £400 were imposed. A number of temporary officials employed by the Department of Agriculture were dismissed as a consequence.[57]

When the Department announced that the entire country was attested free of bovine TB, in October 1965,[58] the incidence of tuberculosis in herds was reported to be just over 2 per cent, compared with 17 per cent in 1953.[59] The main impetus behind the bovine TB eradication campaign had been the threatened loss of the UK market. In 1961 Nagle told British farm leaders that while Ireland was motivated by human and animal health considerations, the prime purpose was an economic one.[60]

THE ADVISORY COMMITTEE ON THE MARKETING OF AGRICULTURAL PRODUCE

The *Programme for Economic Expansion* said very little about the marketing of agricultural produce, probably because the Department of Agriculture had already established an advisory committee on the marketing of agricultural produce and its reports were awaited.[61] The Minister for Finance allocated £250,000 in the 1957 budget to assist in the export marketing of

Irish agricultural produce, and the Minister for Agriculture, Seán Moylan, decided to establish an *ad hoc* advisory committee, to determine how the money should be spent. He decided that the committee should include representatives of the major farming organisations and the agricultural processing industries. Although the Department would provide an office and secretarial services, it would not be represented on the committee; if a Departmental representative objected to some of the proposals that were brought forward, Moylan claimed that 'whatever the merits of the case, his actions would be liable to be misrepresented by outside organisations'. The fifteen-man committee included representatives of the NFA, the IAOS, the ICMSA, the Bacon Curers' Association and the National Executive of the Irish Livestock Trade. Major-General M. J. Costello, the head of the Irish Sugar Company, was asked to act as chairman. When he declined the Department approached Juan Greene, president of the NFA.[62]

This was the first detailed review of the markets for agricultural produce to be conducted since the early 1920s. The committee was authorised to investigate the market for any particular product and to recommend measures to meet the requirements of existing markets or to develop new and expanded markets. By 1959 it had issued reports on the marketing of bacon and pigmeat, eggs, turkeys, dairy produce and livestock and meat.[63] It rounded off its work with a report setting out a broad strategy for Irish agricultural policy, specifically in relation to trade.

In the case of dairy produce, eggs, poultry, pigs and bacon, the committee recommended that powerful export agencies should replace the existing system, where the trade was handled by a large number of exporters. The Pigs and Bacon Commission would become the sole exporter of pigs and pigmeat; at the time exports of Irish bacon to Britain were handled by thirty separate interests. An egg marketing board would fill a similar role for eggs; a turkey marketing board would become the sole exporter of turkeys, although it would also be permitted to sell turkeys on the home market. The Butter Marketing Committee was the sole exporter of butter; the committee recommended that it be replaced by a dairy produce board, which would be responsible for exports of cheese, milk powder (to markets other than Britain), condensed milk and canned cream, as well as butter. The most conservative report related to livestock and beef, perhaps because they were the only products with a secure and profitable market. The committee concluded that a centralised marketing agency for meat would not result in increased exports or higher prices, and recommended no changes in the marketing of store or fat cattle.

The reports went into considerable details on existing and future market prospects in Britain and continental Europe, the importance of trade fairs and exhibitions, and the role of government export agencies. The committee made several recommendations with a view to improving the quality and continuity of supply of agricultural produce. In the case of bacon it recommended that steps should be taken to ensure that 600 tons of bacon were available for export every week; to bring this about it recommended a return to wartime practices where pigs were purchased centrally and distributed to the factories. It proposed some changes in the grading of eggs and bacon and the introduction of guaranteed minimum producer prices for eggs, for grade B bacon (guaranteed prices were already offered for grades A and B1) and for quality turkeys, in order to encourage increased production and more regular supplies.

The *Programme for Economic Expansion* and the heads of agricultural policy drawn up by the Department of Agriculture in 1959 emphasised that cattle should account for most of the increase in agricultural output, and that subsidising agricultural prices was not favoured. However, the report of the advisory committee on general aspects of the marketing of agricultural produce recommended that farmers should be encouraged to produce greater quantities of milk, pigs, poultry and eggs, by being offered guaranteed prices. The committee firmly believed that raising output was a precondition for achieving better marketing, since it would ensure continuity of supplies. The committee also claimed, somewhat implausibly, that Ireland would secure a larger share of the British market if Irish farmers produced more milk, eggs and pigs. In turn this would enable Ireland to exercise more influence over the UK market, and it would reduce the cost of exporting. Although the committee acknowledged that it was improbable that Ireland would be in a position to export butter, pigs and eggs at a profit, it argued that these products provided a decent livelihood for small farmers and helped to maintain employment on the land. For this reason the committee recommended that farmers should be offered guaranteed minimum prices.

On the wider question of the government's trade strategy the advisory committee assumed that Ireland would follow the example of other European countries by moving in the direction of freer trade and closer economic association with Britain and continental Europe. While Britain was the most important market for Irish agricultural produce, the committee noted Ireland's privileged access to the UK market was coming under threat from plans to establish a free trade area, EFTA, and the increase in British agricultural output. It recommended that Ireland enter into an economic association with Britain and that the government negotiate better access for Irish agricultural produce to European markets through bilateral trade agreements.[64] However, the committee was not optimistic about market prospects in continental Europe. It suggested that difficulties such as poor transport facilities outweighed the opportunities.

The Department of Agriculture published a white paper accepting all the major recommendations of the advisory committee, other than the proposal to introduce guaranteed prices.[65] The Department of Finance wanted to set a figure in the white paper of £1.25 million per annum as the maximum cost of export subsidies, but the Cabinet rejected this.[66] The white paper was followed by the 1960 Agricultural Marketing Bill, which contained three sections. One provided for the establishment of an Irish dairy board; a second dealt with the re-organisation of the Pigs and Bacon Commission; the final section provided for the introduction of controls on the manufacture, sale and export of eggs.[67] When the Department of Agriculture produced the initial draft bill, the Department of Finance attempted to have a maximum figure for the cost of dairy subsidies included, but this was over-ruled following objections by the Department of Agriculture.[68] The government subsequently decided to introduce separate bills dealing with the marketing of eggs, dairy produce and pigs.[69] The Agricultural Produce (Eggs) Bill passed both houses in June 1961 without contention.[70] At the time the Department explored the possibility of developing an export trade in broilers (poultry produced in intensive units) but concluded that prospects were unpromising.[71] The Pigs and Bacon Commission was reformed and strengthened in 1964.

The marketing of dairy produce presented particular difficulties. By 1957 the cost of export subsidies was expected to rise to almost £3 million.[72] When the Cabinet asked the Department of Agriculture what could be done to contain the cost, it reported that there was little prospect of exporting butter without a subsidy and it was equally pessimistic about the prospects of increasing the output of cheese and dried milk. The market for chocolate crumb was also under threat. In January 1958 the Cabinet decided that it would meet two-thirds of the cost of the export subsidy in the coming year, with the balance being met by a levy on the dairy industry.[73]

Although the *Programme for Economic Expansion* was determined to limit the cost of agricultural subsidies, it offered no ready solution to the problem of butter exports, other than to suggest that creameries should be encouraged to diversify into producing cheese, and that farmers should feed more whole milk to calves.[74] In February 1959 the Department reported that it was negotiating with a German company about the possibility of opening a cheese factory in Wexford.[75] By the following year the Dairy Disposal Company and Golden Vale Co-Operative were planning to produce cheese.[76] In 1961, however, T. K. Whitaker described milk as 'something of a problem product'.[77] By the late 1950s many European countries were selling subsidised butter on the UK market. In 1958 the British Board of Trade warned the Department of Agriculture that it would introduce anti-dumping duties, unless Ireland agreed to measures to 'regulate' butter imports. The threatened restrictions were prompted by claims from New Zealand that the market for its butter was being undermined by imports of subsidised butter from Ireland, Finland and Sweden. Although Ireland claimed that its right to export subsidised butter to the UK had been acknowledged in the 1938 Anglo-Irish Trade Agreement, and that this had not been altered by the 1948 agreement, Britain did not concede that this was so. On this occasion the threat to Irish butter exports did not materialise. Butter prices on the UK market rose during the winter of 1958 and there were reports of a butter shortage,[78] but the events of 1958 were a foretaste of future developments.

In 1960 the Department introduced legislation setting up a new dairy export board. When the government decided that it should be given an Irish name, the first proposal was An Bord Táirgí Déiríochta, but this was later changed to An Bord Bainne. The bill setting up An Bord Bainne became law in January 1961.[79]

'THE SPECIAL TRADE RELATIONSHIP': ANGLO-IRISH TRADE

One of the main objectives of the *Programme for Economic Expansion* was to increase export earnings, and the market for agricultural produce was an obvious priority. The emergence of two trading blocs in Europe – EFTA and the EEC – posed certain dangers for Irish exports. In July 1959 the committee of secretaries suggested that it was essential to establish closer economic relations with Britain, in order to protect existing economic outlets 'and avoid being squeezed between the emergent trading blocs in Europe'. It recommended that Ireland should attempt to have British price guarantees extended to all the major Irish agricultural exports. In the light of the threat to restrict Irish dairy exports in 1958, the Department of Agriculture was also keen to secure a commitment from Britain that no import quotas would be imposed on Irish agricultural produce, and the continuation of Ireland's existing preferences in the UK market. (Butter from Denmark and other European countries was subject to an import duty, whereas Irish butter was not.) The Department also wanted a commitment from Britain that both countries would confer on future agricultural policies with a view to securing 'balanced agricultural development'. Whitaker told Lemass that Ireland's claim to be included in British agricultural price support schemes should be based on the argument that higher agricultural prices would enable Ireland to increase its imports of British goods.

The Cabinet was divided on this proposal for closer economic relations with the UK. Paddy Smith and James Ryan, the Minister for Finance, were in favour, but the Minister for Industry and Commerce, Jack Lynch, was unwilling to reduce the protection given to Irish manufactured goods in return for concessions to Irish agricultural produce in the UK. Frank Aiken, the Minister for External Affairs, was concerned that any agreement for joint development would imply that Ireland was economically subservient to Britain. Despite these reservations the Cabinet decided to initiate trade talks in the hope that a new trade agreement would provide, 'An assurance of expanding markets in Britain for Irish agricultural products at reasonable and stable prices'. In return Ireland would offer Britain more favourable terms for its industrial products in the Irish market. But two days before the Cabinet took the decision to proceed with trade talks, Britain and Denmark signed a bilateral trade deal. Denmark was a member of EFTA; Ireland was not. Under the agreement Danish agricultural produce would be subject to the same tariffs as produce from Ireland or duty-free access. Britain also gave a commitment that Danish produce would retain its existing share of the UK market and would be given a guaranteed share of any expanding market. If Britain decided to impose quotas on agricultural imports, Denmark would be given a reasonable share of the market. This agreement made it highly unlikely that Britain would agree to a substantial increase in Irish agricultural exports.[80]

The Irish team of Seán Lemass, Paddy Smith and Jack Lynch held exploratory trade talks with British ministers on 13 July 1959 and it was agreed that detailed discussions would continue at official level. On 30 July the Irish authorities submitted a memorandum suggesting that, 'The aim would be the joint and coordinated development of agriculture in both countries'. They claimed there was a stronger case for a common agricultural policy between Britain and Ireland than between the six countries of the EEC. Further trade talks were postponed until after the British general election in October 1959. When Irish and British ministers met in February 1960, Lemass asked whether there was a price that Ireland could pay, which would help to secure what would be tantamount to a 'common market' between Britain and Ireland. Reginald Maudling, the president of the Board of Trade, said that he could not think of any price, which Ireland could pay, that would enable Britain to agree to Ireland's wishes.[81]

The trade agreement signed by officials in April 1960 provided meagre gains for Irish farmers. The 3s 6d differential in the price support for Irish store cattle was abolished for fully-attested cattle, a concession designed to encourage Ireland to speed up the TB eradication programme; and Britain agreed that the price paid for Irish lamb and sheep exported to the UK would continue to be linked to British support prices.[82] Britain agreed not to reduce the preferential terms that Ireland currently enjoyed in the British market without prior consultation. Both governments agreed not to impose special duties or other anti-dumping measures on imports from the other country, unless they were satisfied that the imports would cause material damage to domestic producers or to trade from a third country, and only after first consulting the other country. These provisions brought Anglo-Irish trade relations into line with the practice of GATT.[83] At the time Ireland was not yet a member of GATT. They also agreed to hold annual trade talks.

Although the Department of Agriculture claimed that the 1960 agreement 'stresses the special trade relationship which existed between the two countries and the desire of both Governments to maintain and expand existing trade',[84] the early 1960s saw Britain imposing further restrictions on Ireland's access to its market, particularly for butter and bacon. The introduction of import quotas was a critical component of Britain's plans to reform its agricultural policy. In 1961 Britain issued a white paper on agricultural policy that included a commitment to continue to provide British farmers with favourable prices, but Britain was determined to reduce the cost of exchequer subsidies, by setting a ceiling on domestic agricultural output of some commodities and by limiting imports.[85] The Department of Agriculture also suspected that Britain wished to create a crisis in the UK butter market in order to protect New Zealand and Australia's market shares, in anticipation of Britain applying to join the EEC. Although the Department of Agriculture continued to emphasise the historically close trading links between Britain and Ireland, by the early 1960s these carried little weight in trade talks, when compared with membership of a modern multilateral trading bloc, such as EFTA. Ireland's preferential access to the UK market was being challenged by Denmark, which was demanding similar terms. The contraction of the UK market for dairy produce and bacon was ill timed, since in 1961 Ireland established a modern export marketing agency, An Bord Bainne, and moves were afoot to improve the marketing of bacon.

In March 1961 New Zealand accused Ireland of dumping subsidised butter on the UK market, and asked for an assurance that this would cease. The Department of Agriculture pointed out that Irish butter only accounted for 7,000 tons, or less than 2 per cent of UK imports, whereas New Zealand supplied Britain with 147,000 tons. However, Denmark also alleged that Irish butter imports were 'a material influence' in the present market crisis and threatened to ask Britain to introduce anti-dumping measures against Irish butter and dried milk. Denmark had requested that Britain remove all import duties on Danish poultry, eggs, cheese and canned milk.[86] When the National Farmers' Union and the (British) Milk Marketing Board joined in demands for anti-dumping measures to reduce the over-supply of dairy produce, Britain referred the matter to GATT.[87] Although GATT held a three-day meeting in September 1961 (the prompt action suggests that this was regarded as a serious matter) to examine the problems in the UK butter market, it failed to resolve the matter. The Irish authorities noted that New Zealand appeared to regard the British market as their natural right. They were not prepared to agree to any restrictions on New Zealand butter, but they expected that all other exporting countries would make a sacrifice to enable New Zealand to benefit from higher prices.

On 26 September the British Trade Commissioner in Dublin presented the Department of External Affairs with a proposal that Ireland should reduce its exports of butter between 1 October 1961 and 31 March 1962 to 4,000 tons, or less than half the quantity exported during the corresponding period in the previous year. The proposal involved a reduction in butter imports from every country except New Zealand; if Ireland refused to accede to this proposal, Britain would impose anti-dumping duties on Irish butter.[88] The fact that this quota was determined without prior consultation was in breach of the 1960 trade agreement. On 9 November the Cabinet decided that it should be rejected, and that a white paper should be prepared outlining Ireland's position. It reaffirmed this decision on 21 November in line with the advice given by the Department of Agriculture. Although Britain was also threatening to impose import quotas on Irish bacon, the Department was sceptical that the prospects for Irish bacon would be enhanced if Ireland acceded to Britain's request for a reduction in butter exports.[89] When Ireland refused to accept an import quota of 4,000 tons for the six months to 31 March 1962, Britain imposed a duty on Irish butter.

Talks on future quotas were due to begin in Geneva on 22 January 1962. Although British and Irish officials met in London on 16 January, Britain was not prepared to make any commitments in advance of the GATT talks. The British informed the Irish representatives that the problems of over-supply were expected to continue. If Ireland could make a case in Geneva for a larger quota, Britain would not be obstructionist. The Irish delegation emphasised that Ireland had a special trading relationship with Britain and should therefore be treated in a different manner to other importers. Michael Barry indicated that Ireland was seeking an annual butter quota of 16,000 tons. If the Irish quota was unsatisfactory, he warned that Ireland would be forced to ask 'if the Trade Agreements with Britain meant anything and if our problems had to be settled multilaterally'. The Irish ambassador in London, Hugh McCann, subsequently reported that British officials had indicated that Ireland would have to present a strong case if it were to obtain a higher quota at the Geneva talks. Rumbold, a senior official at the Board of Trade, advised that Ireland should find a formula that would justify an increase, and it should adopt tactics that would secure the support of other affected countries. Nagle described these remarks as 'far from reassuring. In effect he appears to be trying to jettison bilateral obligations and to wash his hands of any definite responsibility towards us in regards to butter.' This was disturbing given the commitments contained in the Anglo-Irish trade agreements that both countries would consult on these matters. Nagle suspected that Britain and New Zealand were in close contact, and that Britain feared that New Zealand would impose restrictions on British imports if Britain imposed a quota on New Zealand butter.[90] He recommended that Ireland should threaten to take similar retaliatory action, but Whitaker believed that this would be unwise. When it became apparent that no agreement would result from the Geneva talks, the task of allocating butter quotas fell to a senior GATT official, Wyndham White. Ireland demanded an annual quota of 15,000 tons. White initially suggested a figure of 9,000 tons. The talks again ended without agreement.

Irish bacon exports were also threatened by anti-dumping regulations. British bacon-curers demanded that the Board of Trade curb imports of subsidised bacon from Ireland.[91] In January 1962 Hugh McCann reported that the British authorities were anxious to discuss the matter. He also intimated that Britain wanted to put pressure on the Danes to restrict bacon exports to the UK. Again the Department of Agriculture pointed out that Irish produce did not account for a significant share of the UK market. In 1960/1 Ireland supplied a mere 7 per cent, and imports were no larger than in 1938/9. The Department also reiterated that Irish agricultural produce had a right to unrestricted entry to the UK market under the terms of the 1938 and 1948 trade agreements. When Duncan Sandys, the Secretary of State for Commonwealth Relations, raised the matter with Hugh McCann, shortly after this, Britain agreed with McCann that the main problem for the UK bacon market was the higher imports from Denmark, but insisted that if Ireland agreed to limit exports, Britain would find it easier to persuade Denmark to do likewise. These developments were unwelcome at a time when the Department of Agriculture was attempting to improve the quality of Irish pigs. As an incentive to farmers to produce better-quality pigs, a new, higher standard of pig, a Grade A Special, was introduced that attracted higher guaranteed prices. By 1960 up to 17 per cent of Grade A pigs were meeting the higher standard.[92]

In March 1962 McCann reported that Britain had decided to introduce a system of import licences for butter and would be asking Ireland to waive the conditions in the Anglo-Irish trade agreements precluding this. When Nagle visited London for discussions with the Board of Trade, Britain offered Ireland an annual quota of 10,000 tons. The Irish response followed the traditional line: Ireland objected in principle to any restriction; it would prefer a voluntary agreement. It also claimed that Ireland's circumstances warranted more favourable treatment. Unless the quota was increased, Ireland would find it difficult to agree to waive the conditions in the Anglo-Irish trade agreements precluding quotas. After these talks Lemass suggested that Smith should travel to London and he asked Britain to defer a decision until the Minister for Agriculture had had an opportunity to present the Irish case. Lemass told the British ambassador that if Irish butter exports to Britain were restricted to the proposed level, this 'could possibly have permanent and detrimental consequences for us when we became members of the E.E.C. and were seeking a higher share of Europe's butter market'. McCann warned that Smith's trip to London would be 'the last throw of the dice' because Britain planned to make an announcement about import restrictions four days later. When Smith met British ministers in London, they raised the Irish butter quota to 12,000 tons. Although Smith dismissed this as unacceptable, Britain held firm. When Britain announced the butter quotas some days later, the Department of Agriculture noted that the Poles had been treated generously, whereas the French had been awarded a smaller quota than under the GATT figures. Agriculture noted wryly that this 'must be regarded as a very courageous decision by the British in present circumstances, i.e. taking into account the Common Market negotiations and the size of French stocks'. The government press statement noted that although the government was not satisfied, Ireland's quota was higher than that originally offered.[93]

The history of Anglo-Irish trade in agricultural produce during the early 1960s indicates that trade negotiations were moving from a bilateral to a multilateral context. Although Ireland continually referred to a 'special relationship' and to the long history of Anglo-Irish trade – the Department of Agriculture told Erroll, the president of the Board of Trade, that Ireland was exporting butter before New Zealand was discovered[94] – the international climate had shifted. At one point in 1962, when the Department of Agriculture was expressing frustration that Britain was not honouring the Anglo-Irish trade agreements, Cornelius Cremin, secretary of the Department of External Affairs, reminded Nagle that Britain's approach to trade had become more multilateral, which did not suit Ireland, because Ireland preferred a bilateral approach.[95] Yet by the early 1960s Irish frustration with the limitations of the UK market was prompting the government to investigate the possibility of EEC membership. However, the government was fully aware that the full benefits of EEC membership for Irish agriculture could only be realised if Britain also became a member.

IRELAND AND THE EEC, 1960–3

On 20 July 1960 Seán Lemass made a statement in Dáil Éireann, outlining Ireland's future policy on Europe. He noted that the first objective would be to protect Ireland's trade relationship with Britain, which he described as 'the keystone of our external trade structure'. A second objective would be to secure markets in Europe.[96] By this time the Department of Agriculture was becoming concerned that the EEC's plans for a Common Agricultural Policy (CAP) would seriously reduce exports of Irish agricultural produce to member countries.[97] On the day that Lemass outlined the government's policy in Dáil Éireann, the NFA issued a statement urging the government to join the EEC without waiting for Britain. Commenting on this statement, *The Irish Farmers' Journal* remarked that, 'By and large, we must choose between the higher prices and stability within the Common Market and a declining market for farm produce in Britain, where dumping from Europe and the rest of the world, is increasingly likely'. According to this article, one factor behind the NFA's announcement was the failure to secure better market opportunities in Britain under the recent trade agreement.[98] Disappointment with the outcome of the 1960 Anglo-Irish Trade Agreement had also prompted several TDs to table questions in Dáil Éireann, asking whether the government planned to apply for membership of either EFTA or the EEC.[99]

The Department of Agriculture dismissed the NFA's position as unrealistic. If Ireland joined the EEC without Britain, it noted that there would be gains for pig and egg producers, and dairy farmers would benefit from higher EEC milk prices. Livestock farmers would be the major losers, since EEC imports of quality beef 'could scarcely absorb our total exportable surplus of such beef'. Livestock exporters would remain dependent on the British market, but with Ireland inside the EEC and Britain outside, it doubted that Britain would maintain the existing link between British and Irish cattle prices. If Britain imposed restrictions on Irish cattle exports the Department concluded that 'we would be in serious trouble'. As the EEC was almost self-sufficient in agricultural produce, Ireland could not assume it would be permitted to expand production as it wished. The Department also expressed fears that the EEC would introduce a programme to consolidate farm holdings and reduce the numbers employed in agriculture. If Britain also joined the EEC and Irish farmers were treated like French and German farmers, 'we should be happy enough', but it feared that 'the Six will not wish to depart from their present delicately balanced agricultural plan', and they might exclude Ireland and Britain from full integration into the EEC's agricultural policy. Given Ireland's lack of a large and expanding home market it was necessary to become associated with a strong industrial economy that could support Irish agricultural incomes. This could not be achieved in the absence of 'some special economic understanding with Britain'.[100] In a later, more detailed response, produced in February 1961, the Department determined that the benefits of joining the EEC (without Britain) would not be comparable to the benefits that would accrue 'from integrating Irish agriculture into the British food production machine'; in the Department's opinion such an arrangement would enable a substantial expansion of Irish agriculture.[101]

By 1961 there were reports that Britain was giving serious consideration to applying to join the EEC. On 27 April Lemass and the ministers for Agriculture, External Affairs, Finance and Industry and Commerce took a decision that if Britain applied to join the EEC, Ireland would do likewise. It was also decided to discuss the matter with the British authorities. Ireland wanted prior notice if Britain decided to apply for membership.[102] Lemass introduced a white paper in Dáil Éireann on 5 July 1961, setting three future trading options for Ireland: an Anglo-Irish trade agreement; membership of the EEC; or membership of EFTA. He informed the Dáil that if Britain applied to join the EEC, Ireland would do likewise.[103] Some weeks later he told the annual summer banquet of Macra na Feirme that Ireland's decision not to join the EEC without Britain had nothing to do with politics, 'but only with the hard inescapable facts of our trade situation'. Britain took 75 per cent of Irish exports.[104]

The Department of Agriculture was concerned about the possible impact of EEC membership on Anglo-Irish trade.[105] When Nagle met Sir Eric Roll, the deputy-secretary at the British Ministry of Agriculture, Fisheries and Food, in June 1961, he commented that Ireland was in the dark about Britain's plans for agricultural imports if it became a member of the EEC. Because EEC membership would present serious difficulties for Irish manufacturing industry, Irish people 'would expect positive evidence as to our agricultural prospects'. Sir Eric Roll informed him that Britain had yet to decide on what should be done about imports of temperate foodstuffs from the Commonwealth in the event of EEC membership. Nagle emphasised that it was important that Britain should open discussions with the Irish government over agricultural trade before it was publicly committed to any arrangements with the European Community. On 21 June Britain agreed to hold early discussions with Ireland on the implications of EEC membership.[106] When Lemass sent an aide-memoire to Ludwig Erhard, the West German Chancellor, in August, a paragraph was inserted on the insistence of the Department of Agriculture, stressing the importance for Irish agriculture of ensuring that negotiations on Ireland's conditions of entry were conducted simultaneously with the British negotiations. This matter cropped up repeatedly in Irish memoranda during the remainder of 1961.[107]

During the autumn of 1961 Ireland began to prepare for talks on its application to join the EEC. Lemass suggested that a competent official, familiar with the agricultural aspects of the Treaty of Rome, should be posted to Brussels on a permanent basis. Smith recommended that this should be Dr D. O'Sullivan, the agricultural counsellor at the Irish Embassy in London. J. O'Mahony, at the time an assistant principal in the Department of Agriculture, was posted to London as agricultural counsellor.[108] In

September Nagle, Whitaker and Cremin travelled to Brussels for informal talks. At the time the EEC was drawing up proposals for a common agricultural policy. When Nagle, accompanied by O'Sullivan and Doherty, met Sicco Mansholt, the EEC Commissioner for Agriculture, the Irish officials referred to Ireland's interest in the CAP and the importance of the British market for Irish agriculture. Mansholt told them that the CAP negotiations could not be postponed until the applications for membership from Ireland, Britain and Denmark had been decided, but he promised that the applicant countries would be kept informed of developments regarding the CAP, and their views would be taken into account. When Whitaker and Con Cremin returned from a tour of EEC capitals, they reported that agriculture did not present a problem in Ireland's application for membership; the main handicap appeared to be Ireland's neutral status.[109]

Lemass had given a commitment that the Minister for Agriculture would meet the farming organisations to discuss the implications of EEC membership, and the Department of Agriculture issued invitations to the NFA, the ICMSA, the IAOS, the Irish Beet Growers' Association and the county committees of agriculture.[110] When they met the Minister, the Department suggested that groups should be established to study the implications of EEC membership for all the major commodities – cattle, sheep, beef and mutton; pigs and pig products; milk and milk products; poultry and eggs; cereals; sugar- beet and horticulture. Each group would examine how efficient its sector was in terms of output and marketing, and future market prospects within the EEC.[111] A similar process was under way for Irish industry. However, the prospective market conditions for agricultural produce remained uncertain until the existing member states reached agreement on the CAP in January 1962.[112] By July 1962 all the study groups had met, and reports on pigs, beef, milk products and cereals were expected by the autumn.[113]

Lemass presented Ireland's application for membership of the EEC in Brussels on 18 January 1962. He opened his speech by referring to Ireland's historic and cultural links with Europe and the political ideals behind the formation of the European Community. When he turned to economic matters he began with agriculture. He mentioned the importance of agriculture to the Irish economy, the expectation that the CAP would provide rational and orderly trading conditions for agricultural produce, and the Community's commitment to maintaining viable family farms. He indicated that Ireland was concerned at how Britain's policy of food imports would be brought into harmony with the EEC.[114] An early draft of this speech referred to the importance of retaining Ireland's bilateral trading arrangements during the transition to EEC membership, but this was removed on the recommendation of the Department of Agriculture.[115]

Although Ireland had formally applied for membership of the EEC, the Commission showed little interest in opening negotiations on Ireland's application. In February 1962 Biggar, the Irish ambassador in Brussels, reported that there was a danger that Ireland's application would be put on the long finger, until the outcome of negotiations on Britain's membership had become clearer.[116] The delay gave rise to concern that Ireland would not be consulted about transitional arrangements for British trade in agricultural produce. It also threatened to exclude Ireland from consultations on the formulation of detailed proposals for the CAP. On 14 January, four days before Lemass' Brussels speech, the Council of the EEC agreed on regulations that would come into force on 1 July 1962 as the first stage in implementing CAP. The process would be completed on 1 July 1969. The arrangements provided for the establishment of a European Agricultural Guidance and Guarantee Fund (FEOGA) to provide refunds on exports of agricultural produce to countries outside the EEC, intervention (floor) prices in the internal market, and money to fund structural changes in European agriculture. The rules of competition would apply to agricultural markets, unless exceptions were agreed in order to assist the establishment of the CAP. Management committees were established to devise regulations governing each commodity; these regulations would provide for target prices, levies, and intervention prices. By the beginning of 1962 the Commission had drawn up detailed proposals for eggs and poultry, pigmeat and wine, but regulations for beef, sugar and dairy produce had yet to be negotiated.[117] On 30 January Biggar reported that the EEC was planning to consult Britain and Denmark (Denmark had also applied to join the EEC) about the CAP proposals for beef, dairy produce and sugar. Nagle urged that Ireland should be included in these discussions; 'our experience of both the British and the Danes is that they are usually very quick to worm their way into discussions of this kind'.[118] When Biggar protested to EEC officials that they were making a distinction between Britain and Denmark, and Ireland, EEC officials reported that the talks were 'simply to amuse the people'. Biggar retorted that 'our people had to be amused too'.[119] He claimed that the Commission tended to regard Ireland's application as an adjunct of the British application.[120]

In March 1962 Nagle and O'Doherty met senior EEC officials in

Brussels, and arranged to supply them with statistics on Irish agriculture, and with a statement setting out the Department's views on the process of harmonising legislation.[121] In return the EEC officials agreed to consult Ireland on an informal basis about the draft CAP regulations governing beef and dairy produce.[122] Ireland received a copy of the proposed regulations on dairy produce some weeks later,[123] but when the Department of Agriculture pressed the EEC to hold informal talks on these regulations, the Commission repeatedly procrastinated, offering a variety of excuses for doing so.[124]

Ireland's other concern was to discover the terms that Britain was seeking for agriculture. In February 1962 Hugh McCann, the Irish ambassador in London, presented a summary of Britain's views on agriculture within the EEC, which was based on his discussions with officials in the Commonwealth Relations Office. He reported that Britain saw market sharing (quotas) as one means of coping with over-supply. The British wished to have an annual review of the agricultural sector, and to retain the right to 'top up' the incomes of British farmers. Britain believed that the EEC was coming to appreciate the need to safeguard vital Commonwealth interests, and hoped that concessions on Commonwealth imports would continue after the end of the transitional arrangements. Britain also acknowledged that veterinary health measures could not be relied on to exclude continental produce in the long term.[125]

When Nagle read this report, he commented that Britain's stance was dictated solely by what was best for British farmers and for the Commonwealth. It showed no real acceptance of the Common Market agricultural philosophy. Britain's objective was to ensure that Commonwealth food would continue to be imported into the enlarged EEC, but the adverse effects of this concession would fall on others. It was in the interests of Irish agriculture that import quotas for Commonwealth produce should be as low as possible. Ireland would not favour any arrangement for Commonwealth produce beyond the transitional period. The request to be permitted to 'top up' farm incomes ran contrary to the basic objectives of the Common Market of equalising prices so that production would be concentrated in the most efficient country. If Britain continued to top up farm incomes this would mean that the increase in Britain's industrial wealth, because of EEC membership, would be used to assist its farmers, not farmers in weaker countries. Britain's request for a long transitional period would be of benefit to Irish horticulture, because it relied on tariff protection, but it would damage all other sections of Irish agriculture. Nagle advised that Ireland should adopt a similar attitude to the Six: 'we would see little reason for concessional terms for British agriculture but would agree that the Community would have to see what it could do to ease the effects of Common-Market policy on exports from New Zealand and certain other major exporters during the transitional period'. He ended by noting that 'the British still seem to want the best of both worlds'. Nagle did not anticipate that Britain would get the deal that it wanted. At this stage he cautioned that there was no need for Ireland 'to enter the lists against them'.[126]

Ireland's application was due to be considered by the Council of Ministers on 24 July 1962, but the Council referred the matter back to their permanent representatives. This meant that any discussion at Council would be deferred at least until September, much to Ireland's annoyance. Nagle was concerned that Denmark would be consulted on the framing of agricultural regulations, whereas Ireland would not. He claimed that some draft regulations, such as those relating to veterinary health, would be disadvantageous to Ireland. By the time that a British entry package had been negotiated, he feared that it would be too late for Ireland to influence the Community's thinking on various agricultural policies.[127] On 23 October Biggar reported that the EEC Council had agreed to open talks on Ireland's application. Nagle met Mansholt three days later to request that Ireland should now be given the same consultation rights as Britain and Denmark.[128] Mansholt agreed to this in principle, and some weeks later the Department of Agriculture sent him a copy of their observations on the EEC's draft directive on the fresh meat trade, asking that its views, which were broadly favourable, should be noted.[129] However, in December Britain protested at Ireland's submitting its views on lamb and sheep to the Commission. The Irish note had pointed out that any concessions to New Zealand and Australia would damage Ireland's interests.[130]

The Department of Agriculture also commissioned a report by Professor Raeburn, an agricultural economist at the University of Aberdeen, who had carried out a survey of Irish agriculture in 1947 on behalf of the British Ministry of Food, and K. E. Hunt, of the Agricultural Economics Research Institute at Oxford, on the difficulties that Irish agriculture might experience in adapting to EEC membership.[131] This report was mainly statistical. It suggested that Germany was the most promising market for Irish produce, and the Department decided that Irish efforts should be concentrated there. The main difficulties were the lack of an efficient distribution system for Irish produce and the high cost of advertising and promotion. The Department recommended that Irish exporters should establish a combined marketing operation, and that efforts should initially be concentrated in one region.[132]

By the summer of 1962 Irish officials were becoming concerned that Britain's application for EEC membership would fail. In July O'Sullivan reported that there were major disagreements between Britain and the EEC over agriculture.[133] Britain was seeking unrestricted entry for Australian and New Zealand beef; the right to operate what the Department of Agriculture described as 'an isolated and protected sheep and lamb market', and the continuation of the Commonwealth sugar agreement.[134] On 3 July the committee of secretaries decided that the task of working out 'fall back positions' if the British application foundered, should be put in hand as a matter of urgency.[135] Yet the rumour mill continued to send conflicting reports during the autumn and winter of 1962. On 6 December J. O'Mahony reported that Lardinois, the agricultural attaché at the Netherlands Embassy in London (and a future EEC Commissioner), had expressed concern that the negotiations between Britain and the six EEC members were on the point of collapse.[136] In contrast, on 22 December Biggar reported that there was an air of 'restrained optimism' in the Commission that a deal could be concluded with Britain on agricultural matters.[137] In early January 1963, with the successful completion of British negotiations apparently in prospect, the Department was pressing for the reports of the commodity study groups to be completed, and it was making arrangements for senior EEC officials to travel to Dublin for talks on the dairy industry.[138] De Gaulle's veto of Britain's application at the end of the month brought these developments to a halt. Although Ireland's application remained on the table, it was generally acknowledged that Ireland would not join the EEC unless Britain became a member. The NFA continued to insist that Ireland should join the EEC independently of Britain, but this was not a realistic option.

Lemass told the Dáil that he regretted the suspension of negotiations on British entry to the EEC, and expressed the hope that a way would be found to overcome the impasse. In the meantime the Irish government would explore the possibility of expanding export markets in Europe and Britain. Ireland would 'be prepared to consider participating in any negotiations for collective arrangements for freer trade involving our principal trading partners'.[139] Ireland's 'fall-back position' was to secure a free trade agreement with Britain. Yet Britain's efforts to protect the position of both its farmers and Commonwealth producers throughout the

371

negotiations on EEC membership, and its refusal to acknowledge the existence of 'a special trade relationship' with Ireland, when it introduced import quotas for dairy produce, were indications of the difficulties that this would entail.

LIVING STANDARDS, ECONOMIC PLANNING AND FARMING ORGANISATIONS

By the end of 1963 the agricultural price index stood at 102.2 (1953=100), whereas the consumer price index had risen to 131.2 (1953=100). Agricultural prices were lower than in 1958. Between 1960 and 1963 store cattle prices rose by only 2 per cent. The poor performance of the livestock trade, which had been regarded as the most promising sector, was further evidence of the difficult conditions that confronted Irish farming during the late 1950s and early 1960s. British farmers were short of fodder in 1958, and as a consequence they bought fewer stores, and the market remained depressed from then until 1961. Sales of Irish livestock in the UK were also damaged by fears that they would re-infect herds with bovine TB.[140] The market for British beef was depressed by higher imports of Argentinian beef and cheap broiler chickens;[141] indeed, British consumption of beef remained below the pre-war level. The British Ministry of Agriculture was encouraging its farmers to produce more livestock in place of milk, which was in over-supply. While this might ensure a long-term market for Irish stores, the market for beef and fat cattle did not appear promising.[142]

Any discussion on agricultural living standards must be set in the context of four factors:

- the widening gap in living standards between the farming and non-farming communities;
- the emphasis that the *Programme for Economic Expansion* placed on agriculture as the key sector in generating economic growth;
- the emergence of more powerful farming organisations and their belief that they should be party to the formulation of agricultural policy;
- the rhetoric of social justice and the importance of preserving the family farm, which featured prominently in government speeches by the early 1960s.

The decade from the mid-1940s to the mid-1950s saw a major expansion in rural and agricultural organisations. They were a logical response by farmers to the growth in government intervention in agriculture, and the realisation that farm prices were increasingly being determined by government. A secondary motive for their emergence was the knowledge that farm incomes were lagging behind other sections of the community. In Britain the National Farmers' Union took part in annual price negotiations with the Ministry for Agriculture.[143] The Irish government's commitment to economic planning in 1958, and Lemass' preference for consulting vocational interests, provided Irish farming organisations with an opportunity to become more assertive.

The negotiations between farming organisations prior to the founding of the NFA in 1955 were carried out on the assumption that the NFA would be a federation, with specialist organisations such as the ICMSA, the Irish Beet Growers' Association, and commodity organisations acting under its umbrella. However, Irish farmers failed to create a unified organisation on the lines of the NFU. In contrast, business organisations, such as the Federated Union of Employers, the Federation of Irish Industries and the Irish Congress of Trade Unions assumed a much higher profile from the late 1950s, as wage and salary negotiations became more centralised. Wages rose by 17 per cent between 1960 and 1964; the increases were negotiated as part of the eighth and ninth wage rounds.[144] The numerous references in speeches by Lemass and other Cabinet ministers to Ireland's new-found economic growth, and the rising living standards, highlighted the growing gap between the farming sector and the rest of the economy. In October 1960, in a speech to the Dublin Chamber of Commerce, Lemass claimed that there was a real prospect of achieving a major expansion in industry that would result in higher employment and improved living standards for the urban population. A rise in exports had eliminated the long-standing problem with the balance of payments; unemployment was declining; but agriculture was going through a difficult transition.

The debate over rural living standards gained added impetus in 1960, when the EEC gave a commitment to safeguard the family farm. Seán Lemass made a reference to this in January 1962, when Ireland formally applied to join the EEC.[145] In 1960 Lemass had told a Macra na Feirme dinner that 'People do not live by economics alone, and the social advantage of an agricultural structure which preserves the family farm are so obvious – at least, to us here in Ireland – that we would, whether within or without the European Community, assert the justification of action by the Government, on behalf of the country, to ensure its maintenance'. He had gone on to say that Ireland's capacity to preserve the family farm would be much greater within an international community such as the EEC, because the EEC accepted the principle that hard-working farmers were entitled to a standard of living comparable to that of the urban population, and the prices of agricultural produce should be set at a level that would make this possible.[146] A 1961 encyclical by Pope John XXIII, *Mater et Magistra*, had stated that governments had an obligation to ensure that families living on the land enjoyed a standard of living comparable to other sections of the population. Lemass had cited this at some length during a speech to the Muintir na Tíre rural week in August 1961.[147] Such statements provided grist for farming organisations. Farm leaders regularly cited *Mater et Magistra* to support claims for additional state funding. The NFA requested and received financial support from the Department of Agriculture to attend a conference in Rome in 1962 that was devoted to this papal encyclical.[148] The ICMSA urged the government to encourage an expansion of pig production in order to provide small farmers with the means to live 'at least in frugal comfort'.[149]

In 1962 an official in the Department of Finance remarked that farmers' attitudes 'will be fortified by Government policy declarations that the farmers, as well as other sections of the community, should share equitably in increases in the national income'. He added that 'the preservation of status relative to other sections of the community was assuming greater importance'. Unless agricultural incomes kept pace with those of other workers, there would be a rise in the numbers leaving agriculture, and this was something that the government wished to avoid until more jobs became available in industry and services. Any further increase in the numbers leaving agriculture would 'be represented as reflecting a cynical attitude by the Government to agriculture'. In his opinion it might be in the public interest to improve farming incomes.[150] In February 1961 T. K. Whitaker suggested that the government should introduce some special measures to assist farming in underdeveloped areas, if only for psychological reasons. Liam Cunningham, Fianna Fáil TD for Donegal North-East, told Lemass in 1962 that small farmers in Inishowen were completely disillusioned because no farm enterprise offered them a decent living. He warned that they would 'grasp at any chance that promises fulfilment of their hopes. They are restless for a change', and they would fight hard to improve conditions. He prayed 'that the party of our choice will give us full support and a fair hearing'.[151]

Demands for direct measures to increase farmers' incomes were difficult to reconcile with the philosophy of the *Programme for Economic Expansion*, which stated that exchequer money should be used to boost productivity and to reduce farmers' costs, not to subsidise farm prices. In March 1960 the Department of Agriculture presented the government with a memorandum, 'Proposed Action to Increase the Incomes of Farmers'. It began by noting that agricultural incomes had fallen during the past two years, at a time when other sections of the community had seen their incomes rise, despite the fact that 'the economic justification is by no means clear'. The Department appended a list of recommended measures designed to raise farmers' incomes, including a subsidy on the price of potash; higher prices for pigs that qualified for the new Grade A Premium category; an export subsidy for reactor cattle (which was presented as part of the government's bovine TB eradication scheme); and a higher milk price. All these measures, with the exception of the increase in the price of milk, could be described as providing farmers with an incentive to improve the quality of produce or raise productivity. Despite the objections of the Department of Finance, the Cabinet approved the package, with the proviso that the increase in milk prices would be met by raising the price of butter, not from the exchequer.[152]

In March 1961 the Department tried to terminate the export subsidy for reactor cattle, because otherwise it feared farmers would come to regard it as a permanent price subsidy, but the Cabinet decided that it should be extended, because the market for Irish livestock in Britain was depressed. When its removal was reconsidered three months later, Ryan, the Minister for Finance, and Smith decided that its removal would lead to a serious depression in the Irish livestock trade. They also agreed that the gradual reduction of the subsidy over several months with a view to winding it up, 'would react adversely on farmers'. Both ministers decided that they would publicise the fact that this was a temporary subsidy linked to the eradication of bovine TB. T. K. Whitaker remarked that it would be 'most unfortunate' if a measure designed to encourage the eradication of bovine TB resulted in exchequer support for 'the last major item of agricultural exports not already subsidised'.[153] Yet the continuation of the subsidy was undoubtedly prompted by the state of the market, not by the wish to eradicate bovine TB.

Milk prices presented an intractable problem. Export subsidies were a costly item for the exchequer and any price increase not linked to improvements in quality or disease eradication was liable to trigger additional demands for anti-dumping tariffs in the UK. In 1962 the Report of the Survey Team on the Dairying Industry, which the Department commissioned as part of the preparation for joining the EEC, emphasised the need to raise standards by introducing compulsory grading of milk and a milk advisory service. The report recommended that dairy farmers should use milk-cooling equipment, and advised that the possible efficiencies from reforming the system of transporting milk to the creameries should be investigated. At the time most dairy farmers brought milk to the creamery every day, often using a horse or a donkey and cart. While this provided quaint photographs for tourists, it was not in keeping with high productivity or modern standards of hygiene and quality. The survey team recommended that grants for farm buildings should be conditional on cow-houses meeting specified standards and that grants for farm water schemes should be reconsidered.[154] The fact that responsibility for rural water schemes was divided between the ministers for Agriculture and Local Government and the Department of the Gaeltacht undoubtedly hindered progress.[155]

Negotiations between the Department of Agriculture, the Taoiseach and farm organisations became much more common from the late 1950s. Although this reflected Lemass' more consultative style of government, it began in response to difficult economic circumstances. In March 1958, while de Valera was still Taoiseach, the Cabinet decided that the Minister for Agriculture should hold an annual meeting with the NFA to review the state of agriculture. This was in line with the practice in Britain, where the Ministry of Agriculture held an annual meeting with the National Farmers' Union to discuss prices during the coming year. The government agreed to this concession when de Valera and Smith met a deputation from the NFA on 13 March 1958. At this time the critical state of government finances had resulted in cuts in the ground limestone subsidy; in the amount of money allocated for land reclamation and farm building grants; and the level of price support for wheat, pigs and feeding barley. Farming organisations were understandably angered at the reduction in government aid to agriculture, and in February 1958 the NFA held an emergency meeting where it passed a motion of no confidence in the government's policy towards agriculture. When de Valera invited a delegation of NFA members to a meeting, it submitted a memorandum demanding that the government give a commitment to introduce measures that would ensure an expansion of agricultural output. It also requested an annual meeting with the Minister for Agriculture to review policy on agriculture.

At a time when finances were tight, this was one concession that did not involve an immediate rise in government spending. However, Smith seems to have been less than enthusiastic about this agreement. He remarked that he had met NFA committees on several previous occasions, and 'such meetings to be useful needed free and frank discussion, but he had discovered that this exposes a Minister to misrepresentation and misunderstanding, when those he meets go outside.'[156] But the report of the meeting between the government and the NFA in *The Kerryman* carried the headline, '"Annual Review" May Bring New Farm Era'.

In March 1959 the *Irish Farmers' Journal* reported that the NFA was conducting a review of every commodity in preparation for the promised annual meeting with the Minister. The NFA submitted a lengthy document to de Valera and Smith some weeks later. This began by emphasising that average farm incomes were lower than the wages of unskilled workers, despite farmers' long hours and a high level of capital investment. The NFA demanded that targets should be agreed for increases in the output of different commodities in coming years, so that farmers would be in a position to make long-term plans for increased production. The document also sought a reduction in taxation, especially agricultural rates; incentives to persuade farmers to eradicate bovine TB; the creation of marketing boards for agricultural produce that would be controlled by farmers; improved access to agricultural credit; price support for dairy produce, bacon and grain; and an aggressive government policy to ensure economic prices for Irish agricultural exports.

The letter accompanying this memorandum noted that in 1958 it had been agreed that the NFA would hold an annual review with the government. However, Maurice Moynihan, the secretary to the government, noted that the agreement had provided for an annual meeting with the Department of Agriculture.[157] When Greene met Lemass and Smith in July 1959, shortly after Lemass became Taoiseach, he again pressed for the review to be held with the government, not with the Department of Agriculture. Lemass suggested that other relevant ministers, such as the ministers for Transport and Power, Industry and Commerce and Finance, might attend part of this meeting, but he was not prepared to agree to a meeting between the NFA and the government.[158] The NFA appears to have drawn a distinction between the Taoiseach and the government as a whole, and the Department of Agriculture, reserving its strongest criticism for the latter. In a supplement to the *Irish Farmers' Journal* published in September 1959, Juan Greene claimed that 'the relationship between vocational farm organisations and the Department of Agriculture has not developed to the point where co-ordinated endeavour has meant in effect that we have been able, even at this late stage, to have defined agricultural policy'. He suggested that the failure to establish a unified vocational voice for agriculture meant that the Department of Agriculture was forced to play a role in farming matters that it had never been designed to play. The multiplicity of voices speaking on the farmers' behalf meant that the Department became the sole arbiter. As a consequence, the Department had developed 'a closed shop mentality'. For many years, he claimed, 'the impression created in the public mind has been that of the farmers and their own State Department in a state of continuous rebellion and constantly at each other's throats'. He believed no other vocational group to be 'so obviously out of tune' with the government department that represented its interests.

Smith refuted Greene's allegations in a letter that included a list of over forty meetings between the Department of Agriculture and the NFA during the previous twelve months. Smith claimed that the NFA used meetings with the Department 'for purely propaganda purposes', and alleged that the NFA engaged in a constant campaign to 'denigrate and besmirch' the Department. If negotiations between the NFA and the Department were to be effective, 'mutual trust and goodwill' would be essential.[159]

Relations between the Minister and the NFA remained cool following this exchange. In March 1960 Greene told Lemass that he had had a long meeting with Smith. According to Greene,

> He didn't appear anxious for the type of review as outlined in my letter to you since it was his opinion that it would be largely repetition of the facts that had been previously presented and which were already well known to him. He also felt that it would draw further undue speculation and that in any case they had hoped to make an announcement at an early date. [This was presumably an announcement of the package of measures described above.]

Greene told Lemass that while the NFA was not pressing for a review of farm prices, he hoped that the government would make 'a substantial contribution towards alleviating this adverse income position'.[160] The package of measures to assist farmers announced by Smith included an increase in the price of butter; higher guaranteed prices for premium pigs; a potash subsidy; an export subsidy for reactor cattle; and rates exemption for new or restored farm outoffices. Greene noted that these concessions were worth £2 million, which was £13 million less than the relative deterioration that had taken place in agricultural incomes over the past year.[161]

Comparisons between farm incomes and those in the rest of the community began to feature strongly in the NFA's communications with the government, whether these were conducted in private or on public platforms. In December 1961 Louis Smith, an economist with the NFA, told Tadhg Ó Cearbhaill in the Department of the Taoiseach that the NFA had calculated that farmers would need an additional £83 million in order to restore agriculture's share of national income to the 1953 level and to compensate for the loss in relative incomes following the eighth round of wage increases. Officials in the Department of Finance described this demand as patently extravagant. By February 1962, however, telegrams were flooding into Merrion Street demanding that farmers' incomes should be increased in line with those of other sections of the community. This campaign was orchestrated by the new president of the NFA, Rickard Deasy. Nagle anticipated that it might be 'one of the opening shots in a wider campaign to press the government for a greater interest in (i.e. assistance to) agriculture'. He reported that during a recent meeting with the Department, Deasy had referred continually to the eighth wage round.[162] These telegrams coincided with a series of protest meetings by farmers in provincial towns.[163]

Farmers were increasingly linking wage and salary increases to those of workers in the other sectors of the economy with demands for higher guaranteed prices for milk, bacon and grain. When the book of estimates for 1962/3 was published in January 1962, showing no increase in milk prices, the ICMSA and the NFA demanded separate meetings with Lemass. In advance of these meetings – Lemass first met the ICMSA because it was the first to demand a meeting – Lemass indicated to Smith that he might consider bringing additional proposals to assist agriculture to the Cabinet. He emphasised that the Department should not be limited to the ideas proposed by the NFA, adding, 'We will get no credit from the N.F.A. no matter what we do'. Smith promised that the Department would respond shortly.[164]

When Smith addressed the Dairy Science Society at UCC some weeks later on the place of dairying in our agricultural economy, he conceded that the government's contribution to providing farmers with higher milk prices had not been 'spectacular', but they had gone 'to the limits of practicability', in the light of the cost to the exchequer and the danger that higher prices would lead to additional restrictions being imposed on Irish dairy exports.[165] On 7 March Smith told the Dáil that he would not concede an increase in the price of milk. When Lemass met the ICMSA the following day, it demanded that the government should continue to support traditional milk producers until the Common Market came to their rescue.[166]

Lemass informed the delegation that the government could not concede an increase in the guaranteed price for milk, because this would only trigger additional anti-dumping measures against Irish produce in Britain.[167]

In advance of its meeting with the Taoiseach, the NFA submitted a four-point programme designed to enable agriculture to prepare for EEC membership. This comprised:

- measures to reduce farmers' costs, including a reduction in taxation;
- ensuring better price competition in rural areas;
- bringing Irish farm prices into line with those in the EEC;
- cash grants to farmers.

The Department of Agriculture noted that in order to prepare for joining the EEC, future assistance to farmers should be directed towards increasing efficiency rather than price supports. The Department would support demands for a further increase in agricultural rates relief, a reduction in the tax on tractors, and extending farmers' entitlement to health benefits, but it ruled out higher milk prices and cash grants. It also conceded that complaints from farming organisations about low farm incomes were justified.[168] When Lemass met the NFA on 19 March 1962 he rejected its attempt to negotiate on the basis of a gap of £83 million between agricultural incomes and the rest of the community. Although he disputed the extent of the income gap, Lemass acknowledged that 'developments adverse to the farmers had recently been taking place'. He recommended that farmers should counter this by higher productivity, and he gave a commitment to review the provisions for agriculture in the forthcoming budget in the light of the overall financial position. He also warned that the government was under pressure to provide additional money for education and social welfare. When Deasy suggested that a further deterioration in farm incomes was imminent, Lemass cautioned the delegation that it would be futile to rely on a statistical approach to the problem. 'No matter what anyone could prove by statistics, it was the practicalities which set the limits in circumstances such as the present'. He warned the NFA that if it engaged in a political strike in an effort to secure further concessions (it was threatening to withhold rates), the government would feel obliged to take strong measures in the public interest. When the NFA delegation referred to the NFA's unsatisfactory relationship with the Department of Agriculture, Lemass rejected the suggestion that the Department was failing to pull its weight in the interests of the agricultural sector. He expressed the hope that misunderstandings might be avoided by better public relations.[169]

These discussions took place at a time when it was widely believed that Ireland was about to join the EEC. When Nagle met Sicco Mansholt, the EEC Commissioner for Agriculture, on 15 March 1962, four days before Lemass met the NFA, he mentioned that Irish farm organisations were demanding price increases in anticipation of EEC entry, and Mansholt indicated that their demands were not unreasonable.[170] In May the producer price for milk fell by 1d a gallon when An Bord Bainne increased the levy on producers to meet one-third of the cost of higher export subsidies, but the government reversed this price cut in June. Otherwise the government persisted in opposing further increases in price subsidies. In August 1962 Lemass told the Muintir na Tíre rural week that the Irish state gave much greater support to agriculture than other European countries, despite the fact that this support rested on a much smaller industrial base.[171] Farm leaders disputed this assertion.

Between 1961, when Ireland announced its intention of applying for membership of the EEC, and January 1963, when General de Gaulle vetoed Britain's EEC membership, both the government and the NFA could view the problem of low farm incomes as a short-term difficulty that would be alleviated when Ireland joined the EEC. Nevertheless, Ireland's application to join the EEC added another dimension to the somewhat-difficult relationship between the NFA and the Department of Agriculture. The NFA expressed frequent criticism both of the extent to which it was being consulted, and the adequacy of measures to prepare Irish agriculture for membership. When Nagle reported to Nicholas Nolan, the secretary of the Department of the Taoiseach, on a meeting with the NFA in April 1962 to brief it on Ireland's negotiations for EEC entry, he remarked that the NFA's attitude was 'a product of

1. their policy not to acknowledge the considerable assistance given to agriculture by the Government;
2. their desire to be the only organisation recognised in relation to discussions on the Common Market;
3. a growing realisation that agriculture in the Common Market is not going to be all fun and games, so that a scapegoat (e.g. the processing industries) must be found in case everything does not go well;
4. a certain immaturity which still afflicts them.'

Nagle recommended that the government issue a press release setting out all that had been done to prepare agriculture for EEC entry, and to counter the NFA's criticism of the Department, which he described as quite unjustified and indeed dishonest. It had complained that the commodity study groups established by the Department to assist Irish agriculture in adjusting to EEC entry were too large and unwieldy. The Department reiterated that it could not deny to interested organisations (which did not accept the NFA as their spokesperson) the right to be represented. It expressed anger at the frequent repetition of allegations in Dáil Éireann, in newspapers and in periodicals, such as *The Economist*, that its efforts to prepare Irish agriculture for EEC membership lagged far behind the work carried out with industry. He pointed out that as key sections of the CAP were only being drafted in 1962, it was difficult to devise an appropriate response.

When Tadhg Ó Cearbhaill read this report, he sent Lemass a memorandum, remarking that 'the public image of the Department is not good'. In his opinion it was not desirable that this unfavourable image should persist, given the promising prospects that EEC entry opened up for Irish agriculture. Ó Cearbhaill noted that there was,

> … a strong element of injustice in the current concept of a cautious, slow-moving, hide-bound Department of Agriculture and one can sympathise with the feelings of exasperation and resentment felt by officers of the Department at this blackguardly treatment – some of it at the hands of persons whose interests the Department are working to serve.

He expressed concern that the criticism would damage morale, and suggested that there was a need for a positive effort to improve the public image of the Department of Agriculture. He recommended that the Taoiseach might intervene in agricultural debates in the Dáil. There was also scope for the Minister and the Secretary and other senior officials to hold press conferences, although he admitted that there might be complications if officials became involved in matters of political controversy. He also suggested that the techniques developed by public relations experts and press officers might prove of value. The Department should also take steps 'to rid itself of any procedures or attitudes which may have contributed to its present unfavourable image'. Lemass followed this with a letter to Paddy Smith, expressing sympathy at the annoying criticism of the Department's work. Lemass cited some recent favourable reports, including a quotation from *The Economist*, that described the Department's preparation for EEC membership as 'a step in the right direction', although it also remarked that 'the department's reputation for energy has not been impressive in the past'. Lemass suggested that this comment raised the question of the general image of the Department of Agriculture. The paragraphs that followed repeated large sections of Ó Cearbhaill's letter, including his comment about 'a cautious, slow-moving, hide-bound Department' and the danger that repeated criticism would damage morale. Lemass noted that the Department's staff already included a public relations officer. He asked what ideas Smith might have to address the problem and 'how the rest of us might help'.

Smith replied, blaming NFA president Rickard Deasy and NFA economist Louis Smith for the negative campaign, and expressing surprise that Garret FitzGerald had repeated the NFA's claims concerning the inactivity of the Department of Agriculture over EEC policy in a recent article.[172] Smith claimed that agriculture was 'always, and in all countries, a target for criticism and a subject for pet theories'. He was uncertain what should be done, although he agreed that further measures were necessary to improve the Department's image and he expressed a willingness to discuss the matter with Lemass. Lemass wrote to Smith three days later, suggesting a meeting, and enclosing a copy of a recent article in the *Irish Press* where the bishop of Cork, Dr Lucey, stated that, 'Irish farming had been lamentably and catastrophically served by the Department of Agriculture'.[173] If Lemass and Smith met to discuss the image of the Department of Agriculture, no record survives and there is no indication of any concerted effort to improve the Department's image at this time.

Although de Gaulle's veto ended the debate over preparations to equip Irish agriculture for EEC membership, it also meant that any resolution to the problem of low farm incomes would have to be found from Irish resources. By March 1963 newspapers were reporting that there was a danger that a dispute over milk prices would erupt between the Minister and the NFA. Farm protests were becoming a more common feature of life in France and other continental countries, which indicated that EEC membership did not offer a complete solution to the problem. The *Sunday Telegraph* suggested that Irish farmers might follow the example of French farmers by blocking public roads.[174]

Smith refuted claims by farm leaders that agricultural incomes had fallen seriously behind those in other sectors of the community. During a speech on the estimate for the Department of Agriculture in March 1963 he reported that income per farm-family-member had increased by 30 per cent between 1953 and 1962, and that agricultural incomes in 1962 were 152 per cent higher than in 1947, whereas non-agricultural incomes had increased by 130 per cent during the same period. However, Smith conceded that farm incomes were exceptionally depressed in 1947, which was his base year.[175] Four days later he presented a memorandum to Cabinet justifying the case for higher milk prices. He acknowledged that 'producers are not mistaken in claiming that only very moderate increases in milk prices have been conceded in recent years, and that the return secured by the non-agricultural sector for its services has gone up by a much higher percentage'. Costs such as wages and rates on agricultural land had risen by much more than the price of milk. Irish farmers received the second lowest milk price in western Europe, after Denmark. Smith claimed that despite the low price there had been 'a remarkable increase both in the volume and efficiency of milk production in the past decade', mainly owing to fertiliser subsidies and the work of the advisory services. (The switch to high-yielding dairy breeds, such as Friesians, was another important factor.) Although conceding higher milk prices would mean an additional cost to the exchequer, he suggested that they were justified by the need to encourage a rise in the livestock herd. Smith claimed that:

> It is not right that the gap between farmers' incomes and the incomes in the non-agricultural sector should be allowed to widen further and that the benefits of improved efficiency in agriculture should be to a large extent neutralised by low prices and increasing costs (including the cost of living). A further widening of this gap will produce serious social tensions which could inflict damage on the whole economy and retard its general advance.

He expressed a wish that any increase in the price of milk should be linked to improvements in quality, with the price increase taking the form of a quality bonus, as recommended by the Survey Team on the Dairy Industry. This would also be consistent with the *Programme for Economic Expansion*. But as the quality bonus could not be introduced for twelve months, he recommended that the government should grant a straightforward price increase, but farmers should be warned that future increases would be linked to improvements in quality. When Lemass and Smith met a deputation of the dairy industry committee (an *ad hoc* body that included representatives of the IAOS, the Irish Creamery Managers' Association and the ICMSA, but not the NFA) on 29 March, they did not announce an increase in the price of milk, although they promised to give serious consideration to some concession at the time of the budget. The Cabinet agreed to a price increase of 1d a gallon shortly after this meeting.[176] The decision to raise milk prices at this time was a response to increased militancy among farmers. An additional factor was Britain's decision to impose quotas on a wide range of imported agricultural produce, which removed the threat that anti-dumping sanctions would be imposed if the exchequer subsidy was increased. The announcement of higher milk prices failed to reduce unrest in the dairy industry. When An Bord Bainne raised its levy on creameries by 1d a gallon some weeks later, in order to meet its share of the escalating cost of export subsidies, the dairy industry committee encouraged farmers to refuse payment. When Lemass met NFA president Rickard Deasy in July, Deasy indicated that he expected pressure to build up during the coming winter for a rise in milk prices. Lemass indicated that the government would oppose a further increase, but Deasy suggested that it should offer farmers an incentive to produce cleaner milk,[177] which was very much in line with what Smith had recommended some months previously.

A Turning Point for Irish Agriculture?

By the summer of 1963 the government was about to unveil the *Second Programme for Economic Expansion*, so this is a useful point at which to examine the state of agriculture. When the *Programme for Economic Expansion* was published in November 1958, agriculture was regarded as the leading sector in the Irish economy. By 1963 net output in agriculture was only 1 per cent higher than in 1957, and less than 15 per cent higher than in 1958, a year when agricultural output fell by 11.5 per cent because of appalling weather.[178] By comparison, in 1963 the output of manufacturing industry was 47 per cent higher than in 1957 and 44 per cent higher than in 1958.

The stagnation in agricultural output was not due to lack of investment. By 1963 public investment in agriculture had reached £12.4 million, almost double the figure that was projected in the *Programme for Economic Expansion*. Agriculture was absorbing 19 per cent of the capital programme and 12.5 per cent of the current budget.[179] Government expenditure on agriculture rose from £21 million in 1958/9 to £39 million in 1963/4. Although the cost of subsidies on dairy produce, bacon and wheat increased, most of the additional spending went towards the cost of eradicating bovine TB and fertiliser subsidies. At its peak in 1961/2 the eradication of bovine TB cost over £9 million, or one-quarter of total government expenditure on agriculture. The government and the Department held firm to the line adopted in 1958: priority was given to investment and measures to raise productivity.

The years of the *Programme for Economic Expansion* brought undoubted technical and scientific advances in Irish agriculture: there was a considerable increase in the quantity of fertiliser being spread on Irish farms; a rapid increase in the number of Friesian cows; 1963 was a record year for milk yields; An Bord Bainne was transforming the marketing of Irish dairy produce; and the research expertise of the Agricultural Institute was beginning to make its impact on the Department's programmes.

Yet these achievements did not result in a significant increase in total output or in farm incomes. If the outcome was disappointing it was primarily due to the extremely difficult market conditions, and this was the primary factor in the widening gap between incomes in farming and the rest of the economy. The Department's firm stance on conceding price increases was costly in many respects. It gave rise to a more militant attitude among farming organisations and to widespread criticism of the Department, despite the fact that responsibility for the tough line on exchequer spending rested with the Cabinet. The changes in the style of government, with greater participation by vocational interests, proved difficult for the Department of Agriculture, particularly because Smith and Lemass had rather different attitudes on this matter. Although the Department would have faced difficulties in adjusting to a more consultative form of administration, irrespective of economic circumstances, these difficulties were compounded by the lack of growth within agriculture.

In September 1963 Jack Nagle told the annual general meeting of the Agricultural Science Association, the body that represented graduates in agricultural science, that 'while the international agricultural situation may be complex and difficult, it does not justify either pessimism or a feeling that our agricultural future is going to be determined by forces entirely outside our control'.[180] Yet the events of the preceding years had indicated that many matters that were critical to the future of Irish agriculture, such as Britain's agricultural policy and Ireland's admission to the EEC, were determined by forces not within the control of the Irish government or the Department of Agriculture.

CHAPTER EIGHT

MAKING BETTER FARMERS: RESEARCH, EDUCATION AND THE ADVISORY SERVICES, 1945–1970s

'It is a matter of the highest national priority to raise the standard of Irish farming skills'. This statement appears in chapter 11 of T. K. Whitaker's *Economic Development*. The chapter went on to note that for many years agricultural education had been the 'Cinderella of the educational household'; it was essential that education should be ' "sold" to rural Ireland'.[1] These objectives recall the original mission of the DATI, and the importance that it assigned to education and the advisory services. Yet from the late 1920s, when a separate faculty of agriculture was established at UCD, and a faculty of dairy science opened at UCC, until the late 1950s, the only notable advance was the introduction of agricultural science as an optional subject in the secondary-school curriculum in 1943.[2]

This lack of development was not unique. Irish education underwent no significant changes between the Vocational Education Act in 1930 and the late 1960s, when a nation-wide scheme of free post-primary education was introduced, and new third-level colleges established. Yet the Department of Agriculture's efforts to improve Irish farming practice in the 1950s ultimately depended on research and education. This chapter examines agricultural research and education in the years between the end of World War II and the early 1970s, together with measures to provide special assistance to small farmers in the west of Ireland. The topics are linked, because the programme to aid small western farmers placed considerable emphasis on the advisory and educational services.

The importance of education and research in agricultural development was highlighted by the Committee on Post-Emergency Agricultural Policy. In May 1945 the Minister for Agriculture, James Ryan, sent a memorandum to government, in which he noted that, 'Agricultural education cannot be a potent factor until agricultural classes and residential schools form part of the normal training of the big majority of farmers in the country. As matters stand at present it cannot be said that we are doing much more than pilot or pioneer work in education'.[3] A report on veterinary services, compiled by the Committee on Post-Emergency Agricultural Policy in 1944, suggested that there was an urgent need to reform the existing services and to provide better facilities for clinical work and for training veterinarians. There was a shortage of veterinarians, and a lack of resources for research.[4] In 1949 Michael Tierney, the president of UCD, complained to the Department about the inadequate facilities available to the faculty of agriculture. He suggested that it should become an independent college within the university, with a much larger budget.[5]

The realisation that there was a need to improve agricultural education was not confined to the Department of Agriculture or to the universities. During the war years a network of young farmers' clubs was founded to provide better education in practical farming. In 1944 several of these clubs came together to form Macra na Feirme. Macra set out to promote agricultural education and to provide better social amenities, so that rural life would become more attractive, especially for younger people. By 1951 the organisation had almost 15,000 members and 400 clubs. Several agricultural instructors, notably Harry Spain, who subsequently became an inspector in the Department of Agriculture, helped to foster this development.[6] The Department supplied lecturers and educational films and paid the salary and expenses of an education officer.[7] Throughout the 1950s Macra na Feirme and other rural organisations such as Muintir na Tíre and the Irish Countrywomen's Association (ICA) expanded their voluntary educational programmes, with the objectives of raising the standard of farming and developing community leadership skills.[8] Their efforts were aided by the ECA office in Dublin, established as part of Marshall Aid, which funded exchange visits between Irish and American rural organisations. In 1950 the first three Macra members travelled to the United States on an exchange visit with members of the 4H Clubs, a comparable US farming organisation. The role of rural organisations in promoting better farming and improving rural living standards was endorsed by the United Nations Food and Agricultural Organisation, which dedicated several conferences to these themes.[9]

Yet, despite the widespread acknowledgement of the importance of education and research, it proved difficult to devise an institutional framework that would meet Irish needs. The Ministers and Secretaries Acts of 1924 and 1928 and the Vocational Education Act failed to determine the relative responsibilities of the Department of Agriculture and the Department of Education for agricultural education. The denominational divisions of Irish university education complicated the task of providing facilities for third-level education in agriculture and veterinary science. There was also a strong current of opinion, exemplified by the 1944 report of the Commission on Vocational Organisation, which objected to the powerful role of the Department of Agriculture, preferring that agricultural services should be controlled by vocationally-elected bodies based around the Catholic parish. Echoes of these ideas can be found in Father McDyer's campaign for pilot areas in the west of Ireland during the early 1960s.

When the Department of Agriculture was established in 1900 its staff complement included the lecturers at the College of Science. The establishment of the faculties of agriculture and dairy science robbed the Department of many of its key research workers, when they transferred to university positions, but no decision was taken at the time as to the respective functions of the universities and the Department in agricultural research. Most of the Department's research was concerned with field trials, to determine which varieties of sugar-beet and other crops were most suitable in Irish conditions; which dressing was most effective in preventing smut on oats; and similar matters.[10] The precise relationship between the Department's research and the research being carried out by the Agricultural Institute became a crucial issue following the establishment of the Agricultural Institute in 1958.

Lack of resources was another factor. In 1938 there were only thirty-eight agricultural advisers employed by county committees of agriculture. While this had increased to eighty-three by 1950, the fact that half of their salaries was met from local authority rates – at a time when there was considerable opposition to rising rates demands – meant that the advisory services remained inadequate, and this problem was most acute in the poorer counties of the west of Ireland.

THE AGRICULTURAL INSTITUTE

In 1949 Joseph Carrigan, the head of the ECA mission in Ireland, recommended to James Dillon, the Minister for Agriculture, that Ireland should adopt the US model where responsibility for agricultural research, teaching and advisory services rested with a single institution.[11] No written account exists of Carrigan's original proposal, but a 1952 report by the Department of Agriculture gives a general outline. The institute would be responsible for all research in agricultural and veterinary science currently carried out by the Department or the universities, and it would extend the range of research being carried out considerably. Buildings and land would be provided at Brownsbarn, Clondalkin, County Dublin. Students of agriculture and veterinary science would spend the final two years of their university education there, having first studied basic science subjects at the NUI or Dublin University. The Albert Agricultural College and the faculty of dairy science at UCC would be absorbed into the new institute.[12] Carrigan recommended a substantial increase in the number of agricultural advisers, including the appointment of one extension worker with responsibility for agricultural education for every six parishes.

Carrigan's plan would have entailed radical changes in the structure of agricultural education and research, and a substantial dilution of the Department's powers. It would also be an expensive proposition. An undated memorandum by Carrigan indicated that the institute would require an annual budget of £400,000, in addition to the cost of extension (advisory) services; the current budget for agricultural research and education was £120,000–£140,000. Consequently the proposal was dependent on funding from the ECA. On 12 May 1950 the Department of Agriculture was informed that the government had given approval in principle to the idea of an agricultural institute, although the 1952 report prepared by the Department noted that the Department had made no submission in writing on the proposal nor, 'so far as it is known', had the Minister for Agriculture made a written submission.[13] All the early discussions took place outside the normal administrative channels, but this was by no means uncommon during the term of the first inter-party government. Records of Cabinet decisions for this government are incomplete and it also tended to hold informal Cabinet meetings.[14]

In July 1950 the Cabinet approved a memorandum to be sent to Carrigan, which stated that it proposed to devote 10 per cent of the money in the counterpart special account (the Grant Counterpart Fund) to capital expenditure associated with tourism. The balance would be used for the expansion and improvement of agriculture, forestry and veterinary research, education and extension services.[15]

At this point the proposal began to disintegrate. Dillon informed Paul Miller, who had succeeded Carrigan as head of the Dublin ECA office, that he did not propose to transfer the advisory service to the new institute. Miller disagreed with this decision. Dillon had already embarked on plans for a new advisory service that would be organised on a parish basis, but there is no reason why the parish plan could not have been implemented under the auspices of the agricultural institute. To placate Joseph Blowick, the leader of Clann na Talmhan, who was the Minister for Forestry, the government decided that the institute would have no responsibility for forestry.

Enthusiasm for a central campus was also waning. Dillon suggested that new buildings should only be constructed as necessary, and that the veterinary college and the dairy science faculty in Cork should remain at their existing locations. This change of mind may reflect concern at the high cost of constructing a central campus. Alternatively, it may have been a response to the growing opposition from the Irish universities. Michael Tierney, the president of UCD, who was a former Cumann na nGaedheal[16] TD, had been keeping a close eye on the plan to establish an agricultural institute. Shortly after Carrigan first mooted the idea, Dillon and Patrick McGilligan, the Minister for Finance, who was a professor of law at UCD, met Tierney in Leinster House to discuss the proposal.[17] On the following day Dillon informed Costello that Tierney was drawing up the heads of a proposed bill. Dillon suggested that the institute should be a recognised college of both the NUI and Dublin University.[18] Costello gave his approval in principle to the idea (although the matter had not yet come before the Cabinet), provided that Dillon secured the support of UCC president, Alfred O'Rahilly, and Dr Alton, the provost of TCD. But the heads of the bill submitted by Michael Tierney on 5 July 1950 envisaged that the institute, to be based at Clondalkin, would be a constituent college of the NUI, but not of Dublin University, and it would be primarily concerned with teaching, rather than research. All the existing faculties of agriculture and veterinary science would be placed under its control, including the dairy science faculty at UCC. Tierney's bill was drafted with the interests of UCD in mind, and it was a far cry from Carrigan's original plan. It was also calculated to arouse opposition from TCD and UCC.

No formal steps had been taken to establish an agricultural institute by the time that the 1951 general election swept the inter-party government from office. The change of government meant that all aspects of the proposal were reassessed, initially by the interdepartmental ERP committee,[19] which was drawing up a list of projects that would be funded from the Grant Counterpart Fund. In August 1951 it discussed how responsibility for research should be allocated between the Department of Agriculture and the universities. When the committee next met on 7 September it added an amendment to the minutes of the August meeting, that 'It was of the first importance that a system of liaison acceptable to all parties should be established between the constituent colleges of the NUI and TCD'. The Department of Agriculture prepared a lengthy report for the committee on the institute, which pointed out that the concept 'involves quite a number of perplexities, uncertainties and controversial points that will have to be resolved before the proposal can be further advanced'.

The US authorities continued to urge the government to press ahead with the establishment of an agricultural institute. When Dean Dexter of the ECA met officials of the Department of Agriculture on 27 October 1951 he emphasised that an agricultural institute was an absolute necessity.[20] The ECA officials in Dublin urged the government to forward detailed proposals as soon as possible, because they wished to have expenditure under the Grant Counterpart Fund approved before Congress went into recess in the summer of 1952. The Mutual Security Act of 1951 had replaced the ECA, and as Ireland had no security agreement with the US (Ireland was not a member of NATO), there would be no MSA mission in Ireland, and the ECA mission would soon end.[21]

Despite the urgency, the Department of Agriculture had not drawn up specific proposals for the agricultural institute by May 1952. Seán Ó Broin informed Charlie Murray of the Department of the Taoiseach that there were several matters of principle still to be resolved, including the question of a central campus; whether the extension services should be transferred to the institute; whether it should be a teaching institute, a research institute or both; the future of agricultural education in the universities if it was decided that the institute should be a teaching institute; and the future of veterinary education and research. By June 1952 the Irish government had submitted nine projects seeking counterpart funding to the MSA, but three proposals, all relating to agriculture, had yet to be finalised: the agricultural institute, the eradication of bovine TB and a subsidy scheme for ground limestone. On 26 June Murray minuted that the agricultural institute 'is making little if any, headway'. One month later Nicholas Nolan, of the Department of the Taoiseach, reported 'no development'.

Some of the outstanding matters were resolved in November 1952 by a sub-committee of the Cabinet, consisting of Ryan, Smith and Walsh – two former ministers for Agriculture and the current Minister. The institute should concentrate on research and higher education; there would be no central campus; it would not control the advisory service; third-level education in agriculture, forestry, horticulture and veterinary science would be transferred to a single unit that would be affiliated to one or both universities; if agreement could not be reached on affiliation, it would become a separate university. In January 1953 the Cabinet accepted these recommendations.[22]

The decision to place third-level education in agriculture and related subjects under the control of the agricultural institute proved highly controversial. UCC protested at the threatened loss of its dairy science faculty.[23] The prospect of students from TCD and the NUI studying together in an institution that would not be under the exclusive control of the NUI prompted complaints from John Charles McQuaid, the Catholic archbishop of Dublin, about the dangers of mixed education removed from a Catholic atmosphere. The Catholic archbishop of Tuam and the bishop of Galway supported the campaign for the establishment of a faculty of agriculture at UCG.

The proposed governing body of the institute was another source of contention. In 1951 the Agricultural Science Association, which represented graduates in agricultural science, expressed its support for the establishment of a national college of agriculture that would be responsible for the extension service, agricultural education, higher education and research, and the education 'of the man who tills the land and rears the stock'. It demanded that the college should be run by a full-time president and an academic council that would be independent of the Department of Agriculture.[24] An undated memorandum from Carrigan emphasised that the governing body should include representatives of the agricultural community, chosen for their expertise and interest; they should not be political appointees. However, in September 1951 the Department recommended that the Minister for Agriculture should appoint the members of the governing body. It suggested that it might consist of seven members: the president of the institute, one representative each from the NUI and TCD, two representatives of the Department, and two representatives of the agricultural industry. In January 1953 de Valera's Cabinet determined that the Minister for Agriculture would appoint a majority of the members of the governing body. This decision gave rise to further objections from the governing body of UCC and the Catholic hierarchy, because it was seen as yet another example of excessive state control.[25] It would also appear that at least one member of the Cabinet shared these reservations. In May 1953 the Minister for Education, Seán Moylan, presented de Valera with a proposal for the establishment of an autonomous agricultural, educational and development board, which would be responsible for agricultural research, training advisers, advisory services, investigation into farm income and management, and advising the government on agricultural policy. The board would also assist in the establishment of a representative farmers' organisation.[26] Moylan's intervention may not have been wholly disinterested, since the departments of Education and Agriculture were often in dispute over who should be responsible for agricultural education.

Efforts to resolve these issues delayed the drafting of legislation, and when Fianna Fáil lost office in 1954, the plans for an agricultural institute were still on the drawing board. The incoming second inter-party government proved to be sympathetic to opposition interests. In 1955 the Taoiseach, John A. Costello, gave a sympathetic hearing to demands from western TDs for the establishment of a faculty of agriculture in Galway that would take account of special conditions in western areas,[27] and he reassured Muintir na Tíre Rural Week that the institute would not be under government control.[28] In 1956 the inter-party government announced that undergraduate education in agriculture would remain with the universities, but it was anticipated that the institute would be responsible for postgraduate education and research.[29] When Fianna Fáil returned to office in 1957 it did not reverse this decision.

The Agriculture (An Foras Talúntais) Act of 1958 established An Foras Talúntais (AFT) as an institute for agricultural research, otherwise known as the Agricultural Research Institute. Moylan moved the first stage of the bill in Dáil Éireann on 6 November, shortly before he died; the second and third stages were moved by Frank Aiken, who was acting Minister for Agriculture; Smith moved the fourth and fifth stages. De Valera introduced the second reading in the Seanad.[30] For the purpose of the Act, agriculture was defined as including horticulture, forestry and bee-keeping 'and facilities, activities and sciences which relate to or tend to promote or improve agriculture'. The institute was charged with promoting and co-ordinating agricultural research, and communicating its findings. Its range of activities would include:

- awarding grants for research;
- funding scholarships and fellowships for researchers;
- organising conferences, lectures, seminars and publishing papers;
- providing facilities for carrying out research 'as it considers desirable';
- the control and administration of agricultural research facilities that might be transferred to the institute;

- 'to consult with and advise' persons engaged in agricultural research in relation to their research;
- advising the Minister for Agriculture on any matter relating to agricultural science or research, on which he requested advice.

The initial funding of £1.8 million was provided by the grant counterparts special account; £1 million was placed in an endowment fund and the balance was used to cover start-up costs. The capital in the endowment fund could only be used to provide new research facilities, but the annual income could be used to meet running costs. The legislation included a commitment that the Department of Agriculture would provide an annual grant, and if research units were transferred to the institute, it would receive any funds allocated to those units. The institute was to be governed by a council, consisting of a chairman, to be appointed by the President, and twelve ordinary members who would be appointed by the government. Five of the ordinary members were to be nominated by agricultural and rural organisations; four were to be university nominees; the remaining three were to be nominated by the Minister.[31] There was to be no representative of the Department of Agriculture on the council. The first chairman was C. J. Litton, a farmer and a member of the NFA, who was one of the founders of the *Irish Farmers' Journal*.[32] Dr Tom Walsh, the head of the Department's soil research division, became the first director.

'Two Departments of Agriculture': the Relationship between the Department and An Foras Talúntais

Despite the long gestation period, many matters remained unresolved when An Foras Talúntais (AFT) was established, in particular whether all the Department's research activities should be transferred to AFT, and the extent to which the Department would oversee its work. The Department had anticipated that AFT would begin by carrying out a survey of existing research facilities, and that it would then submit a detailed research plan to the departments of Agriculture and Finance, which would enable them to assess the financial implications. In December 1958, however, shortly after AFT was founded, Nagle claimed that AFT was determined to take control of all agricultural research activities and it was interpreting the term 'in a very wide sense'. He drew an unfavourable contrast between the attitude of AFT towards budgetary planning and that of the universities, which were equally autonomous. Nagle suggested that AFT should be requested to submit a detailed research programme every year, with an estimate of the cost, which would then be subject to negotiations between AFT and the departments of Agriculture and Finance.

Nagle was particularly concerned about the future of field experiments and other trials currently carried out by the Department of Agriculture, either at the agricultural schools or by the staff of the county committees of agriculture. He recommended that the Department should continue to carry out work of this nature, 'so long as there is a technical staff in the Department of Agriculture', but the trials should be co-ordinated with the research being carried out by AFT. Nagle cited a speech by de Valera on the second reading of the AFT Bill in the Seanad in support of this stance. De Valera had stated that the Institute would be 'the means of co-ordinating the work' carried out by the research units under the Department's control. It would review their work, advise them and consult them. De Valera expressed the hope that AFT would secure 'the goodwill of the existing institutions, so that they will be ready to co-operate, so that they will listen to any advice and so that they, in return, may make suggestions to the Institute'. AFT had requested that all institutions under the Department's control that were engaged in research and experimental work should be transferred to AFT. Nagle suggested that this did not 'seem to be a reasonable interpretation of "co-ordination"'. Nevertheless, the Department had agreed to this in principle, and plans were being drawn up to place under AFT's control the Department's farm at Grange, County Meath, which would be the headquarters for the Institute's research into animal breeding; Johnstown Castle in County Wexford; and the experimental stations at Glenamoy, Clonsast and Derrybrennan.

However, the future of the plant breeding and seed propagation work at the Department's farm at Backweston, County Dublin, was a matter of dispute. This work was directed by John Brady, who was a senior inspector in the Department. In 1953 this station introduced a certification scheme for seed wheat. Before this work began the quality and purity of the Irish wheat crop was deplorable, but by 1956 it was possible to provide sufficient high-quality certified seed oats, wheat and barley to meet the country's needs. The station also bred new varieties of grass seed, and Brady's expertise was widely recognised. He claimed that the success of this work was dependent on unified control of all the essential elements: 'variety and strain testing, seed propagation, crop inspection, supervision of seeding processing and certification'. It would be impossible to divide the station's work in propagating seed (which was expected to remain the Department's responsibility) from research trials into varieties. The statistical results of trials carried out at the station were sent to the agricultural advisers at the end of every season, so that they could advise farmers on the most successful varieties of seed. Brady claimed that if this arrangement were altered, Irish grain yields would decline. By 1958 the unit had begun to propagate root crops. As Brady refused to consider transferring to a senior research appointment at AFT at an increased salary (Nagle noted the fact that Brady had once been Walsh's superior was a consideration), Nagle suggested that he should continue to conduct both the research and the experimental work at Backweston as an inspector of the Department.[33] The impasse over Backweston was a direct consequence of the delay in establishing AFT, because in 1952 the Department had listed research of this nature as a priority for the Institute.[34] Nagle recommended that a series of committees should be formed to co-ordinate the work of AFT and the Department.[35]

During the following weeks the future of the Backweston farm and the question of reviewing the annual budget of AFT were the subject of several meetings between representatives of the Institute and the ministers for Agriculture and Finance. But when the council of AFT met on 17 February 1959 it passed a unanimous resolution:

> That in view of certain fundamental differences of opinion between the Department of Agriculture and An Foras Talúntais on matters relating to the functions, work and responsibilities of An Foras Talúntais that this meeting stands adjourned pending a decision on these matters by the Government.

The council requested a meeting with the government so that it could explain these differences.[36] In a note to Maurice Moynihan, Nagle summarised the items in dispute as Backweston 'and the plant breeding question', progeny testing (the Department planned to carry out research in this area and to establish a meat research centre), Johnstown Castle, and 'general procedures for co-ordinating their activities and those of this Department'. He added that 'until they specify the points with which they are concerned we cannot be certain'. He accused AFT of a 'monopolistic' outlook, 'even dictatorial. They seem to think that once they make decisions, everyone must conform'. He expressed regrets that the Department was not represented on the council of AFT, and consequently it did not know 'the atmosphere at Council discussions'.

De Valera agreed to meet a deputation from AFT, but he asked them to present him with a statement in advance, setting out 'the fundamental differences of opinion' that were mentioned in the council's resolution. The key issue was whether AFT should be given responsibility for agricultural research. Walsh claimed that the chairman and council of AFT had taken office on the understanding that they would be solely responsible for agricultural research at a national level, and that all research funds would be at their disposal. He alleged that the Department of Agriculture had constantly questioned this assumption. In response to this, Nagle noted that 'from an early stage' the council adopted a course of action that was very different from what the government had intended and he cited speeches by Aiken and de Valera during the passage of the bill, indicating that it was the government's intention that AFT should 'try and get as much research as possible done by existing institutions'. In his speech on the second reading of the bill in the Seanad, de Valera indicated that the first task of the Institute would be to co-ordinate and review the work carried out by existing research units; establishing its own research units would be 'the next thing'. However, in the next sentence, de Valera stated that AFT should establish its own research units, 'if the governing body of the institute is of opinion that this is the best way in which the particular investigation … should be carried out'. Nagle claimed that the difficulties sprang from 'a doctrinaire concept' that all agricultural research and experimental work, including simple field trials, should be controlled by one central organisation. He pointed out that there were 'extensive borderlands' between research, developmental and educational work. Nagle ended on a conciliatory note, emphasising that the Minister and the Department would need AFT's help in formulating a development policy for agriculture, and the technical officers of the Department would need AFT's assistance in grappling with day-to-day problems. 'It would be tragic if a workable system of co-operation cannot be made a reality'.

When de Valera and Smith met a deputation from the council of AFT on 25 March 1959, de Valera insisted that there was nothing in AFT's charter to support the view that the Institute should have sole responsibility for agricultural research. He suggested that AFT should aim at co-ordinating rather than controlling research. But Litton, the chairman of AFT, countered that this would be extremely difficult, and that the greatest economy would be achieved if all major research were conducted by one organisation. He did not envisage that there would be any difficulties in co-ordinating the work of AFT with that of the universities, but in the case of the Department of Agriculture, 'there was a danger of over-lapping and duplication'. Walsh claimed that the Department had failed to inform AFT of its research plans, or had only done so at the last moment. He referred to the Department's plan to establish a meat research centre.

This meeting failed to resolve the issues that were in contention, and arguments over the role of AFT revived when the Department received a draft of AFT's first annual report in October 1959. This contained the statement that the functions of AFT included 'the most efficient use of State finances available for agricultural research' and creating 'a strong unified research organisation into which the activities of existing organisations could be properly integrated and unified'. Nagle pointed out that neither of these was listed among its statutory functions. The Department was also upset that reports of the disagreements between the Department and AFT had appeared in the press. Nevertheless, the atmosphere was cordial when Smith and senior officials met Walsh and Litton some days later. Walsh promised that there would be close liaison between AFT and the Department over AFT's new veterinary research. Both sides agreed to meet to determine priorities for AFT's research programme. No mention was made of the annual report, much to Smith's puzzlement, because as he told Lemass, one of the purposes behind the meeting had been to discuss 'some objectionable features' of the report. Shortly after this meeting, 'in deference to the wishes of the Minister', the council of AFT conceded that the Department should continue to carry out research in plant breeding, but it requested that the research should be co-ordinated with AFT's work. In recognition of the improved relations between AFT and the Department, Lemass and Smith agreed to meet a deputation from AFT. After this meeting Walsh informed Lemass that the council of AFT had agreed to remove a contentious paragraph from the annual report, which noted that the financial allocation provided for AFT was 'inadequate to meet the programme of development considered desirable' and it had been forced to curtail its development programme as a consequence.

Relations between the organisations improved somewhat once these matters had been resolved. But when Nagle demanded that AFT submit estimates for expenditure for 1960/1, Walsh demanded to be provided with details of the Department's research programme at Backweston. Although the Department and AFT established a number of liaison committees to discuss research, AFT remained reluctant to provide the Department with information, because it believed that this would lead to further interference by the Department. Veterinary research became a new cause of contention; the Department claimed it did not fall within the remit of AFT.

There were also disagreements over funding. In March 1960 Walsh complained to Smith that AFT had only been allocated £400,000 to meet current expenditure for 1960/1. This was two-thirds of the sum it had requested; moreover, the provision for capital expenditure was inadequate. The Department replied that the budget had been agreed by the ministers for Agriculture and Finance. For the year 1961/2 AFT could expect to receive £450,000 for current expenditure, and plans should be drawn up on this basis. As for capital investment, AFT was expected to meet all capital expenditure for at least the next five years from the £1 million capital fund that was provided under the Act.[37] Walsh responded to this news, which came in a letter from Michael Barry, assistant secretary of the Department of Agriculture, by claiming that 'There is in fact no mention in the Act of the Department of Agriculture as such, having a statutory function with regard to An Foras Talúntais. … This is a function of the Minister', which would seem to indicate that he did not understand the terms of the 1924 Ministers and Secretaries Act. Nagle informed him that 'under existing law the Department of Agriculture and the Minister for Agriculture may not be regarded as separate and distinct units each with its own separate powers, duties and functions'.

The AFT submitted an estimate of expenditure for the year 1961/2 totalling £647,000, which was £200,000 more than the amount indicated by Barry. In a note to Smith, concerning this estimate, Nagle recalled that he had warned two years earlier about 'the difficulties which could arise if An Foras Talúntais were given their head'. His foreboding had been justified, and there was now 'an even greater danger of having in effect, two Departments of Agriculture in the country'. He claimed that the tactics being adopted by AFT were 'those of a pressure group rather than of a learned body'; unless AFT was made to act 'in a reasonable and responsible way, the position is going to become a lot worse in the future'. When Lemass met representatives from AFT on 2 February, in an effort to resolve the dispute over the budget, he expressed concern over the poor relations that existed between the Department and AFT. He noted that 'the fault did not seem to me to rest with the Department of Agriculture and was in part attributable to the atmosphere of Empire-building which has surrounded the Institute and to the pressure tactics used to get a larger grant'. While the government would wish to provide the Institute with more money, the Institute 'could not expect to write their own check [sic]'. He told Litton that AFT's budget for the coming year would not exceed £450,000. It eventually received £500,000.

The impression that AFT was engaging in 'empire-building' was strengthened by its reaction to a report that the UCC dairy science faculty planned to expand its research. Walsh expressed 'surprise and bewilderment' at this announcement. He claimed that UCC would duplicate work being carried out by AFT. Litton wrote to Smith demanding to be informed about UCC's plans. Smith replied that there was no question of UCC's receiving a research grant from the Department; research was a necessary and a normal part of a university's activity.[38] In November 1960 UCD president Michael Tierney drew Nagle's attention to an entry in the Dublin University calendar for 1960/1 for a BA degree with a moderatorship (honours degree) in agriculture. The calendar noted that, 'In dealing with this subject the University has the assistance of the Research staff of the Agricultural Institute'. Tierney announced that if this degree were allowed to proceed he would request the governing body of UCD to refuse to accept students from TCD into the third and fourth-year classes in agriculture.[39] The archbishop of Dublin, John Charles McQuaid, contacted Nagle and T. Ó Raiftearaigh, the secretary of the Department of Education, on this matter.[40] The proposal was dropped.

By 1963/4 the annual budget for the Institute had reached £850,000, which was substantially greater than the amount allocated to the faculties of agriculture and dairy science at UCD and UCC or the agricultural advisory service. In a note prepared for Lemass in the spring of 1963, the Department of Agriculture suggested that the Institute should be asked to provide clear evidence that the practical results were commensurate with expenditure.[41] AFT's research priorities reflected the overall plans for agriculture outlined in the *Programme for Economic Expansion*. Research into animal production, including dairying, was regarded as the most important matter. Other priorities were research into soil resources and land-use potential; plant sciences and crop husbandry; agricultural engineering and farm buildings; horticulture; the economics of farm management, including home economics and rural sociology and the marketing of agricultural produce. AFT also pioneered a new system of evaluating research that would enable it to decide which projects should be given priority. The evaluation was carried out by panels of experts from Ireland and overseas, and every project was evaluated under a number of criteria, including the ratio of benefit to cost.[42]

Relations between the Department and AFT remained stormy. In addition to matters concerning the co-ordination or duplication of research, the comparative salaries of senior officials at AFT and those of the Department – the salaries offered by the Institute were higher – was probably the most contentious issue. When Charles Haughey met Walsh and Litton for the first time after his appointment as Minister for Agriculture, late in 1964, he expressed the wish that relations between the Department and AFT should be on more clearly-defined terms, yet when Nagle and Walsh met to discuss this in May 1965, both parties rehearsed many old grievances and some new ones. Walsh protested that AFT had not been consulted about the proposal in the *Second Programme for Economic Expansion* to appoint specialist advisers to work with the local advisory services. Other matters in contention included AFT's desire to have the cereals station at Ballinacurra and the Department's veterinary research laboratory transferred to AFT. This latter claim smacked of further empire-building, since the work at the veterinary research laboratory was not concerned with basic research, but rather with the Department's responsibilities in relation to quality control of meat, and the eradication of bovine TB and brucellosis.[43] Ballinacurra remained under the direct control of the Department.[44] The *Second Programme for Economic Expansion* announced that a meat research unit would be established, with funding from the Department and the meat industry. The idea had been under consideration since 1960, and the Department was determined that this unit would be independent of AFT. Although the annual report of the Minister for Agriculture for 1963/4 noted that 'protracted negotiations' had taken place on the matter, the research unit was never established.[45]

When the Devlin Commission examined the organisational arrangements of the Department of Agriculture some years later, it remarked on the failure to integrate the research activities of AFT within a national plan for agriculture.[46] Yet, despite these administrative difficulties, mainly caused by the failure to determine the precise role of AFT and its relationship with the Department before it was established, AFT made a significant contribution to the development of Irish agriculture during the 1960s and afterwards. Correspondingly, the delay in establishing AFT retarded progress in agriculture during the 1950s.

AGRICULTURAL ADVISERS, VOCATIONAL INTERESTS AND THE PARISH PLAN

AFT was merely one element in the overall programme of agricultural education and research, although if Carrigan's original plan had been followed, AFT would have controlled the entire range of educational and advisory services. Yet the proposal to place the advisory service under AFT was dropped at an early stage. By the early 1950s the advisory service had been in existence for almost fifty years. The last major changes had taken place in the 1920s; they were concerned with superannuation and permanent appointments, and the creation of chief agricultural officers, rather than with the nature of the job. No major review of the advisory service was carried out until the mid-1960s, although the Committee on Post-Emergency Agricultural Policy and Carrigan had both recommended a substantial increase in the number of advisers.

In 1948 James Dillon, the Minister for Agriculture, announced the creation of a new advisory service, which would be provided by parish agents. The name was modelled on the US term for an agricultural adviser – the county agent. The parish agent would be a 'competent highly-trained graduate in agricultural science', who would be at the disposal of every farmer in the parish. He would be expected to make the acquaintance of every farmer and to impress on him, that 'he is their servant and is anxious to be called upon to afford any assistance'. Dillon drew a contrast between the parish agent, who would respond to the needs and wishes of local farmers, and the existing instructors, who were 'in the service of the county committees', although he expressed the hope that the county committees would lend instructors to the scheme. Like Patrick Hogan, Dillon had a rather low opinion of the county committees of agriculture.[47] Dillon's plan fitted into Muintir na Tíre's proposal to reorganise local government by basing it on the parish.[48] He claimed that he had devised the scheme with advice from Muintir na Tíre's founder, Canon Hayes. The 1944 *Report of the Commission on Vocational Organisation* had recommended that the county committees of agriculture should be superseded by agricultural services organised around the parish, and by county boards of agriculture, whose members would be elected by vocational interests.[49] The parish plan tried to capitalise on Macra na Feirme's enthusiasm for agricultural education and community action. Dillon's biographer, Maurice Manning, noted that 'the cabinet took the unusual step of allowing Dr Harry Spain, one of the founders of Macra na Feirme, to implement the proposals. Spain became closely identified with the Parish Plan, and he toured the country with missionary zeal, urging communities to take part in it'.[50] Agents would be appointed following an application by a parish, a co-operative or a rural organisation, such as Macra na Feirme or Muintir na Tíre. The first agent was appointed in 1948 in Bansha, County Tipperary, the parish of Canon

Hayes. Two others were appointed, in Tydavnet in County Monaghan and Ardee in County Louth in 1949.

The parish scheme encountered numerous obstacles. To begin with, there was a contradiction at its heart. Although responsibility for agricultural instruction was ostensibly being transferred from the county committee to the community, parish agents were appointed by the Department of Agriculture, and the Department paid their entire salary. For this reason they could be regarded as an example of increased Departmental control. The existing agricultural instructors were appointed by the county committees of agriculture, and half their salaries was met from the rate in aid of agriculture. Patrick McGilligan, the Minister for Finance, protested that parish agents would weaken the capacity of the county committees of agriculture to provide local leadership; furthermore it would be 'a blow to the system of representative local government and a notable step further to the direction of a highly-centralised state'.[51] Cork County Committee of Agriculture, which was predictably opposed to the idea, because it would weaken its authority, dubbed the parish plan the 'Merrion St. Parish Plan'. Macra na Feirme announced that it would oppose the plan because it was state-controlled. It objected to agents being appointed by the Civil Service Commission, and not by the local sponsors. The bishop of Cork, Dr Lucey, suggested that it would be preferable if a parish paid its instructor, rather than take one 'who would dance to the departmental tune',[52] but this was a utopian suggestion.

In 1950, when Dillon was on the point of extending the parish plan from its pilot phase, the Agricultural Science Association instructed the twenty-seven parish agents, who had been notified of their appointment, not to take up duty. At the time the association was negotiating improved pay and promotional conditions for its members who were employed by the county committees of agriculture. It was dissatisfied with the salaries being offered to parish agents; it also feared non-graduates might be appointed to these posts. Dillon told the annual Muintir na Tíre rural week that the parish plan he had devised with Father Hayes had gone 'up the spout', because of the opposition from the Agricultural Science Association.[53] In 1952, when he was out of office, he claimed that the first parish agent appointed in Bansha, County Tipperary, had succeeded in having the soil of nearly every farm tested within eighteen months and in persuading farmers to use more fertiliser and to make silage.[54]

One of the puzzling features of the parish plan was Dillon's refusal to consider placing the parish agents under the control of the Agricultural

Institute. In September 1951, by which time Dillon was in opposition and Walsh was the Minister for Agriculture, a Department of Agriculture memorandum noted that Dillon had opposed the suggestion that the advisory service should be transferred to the proposed agricultural institute. The Department described this idea 'as a retrograde one', which would be 'tantamount to the abdication by the Minister of functions which are now regarded as appropriate to the Government and not to a body having no responsibility to Parliament'. It noted that the US extension service was a purely advisory service, whereas in Ireland the agricultural instructors administered a large number of subsidy schemes. It would not be possible to divide the role of the instructors between advisory work, which would be carried out under the direction of the Agricultural Institute, and administering the Department's schemes. The Department claimed that the instructors and the parish agents 'would carry far more popular appeal' if they were in a position to assist farmers in obtaining grants, than if they were purely advisory agents.[55] This was a somewhat spurious argument, since many schemes that were grant-aided by the Department, such as farm buildings, were operated by the Department's staff, not by the advisory service. It is more probable that Dillon and Walsh were reluctant to relinquish control.

Although Walsh, who was a former member of Kilkenny County Committee of Agriculture, wished to retain the existing advisory system, other members of the government were in favour of reorganising the service. In April 1953 Seán Moylan recommended that it should be placed under an autonomous board that would be responsible for all agricultural research and education. He suggested that the advisory service should be expanded considerably, and that a new grade of specialist advisers should be appointed, who would work closely with the research organisation to assist with problems beyond the competence of the existing staff.[56] One month later Erskine Childers, the Minister for Lands, presented the Cabinet with a report, which recommended that the advisory service should be placed under a special board that would be chaired by General M. J. Costello, the head of the Irish Sugar Company. Childers claimed that the county committees of agriculture had,

> … no activating enthusiastic week to week influence on the Advisors in rural areas. The whole of the co-ordinating arrangements between the farmers' organisations and the advisory work of the Department should be completely changed so that the Advisors from the top to the lowest rank should associate with farmers.[57]

The parish plan was revived by the second inter-party government. In October 1956 John A. Costello gave a commitment to appoint one parish agent for every thousand farms.[58] But when Fianna Fáil returned to office in 1957, the parish plan was abandoned. *Economic Development* provided a diplomatic obituary. It noted that the OEEC had described the proposal as 'a most forward step in the improvement of agricultural advisory work in Europe', but it warned that there was a considerable risk of duplication and friction between the Department and the county committees. Any improvement in farming skills in the immediate future would have to be achieved through the advisory services. The objectives of the parish plan could probably be met by strengthening the existing services. The fact that the parish scheme was wholly funded by the Department, whereas the cost of the advisory service was shared with the local authorities, may have been a determining factor, given that *Economic Development* was determined to secure better value for existing exchequer spending on agriculture.

In 1958 there were 200 general advisers and 23 parish agents – one for every 1,200 farmers. One hundred additional advisers would be needed if Ireland were to achieve the British ratio of one adviser for every 800 farmers.[59] Although the 1958 figure was inadequate, it was a substantial advance on the position in 1950, when there were only eighty-three agricultural advisers; forty-nine advisers in horticulture; and eighty instructors in poultry-keeping. The expansion in the number of advisers in horticulture and poultry did not keep pace with the growth in agricultural advisers. In 1960 there were seventy-seven poultry instructresses, three fewer than in 1950, and sixty-two horticultural instructors.[60] *Economic Development* recommended that the advisory services should be reorganised, with individual instructors subject to greater supervision, and additional specialist advisers being appointed,[61] but no changes were introduced during the years of the First Programme for Economic Expansion.

Because of the uncertainty over the proposed structure of the agricultural institute, all major capital investment in university facilities for agricultural education was delayed, as was the establishment of specialist courses in agricultural engineering and agricultural economics. The Department of Agriculture had remarked on the need for such courses in 1951.[62] The number of students studying degree courses in agricultural science began to increase during the late 1950s, in response to a growing demand for graduates in agricultural science. This gave added life to the campaigns being orchestrated by UCC and UCG for faculties of agriculture. Cork's demand received the support of the Department of Education, but was predictably opposed by the Department of Finance, which feared that it would only lead to demands for faculties of agriculture to be established in UCG and TCD. The proposal to establish a faculty of agriculture at UCC was withdrawn from Cabinet in February 1959 and did not reappear; the UCG campaign also petered out.[63] Most of the expansion took place at UCD. In 1961 UCD introduced the first specialist degrees in agricultural science – in crop production; animal production; biological sciences; and production and distribution in agriculture. In the following year UCD bought the Lyons Estate at Celbridge, County Kildare, to provide more space for the practical aspects of the degree course. The Albert College at Glasnevin, which had provided training in agriculture since Victorian times, was sold to Dublin Corporation for housing.[64]

The rival interests of UCD and TCD, and the determination of the Catholic hierarchy to preserve the denominational character of Irish universities, hindered advances in veterinary education. The British 1948 Veterinary Surgeons Act gave the Privy Council power to recognise university degrees in veterinary science, and it provided for the reconstitution of the Veterinary Council. Although Irish students would continue to receive a diploma from the Royal College of Veterinary Surgeons, this was only an interim arrangement because Irish veterinary students wanted to be awarded a university degree like their counterparts in Britain. The Department of Agriculture suggested that the Veterinary College should remain under the Department's control. All students would attend courses in general science either at TCD or NUI, moving to the veterinary college for the later years of their course. Students would be awarded a degree by either Dublin University or NUI.[65] The Department assumed that all students at the veterinary college would be taught together, but throughout the 1950s students from UCD and TCD attended separate classes, with the premises being shared by both colleges. In 1967 the Commission on Higher Education commented that the arrangements for veterinary education,

> … cannot be regarded as satisfactory. There is no need for two schools of veterinary medicine to deal with an annual intake of 60 students. It is a wasteful arrangement and all the more grievous as improvements in accommodation, equipment, and staffing are required. Moreover, the efficient and economical administration of the Veterinary College is made more difficult by basic differences between university and civil service administrative procedures. Altogether, the participation of three distinct bodies in the provision and management of a relatively small

sector of higher education is educationally and administratively indefensible.[66]

The commission recommended establishing a national college of agricultural and veterinary sciences with responsibility for agricultural and veterinary research, for professional training in agriculture, dairy science, horticulture, forestry and veterinary medicine, and for new branches of higher agricultural education, such as rural home economics. The college would be a fully-integrated teaching and research organisation of university standing, with a governing council that would have full responsibility for the entire organisation. The commission's objectives were to link higher education in agriculture with research; to place higher education in agriculture on a firm scientific basis; and to achieve greater unity in higher agricultural education.[67] Its recommendations had much in common with Carrigan's original plans for an agricultural institute, and, as happened on the previous occasion, they were ignored. The only substantial change after the publication of this report was the transfer of the veterinary college to UCD, where it was constituted as a separate faculty.

EDUCATING FUTURE FARMERS

Agricultural education is not held in high esteem by the farmer. He considers that traditional methods are better than those learned at an agricultural college, or from the local instructor. The agricultural colleges and the instructors are accused of being too theoretical, or working under ideal conditions, of not making due allowance for local conditions of soil and climate and of not appreciating the practical and economic difficulties which the farmer must over come.

This claim was made by the Limerick Rural Survey, which carried out fieldwork in 1958/9; it was financed by a technical assistance grant from the US and administered by the Department of Agriculture. A majority of farmers surveyed agreed with the statement that sons who returned to the farm after attending an agricultural college were 'cocky and want to change everything'. They questioned their fathers' judgements, and perhaps their authority. Consequently most farmers were not simply indifferent to agricultural education; they were positively opposed to it.[68]

Attendance at the agricultural colleges controlled by the Department remained low. In 1926/7 39 male students attended the colleges at

Ballyhaise and Clonakilty, and 106 women enrolled at the Munster Institute. By 1956/7 Ballyhaise, Clonakilty and Johnstown Castle attracted a total of 74 male students, and 79 women studied at the Munster Institute. The largest attendance was at the Athenry agricultural college, which provided short-term courses for 126 students.[69] A further 700 students attended private agricultural colleges that were in receipt of funding from the Department of Agriculture.[70] Most courses were of one year's duration, although a minority of students attended two-year courses. Many students were funded by scholarships awarded by the county committees of agriculture.[71] Few graduates of the agricultural colleges became fulltime farmers and only 30 per cent of male students who attended a vocational school returned to farming.[72] A survey carried out by AFT of farmers in West Cork revealed that only 4 per cent had received any fulltime post-primary education; 1 per cent had attended an agricultural college. Yet farmers who had received post-primary education were much more likely to adopt new farming practices than those who had only attended primary school. The most innovative farmers were those with post-primary education, who then attended an agricultural college.[73]

The difficulty in developing an appropriate educational programme for future farmers was compounded by a lack of clarity over the respective roles of the Department of Agriculture and the Department of Education. *Economic Development* noted that the Department of Agriculture was 'almost completely divorced' from the vocational schools. Adult education classes in agriculture were organised by the county committees of agriculture through the advisory service, and they were generally held in national schools, whereas day-time rural science classes in vocational schools were organised by the vocational education committees (VECs). It added that, 'It cannot but be a cause of national concern that the Department responsible for agricultural policy is not more closely associated with the furtherance of agricultural knowledge in these schools, or that, in the past, some of the most successful projects in these schools have had to be introduced almost by subterfuge'.[74]

Many of the rural science teachers employed in the vocational schools were graduates in agricultural science, and they often worked closely with local advisers to promote Macra na Feirme and other educational programmes,[75] but the formal relationship between the two departments was less amicable. In 1964 the Department of Agriculture noted that the Ministers and Secretaries Act of 1924 did not list agricultural education as a function of the Department of Education, 'though several other types of

education and training are mentioned as functions of that Department',
whereas the Ministers and Secretaries (Amendment) Act of 1928 included
'education in agriculture and in subjects relating thereto' as one of the
functions of the Department of Agriculture, and the Agriculture Act of
1931 required every county committee of agriculture to prepare an annual
'scheme … for giving assistance and instruction for the purposes of
agriculture and rural industries in its county'.[76]

The inadequate state of agricultural education, particularly the education of men and women who would remain on the land, was in conflict
with the commitments given by successive governments to protect and
preserve rural Ireland. In 1949 Dr. P. E. Ó Suilleabháin, the chief inspector
in the technical instruction branch of the Department of Education, told
the Commission on Emigration that 'the whole aim and idea of our schools
is to train people to stay on the land'. This was both a cultural and an
economic issue. All male students who attended vocational schools in rural
areas and small towns studied rural science.[77] When Fianna Fáil was out of
office between 1954 and 1957, a sub-committee of the party's national
executive drew up plans for a major expansion in second and third-level
education, including major provisions for vocational education and
additional places in agricultural schools and colleges.[78]

In 1959, as part of the Programme for Economic Expansion, the departments of Agriculture and Education joined forces to establish winter farm
schools designed for teenagers who had left school to work on the family
farm. Classes were held in rural vocational schools during winter months,
with instruction provided by the agricultural adviser or by the rural science
teachers attached to the vocational school. Nagle cautioned that it would
take time to build up attendance; for the first year it was hoped to attract
an attendance of 600 to 800. He believed that the success of these winter
schools would depend very much on the co-operation of rural organisations.[79] In 1959/60 winter farm schools were held at thirty-seven centres
in twenty-six counties, and 839 pupils attended. However, by 1963/4
attendance had dropped to 497, and only seventeen counties were holding
classes. The Department claimed that there had been a definite switch
from day to night courses, because the day courses were 'top-heavy with
subjects which have little relevance to agriculture and farmers have not
been prepared to leave their farms during the day to attend such courses'.
If the winter farm schools were to prove successful it was essential that the
courses should be organised by the county advisory service, 'who were
conversant with farming needs', and not by the vocational education

committees. The Department anticipated no difficulty in running winter farm schools without the co-operation of the VEC.[80]

The matter came to a head in July 1963 when Part I of the *Second Programme for Economic Expansion* was being finalised. A Cabinet committee, consisting of the Taoiseach and the ministers for Finance, Agriculture and Industry and Commerce, decided that the reference to the possibility of introducing a scheme of part-time education for young farmers should be deleted from the *Second Programme*, at the request of the Minister for Agriculture.[81] When the final draft of Part II of the *Second Programme* was being agreed in May 1964, the Minister for Education, Patrick Hillery, wrote to Lemass objecting to the inclusion of a statement that 'the responsibility for agricultural education rests essentially with the Minister for Agriculture'. He was prepared to agree to a statement that the Department of Agriculture and the county committees of agriculture have 'a special position and responsibility in regard to agricultural education', provided that it included a reference to the responsibilities of the Department of Education and the VECs 'to the extent that instruction bearing on agriculture is provided in secondary and vocational schools'. The Department of Agriculture claimed that the vocational education committee's role was restricted to providing continuing education for young persons between the ages of fourteen and sixteen and 'subjects bearing on or relating to agriculture cannot be included in technical education, except in accordance with an Order made after consultation with the Minister for Agriculture'. The Department expressed concern that the one-month farm apprenticeship courses being organised by the VEC, which attracted boys between the ages of sixteen and eighteen years, were catering for the type that normally attended winter agricultural classes and winter farm schools, and demanded that attendance should be restricted to boys who had just completed their continuation education.[82] The first course of this nature was introduced in 1961 by Elphin vocational school in County Roscommon. Students were instructed in rural science, construction of farm buildings and the maintenance of farm equipment and they visited neighbouring farms.[83]

Women and Agriculture

Until the 1950s most references to the role of women in Irish agriculture were concerned with poultry, and perhaps with butter-making. When the Department of Agriculture proposed to establish a commission on agriculture in 1938, it decided to nominate one woman, who would act as a representative for both women and the poultry sector, but she was dropped from the final list of members. After World War II, however, there was a growing awareness in Ireland, and elsewhere, that women were central to the survival of family farms. The high rate of female emigration from rural Ireland give rise to fears that the family farm would collapse because of a shortage of wives. The Commission on Emigration suggested that the lack of electricity and running water were among the factors deterring young women from marrying farmers. Another was the late age at which farms were inherited.[84] When Leitrim Vocational Educational Committee ran a course in home economics for farmers' daughters in the early 1950s, the cookery classes were conducted over an open fire.[85] By the late 1950s most farm-houses had electricity, but only a minority had adequate running water or bathroom facilities.[86] Patrick McNab described farm-houses in County Limerick as giving 'an impression of comfort and well-being' from the outside; 'The interiors, however, do not live up to expectations'.[87]

The ICA was the main source of education in home economics for rural women until the 1960s. The organisation appointed four home economics advisers, who had been trained in the United States under ECA grant counterpart schemes.[88] In 1959 the ICA convened a conference on 'The Rural Family', attended by representatives of the departments of Agriculture and Education, where the value of a rural home economics advisory service was among the topics under discussion.[89] The Department of Agriculture appreciated the value of the work being carried out by the ICA, and in 1961 demanded that the Department of Finance increase its annual grant. When Finance refused, the Department enlisted the support of Lemass to have this decision reversed.[90]

In 1960 an international conference on agricultural advisory services, organised by the OEEC, recommended that ministries of agriculture should include a rural home economics advisory service as an integral part of the advisory service.[91] The idea gained additional support in 1962 when the report of the Inter-Departmental Committee on Small Western Farms recommended that a pilot programme of home economics advisers should be established in western counties.[92] Smith sent Lemass a detailed memorandum, arguing that it should become part of the agricultural advisory service. Most farmers' wives were involved in making decisions on the running of the family farm, and any training programme should take this into consideration. It should equip them to take a hand in developing progressive ideas in the rural community, and it should impress on them that farming was 'a good and satisfying vocation'. The memorandum noted that it was becoming increasingly difficult for farmers to find suitable wives.

As a first step towards introducing a farm home advisory service Smith suggested that a small group of poultry instructresses should be given an intensive training course of six to twelve months in farm home management. This was not a novel proposal. In 1957 the Cork County Committee of Agriculture had suggested that poultry and butter-making instructresses should provide advice on home management, and in the following year the Irish Agricultural Officers' Organisation, which represented all categories of instructors and instructresses employed by the county committees of agriculture, took up this demand.[93] By 1960 county committees of agriculture employed fewer poultry advisers than in 1950,[94] and this trend seemed likely to continue, as poultry production switched from small farms to large commercial enterprises. Retraining the poultry instructresses as home economics advisers would equip them with skills that seemed more relevant to the needs of modern farm women.

When Lemass read the proposal that Smith submitted, he indicated that it made 'a very convincing case for developing this service from the Agricultural Advisory Service'. He urged the Minister for Education, Dr Patrick Hillery, to support the proposal unless he saw 'very strong objections in principle'. When the chief educational officers of the VECs learned of the proposal they demanded that the new service should operate under their control. They claimed that several VECs were already providing suitable courses. On 27 July 1962 Dr Hillery informed the Department of the Taoiseach that their views had convinced him that 'the entry of the Department of Agriculture into this activity will be to the detriment of rural families'.

The Department of Agriculture had already announced that the first intensive training course for rural home economics advisers would begin in the autumn at the Munster Institute. The course would be organised by a senior member of the home economics advisory course of the state of Nebraska, and by an official from the rural home economics service in the state of Bavaria. Both of these women were selected because they were Catholics.[95] In the light of the 'sharp conflict' of opinion that existed between the two departments, the Department of the Taoiseach referred the matter to a sub-committee, with representatives from the departments of Agriculture, Education and Finance, although it was agreed that the pilot training course would go ahead.[96] In an astute piece of public relations the Department of Agriculture arranged for members of the ICA to visit the training course.[97]

In October Tadhg Ó Cearbhaill informed Lemass that there was 'scarcely any hope' that the sub-committee would reach agreement. Whitty, the Department of Finance representative, had informed him in confidence that the representatives of the Department of Education were operating under very rigid instructions.[98] When the draft report of the interdepartmental committee was sent to the relevant departments for consideration, in January 1964, Whitty informed Ó Cearbhaill that 'the reaction of the Agriculture member was pretty strong'. Whitty anticipated that he might be the sole signatory. He also noted that the OECD would probably consider the report of the interdepartmental committee.

The disagreement between the departments of Agriculture and Education over who should be responsible for training in farm home economics escalated during 1964 when the Offaly VEC refused to permit the county committee of agriculture to hold classes in farm home management in Shinrone vocational school. Harry Spain reported that the Department of Education had instructed the CEO that he should not make the school premises available. This was particularly ironic as Telefís Éireann had been planning to make a programme about community co-operation in Shinrone. Smith used the incident as an opportunity to reiterate the Department of Agriculture's claim that it should have overall responsibility for agricultural education. He reminded Lemass that the Department of Agriculture had been responsible for agricultural education since its inception. Its task would be much easier if young people entering farming had received a good continuation course after primary school and he suggested that the Department of Education should direct its energy towards doing this, 'rather than attempting work which does not come within their function at all'. He demanded that the *Second Programme for Economic Expansion* should contain a clear statement indicating where responsibility for agricultural education and rural home management rested.

It emerged that the decision to deny the county committee of agriculture the use of school premises was prompted by the threat of publicity on television. The secretary of the Department of Education, T. Ó Raiftearaigh, told Nagle that

> ... given a proper spirit between our two Departments, this whole affair, with all it entails, would never have arisen. It is a pitiable state of affairs between the two Government Departments. What an example to those concerned throughout the country.

Nagle responded warmly to this message, and within days both secretaries had agreed on the responsibilities of their respective departments and on future co-operation. The relevant paragraphs in the draft of the *Second Programme* were altered accordingly. The revised version of paragraph 45 stated that the Department of Agriculture had 'a special position and responsibility in regard to agricultural education'. The Department of Education and the VECs had a responsibility for education 'bearing on agriculture in primary, secondary and vocational schools'.

The private agreement fleshed out the details. Winter farm schools would be organised by the county committees of agriculture with the co-operation of the VECs. The farm home advisory service would be developed within the general framework of the agricultural advisory service, and it would be extended to all counties. The Department of Agriculture agreed to co-operate fully with the Department of Education on the use of buildings or staff of the VECs. The senior technical staff of the two departments would confer on the curriculum of the winter farm schools. At the suggestion of T. K. Whitaker, the Department of Agriculture agreed to consider the possibility of using the domestic science teachers attached to the VEC in connection with the rural home advisory service. The draft report of the interdepartmental committee was abandoned. Nagle concluded that although the talks had been 'a painful and delicate process' they had been 'a prerequisite to genuine co-operation'.[99]

In 1965 the Department reopened the agricultural schools at Athenry and Clonakilty, which had been modernised and extended. Yet by 1969, only 550 of the 4,000 boys who took up farming every year had completed a course at an agricultural college. A further 250 attended a winter farm school. The *Third Programme for Economic and Social Development* claimed that the low proportion of farmers, trained at an agricultural college was due to a lack of places, and it gave a commitment to create 300 additional places and to provide more scholarships. It announced that in future, winter farm schools would operate from the farm training centres. The Department planned to establish 100 throughout the country; where possible, they would be located beside vocational schools. The farm centres would provide courses for men and women engaged in farming.[100] The decision to provide farm centres removed agricultural education from the vocational schools and placed it under the control of the county committees of agriculture. By 1969 there were practical reasons for this: the introduction of free second-level schooling in 1968 meant that many vocational schools were overcrowded, and they were unlikely to be in a position to provide space for agricultural classes.

The Farm Apprenticeship Scheme

The farm apprenticeship scheme was an earlier attempt to provide a training programme for future farmers and a means of providing them with land at an early age. It was prompted by concern over the low educational standard among farmers and the late age of marriage and land inheritance. Éamon de Valera had tried to provide a solution to the problem of rural marriages in the 1940s, when he proposed that the government should finance the construction of dower-houses on farms, to permit earlier marriages by inheriting sons. His plan came in for severe criticism from an inter-departmental committee of civil servants, and was never implemented.[101]

The idea for a farm apprenticeship scheme originated with Macra na Feirme. In 1952 P. M. Quinlan of Macra na Feirme sent John A. Costello a copy of a paper he had written with the title 'Own Your Own Farm At Thirty, an Incentive for Rural Education'. He suggested that young men who completed an apprenticeship programme should be provided with a government loan that would enable them to buy a farm. Young women who underwent a training scheme in farm home management would be given a marriage bonus, a cash grant that could be used for poultry development, and some electrical appliances.[102] In a separate development the Agricultural Association, a group of farmers based in County Dublin, met James Dillon in 1954 to discuss the possibility of setting up an apprenticeship scheme to train workers for glasshouse enterprises. This prompted the Department to investigate the agricultural apprenticeship schemes that existed in other European countries. It concluded that there was no great need for apprenticeship training in Ireland because of the large number of family farms.

Nevertheless the concept began to attract attention. The Report of the Commission on Emigration drew attention to the high average age of farmers. In 1951 the average male farmer was aged fifty-five, the average woman farmer was sixty-two. The commission recommended that the government examine the possibility of providing farms for young credit-worthy farmers, and other measures that would reduce the age of succession to farms, and improve the marriage patterns of rural communities.[103] In 1956 the Kildare branch of the newly-formed NFA recommended a five-year apprenticeship programme, that would include attendance at an agricultural college and practical experience on different types of farm. But when the Minister for Finance, Kildare TD Gerard Sweetman, met a deputation from the Kildare NFA to discuss the idea, officials in the Department of Finance echoed the views of their colleagues in the

Department of Agriculture, that 'most boys reared on Irish farms have already served an apprenticeship course to farming by the time that they leave school'.[104] Nevertheless the proposal gained the support of the Taoiseach, John A. Costello. In January 1957, in the course of a speech at the agricultural college at Palleskenry, he expressed fears that the high average age of Irish farmers would retard agricultural development, and he spoke about the need to provide farms for young credit-worthy farmers. He indicated that this could not be done through the Land Commission, because its task was to complete land purchase and relieve congestion. The solution might lie in establishing a company that would buy and lease land to young farmers on a business basis.[105]

Costello's speech may have encouraged the NFA and Macra na Feirme to submit a joint proposal to the Department. This suggested that the Land Commission should provide fifty-acre holdings to young men who had completed a five-year apprenticeship. Initially they would rent these holdings, with the possibility of purchasing them in time. No holdings would be allocated to anybody who had inherited land unless they disposed of the other farm. They claimed that the scheme 'will initiate a new trend in the land-ward direction, it will give a reasonable promise of greatly improved husbandry, it will foster early marriage where at present there is an inordinate proportion of bachelor and spinster households, and it will limit if not entirely eliminate, undesirable forms of speculation in land and land purchase'. John Dempsey, the secretary of the Department of Agriculture, described the proposal as 'very good if a little ambitious'. The cost of providing a fifty-acre farm would be approximately £3,400, which was similar to the cost of resettling migrants from the congested districts. Dempsey noted that 'this scheme is really an extension of the existing scheme for migrants', with the addition of an intensive training programme. 'In effect, it would seem that it does no more than introduce a new method of selection of migrants. This may be desirable'. Other officials in the Department of Agriculture were less enthusiastic. Daniel Hoctor suggested that this was a matter for the Department of Lands. He believed that sons from well-managed farms who had spent some time at agricultural colleges would be equally suitable candidates for new holdings as men who had undergone a five-year apprenticeship.

The proposal had captured the public imagination at a time when there was growing concern over the future of rural Ireland. It was widely discussed in newspapers and it formed the theme of a weekend conference organised by *Tuairim*,[106] where the idea was strongly pressed by Reverend Dr Daniel

Duffy, a curate from Carrickmacross, County Monaghan, and Dr R. O'Connor, the chief executive officer of the County Monaghan VEC. Bob O'Connor, an agricultural scientist, claimed that, 'Only the central authority had the power and the means to effect a change in land acquisition and tenure which would break the present impasse as far as their young people were concerned'.[107]

In November 1958 the Land Commission suggested that it might allocate a small number of farms for farm apprentices as its contribution to the Programme for Economic Expansion. *Economic Development* had stated that action should be taken to increase the number of farms on the market that were available to young farmers. According to the Land Commission, creating 'scholarship farms' would provide propaganda for the expansion programme and initiate a much-needed trend in the commission's work. The scheme could be limited to small farming counties. Decisions on awarding 'scholarship farms' would be made by a board similar to the Local Appointments Commission. The Department of Agriculture claimed that the Land Commission's proposal would do nothing to increase agricultural output and would not end the flight from the land. In the Department's opinion it would be highly regrettable if the proposal diverted the Land Commission's attention 'from the pressing problem of relieving congestion and of transforming our numerous uneconomic holdings into viable units'.[108]

When Lemass met the joint Macra/NFA farm apprenticeship committee in February 1960, he indicated that although the government was sympathetic to its objectives, there were some fundamental problems with the idea. The Land Commission had a statutory duty to relieve congestion and he anticipated widespread protests from farmers in congested areas if it decided to allocate farms to qualified farm apprentices. Although it would be impossible for the government to provide farms for qualified apprentices, he indicated that it might be possible to offer loans to enable them to buy a farm, and they could possibly be given safeguards against artificial land values.[109] Lemass remained sympathetic to the general proposal, and in August 1962 he asked his colleagues for suggestions as to how it might be advanced. Smith's reply was uncompromising:

> I had been hoping for some months passed that this scheme was dead. I had forgotten the old saying 'It is hard to kill a bad thing.' Hard and all as it may be I think there is little life left in it now le conghamh Dé [please God].[110]

418

Lemass asked the farm apprenticeship committee to revise its proposals. The new submission conceded that there was no prospect that the government would provide farms for apprentices who completed the course. Apprentices would spend one year at an agricultural college, and a further four years working on selected farms; at the end of this period, they would sit an examination at an agricultural college, and would be awarded £2,000 on completing the programme. The scheme would be administered by a private limited liability charitable company, whose shares would be held by the NFA, Macra and the ICA. The administrative costs would be borne by the government.

The Department of Agriculture remained sceptical about the merits of a farm apprenticeship scheme. It informed the Department of the Taoiseach that the scheme would be very expensive for the state and would not provide a solution to the social problems of rural Ireland. It believed it would be more beneficial to use the money to strengthen the advisory and educational services. Harry Spain commented:

> Personally I see very little value in the proposal from this point of view compared with what our advisers can accomplish by working with existing suitable farmers and farmers' sons, individually and in groups. Because of our poor tradition in intensive farming, this demands a long and concentrated effort, but the presence of excellently run farms of all sizes in all kinds of situations, through the country, shows that some progress is being made. If funds are available, I would back their use in strengthening the advisory service at all levels, to give much better long-term results than in subsidising the purchase of a few farms. We should avoid at all costs creating a situation where farmers, instead of being leaders in the social life of their communities, are objects of jealousy.

He would prefer young farmers to spend two years at agricultural college.[111]

When Lemass met the farm apprenticeship committee in December he informed it that he was referring its document to an interdepartmental committee; 'the officials appointed would have the task of finding out every possible defect in their scheme, but would approach the task on the basis that the Government were agreeable in principle … if it could be shown to be soundly conceived and workable'. After this meeting Lemass wondered whether the Department of the Taoiseach should be represented on the committee to ensure 'that it functions with reasonable expedition', but the secretary of his Department, Nicholas Nolan, advised against this. Lemass insisted that an understanding should be reached that the reservations which the Department of Agriculture harboured concerning the farm apprenticeship scheme would not be permitted to result in 'a negative approach' by its representative on the committee, or any delay in completing the task. Nagle replied that while the Minister for Agriculture had some reservations about the scheme, once the Taoiseach had indicated that the government supported the proposal in principle, 'there would be no danger of any lack of a constructive attitude towards it so far as his Department was concerned'. The Department was about to receive a visit from an OECD committee that was examining farm apprenticeship schemes in member countries, and Nagle hoped to be in a position to inform them of the Irish proposals.[112]

When the Macra/NFA committee examined the recommendations of the interdepartmental committee, it claimed that they amounted to a radical altering of the scheme, and asked on what basis the committee had approached the proposal. Daniel Hoctor, who chaired the interdepartmental committee, replied that the committee had viewed the farm apprenticeship scheme as 'essentially … a training scheme, not a land settlement scheme', and it had set out to devise a scheme that would supplement existing provisions for agricultural education. Both parties disagreed about the number and value of the prizes to be awarded. Nagle suggested that an award of £2,000 for completing the farm apprenticeship programme was too generous; he recommended a limited number of prizes, £500 for those who achieved a merit award in the apprenticeship tests, and up to fifteen awards of £250 each for those with lower achievements. The NFA/Macra committee saw the scheme as a means of assisting sons of small farmers, and it recommended that it should be means-tested; the interdepartmental committee disagreed.[113] Although the farm apprenticeship committee modified its proposal to comply with most of the recommendations of the interdepartmental committee, it remained determined that scholarships should be means-tested and distributed on a regional basis, with at least 75 per cent going to lower income groups. Seán Healy, who represented the NFA on the committee, added that, 'To us the fundamental point is that apprentices, having served practical training, will not find their abilities frustrated, but will be assisted in putting their training into practical application as independent farmers or farm managers.[114] When Dr Daniel Duffy met Hoctor he emphasised that when he devised the scheme, he had been thinking of something that would lead 'to a farming ladder and land settlement rather than one whose objectives were primarily educational'. He was reluctant to abandon this idea, but when he discussed it with the Monaghan County Committee of Agriculture he got no encouragement. By June 1962 most of the outstanding details had been agreed: the government would provide thirty awards of £500 each to those who completed the apprenticeship with special merit, and it would meet the cost of fees and travelling expenses for apprentices attending courses at agricultural colleges.[115]

The farm apprenticeship scheme was eventually announced in May 1964 with an initial eleven apprentices. It was organised by a board consisting of representatives of Macra na Feirmc, the NFA, the ICA and the Federation of Rural Workers. There were some teething problems. In April 1967 Rory Murphy, the chairman of the Farm Apprenticeship Board, claimed that the lack of support staff meant that there were problems in the selection of suitable farmers and apprentices. Some apprentices dropped out because of poor relations between master farmers and apprentices. By 1966 there were fifty-three apprentices; sixteen had been recruited in 1964; twenty-one in 1965 and sixteen in 1966.[116]

Several of the issues raised by the Farm Apprenticeship Scheme – the involvement of outside groups in formulating proposals; the question of land settlement; the involvement of Seán Lemass; and the inter-departmental aspects of the proposal – also crop up in relation to the inter-departmental committee on small western farms.

SMALL WESTERN FARMS

There was no tradition of a regional policy in the Department of Agriculture. Horace Plunkett had believed that the problem of small farms was not a regional matter; it existed throughout Ireland. During the 1930s the Department provided grants for land reclamation in the former congested districts, and in 1949 James Dillon announced special aids to develop poultry production and glass-houses in Gaeltacht (Irish-speaking) areas. The Fianna Fáil government of 1951–4 expanded the range of incentives offered for glass-house enterprises in the Gaeltacht, and established a state-owned grass meal factory in County Mayo, to process grass grown on cutaway bog. None of these schemes originated in the Department; they were supported by interests whose primary purpose was to protect the Gaeltacht, not to develop agriculture. The Department of Agriculture advised against the glass-house scheme, because it believed it would be expensive and would have little prospect of success, and this proved to be correct.[117] It was equally critical of the grass meal project, and throughout the 1950s repeatedly advised that it should be wound up, although the Department's advice was rejected.[118]

The decision to examine the needs of western small farms was taken by Seán Lemass. It was prompted by his concern that all sections of the community should share in the benefits of economic growth. In 1961 he told James Ryan, the Minister for Finance, that:

> In my view the main, if not the only question arising in national economic policy to which we have not yet found a satisfactory answer, is how to deal with the problem of the small (mainly western) farms, and to ensure reasonable standards of income for those who live on them.

The National Farm Survey for the years 1955–8 revealed that the average income over the three years on all farms in the north and west averaged £180, compared with £193 in the east and midlands and £311 in southern counties.[119] Lemass wished to establish whether the government should encourage the amalgamation of small farms, and the social consequences if this were done; the economic potential offered by forestry; whether some forms of state aid could reduce the cost of production on these holdings; and whether small farmers should be encouraged to embark on new enterprises. Lemass raised these questions with T. K. Whitaker, who suggested that a 'super-organiser' should be sent into the underdeveloped areas to encourage local and community initiatives.[120]

The Department of Agriculture was extremely wary about the idea of a 'super-organiser'. Nagle remarked that it would be 'very like a resuscitation of the Parish Plan, as against the advisory services provided by the County Committees of Agriculture with our co-operation'. In his opinion it would be preferable if the county committees of agriculture directed special attention to the underdeveloped areas. This might be done by establishing special committees in each area, consisting of the chief agricultural officer, local instructors, and representatives from the Department of Agriculture. Smith suggested that measures might be introduced to improve hill-grazing and to extend dairy farming, but this proposal caused alarm bells to ring in the Department of Finance because it would raise the cost of dairy subsidies. Whitaker remarked that milk was 'something of a problem product – hardly suited to problem areas!' Smith was keen to have the matter examined by an interdepartmental committee, so that the prospects for creating employment in tourism, fishing and manufacturing industries could also be investigated.

Lemass was reluctant to agree to an interdepartmental committee, because he feared it would delay government action, but when Ryan and Whitaker expressed their support for the idea, he conceded. He asked the Economic Development Branch of the Department of Finance to take charge, in order to eliminate 'some of the inevitable delays' and to resolve differences between departments. However, Ryan suggested that the committee be chaired by a representative from the Department of Agriculture and it should report jointly to the ministers for Agriculture and Finance. While Lemass wanted the committee to be confined to examining agricultural problems, Ryan argued that this would be unduly restrictive. In his opinion the problem was 'probably not soluble on an exclusively agricultural basis' and it would be necessary to consider prospects in tourism and industry.

Lemass announced the appointment of the interdepartmental committee at the annual general meeting of the ICA on 11 April 1961. In a speech, which received widespread and favourable press coverage, he placed rural development at the heart of the government's economic and social policy. Lemass noted that an improvement in rural conditions,

> ... is a real test of our capacity as a nation to organise ourselves on a sound basis and to give the country economic foundations which will be strong enough to withstand all the vicissitudes which changing world conditions can produce. A country whose economy is founded in a well-organised diversified agriculture is always a happy country. The chief aim of all our endeavours is to bring that situation into reality in Ireland and to establish its entitlement to that description.

He mentioned that the Minister for Agriculture was hoping to extend the creamery system in the west of Ireland to give small farmers a new outlet for milk, and he referred to the importance of educational and advisory services and the role of voluntary organisations such as the ICA.

The committee, which was chaired by Michael Barry of the Department of Agriculture, consisted of Daniel Hoctor (Agriculture), Tom Walsh (AFT), M. D. McCarthy (CSO), D. P. O'Sullivan and S. P. Mac Piarais (Lands), J. F. Harman (Finance), and S. MacFhloinn (Gaeltacht). In June 1961 the committee circulated a report, noting that every idea it had examined, had presented serious problems. Michael Barry acknowledged that it 'does not look like real progress'; 'the more we dig into this matter the more complex it becomes'.

These complexities were highlighted in the final report, which was published in April 1962. This noted that the economic backwardness of the region could be explained by four factors:

- a disinclination on the part of young people to remain in the area, when high living standards were available elsewhere;
- western farmers did not benefit from the price guarantees offered on wheat, barley, butter and milk;
- pigs, poultry and eggs, the traditional sources of income on small western farms, were no longer profitable;
- lack of industry reduced the prospects for employment outside farming.

Emigration did little to solve these problems: it did not result in the consolidation of land holdings, and it sapped community spirit and initiative. However, these problems were not unique to the west of Ireland; similar conditions could be found in many parts of Europe. The EEC had stated that 'safeguarding of the family farm' was a long-term objective of agricultural policy. The committee concluded that price supports would not bring a permanent improvement in the position of small farms. It recommended action under four headings:

1. Structural Policy
2. Production and Marketing
3. Educational and Social Policy
4. Industrialisation, Tourism, Fisheries, and other Ancillary Matters

When the report of the committee was considered by the government, most of the discussion centred on the question of land structures. The recommendations on land policy dominated press coverage of the report.[121]

One-quarter of holdings in Ulster and Connacht were between one and fifteen acres, and these were uneconomic. In such circumstances the future lay in creating jobs outside agriculture. Small farms should be capable of supporting two adult males, if family and community structures were to be maintained. As many farms would not meet this criterion, employment must be developed in tourism, forestry and industry. The published report recommended a range of measures that would increase the supply of land for redistribution: giving the Land Commission the power to acquire land that had been derelict or abandoned for five years; encouraging elderly farmers to transfer their land to the Land Commission in such a way that they could retain their home and their old age pension; providing loans for larger western farmers to buy farms elsewhere in the state.[122]

Although the Land Commission had been redistributing land for many decades, its practice was to divide any available land among the adjacent farmers. This meant that the enlarged holdings remained too small to be economical, but any decision to give an entire farm to one claimant would be politically controversial.[123] For this reason the published report merely indicated that this was 'an opportune time to review the present size of standard holdings, and the policy of excluding from allotment holdings which have been created or brought up to a previous standard'.[124] At the time the Land Commission defined viable holding as thirty-three acres of good land. The files indicate that the interdepartmental committee was in favour of forty to forty-five acres as the new minimum size and that it wanted to see land available for redistribution given only to farmers with a proven record of good husbandry.[125]

A minority report by McCarthy and Harmon claimed that any attempt by the Land Commission to restructure landholdings would be a waste of money. It would also deter farmers from acquiring land by their own efforts. They suggested that the transfer of land should be left to market forces, with the government's role limited to ensuring that young farmers were provided with credit to enable them to buy land. J. O'Brien, the secretary of the Department of Lands, claimed that this report was unjustifiably critical of land policy, but emphasised that his remark did not indicate that he opposed the publication of the minority report.[126] It was published, but the authors were not identified at that time.

The Minister for Agriculture, Patrick Smith, also expressed private reservations about the recommendations concerning land redistribution, although his concerns were utterly at variance with the views expressed by McCarthy and Harmon. In June 1962 Smith sent a letter to James Ryan, the Minister for Finance, arguing that it should not be assumed that the existing farm structure was necessarily uneconomic, although he was prepared to agree to the Land Commission's raising the size of its standard holdings, perhaps to fifty acres.[127] But in January 1963 Smith demanded that the Land Commission continue to divide vacant land among all qualified applicants, whereas the Land Commission itself wanted to create minimum holdings of forty to forty-five acres. Although Smith eventually dropped this demand, following a meeting with Michael Moran, the Minister for Lands, he added that 'as in the case of a woman, my last word is I like my draft best'.[128] Smith's attitude was obviously coloured by personal experience. During his speech on the 1963/4 estimate for the Department of Agriculture, he mentioned that he had spent his life in a community that consisted of small farms ranging from ten to forty acres, and he believed 'that they maintain a social pattern far superior to that obtaining in countries where there are large blocks of land run by advanced methods of mechanisation, which eliminate the human element practically entirely'. He believed that the farm structure found in counties Cavan and Monaghan, and the west of Ireland, was viable; it would be 'a great treason to our whole outlook on life if we accepted the doctrine that our future policy in regard to agriculture should be founded on the conviction that that social pattern is fated to go'.[129] Smith and Erskine Childers, TD for Monaghan, succeeded in having counties Monaghan, Cavan and Longford included in government measures to assist western farms.[130]

The interdepartmental committee recommended that the land project should be transformed into a farm rehabilitation scheme, with land project staff working closely with the advisory service. Participating farmers would be provided with credit to enable them to stock their lands, but they would be under an obligation to ensure that reclaimed land was properly maintained. Land rehabilitation should begin on a trial basis in a number of pilot areas, with priority being given to group projects; Harmon and McCarthy suggested that the effectiveness of the land project should first be investigated.

The section relating to agricultural production and marketing recommended that farmers should concentrate on traditional intensive lines of production, such as pigs and poultry, rather than trying to make a living by 'ranching without ranches'. EEC membership would bring higher prices for pigs, poultry and eggs and farmers should expand these products in advance of Irish membership. Pig and poultry farmers should establish co-operatives to handle marketing and supplies of feed. There seemed to be potential for developing an export trade in bull beef, high-grade mountain lamb, and wool. The interdepartmental committee supported the Department of Agriculture's plan to expand dairy farming, which would provide farmers with a regular cash income. Many of these proposals were dependent on developing a strong co-operative system, which would make farming more profitable and reduce farmers' dependence on the state. The Department agreed with most of the proposals, although officials expressed reservations about the plan to carry out demonstrations of surface seeding on blanket bog. This was a modified version of the 1950s project to produce grass meal on blanket bog, which the Department had consistently opposed.[131] It also warned about the difficulties in marketing horticultural produce from remote areas, and again its reservations were based on the failure of earlier horticultural projects in Gaeltacht areas.

On education and social policy the interdepartmental committee recommended offering more scholarships to agricultural colleges and developing short courses that would be suitable for future farmers. It recommended that the advisory service should be strengthened in western areas, with a target of one adviser for every 800 farmers, and the establishment of a farm home advisory service. Western counties had the lowest ratio of advisers to farmers; the highest ratios were found in prosperous counties such as Meath, Wexford and Kildare.[132] The imbalance was due to the fact that the number of agricultural advisers was determined by the county committees of agriculture. Half of the cost of salaries was met from the county council rates, and because the Department did not specify a minimum number of advisers, or a maximum number of farms per adviser, provisions varied widely between counties. In 1959/60 the highest rateable valuation per capita was in County Meath, the lowest in Mayo. The lowest rate in the pound was levied in County Meath, and the highest in County Donegal, closely followed by County Mayo.[133] When local finances were under strain, economies in the local advisory services were a favourite target, hence the inadequate numbers in the poorer counties.[134] The interdepartmental committee recommended that the government pay a higher proportion of the cost of advisers' salaries in the poorer counties.

When the report of the inter-departmental committee was circulated to the Cabinet, ministers were provided with copies of papers written by agricultural economists Rosemary Fennell and E. A. Attwood. According to Fennell, the imbalance in the economy of the west of Ireland was caused by a lack of industry and an almost complete dependence on agriculture.[135] Attwood claimed that the assistance currently provided to small western farms was too diffuse. In the past, the economic problems of individual farms had been viewed as a variety of distinct problems, not as a single entity. Farmers had not been encouraged to accept that the onus for raising agricultural output rested with them. The state had a responsibility to provide them with expert technical advice, and some of the necessary capital, but it should not absolve the farmer from his essential function of risk-taking and decision-making.[136] Attwood's paper reflected the broad philosophy behind the report of the interdepartmental committee, with its emphasis on measures to promote co-operation and personal initiative. The committee recommended that the unemployment assistance scheme should be revised so small farmers would not be deterred from efforts to raise output by fears that they would no longer be eligible for a benefit.

Many of the committee's recommendations were implemented within a short period. The government agreed to contribute 75 per cent of the salaries of advisers in western counties.[137] In November 1963 the Minister for Agriculture gave a commitment to increase the number of advisers in western counties from 102 to 183.[138] County development teams were established to co-ordinate the activities of government departments and local authorities, as the interdepartmental committee recommended, and they took on the task of promoting tourism and industry.[139] The Department of Social Welfare began the review of its means-testing regulations relating to agriculture.[140] In 1965 legislation was introduced providing for a farmers' dole.[141] But the interdepartmental report indicated that there was no single, simple solution to the problem of western farms.

The committee stressed the importance of encouraging local community initiative, and Lemass was very keen to involve rural voluntary organisations in the government's western development programme. But in December 1962 the Department of Agriculture informed the Department of the Taoiseach that it had not yet contacted voluntary organisations 'because of the probability that the main and only result would be far-reaching demands by them for increased financial assistance for farmers, rather than effective help in achieving the objective aimed at'.[142] Tadhg Ó Cearbhaill remarked that 'the record of the agricultural organisations … does not reflect any keenness to get involved even though the subject is of vital interest to the farming community'. The ICA was the only rural organisation to submit its views to the committee before the report was completed.

'Hatcheries for Ideas': the Pilot Area Programme

This lack of interest on the part of farming organisations (Mayo-born journalist John Healy was very critical of the NFA for this reason)[143] created an opportunity for an *ad hoc* pressure group to emerge, and it promptly came up with the simple panacea that the interdepartmental committee had eschewed – pilot areas. The campaign was led by a County Donegal priest, Father James McDyer, who was well known for his work in establishing a vegetable-growing and processing co-operative in Glencolumbkille. In

June 1963 Father McDyer organised a meeting in Charlestown, County Mayo, which called for the extension of the Glencolumbkille model to pilot areas. The meeting asked the government to instruct the Irish Sugar Company to co-operate with local vegetable-producing schemes, and demanded a more lenient approach to means-testing small farmers when they applied for unemployment assistance (this was already being examined).

Lemass agreed to receive a delegation from the Charlestown meeting. This consisted of four priests and nine laymen, among them, Father McDyer, Father Browne, the president of Muintir na Tíre, and the socialist writer Peadar O'Donnell, who had been a member of the Commission on Emigration. They demanded that the government establish twelve pilot areas modelled on Father McDyer's Glencolumbkille project; some would concentrate on pigs or dairy farming, others on vegetables. Lemass indicated that he would reconvene the interdepartmental committee to examine this proposal.

The reconvened interdepartmental committee visited Glencolumbkille in October 1963, and met Father McDyer and his group in Carrick-on-Shannon. Tadhg Ó Cearbhaill told Lemass that Michael Barry had expressed considerable disappointment at the outcome of this meeting. The discussion was dominated by Peadar O'Donnell, who demanded that the committee agree to the establishment of twelve fruit and vegetable processing plants, at centres to be selected by local groups. If the committee did not approve this plan, O'Donnell indicated that the Charlestown group would be left with only 'the open road to public agitation'. Barry reported that Father McDyer's group consisted of four priests, one veterinary surgeon, a baker and Peadar O'Donnell, but no farmers.[144] When the interdepartmental committee failed to give the assurance that O'Donnell demanded, the group began a series of protest meetings. At a mass meeting in Charlestown, one speaker drew an unfavourable contrast between the 'the group of back-room boys' on the interdepartmental committee, and the 'bunch of ordinary men' associated with Father McDyer. On 30 November the *Roscommon Herald* reported that 500 farmers had attended a meeting in Castlerea addressed by Father McDyer.[145]

Lemass had given Father McDyer a commitment that the interdepartmental committee would meet him once more, before finalising its report, and on 5 February it met a delegation, which included the bishop of Achonry, Dr James Fergus. Father McDyer wanted the selection of pilot areas to be made by a board, on which his group would be in a majority.[146] However, the committee recommended that the selection should be made by the Central Development Committee (CDC), a committee of civil servants who would evaluate the proposals submitted by the county development teams, which would oversee the pilot areas programme.[147]

The interdepartmental committee recommended that there should be one pilot area in each of the twelve western counties. The areas selected should be representative of small farm areas in the counties, with holdings of a sufficient size to provide an adequate family income, if properly developed. They should be small homogeneous communities, consisting of 200–400 farms, where the problems of development could be treated in a flexible, experimental manner. A full-time adviser would be assigned to each area. The programme would emphasise self-help and community effort, and the IAOS would be encouraged to run programmes for co-operative education. While special grants would be provided, this would be done on a selective basis, and the local adviser would ensure that all capital was used effectively. The areas would demonstrate what could be achieved by community effort to develop available resources to the full; other areas would be encouraged to apply the lessons. In the short term the emphasis would be on agriculture, but in the longer term other sources of income would be developed.[148]

When the report on the pilot areas was published, Father McDyer congratulated Lemass on the courageous decision to establish pilot development schemes but according to the *Irish Press*, he was 'keenly disappointed' by the report. He demanded that the pilot areas should be selected on the basis of 'local initiative'. He wanted ultimate control to rest with voluntary bodies, and he demanded the formation of a western council. In May 1964, after another meeting with Lemass and Smith, Father McDyer announced that his group had disassociated itself from the pilot areas scheme. However, the president of Muintir na Tíre, Father Browne, informed Lemass that this decision would be revoked if the Charlestown group were given representation on the CDC, which was responsible for the pilot areas programme.

In the light of this olive branch Charlie Murray of the Department of Finance indicated that some form of association could be worked out between the CDC and the Charlestown group, although he noted that the Department of Agriculture was opposed 'even to the idea of meetings between the Central Development Committee and the Charlestown Group' because this would give the group unwarranted status. The Department of Agriculture was concerned that this concession would encourage other local groups to bypass the county development teams and the Department of Agriculture, in search of special concessions from the CDC. When Barry was informed of Murray's suggestion, he indicated that if voluntary groups were to be included in the CDC, many organisations had greater claims to membership, such as the county committees of agriculture. He warned that this proposal raised questions about the relationship between the CDC and the Minister and the Department of Agriculture. Nagle suggested that the problem could be resolved by arranging occasional meetings between rural organisations and the county development teams.

Lemass, on the other hand, was very much in favour of Murray's proposal, and he asked Smith to reconsider his attitude. But Smith queried whether the Charlestown group represented the views of any organisation except the Catholic hierarchy in the west of Ireland. He doubted that the NFA or other rural organisations would acknowledge them as the accepted spokesmen on small-farming problems. If this group was accorded representative status, Smith claimed that it would damage the status of the county committees of agriculture, who would run the pilot areas pro-gramme. If the composition of the CDC were altered to include outside bodies, Smith warned that 'my position and that of my Department will become very difficult. Do we get proposals for agricultural development from the Central Development Committee or do we negotiate, as we have up to now, direct with farmers' organisations?' He conceded that his views might appear to be rather negative, but he was anxious to ensure that the Charlestown group did not achieve a special place to the detriment of other bodies, 'just because they are good publicists'.

By 1964 the debate over the future of small farms had become bound up with the *Second Programme for Economic Expansion*, which projected a substantial decline in the numbers employed in farming by 1970. The statement of support for the small farming community that the western bishops sent to Lemass should be read in this context. According to the bishops, 'it would be an irreparable loss to the nation and to the Church if they were left to thin themselves out under the merciless operation of economic laws'. They referred to the Charlestown group, 'which is close to the people and representative of all sections, and which seems to us to have come to grips with the problem in a practical way'. Lemass sent a copy of this statement to Smith, reminding him that 'ensuring the fullest co-operation and good-will for this scheme is an over-riding consideration'. If it proved impractical to grant the Charlestown group permanent membership of the CDC, a preliminary conference attended by the county committees of agriculture and 'all appropriate organisations' would serve a useful purpose. Smith informed Lemass that if the bishops wanted the Charlestown group to be represented on the CDC, he would be completely opposed to the proposal. He was willing to bring the rural organisations together in order to win their support, but as the programme was almost exclusively concerned with agriculture, it should be his responsibility.

James Ryan succeeded in resolving this difference of opinion between Smith and Lemass. In August 1964 Smith invited representatives of the county committees of agriculture, the NFA, the IAOS, the ICMSA and the Charlestown group to a meeting to discuss the pilot areas scheme. Father McDyer demanded that rural organisations should have at least two representatives on the committee to oversee the pilot areas programme, but Smith rejected the idea; he suggested that the local committees were the most important bodies. After this meeting Father McDyer dismissed the pilot areas scheme as only a face-saving device.[149] In November 1964 the Charlestown group published a broadsheet noting,

> Government plan for Economic Expansion:
> 43 per cent increase in the number of cattle.
> 17 percent fall in the country population
> which will affect the West to not less than a 30 per cent fall in small farm population.
> The truth is industry, banking, big business have taken over the State. They speak through the civil servant cadres, who preserve the appearance of democratic government by using Ministers as their public relations officers.[150]

In January 1965 the Charlestown group changed its name to the Committee for the Defence of the West and marked its reincarnation by issuing a ten-point plan. Most of the proposals involved new or substantially-higher government grants, but it also proposed subdividing common land. Coincidentally, the week before this plan appeared, the new Minister for Agriculture, Charles Haughey, visited the west to gain first-hand knowledge of the area's problems.

Haughey proved to be more receptive to Lemass' views than Smith. He reported that there was considerable scope for raising output on western farms by 300 to 400 per cent and he expressed amazement at the advanced thinking of many of the farmers. There were, however, some obstacles to progress, notably the 'strident publicity of the "Charlestown Committee"'. Although its ideas were 'off the ground', the committee was influential

432

and consequently the NFA and other organisations were 'inclined to go along with it'. Haughey suggested that a small team consisting of an adviser, a farm buildings expert and a land project official should be established in each pilot area, who would report to the chief agricultural officer of the county committee of agriculture. He was also giving consideration to decentralising some of the Department's services, including land reclamation, buildings and veterinary services, and establishing a special office in Galway to 'coordinate and push' the services of the Department and the county committees of agriculture in the west of Ireland and particularly in the pilot areas.

Lemass described the pilot areas as 'hatcheries for ideas' that would have general application throughout the west. He reminded Haughey that his task was to demonstrate the government's determination to provide 'a new deal for small western farmers', that would be based on self-help. Lemass criticised the Charlestown group for 'spreading an atmosphere of defeatism and the fostering of belief in dependence on Government doles rather than on local effort'.[151] The Department's response to their ten-point plan noted that,

> A plethora of grants and subsidies, even if they result in increased output, do not represent a sound agricultural policy even for depressed areas. … Neither co-operation nor the pumping in of Government subsidy will save farms which are chronically non-viable.

It reiterated that forty to forty-five acres of good land was necessary to earn

> … an acceptable livelihood. While nobody wishes to see farmers leaving the land is it not better to aim at a reduced number of viable farmers who we can support and hold as an alternative to the wholesale emigration of a large number who find their position chronically uneconomic.

In March 1965 Haughey announced the appointment of Dr John Scully as the Department's first western regional officer, based at the agricultural college in Athenry. Scully had served for six years as a parish agent in Bansha and he then completed a PhD at the University of Illinois. He was an appropriate choice, since there were many similarities between the pilot areas programme and the parish plan.[152] Haughey also went to considerable efforts to placate the Committee for the Defence of the West by appointing a consultative council for the west, which he chaired. Father McDyer was among the thirty-nine members. McDyer was further placated by the Department's decision to establish a special experimental scheme in Glencolumbkille to investigate the possibility of creating viable farming units in an area where the soil and climate were especially inhospitable. The Ballina-based *Western People* claimed that Mr Haughey had kept faith with the western lobby. These initiatives were not unconnected with the 1965 general election campaign. After the election Lemass appointed Paddy Lalor as parliamentary secretary with responsibility for the west.[153]

When Haughey reported on the outcome of the first year's operations in the pilot areas, to a meeting of the western consultative council in Athenry in August 1966, he told them 'that it would be wrong to assume that we know all the answers'. Further research was necessary to provide comprehensive solutions. Nevertheless, the report recorded an impressive increase in livestock numbers and in the amount of building and drainage work that had been completed. When the Department of Agriculture presented a similar report to the Cabinet, it suggested that the scheme was meeting the special needs of western counties where farmers had gained little from price support schemes. It also outlined proposals for future developments. These included expanding the pilot areas to three times their existing size; a special hill-sheep pilot area in Ballycroy, County Mayo; and a supplementary heifer grant and measures to assist western farmers living outside the pilot areas, on condition that they drew up development plans.[154] These recommendations were approved early in 1967. By that time Jack Lynch had succeeded Lemass as Taoiseach and Neil Blaney was Minister for Agriculture. The government was coming under pressure to extend the pilot areas to include the entire west of Ireland. Leitrim County Council called for the entire county to be deemed a pilot area.

In 1971 John Scully published a report on agriculture in the west of Ireland that included a comprehensive review of the pilot areas programme. In some respects the scheme had been extremely successful. Gross margins on farms in the pilot areas had increased by 40 per cent between 1964/5 and 1969/70. This was five times the rate of increase in the twelve western counties between 1959 and 1969. Over the five-year period the proportion of viable or potentially-viable farmers in the pilot areas rose from 23 to 38.5 per cent; cow numbers increased by 32 per cent; other cattle by 30 per cent. Although farmers in pilot areas were eligible for much more generous capital grants than other farmers, expenditure on grants for farm buildings and reclamation was relatively modest, because grants were only approved if they were a necessary part of an overall farm development plan. This suggests that Lemass' hope that the pilot areas programme would help people to help themselves was being fulfilled.

Nevertheless, Scully reported that the majority of farmers in many pilot areas had benefited very little from the available assistance. This was not due to any inadequacies in the programme, but to poor quality of land, the large number of unviable farms, and the high proportion of elderly farmers. The farmers who had achieved a substantial increase in their gross margin were not hindered by these factors. His recommendations for the future were for the continuation of existing policies: structural reform leading to larger farms; improvements in agricultural education and advice; and a farm development scheme.[155]

The Agricultural Advisory Services during the 1960s

The report on the pilot areas programme was an indication of what could be achieved by an intensive advisory programme, given farms of economic size and reasonable quality of land. Between 1956 and 1966 the number of agricultural advisers employed by county committees of agriculture doubled from 152 to 302. By the end of 1966 the Department of Agriculture had met its target of one adviser for every 800 holdings over ten acres in the underdeveloped western counties, and additional money had been provided to the universities to expand provisions for agricultural education.[156]

The *Second Programme* gave a commitment that the basic structure of the existing advisory service would remain unaltered. The primary responsibility for the advisory service would remain with the county committees of agriculture; the Department of Agriculture would ensure that the service was satisfactory. The main contact between the Department and the local advisory service was through the Department's district inspectors. They were responsible for ensuring that the advisory service was efficient, and that advisers were implementing the Department's policies. District inspectors examined the annual estimates for every county committee of agriculture, and they presented the estimate to the county committee jointly with the chief agricultural officer.[157] Yet, as there were only three district inspectors to cover the entire country before 1958, the Department's oversight must necessarily have been limited, and the doubling of the number to six in that year is unlikely to have transformed matters. In addition, all chief agricultural officers attended two conferences every year at the Department, lasting several days, where they were briefed on current agricultural matters and any new schemes that were being implemented. A conference in December 1958 concentrated on examining the agricultural policies outlined in the *Programme for Economic Expansion*.[158]

In 1966 the Minister for Agriculture, Charles Haughey, commissioned a review of the agricultural advisory services by W. Emrys Jones and Albert Davies, who were respectively the director and chief farm management adviser of the National Agricultural Advisory Service of England and Wales. This was the first comprehensive review of the service since its creation. Jones and Davies reported that the advisory staff were able, and the majority were well trained. The main weakness continued to be the wide variation in the service provided in different counties. Although the government had substantially increased the money provided for advisory services in western counties, the richer counties of the east and the south continued to have the most favourable ratios of advisers to farmers. Jones and Davies expressed concern at the failure to achieve more uniform standards throughout the state. Although the chief inspector in the Department of Agriculture was nominally responsible for the advisory service, he lacked the executive authority and the financial powers to carry out the task, and much of his time was devoted to other duties. Relations between the advisory service and the Department were reported to be good, but the lack of overall direction meant that each county decided on its own programme (this had been so from the beginning), which they pursued 'with varying degrees of vigour'. Jones and Davies claimed that much of the advisers' time was spent administering the Department's grant and development schemes. When instructors were overworked, the educational services tended to suffer.

Jones and Davies suggested that the function of the advisory service should be to advise farmers, and to enable them to make the most profitable use of the available resources. To achieve this, advisers would need to be up to date on the technological, social and economic aspects of their work. Advisers should work in co-operation with other organisations in the agricultural sector, and they should advise the government on the technical implications of agricultural policies. But this would require a fundamental change in the organisation of the services. They recommended that:

- the Department set a new target of one adviser for every 600 farms;
- there should be greater interchange of staff between the county committees of agriculture and the Department;

- a new grade of senior instructor should be created;
- deputy chief agricultural officers should be appointed in every county;
- more resources should be provided for in-service training;
- a national agricultural advisory service should be established.

Jones and Davies believed that clearly-defined objectives could only be met through a national advisory service, and they explored a number of possible administrative structures. They rejected the idea of linking AFT and the advisory service in one organisation. This left two options: creating an autonomous semi-state institution, similar to AFT, or placing the advisory service directly under the Department of Agriculture. They eventually recommended the latter option, provided that the officers were 'not hampered by a civil service culture and [are] not burdened with non-advisory and executive duties'. Provincial centres, with provincial directors and specialist staff, would act as a bridge between Dublin and the local advisers. All horticultural services should be concentrated south of a line drawn from Dundalk to Limerick. The number of poultry instructors should be permitted to decline, because the industry was now on a commercial basis. National and county agricultural advisory councils would replace the county committees of agriculture, but they would not have any administrative responsibilities.[159] These recommendations would involve radical changes in a long-established system, and discussions and consultation on the proposals proved to be lengthy. A full-scale reform of the advisory service was not carried out until the 1980s. In 1967, however, the faculty of agriculture at UCD established a post-graduate training programme for agriculture advisers, with financial aid from the Kellogg Foundation in the United States.[160]

These organisational changes were being recommended at a time when the advisory service was being asked to carry out more complex tasks. Scully noted that farm planning had come to be accepted as a fundamental aspect of advisory work in all counties. Advisers were increasingly being asked to undertake duties that were very different from their traditional role, such as promoting and organising group activities in rural communities. He suggested that they would need intensive training in group dynamics and behavioural sciences. Some of these needs were being met by work being carried out by AFT, the Economic and Social Research Institute and the Kellogg Agricultural Extension Centre at UCD. Farmers had other sources of information at their disposal. A survey carried out in the early 1960s revealed that agricultural radio programmes were the most commonly-mentioned source of information, followed by the advisory service and farming papers. Telefís Feirme, a unit dedicated to producing farming programmes, soon became an important source of information. Agricultural advisers set up viewing groups to take full advantage of these programmes.[161]

THE DEPARTMENT RESPONDS TO CHANGING NEEDS

What conclusions can be drawn from the issues that have been discussed in this chapter? It is evident that agricultural research and education and the advisory services were not provided with adequate money, and that these services should have been reviewed and modernised during the years immediately after World War II. However, this neglect was not unique to agriculture; it applied to all aspects of education and research. Although the role played by the Danish Folk Schools in developing a modern successful agricultural sector was often cited, this lesson was not applied to Ireland. There were many reasons for this: lack of exchequer resources; reliance on local authority rates; and the reality that any development in education had to contend with difficulties in the area of church-state relations. As the benefits from investment in education were not immediately evident, they may have been under-valued. The rivalry between the departments of Education and Agriculture contributed to the neglect, as did the widely-held assumption that education was not relevant to a career in farming. As the Limerick Rural Survey noted, 'The sons who do not show scholastic ability become farmers by default'.[162] By the 1960s it was evident that living standards in agriculture were lagging behind other sectors of the economy, and this discouraged young men and women from embarking on agricultural education.

Many of the factors mentioned above were outside the control of the Department of Agriculture. Nevertheless, after the Plunkett years, education does not seem to have been a major preoccupation for the Department. The fact that responsibility for the advisory and educational services rested with the local authorities may be an important factor, because after Independence there was widespread resentment in provincial Ireland at excessive control by the government in Dublin, particularly in matters concerning local government. Hence, the best option for the Department of Agriculture was not to adopt a heavy-handed approach with the county committees of agriculture.

The story of the protracted origins of the AFT is an indication of the extent to which during the 1950s, new ideas were blocked by vested interests. This decade was marked by cultural and economic protectionism, including a wish to protect the status quo against change. Such sentiments were reinforced by the depressed economic conditions. Yet they only served to exacerbate the economic and social problems of the time, and to delay the reforms that were necessary if conditions were to improve.

Ireland depended on the state to provide the dynamic for economic development. This meant that there was a need to develop administrative structures that were somewhat different to the traditional model of a government department. Government programmes, such as western development, agricultural education, the farm apprenticeship scheme and rural water, increasingly demanded the co-operation of more than one department, if they were to be effective. The troubled relationship that existed between the Department and AFT after its foundation is an example of the difficulties that were involved in the transition from a departmental administrative system, and its tradition of detailed scrutiny of all expenditure, to a more autonomous semi-state agency, and an appropriate relationship between the two. Yet there is little doubt that AFT was also stretching its statutory powers to the limit and beyond, and its wish to control all agricultural research was misguided.

The Department of Agriculture also found it difficult to cope with the insistence by the Charlestown group that it should play a major role in formulating policy for the west of Ireland. Part of the problem stemmed from the fact that it was a self-appointed group, but again the traditional departmental structures did not accommodate themselves easily to outside involvement in policy-making. Additional difficulties stemmed from the fact that the process of economic development threatened the survival of traditional Irish farming structures. The pilot areas programme in western counties was well designed, and in many respects highly successful. It enlisted the support of local community organisations; with an office in Athenry, it was a pioneering example of the decentralisation of government services; and it worked by encouraging self-help rather than massive price subsidies or grants. The pilot areas programme was devised on the assumption that better advice, access to credit, co-operative marketing schemes, and slightly larger farms, say forty to forty-five acres, would ensure the survival of the traditional agrarian society of the west of Ireland. Yet it demonstrated that many farms in western areas were not viable, even with the best efforts of their owners and the government. Agricultural policy had to try to reconcile the conflicting pressures of raising productivity and preserving a life-style that was believed to embody the core values of the Irish nation. In June 1964 the western bishops wrote to Seán Lemass on this topic:

> The people of the small western farms are in a special way representative of the nation inasmuch as they have clung longer than people in other parts of the country to the traditions which are characteristic of the Irish way of life and of Irish culture including the native language. Even if this can be attributed in large part to an accident of history, it is nevertheless a fact. Moreover, their homes have always been nurseries of religious vocations, thus contributing to the building up of Ireland's spiritual empire. We believe that it would be an irreparable loss to the nation and to the Church if they were left to thin themselves out under the merciless operation of economic laws.[163]

CHAPTER NINE

A CHANGING WORLD, 1963–1973

The ten years between the collapse of Ireland's first application for EEC membership and eventual accession on 1 January 1973 presented many challenges for the Department of Agriculture. The *Second Programme for Economic Expansion* set the objective of a 50 per cent increase in gross national product over the 1960s. Agricultural output was expected to rise by one-third, and detailed targets were set for all the major products. The statistical targets given in the *Second Programme*, and its less ambitious successor, the *Third Programme for Economic and Social Development*, covering the period 1969–72, figured prominently in trade negotiations with the UK, and in the Department's relationship with farming organisations.

The growth target for Irish agriculture in the *Second Programme* was unduly ambitious, given that Irish produce was being progressively excluded from the EEC market, and additional restrictions were being placed on exports to the UK. The 1965 Anglo-Irish Free Trade Area Agreement brought some improvement, but within three years Irish cheese exports to Britain were curtailed, and there was a threat to livestock exports. However, the formal opening of talks on Ireland's accession to the EEC in 1970 appeared to offer a long-term solution.

The mid-1960s saw the relationship between the government and the National Farmers' Association deteriorate, culminating in the farm dispute of 1966/7. Although the ostensible cause was NFA's demand to be acknowledged as the representative of the farming community, and to play a formal role in determining agricultural policy, the fact that agricultural incomes had not risen in line with expectations was also a major factor. Agricultural policy was also influenced by social factors, such as the campaign to raise the living standard of small farmers. In 1967 the government introduced a two-tier milk price, giving small producers a higher price per gallon. Garret FitzGerald remarked that, 'Even in the 1967 budget, when the only buoyant element in farm output – the cattle trade – was seriously threatened, the additional aid given to agriculture was predominantly social in character'.[1] The two-tier milk price and the extension of dairying in the west of Ireland were in direct conflict with the objective of raising productivity. The mid and late 1960s saw important advances in Irish agriculture, such as the first steps towards rationalising the creamery sector, the beginnings of Ireland's modern cheese-processing and a substantial expansion in meat-processing, but these achievements were dwarfed by the problems of disposing of agricultural produce, especially dairy produce. Price supports accounted for an ever-increasing share of public spending on agriculture as the government tried to meet farmers' expectations of rising living standards, despite the difficulty in finding profitable markets for agricultural produce. Irish farmers came to see it as their right to share in the incomes policies and regular wage increases that had become the norm for other workers. The announcement that Ireland would join the EEC in 1973 brought widespread relief, since it meant that the cost of price supports would no longer fall exclusively on the Irish exchequer.

The mid-1960s saw a rapid turnover of ministers. In October 1964 Patrick Smith resigned from the government because he disagreed with the decision to intervene in a labour dispute – a disagreement that epitomised the differences over policy and style of government between Smith and the Taoiseach, Seán Lemass. He was succeeded by the Minister for Justice, Charles Haughey, a Dubliner who was the son-in-law of Seán Lemass and a future Taoiseach. On 8 October 1963, the day that Haughey was appointed as Minister for Agriculture, Lemass advised him to invite all the rural organisations to meet him for discussions; he should also talk to deputies who were interested in agricultural matters. Lemass specifically mentioned Jim Gibbons, a Kilkenny TD, who became Minister for Agriculture in 1970.[2]

When Lemass resigned as Taoiseach in November 1966, his successor, Jack Lynch, appointed Haughey as Minister for Finance. Neil Blaney, a Donegal TD, who had succeeded Smith as Minister for Local Government in 1957, became Minister for Agriculture. The son of a Fianna Fáil TD and a founding member of the party, Blaney was first elected to Dáil Éireann in 1948 in a by-election following the death of his father. Like Haughey, he belonged to a younger political generation than Smith. Blaney served as Minister until 1970, when he was dismissed by Jack Lynch. He was succeeded by James Gibbons, a Kilkenny farmer, who remained Minister for Agriculture until the change of government in the 1973 general election.

Economic Planning: Consultation and Relations with Farm Organisations, 1963/4

When the *Programme for Economic Expansion* was published in 1958 it anticipated that agriculture would be the leading sector in Irish economic growth. By 1963, when part I of the *Second Programme* was published, this role had passed to manufacturing industry, and if agriculture had failed to meet its growth target, the *Second Programme* suggested that the growth rate for manufacturing industry should be stepped up.[3] Work on the *Second Programme* began in the summer of 1961. The initial draft, compiled by the Economic Development Division of the Department of Finance, was circulated to other government departments for comment in June 1963.[4] When the Minister for Finance, James Ryan, forwarded a copy to Seán Lemass on 10 July 1963, he remarked that,

> The contemplated target for agriculture – an annual increase of 2.8 per cent [this figure was later rounded up to 2.9 per cent] – is an optimistic assessment of the prospects for Irish agriculture. It raises two inter-related issues: (a) the physical problem of increasing output, and (b) the marketing problems of selling the additional output. While the first problem arises mainly in relation to cattle, its importance can be gauged from the fact that cattle and cattle products account for over one-half of total agricultural output and for about 70 percent of the total increase projected between 1960 and 1970.

Ryan noted that in order to achieve this target it would be necessary for cattle numbers to rise by an average of 83,000 every year from 1964 until 1970. As cattle numbers only increased by an annual average of 15,000 between 1952 and 1962, he concluded that this 'would be a major task'. Moreover, export outlets would have to be found for virtually all the additional output. Ryan noted that EEC agricultural commissioner, Dr Mansholt, had warned that if present agricultural policies remained unchanged, the OECD countries would be unable to dispose of surplus stocks of several commodities.

> The general surplus of agricultural commodities in international markets, the break-down in the EEC negotiations and the likelihood that Britain will introduce further quota arrangements for products of importance to this country, illustrates the difficulties in increasing agricultural exports.

On 15 July 1963 Ryan recommended that this draft of the *Second Programme* should be published; a more detailed version, which became part II, would appear at a later date.[5] At this point Smith voiced strong objections to several aspects of the draft, and a Cabinet committee, consisting of the Taoiseach and the ministers for Agriculture, Finance and Industry and Commerce, decided that the entire section relating to agriculture should be rewritten. One matter in dispute was the section dealing with the provision of part-time education for young farmers, and a second related to price subsidies. The Department of Agriculture suggested that the *Second Programme* should refer to price subsidies as evidence of the government's commitment to farming. The departments of Agriculture and Finance were both in agreement that the priorities for agriculture under the *Second Programme* should be:

- to negotiate a trade agreement that would provide a more secure market for Irish agricultural exports;
- measures to increase efficiency;
- the creation of viable farming units.

However, the Department of Finance was less optimistic about Ireland's prospects of joining the EEC before 1970. Although Whitaker indicated to Nagle that the differences between the two departments could be resolved by rearranging the text, he wondered,

> … whether the net effect of the additions and omissions is not to create a greater sense of optimism than the realities of the situation warrant and thus to weaken the Government's defences against the pressures of the NFA and other farming organisations for incomes support out of line with economic facts. Some road-blocks of realism appear to be desirable. The repeated and unqualified assumptions about membership of the EEC are particularly open to question. Even admission to the EEC may not solve our agricultural problems.

Despite the reservations expressed by the Department of Finance, part II of the *Second Programme*, which was published in 1964, raised the target growth rate for agriculture for 1960–70 from 31 to 33 per cent.[6]

Whitaker's comment indicates the extent to which the government's relations with farming organisations influenced the drafting of the sections relating to agriculture in the *Second Programme*. The decision not to include representatives from the agricultural sector in the National Industrial and Economic Council (NIEC) served to isolate economic planning in relation to agriculture from the overall process. The NIEC was established in the autumn of 1963, and became a key agent in the formulation and implementation of policies under the *Second Programme*. Its genesis lay in the development of more centralised wage-bargaining and the government's fear that excessive wage increases were fuelling inflation and damaging the economy. In February 1963 the government published a white paper entitled *Closing the Gap* – the title referred to the widening gap between the increase in incomes and the increase in productivity – which called for wage restraint and suggested that some mechanism should be devised for negotiating an incomes policy.[7] The outcome was the NIEC, an organisation that would report to the national Employer–Labour Conference[8] and to the government on the development of the economy, and the realisation and maintenance of full employment and a wages policy. The membership would include representatives of employers, trade unions and government nominees, but no farmers.[9]

Farming was not represented on the NIEC because it was regarded as structurally different, and because agricultural incomes were determined in a different manner to incomes in manufacturing industry.[10] However, the Department of the Taoiseach decided that one of the government's eight nominees should be from the agricultural sector. Tadhg Ó Cearbhaill suggested Dr Tom Walsh, the director of the Agricultural Institute, but Nagle informed him that this would be 'embarrassing to this Department [Agriculture] as it would convey the impression that the Institute, which is concerned only with agricultural research, has direct and active functions in the working out of national economic policies'. Nagle recommended several alternative names: Reverend P. Collins, the director of Warrenstown Agricultural College; Juan Greene, the former president of the NFA, who 'would take a broader and more rational view of things' than the current president, Rickard Deasy; Dr Henry Kennedy, the former secretary of the IAOS. Although Nagle claimed that Kennedy was not the easiest man to get on with, because he held rigid views, he regarded him as most intelligent, highly experienced and a man of the utmost integrity. The two final names on Nagle's list were Father Browne, the national chairman of Muintir na Tíre, and Lieutenant General Costello, the head of the Irish Sugar Company. Nagle sized up Costello as 'an easy man to quarrel with and can be difficult and unpredictable, [but] his standing in rural areas is good and he is something of a national personality'. Nagle would have preferred him to Walsh, 'even if, as is always possible, we in this Department at some time or other may "get in his hair" '.[11] The government nominated Patrick Kelly, Kennedy's successor as secretary of the IAOS.

When the membership of the NIEC was announced in October 1963, John Feely, the chairman and secretary of the ICMSA, demanded that farmers should be represented. He claimed that their omission was evidence of 'the unnatural dichotomy in economic thought and planning in this country' and an indication that the government did not take account of the interdependence of agriculture and industry. If agricultural policy was to be excluded from the NIEC, the ICMSA wanted a separate council for agriculture.[12] When Lemass addressed the first meeting of the NIEC on 9 October 1963, he informed them that their first task would be to examine the non-agricultural aspects of the *Second Programme for Economic Expansion* and to advise on how the targets could be realised, and if possible, surpassed. Agriculture was not represented on the NIEC because 'agricultural policy is determined to a large extent by external conditions, which we cannot hope to alter by discussions taken here'.[13]

This statement exaggerates the difference between agriculture and manufacturing industry, and it was inconsistent with the views that Lemass had expressed to a meeting of the Dublin North-East Comhairle Ceanntair of Fianna Fáil on 19 April 1963, when he suggested that wage and salary-earners should benefit from regular income increases, which would raise their real purchasing power by a percentage figure that would be justified by the growth of the economy. A similar principle should apply to farmers, although the increase might be delivered by budgetary measures to reduce farmers' costs and increase the guaranteed prices for milk, wheat, barley and pigs. Lemass expressed the hope that a farmer who worked his land fully and efficiently would be in a position to share in national prosperity to the same degree as wage and salaried workers.[14] If farm incomes were to increase in line with the rise in national income, by means of budgetary measures, it would seem appropriate that farmers should be represented on the NIEC, given the NIEC's role in advising the government on economic policy.

Two weeks after the first meeting of the NIEC, Nagle informed Lemass' private secretary that

> ... farmers could not be expected to view with equanimity the estab-lishment of a new body which might appear to have the function – in a broad general way of course – of approving, as economically justifiable, increases of remuneration in the non-agricultural sector in relation to

a specific rate of growth of the economy, while similar machinery did not exist for agriculture.

Nagle reported that the Minister for Agriculture was not in favour of creating a separate council for agriculture, because he feared that it would turn into 'a pressure group' that would demand higher guaranteed prices and other concessions. Smith believed that representatives of the producers' committees, which acted as consultative groups over Ireland's entry to the EEC, should be members of the NIEC. This would have the added advantages that employer and labour representatives would learn about the special problems and conditions of agriculture, and farmers' representatives would derive 'some salutary experience from such an arrangement'.[15]

Smith believed that admitting farming representatives to membership of the NIEC would provide the most suitable mechanism for consulting them on economic matters; it would also reinforce the view that agriculture had a central role to play in economic policy. When the question of agricultural representation on the NIEC surfaced in the autumn of 1963, the relationship between the Department and the NFA was under considerable strain. There were several issues at stake, including the question of farm incomes, and nominations to committees or boards controlled by the Department. When the Department announced its intention to alter the composition of the Pigs and Bacon Commission in 1961, the NFA had objected to three of the six places being allocated to bacon-curers. In order to placate them the Department reduced its representation to one, giving the additional place to a farming representative.[16] By 1963 the matter in contention was membership of An Bord Gráin. The board was established in 1959 to handle the purchase and disposal of Irish wheat. In 1963 its functions were extended to include responsibility for the barley crop and the import of coarse grains, and the membership was revised.[17] When Smith informed NFA president Rickard Deasy that he planned to appoint four traders, two representatives of the NFA, one representative of the co-operatives and one member representing pig farmers, the NFA demanded that they should select the representative of the pig farmers,[18] but Smith nominated a representative of the county committees of agriculture to fill this role.[19] It appears that this dispute resulted in a breakdown in relations between Smith and the NFA, because in a departure from previous practice, when Lemass and Deasy met in November and December 1963, Smith was absent, although Lemass kept him abreast of developments. On 5 November Lemass sent Smith a report of a meeting on the previous day.

> I told Mr. Deasy that it was your desire to promote closer co-operation with the N.F.A. in constructive development work for the benefit of farmers, and that, if the organisation desired this and conducted their activities on this basis, the tensions and difficulties which have recently developed could quickly disappear, and this would be in accord with your wish.

Lemass added that he had informed Deasy that the NFA 'could not ride two horses at once, and a wish for closer co-operation with the Department of Agriculture could not be reconciled with a course of action which would make conflict with the Government inevitable'. (This was a reference to the rates strike that was being mounted by members of the NFA in County Kilkenny.) Lemass continued:

> I know that it will be your desire to be as oncoming as possible in this matter, that you will instruct your officers that constructive proposals from the N.F.A. should be examined sympathetically, and that as occasion offers you will confirm to the N.F.A., subject to the conditions I stipulated, the views which I attributed to you regarding co-operation with them.[20]

Smith did not reply for more than two weeks. While he acknowledged that closer co-operation with the NFA would be desirable, not least because 'it would make life more pleasant for me and my officials', he claimed that it was difficult to find a basis for fruitful co-operation 'while the NFA reserve the right to be destructively critical of every move made by me to help farmers, and to use meetings with me and my officials as the basis for biased attacks on us and on Government policy'. He claimed that the two large farming organisations, the NFA and the ICMSA, regarded the Department of Agriculture and the Minister as 'just tools to be used for furthering their sectional interests'. It was his policy that officials should always be available to meet delegations from farming organisations to discuss matters of mutual interest.[21] At this time Rickard Deasy was in regular contact with Lemass over a number of minor matters, such as an invitation for Deasy to address the agricultural committee of the British Labour Party, or Deasy's report on a recent meeting of the International Federation of Agricultural

Producers in Rome. On 14 December Lemass informed Smith that he had given a commitment that Deasy could submit 'an agenda of matters in respect of which he thinks the N.F.A. have any reason to feel that they are not meeting with a fully cooperative and reasonable attitude in the Government or in your Department', provided that they first called off their anti-rates protest. Lemass had agreed to discuss this agenda of grievances with a deputation from the NFA; if necessary he would devote an entire day to the talks.[22]

On 2 January 1964 the NFA submitted a twelve-item agenda. Item one was 'An apparent lack of appreciation by the Government of the function or system of farmer organisation'. Among the other items were, 'No recognition of the NFA; no regular mechanism for negotiation; lack of true consultation before schemes are introduced; the Department's conservatism'; the 'paternalism' of the Government; the need for a 'new attitude of leadership to farmers' on the part of government ministers; and the need for the government to project a new positive image in relation to farming. The most specific grievances related to the poor quality of statistical data relating to agriculture; the NFA demand for an annual review of agricultural policy; and the composition of marketing boards.

The NFA claimed that farmers believed that the government's attitude was 'one of instinctive hostility'. It criticised the failure to devolve more responsibility for agricultural policies to farmers, and suggested that other departments had a much better working arrangement with voluntary and professional organisations than the Department of Agriculture. The Department refused to consult the NFA on 'general issues, such as the levels of income', and it was only consulted on specific matters, such as the eradication of bovine TB when a scheme was about to be announced. It wished to be involved at the planning stage.

The Department of Agriculture began by noting, quite correctly, that the draft agenda consisted almost entirely of generalisations. Thereafter, it concentrated its attack on the underlying assumption that the NFA should be recognised as 'a kind of agricultural cabinet whose views should determine the Government's decisions'. The Department suggested that the ICMSA was probably more representative of small farmers than the NFA. In its opinion the NFA was 'unfortunately, still at an immature stage ... its claims and assertions are quite out of proportion to its real performance'. If the government allowed itself to be led by agricultural pressure groups, 'it would quickly find itself tied hand and foot in respect of agricultural policy'. An annual price review, on the British model, could not be countenanced, unless the government were prepared to accept annually 'a bigger and bigger bill for agriculture, while having less and less say in the matter'. However, the Department was not opposed to an annual meeting 'to survey the whole of the agricultural scene', provided it was not conducted exclusively with the NFA.

Lemass' outline response to the NFA document, which was drafted before he had been apprised of the views of the Department of Agriculture, was a much more emollient document. John Horgan remarked that, 'Lemass had to balance his impatience with farmers with his need to identify an organisation that could speak authoritatively for them at the negotiating table. The only serious candidate for this role was the NFA'.[23] Lemass noted that it was the government's policy to co-operate with vocational organisations 'in all spheres', although the large number of agricultural organisations made this difficult. The government recognised that the NFA was a major farming organisation and it never refused to consult it. While the government had no objection to an annual review, it could not be a British-style price review. There was an expectation that the Minister for Agriculture would always take the views of the NFA into account.

Smith remarked that the tone of this reply was too defensive; it appeared to imply that the government's attitude towards the NFA had been 'faulty' in the past. He reminded Lemass that, 'The NFA is – and its predecessors always were – composed of and controlled by people who never had a friendly attitude to us as a party'. The ICMSA was an older organisation that was equally representative of farmers, although 'there is plenty of rascality and tangling in this organisation too'.[24] Smith outlined various instances of 'hookery' involving the NFA and counselled Lemass against adopting a course of action which would imply that the NFA were being 'picked out by the Government as the leading farming organisation'. Although he acknowledged that Lemass and other members of the government believed that he was 'a bit fiery on the subject', Smith claimed that if any other member of the government had been in his shoes, 'he would have lost his temper and denounced the NFA publicly a hundred times over'.

When Lemass and Smith met a delegation from the NFA on 9 January 1964, Lemass made it clear that the government would continue to meet other organisations. However, the NFA continued to press for exclusive negotiating rights. Rickard Deasy claimed that 'logically the NFA should be the organisation to deal with all farming matters – with seats on their Council for commodity organisations'. Another delegate suggested that if another organisation wished to discuss potatoes with the Minister, that they should be informed that the matter was under discussion with the NFA. The NFA rejected the Department's proposal of joint meetings with the ICMSA and the NFA to discuss milk prices. Lemass told Smith after this meeting that he believed that the NFA was mainly concerned with recognition and that the government could go some way to meet their demands. Smith sent Lemass a draft letter, which Lemass broadly approved, although he suggested that the phrases italicised in the following paragraph should be removed:

> … in pursuance of the common desire of the Government and the NFA to promote greater unity among farmers' organisations, the Minister for Agriculture, will by agreement with the NFA, invite representatives of the ICMSA and other interested farm organisations to attend, as observers, discussions between him and the NFA. Similarly, he will intimate to the ICMSA and other farm organisations concerned, that, *by agreement with the ICMSA or such other organisations*, he would wish to invite representatives of the NFA to attend, as observers, discussions held by him with the ICMSA or other organisations. The foregoing arrangement will apply particularly to matters relating to creamery milk *and to other matters of substantial importance in relation to Government agricultural policy.*

The amendments suggested by Lemass indicate that he wished to confine negotiations with other farming organisations to the question of milk, and that he was prepared to give the NFA observer status at all meetings with other farming bodies, while others could only attend talks between the government and the NFA with the latter's permission. Smith informed Lemass that he was reluctant to make the changes sought, because they would circumscribe the ability of the Minister for Agriculture to meet 'whoever he wants, whenever he wants either separately or jointly'. Lemass did not press the point.

When the NFA was presented with a copy of Smith's letter, it expressed its satisfaction with every section except the paragraph quoted above. Nicholas Nolan, the secretary of the Department of the Taoiseach, again asked the Department of Agriculture to reconsider the possibility of amending this paragraph to take account of the NFA's objections, but Nagle retorted that any change would damage the relationship between the Minister and the ICMSA. Lemass tried to persuade Smith to restrict the consultative role of the ICMSA to matters relating to the dairy industry, but he refused, and on 29 January 1964 Lemass sent the NFA a copy of the agreement that included an unchanged version of the contentious paragraph. He informed Deasy that,

> This document may now be regarded as expressing the Government's views and intentions. While it may not be fully as your organisation would wish to have it, I hope that it will be accepted as a satisfactory working foundation, and that as a result of it, relations between the Department of Agriculture and the N.F.A. will develop in a constructive manner to the advantage of all concerned, particularly the farmers.[25]

The document began by noting that the lack of unity among farming organisations, particularly between the NFA and the ICMSA, had created 'practical difficulties in making satisfactory arrangements for that degree of close and regular consultation with farmers' representatives which they consider desirable and wish to have established'. The government would continue to urge the NFA and the ICMSA to resolve their differences, 'and so facilitate the holding of full and effective consultations with the Government on behalf of farmers generally'. The government welcomed the prospect of 'regular and comprehensive discussions with the NFA in the formulation of agricultural policy in the broadest sense, as well as their practical cooperation in respect of specific aspects of Agriculture'. They would take the NFA's comprehensive interest in agricultural policy into account when making appointments to boards and committees. The government and the NFA would hold an annual meeting to carry out a 'broadly-based annual review of agricultural progress and prospects, but it would not take the form of a price review along the lines of the annual meeting between the NFU and the British Ministry of Agriculture'. In the normal practice the Minister for Agriculture would inform the NFA about pending changes in the Department's policy, and the Department would consider any representations from the NFA on such matters, but the Minister would be not be required to divulge confidential information on matters such as negotiations with other governments. The government would continue to provide financial assistance for NFA representatives to attend international conferences. The final paragraph noted that the government would welcome the assistance of the NFA 'in the application of particular plans for the improvement of agriculture, when widespread understanding of the aims to be achieved and the co-operation of farmers

Avondale Forestry Station – Apprentices at work planting – 1906

The Dead Meat Trade – Leaving the Slaughter House – 1908

Disinfecting before leaving an infected place – Foot and Mouth Disease
outbreak Swords, Co Dublin – 1912

The Department's Fishery Cruiser "Helga" – 1908

The Dublin Cattle Market – Cattle being driven through city to
North Wall for export – 1916

Growing of crops for silage – cutting silage crop with reaper and binder at
Albert Agricultural College – 1923

Seed Potato Exhibit staged by Department at Royal Horticultural Society's
Great Autumn Show London – 1935

Harvesting crop of oats at farm in Clonsilla, Co. Dublin
(Photo credit: Teagasc) – 1947

Tractors at work on the newly acquired experimental farm in Mitchelstown,
Co. Cork (Photo credit: Teagasc) – 1950s

Minister Hillery and an Taoiseach Jack Lynch signing Treaty of Accession to
the European Communities (Photo credit: Pat Langan, Irish Times) – 1972

Minister Walsh and Department team returning from CAP reform negotiations
(Mac Sharry Reforms) (Photo credit: Irish Farmers Journal) – 1992

DAFRD Centenary Conference, Dublin Castle
Mr. John Malone, Secretary General DAFRD; Mr. Franz Fischler, EU
Commissioner for Agriculture; Mr. Joe Walsh TD, Minister for Agriculture,
Food and Rural Development; Mr. Miguel Rodriguez Mendoza,
Deputy Director WTO; Mr. Donal Creedon, former Secretary, DAFRD
(Photo credit: Fennell Photography) – 2000

Government Buildings, Merrion Street, location of Department to 1974

Agriculture House, Kildare Street, current HQ

is important for success'.[26] This agreement marked a substantial strengthening of the NFA's role. When T. K. Whitaker discussed the matter of agricultural representation on the NIEC with Nagle in March 1964, he reported
that Rickard Deasy had not expressed any great interest because membership of the NIEC might 'interfere ... with the annual price review'.[27]

On 27 January, two days before this agreement was finalised, Deasy
sent Lemass an advance copy of an NFA report 'Farm Income and
Agricultural Development 1964/70'. The title and the timeframe indicate
that this was the NFA's version of an agricultural policy during the term of
the *Second Programme*. The accompanying letter adopted a conciliatory tone.

> In putting forward this document, we recognise that our governments
> have for a long period provided very large sums by way of State assistance
> to agriculture. We recognise also that ultimate policy decisions are,
> and must always remain, the prerogative of government.

The NFA's conciliatory atttitude did not extend to the Department of
Agriculture, because it failed to provide the Department with copies of the
report and when the Department tried to purchase the report, it was
informed that it was out of print. (The Department eventually managed to
buy twelve copies.) The NFA set out detailed proposals relating to
agricultural prices, credit, taxation, marketing boards, veterinary services,
small farms, grant schemes for farm buildings, fertilisers, drainage and
equipment.

Lemass suggested that a Cabinet committee should be established to
consider the report. He recommended that Smith might arrange a suitable
occasion to make a comprehensive speech on the document, indicating
that it was receiving his consideration. Smith informed Lemass that a cursory
reading indicated that if all the NFA proposals were implemented, the
additional cost to the exchequer would be 'frightening'. Smith recommended that a Cabinet committee consisting of the ministers for Lands,
Local Government and Finance should scrutinise the NFA document.[28]

The NFA accepted the target that the *Second Programme* set for a rise in
agricultural output, although the NFA wished it was higher. It also approved
the 1970 target for an annual cattle output of 1.5 million head, and the
proposals contained in the *Second Programme* for agricultural research and
education, the advisory service and the expansion of agricultural co-
operation.[29] However, the Department of Agriculture reported that there
was scarcely a chapter in the NFA document that did not contain proposals

for additional state expenditure. The Department was highly critical of NFA calculations, which suggested that farmers would contribute two-thirds of capital expenditure over the years 1964–70, with the balance coming from the exchequer. This figure was achieved by including existing and future contributions by farmers in estimates for capital expenditure, while ignoring existing capital expenditure by the state.

One of the longest sections in the document dealt with marketing boards. The NFA was demanding that the government establish marketing boards for all major commodities. At least half the places would be filled by farmers' representatives, who would be elected by a register of producers. One place would be allocated to the government, with the remainder filled by marketing and processing interests. The meat marketing board would develop markets for beef and lamb; provide an improved wholesaling and delivery service for Irish meat in Britain; and assist in developing the meat-processing industry. More controversially, it would operate an intervention scheme, buying cattle and sheep at agreed prices. The potato marketing board and the wool marketing board would fulfil similar functions. A strengthened pigs and bacon commission, controlled by producers, would centralise the purchasing of pigs and offer fixed floor prices for all grades.[30] The Department described the proposed marketing boards as a device 'to enable the farmers to spend large amounts of money raised by taxation while the Government would have a minimum say in such expenditure'. It also criticised the NFA for failing to indicate which schemes it regarded as a priority, despite the fact that it must have known that the government could not afford to concede the entire package.

Lemass used the somewhat unlikely venue of a Fianna Fáil convention to select candidates for the forthcoming Dublin County Council election to launch an attack on the NFA document. He warned that an improvement in the relative incomes of farmers could not be achieved by higher government subsidies. The government was giving the NFA document 'full and sympathetic consideration', despite the fact that the cost was beyond the realms of financial possibility. In a light-hearted vein he suggested that while the NFA committees had

> … a most enjoyable time, putting down on paper all the different ways in which more public money could be spent for the benefit of farmers, some of them must have had an inkling, that, unless the Bog of Allen turns into gold, they were more often than not day-dreaming instead of preparing practical plans.

He warned the NFA not to pursue its threat to take action unless the government assented to all these proposals within three or six months. 'As a Government we are answerable to the people and not to the N.F.A. or any other sectional organisation'. This strong line was reinforced in a speech by Niall Blaney, the Minister for Local Government, in Dáil Éireann, where he made it clear that the government would not tolerate an organised campaign to withhold rates.

When officials in the Department of Agriculture met a delegation from the NFA on 9 April 1964, to discuss target growth rates and policies under the *Second Programme*, Nagle reported that the NFA wanted a more rapid rate of increase in agricultural output than the government had projected. It also demanded higher guaranteed prices for pigs, milk, wheat and barley to compensate for increased costs and for the ninth round of wage increases; a levy on imported wheat; and measures to stabilise the cost of agricultural rates. When the NFA met Smith, Lemass and Nagle on 10 April it raised the question of marketing boards, but Lemass stated that the government could not agree to the creation of boards over which it had no effective control, and where its role would be confined to levying the taxes necessary to finance the operation. A government press-release after this meeting stated that the NFA proposals would be 'carefully considered in the light of the Budgetary position'.[31] When the Minister for Finance, James Ryan, presented his budget four days later, he announced a package of measures to assist farming, amounting to £9 million. This included higher prices for milk and pigs, and additional rates relief. Ryan reminded the Dáil that the government had already announced higher prices for barley and sugar-beet.[32] John Horgan has described the 1964 budget as 'the farmers' budget'.[33]

THE 'BROWN BOOK'

Agriculture and the Second Programme, or the 'Brown Book' as it is known, from the colour of the cover, was published in the summer of 1964. It contained the detailed projections and policies for Irish agriculture during the period covered by the *Second Programme*. With an anticipated annual growth rate of 3.8 per cent during the years 1964–70[34] and an expected decline in the numbers engaged in agriculture from 390,000 in 1960 to 303,000 in 1970, gross product per person in farming was expected to rise at an annual rate of 5 per cent or by 60 per cent over the decade, which was substantially higher than the 40 per cent increase anticipated for non-agricultural workers. More than 60 per cent of the increase in output was expected to come from cattle and meat.

The 'Brown Book' contained a commitment that the government would continue to offer guaranteed prices for wheat, feeding barley, milk and pigs 'in order to maintain a certain stability in farming incomes'. Government policy would be guided by the general principle that 'farmers who work their land fully and efficiently should share equitably in the growing national prosperity and that a reasonable relationship should be maintained between farm incomes and incomes in other occupations'. It noted that many western governments supported farm incomes through subsidies or fixed prices, because they believed that it was desirable for reasons of equity to maintain a balance between relative incomes in farming and other sectors of the community. However, *Agriculture and the Second Programme* emphasised that increases in farm incomes would be achieved through higher output, not through additional exchequer support.

The report examined the market prospects for agricultural produce in detail, using FAO estimates for future world demand. Developed countries would have ample supplies of all major food items other than beef for the remainder of the 1960s, and this would make it increasingly difficult to dispose of surplus produce on export markets. Despite these unpromising market prospects, the report claimed that Irish agriculture could achieve a substantial growth in output, firstly because there was considerable scope for more intensive agricultural production, and secondly, because it anticipated that Ireland would join the EEC during the second half of the 1960s. EEC membership would mean higher prices and a substantial improvement in export markets and this would encourage farmers to increase output. It also anticipated that in the near future there would be 'better management of supplies and markets and high and firm prices', thanks to the working groups recently established by the GATT.

Investment in agriculture under the *Second Programme* was very much a continuation of the *First Programme*, with the emphasis on raising efficiency and reducing the cost of production. With the bovine TB eradication scheme apparently winding down, the eradication of brucellosis, sheep scab and warble fly infestation became the primary objectives for veterinary health. Reducing the number of livestock lost through brucellosis and calf mortality was one of the most effective means of raising livestock output.[35] The *Second Programme* gave a commitment to extend the Department's veterinary services by establishing regional laboratories. Performance testing and progeny testing of livestock would be expanded, with livestock research being carried out by the Agricultural Institute, the Department of Agriculture, the universities and the Meat Research Institute.

In 1965 the Minister for Agriculture, Charles Haughey, told the Dáil that *Agriculture and the Second Programme* 'commanded general acceptance from farming and rural organisations'.[36] The report stated that the annual reviews 'in consultation with the National Farmers' Association' provided 'a useful framework for a period survey' of agricultural policy, although it reiterated that this was not 'a price review'. When Rickard Deasy addressed the annual general meeting of the NFA in July 1964, shortly after the report's publication, he spoke approvingly about the agricultural aspects of the *Second Programme for Economic Expansion*. He told the gathering that, 'while some differences existed between the Association and the government, particularly on the question of farm costs and prices', there had been a considerable improvement in relations between the NFA and the Minister for Agriculture and his Department. He paid a personal tribute to the part that Lemass had played in bringing this about.[37]

When Patrick Smith presented the estimates for the Department of Agriculture to Dáil Éireann in June 1964 he remarked that in addition to the higher guaranteed prices announced in the budget, farmers were also benefiting considerably from higher cattle prices. There was a shortage of beef throughout Europe, and although some of the reasons for this were temporary, Smith was confident that the outlook for agriculture remained promising.[38] In 1964 net agricultural output rose by almost 15 per cent, and farm incomes by 20 per cent per capita. Higher beef prices, and the increases in the guaranteed prices for sugar-beet, feeding barley, pigs and milk, meant that the agricultural price index rose by 11 per cent, whereas it had only increased by 2.6 per cent between 1960 and 1963.[39] Smith told the Dáil that the concessions granted to agriculture in the 1964 budget were prompted by a wish to raise farmers' incomes and to maintain a 'reasonable relationship' with incomes in other sectors of the economy.[40]

The concessions should also be seen in the context of the ninth wage round, which was agreed in January 1964. This gave most wage and salaried workers an increase of 12 per cent over the following two years.[41] The government took part in the wage negotiations as an employer, and Lemass was personally involved in negotiating the final figure. John Horgan has suggested that the agreement was unduly generous, either because Lemass was over-optimistic about the prospect of Ireland joining the EEC (this seems unlikely, since there is no evidence of any movement to reopen negotiations at this stage) or because he shrank from confrontation, and therefore capitulated too readily to trade union demands.[42] Although agricultural labourers were not included in the ninth wage round, in February the Cabinet instructed the Minister for Agriculture to inform the chairman of the Agricultural Wages Board that the minimum wage recently set for farm labourers was 'entirely inadequate ... in the circumstances now prevailing', and they were awarded a wage increase of 15 per cent.[43]

Although Seán Lemass expressed the hope that the 1964 pay agreement 'signalled the end of the class war', the year was marked by several bitter strikes, as workers attempted to gain more than the terms that had been offered. Dublin building workers went on strike in August, demanding a reduction in their working hours from 42½ to 40 hours. By October the strike remained unresolved, and there were fears that it might spread throughout the state, until Jack Lynch, the Minister for Industry and Commerce, intervened and agreed to their demand for shorter working hours.[44]

THE RESIGNATION OF PATRICK SMITH

Lynch's concession led to the resignation of Patrick Smith. In his letter of resignation to Lemass on 7 October 1964, Smith claimed that Ireland was faced not only with 'tyranny but a dishonest incompetent one'. He condemned the trade unions for disregarding the national wage agreement and the 'utter lack of leadership' shown by their leaders. He called for the government to fight the plague of militant trade unions. On the day after Smith's resignation the *Irish Independent* suggested that a Cabinet reshuffle had been on the cards and that Smith would have been removed,[45] but no evidence has emerged to confirm this point of view. Relations between Lemass and Smith were often difficult; Smith was not altogether in sympathy with Lemass' style of government. He disagreed with Lemass' wishes to grant the NFA privileged status as spokesman for agricultural interests, and to give Father McDyer and the Charlestown group a role in framing policy on pilot areas and small western farms.

On the whole, Smith adopted an austere approach towards farmers' demands for price support from the exchequer; his views on public spending were conservative, although he pressed determinedly for an expansion in dairy farming in western counties, despite opposition from the Department of Finance. He believed that agricultural policy should be determined by the Department of Agriculture, not by farming organisations. If farming interests were to be consulted or represented, he would prefer that this should be done through the county committees of agriculture. In 1964 Smith introduced legislation designed to make the county committees of agriculture more representative of the farming community, by requiring that 50 per cent of the members should not be county councillors. He hoped that this would encourage the nomination of people active in farming organisations. His commitment to the county committees of agriculture reflected his long career in local government. He had served for many years as chairman of Cavan County Council. Smith emphasised that as Minister for Agriculture he represented the government, not the farmers, and his duty was to the government and to the public. Despite the somewhat acrimonious relationship between Smith and the NFA, it expressed regret at his resignation. Louis Smith and Seán Healy claim that by resigning he gave up a position of influence, which he could use on the farmers' behalf.[46]

Anglo-Irish Trade, 1963–5

In January 1966, during the debate on the 1965 Anglo-Irish Free Trade Area Agreement, Charles Haughey remarked that when he was appointed Minister for Agriculture in the autumn of 1964, he was struck by the fact that the Department was planning for 'major increases in our agricultural production and exports under the *Second Programme* while the markets in which we could dispose of them were becoming more and more restricted'.[47] In January 1963, after de Gaulle's veto had ended any immediate prospect that Ireland would become a member of the EEC, the Department of Finance noted that the prospects of maintaining 'even our modest level of agricultural exports' to EEC member countries were 'uniformly poor' for every product except beef.[48] In a separate report the Department of Agriculture acknowledged that there was no prospect of free trade being extended to agriculture on a similar basis to industrial goods; the GATT and other major trading groups had adopted the principle of negotiating 'reasonable access' as an alternative. (The *Second Programme* gave a much more promising interpretation of the prospects of GATT opening up trade in agricultural produce.)

In the early 1960s Britain and the EEC accounted for two-thirds of world imports of dairy products; three-quarters of world meat imports; one-third of sugar imports; and half of the world's commercial imports of wheat. The Department of Agriculture believed that the best option for Ireland was to attach itself to 'one of the price supported blocks' – the EEC or Britain; in order to achieve this, Ireland should be prepared to reduce tariffs on manufactured goods in return for market concessions for agricultural produce.[49] On 21 January 1963, within days of de Gaulle's veto on Britain's EEC membership, the committee of secretaries recommended that Ireland should explore the prospects of securing an Anglo-Irish free trade agreement.[50]

Ireland had already failed to secure this type of agreement in 1959/60 and the prospects of success on this occasion appeared even less promising. In February 1963 the British Prime Minister, Harold Macmillan, told the House of Commons that the British exchequer's open-ended support for agriculture must be controlled. The details of the new agricultural policy had yet to be worked out. Tadhg Ó Cearbhaill also questioned the wisdom of trying to negotiate a long-term trade agreement in the run-up to a British general election.[51] Nevertheless, the Irish government pressed ahead with trade talks. On 26 February Cornelius Cremin, the Irish Ambassador in London, reported that Christopher Soames, the British Minister for Agriculture, Fisheries and Food, had told him he would be embarrassed if the Irish Minister for Agriculture accompanied Lemass at these talks because he (Soames) had nothing to offer. Soames indicated that talks were premature.[52] Hugh McCann, secretary of the Department of External Affairs, warned that the Danes were demanding further concessions on their agricultural exports to Britain, as fellow members of EFTA.[53] This was confirmed by D. O'Sullivan, the agricultural counsellor at the Irish Embassy in London; Arthur Propper, the permanent under-secretary at the Ministry of Agriculture, Fisheries and Food (MAFF), had informed him that Britain regarded Denmark as a special case. Denmark had been severely hit by the collapse of the negotiations on EEC entry,[54] and it would be impossible for Britain to refuse them compensation, whereas Britain believed that the collapse of the EEC entry negotiations would have little impact on Ireland. Propper also remarked that 'EFTA considerations made it imperative' that Britain should give special consideration to Denmark.[55]

Bilateral trade talks between Denmark and Britain were scheduled for 13 March,[56] five days before ministerial talks on Anglo-Irish trade. When Lemass and Aiken, the Minister for External Affairs, arrived in London, Britain informed them that Denmark was demanding the removal of the 15s-per-cwt duty on butter imported into Britain, from which Ireland was exempt. Britain had agreed to remove the butter duty from all EFTA members. It claimed that this would have no impact on Ireland because butter imports would be restricted by quota. Nagle noted that while Britain retained all its existing advantages in the Irish market, the position for Irish agricultural exports in Britain had deteriorated considerably in recent years; the proposal to lift the tariff on Danish butter would add to the inequitable advantage that Denmark had gained through a generous butter quota. Britain later decided to remove all import duties on butter, irrespective of the country of origin, as long as quotas remained in operation. This concession would benefit New Zealand and Australia, while placing Irish butter at an even greater disadvantage. The Irish authorities noted that it would lead to pressure from Australia and New Zealand for quotas to be continued indefinitely.[57]

In May 1963 the Irish government received an advance copy of the British statement on future agricultural policy. Britain was determined to limit the cost of price supports for agricultural produce by setting a limit on the quantities of produce that would qualify for price support, including livestock and sheep. Before the new regulations came into effect on 1 April 1964, Britain planned to hold talks with the main overseas suppliers to limit imports of meat and cereals, either by quotas or through minimum prices. Officials in the Department of Agriculture feared that the regulations would include a limit on the quantity of Irish stores that would qualify for price guarantees.[58]

In August Britain wanted to open bilateral talks with Ireland on the implications of the reforms in agricultural policy for Ireland's trade in livestock, meat, bacon and cereals. But Irish ministers wanted any talks to concentrate on Lemass' proposals for 'a two-country common market concept.'[59] The Cabinet decided that the Irish authorities should refuse to engage in talks on the proposed withdrawal of price guarantees on livestock unless Britain agreed to discuss the possibility of creating an Anglo-Irish free trade area. But Whitaker reported two days later that his talks with British officials indicated that 'there is no likelihood of any flexibility in the British Government's agricultural policy'.

When officials at the Department of Agriculture met their counterparts in MAFF for talks on 23 September, MAFF indicated that it was under considerable pressure from farming interests and exporters to reach agreement on measures to control imports of livestock and meat. It claimed that the proposal to introduce 'market stabilisation', quotas for meat and livestock, would be in everybody's interest, and it refused to give a guarantee that Irish store cattle would be exempt from the proposed changes. Britain wished to maintain a fair balance between domestic production and imports of fat cattle and meat, and this would involve some regulation of imports. The Department of Agriculture noted that MAFF officials had expressed concern at the planned increase in Irish cattle output under the *Second Programme*. The Department replied that these targets had been set in the expectation that Ireland would join the EEC. If Britain imposed controls on livestock and beef, this would damage the Irish livestock industry, and reduce the prospect that numbers would expand at the rate envisaged in the *Second Programme*. At the end of these talks Nagle reached the conclusion that the new British agricultural policy would freeze agricultural production and trade in its existing pattern, with no scope for an expansion in Irish exports. The only minor cause for optimism after these talks was the prospect that Ireland's quota for pork and bacon would permit some expansion in that sector. Britain gave an undertaking some weeks later not to limit imports of Irish pork for the next five years; the Irish bacon quota would be reduced slightly from its current level.[60]

Talks on the proposed Anglo-Irish free trade area finally opened under the auspices of the Anglo-Irish joint committee (a committee consisting of British and Irish officials that met annually under the 1960 trade agreement) on 26/7 November, more than six months after Lemass broached the idea. Ireland was prepared to reduce its tariff on British manufactured goods; in return it wanted a gradual harmonisation of agricultural prices and production in Britain and Ireland. Specifically, Ireland was demanding a sizeable increase in the butter quota; the elimination of the requirement that Irish cattle had to be in Britain for three months before they qualified for fat-stock price guarantees; an assured market for Irish beef; and price arrangements and improved market shares for cheese, pigs, bacon, eggs and poultry.[61] Although British officials described the Irish proposals as 'imaginative and important', they warned it would be difficult to reconcile them with Britain's obligations to third countries and with Britain's new agricultural policy, because they would involve discriminating between Irish suppliers and others. Britain was also worried at the prospect of having to absorb the large increase in Irish agricultural produce that was projected in the *Second Programme*. British officials suggested that this difficulty would be considerably eased if the Irish proposals provided for some limit on agricultural exports to Britain, in line with Britain's planned limits on domestic agricultural production. Irish officials tried to allay British fears about a substantial rise in Irish agricultural exports: they claimed that the

Second Programme contemplated only 'a modest rate of agricultural expansion'.

These were only opening gambits, and their significance was dwarfed by the changes under way in British agricultural policy. On 4 December MAFF informed the Department of Agriculture that Britain would be forced to admit a token quantity of livestock from the Continent; in the past they had excluded continental livestock on health grounds, which had given Ireland a *de facto* monopoly of livestock imports to the UK.[62] A month later MAFF floated two proposals for the future regulation of Irish livestock and cattle exports to the UK. Britain would set a global figure for all types of cattle exports from Ireland. Under this arrangement the composition could shift between beef, fat-stock and stores, provided that the total remained below the quota. Alternatively, Britain would set maximum and minimum import figures for store cattle. If imports exceeded the maximum limit, Britain would restrict imports of fat-stock and beef; if they fell below the minimum level, Ireland would be permitted to increase its exports of fat-stock and beef. Any arrangements for beef quotas would be 'entirely without prejudice' to the proposals that Lemass had made to the British government. Irish officials reiterated that the 1948 trade agreement gave Ireland a guarantee of entry to the British market, free of quotas. Nagle stressed that one of the major objectives of Ireland's current programme for economic development was to increase the output of livestock, which was 'the main pivot of our economy'. Ireland was only asking that the extra production should be 'accommodated by the United Kingdom, not that we should get theoretical or imaginary quotas which in all probability we would never expect to fill'. He claimed that Irish livestock output would have been considerably higher in the early 1960s, were it not for the bovine TB eradication scheme.

These inconclusive talks were followed by multilateral talks on meat and cattle between Britain, Ireland, Australia, New Zealand, Argentina and Uruguay. Nagle reported that the atmosphere at these talks was sour. The Australians demanded that the Irish store trade to the UK should be investigated. There seemed little prospect of an agreement being reached on quotas for beef and livestock.[63] Ireland was in a difficult position at these talks. If Britain expanded its domestic livestock sector, Ireland would gain from an expanding trade in store cattle, but this would reduce the prospective market for fat cattle and beef. Other overseas participants were only interested in securing the maximum market for beef.[64] The talks ended in early February without reaching agreement. Nagle believed that they collapsed because of pressure from the NFU.[65] It later emerged that the talks ended because Britain was concerned about a significant reduction in supplies of beef from the southern hemisphere.[66]

The break-down of the multilateral talks was probably to Ireland's advantage. When Lemass travelled to Britain for St Patrick's Day in 1964 he brought a new draft from the Department of Agriculture on the implications of Ireland's request for improved agricultural outlets in Britain. This claimed that it would be possible to initiate a free-trade-area arrangement that would not impose a major financial burden on the British government, 'provided the latter recognise the need to permit a steady expansion in our agriculture and show themselves willing to translate this concept into action as circumstances permit'. Ireland wanted the three-month residential qualification for Irish cattle in the UK to be replaced by an agreement providing for the free movement of cattle, 'with prices being formed and the age or stage of animals exported being determined by the natural inter-play of market forces', and the harmonisation of cattle production policies in Britain and Ireland. Ireland hoped that Britain would assist if it got into difficulties with excess butter stocks, but Ireland was prepared to restrain dairy production, relying on higher cattle prices to increase the incomes of farmers, including the dairy farmers who produced the calves.

By April 1964 beef was in short supply in the UK and efforts were made to import additional quantities from Ireland. Patrick Smith wrote to his British counterpart, Christopher Soames, suggesting that this offered an opportunity to establish closer links between the cattle industries in both countries.[67] Soames rejected the idea, telling Smith that it would entail giving Ireland a straight import subsidy that would not apply to other suppliers.[68] When Lemass planned a unilateral 10 per cent cut on all Irish import duties, Smith argued that the concession should be restricted to Britain, provided that Britain agreed to end the three-month waiting period for Irish livestock. Smith claimed that Ireland would not achieve 'real economic progress simply by slashing tariffs against all and sundry'. Such actions tacitly implied that agriculture would be of little importance in the future. He wanted to encourage co-operation between Britain and Ireland on a range of matters, including the development of meat-processing plants in Northern Ireland and the Republic.[69] The shortage of beef made Ireland more optimistic about the prospect of securing a trade agreement with Britain.

Any agreement was likely to be delayed by the upcoming British general election. In December 1963 J. O'Mahony, the agricultural attaché in

London, reported that Fred Peart, the Labour party spokesman on agriculture, had admitted that the Labour party's policy was similar to that of the Tories, although he made positive noises about a special relationship with Ireland.[70] The general election in October 1964 saw the return by a narrow margin of a Labour government. Shortly after the election the new government imposed a 15 per cent surcharge on all imports of manufactured goods, in order to strengthen sterling and reduce the balance of payments deficit. Lemass protested to the British ambassador at the setting aside of the Anglo-Irish agreements and he demanded a meeting with the British prime minister, Harold Wilson.[71] At this meeting Wilson and Lemass agreed that talks should begin on a new Anglo-Irish trade agreement, and Lemass confirmed this in a letter. Although he pressed for talks at ministerial level, Wilson refused, because he claimed that his ministers were not yet ready.

In preparation for the re-opening of talks Nagle drafted a revised statement setting out the Department of Agriculture's demands. The main requirements were access to British prices for fat cattle, sheep and beef, and larger quotas for butter and bacon. Nagle was emphatic that Ireland should not give any written commitment at this stage to limit its future agricultural exports to Britain.[72]

When the talks opened on 17/18 December 1964, British officials indicated that while Britain welcomed the idea of a free trade area in principle, it was determined to keep any concessions to Irish agriculture to a minimum. Britain's agricultural policy was designed to keep the volume of agricultural imports at current levels, while creating stable markets. Concessions to Ireland would only be possible in the case of produce, such as livestock and meat, where the demand for imports was expected to increase, but Britain would be more willing to grant concessions for store cattle than for fat cattle. They claimed that extending British price support to Irish produce was out of the question because there would be 'unpredictable effects on the rate of expansion' of Irish imports and on the British market, unless limits were imposed on livestock numbers and prices. Linking Irish agriculture to the British price system 'would mean, in effect, rewriting the British Agriculture Acts'. Any assistance for Irish butter exports would have to be 'on the margin'; in other words, Britain would occasionally take an additional 1,000 tons or so. There was no scope for expanding the Irish egg trade to the UK, and Irish potatoes would have to share the disadvantages of levies and acreage quotas that applied to British farmers.

On 23 December Hugh McCann sent Nagle, Whitaker and J. C. B. McCarthy his assessment of the negotiations to date. Britain was demanding that Ireland should dismantle all protection for 85 per cent of its trade within five years. In return it would reduce the waiting period for store cattle from three to two months, and remove duties on the limited range of manufactured goods that were not already duty-free. McCann was emphatic that Ireland should reject Britain's opening bid. If Ireland secured further concessions for agriculture, at the cost of a reduction in the growth of Irish industry, in his opinion it would be 'a retrograde step', given that industry was generally seen as the key to higher living standards for the Irish people. Nagle responded that McCann had oversimplified the roles of agriculture and industry in Irish economic development. If the export targets in the *Second Programme for Economic Expansion* were to be achieved, it would be necessary to raise agricultural exports by approximately £40 million. Most of this would have to be sold in Britain. This would bring an increase in national income. He reminded McCann that one-third of the working population depended on agriculture.

Nagle went on to set out his vision for the Irish economy, and for Anglo-Irish relations. He hoped that any agreement on an Anglo-Irish free trade area would include provision for an Anglo-Irish economic development committee. Ireland should aim to become part of the British agricultural support system, and the two countries should develop a joint policy for industrial development that would bring British capital and industrial skill to Ireland in an orderly fashion. He did not believe that Ireland could solve its economic problems 'except in cooperation with Britain'. If greater economic co-ordination was not achieved between Britain and Ireland, there was an acute danger of over-capacity in meat-packing plants north and south of the border, and unco-ordinated projects for aeroplanes and shipbuilding – a reference presumably to the planned Potez aerospace plant outside Dublin, and the Verolme shipyard in Cork. Nagle drew a link between Anglo-Irish economic co-operation, the discrediting of 'tribal nationalism' and a growing realisation that the fortunes of both countries were interdependent. He believed that if Ireland approached the forthcoming trade talks with 'goodwill and purpose they may well prove to be the beginning of an important new orientation in British-Irish relations'. A common-market type arrangement with Britain would go some way to resolving 'the most important problem facing the Government' – partition.[73] On many occasions from the late 1940s, when he first became involved in Anglo-Irish trade negotiations, Nagle expressed a more benign view of

Britain's intentions than the evidence might warrant, and this was one such occasion. Nevertheless, his statement indicates that economic and political relations in the 1960s cannot be treated in isolation. The committee of secretaries, of which Nagle was a member, dealt with all of the key aspects of Irish policy at the time, including Northern Ireland and Irish foreign policy.

McCann was less sanguine about the merits of an Anglo-Irish trade agreement than Nagle; he preferred a multilateral approach to trade relations. Putting all trade eggs in the British basket (John A. Costello had used an identical phrase during the 1948 trade talks) would leave Ireland vulnerable to pressure from London. He also feared that it might damage Ireland's image within the EEC because it would be seen as less European and more Anglo-Saxon. While a trade agreement might bring economic benefits, McCann believed that in national terms it would be a retrograde step. McCann was out of line with Whitaker and Nagle. Whitaker retorted that economic strength would enhance Irish political influence, and any trade agreement that was economically beneficial would bring political dividends.[74] Although the Department of External Affairs remained unenthusiastic about what was on offer, on 19 February 1965 the Cabinet gave its approval for further talks, but insisted that the removal of the waiting period for Irish cattle should be a key objective.[75]

When talks resumed on 25/6 March 1965, Britain accepted Ireland's offer to cut tariffs on industrial goods by 10 per cent each year. In return Ireland would be given unrestricted access for 85 per cent of agricultural exports; the exceptions were bacon, main-crop potatoes, butter and sugar. Bacon was covered by the agreement reached in the autumn of 1963. Ireland also had an export trade in sugar to the UK during the late 1950s, but this had been damaged when Britain imposed an import levy in December 1961. Ireland had been compensated for this under an agreement in 1962. Ireland also began to export sugar to the United States in 1962, thanks to the assistance of US President John F. Kennedy in securing a modification of US trade regulations.[76]

In the case of livestock Britain's primary concern was to secure an adequate supply of store cattle. It demanded that Ireland give a commitment to supply a minimum number of store cattle every year, but any agreement on price would be relegated to an annexe to the agreement. The future market for Irish stores was increasingly uncertain because Britain had recently introduced a calf subsidy that would be paid when the animal was slaughtered; this subsidy did not apply to imported livestock. Britain was only prepared to reduce the residence period for Irish cattle and sheep by one month. If the waiting period ended, Irish fat cattle would qualify for British price guarantees, and the incentive to export stores would be lessened. Britain was only prepared to offer a price guarantee on 20,000 tons of carcase beef, roughly equivalent to the current Irish exports to the UK, again because of fears that a higher quantity would reduce the number of stores being shipped to the UK. Indeed, Britain displayed a rather hostile attitude towards the Irish meat-processing sector. Irish officials were questioned about the amount of state aid that it had received. Michael Barry informed them that the rapid expansion in recent years had taken place without any special state aid. (Improvements in transport, particularly the introduction of modern ferries, were a major factor.) He also reported that three of the largest factories could supply 20,000 tons in twenty weeks; there was ample scope for an increase in exports.

Ireland wanted a minimum annual quota of 25,000 tons of butter (the current figure was 16,000), and an orderly increase to take account of the expected rise in Irish milk output. It also demanded an immediate doubling of the quantity of meat that would qualify for price guarantees, and a gradual rise in later years in line with Ireland's expanding output of livestock. Nagle and Barry tried to convince the British officials that the planned expansion in Irish livestock numbers would ensure adequate supplies of stores, fat cattle and beef. A deal on lamb presented even greater difficulties, because Britain claimed that it would provoke criticism from New Zealand and from British farmers. The other stumbling block was Ireland's demand that Britain should give a clear undertaking that Irish agricultural exports, other than butter, bacon, sugar and potatoes, would have unrestricted access to the British market in the future.[77] Britain wanted to be free to limit imports from Ireland if they were restricting output by UK producers. Ireland was only prepared to accept restrictions in the context of an international commodity agreement.

As the British Labour government had only a tiny majority, another British general election was expected shortly, and Lemass was eager to conclude an agreement before this happened. On 21 June Britain handed over what Hugh McCann described as its maximum concessions. It granted unrestricted access to Irish agricultural produce (other than butter, bacon, potatoes and sugar), subject to whatever provisions were made for the agreement to be reviewed, and subject to general GATT exceptions.[78] Britain did not anticipate imposing any further restrictions on Irish agricultural exports before 1970. Ireland demanded clarification on these matters; it was especially concerned to secure a commitment to increased quotas for bacon and butter in future years.[79] Britain indicated that it might make further concessions in the case of sheep and beef, but there was no prospect of Irish animals qualifying for the British calf subsidy.[80]

When British and Irish ministers met for talks on 26 July 1965, Lemass' opening statement noted that all the outstanding issues concerned agriculture, which was 'the pivot on which the development of our economy as a whole depends'. He pointed out that with the exception of store cattle, Britain's guarantee of access for Irish produce was only similar to what was offered under the most-favoured-nation treatment in the GATT agreements. He indicated that 'presentationally and in substance, something more is called for in a free trade area'.[81] Lemass pressed for a minimum of 35,000 tons of beef to be included in the British deficiency payments, but Britain held firm. When Harold Wilson joined the talks at lunch-time, he offered to include a good-will clause on butter in the agreement and to extend deficiency payments to 5,000 tons of lamb.[82] At this meeting both governments agreed to establish a group to draft the treaty but progress was slow, mainly because of continuing disagreements over the agricultural clauses.

The agreement was eventually signed on 14 December 1965. Britain agreed to remove all protective duties on Irish manufactured goods imported to the UK from 1 July 1966. In return Ireland would remove all protective duties on British manufactured goods over the next nine years. The waiting period before Irish cattle qualified for British deficiency payments was reduced to two months. Britain agreed to pay the Irish government an annual sum equal to the UK fat-stock guarantee on 25,000 tons of beef and 5,500 tons of carcase lamb. The Irish government undertook to use their best endeavours to ensure that the number of store cattle exported from Ireland to the UK in any calendar year would not fall below 638,000 head, and that at least 25,000 tons of beef and 5,000 tons of lamb would be exported annually to the UK. Ireland was given a firm guarantee that no restrictions would be imposed on Irish store cattle exports, which accounted for 40 per cent of agricultural exports to the UK. Imports of bacon, butter and cereals into the UK would continue to be governed by multilateral arrangements. Ireland's butter quota was raised to 23,000, which according to Irish officials was 'sufficient to absorb anticipated exports'.

In an exchange of letters, associated with the treaty, the UK government gave Ireland an assurance that it would try to provide opportunities for growth in agricultural exports, and it would take account of Ireland's projections for increased dairy output under the *Second Programme*. In the case of other agricultural produce, exports would only be regulated in the context of a multilateral commodity agreement or another international agreement. If this happened, Britain would be obliged to consult the Irish government in advance and to take account of the quantities that Ireland expected to have available for export under the *Second Programme*. Ireland's quota for any particular product would be no less than the volume exported to Britain during a recent representative period, and it would be Britain's intention to provide Irish producers with opportunities to expand output on no less favourable terms than those given to British farmers.[83]

When Charles Haughey addressed the Dáil on 5 January 1966 during a debate on the Anglo-Irish Free Trade Area Agreement, he noted that prior to this agreement Ireland was in

> ... a very vulnerable position in respect of one of our most important forms of economic activity – our agricultural exports ... the truth of the matter is that during the past decade or so our Irish agricultural production has been carried on under the shade of disorganised and uncertain export markets.[84]

The agreement was a triumph for Irish persistence over British indifference. In 1969 Lemass remarked that the agreement had been continually hindered by British procrastination, although the Labour government proved more responsive than the Conservatives.[85] In Ireland the agreement was widely condemned as marking the end of Irish economic independence. The leader of the opposition, Liam Cosgrave, described it as an unbalanced agreement: 'in return for limited and doubtful agricultural gains' virtually the entire Irish market for manufactured goods would be exposed to 'high-powered competition from British industry'. However, the Conservative spokesman on agriculture in the UK was also highly critical of the agreement. For this reason Lemass dissuaded Lord Killanin from raising the matter in a debate in the House of Lords.[86]

THE ORIGINS OF THE 1966 FARMERS' DISPUTE

The 1965 Anglo-Irish agreement was negotiated during a difficult period for the Irish economy. In March 1965 the NFA and the Department of Agriculture carried out their annual agricultural review, which involved between ten and fifteen meetings. Five meetings were attended by the

Minister for Agriculture.[87] When the review was in progress, the government announced higher prices for cereals and liquid milk, and a new quality milk bonus. In addition, the Minister for Agriculture gave a commitment to increase pig prices in the autumn and to review the level of grants for the land project.[88] When Lemass addressed the final session of the annual review, he commented that it had been conducted in a greatly improved atmosphere. In its closing remarks the NFA noted that there was a continuing need to raise farmers' incomes and to offer a higher price for milk; it was also demanding further concessions on agricultural rates relief.[89]

When Charles Haughey presented the annual estimate for the Department of Agriculture to the Dáil on 29 April, he expressed confidence that 1965 would prove to be another good year for Irish farmers. Cattle and beef prices were expected to remain buoyant; given suitable weather he anticipated a further rise in milk output; sheep production was at a record level; pig numbers were showing signs of record expansion; higher prices had already been announced for sugar-beet, malting and feeding barley and wheat.[90] When the 1965 budget gave no further concessions to farmers,[91] the NFA denounced it as 'a completely negative document as far as agriculture is concerned', and demanded an immediate meeting with the government. The Department of Agriculture responded by listing the numerous concessions that had already been announced, adding that the fortunes of Irish agriculture during 1965 would be determined mainly by cattle prices.

The main point of contention between the NFA and the government concerned the estimates for agricultural income during the current year.[92] In 1964 farm incomes rose from £120.5 million to £142.5 million, or from £458 to £537 per family-farm-member. Higher cattle prices accounted for most of the increase.[93] On 28 June 1965 Deasy informed Lemass that the NFA had submitted 'an unchallenged prediction' during the 1965 annual review, that farm incomes would fall by £2 million during the coming year, whereas shortly after the review had ended, the government published an estimate showing farm incomes rising by £12 million. Farmers believed that the budget had been devised on the basis of this 'grossly optimistic' estimate. Deasy also claimed that there was a general feeling among farmers that 'certain aspects of the Review must be regarded as a continuous process'. Farmer confidence could only be restored 'if the mechanism is seen to work smoothly and effectively'. Lemass informed him that the statistics on farm income would be examined, but this would take time; it was 'quite erroneous' to suggest that the estimates for agricultural incomes had determined the shape of the budget.[94]

Retrospective calculations carried out by the CSO indicated that the NFA projection was much closer to the actual outcome than the government's figures. In 1965 aggregate farm income was £142.4 million, almost identical to the 1964 figure of £142.5 million. Income per family-farm-member was estimated to have increased from £537 to £562 per capita, but the improvement was due to a decline in the numbers engaged in farming.[95]

In 1964 exports of livestock and beef were the equivalent of 1,078,000 cattle. In the following year this declined to 886,000, and the value fell from £70.9 million to £62.2 million.[96] The deterioration in the livestock trade was evident early in the year. In February 1965 the government introduced a temporary export subsidy for carcase meat, that was due to last until June.[97] Exports of manufactured goods also fell as a result of Britain's decision to impose a 15 per cent surcharge on all imported goods. Meanwhile, the Irish import bill increased because of the economic boom that followed the generous wage settlements. The higher balance of payments deficit prompted the Central Bank to place curbs on bank credit in May 1965, and this had a severe impact on farmers. In July the government announced price controls, restrictions on any additional public spending, and cuts in the public capital programme.[98] By the end of the year stock numbers on Irish farms had risen sharply owing to the depressed market.

In the spring of 1966, for the first time the Department of Agriculture and the NFA reached agreement on projections for agricultural output and income for the coming year. Farm incomes were expected to rise to £150.7 million compared with £145.2 million for 1965. During the review the government agreed to make a number of changes to the land project and the farm buildings scheme. The 1966 budget, which was introduced at an unusually early date in March, announced several measures to assist farming:

- New or improved farm buildings would be permanently exempted from an increased valuation (the exemption had previously been limited to twenty years).
- All exports of carcase beef and lamb to the UK would qualify for British guaranteed payments. Under the 1965 Anglo-Irish agreement, which was due to come into effect in July 1966, these guarantees only applied to 25,000 tons of beef and 5,500 tons of lamb; the Irish government would meet the additional cost.

- The value of grants for pig farrowing and fattening houses on small farms was increased.
- The Minister for Finance gave an undertaking that if farmers' incomes deteriorated during the coming year, the government would review the situation in the light of prevailing circumstances.[99]

The early date for the 1966 budget reflected the difficult economic circumstances. Overall, the budget was deflationary; taxes were raised and the amount allocated for public capital spending was less than in 1965.[100] Given these circumstances, the package of measures announced for farmers was relatively generous. Yet farm prices remained depressed, and the cattle trade was particularly slow, despite the anticipated benefits from the Anglo-Irish trade agreement. By the end of March there were reports that the NFA was planning a series of commodity strikes in protest at the government's failure to bridge the gap between agricultural and other incomes.[101] In May the Department of Agriculture reduced its estimate for farm income in 1966 by £2.8 million, because it anticipated that the wet spring weather would mean poor crop yields, and a below-average quantity of milk.

Charles Haughey publicly acknowledged the difficult economic circumstances. Opening the debate on the estimate for the Department of Agriculture on 11 May 1966, he told the Dáil that the government would shortly announce new measures to raise farm incomes to the levels projected.[102] On 26 May, in the closing stages of the debate on the agricultural estimate, he announced an immediate increase in the price of milk of 2d per gallon; an increase in the quality premium from May 1967; a new scheme of headage payments for farrowed sows; grants for hill sheep; and a new scheme for agricultural credit.[103] The Department estimated that these measures would raise farm incomes by £5.5 million in a full year, and that the figure estimated at the beginning of the year would be reached.[104]

Despite these additional concessions, Haughey tried to dampen farmers' expectations that price supports offered a realistic mechanism for raising farm incomes. He cautioned that in a country such as Ireland, where over 30 per cent of the population made their living on the land and a high proportion of agricultural produce was exported, there was 'a very real limit to what can be done by way of direct support from the Exchequer'. In the long term, 'the real breakthrough must come from helping farmers to increase their incomes by increased production and higher productivity. Anyone who preaches any other gospel is only deceiving our farmers and storing up trouble for the future'. He criticised farm leaders for suggesting that the Department should reduce expenditure on fertiliser subsidies in order to provide more generous price support. There was a danger that 'agitation directed only to getting higher prices may develop a kind of dole mentality which would eventually make agriculture subservient to the State'. He wanted to see 'a self-reliant, independent and progressive agriculture, fully backed up by, but not utterly dependent on, the State'.[105]

Haughey's speech must be read in the context of growing farm protests. These were prompted by the combination of difficult economic circumstances and the on-going battle between the ICMSA and the NFA for the right to represent farmers. The two issues were not unrelated, since the depressed state of agriculture provided both organisations with an opportunity to prove their claim to be the most effective representative of the farming community. In April 1966 the ICMSA placed a picket on Government Buildings and Leinster House, in protest at the involvement of the NFA in discussions on the future of the dairy industry, and in order to press their case for the introduction of a two-tier milk price that would give a higher price per gallon to small producers. Louis Smith and Seán Healy suggest that the ICMSA picket was responsible for the 2d a gallon increase in the milk price that was announced on 26 May, and this convinced the NFA that militant action was more effective than talks.[106]

In his opening address to the fifth congress of the European Society for Rural Sociology, at Maynooth College, on 22 August 1966, Charles Haughey remarked that although living conditions in rural areas had improved in recent years, 'there is probably a great deal more dissatisfaction and agitation than there was in the 1930s when things were a great deal worse'. The growing dissatisfaction was caused by the practice of drawing comparisons between rural and urban living standards, and the fact that when farmers gained some of the benefits of modern living they wanted more. In his opinion this was 'a perfectly natural development and not something to be resented or complained about. Rather it is something to be accepted as inevitable and sensible provision made for it in our social and economic planning'.[107] The economic climate was extremely volatile during the summer of 1966. In June the government announced further tax increases on petrol and tobacco, and a new wholesale tax of 5 per cent.[108] The Irish banks began a lengthy strike on 5 May, and a UK shipping strike that lasted from 15 May until 1 July disrupted the cattle trade. The tenth round of wage increases, which was negotiated during the summer months, reinforced the contrast between the regular increases in income awarded to wage and salaried workers, and the more uncertain circumstances of farmers. Cattle prices fell sharply because the EEC market was closed off by punitive import duties. The EEC Council of Ministers rejected a request by the West German government to import a quantity of Irish beef free of import levies. Record livestock numbers in Britain reduced the demand for Irish cattle. Credit restrictions and the British shipping strike added to farmers' woes. On 31 August, in an effort to offset falling cattle prices, the Department introduced another temporary scheme of headage payments on fat bullocks and heifers exported to Britain until the end of the year. This gave Irish farmers a price equal to the guaranteed price paid for British fat-stock.[109] The fall in cattle prices, coupled with a low milk output, and an unpromising tillage season, resulted in a further downward revision of estimates for farm income, despite the additional assistance given in May. By the autumn, the Department of Agriculture conceded that the commitment to reduce the gap between farm incomes and incomes in other sectors of the economy would not be fulfilled during 1966.[110]

At the annual general meeting of the NFA on 25 August 1966, Rickard Deasy accused the Minister for Agriculture of 'rushing from one expedient (whether political or economic) to another, while all the time shying away from the key decisions and even from key discussions on fundamental policy issues'. He demanded that the government establish a meat marketing authority to give some stability to the livestock and meat trade. Deasy claimed that the Minister for Agriculture was in favour in principle of establishing a meat marketing authority, but his officials were not. 'In this he is in advance of his Department, which still blindly adheres to a dyed-in-the-wool belief in the Victorian doctrine of the right of the entrepreneur'.[111] Deasy, who was coming to the end of his term as president, suggested that farmers must prepare 'for a renewed militancy', although he cautioned that 'militancy is a weapon not an end, even if it is forced underground, constructive work must continue because in the ultimate the conference table is inevitable'. A militant who arrived at the conference table without constructive plans would ultimately be the loser.

The NFA telephoned the Department of Agriculture on the day of Deasy's speech to request a meeting with the Minister on the following day. Charles Haughey initially agreed to a meeting, but cancelled the appointment when he learned of the contents of Deasy's speech. When the council of the NFA met on 17 September, it announced a protest march to Dublin, and demanded a meeting with the Minister for Agriculture and the Taoiseach when the march arrived. On 17 October, before the marchers reached Dublin, the Minister's private secretary informed the NFA that if it submitted a memorandum, it would receive careful consideration and a meeting between the NFA and the Department would be arranged in due course, if this was considered desirable. On 19 October the NFA held a rally in Merrion Square, close to the Department's offices. At the end of the rally it demanded a meeting with the Minister, and when this was not granted began a sit-down on the steps of the Department of Agriculture and Government Buildings.

The NFA also issued a declaration of farmers' rights, which noted that the Irish government had accepted Pope John XXIII's objective of preserving the family farm, and included a reference to the commitment in the 1916 Proclamation giving equal right to all citizens. The NFA claimed that this right could not be achieved until 'the farmer is put in a position to earn an income high enough to support standards of social and educational progress, social security, home amenities and leisure equal to the rising standards achieved by comparable workers in the other sectors'. These standards were not being met for a majority of the rural population. An improvement in rural living standards was dependent on effective farm policies to raise productivity, and 'on the full development and efficient operation of the supply, processing, and marketing arms of Irish agriculture'. The NFA presented eleven demands to the government.

1. The right to an incomes policy which would effectively close the gap between farmers' incomes and those in other sections of the economy.
2. The right of small farmers to a well-planned system of production incentives that would be available on equal terms to all potentially viable small farms.
3. The right of communities in underdeveloped rural areas to a comprehensive rural development programme.
4. The right to social security and retraining opportunities equally with other citizens.
5. The right to immediate commodity price and credit policies, so as to ensure the real availability, proper employment, and fair remuneration of all the factors of production, including working capital.
6. The right to professional agricultural training.
7. The right to a financial and legal framework – affording to all farmers encouragement and opportunity of involvement in the full development of the co-operative movement.

8. The right through their representative organisations to full consultation and involvement in the formulation and putting into effect of agricultural policy.
9. The right to protection against the effects of unchecked vertical integration or foreign control whether in the supply, processing, or marketing arms of agriculture.
10. The right to effective participation in the marketing of agricultural produce.
11. The right to carry no more than the fair share of taxation; in particular the right to relief from systems of taxation such as local rates which are not proportionate to the ability to pay.

Although many of these demands were within the remit of the Department of Agriculture, others, such as taxation and social security, were not. As we saw in the previous chapter, the government had already introduced measures to assist small farmers and communities in underdeveloped rural areas, without any input from the NFA. Despite this long list of demands, Seán Lemass believed that the issue at stake was who should determine Irish agricultural policy. In a letter to John B. Murphy, the secretary of the Seán Moylan Cumann of Fianna Fáil, in Kiskeam, County Cork, he remarked that the government regarded the NFA campaign 'as an attempt to undermine the authority of the elected Government and to make it subservient in regard to agricultural policy, to the NFA leadership'. Lemass claimed that the government had taken the only possible stand in the circumstances, by refusing to meet the NFA leadership. He sent a similar message to Deasy some days later. [112] A secondary theme in the government's response was the suggestion, which had often surfaced in the past in memoranda from Patrick Smith, that the NFA was not fully representative of Irish farmers. On 28 October Lemass told the Dáil that, 'we are not being asked to meet the Irish farmers. This is a small group of ambitious men who want us to forego our responsibility for agricultural policy'. Haughey made both these points when he told the Fianna Fáil National Executive that the protest concerned a leadership struggle between the NFA and the ICMSA, but 'a responsible organisation could not and should not be allowed to usurp the functions of government'.[113]

The character of the NFA protest and the government's tough stance were consistent with the state of industrial relations in the mid-1960s. The number of days lost through strike action rose sharply between 1962 and 1964, and increased further in 1965 and 1966. The economic recession that began in 1965, and continued into 1966, prompted the government to take a tough stand on wage demands, but with limited effect. In 1966 only 49 per cent of Labour Court recommendations were accepted by workers, compared with 80 per cent in 1961. Some disputes became extremely militant. In 1965 a dispute by telephonists over trade union recognition led to sympathetic strikes, protest marches and hunger strikes. When ESB fitters went on strike during the summer of 1966, the government introduced emergency legislation outlawing strike action. The Labour Court noted that pay claims in 1966 'were fought with a tenacity seldom previously experienced'.[114] Any concessions to the NFA would have had repercussions for incomes policy and industrial relations throughout the economy.

On 2 November the *Irish Press* reported that Seán Lemass was planning to retire as Taoiseach.[115] He tried to use his time as caretaker Taoiseach, before the election of his successor, to broker a settlement with the NFA, and for a time this appeared to be successful. The NFA ended its sit-down protest; it had a meeting with Lemass and Haughey, and Lemass promised that his successor would also meet them. The new Taoiseach, Jack Lynch, and the new Minister for Agriculture, Neil Blaney, met a deputation from the NFA on 21 November. But when the NFA demanded a further meeting with the Taoiseach, four days later, Lynch refused the request. He informed the NFA that any further meetings should be with the Minister for Agriculture. Lynch and Blaney met the ICMSA on 30 November, and on the following day the NFA resumed its sit-down outside the offices of the Department of the Taoiseach and the Department of Agriculture. The pickets remained in place until 19 December, when the NFA escalated its protest by blocking roads with farm machinery. Most major national routes were blocked on 9 January. With no end to the dispute in sight, an inter-departmental committee met at the Department of Justice to consider what actions should be taken. It discussed a number of options, such as removing future roadblocks and seizing cattle in lieu of unpaid rates.[116] By the end of February a total of thirty-eight members of the NFA were in jail and Fine Gael TD Gerard Sweetman approached Lynch seeking a settlement, but the Taoiseach adopted a tough line: 'the situation could be ended, not by Government action but by the Association reverting to methods which are within the law'. Lynch reiterated Lemass' line that the government must be free to determine policy without pressure from any section of society.[117]

Blaney took advantage of the dispute to revise the Department's procedures for consultation with farm organisations. In January 1967 he announced that he planned to establish a national agricultural council, which would play a similar role in relation to agriculture to the NIEC.[118] He submitted a memorandum to the Cabinet some weeks later, recommending that the government should withdraw the agreement that had been reached with the NFA in 1964. In its place he proposed to establish a national agricultural council. The fourteen-member council would comprise two representatives each from the General Council of Committees of Agriculture, the NFA, the ICMSA, the Irish Beet Growers' Association and six ministerial appointees, who would be drawn from interest groups not adequately represented by the four main organisations, such as liquid milk producers, sheep farmers, and small farmers from northern and western counties. The council would become a national forum for discussions on agricultural policy between representatives of the farming community and the Minister. This would include an annual review of the position and prospects for agriculture, replacing the review that was previously conducted with the NFA. However, the existence of the council would not preclude meetings between the Minister and individual farming organisations. Blaney expressed a wish to see the national agricultural council nominate a member to the NIEC. If this happened the Department would appoint an official to serve on the NIEC, which would be transformed into the National Economic Council.[119]

On 5 March the NFA announced that it was embarking on a commodity strike, but this was abandoned on 11 March. Other protests ended three days later, and sixty-five farmers were released from prison. The Government Information Bureau issued a statement welcoming the end of the dispute, and noting that the way was now open for a meeting between the Minister for Agriculture and the NFA.[120] When Lynch and Blaney met the NFA on 21 March – a meeting that lasted seven hours[121] – the national agricultural council was one of the items under discussion. Two days later the council of the NFA announced that it could not accept the government's unilateral decision to end the arrangements for an annual review of agriculture, which were agreed in January 1964. Although the NFA protested that it was willing to co-operate with the ICMSA and other producer organisations in establishing representative negotiating machinery, it was not prepared 'to be manoeuvred into participation in an NAC about which little is known except that it seems to be open to political influence and to lack independence'. However, a private letter from Deasy to Blaney, that accompanied this statement, adopted a more conciliatory tone:

> I find it hard to understand why you were so insistent that we should have welcomed your proposal for a National Agricultural Council. I would have thought that you would have attached greater weight to a welcome from us if we had received sufficient information on the proposal to enable us to welcome it in good faith and with a full understanding of the proposal under consideration.

This suggests that the national executive of the NFA was adopting a more militant line than the president, and this interpretation is supported by the press release that the Department of Agriculture issued in response to the NFA statement. The Department claimed that on 21 March the NFA delegation had agreed that a pre-budget review should be conducted with the Minister on an *ad hoc* basis by convening the National Agricultural Council; it had also agreed to recommend to its executive that it should announce an end to the NFA rates campaign.[122]

The National Agricultural Council (NAC) met on two occasions in the run-up to the 1967 budget, but NFA members did not attend and the NFA rates protest continued.[123] On 11 April Charles Haughey, introducing his first budget, announced that all agricultural holdings with a valuation of less then £20 would be de-rated, and scaled relief would be granted to all holdings with a valuation from £20 to £33.[124] When this failed to bring the rates protest to an end, Lynch made a television broadcast on 24 April, reiterating that the law of the land would be upheld. The NFA called off the dispute four days later, but a number of individual farmers continued to defy rates demands.[125] The NFA continued to boycott meetings of the NAC. In August 1968 the Cabinet decided that the NAC should be discontinued when its two-year term ended early in 1969.

> The general feeling seemed to be that the best line would be for the Minister, at an appropriate stage to issue a statement indicating that the Council as at present constituted has done excellent work, that he still considers that it is the best and the most appropriate form of organisation for the purpose it is meant to serve, but if all the major farming organisations are not prepared to join it, he would appeal to them to set about forming their own organisation, with a view to its succeeding the Council when the latter's two-year term of office expires in February next.[126]

The final meeting of the NAC took place on 22 August 1968.[127] In January 1969 Jack Lynch held a surprise meeting in Cork with NFA president

T. J. Maher, in an attempt to re-establish regular consultation between the NFA and the government. However, relations did not proceed smoothly. The *Irish Press* reported that 'The NFA has been guaranteed access to the Department of Agriculture and full rights to negotiate and consult with the Government in planning future farming policies'. The article quoted a remark by T. J. Maher that, 'As of today, I can walk into the Department and meet the Minister man to man'.[128] A bulletin issued to NFA members claimed that the NFA had been granted the right of consultation on all commodities, and 'on all problems of concern to the 80,000 dairy members of the Association'. Neil Blaney was clearly uncomfortable with the NFA's claim to represent all farmers, and the belief that the organisation had the right to meet the Minister and officials of the Department of Agriculture at will. On 3 March he informed Cabinet colleagues that the NFA had demanded three meetings in an eight-day period, and he was not prepared to concede their demands; to do so would be to revert 'to the ridiculous situation of the mid-60s'; he was determined to establish 'proper consultation machinery'. Blaney drew a distinction between negotiation and consultation. The Department was not prepared to negotiate agricultural policy with the NFA, but it would agree to consultative meetings, provided that they followed agreed arrangements. Although Blaney met the NFA and the ICMSA on several occasions in the following months, he refused to negotiate on agricultural policy. When he announced a revised scheme of milk prices in October 1969, without first consulting the NFA, Tom Blake, the acting president of the NFA issued a press release claiming that 'Mr. Blaney believes in dictation not in consultation'.[129] The fall-out from the 1966/7 dispute dissipated very slowly.

One feature of the farmers' dispute that concerned Nagle was 'the persistent attacks on Civil Servants'. He feared that 'once begun, this practice could spread'. In November 1966 he sent Whitaker a selection of press-cuttings from national and provincial newspapers, suggesting that it would be desirable if the Department of Finance, which was responsible for personnel throughout the civil service, issued a statement setting out the government's attitude to campaigns against civil servants, who were unable to reply to public criticism. The press-cuttings consisted of reports of speeches and statements by NFA leaders and letters to the editor, and all placed the responsibility for the difficult relationship between the NFA and the Department on civil servants. A correspondent in *The Irish Times* suggested that what was needed 'and what we have never had in Upper Merrion Street, is a Minister with enough guts to tell the secretariat he will handle the problem his way'. Rickard Deasy claimed that Nagle and the deputy secretary, Michael Barry, had 'doctrinaire objections to marketing boards and doctrinaire objections to farmers having anything to do with them'. He also claimed that good ideas originating in the Agricultural Institute had been 'put-down by Victorian-minded civil servants'.[130]

The dispute between the NFA and the government erupted during an agricultural recession. Gross agricultural output fell by 4.5 per cent during 1965; in 1966 it rose by only 0.5 per cent and cattle prices fell by 5 per cent.[131] The depressed market for cattle had a particularly severe impact on small and medium-sized farmers who were forced to carry excess numbers of cattle through the winter because they were unable to sell them during the autumn. The Department of Agriculture wanted to introduce a temporary scheme to provide farmers with animal feed at reduced cost, and a special subsidy for spring nitrogen to encourage early grass, but the government refused. According to the Department of Finance,

> To carry out within the year a third salvage operation [this was a reference to the extension of the price guarantees for beef; the measures introduced in May 1966 and the temporary headage payments for fat cattle] on behalf of agriculture, which is essentially subject to seasonal hazards, would in the view of the Minister for Finance be a bad precedent, apart from being unwarranted on the facts of the feed situation.[132]

When the Department of Agriculture carried out a review of the *Second Programme for Economic Expansion* in April 1967, it noted that agricultural output had shown very little increase between 1964 and 1966. If the projected rate of expansion in the *Second Programme* was to be achieved, it was critical that Ireland join the EEC before 1970. However, it insisted that the revised projections should continue to be based on the assumption of EEC membership, despite the fact that the Department of Finance considered that 'this assumption would be unrealistic and lead to embarrassing results'. Even if Ireland joined the EEC before 1970, which Finance considered improbable, there would be a transitional period during which agriculture would not enjoy the full benefits of membership. Finance wished to revise projections for the growth of agricultural output downwards to an annual rate of 1.5 per cent, which was less than half the figure given in the *Second Programme*. Agriculture countered that a revision of this order would amount to an open admission that EEC entry was unlikely, and that the

Anglo-Irish Free Trade Area was of little value. It 'would be construed as an admission on the part of the Government of lack of confidence in the effectiveness of their agricultural policy, especially as the targets are aims not forecasts'. Agriculture claimed that large fluctuations in output were a feature of agriculture: 'a couple of good years could alter the position dramatically', and the cumulative effects of greater efficiency were likely to lead 'to a gathering momentum'. Reducing the target growth rate would have 'an adverse psychological effect on farmers and would lead farm organisations to push for more state assistance'. Agriculture claimed that even the expectation of EEC membership in the near future would spur farmers to greater productivity. If the government decided to rule out the possibility of joining the EEC before 1970, it recommended that the target annual growth rate for agriculture for the years 1967–70 should be 'at least 5 per cent'.[133]

But the Department of Finance stuck to its guns. It reiterated that, 'If a review is to be effective then it must be realistic'. This was preferable to 'excessive optimism'. However, the Finance memorandum was withdrawn from Cabinet on 9 May. Newspaper reports suggested that the *Second Programme* had been 'abandoned'.[134] The *Review of Progress, 1964–67*, published in the summer of 1967, revealed that all three sectors of the economy had fallen short of their targets. Agricultural output had risen by less than 2 per cent between 1964 and 1967, compared with a target of 16 per cent;[135] this was an average annual increase of 0.9 per cent.[136] However, agricultural incomes rose by an estimated 10 per cent in both 1967 and 1968, which suggests that the optimism expressed by the Department of Agriculture was not unjustified. In December 1968 Blaney told the Dáil that 'the trend in total agricultural income in 1967 and in 1968 has matched the trend in other sectors during these years, and the higher total income was shared by a lesser number of people'. He reiterated the commitment given in the *Second Programme* that all farmers who worked their land fully and efficiently 'will share equitably in the growing prosperity of the nation'.[137]

LIVESTOCK

In the late 1950s the number of cows fluctuated around a figure of 1.2 million, which was similar to the figure on the eve of World War I. By 1970 it had increased to 1.7 million. The increase in numbers was largely due to the calved heifer subsidy scheme, introduced in January 1964, which gave farmers a subsidy of £15 for every additional heifer in their herd.[138] By June 1964, six months after it had been introduced, Paddy Smith estimated that 75,000 animals would qualify for subsidies during the current year; a supplementary estimate would be necessary to meet the additional cost.[139] By the end of 1964 the number of milch cows and heifers in calf had increased by 151,000. In 1966 Charles Haughey, the Minister for Agriculture, told the Dáil that, thanks to the calved heifer scheme, 'we have at last broken through the hitherto seemingly impenetrable ceiling of around 1,200,000 cows which had persisted for nearly a century'.[140] When the scheme was discontinued in June 1969, the cow population was approximately 1.66 million, compared with 1.28 million in June 1960. However, the cost of adding an extra cow to the national herd was £34, more than twice the anticipated figure, since some farmers only increased their herds temporarily to take advantage of the subsidy, and others reduced cow numbers during these years. More intensive stocking rates created a need for more winter feed, at a time when the acreage of barley and root crops was declining. Agricultural advisers had been urging farmers to make silage since the early 1950s, and farmers were beginning to heed the message, but in 1966 the output of silage amounted to roughly one-seventh of the output of hay.[141]

The increased cow herd brought a substantial expansion in livestock output. In 1967 exports of cattle and beef were the equivalent of 1.4 million animals; the previous record was 1,077,000 in 1964. The Irish government's decision to extend British deficiency payments to all beef exports resulted in a substantial rise in beef exports, but the subsidy almost wiped out exports of fat cattle. In 1967 they totalled a mere 27,300, compared with over 205,000 in the previous year, while exports of carcase meat more than doubled from 69,000 tons in 1966 to almost 146,000 tons.[142] Ireland became the largest exporter of carcase beef to Britain for the first time in 1967, and imports of livestock from Northern Ireland rose sharply to meet part of the demand.[143] When an outbreak of foot and mouth disease was reported in Britain in the winter of 1967, the government imposed a complete ban on livestock imports and anyone entering the country from Britain was prohibited from visiting farming areas for twenty-one days. Vaccination against brucellosis was suspended, and the staff redeployed to confront the threat of foot and mouth disease. Many Irish emigrants responded to the government's call not to travel home for Christmas for fear of spreading the disease.[144] The improvement in the livestock trade continued in 1968, when livestock prices reached an all-time high. Yet the higher prices were mainly due to exchequer price supports, which cost almost £4.7 million by 1967/8, compared with £43,000 in 1964/5.[145] Livestock and beef exports were almost wholly reliant on the UK market; exports to EEC countries had almost disappeared. The US was the second most important market, accounting for 34,000 tons of manufacturing-quality cow beef in 1967. By 1968 imports of Irish beef to the US were subject to voluntary restrictions, and mandatory controls were in prospect. Store cattle exports failed to meet the 1965 target figure of 635,000.[146]

The growing diversity of Irish livestock breeds, which began in the early 1960s, continued. By 1972, in addition to Charollais, the Irish cattle herd had added several new species, such as Limousin, Pie Rouge, and Fleckvieh, also known as Simmental, and Charollais and Fleckvieh breeds had also been added to the herds at the AI stations. In 1965 two-thirds of cows inseminated at the AI stations were inseminated by dairy bulls, but the proportion inseminated by beef bulls increased in later years; by 1969 and 1970 they accounted for a majority of inseminations. The change probably reflected a growing awareness of over-supply of milk and the introduction in 1969 of a beef incentive scheme. In 1968 Hereford cattle displaced Friesians as the most popular breed. The wider range of breeds on offer prompted efforts to raise the standard of Shorthorn cattle, by creating pedigree herds in co-operation with the Irish Shorthorn Breeders' Association. In 1972 the Department introduced grants in respect of the progeny of selected Shorthorn cows, but in the first year only seventy-two payments were made. Despite the growing popularity of AI, the county committees of agriculture continued to operate their bull premium scheme, which had been in operation since the foundation of the DATI.[147] Scrub bulls continued to damage the quality of Irish livestock and in 1967 the Department ordered an intensive campaign to find these animals and legal proceedings were taken against the owners of 483 unlicensed bulls.[148]

The *First Programme for Economic Expansion* had highlighted the value of progeny testing as a means of improving the quality of livestock, but there was considerable scope for extending and refining its use, particularly in the evaluation of dairy traits. A 1966 paper by E. P. Cunningham to the Statistical and Social Inquiry Society of Ireland set out how this could be done, using a protocol devised by the Agricultural Institute that used statistical techniques developed by the US space programme. Perhaps the most interesting statement in this paper, given the long debate over dual-purpose cattle, was that 'the weight of contemporary evidence indicates no antagonism between beef and dairy traits – in other words that true dual-purpose cattle can be bred'.[149] A new programme for progeny testing of dairy bulls was introduced in 1969, following the model outlined in this paper. A new milk recording scheme began in 1972, and up to 6,000 pedigree animals were assessed every year in a weight-for-age record scheme.[150]

'THE RISING TIDE OF MILK'[151]

Milk prices had remained stable throughout most of the 1950s, and rose by less than the rate of inflation during 1958–63. The rate of price increase accelerated after 1964, and by 1968 farmers received one-third more for their milk than in 1960. These price increases were conceded, despite the growing difficulty in disposing of dairy exports. A higher milk price was one of the most common ways of placating farmers' grievances; dairy farming was regarded as the lynchpin of the Irish family farm, and higher prices were justified as an income supplement to farm families. The National Farm Survey for the years 1955–8 had revealed that dairy farming offered the best incomes for farmers on any given acreage.[152] By the late 1960s milk with its guaranteed price and monthly creamery cheques offered farmers a much more reliable income than the livestock trade, which was at the mercy of the volatile UK market. Although Paddy Smith encouraged the extension of dairy farming in western areas as a practical means of raising farm incomes, Munster remained the heartland of the dairy sector, and milk yields and herd sizes in Ulster and Connacht remained below the national average.[153] The expansion of dairy farming in western counties brought obvious benefits to individual farmers, but it exacerbated the problem of low productivity, which the Department was trying to alleviate.

In 1962 the Report of the Survey Team on the Dairying Industry indicated that it was essential to raise standards if the industry was to prosper within the EEC.[154] In 1965 the Department of Agriculture introduced a bonus payment for milk that met specific quality standards and by 1968 two-thirds of milk supplied to creameries qualified for this payment. The 1962 report also noted that the small size of creameries made it difficult to introduce modern management techniques, and it recommended that creameries should be rationalised into fewer and larger units.[155] This prompted renewed interest in the co-operative movement, as did the recommendation of the interdepartmental committee on small western farms that the creamery industry should be encouraged to expand in western counties. In 1960 almost two-thirds of the 188 co-operative creameries were located in Munster.

When the Department of Agriculture reviewed the Irish creamery sector in September 1962, it noted that the long-standing weakness of the Irish co-operative movement remained evident. Few milk suppliers were share-holders; the committees of co-operative societies tended to remain in the hands of the same families for generations and the success of any co-operative was largely determined by its manager. The lack of an educational foundation 'conducive to the development of a high sense of rural values' and the shortage of agricultural advisers were among the factors that had prevented the development of a strong co-operative movement. In sentences that could have been written by Horace Plunkett the Department noted that,

> A vigorous campaign appears to be necessary now to promote a healthier outlook towards cooperation and to arouse the interest of farmers generally in the potentialities of cooperation for the improvement of their lot. A greater sense of solidarity and common purpose is required throughout the whole cooperative movement.

The first step should be to create an effective co-operative council. The regulations governing co-operatives should be brought into line with modern practices elsewhere. The Department recommended that an independent survey of the co-operative movement should be carried out by a recognised expert from outside Ireland. This would stimulate discussion on co-operatives and provide a guide to future actions.

When Lemass met Henry Kennedy, the general secretary of the IAOS, to discuss the possible reform and expansion of the co-operative sector, Lemass told him that the government would not hesitate to provide money to encourage an expansion of the co-operatives, 'if it were convinced that the right kind of leadership would be available'. When Lemass raised the question of appointing an outside expert to report on the co-operative movement, Kennedy offered to suggest a name. Yet when he discussed the matter later with Nagle, Kennedy expressed doubts about the value of bringing in an outside expert. He claimed that 'all that is needed are the resources'. But Nagle was keen to commission a report and Kennedy suggested the name of Dr Joseph Knapp, who was employed by the Farmer Co-operative Service of the US Department of Agriculture. Knapp arrived in Ireland in June 1963, and completed his report by the following December.[156]

Knapp recommended that the IAOS should be reorganised so that it could provide stronger leadership and better technical services to the agricultural community. The IAOS should be given full responsibility for restructuring the dairy industry; the Dairy Disposal Company should be transferred to co-operative ownership; and the IAOS should broaden its activities to include all forms of agricultural co-operation. In order to achieve these objectives Knapp recommended that the annual government grant to the IAOS should be increased to £100,000, or nine times the current figure.[157]

Lemass gave the Knapp report his public support in a speech to Bally-clough Co-Operative Society. He expressed the hope that it would 'herald the beginning of a new era of Irish cooperation and Irish farming'. The report was welcomed by the NFA and the National Co-Operative Council, and it was endorsed by the annual general meeting of the IAOS. In May 1964 Lemass asked the Department of Agriculture for a progress report on its implementation. Michael Barry replied that the Department was encouraging the IAOS to reorganise itself as a first step. However, he warned that, in the Department's view, the society was devoting too much attention to providing engineering and architectural advice to co-operatives, and too little attention to providing basic education in the principles of co-operation. Barry added that co-operatives in counties Limerick and Kerry claimed that they would not proceed with any restructuring until the future of the Dairy Disposal Company had been settled. In the Department's opinion the transfer of the Dairy Disposal Company to co-operative ownership was 'a very complex matter' that should be postponed until the IAOS and the co-operatives had put their own houses in order.

Barry's comments indicated some reluctance within the Department of Agriculture to transfer the Dairy Disposal Company to co-operative ownership. In a memorandum submitted to Cabinet on the Knapp report in June 1964, the Department of Agriculture suggested that Knapp had been somewhat partisan in his research into the history of the Irish dairy industry, and that he had relied almost exclusively on the annual reports of the IAOS. It rejected Knapp's assumption that the Irish dairy industry consisted of two opposing blocs – the co-operatives and the Dairy Disposal Company. It claimed that the two often worked in co-operation. It was critical of Knapp's statement that 'the Dairy Disposal Company cannot be continued indefinitely as a Government enterprise if the Irish Government is to accept fully the encouragement of agricultural cooperation as a part of its national agricultural policy'. Knapp had recommended that the Dairy Disposal Company should be liquidated and its enterprises handed over to co-operative ownership, without any study of the company's current operations. This recommendation was backed up with vague statements, for example, 'that the efficiency of many Irish co-operatives already demonstrates that co-operatives have the management capability to take over these operations and run them efficiently'. Knapp failed to recommend whether the company should be replaced by one large co-operative, or by a number of co-operatives; all the detailed planning had been left to the IAOS. The Department suggested that any alteration in the structure of an organisation as large as the Dairy Disposal Company should not be undertaken lightly. The current trend was towards larger units, and the Report of the Survey Team on the Dairying Industry had recommended that creameries should be amalgamated. A decision to break up the largest unit in the Irish dairy industry – the Dairy Disposal Company processed 20 per cent of national milk output – would be a retrograde step.[158]

When Lemass was questioned in Dáil Éireann about the proposal to transfer the Dairy Disposal Company to co-operative control, he replied that the government did not object in principle to the proposal, but the practical difficulties were greater than Knapp appeared to appreciate.[159] The Dairy Disposal Company subsidised its smaller creameries from the profitable larger units; if the company was broken up there was a real danger that the smaller creameries would close. However, in the following year Haughey noted that the government had accepted the Knapp report, and a substantial grant would be given to the IAOS to enable it to reorganise its activities.[160] The rationalisation of creameries began in 1964 with the merger of Suirvale and Mitchelstown co-operatives. Seven independent creameries in South Tipperary merged in 1966 to form the South Tipperary Farmers' Co-Operative, and Ballyclough Creamery in north Cork absorbed several smaller creameries in the adjoining areas. Bulk collection of milk began in 1964/5 when the Department gave Waterford Co-Operative a grant to carry out a pilot scheme which was monitored by the Agricultural Institute.

The NAC commissioned a further report on the organisation of the Irish dairy industry in 1968. The authors were Hugh Cook, professor of agricultural economics at the University of Wisconsin, who was a noted expert on the marketing of dairy produce, and Gordon W. Sprague, who had worked for many years as an economist with a large dairy products co-operative in Minnesota. They reported that Ireland possessed the resources and the technology to create a modern dairy industry. There were farms with large dairy herds, modern milking parlours, and equipment for winter feeding, milk handling and refrigeration, which were comparable to those in any other major milk-producing country. But the scope for greater efficiency was limited by the small size of herds, which made it unprofitable to introduce milking machines and bulk collection. Seasonal fluctuations in milk output were another factor that reduced productivity. Cook and Sprague anticipated that the 1970s would bring further substantial increases in output, owing to continued improvements in grassland production, the expansion of dairying in western and northern counties, and higher yields per cow.[161]

Recent technological developments meant that the optimal size of a creamery was much larger than it had been in the early 1960s. There was a close association between the size of creameries and overall productivity: the most efficient dairy farmers were those that supplied the larger creameries, because large creameries offered better facilities. Cook and Sprague recommended that Irish creameries should be reorganised into units with an annual minimum supply of 1 million gallons of milk; this would bring major savings in the cost of production and improvements in quality. The restructuring should take place as quickly as possible, 'with the maximum of local initiative and leadership', but they acknowledged that 'this may require national programmes to develop and nurture' such leadership. Like Knapp they assumed that the reorganisation should be carried out through the co-operatives, with the Department of Agriculture and the IAOS working together through a co-ordinating committee. Within three years they wanted to see an end to the practice of returning skim milk to farmers; all milk should be cooled before collection and milk should be collected by hauliers, not delivered by individual farmers. Federated creameries should be established as a transitional step towards full mergers. Cook and Sprague recommended that the Dairy Disposal Company should continue in existence, with responsibility for developing dairying in western areas – the NFA had apparently objected to this proposal some years earlier[162] – and promoting increased consumption of dairy products in the Irish market in conjunction with An Bord Bainne.

The rationalisation of the creamery system proved to be a complex task. There was considerable local opposition to the closure of small local co-operatives, and the Minister set up a special group to advise him on the economic and social implications of the planned changes. By the early 1970s the process of rationalisation was gathering pace. In 1972, after several years of negotiation, which was brokered by the IAOS, four co-operative societies in counties Mayo, Sligo, Roscommon, Leitrim and Galway, came together to form North Connaught Farmers Ltd. Many smaller creameries had also closed or amalgamated in the dairy heartland of Cork, Waterford, Tipperary and Limerick, and the long and complex process of transferring the creameries owned by the Dairy Disposal Company to co-operative ownership was under way, but this was not completed for some years.[163] In 1971 the Pigs and Bacon Commission began to carry out a similar rationalisation of pig factories,[164] which had been first mooted during the 1930s.

One of the other major developments during the 1960s was the substantial rise in the amount of cheese produced. The total output of milk increased from 480 million gallons in 1960 to 775 million gallons by 1970, and the Department encouraged more creameries to produce cheese in order to reduce the butter surplus, which could only be exported at considerable cost to the exchequer. A system of cheese grading introduced in 1966 ensured that Irish cheese achieved premium prices in the UK market. By 1967 the quantity of cheese produced in Ireland was eleven times greater than in 1958 and there was a substantial rise in the output of skim milk powder. At the end of the 1960s, however, butter continued to account for three-quarters of the milk processed by Irish creameries.

In September 1968 the Department of Agriculture agreed to pay an additional 1d a gallon on the first 7,000 gallons of milk delivered by each supplier to a creamery. The ICMSA had been demanding a two-tier milk price for several years but the Department was opposed to its introduction. In May 1966 Charles Haughey told the Dáil that apart from the matter of cost – the higher price would apply to the majority of milk supplies – the Department believed that it would discourage farmers from increasing productivity. Where two-tier milk prices existed in other countries they were designed to restrict milk output, not to encourage an expansion.[165] In 1966 the Department commissioned a study on the matter by Lieutenant General M. J. Costello; E. A. Attwood, an economist attached to the Agricultural Institute; A. J. O'Reilly, the managing director of An Bord Bainne; Paddy O'Keefe of the *Irish Farmers' Journal*; and J. J. Scully, the Department's officer in charge of western development. They reported that the disadvantages of a two-tier milk price outweighed the advantages. If the government wished to provide special assistance to small farmers, they recommended that it should be done through a bonus incentive scheme for low-income farmers who drew up a farm development plan. This scheme would apply to all farm enterprises. To qualify, a dairy farmer would have to produce a plan showing that he was in a position to raise his output to at least 7,000 gallons of quality milk.[166] These recommendations were in line with the development plans that farmers in pilot areas were being encouraged to adopt, and a small farm incentive bonus scheme was introduced in 1968.[167]

The decision to introduce a two-tier milk price in September 1968, despite strong advice to the contrary from this inquiry team, was an attempt to stifle a campaign for higher milk prices. On 30 August the ICMSA announced it would launch 'the biggest campaign the country has ever seen' in support of its claims for an increase of 4½d per gallon in the price of milk, and this demand was supported by the NAC.[168] The ICMSA and the NFA placed pickets on Government Buildings in September 1968, in protest against an increase in the levy on milk producers by An Bord Bainne to meet the cost of export subsidies; under an arrangement introduced in 1958, one-third of the cost was borne by the industry, the balance by the exchequer.[169]

This protest at an increase in the milk levy reflected the growing problem in disposing of the dairy surplus. The 1965 Anglo-Irish Free Trade Area Agreement included a commitment that no restrictions would be imposed on Irish exports, other than butter, bacon, potatoes and wheat, without prior consultation. In August 1968 Britain asked all the countries that exported cheese to Britain to introduce voluntary restrictions on cheddar or cheddar-type cheese. The Irish authorities pointed out that An Bord Bainne only shipped cheese to Britain to meet agreed orders. Consequently, Ireland was not responsible for the rising stocks of unsold cheese, and Irish cheese was selling at higher prices than its competitors.[170] Cheese was not the only product under threat. An import levy on beef was being mooted, and MAFF had recently announced a further programme to expand UK farming. Britain had also introduced an import deposit scheme on all manufactured goods, without prior consultation, which was in breach of the 1965 agreement.

When Jack Lynch, accompanied by Nagle, met the British Minister for Agriculture, Food and Fisheries, Cledwyn Hughes, in November 1968, the Irish party set out two heads for discussion. The first was a request, yet again, that Britain and Ireland should be regarded as a single market for the purpose of cattle and beef. The second concerned Britain's proposal to restrict Irish cheese imports to 30,100 tons over a two-year period ending on 31 March 1970. Lynch demanded a minimum quota of 37,000 tons. He remarked that when the 1965 agreement was being negotiated the Irish team had not been given any indication that restrictions might be imposed on cheese. Cledwyn Hughes offered a cheese quota of 33,000 tons. He pointed out that Ireland's agricultural exports to Britain had increased from £105 million to £135 million between 1965 and 1968. He also indicated that Britain was demanding that Irish cattle shipments should be phased.[171]

Ireland continued to demand a minimum quota of 37,000 tons. In January 1969 Hugh McCann, the secretary of the Department of External Affairs, told the Irish ambassador in London that cheese had become 'a touchstone to the whole agricultural side of the Anglo-Irish Free Trade Area Agreement'. Anti-agreement feeling was mounting in Ireland and it would increase if Britain imposed anti-dumping measures on Irish cheese. When the British Board of Trade applied for the imposition of anti-dumping measures against Irish cheese, the Department of Agriculture presented a strong counter-case. It pointed out that New Zealand cheese was not treated as causing material injury to the British domestic industry, despite the fact that it sold at £5 per ton less than Irish cheese, and it received state assistance. Norwegian and Danish cheeses were not mentioned either, although they also received state assistance and commanded even lower prices. An increased milk output was a necessary by-product of higher cattle numbers, and Irish livestock output had expanded to meet British market needs. In February Nagle informed the British ambassador, Sir Andrew Gilchrist, that 'everybody on the Irish side was very fed up' over the manner in which Britain had handled Irish cheese exports. Some weeks later it emerged that Britain was also planning to reduce the Irish butter quota from 26,000 to 23,000 tons. The Department complained that British butter output was rising sharply, but Ireland was not being given its fair share of the market as agreed in 1965.

The reduction in the butter quota was announced at a time when Ireland was preparing for talks with Britain on the cattle trade. The Department of Agriculture wanted to introduce a system of deficiency payments that would be similar to the British fat-stock guarantee scheme, but with a lower guaranteed price. The scheme would be jointly certified by Britain and Ireland, and they would share the cost. The Department had been considering such a scheme for some time. It believed that a deficiency payments scheme, coupled with a guarantee of full and unimpeded access to the UK market, was essential to secure a long-term expansion of livestock output. It also claimed that this was the opinion of the farm organisations. If farmers were given greater security about markets and prices, beef would provide 'a very necessary counter-attraction to milk'. Most Irish livestock was sold in the autumn and Britain was threatening to impose a variable import levy on imports of livestock and beef, ostensibly to encourage a more even flow throughout the year. The Department of Agriculture claimed that deficiency payments could be used to similar effect, and it believed that their introduction might avert the threat of UK import levies. As the Irish government had been funding deficiency payments on all Irish beef exported to the UK since 1966, the Department's proposal should be seen as an extension of the existing price supports for beef.

When British and Irish ministers met for trade talks in London on 27/8 February 1969 no progress was achieved, although Harold Wilson ended Ireland's annual payment of £250,000 in reparation for damage to property during the Irish War of Independence. These payments had been due to continue until 1985.[172] A meeting in Dublin some weeks later proved more fruitful. Britain confirmed Ireland's right of access to the British market for agricultural produce; Ireland's butter quota was confirmed at 26,000 tons, with a secret undertaking of an additional 1,000 tons later in the year; and the cheese quota was set at 35,000 tons over two years. However, Neil Blaney warned that if the restrictions that had been applied to cheese were extended to other commodities, the 1965 agreement would become worthless for Ireland.[173]

In February 1969 the Department introduced a beef cattle incentive scheme, designed to encourage an expansion in the number of beef cattle without a corresponding increase in milk. Grants of £12 were provided for the third or additional cow that was matched by a calf on holdings that did not produce milk on a commercial basis. Neil Blaney claimed that the scheme was designed 'to provide some reasonable counter-attraction to milk',[174] at a time when the cost of disposing of dairy produce was rising. Yet the Department was increasingly concerned to ensure the future of Irish beef and livestock exports to the UK. Britain had rejected all Irish proposals concerning livestock and beef during the talks in Dublin in March 1969, and the Department believed that it was planning to introduce some form of import levy on beef. When British and Irish officials met for trade talks in October 1969, the British proposals turned out to be similar to what the Department of Agriculture had anticipated: variable levies on beef imports, and a corresponding measure of price discipline for domestic producers. Britain indicated that the talks were purely exploratory, but contested the Irish claim that the proposals would be contrary to the 1965 agreement.[175] Britain offered to exempt Irish beef exports, on condition that Ireland agreed to the support price for Irish beef, provided under the 1965 agreement, being abated. When the committee of secretaries discussed this proposal, Nagle claimed that it was inevitable that Irish beef would be subjected to import levies, although the effects could be largely offset by deficiency payments. Nagle argued that it would be advisable to reach an agreement on agricultural trade with Britain, because a general election was expected within the next twelve months, and he feared that a Conservative government would be less accommodating.

When the Anglo-Irish Economic Committee (a committee of senior officials) met on 13/14 November 1969, the Irish delegation expressed dissatisfaction with the market for agricultural exports. Irish officials noted that 'our agricultural gains under the Agreement had been limited, contrary to expectations, and the recent trend towards restrictions on agricultural imports by Britain was a cause of concern to us'. The deficit in the Irish balance of trade with Britain had been increasing for several years, which suggested that Britain had been the main beneficiary from the 1965 trade agreement. When British and Irish ministers met in December, Haughey protested at 'the failure of the British Government to recognise that access to the British market for Irish agricultural products was an essential and fundamental element in the operation of the Agreement'. Such protests were of little more than symbolic value; Britain deferred detailed discussions on beef until the following year.[176] In 1970 Britain announced that it would introduce variable import levies on imports of cattle, beef, mutton and lamb, and on milk products other than butter and cheese, which were already controlled by quota. There were lengthy negotiations between British and Irish officials on this matter, with Irish officials reiterating Ireland's rights under the 1965 Anglo-Irish Free Trade Area Agreement. In the end it was agreed that the new provisions would not be applied to Ireland provided that Ireland's subsidies for beef were kept in line with payments under the British fat-stock price guarantee. In the case of dairy produce other than cheese and butter, Ireland gave an undertaking to keep exports at existing levels, which was very similar to the voluntary agreement of 1958. In return Britain agreed not to impose import levies on Irish dairy produce.[177]

The decision in 1969 to establish Córas Beoistoic agus Feola (CBF), the livestock and meat marketing board, must be seen in the context of the Department of Agriculture's strategy for the Irish beef and livestock trade in the UK. The Report of the Store Cattle Study Group recommended that the government should establish a livestock promotion authority.[178] The NFA did not approve of the decision to make CBF responsible for promoting both livestock and beef, and it also objected to the fact that unlike An Bord Bainne and the Pigs and Bacon Commission, CBF's role was entirely promotional; it took responsibility for stands at trade fairs, and other activities that had previously been carried out directly by the Department of Agriculture.[179] If the Department's views had prevailed, CBF would have functioned along similar lines to the other organisations, operating a deficiency payments scheme for Irish beef.

THE *THIRD PROGRAMME FOR ECONOMIC AND SOCIAL EXPANSION*

The negotiations over Irish agricultural exports to the UK became closely embroiled with the development of the final draft of the *Third Programme for Economic and Social Expansion*. When the *Second Programme* was abandoned in 1967, the Department of Finance began work on its successor, the *Third Programme*, covering the years 1969–72, which would not include targets for individual commodities. The Department of Finance projections provided for an annual rise of only 1 per cent in agricultural output, but the Department of Agriculture pressed for a target growth rate of 2.5 per cent. The first draft compromised on 1.75 per cent, but Agriculture refused to accept a figure below 2 per cent. It claimed that many of the factors that reduced the growth rate during the *Second Programme*, such as bad weather, the collapse of the British livestock market in 1966, and credit restrictions in Britain and Ireland in the mid-1960s, were unlikely to recur. A growth target of 1.75 per cent appeared extremely low, when industrial output was expected to rise at an annual rate of 6.5 per cent; 2 per cent was 'presentationally better'. If Ireland published a low growth target for agriculture, the Department feared that Britain would use it to impose further restrictions on Irish agricultural exports, because in the 1965 trade agreement Britain had agreed to take the targets in the *Second Programme* into consideration when regulating agricultural imports. Finance insisted that 1.75 per cent was 'the very upper limit'. It pointed out that the figure related to physical output, not farm incomes. Price changes and falling employment in agriculture would ensure that average incomes would rise at a much higher rate. On 3 January 1969 the Cabinet accepted the target growth rate of 1.75 per cent.[180]

The *Third Programme* set six objectives for agricultural policy:

1. Increasing the efficiency in the production, processing and marketing of farm products;
2. Ensuring that agriculture made the highest possible contribution to economic and social progress;

3. Ensuring that farmers who worked their land fully and efficiently would share in the growing national prosperity and that a reasonable relationship would be maintained between farm incomes and incomes in other sectors;
4. Improving the structure of agriculture and strengthening the competitive capacity of viable family farms;
5. Aiding smaller and more vulnerable farms to secure an acceptable level of income;
6. Improving the conditions of access to external markets for agricultural exports.

These objectives were very much a restatement of agricultural policy over the preceding decade, although the first objective, linking production, processing and marketing as integral elements in an agricultural policy, indicates a move away from the older emphasis on commodities towards a modern food and agricultural industry. The objectives set out above were also consistent with the CAP and the Mansholt Plan for European agriculture, which was published in December 1968.[181]

On 27 January 1969 the secretary of the Department of Finance, Charlie Murray, sent Nicholas Nolan a memorandum on the *Third Programme*. This noted that it had been agreed to consult the NFA and the ICMSA on agricultural aspects; any resulting changes would be brought to the government's notice. Murray informed Nolan that the Department of Finance wished to include a paragraph setting out the extent to which dairy exports were currently subsidised and estimates of the future cost of dairy subsidies. However, the Department of Agriculture was insisting that this paragraph should be removed, because it was concerned that the information would be used to justify the introduction of anti-dumping measures against Irish dairy produce in Britain.[182] Agriculture later claimed that the estimates for the future cost of dairy subsidies failed to allow for the possibility that agricultural market conditions and prices would improve. Price subsidies were extremely high at the time because of the 'exceptionally depressed state of the dairy products market'. In the Department's opinion,

… a real imponderable is the extent to which increased financial subvention to agriculture will be necessary to implement the Government's commitment on income relationships. This will depend not only on output, input and price movements in agriculture but also on the degree of success attending income restraint policy in other sectors.

The Department recommended that the *Third Programme* should only include broad indications of the future cost of price subsidies,[183] and its view prevailed: the published version of the *Third Programme* followed the lines favoured by the Department of Agriculture.

By 1970 the estimate for the Department of Agriculture was the largest of any government department. Price subsidies accounted for £36.5 million, almost half of total expenditure. The £30.5 million bill for dairy subsidies presented the greatest headache. In 1960/1 dairy subsidies cost the exchequer £4.7 million, or 3.7d of the average price of 19.63d per gallon of milk. In 1968/9 this had increased to 11.7d per gallon, more than 40 per cent of the total price of 25.71d. The price of milk, minus subsidies, was lower than in 1960.[184] With quota restrictions on sales of butter, skim milk and cheese to the UK, export markets had to be found for the equivalent of 150 million gallons of milk, often at a considerable loss.[185] Exports of butter to markets other than the UK earned an estimated 3.3d per gallon of milk, when the cost of manufacturing the butter was taken into account.[186] The Department wanted farmers to increase the quantity of milk that was fed to pigs and calves, but ironically during the 1960s less milk was used as animal feed than before, because creameries began to process skim milk for export, and the change to bulk collection meant that skim milk was no longer being returned to farmers.[187] The Department urged the Cabinet to approve regulations banning the advertising of margarine, and requiring margarine manufacturers to use butterfat as a raw material. But these proposals were opposed by the Department of Industry and Commerce and the Department of Health (both mentioned the word cholesterol) and the proposals were withdrawn.[188] Nevertheless, they indicate the desperate need to find outlets for milk.

In October, with Fianna Fáil safely returned to power in the 1969 general election, the Department announced a new, more complex structure for milk prices, which was a development of the two-tier milk price introduced the previous year. The highest price was again offered for the first 7,000 gallons, with tiered price reductions for larger amounts. A producer would receive no price support from the exchequer for an annual output in excess of 60,000 gallons.

Although the increased output of milk was an inevitable consequence of rising livestock numbers, it also reflected the positive benefits of dairy farming. Dairy farming provided a satisfactory income on medium-sized farms, plus the security of a monthly milk cheque, which brought farming households into closer conformity with the income patterns of wage and salaried workers. In 1970 Bob O'Connor, an agricultural economist at the ESRI, noted that the expansion in milk was achieved at the expense of a declining output of sheep and wheat – products that attracted smaller exchequer subsidies. Although wheat prices rose during the 1960s by almost the same amount as milk prices, farmers opted for milk because production was less vulnerable to bad weather.

In 1970 the Department published a review of state expenditure on agriculture to see how far it conformed with the objectives set out in the *Third Programme*. It recommended that expenditure should be concentrated on measures that would increase economic growth; less money should be spent on milk subsidies, more in assisting farmers to produce products for which there was a profitable market. The range of subsidies should be reduced, and they should be allocated on a more selective basis. Grants and subsidies should be directed towards farmers who had prepared a comprehensive farm development scheme, which showed that they were capable of achieving a substantial increase in output. Farmers who were not regarded as potentially commercial should be given financial induce-ments to retire. Work on this report began in 1967. By the time it was completed, Ireland had been accepted as a future member of the EEC, which meant that the Irish exchequer would not have to meet the full cost of supporting agriculture in the long term. Nevertheless, the government decided to publish the report in the hope that it would stimulate discussion on issues that would remain relevant after Ireland's entry to the EEC.[189]

The first tentative steps towards Ireland's renewed application for EEC membership were taken when Neil Blaney met the EEC's Com-missioner for Agriculture, Sicco Mansholt, in January 1967.[190] Ireland's application was formally reactivated in May 1967. The EEC member states agreed in principle on the enlargement of the EEC in December 1969, and negotiations opened in June 1970. In April 1970 the Department of Agriculture published a report entitled *Irish Agriculture and Fisheries in the EEC*,[191] and the government issued a white paper on the implications of EEC membership. The Department's main concerns related to transitional arrangements for Irish agriculture, Anglo-Irish trade during the transitional period, and measures to protect animal and plant health.[192] It anticipated that most Irish agricultural exports would continue to go to the UK, although exports of beef and livestock to other EEC member countries were expected to rise. The Treaty of Accession, signed on 22 January 1972, provided for a five-year transition. During this time agricultural prices would adjust to EEC levels; internal tariffs with other EEC members would be removed; and external tariffs would be adjusted to the EEC's common external tariff. The Department secured important derogations on the import of live animals and meat, in order to protect animal health.[193]

Administrative Reforms

In 1965 the Minister for Agriculture was given responsibility for fisheries and the title of the Department was changed to the Department of Agriculture and Fisheries, the first change in title since the 1930s. By the late 1960s the Department consisted of two principal administrative divisions and three technical branches, with a staff in excess of 3,000. The structure had evolved in a largely *ad hoc* manner.

According to the Devlin Commission on the Organisation of the Public Service, which was published in 1969, 'The distribution of work arose through experience of the individuals and has been re-arranged from time to time to suit changes at Assistant Secretary level'. There was no functional uniformity in how responsibilities were grouped. When a second post as deputy secretary was created in 1965, the new appointee took responsibility for supervising two divisions with which he was already familiar. Each deputy secretary was concerned with the development of farm facilities, farm output improvement, commodity market control, and economic considerations of agriculture. The Devlin Report claimed that the task of co-ordinating the Department's wide range of responsibilities was forced up to the highest level, which meant that the secretary was 'over-burdened with detail' (this problem was not unique to the Department of Agriculture). Professional and technical staff had no executive power: they made recommendations, but the decision to implement, or not, was taken by administrative staff; this led to duplication and delay. The Devlin Report concluded that the Department's work was impaired by a lack of co-ordination, both internally, and between the Department and outside bodies. Although many of the Department's schemes had been effective in raising output and improving the quality of agricultural produce, some of these had been introduced hurriedly 'through pressure from the farmers'. The Devlin Commission recommended that all schemes should be subject to review and properly integrated within a national plan for agriculture, together with the research carried out by the Agricultural Institute and the work of the county committees of agriculture.

The Devlin Report recommended that the Department's activities should be grouped on a functional basis, with the administrative and technical elements being integrated within each functional area. Special units would be responsible for planning, finance, personnel and organisation. Separate units should be developed in the Department and related bodies to co-ordinate plans; the execution of agreed plans should be delegated to properly staffed units. The respective roles of the Department and the county committees should be clarified. The Agricultural Institute would report directly to the secretary, while the head of the Department's planning unit would serve on the council of the Agricultural Institute.[194]

One of the most important recommendations in the Devlin report was the merging of the Department of Agriculture and the Department of Lands in a new Department of Agriculture and Lands. Devlin anticipated that the Farm Improvement Service would be the largest unit in the new department, with a staff of 1,000. The new service would be responsible for farm buildings, credit, pilot areas, western development, livestock breeding and inspection, eggs, poultry and dairy produce, cereals, fertiliser and horticulture. It would also be responsible for agricultural education and for an expanded and reformed advisory service.[195] The central role given by the Devlin Report to the Farm Improvement Service, and the recommendation for a merger of the departments of Lands and Agriculture, is evidence that farm structures had come to be seen as one of the most critical aspects of agricultural policy.

IRISH AGRICULTURE ON THE THRESHOLD OF EEC MEMBERSHIP

In April 1968 the Agricultural Adjustment Unit at the University of Newcastle-on-Tyne organised a conference on 'Irish Agriculture in a Changing World'. In a postscript to the book of the same name, which contained the conference papers, the editors, I. F. Baillie and Seamus Sheehy, remarked:

> As speaker succeeded speaker, a sense of gloom and pessimism seemed to settle over the conference. While the inevitability of change and the need for readjustment were accepted, there was a feeling of helplessness. Ireland appeared to be trapped by remorseless economic and social pressures from within and without, and little hope was seen of changing the direction of existing policies or of influencing the formulation of new policies.[196]

This was typical of the response to Irish agricultural matters on the eve of Ireland's entry to the EEC. These were years of immense change: the breeding stock was undergoing a major transformation; the dairy industry was responding to market pressures by developing new products, such as quality cheese; rapid mechanisation of the Irish grain harvest meant that millers could no longer cope with the pressure from farmers to provide storage and drying facilities;[197] the horticulture sector, which still benefited from a protected market, was supplying a record 70 per cent of fruit and vegetables in the processing industry, and over 90 per cent of the domestic market;[198] and the co-operative movement was undergoing a major programme of reform. The extensive list of reports commissioned by the Department of Agriculture indicates that a greater range of policies were under review than ever before. The first sustained analysis of structural problems in Irish farming was initiated in the 1960s, and the first major review of the advisory service.

Between 1960 and 1968 family farm income rose by 52 per cent, the number of family-farm-members fell by 17 per cent and the average income per head by 82 per cent in current prices; real incomes rose by 33 per cent. The Annual Report of the Minister for Agriculture and Fisheries for 1973/4 remarked that:

> Over the past decade agricultural production has tended to become more specialised, both at the industry level with the growing concentration on cattle and milk and at the individual farm enterprise. This is part of the general move towards a more commercial system of agricultural production. It is evident that the development of more intensive farm enterprises will proceed further in the coming years.[199]

How do we reconcile these significant developments, with the sense of pessimism? One factor that contributed to the prevailing gloom was the preoccupation with economic programmes that set out policy objectives and statistical targets by which success or failure were measured. Target growth rates came to be seen as an indication of agriculture's standing in the wider economy. In February 1969, when NFA leader T. J. Maher met Neil Blaney to discuss the sections concerning agriculture in the *Third Programme*, he described them as 'totally inadequate', and asked to be supplied with detailed growth targets for individual commodities. Blaney informed him that the government did not plan to set targets for individual commodities, because the targets in the *Second Programme* had led to an 'undue preoccupation with statistical detail rather than policies'.[200] A preoccupation with statistical detail, and with comparative statistics, was very much a feature of this period.

The practice of drawing comparisons between urban and rural incomes, and relative increases, also contributed to dissatisfaction among farmers. Irish farm organisations wanted to engage in price negotiations, similar to the British NFU, or in negotiations that would be akin to the wage bargaining of modern trade unions. But successive ministers for Agriculture were keen to point out that farmers were not wage-earners, and the relationship between the Department and the farmers was not one of employer and employee. In 1968 Neil Blaney remarked that 'farmers are businessmen or entrepreneurs and they are not employed by the Government in the same way as a trade union member might be employed in an industry'.[201] Nevertheless, during the 1960s, government ministers and officials in the Department increasingly drew a distinction between agricultural output and farm incomes, and government expenditure accounted for the largest share of the increase in farm incomes during that decade.[202]

The most intractable problem facing Irish agriculture was its long-term future. The numbers engaged in farming were declining throughout the developed world, and markets were over-supplied with produce. Between 1961 and 1971 the numbers employed in agriculture and forestry fell by more than one-quarter, and the pattern in other European countries indicated that this process would probably continue. Although EEC membership would reduce Ireland's dependence on the UK market, and it promised substantially higher prices for farm produce, it would not resolve the long-term problems of structural adjustment and a declining workforce in farming. In December 1968 the EEC published the Mansholt Plan, which set out a long-term programme for structural reform. The plan anticipated that 5 million people throughout the EEC would leave farming during the 1970s.[203] EEC membership therefore presented a major challenge to the Department of Agriculture and to Irish farming, not least the need to bring about a transformation of Irish agriculture that would be acceptable to Irish farmers and to the wider community.

CHAPTER TEN

FROM MANSHOLT TO MACSHARRY: 1973–2000

The impact of Irish membership of the European Economic Community (EEC)[1] on the Department of Agriculture deserves a separate book. This chapter can only provide a brief outline. Until Ireland became a member of the EEC in January 1973, agricultural policy was formulated exclusively by the government on the advice of the Minister for Agriculture and his Department. Of course, policy decisions had to take account of conditions in the major export markets, particularly the United Kingdom. Farm organisations also gained increased influence over agricultural policy during the 1960s. But any request by the Department of Agriculture for an increase in the agricultural estimate, had to compete with the demands of other government departments. In 1962, for example, Seán Lemass told farming representatives, who were pressing for additional assistance, that the needs of agriculture had to be balanced against demands for higher spending on education and social welfare.[2]

The EEC's Common Agricultural Policy (CAP) was the framework within which farm policy and, in particular, price and market policy was conducted, and most of the funding for agriculture began to come from Community resources. In the financial year 1973–74, Ireland's first full year as a member of the EEC, the estimate for the Department of Agriculture fell by almost £20 million to £59.5 million; it fell by a further £10 million in the following year. By 1978, which was the end of the transitional period, the EEC paid for 70 per cent of Irish public expenditure on agriculture, and this had increased to 88 per cent by 1988.[3]

One former secretary of the Department of Agriculture has remarked that once Ireland joined the EEC, the major policy decisions were taken in

Brussels, although the Department had 'a certain degree of discretion' in deciding how they should be applied in Ireland.[4] However, this statement underestimates the Department's role in formulating agricultural policy. Since 1973 Irish ministers for agriculture and senior civil servants have played a prominent role in all negotiations concerning the Community's agricultural policy, and in determining agricultural prices for the coming year.

The main economic purpose behind Ireland's application for membership of the EEC was the belief that it would bring major benefits to Irish agriculture and a significant rise in farm incomes. Once Ireland became a member of the Community, the Department of Agriculture set out to ensure that the anticipated benefits were realised to the full. All the major Irish political parties supported the CAP, so that changes of government during the 1970s, 1980s and 1990s had little impact on Ireland's stance in EEC farm talks. The financial benefits of EEC aid for agriculture proved to be considerable: between 1973 and 1999, net CAP transfers to Ireland totalled £22 billion, bringing about a significant improvement in rural living standards.[5] For the years 1979–86 they amounted to an average 7 per cent of GNP.[6]

In 1973 the CAP accounted for two-thirds of the total EEC budget[7] and the Community's policy towards agriculture was much more developed than policies towards industry, the environment, education and social welfare. The Department of Agriculture had stationed a representative in Brussels since the early 1960s, and the Department played an important role in negotiating Ireland's terms of entry, so it was already familiar with the workings of the Community when Ireland became a member.

The change from a national agricultural policy to one that was Community-based presented an immense challenge for the first generation of ministers and officials. The Department of Agriculture probably had greater experience of international negotiations than any department, other than External Affairs; trade talks with Britain had been a regular feature of the Department's work since the late 1930s. However, Britain had held the trump cards in those talks, whereas EEC agricultural policy was determined mainly by the Council of Ministers (ministers of agriculture from all the member countries), and Irish ministers and officials were negotiating on much more equal terms than before. During the 1950s and the 1960s the Department had regularly expressed a preference for bi-lateral negotiations and agreements,[8] but in the EEC, farm policy was negotiated through multi-lateral talks. Reaching agreement on EEC farm prices, or on changes to the CAP, tended to be a lengthy process, because the interests of pre-dominantly industrial countries such as the United Kingdom and Germany – the largest contributors to the EEC budget – differed from those of more agricultural countries such as Ireland and France, and every agreement involved compromises between the diverse interests of member states. Irish politicians and officials rapidly learned the importance of forming alliances with other member states. The Department of Agriculture became knowledgeable about market and production trends for commodities that had not traditionally figured on its agenda, such as wine, olive oil and tobacco; it was conscious that Irish interests would not be taken seriously if Irish representatives did not display a corresponding interest in the problems of other member states.[9] EEC agricultural negotiations are very time-consuming. In 1992 the Minister and officials in the Department of Agriculture and Food attended a total of 922 EC meetings, consisting of 13 Council of Minister Meetings; 2 Informal Councils; 1 General Affairs Council; 29 Special Committees on Agriculture; 2 Informal Committees on Agriculture; 4 High Level Working Groups; 279 Council Working Group Meetings and 592 Commission Meetings.[10] The Department has also been extremely effective in placing national experts in key units within the Agricultural Directorate.[11] Its skill in advancing Irish interests within the EEC is widely acknowledged. One writer has remarked that, 'The Irish Department of Agriculture has some of the most resourceful and competent civil servants in the entire public service. Their skills have been honed in many late-night battles in Brussels, seeking to nudge yet another concession to Irish farming out of their partners'.[12] A recent study of how Irish government departments relate to the EU concluded that the Department of Agriculture and Food 'has the clearest and most focused competence in relation to EU issues'.[13]

In March 1999 Minister of Agriculture Joe Walsh reported to the Seanad on the triumphant conclusion of the Agenda 2000 CAP reform. The original proposals, presented to the Council of Ministers in September 1997,[14] would have resulted in an estimated loss of £226 million a year to Irish agriculture; whereas it was estimated that the final agreement would bring an annual gain of £7 million, when the changes were fully implemented in 2007. Faced with 'an uphill battle' to persuade EU farm ministers and the Commission to modify the proposals, the Minister argued the Irish case at every possible opportunity: at meetings of the Council of Ministers, and in a series of bilateral meetings with the Agricultural Commissioner, Franz Fischler, and other ministers for agriculture. In the run-up to the decisive European Council meeting in Berlin, on 24–25 March 1999, the Minister met Commissioner Fischler and the President of the Council of Ministers on several occasions; his officials met their opposite numbers in other EU ministries of agriculture to press the Irish case.[15] The Department of Agriculture regarded the agreement as especially favourable to Irish interests.

The changes in the title and the remit of the Department of Agriculture since 1973 have followed changes in the administrative structures of the Community's farm policy. In 1977 the Department was given responsibility for land policy. Although this had been recommended in the 1969 Devlin Report,[16] it was also consistent with the EEC's structural programme. The EEC Agricultural Directorate regarded food and agriculture as two aspects of a single industry, and in 1987 the Department of Agriculture became the Department of Agriculture and Food.[17] The 1987 decision to make the Department responsible for rural development – although not reflected in the Department's name until 1999 – was also in line with Community policy.[18]

THE COMMON AGRICULTURAL POLICY (CAP): PRICE SUPPORTS AND INTERVENTION, 1973–92

When Ireland joined the EEC in 1973, the CAP had two main components: the FEOGA Guarantee Fund, which provided price and market support for agricultural produce, and the FEOGA Guidance Fund, which assisted investment and structural changes in farming and food processing. Initially it was intended that 70 per cent of expenditure would be allocated to the Guarantee Fund, with the balance going to structural programmes, but expenditure on structural programmes has never reached 10 per cent of the total.[19]

The CAP began to apply to Ireland from 1 February 1973, one month after Ireland's accession. Although Irish agricultural prices rose sharply between 1968 and 1972, in anticipation of EEC membership,[20] in 1973 they were still substantially below the EEC average. The transitional arrangements were designed to bring Irish farm prices into line with Community prices by the end of 1977. From February 1973 the price supports that the Irish government had offered for wheat, barley, sugar-beet and milk were replaced by FEOGA guarantees.[21] As there was no longer a role for An Bord Gráin, it began to wind up its operations, and it ceased to function in

1975. In 1973 An Bord Bainne was transformed into a co-operative to conform with EEC regulations.[22]

The FEOGA Guarantee Fund gave Irish producers support for all major products except sheep, potatoes, poultry and eggs. The intervention system set a floor price for produce such as beef, pigmeat, skim milk, butter and grain; when prices fell to this figure, the EEC's intervention agent bought produce and removed it from the market. Imports from non-EEC countries were subject to import levies, and they were only permitted if EEC prices were above a determined minimum import price.[23] EEC exporters received subsidies on agricultural exports to third countries to bridge the gap between EEC prices and world prices.

As the official intervention agent for the EEC, the Department of Agriculture was responsible for buying beef or dairy produce and placing it in intervention; making payments to processors and exporters in the form of Aids to Private Storage (APS); and paying export refunds and monetary compensation amounts. The Department had to meet the cost of buying beef and dairy produce into intervention, borrowing the necessary bridging finance, subject to the consent and guarantee of the Minister for Finance. FEOGA advances covered the cost of storage and insurance, and FEOGA reimbursed the Department for losses on the sale of intervention stocks.[24]

Before Ireland joined the EEC, the Department of Agriculture had assumed that aids and subsidies, rather than intervention, would be the most common form of price support, and for this reason it was decided not to establish a separate intervention section. The administration and supervision of EEC support schemes was handled by the individual commodity divisions, so that the dairy division was responsible for dairy intervention and the beef industry division for beef intervention.[25]

The oil crisis that erupted in the autumn of 1973, following the Arab–Israeli war, ended the long period of economic growth in the developed world that began in the late 1940s. After 1973 western Europe experienced two decades of high unemployment, inflation, volatile currencies, and low growth in output and incomes. The recession reduced the demand for agricultural produce in the EEC and throughout the developed world. The workings of the Community's price support schemes were further complicated by currency fluctuations. Implementing the EEC's support schemes would have presented a major challenge for the Department of Agriculture in normal circumstances; EEC regulations were detailed and complex, and their interpretation could be a matter of dispute. But the timing of Ireland's accession to the EEC made the task much more difficult.

For Irish farmers, 1974 was the year of 'the cattle crisis'; prices offered for fat cattle fell by one quarter between the autumn of 1973 and the autumn of 1974.[26] This unexpected collapse in cattle prices tested the Department's capacity to administer the intervention system. When prices for beef or dairy produce fell to the intervention price, the Department entered the market, buying up produce, and arranging for its storage and eventual sale. This direct involvement in the market was a new departure. Although the Department had bought old cattle for slaughter during the 1930s, buying, storing and selling beef became a regular part of its activities for the first time. A small quantity of Irish beef was bought into intervention in the autumn of 1973, and by 31 March 1974, intervention stocks had reached 10,000 tons.[27] In 1974 over 40 per cent of cattle slaughtered were bought into intervention – a figure that was not exceeded until 1990.[28] This was far in excess of Ireland's cold storage capacity, so the Industrial Development Authority (IDA) introduced grants for the construction of additional storage, and the EEC authorised the de-boning of intervention beef in order to conserve space. By the end of 1974 the quantity of boneless beef in intervention stores in Ireland had increased to 40,000 tonnes, although the Department had succeeded in selling 50,000 tonnes of bone-in beef from intervention stocks.[29] In 1975, 19 per cent of livestock output ended up in intervention, as did 42 per cent of skim milk. The first stocks of butter were sold into intervention in 1979; the proportion of butter entering intervention rose in subsequent years and between 1983 and 1987 it ranged from 22 to 45 per cent of total output.[30]

Between 1973 and 1992 the Department of Agriculture supervised the slaughter, processing and export of 7.3 million tonnes of beef, the equivalent of 20.5 million animals, and it was responsible for total payments to the industry in excess of £8.5 billion.[31] Over 2 million tonnes of beef were bought into intervention at a cost of over £4 billion. As the beef mountain increased, and Irish storage outlets became saturated, the Department rented space in the United Kingdom, in continental Europe, and on ships berthed at Foynes in the Shannon estuary.[32] The post-1973 oil crisis brought new wealth to oil-producing countries such as Iraq and Libya, and these markets accounted for a substantial share of the sales of intervention beef. By 1980, 30 per cent of Irish beef exports were going to markets outside the EEC, mainly to the Middle East. In 1990 the Iraqi invasion of Kuwait, political and economic uncertainty in eastern Europe, and the health scare caused by BSE, resulted in the collapse of export markets for Irish beef. The volume of beef going into intervention in 1990 was in excess of 230,000 tonnes, which was 94,000 tonnes higher than the previous peak in 1975, and substantially greater than the quantities bought into intervention during the 1980s.[33]

Intervention was important primarily for beef and dairy produce. EEC price supports for pigmeat were less favourable. On several occasions when the market was slack, the EEC introduced temporary Aids to Private Storage (APS); this meant processors were subsidised to store pigmeat until market conditions improved. Responsibility for storing and disposing of pigmeat in APS rested with producers not with the Department.[34] APS were also used to store surplus beef at a cost of almost £196 million between 1973 and 1992.[35]

When Ireland joined the EEC in 1973, the CAP did not apply to sheep. France, the largest continental market, continued to deny free access to Irish lamb and sheep, which meant that Irish producers could not take advantage of high French prices.[36] In 1977 Ireland took France to the European Court in order to force them to drop restrictions on lamb and sheep imports, and France agreed to concede free access from the end of that year.[37] When Ireland and France asked the Community to introduce a market support scheme for sheep, other member countries objected, but it was eventually introduced in October 1980.[38] The Community was not self-sufficient in sheep, and the United Kingdom continued to import large quantities from New Zealand. However, a ewe premium, introduced primarily to improve the incomes of sheep farmers, brought about a substantial increase in sheep stocks; Irish sheep numbers rose rapidly during the 1980s.[39]

THE BEEF TRIBUNAL

The Department's performance between 1973 and 1992 as the EU's intervention agent was scrutinised in detail by a tribunal, established by the Minister for Agriculture and Food on 31 May 1991, to inquire into 'allegations regarding illegal activities, fraud and malpractice in and in connection with the beef processing industries'. The tribunal was established in response to a *World in Action* programme, transmitted by the British television company ITV on 13 May 1991, which made serious allegations concerning Ireland's largest beef-processing company, Goodman International. The allegations that directly concerned the Department of Agriculture related to abuses in the intervention system, the export refund scheme and APS. Similar allegations had already been made by opposition deputies in Dáil Éireann, and these allegations were also investigated by the tribunal. As the EU's intervention agent, the Department of Agriculture and Food was responsible for ensuring that all claims for EU support schemes complied with the regulations. The tribunal also examined allegations relating to abuses of the export credit insurance scheme, and allegations that political influence in favour of the Goodman group led to an alteration of the conditions attached to the export credit insurance scheme.[40] The tribunal, with the President of the High Court, Mr Justice Hamilton, as its sole member, sat until June 1993; his report was issued in the summer of 1994.

The report confirmed that fraud and malpractice had taken place under the various EC schemes, although the evidence given by the Department of Agriculture showed that the EC had disallowed only £3.07million, or 0.04 per cent, of the claims submitted by the Department between 1973 and 1992.[41] The tribunal concluded that the malpractices had happened because of the inadequate control system laid down by EC regulations and by the Department of Agriculture; the inadequacies in the Department's controls were 'due mainly' to a shortage of Department of Agriculture officials in the meat factories. Mr Justice Hamilton referred to the difficulty of inspecting the huge volume of meat passing through the boning plants, noting that the task was made more difficult because most animals were slaughtered during the autumn.[42]

During the course of the tribunal, it was suggested that there might be a potential conflict between the Department of Agriculture's role as the intervention agent, which required them to police the beef-processing industry, and its efforts to develop the Irish beef sector,[43] and that it might be advisable to transfer responsibility for intervention to a separate agency.[44] The Secretary of the Department of Agriculture, Michael Dowling, told the tribunal that the Department had established a separate Intervention Unit in 1990, in order to cope with the large increase in produce going into intervention, and additional staff were allocated to the new unit to cope with the increased work. As part of the administrative overhaul, the Department had introduced new contracts, which placed the obligation for conforming with EC regulations on the meat-processing firms; control structures were reformed; staff involved in monitoring intervention were given additional training; and a new system of surprise inspections was introduced.[45] Michael Dowling claimed that the new unit had all the benefits of a separate intervention agency, without the possible disadvantages: the unit was separate from the Department's policy activities, but potential difficulties relating to staffing were avoided by keeping it within the Department.[46] The reforms that the Department introduced in 1990 convinced Mr Justice Hamilton that there was no need to establish a separate intervention agency. He noted that the administrative changes 'have rendered unnecessary many of the recommendations which might otherwise have been made by the Tribunal'. His report recommended only minor modifications in the Department's monitoring procedures.[47]

THE GREEN POUND

The difficulties of administering the FEOGA Guarantee Fund were exacerbated by fluctuating exchange rates, and the Department of Agriculture had to develop an expertise in international monetary matters. The common price arrangements for agricultural products were operated by fixing amounts in terms of a notional accounting unit, called the unit of account, which was converted into the national currencies of member states, not on the basis of the current value of the currency, but at a fixed official rate. The Irish green pound was the name given to the notional value assigned to the Irish currency, the word green referring to agriculture, not to Ireland's national colour. As the market exchange rates for most Community currencies diverged from the CAP green rates, a system of monetary compensation amounts (MCAs) was introduced to prevent the price arrangements under the CAP being distorted, and to deter member countries from trying to gain a market advantage through currency devaluation. Member states, whose currencies had floated downwards, such as Ireland, the United Kingdom, Italy and France, had to pay MCAs on all produce shipped to countries with appreciating currencies such as Germany. On the other hand, German exporters received a grant on produce shipped to Ireland and other states whose currencies were depreciating. Responsibility for administering MCAs fell on the Department of Agriculture.

Between the summer of 1973 and the summer of 1974 the Irish green pound rate was approximately 15 per cent above the actual market rate for the Irish currency, and Irish agricultural exports to all markets other than Britain were subject to MCAs.[48] Farm incomes suffered because the high rate for the green pound reduced the value of EEC prices to Irish farmers. In October 1974 the Minister for Agriculture and Fisheries secured a devaluation of the Irish green pound. There were three further devaluations of the Irish green pound in 1975, three in 1976 and three in 1977.[49] Each devaluation entailed hard bargaining by the Department, but these concessions ensured that Irish farmers gained significant benefits from higher EEC prices. As Britain did not devalue its green pound in line with the Irish green rate, the values of the two currencies as calculated for agricultural trade purposes, widened considerably, providing better market opportunities for Irish agricultural exporters in the United Kingdom, but also new scope for cross-border smuggling. Ireland joined the European Monetary System (EMS) in 1979, which made the option of regular green pound devaluations more difficult, although the Irish currency was realigned with other EMS currencies in 1981, and further changes in the green pound rate between 1984 and 1987 gave Irish farmers a nominal increase of 12.1 per cent in farm prices, at a time when EC support prices did not rise.[50] Although MCAs were abolished in January 1993, and changes in the green rates were restricted[51] as the Community began the process of establishing a common currency, the agri-monetary system – the term used to cover MCAs and changes in green currencies – remained a feature of the Community's agricultural policy until the introduction of the euro in the year 2000.

The 'Prudent Price Policy' and Milk Quotas

In 1975 a 'stocktaking report' by the European Commission on the CAP concluded that it was succeeding in its objective of narrowing the gap between farm incomes and those in other sectors of the economy, and should therefore be continued.[52] But the cost of price supports rocketed during the 1970s as farmers lobbied for price increases that would compensate them for double-digit inflation. In 1977, in an effort to control costs, the Commission introduced a 'prudent price policy'. In future, support prices would not keep pace with inflation, but would be permitted to fall by 3 per cent per annum in real terms. Irish farm incomes rose during the 1970s in every year except 1974, but real farm incomes through-out the 1980s were lower than in the 1970s as a consequence of the 'prudent price policy'.[53]

By 1984 the Community had an excess supply of all the main farm produce, except fruit, vegetable oils and sheepmeat.[54] Although measures were introduced in 1977 to curb the increased output of milk, they had not proved successful.[55] In an effort to reduce the quantities of dairy produce going into intervention, the European Council (the prime ministers of member states) agreed to introduce a superlevy on milk, which came into effect in April 1984. Each country was allocated a national quota; any milk in excess of this amount would be subject to a superlevy or a punitive tax. Ireland demanded to be treated as a special case: the Irish dairy sector was underdeveloped and should be permitted to expand; moreover, quotas would have a much greater impact on Ireland than on other member states because of the large share of national and agricultural income derived from dairy produce. Although government and opposition were united against the proposed milk quotas, the Minister for Agriculture, Austin Deasy, cautioned that for the Community, the only alternative to the superlevy was a cut in price support for dairy produce, and he believed that this would be 'much more detrimental to agriculture and to the economy'. The government made considerable efforts to have Ireland exempted from the first round of quotas, which would apply until 1988, in the hope that the milk surplus might have disappeared by then,[56] but this was rejected. Nevertheless, the campaign by the Taoiseach, Garret FitzGerald, the Minister for Agriculture, Austin Deasy, and officials in the Department of Agriculture did bear fruit.[57] The 1984 milk quotas provided for a reduction of 7 per cent on the 1983 Community milk output, and most member states received a national quota equal to their 1981 output,[58] but Ireland was granted an increase of 4.63 per cent. FitzGerald's strong defence of Irish interests even attracted the admiration of British Prime Minister Margaret Thatcher.[59]

The superlevy was the first in a series of measures designed to reduce the surpluses of agricultural produce in the Community. At the end of 1986 it was announced that, in future, intervention would be suspended when the quantity of butter or skim milk in storage reached a specific level. In the following year measures were introduced to stabilise the output of most major commodities at the existing level. If output exceeded the quota, producers would be penalised by substantially lower prices.

The introduction of milk quotas presented the Department with new administrative challenges. Each member country was free to determine how a national quota would be assigned. The Department distributed the national quota (5.2 million tonnes, plus 303,000 tonnes from a Community Reserve quota) between the milk purchasers – creameries and dairies – and they collected the superlevy from those who exceeded the quota. The additional quota was targeted towards smaller producers. Milk purchasers could take an additional 497 gallons from each supplier who had delivered less than 14,000 gallons in 1983, plus an additional 3.53 per cent from larger suppliers, based on their 1983 output. The creameries and dairies were responsible for allocating quotas to individual suppliers and keeping records of their output.[60] If a creamery failed to meet its quota, the unused quota could be transferred to another creamery.

The 1984 provisions were intended to run for five years, but they have been repeatedly extended, most recently until 31 March 2008. By the late 1980s, following consultation with the dairy industry, measures were introduced enabling quotas to be leased and sold,[61] and this made it possible to bring about some restructuring of dairy farming. In 1983 more than a quarter of suppliers to Lough Egish and Killeshandra Co-Operatives (now Lakelands Co-Operative) in counties Monaghan and Cavan, supplied less than 12,800 gallons; by 1995/6 only 7.5 per cent of suppliers fell into that category, and the proportion of farmers supplying from 20,000 to 60,000 gallons had doubled, from 17 to 35 per cent.[62]

STRUCTURAL POLICIES: THE MANSHOLT PLAN

The FEOGA Guidance Fund provided aid for investment and structural reform in farming and food processing. The 1968 Mansholt Plan, which the EEC adopted in 1972, was designed to bring about a substantial fall in the numbers employed in farming, while ensuring that those remaining would be capable of earning comparable incomes to workers in industry and services. Landholdings would be consolidated to create larger farms, with special aid provided for farmers who were regarded as capable of becoming commercially viable. When the Mansholt Plan was drafted, most EEC member states enjoyed full employment, and the European Commission was keen to encourage workers to move from agriculture into sectors of the economy that were experiencing labour shortages. Such a policy was not appropriate for Ireland, because there was little immediate prospect that industry could provide jobs for any substantial number of agricultural workers, and proposals for a deliberate reduction in the farming population would have been politically unacceptable. When Mansholt visited Ireland in November 1970, farmers from Land Commission holdings in Kildare and the Meath Gaeltacht greeted him with placards that read 'Go Home Cromwell'.[63] Farm organisations in other member states were also opposed to the Mansholt Plan.[64] In the event, the Farm Modernisation Scheme that was introduced in 1974 was much more in tune with Irish requirements. Farms were divided into three categories:

- Development Farms, where the income per labour unit was below that of non-farm workers, but was capable of being increased; development farmers were required to draw up a six-year development plan with the assistance of an agricultural adviser and to keep detailed accounts;
- Commercial Farms, where income per labour unit was already above the average for non-farm workers;
- Others – a category that included those with low incomes that were not capable of being increased.

All three categories could apply for grant assistance for land improvement, farm buildings, capital equipment, horticultural projects, and keeping accounts, although the rate of grant assistance varied between the different categories. Development farmers could also claim grants towards the cost of purchasing additional stock, provided that they had drawn up a livestock development plan, and they were eligible for premium payments on livestock and sheep.[65] The EEC met the cost of assisting development farmers; the cost of providing grants for commercial and 'other' farmers was met by the Irish exchequer.[66]

The Farm Modernisation Scheme came into operation on 1 February 1974, and all existing Department schemes for land drainage, farm buildings, and capital equipment were subsumed under the scheme.[67] By 1982, over 115,000 farmers were participating in the scheme: 4,643 farmers were classified as commercial, 26,745 as development farmers, but the overwhelming majority, 84,000,[68] were classified as 'other'. Some farmers decided not to apply for development status, because they believed that the value of the additional grants was outweighed by the requirement to follow a development plan and keep detailed accounts. Only 34 per cent of land drainage assisted under the Farm Modernisation Scheme was carried out on development farms, compared with 56 per cent on 'other' farms.[69]

In 1975 the EEC introduced the Disadvantaged Areas Scheme. One agricultural economist has described this as 'a U-turn', since it offered incentives for non-viable farmers to remain on the land, whereas the original intention of the Mansholt Plan had been to encourage them to leave farming. The 'U-turn' was prompted by opposition to the original plan, and by the rising level of unemployment throughout the Community; by 1975 it was no longer desirable to encourage a mass exodus from farming.[70] The introduction of the Disadvantaged Areas Scheme removed one of the major criticisms directed against EEC farm policy – the absence of a regional dimension. This criticism was particularly pertinent in Ireland, where a pilot areas programme in western counties had been in operation since the 1960s.

The Disadvantaged Areas Scheme introduced a special cattle headage payment. In order to qualify, farmers had to give an undertaking to remain in farming for the next five years.[71] The range of special incentives offered to farmers in disadvantaged areas was extended in later years, as was the proportion of land that qualified for disadvantaged status. Grants for mountain fencing, mountain grazing, tourism and craft projects were announced in 1976.[72] In 1979 eleven counties were designated as eligible for special field-drainage grants and arterial drainage schemes under the western drainage scheme, with the EEC meeting half the cost.[73] In 1981 a special western development programme was introduced for full-time farmers, who were ineligible for the Farm Retirement Scheme, and failed to qualify for development status.[74] A leading authority on European agriculture has claimed that the Department of Agriculture secured additional aid for farmers in disadvantaged areas in return for agreeing to lower price increases in annual farm talks,[75] but this claim has been firmly rejected by a senior official in the Department who took part in these negotiations. Structural schemes, such as the Disadvantaged Areas Scheme, were much more effective than higher prices in increasing the incomes of small farmers.

In 1985 the Farm Modernisation Programme was replaced by a more flexible Farm Improvement Programme, where any low-income farmer who agreed to draft a development plan and to keep simplified accounts would qualify for investment aids.[76] A new scheme of 'Installation Aid' was introduced for farmers aged under 35 who became the owner or the long-term lesseee of a farm.[77] In order to qualify, a new farmer had to hold the Teagasc Green Cert, or an equivalent qualification; the farm had to be capable of supporting a full-time farmer; and the incoming farmer had to give a commitment to farm on a full-time basis for at least five years.[78] The 'Installation Aid' was designed to encourage the transfer of holdings to younger farmers; the voluntary Farm Retirement Scheme established as part of the 1974 Farm Modernisation Scheme had attracted few takers. The Department's 1990 *Agriculture and Food Policy Review* remarked that 'it was not designed to accommodate the social processes and realities of Irish agriculture'. The terms were not financially attractive, and farmers were afraid that they would be deprived of their old age pension. Moreover, land ownership remained an important indicator of social status in rural Ireland.[79] The Irish experience was mirrored throughout the Community.

Although the number of farmers on holdings of less than 30 acres (12 hectares) was more than halved between 1971 and 1986, most of the land vacated was retained by the immediate family, and it was either farmed on a part-time basis, or let as conacre. Again, the Irish experience did not differ significantly from the rest of the EU. Development farmers acquired very little of the land that came on the market throughout the EU.[80] A 1989 report by the National Economic and Social Council (NESC) identified three reasons for the absence of significant changes in ownership and control of farmland:

- the inadequate level of EU funding for structural programmmes, particularly when this was compared with the amount that was spent on price and market supports;
- EU price and market support schemes, which may have exacerbated structural problems because large farmers benefited to a dispropor-tionate extent;
- the absence of a national socio-structural policy, especially a coherent land policy.[81]

Payments from the FEOGA Guidance Fund exceeded 10 per cent of Ireland's receipts from the EU farm budget on only two occasions during the 1980s – in 1982 and 1983.[82]

REFORMING THE COMMUNITY'S AGRICULTURAL POLICY

The Single European Act

The late 1980s proved to be a critical turning-point for the Irish economy. The 1987 *Programme for National Recovery*, which was drawn up following lengthy consultation between the government, farm organisations, industry and trade unions,[83] set out a strategy for transforming the Irish economy. The EEC was conscious of the contrast between the booming US economy and the stagnant European economies, and it proposed the creation of a Single European Market by 1992, replicating the trans-continental economy of the United States. This involved removing a range of non-tariff barriers to trade and competition within the Community.

The GATT Uruguay Round

A significant number of countries who were contracting parties to the GATT were determined that the Uruguay Round of trade talks, which opened in 1986, would free up world trade in agricultural produce. They demanded that the EEC cease selling surplus agricultural produce on world markets at highly-subsidised prices. In 1988 the EC agreed to freeze its price support at the 1984 level, and to reduce it in the long-term; the Community also agreed to reduce barriers against imports of food from non-member countries.[84] In 1995 the Uruguay Round global trade agreement brought world trade for agriculture and food under global rules for the first time. Negotiations on further reform of world trade in agriculture commenced in 1999 under the World Trade Organisation (WTO), the successor organisation to GATT.[85] By the 1990s the annual reports of the Department were giving considerable attention to developments in GATT – an indication of the growing influence that GATT was exercising over EU farm policy.

The 1992 CAP Reforms

With the moves towards a Single European Market and a liberalisation of world trade in agriculture, and for other reasons, such as a renewed upward trend in intervention stocks of cereals, beef and dairy produce (between 1990 and 1991 the cost of market support schemes rose by 32 per cent),[86] it became essential to carry out a radical reform of the farm support system and the Community's structural programmes. The MacSharry (Ray MacSharry was Commissioner of Agriculture from 1989 to 1993) proposals for reforming the CAP had three main objectives:

- to retain the common price system, Community preference regarding imports, and free movement of products within the Community;
- to preserve full Community financing of market measures;
- to increase price competitiveness, reduce surpluses and provide farmers with realistic alternatives to increasing food production.[87]

In February 1991 the European Commission issued a Reflections Paper on 'The Development and Future of the CAP', setting out key objectives for future policy. These included:

- retaining a sufficient number of farmers on the land;
- ensuring that in future farmers would have a dual role of producing

food and protecting the environment in the context of rural development;

- controlling agricultural production so that markets were brought back into balance.[88]

The reforms were approved by the Council of Ministers for Agriculture in May 1992, after nine months of negotiations. Joe Walsh, the Minister for Agriculture and Food, told the Dáil that Ireland had secured all its main objectives during the talks.[89] The reforms involved a partial shift of EU farm aid from market support to direct payments, or premia, that would be targeted at farmers in greatest need. Price supports were modified to favour smaller producers and disadvantaged regions; in the past, 20 per cent of farmers accounted for 80 per cent of CAP expenditure.[90] The quantity of beef, sheep, cereals and oilseed qualifying for price support was capped, and the support prices for cereals, beef and milk were reduced.[91] Farmers were compensated for the reduction in support prices by an increase in the suckler cow premium, and the introduction of a new male beef premium and a premium to encourage extensive beef production. Direct payments were made to arable farmers in return for agreeing not to cultivate land: this became known as set aside.[92] Measures were introduced to encourage farmers to divert land to forestry, and a more generous scheme for early retirement was introduced. The Rural Environment Protection Scheme (REPS), which was introduced in 1994, offered farmers a fixed annual payment per hectare for five years, in return for a commitment to adopt environmentally-friendly farming practices.[93]

In his Dáil speech Minister Joe Walsh highlighted the fact that intervention would continue: the satisfactory level set for beef premia, and the introduction of specific aids for extensive beef production, were seen as major gains for Ireland. The retention of the Community milk quota at its existing level, instead of the proposed cut, and a much lower reduction in milk prices than was initially proposed, were also in Ireland's interests.[94] The 1992 reforms made it easier for the Community to accept the Uruguay Round.

The 1992 CAP reforms resulted in a substantial shift in EU farm payments from price supports to direct payments to farmers. The Department was under considerable pressure to introduce the new payments as rapidly as possible, and to ensure that the money reached the farmers, because farm organisations had predicted that the changes would have a disastrous impact on farm incomes; in the event, farm incomes rose.[95] The increasing use of direct payments as the main source of EU farm support created further demands on the Department's administrative skills. In 1996, for example, it processed over half a million claims for animal premia alone. According to Brigid Laffan, when direct payments were first introduced, the Department lacked the management capacity to handle the change, 'and has struggled to develop this capacity since then'.[96] The European Court of Auditors has acknowledged that it is extremely difficult to monitor payments under the EU agricultural programme. Two-thirds of payments are made on the basis of information supplied by recipients. In 1997 the Court of Auditors determined that the rate of substantive errors involving payments under the agricultural guarantee funds was 3.3 per cent.[97] New monitoring practices have been introduced to ensure compliance with farm support schemes. Set aside is monitored through detailed mapping, and by satellite imagery. Farmers who entered the REPS scheme (45,000 had done so by 1999) are inspected, and are subject to fines if they fail to meet the necessary conditions, such as maintaining hedgerows and stone walls, and preventing watercourses being polluted by livestock.[98]

By 1998 direct payments to farmers accounted for 56 per cent of aggregate farm income.[99] As the share of farm income coming from direct payments by the Department has increased, so have requests for information about the various programmes, and demands from farmers, farm organisations and TDs to ensure prompt payment of claims. When he took office as Minister for Agriculture in 1995, Ivan Yates gave a commitment to implement a Charter of Rights for Farmers, which would provide farmers with confidential, effective and efficient services. Under the Charter of Rights the Department gave a commitment to set specific targets for making payments under the various farm programmes. An independent Headage and Premia Appeals Unit was established, and the Department introduced a new telephone information service in all local offices.[100] In 1998 the Department inaugurated a well-publicised complaints procedure.[101] The commitment to provide farmers with a high-quality service was re-emphasised in 1999 when the Department's Partnership Committee produced an Action Programme for Modernisation, which involved the introduction of a performance management system. This prescribed very specific standards of service in matters such as responding to queries and requests for information, and making payments under the various programmes. The Appeals Unit received 2,781 appeals between 1995 and 1999, and there were 202 complaints to the Quality Unit in 1999.[102] In 1999 more than 90 per cent of income payments to farmers were made within the specified time period; the only payments that fell short of the 90 per cent target were goat headage payments; 95–100 per cent of market support payments were made within the target period, with the exception of export refunds for beef.[103]

Agenda 2000

The most recent reform of EU agricultural policy, under Agenda 2000, reaffirmed that direct payments would continue to form a major part of farm support at the beginning of the twenty-first century. The reforms, which were seen as a continuation of the changes introduced in 1992, were prompted by the need to prepare for the enlargement of the EU and the next round of WTO trade talks. The proposals tabled by the Commission in 1997 and 1998 posed a major threat to the livelihood of Irish farmers, because they involved substantial reductions in prices and premia for livestock and dairy produce, including a 30 per cent reduction in feed prices and an end to intervention beef. The European Commission was keen to decentralise farm supports, and it proposed that, in future, up to 50 per cent of EU agricultural support would come in the form of 'national envelopes', a sum of money based on national output, given to each member state. Each member state would be free to determine what form these supports would take, but the amount provided in the 'national envelope' would not compensate Irish farmers fully for the loss of income.[104]

The final package agreed in March 1999 was much more favourable to Ireland than the original proposals. Beef prices would be reduced by 20 per cent, and the intervention safety-net for beef was reinstated, although at a lower level. Ireland secured a higher milk quota, whereas the original proposals left the quota unchanged, and the threatened reduction in milk prices was deferred until 2005. Beef and cow premia were increased; the qualifying conditions for the extensive beef premium were eased (the original proposal would have disqualified one-third of Irish beneficiaries); and the threatened cut in the suckler cow quota was removed. The Minister claimed that these changes meant that beef farmers were fully compensated for the reduction in prices; this had been one of the key Irish objectives during the talks.[105] 'National envelopes' did not disappear, but they would form a much smaller share of the EU farm budget than originally planned. Joe Walsh told the Seanad that during the years 2000–2006, Irish farmers would benefit by almost £400 million from the agreement. He described the outcome as 'the best possible deal that could have been achieved'.[106]

Research, Education and the Advisory Service

Although the Community's farm policy did not embrace agricultural education and research, Ireland's accession to the EU resulted in major changes in these areas. There was a well-established tradition of close links between Irish agricultural scientists and colleagues in the United States, Britain and New Zealand; after 1973 these international contacts were extended into Europe, and staff at AFT became involved in collaborative research projects through the EU Standing Committee on Agriculture Research.[107]

The Farm Modernisation Scheme transformed the advisory service: the advisers assisted development farmers in drawing up farm plans; they were responsible for monitoring the farmers' progress in achieving these plans, and for handling most of the paperwork. Many Irish farmers lacked the skills to operate a farm plan or keep proper accounts. It was equally evident that more specialised advisers would be needed if Irish farmers were to benefit fully from the opportunities presented by membership of the EEC. The 1966 report by Jones and Davis, and the 1969 Devlin report on the reorganisation of the public service,[108] had recommended changes in the structure of the advisory service, while Devlin also favoured some alteration in the administrative control of AFT. The Minister for Agriculture, James Gibbons, circulated the heads of a bill to reorganise agricultural educational and advisory services to the Cabinet in 1973, shortly before Fianna Fáil lost office in the general election.[109] In 1976, following lengthy consultation on the matter, Mark Clinton, the Minister for Agriculture in the Fine Gael/Labour Coalition government, introduced a bill establishing a National Agricultural Advisory, Education and Research Authority. This became law in 1977, shortly before Fianna Fáil was returned to office in a general election. Fianna Fáil had been very critical of the proposed changes; while in opposition, James Gibbons had described the bill as 'infested with the notion of the parish plan'.[110] When he was reappointed as Minister for Agriculture, he announced that the new authority would not be established; he planned to introduce amending legislation.

The legislation introduced by Mark Clinton was very close to the spirit of the original Agricultural Institute. The National Agricultural Advisory, Education and Research Authority would be responsible for all the research work being carried out by AFT and by the Department, and for the state-owned agricultural colleges and the advisory service. The authority would be an executive agency, as defined by the Devlin report, which meant that it would not be subject to detailed scrutiny by the Department. The twenty-four-person board would include nominees of the General Council of Committees of Agriculture, agricultural and rural organisations, the universities, state-owned agricultural colleges, and any other agricultural interests that might be prescribed in a statutory order. The role of the county committees of agriculture would be reduced to monitoring the work of the new authority at local level, and devising an annual educational and advisory programme for the county, which would be approved by the new authority. At least half of future members of the county committees of agriculture would be drawn from farming and rural organisations.

Under the 1978 Act introduced by Fianna Fáil, AFT remained an autonomous research body. The Act also established An Chomhairle Oiliúna Talmhaíochta (ACOT), with functions similar to those granted to the National Agricultural Advisory, Education and Research Authority, other than research. While the 1977 Act had transferred the Department's veterinary and cereals research units to the new authority, and the original version of the 1978 ACOT bill provided for their transfer to AFT, this was amended while the bill was going through the Oireachtas, and the veterinary and cereals research stations remained under the Department's control.[111]

ACOT was established in 1980. By 1984 the advisory and educational services had been grouped into five regions and sixty-seven districts. Each adviser concentrated on one main enterprise, although he/she was expected to provide general advice on all aspects of agriculture. A team of specialist advisers and a full-time education officer were appointed in each region. In 1983 a Western Resource Centre opened in Athenry to provide further training for advisers in the special needs of western farming; the centre also carried out research and pilot studies on new farm programmes. With ACOT services operating on a regional basis, the county structures became redundant. By 1985 the annual budget for the county committees of agriculture was only £0.4 million, and most of this went on travel and administration.[112]

In 1982 ACOT introduced a Certificate in Farming, which became popularly known as the Green Cert. This was a three-year course, partly funded by the Youth Employment Agency, and later by the European Structural Fund, which combined work experience with formal course work at agricultural colleges or at ACOT training centres.[113] By 1990 up to 90 per cent of those entering farming had enrolled in this programme. The farm apprenticeship scheme, operated by the Farm Apprenticeship Board, had carved out a separate role, as a training course for farm managers, with an annual enrolment of 100.[114]

By 1985 AFT had a total staff of almost 1,200 and an annual budget of almost £25 million; 70 per cent of the money was provided by the exchequer, the balance coming from consultancy fees and small levies on milk, pigs, sugar-beet and grain. Seven major research centres were responsible for 600 projects in fifteen programme areas: food, beef cattle, dairy cattle, sheep, pigs, grassland, tillage crops, horticultural crops, land resources use and development, agricultural economics and sociology, engineering and machinery, energy, environment, biotechnology, and other services.[115] According to a study carried out by an economist at AFT, that 'consciously attempt[ed] to impart a downward bias to the benefits of agricultural research', the application of earlier research findings was responsible for raising agricultural output by 5 per cent, or more than £100 million, in 1983.[116] Government expenditure on agricultural research and development had risen steadily during the 1970s, but the real value of the government grant to AFT fell in 1983 and 1984.[117] In 1985 the Minister for Agriculture, Austin Deasy, appointed a working group to review the services provided by ACOT and AFT, with a view to establishing 'the fullest possible degree of co-ordination between the services and ensuring that the resources that can be made available are used to the best advantage in helping the agricultural industry to expand'.[118] This review was prompted by two factors: the changing needs of Irish agriculture, and exchequer finances. Developments in biotechnology, genetics and other scientific research made it essential to ensure that farmers and advisers kept up to date with new findings. Agricultural research programmes would also have to take account of the implications of EEC restrictions on production, such as milk quotas. The high level of government borrowing and the need to reduce current budget deficits meant that all exchequer programmes were being scrutinised with a view to possible savings. There was a freeze on recruitment in the public service, and plans to reduce public service employment were under consideration. As most of the funding for agricultural research and the advisory services came from the exchequer, not from the CAP, these programmes became obvious targets for savings on the Agriculture estimate.

The review group recommended that ACOT and AFT should report to a single board of directors; a decision on merging the two organisations would be deferred for five years.[119] However, this recommendation was superseded in 1987, when the incoming Fianna Fáil government launched its *Programme for National Recovery*, which included a major reduction in public service employment: between 1987 and 1990 the numbers employed throughout the civil service fell from 35,5000 to 28,500.[120] In 1988 ACOT and AFT were amalgamated in a new organisation called Teagasc, with an annual budget of £20 million, a reduction of more than 40 per cent on their combined budget of £35 million. The merger resulted in a substantial fall in staff numbers. The 1988 Act also marked the end of the county committees of agriculture.[121] Teagasc was expected to develop a strong commercial orientation, supplementing its exchequer grant with a substantial income from its consultancy and advisory work.[122] In 1987 legislation had been introduced enabling ACOT to charge farmers for advice and professional services,[123] and by 1990 fee income had risen to £2.3 million. The former AFT research stations were increasingly engaged in contract research on behalf of food companies.[124] In 1990 the Agriculture and Food Policy Review, carried out by the Department of Agriculture and Food, recommended that publicly-funded research should concentrate on low-cost enterprises and on measures that would improve quality, as opposed to raising output. Other priorities included environmentally-friendly farming, on-farm diversification and biotechnology.[125]

Animal Health and Disease Control

During the 1950s Irish free-range eggs were unable to compete with large, intensive UK producers, but by the 1980s organic and free-range produce were coming back into fashion, and there was growing concern over the health and environmental risks from the excessive use of fertilisers, weed-killers, pesticides and antibiotics. In April 1984 heavy fines were imposed on producers of liquid milk that was shown to contain residues of antibiotics,[126] and in 1986 a Central Meat Laboratory assumed responsibility for tests for residues of antibiotics and growth hormones in meat, and monitoring the level of water and brine in ham and processed meats.[127] The Department's tests of the levels of growth hormones in meat predated the introduction of EEC controls on the use of growth hormones in 1988.[128] A number of Irish farmers continued to use banned growth promoters, such as 'angel-dust', but a series of well-publicised prosecutions by the Department brought the problem under control. A much more traditional problem – bovine TB – continued to cause concern. In 1985, twenty years after the intensive campaign to eradicate the disease ended, 3.19 per cent of herds were infected with the disease, which was higher than the 1966 figure of 2.8. per cent.[129] It proved equally difficult to eradicate brucellosis.[130] In 1988 responsibility for the eradication of bovine TB and brucellosis was given to a new agency, the Eradication of Animal Diseases Board (ERAD), and a vigorous four-year programme to tackle the disease was announced.[131] Bovine TB continues to blight the Irish veterinary health record. The Agri Food 2010 report, published by the Department of Agriculture, Food and Rural Development in March 2000, stated unequivocally that the level of TB and brucellosis was unacceptable, and the Programme for Prosperity and Fairness (PPF), launched in 2000, set targets for halving the incidence of TB and for making considerable progress towards eradicating brucellosis within the next four years.[132] However, the most immediate health issue facing the Department is the eradication of BSE, a disease whose long-term implications for human health are as yet unknown. Fears about BSE have created major problems for Irish beef exporters.

A MINISTRY OF FOOD

Although food and drink accounted for a substantial share of Irish manufacturing output and exports, there was no national strategy for this sector until the late 1980s.[133] Responsibility for the food industry was divided between the Department of Agriculture and the Department of Industry and Commerce, and this appears to have retarded the development of a coherent policy for production and marketing. CBF, which reported to the Department of Agriculture, and An Bord Bainne, which was a co-operative organisation, were responsible for marketing livestock and beef, and dairy produce, but the market promotion of other food products was handled by Coras Trachtála Teoranta (CTT), which reported to the Department of Industry and Commerce.

The EEC regarded food and agriculture as two aspects of a single industry; export and import trade in food products such as confectionery and chocolate were subject to import levies, export refunds and compensatory payments on their agricultural content, just like cheese and bacon.[134] Food-processing plants were eligible for grant-assistance from the FEOGA Guidance Fund, and these applications were handled by the Department of Agriculture and the IDA. In 1983 FEOGA assisted fifty-eight investments in the Irish food industry, with grants amounting to almost £15 million. Almost half the money went to meat-processing plants; the remainder was divided between dairy processing, poultry, egg grading, fish and vegetable processing.[135] In 1989 FEOGA provided grants totalling £25.4 million.[136]

In the 1970s the Department of Agriculture began to display a growing interest in food. Every annual report from 1973/4 included a section outlining recent developments in the industry.[137] The 1976 bill establishing a National Agricultural Advisory, Education and Research Authority broke with tradition by using a definition of agriculture that included the processing of agricultural products.[138] AFT established a national food research station at Dunsinea in 1986. The 1987 *Programme for National Recovery* claimed that there were 'significant opportunities' for increasing output and employment in the Irish food industry, and it gave a commitment to establish a special Ministerial Office for Food. Michael O'Kennedy became the first Minister for Agriculture and Food, and two quasi-autonomous offices with responsibility for food and horticulture were established in the Department, each controlled by a minister of state – Joe Walsh (Food) and Seamus Kirk (Horticulture).[139] The Office of the Minister for Food co-ordinated the work of the government agencies responsible for the food sector. By the end of 1987 the IDA and the Office for Food had drawn up a five-year plan covering the years 1988–92.[140] The main objective was to reduce the industry's reliance on commodity products, and to encourage firms to develop non-traditional products that appealed to consumers, such as prepared meals, and new meat and dairy products. A major investment programme by Goodman International, Ireland's largest meat-processing company, formed part of this plan.

In 1989 a report by NESC noted that the agriculture and food sectors were now being forced to make the adjustments that Irish manufacturing industry had faced during the 1970s.

> The crucial difference between the Irish industrial and agricultural sectors in the EC has been that the Community system from 1973 to the early 'eighties was one which had made adjustment in industry unavoidable; and if that adjustment had some severe negative consequences (as indeed it did) then the need for national policy and/ or supplementary Community policy was brought to light. The Community system in agriculture was one which made adjustment partially avoidable, while at the same time rewarding the strong far more lavishly than the weak. While this system had much to recommend it, it had one unfortunate consequence. It could conceal the need for a range of long-term national policies concerning the role of agriculture

in the overall development of the economy, and the need for national policies to achieve agricultural objectives which were not, and probably could not, be addressed by the CAP.[141]

NESC believed that access to intervention had retarded the development of the Irish food-processing industry.[142] In 1988, 61 per cent of Irish milk was used to manufacture butter, a product that was very dependent on intervention, compared with 40 and 38 per cent of milk in Denmark and the Netherlands.[143] But the planned CAP reforms meant that intervention was no longer assured, and the introduction of the Single European Market would remove numerous veterinary and plant health regulations that had restricted imports of produce and livestock into Ireland, providing indirect protection for the Irish food sector.[144] The Single European Market would also eliminate other non-tariff barriers to trade within the EC; national regulations on food labelling, packaging, storage and standards would be superseded by Community-wide regulations.

The Agriculture and Food Policy Review, published by the Department of Agriculture and Food in December 1990, stated that the first objective of a national food policy should be to respond to the market, by producing food that could be sold at a profit. It recommended that, in future, state assistance should only be given to projects with a profitable market.[145] Given the urgent need to prepare the Irish food industry for the introduction of the Single European Market, it recommended that a decision to establish a single agency to promote Irish food should be postponed until after 1992. An Bord Bia was established in 1994.[146]

By the late 1980s it was widely anticipated that the increased competition in the production, wholesaling and retailing of food, following the introduction of the Single European Market,[147] would lead to a wave of mergers throughout the industry and the creation of large international firms similar to the giant US food companies.[148] There were fears that Irish food-processing firms would be especially vulnerable to competition because they were much smaller than their European and US competitors.[149] For this reason the five-year plan for the food industry drawn up in 1987 encouraged firms to merge or to engage in joint ventures with overseas companies.

The first wave of creamery amalgamations took place during the 1960s; they continued during the 1970s and 1980s with the aid of grants from FEOGA and the IDA. The pace quickened following the introduction of milk quotas, because mergers and rationalisation offered the only prospect of achieving future economies of scale.[150] By 1990 there were 33 dairy co-operatives, compared with 150 in 1973, and some co-operatives were being transformed into publicly limited companies (PLCs), because this appeared to offer the best prospect of raising additional capital for development. The removal of the preferential tax status of co-operatives in 1976 also made privatisation a more attractive option.[151] The trend began in 1988, when the debt-ridden Bailieborough Co-Op[152] in County Cavan voted to accept a takeover offer by Goodman International.[153] In January 1990 *The Irish Times* suggested that 'the spectre of obsolescence' loomed for co-operatives, because they had 'ignored commercial realities'.[154] The wave of mergers also created a number of food conglomerates with investments in pig processing, dairy produce, beef and other food products. By the mid-1990s several of the new PLCs, such as the Kerry Group, which included former Dairy Disposal Company creameries, had responded to the globalisation of the food sector by becoming multi-national companies, with sales and manufacturing operations throughout the world.

RURAL DEVELOPMENT

In 1988 the EC issued a report called *The Future of Rural Society*, which indicated the need for an integrated rural policy that would create alternative sources of income in rural areas. Irish government policy was abreast, or even slightly ahead, of developments in Brussels, because the 1987 *Programme for National Recovery* had given a commitment to launch a pilot programme of integrated rural development, and in February 1988 the Minister for Agriculture and Food, Michael O'Kennedy, informed the Dáil that he had 'deliberately' expanded the definition of agriculture to include agricultural economics and rural development.[155]

The two-year pilot programme for integrated rural development, which O'Kennedy launched in October 1988, had many features in common with the pilot areas programme of the 1960s. Twelve areas, with populations ranging from 6,000 to 15,000, were selected. The programme was designed to enable local communities to devise and implement their own development plans. No new grant aid was provided, but a rural development co-ordinator, attached to each pilot area, would give advice on how to make use of the existing state services. A majority of the projects were in tourism and agriculture; cultural and community development schemes were also promoted. This pilot effort was subsumed into the EU's Community Initiative for Rural Development – the LEADER programme.[156]

Funding for rural development received a major boost in 1988 when the EC decided to double the budget for structural funds: the FEOGA Guidance Fund, the Structural Fund, and the Regional Fund.[157] There were widespread fears that the planned reform of the CAP and the introduction of a Single European Market would have a devastating effect on living standards and prospects for growth in the peripheral regions of the Community, and the expanded Community Structure Funds (CSF) was designed to prevent this. In order to qualify for assistance under the CSF, projects were required to address one of five objectives. Objective 5 was to (a) speed up the adjustment of agricultural structures and (b) promote the development of rural areas.[158] The programmes submitted for CSF funding by the Department of Agriculture included:

- measures to encourage greater competitiveness in food processing;
- diversifying farm production;
- encouraging agri-tourism and other non-farming economic developments in rural areas;
- protecting the environment, including environmentally-friendly farming practices;
- supporting farm incomes through increased compensatory payments under the disadvantaged areas scheme, which now included three-quarters of agricultural land;
- forestry and fisheries development.[159]

Ireland was allocated £2,280 million, or over 10 per cent of the CSF budget under the first fund, which covered the years 1989–93,[160] and more than double that amount, £4,655 million, from the second CSF budget, for the years 1994–99.[161] One-sixth of Ireland's allocation from the second funding round went to the Department of Agriculture, Forestry and Rural Development, and an additional 4.5 per cent was earmarked for investment in the food industry.[162]

When the Economic and Social Research Institute (ESRI) reviewed the 1989–93 Structural Programme, it concluded that, although farm incomes would increase as a consequence of the structural aids to agriculture, there would be 'little or no impact' on output.[163] Likewise most of the money allocated to the Department of Agriculture, Forestry and Rural Development in the second CSF budget went to support farm incomes, not to promote rural enterprise. Almost half (47.6 per cent) went on headage payments; 20 per cent on subsidies for animal welfare, dairy hygiene, and control of farm pollution; only 3.5 per cent was allocated to programmes encouraging farmers to diversify into organic farming, agri-tourism, or other activities such as raising greyhounds or horses.[164] The large share of the budget devoted to headage payments reflected the Department's view that the first requirement in a rural development policy should be to maintain farmers' incomes.[165]

Agenda 2000 recast all the rural development schemes within a single framework that placed an increasing emphasis on protecting the environment. It allocated extra resources for environmentally-friendly farming methods, and setting the objective of devoting a greater share of agricultural spending to nature conservancy and spatial development than in the past.[166] Under Agenda 2000, compensatory allowances to farmers for adopting environmentally-friendly farming methods would be paid per hectare, not on a per animal basis as before. During the Agenda 2000 negotiations, Minister Joe Walsh emphasised 'the need to have as broad a coverage as possible for aid for rural development activities on and off the farm'. The agreement left national governments with considerable discretion in devising programmes for rural development.[167]

CONCLUSION

Any evaluation of the performance of the Department of Agriculture since 1973 must begin by acknowledging that policy was formulated in Brussels, and furthermore that the main features of the CAP were already in place when Ireland became a member of the EEC. Under the CAP Irish farmers received prices for their produce that were considerably above world market prices, and the intervention system reduced the possibility of acute falls in prices for dairy produce and beef. The benefits of the CAP proved particularly valuable to an agricultural exporting country like Ireland, given the unstable economic conditions that prevailed after 1973. However, the CAP did not give farmers the income stability that they wished for. Farm incomes continued to be vulnerable to bad weather, changing market demand, health scares, and international political and economic crises. But if Ireland had not joined the EEC in 1973, living standards would have been significantly lower for farmers and non-farmers alike, and the levels of emigration and unemployment would undoubtedly have been higher. The CAP increased the value of Irish agricultural exports, and by relieving the exchequer of most of the burden of agricultural expenditure, it made it possible to introduce major improvements in health, education and social welfare.

The Department of Agriculture has consistently seen its role as ensuring the survival of the CAP; maximising Irish gains under its programmes; and securing the highest possible incomes for Irish farmers, with particular attention being given to the incomes of smaller farmers. In 1976 the Minister's annual report drew a distinction between the commercial farming of the south and east of the country, and 'the subsistence struggles' of the west.[168] The growing emphasis since 1992 on direct payments to farmers and the targeting of low-income farm households is consistent with the Irish philosophy of ensuring the survival of small family farms – an objective that was highlighted when Ireland first applied for EEC membership in the 1960s. Membership of the EU has helped the Department to achieve other objectives, such as reducing the dependence of Irish agriculture on the British market; creating a substantial beef-processing sector, and developing food products that are comparable to the best in Europe.

Nevertheless, since 1973 Irish agriculture has generally proved more responsive to EU price and income supports than to consumer demand. One former secretary of the Department commented that the intervention system provided Irish agriculture with 'a soft cushion';[169] it often proved more profitable to sell beef into intervention than to develop new markets in EC countries other than the United Kingdom. The Department's 1990 Review of Agricultural and Food Policy concluded that 'the Irish food industry has been, to a considerable degree, support led rather than market led in its behaviour since its entry to the EC'. Intervention encouraged continuation of the seasonal pattern of Irish livestock production. The autumn cattle glut could be processed and sold into intervention, preventing autumn prices from falling. Consequently, farmers gained very little price advantage from producing finished cattle in the spring. Intervention also prevented structural change in cattle production. A large number of farmers, many of them elderly or part-time, continued to produce a small number of cattle every year,[170] in the knowledge that they would find a market. Since 1990 the EU support system has been altered, but this has brought about other distortions. Headage and premium payments take no account of quality, with the result that the proportion of cattle inseminated by artificial insemination has been declining during the 1990s, as has the overall quality of the Irish livestock herd.[171]

While the various support schemes for cattle and beef have undoubtedly boosted farm incomes, they probably militated against the efforts of CBF, and more recently An Bord Bia, to promote a quality Irish beef sector.[172] EU milk quotas have made it more expensive to create the efficient dairy units that will be needed in future; by 2010 it is projected that 70,000 gallons of milk will be the minimum viable output for a dairy farm, but only 3,000 farms reached that figure in 1999.[173] The conflicts that exist between the objectives of boosting farm incomes, and creating a modern high-quality agricultural and food sector, are not of the Department's making: they are a reflection of the distortions created by the CAP, and the strong political pressures on the Department from farming interests. The influence of Irish farm organisations on agricultural policy undoubtedly increased after Ireland's entry to the EEC, since the strongest card used in the past to reject farmers' demands – the cost to the exchequer – no longer applied. The official history of the NFA claimed that once Ireland became a member of the EEC, 'farmers and the Government could be seen to be on the same side'.[174]

Although the remit of the Department has been extended to include food and rural development, the Department's primary concerns remain with farming, animal health and food safety. A list of the weaknesses of the agriculture and food sector, compiled by the Agri Food 2010 Committee, began by noting the weak links to the consumer.[175] Most expenditure under the CSF went on agriculture and forestry; very little on food and rural development. A mid-term evaluation carried out by the ESRI concluded that 72 per cent of CSF spending on agriculture, forestry and rural development went on measures that would redistribute farm income rather than promote development. A statement of the Department's future strategy for the years 1995–2000 included a commitment to 'a broad view of rural development, encompassing both farm and other enterprises', but the only measure mentioned in the summary statement was 'income support for farmers'.[176] The 1999 White Paper on Rural Development, which was framed in the context of Agenda 2000, set out a more ambitious strategy, involving measures to improve infrastructure and services in rural areas, providing better opportunities for training and education, and promoting sustainable development.[177] But many of these measures will be handled by other government departments or agencies, such as the Department of the Environment and Local Government, or Fás – the government training agency. Under the National Development Plan (NDP) for 2000–2006, the budget for investment in agriculture, rural development and the food industry showed a rise of only 0.6 per cent in real terms, compared with a rise of over 73 per cent in the budget for REPS, headage payments and early retirement schemes[178] – measures that were primarily designed to boost farm incomes. As for REPS, a scheme designed to encourage farmers to take greater account of the environment, a study concluded that the environmental benefits were few; it operated mainly as a form of income support.[179]

The Department of Agriculture has been consistent in its primary objective of raising farm incomes, and it has received considerable assistance from the CAP in achieving this. Between 1970 and the mid-1990s real incomes of those working in agriculture trebled.[180] By the late 1990s the total income of farm households was above the national average,[181] while the proportion of farm households in poverty was below the national average.[182] The CAP regulations that have been imposed since the mid-1980s impose serious constraints on further increases in output, so the emphasis on raising farm incomes through direct payments may well be both necessary and justifiable. Yet there is a real danger that the Department of Agriculture may be left administering a series of quasi-welfare payments and monitoring the labyrinthine EU regulations, while other sectors of a dynamic Irish economy concentrate on growth targets, productivity and technological development. In 1997 the ESRI commented on the contradiction inherent in the Community Structural Fund's objective of closing the gap between average living standards in Ireland and the more developed parts of the EU by measures that were designed to raise output and productivity, and the agricultural schemes funded under the CAP, that were designed to encourage small farmers to stay in production. They continued:

> This contradiction is probably inherent in the CAP itself, but it also reflects an unresolved tension between the national drive for well-paid employment growth based on productivity on the one hand and a perception that rural areas need to be populated by active farmers. Whether a viable and acceptable alternative solution can be found to the rural development problem remains unclear.[183]

With the planned enlargement of the EU to include a number of large agricultural producers, such as Poland, there is a real danger that the cost of farm support programmes will be transferred from the EU to national exchequers. This was an underlying issue in the proposal for 'national envelopes', advanced as part of Agenda 2000. Although the move to renationalise agricultural support programmes was defeated, mainly because of strong opposition from France and Ireland,[184] it will undoubtedly resurface in the future.

Meanwhile the globalisation of the food industry continues. At a conference in Dublin Castle to mark the centenary of the DATI, the managing director of Kerry Group PLC, Denis Brosnan, predicted that the tendency for food companies to merge into ever- larger global companies will continue.[185] The Department of Agriculture, Food and Rural Development has to face the difficult task of balancing the needs of farmers, food processers, consumers, and the general public on issues of food safety, land-use and pollution, while securing the survival of family farm units in the twenty-first century.

CHAPTER ELEVEN

THE DEPARTMENT OF AGRICULTURE
1900–2000

The past 100 years have brought a revolution in farming, and the pace of change has accelerated since the end of World War II. Crop yields have increased enormously, and losses because of animal and plant disease have been dramatically reduced thanks to the application of modern science and technology. Food shortages have given way to surpluses, and seasonal scarcities of eggs, milk and vegetables have either disappeared or are much reduced. A product such as chicken, formerly regarded as a luxury, is a regular item on the dinner table, and the real cost of providing a much richer and more diverse diet is lower than ever before. In the developed world the battle to produce sufficient food to prevent famine and starvation, which preoccupied farmers through the ages, is a thing of the past.

The agricultural revolution of the twentieth century has posed a major challenge for the farming community and for the wider society. Modern farming requires considerably fewer workers than in the past. In 1926, 571 out of every 1,000 men at work in the Irish Free State were engaged in farming; while the proportion had declined by 1961, at 426 per 1,000, farming remained the largest single source of male employment, but by 1996 only 126 out of every 1,000 men earned their livelihood from farming.[1] The changes in agriculture threaten the survival of family farms and the rural communities that depend on them. Over the past 100 years governments throughout the world have become involved in regulating the market for agricultural produce and supporting farm incomes. In Ireland more than half of farming income is now provided by direct payments from the Department of Agriculture, Food and Rural Development.

The idea of establishing an Irish department of agriculture emerged at the end of a twenty-year period of agricultural depression. This agricultural

537

depression, which lasted approximately from 1876 to 1896, prompted several European governments to establish ministries of agriculture in order to assist farmers in improving their incomes. The French Ministry of Agriculture was established in 1881; Denmark set up a separate Ministry in 1894.[2] Having examined what continental states were doing to assist agriculture, the Recess Committee summarised the findings in three words: 'Organization, Representation, Education'.[3]

Education and the application of scientific principles to farming formed the core of the programme pursued by the new Irish Department of Agriculture and Technical Instruction (DATI). Plunkett hired a team of agricultural experts to advise on best farming practices; the DATI established a four-year programme in agricultural science at the College of Science, including a generous allocation of scholarships. Itinerant instructors advised farmers on better farming practices, and the DATI distributed leaflets on crop disease, livestock breeding and other relevant topics. Plunkett regarded the co-operative movement as an adjunct of the DATI, because co-operatives could improve farmers' profit margins by eliminating middlemen from the sale of farm produce, and they would provide farmers with cheaper and better fertiliser and more accessible credit. The Council of Agriculture and the county committees of agriculture provided channels for information between farmers and the DATI. Finally, the DATI set out to promote Irish agricultural exports by enforcing quality controls; negotiating better terms and facilities with the transport companies; and financing trade stands at international fairs. These remained the main activities of the Department until the early 1930s.

At first sight this programme seems modest, particularly when compared with the wide-ranging activities of today's Department, but in reality it was an extremely ambitious programme, because the DATI was attempting to bring about radical changes in rural Ireland. Itinerant instructors might recommend the abandonment or modification of traditional farming practices. Breaking with tradition, by following the advice of a stranger rather than the long-established farming practices of neighbours or a parent, or applying scientific principles in place of custom, struck at the heart of peasant society. Many farmers feared that the cost of additional credit or fertiliser would leave them without sufficient money for basic requirements, or that experimental crops or strains of seed might fail and plunge the family into destitution. For these reasons they were often slow to heed the advice given by agricultural scientists.[4] The relationship between the DATI and the co-operative movement was complicated by political issues, particularly the relationship between the Irish Parliamentary Party and local traders, but again the difficulties in establishing agricultural co-operatives were not unique to Ireland.[5]

When the DATI was founded in 1900 Irish agriculture operated in a free market. Prices for produce and raw materials were set by supply and demand. Farmers could buy fertiliser, grain and machinery at world prices. Irish butter, eggs and livestock had to compete with produce from other countries, both at home and in the British market. The DATI exercised no influence over agricultural prices; the only subsidy given to agriculture was the partial de-rating of agricultural land, which was introduced in 1898 as a benefit to landlords, not to farmers.

The ownership and distribution of land was the responsibility of the Land Commission and the Congested Districts Board, not of the DATI. However, land policy became the principal task of the Dáil Ministry of Agriculture during 1919–22, and Patrick Hogan, the Minister for Agriculture and Lands in the Irish Free State, introduced the 1923 Land Act, which transferred the remaining estates from landlord control. Once this was out of the way, however, the post-Independence Department continued very much along earlier lines, concentrating on measures to reduce farmers' costs or improve the quality of Irish agricultural output and exports. Patrick Hogan was a strong advocate of free trade and the market economy; agricultural rates relief – the Agricultural Grant – remained the only significant subsidy provided for agriculture, although the price of sugar-beet was supported by tax concessions and consumers.

By the end of 1931, however, the collapse in world agricultural prices forced the Cumann na nGaedheal government to abandon its previous policy of free trade; tariffs were imposed on imported butter, bacon and oats to prevent dumping.[6] Fianna Fáil came into office in February 1932 with a programme of self-sufficiency in agriculture and industry that was designed to reverse the prevailing pattern of Irish agriculture since the Famine, by breaking the dependence on the British market and reducing or obliterating the dominance of livestock farming. This programme was very much at variance with the policies previously pursued by the Department of Agriculture; when a committee of senior officials presented a report on wheat-growing to the Minister for Agriculture, James Ryan, in the summer of 1932, it began by noting that it had not been asked to determine whether it was desirable for Ireland to grow more wheat, and it had not considered this matter.[7] Nevertheless, the Department of Agriculture played a key role in the self-sufficiency programme of the 1930s, by encouraging farmers to plant wheat, sugar-beet and tobacco; supplying technical advice on cultivating these crops; and determining which seed varieties were appropriate for Irish conditions. At the same time the Department of Agriculture tried to restrain the more extreme aspects of the self-sufficiency programme, such as the proposals for a radical cull of livestock. The 1938 Anglo-Irish Trade Agreement marked the end of Fianna Fáil's intense ideological commitment to self-sufficiency. However, during the Emergency the Department of Agriculture had the critical task of keeping the country fed, while again ensuring that the long-term interests of Irish agriculture were not damaged, and that long-standing trading links to the United Kingdom were not sacrificed for short-term gains.

The early 1930s were a watershed in the history of the Department of Agriculture. In 1931 Britain abandoned free trade in agricultural produce. In the following year the Fianna Fáil government introduced export bounties for cattle; it fixed the price for Irish-grown wheat, and Irish millers were required to use a specified quantity of Irish wheat in flour. Imports of farm machinery were taxed, and the use of imported maize as animal feed was restricted. The 1930s marked the end of free market conditions for Irish agriculture. Since that time the government, and latterly the EU, have provided some degree of price support for Irish farm produce. Ireland is not unique; by the late 1950s every country in western Europe was subsidising farm prices.

The early 1930s also marked the end of the free access to the UK market that Irish farmers had enjoyed since the 1820s. In 1931 Britain reversed the policy that it had followed since the 1840s of buying food on the world market at the cheapest prices, irrespective of the consequences for Irish and British farmers. Britain set out to reduce its reliance on imported food by offering farmers secure markets and higher prices. If Ireland had remained part of the United Kingdom, this change of policy would have been very advantageous to Irish farmers. But the Irish Free State was independent, and from 1938, when the Economic War came to an end, the terms on which Irish produce was admitted to the United Kingdom were determined by trade negotiations between the Department of Agriculture and the British authorities. After World War II farmers in Britain and Northern Ireland supplied a growing share of UK food requirements. Ireland, Denmark, New Zealand and other exporters competed for a declining market, where the prices often failed to cover the cost of production, and the terms and conditions were liable to be altered at short notice. EEC membership admitted Ireland to one of the world's most privileged trading blocs, and it brought an end to the often-damaging competition with European and Commonwealth producers for a share of the UK market. But trade negotiations remained an important part of the Department's work, although they were now concerned with sales to the Middle East and other markets outside the EU.

The changes that took place during the 1930s transformed the work of the Department of Agriculture. Its original role of providing advice, technical assistance and education took second place to the more immediate pressures to set wheat prices; to allocate pigs to bacon factories; to ensure that the target acreage of sugar-beet was achieved; to dispose of unwanted cattle; to restore grain mills in County Leitrim; or to negotiate a trade agreement with Britain.

When the DATI was established, Horace Plunkett made a determined decision to fill senior positions in the Department with qualified scientists. In 1916 the Agriculture Branch of the DATI was headed by J. R. Campbell, a former professor of agricultural science; the Agricultural Branch consisted of fifty-one men and women with scientific or technical qualifications and forty-eight clerks. The changes in agricultural policy during the 1930s were prompted by political and economic developments in Ireland and the United Kingdom. Although the Department's agricultural experts provided technical advice – on which soils and micro-climates were suitable for growing sugar-beet, and on the most suitable varieties of winter wheat – most of the additional work called for administrative rather than scientific skills, and the number of administrative and clerical staff rose substantially.

In 1935 the Department consisted of four divisions, each headed by a principal officer, with responsibility for implementing and enforcing a range of legislative and administrative measures. For example, Division One was responsible for the Dairy Produce and Eggs Acts, Marketing, Export Bounties on Dairy Produce, Eggs and Poultry; Cereals and Tobacco Acts; the Potato Act; and the Weeds and Seeds Act. In the new administrative structure agricultural scientists and veterinarians were listed under the heading Inspectorate, and it appears they had no role in implementing the specific programmes. The structures that evolved to cope with the Economic War and the self-sufficiency drive of the 1930s were largely unchanged when the Devlin commission on the reorganisation of the civil service reported in 1969. The commission noted that the Department's professional staff had no executive authority; they could only give advice. Although the commission recommended that the distinction between the administrative and the professional staff should end, it has remained to the present day.

The place of agricultural research and education in the work of the Department had already been eroded during the 1920s, when the College of Science was transferred to UCD, thus robbing the Department of Agriculture of many leading researchers. The creation of the Department of Education led to confusion over who was responsible for agricultural education. Although there was an attempt to establish a coherent structure for these services in the early 1950s, when the idea of an agricultural institute was first mooted, this was not achieved until Teagasc was established in 1988.

When the Economic War came to an end in 1938, the Department recommended that a commission be established to investigate Irish agriculture. It was insistent that the commission should be 'purely technical in its aspects and composed only of agricultural experts. The problem is to increase the volume, value, and profitability (consistent with retaining, at least, the present agricultural population). The problem is technical and not economic.' In its opinion a commission composed of bankers, business-men and labour members would be of little use.[8] But by 1938 policy was being driven by political and economic forces rather than by agricul-tural science. In 1945 the Committee on Post-Emergency Agricultural Policy, which was dominated by agricultural experts, set out a long-term programme for investment in agriculture. Its priorities included better veterinary services, soil improvement, and other technical advances. However, the committee could not agree whether post-war agriculture should continue to rely on self-sufficiency and tillage, or encourage an expansion of grassland enterprises that would cater mainly for export markets. Although the broad outlines of agricultural policy were determined by political and economic factors, the details should have been guided by agricultural research, but this did not necessarily happen.

The delay in establishing an agricultural research institute was a major handicap to Irish agriculture during the 1950s, because it meant that agricultural policy was rarely guided by research. The protracted debate on the merits or defects of 'the dual-purpose cow' was dominated by the opinions, even the prejudices, of politicians, and by the vested interests of the breeders' associations, without reference to data on milk yields, beef quality or the relative prices of different breeds. Decisions on milk prices during the 1950s were made on the basis of budgetary considerations, farmers' lobbies and political expediency, not on accurate data about the cost of producing milk, and no evaluation was carried out of the land rehabilitation project until the 1980s. The Department's soil laboratories and grassland research unit at Johnstown Castle demonstrated conclusively that Irish farmers needed to spread substantially larger quantities of fertiliser to eliminate soil deficiencies and to increase yields. However, it was difficult to persuade farmers to follow this advice, given the high cost of fertiliser because of the tariffs imposed by the Department of Industry and Commerce to protect Irish fertiliser manufacturers. The findings of the soil research unit ultimately bore fruit in 1958, when the *Programme for Economic Expansion* cited its research to justify the case for providing a substantial price subsidy for fertilisers. By the 1960s the government's commitment to economic planning and the establishment of the AFT meant that policy on matters such as livestock breeding or western development was increasingly being influenced by research findings. If agricultural policies in recent decades have not always been consistent with the advice of agricultural scientists or agricultural economists, this is generally because this advice conflicts with social and political pressures, or the views of farm organisations, not because of a lack of scientific or economic knowledge.

The effectiveness of many of the Department's programmes has always depended on the local advisory service, and ultimately on whether Irish farmers were receptive to advice on agricultural matters. The Minister for Agriculture could announce a programme for soil testing; he or she could urge farmers to produce silage rather than hay, to spray their crops and inoculate their livestock in order to reduce the incidence of disease. However, the ultimate success of these measures depended on whether the advice reached the farmers; whether they understood the message and were persuaded of the benefits; and whether the advice translated into higher farm incomes. In 1938 the chief agricultural officer for Wexford, M.T. Connolly, wrote that,

It is now an everyday experience to be called in to advise on ordinary farm problems in relation to farm management. The day of 'what do they know' is gone and much credit goes to those few progressive farmers who were to be found in every area of the state: they were, so to speak, the pioneers. In the early days they adopted the methods as advised by the Instructors often at the ridicule of certain of their neighbours. Results, however, are louder than words and it was soon seen that these farmers were obtaining better yields, producing crops of better quality, using manures more intelligently and economically, carrying more and better class of livestock per acre, and in short were more successful than their neighbours.[9]

Despite this statement it would be unwise to assume that a majority of farmers followed the advice of their advisers in 1938 or at a later date. Irish farmers had a low standard of general education. Several witnesses told the 1907 inquiry into the DATI that they could not understand some of the lectures that had been organised by the advisory service, and many of the leaflets supplied by the DATI were beyond their comprehension. Although compulsory schooling was introduced in 1926, the Department of Education adopted an extremely lenient attitude towards absences by farmers' children if they were needed to help out on the family farm.[10] There is widespread evidence that the designated heir was often given less formal schooling than his siblings, or that he inherited the family farm because he had shown little aptitude at school. Many farmers were reluctant to permit their sons to apply for scholarships to agricultural colleges.[11] The development of agricultural education was damaged by the rivalry between the departments of Agriculture and Education, and because the Department of Agriculture claimed overall responsibility for agricultural education it tended to be divorced from the wider educational policy. The OECD report *Investment in Education*, which provided the blue-print for educational reforms during the late 1960s, contained no recommendations for developments in agricultural education,[12] despite the economic importance of agriculture. The Agri Food 2010 report, published in 2000, has recommended that agricultural training should be integrated with mainstream education. This recommendation was accepted by the Minister,[13] and has been put into effect. In 2001, for the first time, applications for places at agricultural college will be handled along with other third-level places by the Central Applications Office.

Responsibility for agricultural education and the advisory services rested with the county committees of agriculture until the 1980s. Horace Plunkett commented that the Recess Committee was extremely conscious that 'the greater part of its work ... would relate to special localities', and that it would only succeed if it had local support.[14] At local level most agricultural services were provided by the county committees of agriculture. The Department supplied them with advisory leaflets, circulars, notices of changes in departmental regulations, and a substantial proportion of their overall funding; it scrutinised the annual budgets of the county committees, and the schemes that the committees wished to promote; the Department's

inspectors visited the chief agricultural officers and the advisers on a regular basis; they attended meetings of the county committees. Chief agricultural officers travelled to Dublin once or twice a year for a briefing by the
Department. Unfortunately, the records to hand give very little indication
of the relationship between the Department and the county committees
or the chief agricultural officers. We do not know if the Department
reprimanded county committees who adopted a lax approach to disease
and weed control.[15]

The Agriculture Act of 1931 required that all local schemes be administered through the county committees and made it obligatory for each
local authority to raise an agricultural rate of 2d in the pound.[16] In 1948
the maximum agricultural rate that county councils could levy was increased
from 4d to 7d in the pound; in 1955 it was increased to 10d, and in 1958 to
15d in the pound.[17] Yet the reliance on local funding meant that services
varied between counties and the poorer western counties had the worst
ratios of advisers to farmers. In 1944 the Minister for Agriculture was
empowered to dissolve a county committee of agriculture even if the county
council had not been dissolved,[18] but these powers were never used, and
there is no evidence such action was ever contemplated. Given the often
turbulent relationship between local authorities and the Department of
Local Government, such harmony suggests that the Department of
Agriculture intruded less into the work of the county committees of
agriculture; it may also suggest that local agricultural services were regarded
as less important than Plunkett had envisaged. Although the county
committees of agriculture remained in existence until 1988, and most local
services were administered under their auspices until the early 1980s, they
failed to evolve to meet the changing needs of Irish agriculture. On the
two earlier occasions when a reform of the advisory service was considered
– the parish plan of the 1950s, and the proposed establishment of a National
Agricultural Advisory Education and Research Authority in 1977 – opinions
were divided on the basis of party politics, and little attention was paid to
the quality of the service. Like the Department, the advisory service was
increasingly saddled with administration of schemes, particularly following
the introduction of the Farm Modernisation Scheme in 1974.

Representation was one of the three objectives for a department of
agriculture listed by the Recess Committee, and this was achieved through
the county committees of agriculture, the Council of Agriculture and the
Board of Agriculture. Despite their limitations, the Council and Board of
Agriculture provided a voice for agricultural interests and they exercised

some influence over policy. When the Irish Free State came into existence, authority was centralised in the minister; the Council and the Board of Agriculture were not reconvened, and were abolished in 1931. The annual meeting of the county committees of agriculture became the only national forum for discussing agricultural policy other than Dáil Éireann, but it failed to develop into an influential platform. Although the Department established a number of consultative committees during the 1920s and 1930s to advise on specific aspects of agricultural policy, they met infrequently, and only when summoned by the minister. In the Dáil and Seanad, opinion on agricultural policy was polarised on party lines, with the result that debates on the Agriculture estimate tended to be dominated by political rhetoric; otherwise deputies were primarily concerned with making representations about local schemes, rather than offering a detailed critique of the work of the Department.[19]

Once the Department of Agriculture began to determine agricultural prices and provide subsidies for land drainage and farm buildings, it was inevitable that farming organisations would emerge to lobby the Department on these matters. The Nobel-prize-winning economist Douglass North noted that 'the larger the percentage of society's resources influenced by government decisions (directly or via regulation), the more resources will be devoted to such offensive and defensive (to prevent being adversely affected) organizations'.[20] It is no coincidence that the Irish Beet Growers' Association was the earliest modern farming organisation to emerge. Beet prices were determined by the monopoly producer: the state-owned Comhlucht Siúicre Éireann Teoranta, and it was very much in farmers' interests to establish a strong negotiating body. The formation of the ICMSA in the early 1950s was a reflection of the fact that the producer price of milk was now fixed by the Department of Agriculture, and that this would probably continue. The scope for agricultural pressure groups to influence policy was further enhanced after World War II when policy was no longer polarised on party political lines, as it had been before 1939. This meant that Fianna Fáil and Fine Gael had to differentiate themselves to the farming electorate in other ways, by being more responsive to demands for farmers' representation, or by promising concessions on farm prices or the agricultural grant. As a consequence, the number of agricultural grants and schemes began to proliferate during the 1950s; they were often introduced to assuage farmers' demands, or as *ad hoc* solutions to agricultural crises. By 1958 the Department of Agriculture operated five separate loan and grant schemes for fertilisers.

The emergence of strong farming organisations has been a European-wide phenomenon; they developed in parallel with increased state support for agriculture. By the 1950s many farmers were coming to regard lobbying for higher prices or lower taxes as a more reliable method of securing higher incomes, than carrying out a programme of investment. Irish farm organisations were conscious of the methods and the achievements of their counterparts in other countries. The militant protests of the 1960s were modelled on the actions of French farmers,[21] and the NFA's demand to engage in annual price talks with the government was an effort to achieve the privileged status that the British Ministry of Agriculture had accorded to the NFU. One British historian claimed that, 'The effectiveness of agricultural lobbying after 1940 is almost legendary, the NFU for a period before 1960 was almost an equal partner with the Ministry of Agriculture in determining policies.'[22] In Britain farmers were a small minority of the population, and agriculture accounted for a relatively low proportion of national income compared with manufacturing and services, so British governments could afford to treat their farmers in a generous fashion. Such generosity was offset by Britain's ability to import most of its food from Ireland, Denmark and the Commonwealth at low prices; indeed, UK food prices were subsidised by Irish taxpayers and consumers. The dominant place of agriculture in the Irish economy, however, meant that even modest concessions proved extremely expensive. Nevertheless, as national income increased during the 1960s, the government was careful to ensure that farmers shared in the national prosperity. During the 1960s the growth in farm incomes gradually became detached from trends in agricultural output, and this process accelerated after Ireland became a member of the EEC.

Since the 1980s the major social and economic programmes have been the subject of lengthy negotiations between the government and the social partners – farmers, trade unions, employers, and other interest groups – and it is widely acknowledged that this has been a major factor in Ireland's economic success. However, the emergence of social partnership was a gradual process. Although Seán Lemass proved very willing to meet delegations from farming organisations and other interest groups when he became Taoiseach, when he served as Minister for Industry and Commerce he resisted demands by Irish manufacturers to be consulted about industrial policy.[23] Indeed, the regular meetings that took place between ministers for Agriculture and the county committees of agriculture or other farming bodies during the 1940s and 1950s were exceptional in

Irish political life at the time. Yet, the underlying tensions that existed between the Department and the farming organisations during the 1950s and 1960s were probably inevitable; farmers' aspirations were rising at a time when agricultural employment was falling and the outlets for Irish agricultural produce were limited. No Irish government would have been in a financial position to meet farmers' demands.

One of the key questions that must be addressed is what is the precise role of a Department of Agriculture? Should it represent the interests of Irish farmers, even at the expense of the interests of taxpayers, consumers and manufacturers? Such a question would have presented no difficulty for Patrick Hogan, because he believed that the interests of Irish agriculture and the Irish nation were identical. On this basis he opposed any change in government policy that threatened the competitiveness of agriculture. But as government intervention in the economy increased during the 1930s, with industrial protection and legislation regulating the wages and conditions of urban workers, there was much greater potential for conflicts of interest between farmers and other sections of the community on matters such as producer prices or taxation. Irish farm organisations appear to have assumed that the Department should represent farming interests without qualification. Patrick Smith, Minister for Agriculture from 1957 to 1964, once reminded farm leaders that he was 'Minister *for* Agriculture, a representative of the Government not of farmers. His duty was to the Government and to the public'.[24] Nevertheless, it is evident that the Department has traditionally looked at agricultural matters from the perspective of the producer rather than the consumer. Consumer interests were obviously a key consideration in the enforcement of health and hygiene regulations, but the Department of Agriculture generally took little account of the impact of higher grain or milk prices on the cost of living when making the case for price concessions in Cabinet. Within the EEC the Department has consistently worked to maximise the benefits to Irish farmers from the CAP, and in this instance has probably echoed Patrick Hogan's belief that the interests of Irish farmers and the national interest are identical.

But this identity of interests does not necessarily apply on issues such as food policy or the environment, and as the contribution made by agriculture to employment or GNP continues to fall, there will be a greater need to take non-farming interests into consideration. The Statement of Strategy for the Department for the years 1995–2000 conceded that its traditional focus had been on agricultural production. It indicated that future policies would be designed to develop 'a strong consumer-oriented food industry'.[25]

While there have been difficulties in reconciling the needs of the agriculture and food sectors in a single Department, the Government decision taken in 1987, to transfer responsibility for food from the Department of Industry and Commerce, was a reflection of the view that the development of the agriculture and food industries is inextricably linked.

When the DATI was established, its responsibilities ranged from agriculture to technical and scientific education and rural industry, but the departmental structure that was introduced by the Irish Free State confined its activities to the narrower question of agriculture. It is worth considering whether the departmental structure established during 1922 was the most appropriate to Ireland's needs. Its greatest merit was that it ensured tight financial control at a time when the solvency of the new state was extremely precarious. However, interdepartmental rivalries and competing interests between departments proved a liability on several occasions, and a more holistic approach towards agriculture and the rural economy might have been desirable.

One obvious gap has been the failure to integrate policy on land with agricultural policy. When the DATI was founded in 1900, most Irish farmers firmly believed that the obvious answer to their difficulties was peasant proprietorship and the redistribution of land occupied by landlords and graziers to small farmers and landless men. In 1900 many agricultural holdings were so small, or the land of such poor quality, that they could not provide their occupants with a decent livelihood, even with the most dedicated attention to the advice given by the DATI. Plunkett, who was a member of the landlord class, regarded demands for the reform of land ownership and distribution as a precondition for modernising Irish agriculture, as a red herring. He consistently argued that the solution to the underdeveloped state of Irish agriculture rested with science and education, not with land reform. Although the Irish Free State initially placed land and agriculture within a single ministry – a quasi-merger of the DATI and the Dáil Ministry of Lands and Agriculture – the Land and Agriculture portfolios were separated in 1928, and this remained the case until 1977. Between the late 1920s and the early 1960s, when the interdepartmental committee on small western farms investigated agricultural policy and farm structures as part of its comprehensive study, the Department of Agriculture appears to have paid minimal attention to farm structures or regional matters. Equally there is no indication that the Land Commission's policy on resettlement or redistribution was influenced to any extent by agricultural considerations.

Today structural problems, such as small farms, poor quality of land and ageing farmers, are widely recognised as some of the major causes of low farm incomes. Would a Department of Agriculture and Lands that took structural problems into consideration when devising and implementing agricultural policies, have been more effective in raising output and farm incomes? Probably not. Eliminating the smallest and most uneconomic farms might have resulted in a more efficient Irish agriculture, but any proposal to consolidate holdings would have been political suicide. Since Independence most criticism of land policy has focused on the limited number of new holdings created by the Land Commission, and the failure to placate the demands of landless men and farmers' sons throughout rural Ireland. There has been no political pressure for the consolidation of farms. The manifesto of Fianna Fáil, Ireland's largest and most successful political party, included a commitment to keep the maximum number of families on the land,[26] and this principle was affirmed in the Directive Principles of Social Policy that were contained in the 1937 Constitution.[27] Most statements on economic and agricultural policy issued by political parties until the 1960s contained a commitment to reverse, or at least halt, the flight from the land. Any question of depriving elderly or inefficient farmers of land, or imposing a land tax to promote greater efficiency – as Raymond Crotty controversially proposed[28] – would have been tantamount to political suicide, given the history of land agitation and the protection given to property rights in the Irish Constitution. In Article 40 of the 1937 Constitution the state undertook 'to vindicate the ... property rights of every citizen', and in the section dealing with Fundamental Rights, the state guaranteed 'to pass no law attempting to abolish the right of private ownership or the general right to transfer, bequeath, and inherit property.'[29] Folk memories of evictions, land-grabbers and bailiffs continued to exercise a powerful influence. Moreover, any attempt to promote more mechanisation in farming, or the consolidation of farms, would have resulted in higher emigration and unemployment. There was also a lack of awareness of the social dimensions of agriculture and rural life until the 1960s, when the Rural Economics section of AFT and the Economic and Social Research Institute began to examine such questions. This omission was not unique to the Department of Agriculture: social investigation in Ireland, and training in the social sciences other than economics, were very slow to develop. The Limerick Rural Survey, funded by the Department of Agriculture, was the first major study of rural social problems to be conducted by Irish researchers.[30]

Structural reform and the number of farmers remain sensitive issues, even in the year 2000. A report by Agri Food 2010 (a group of experts commissioned by the Department to propose a strategy for the development of Irish agriculture and food over the next decade) predicted that by 2010 the number of full-time farmers would have fallen to 20,000, with a further 60,000 part-time farmers and 20,000 transitional farms.[31] The government's response to this report, which was published some months later, following widespread consultation, omitted these statistics in favour of a statement that 'The Government is committed to maintaining the greatest number of family farms. This will involve the development of a core of full time farmers, while at the same time ensuring that smaller farmers have the opportunity to supplement their income through off farm work'.[32] This reads very much like an updated version of the commitments given by previous Irish governments to maintain the agricultural population at its existing size.

In 1995 the mission of the Department was 'to develop the agriculture, food and forestry sectors in a manner which will maximise their contribution to the economy and to sustainable employment, while protecting the environment, advancing food safety and animal health and welfare, and promoting rural development'.[33] The EU now recognises that the development of agriculture is not sustainable without taking into account the need to protect the environment, food safety, animal health/welfare and rural development. Agriculture policy has therefore become even more complex and Agriculture Departments in all developed countries have had to readjust to this more complex policy environment. The reorganisation of the Department as set out in the recently published Statement of Strategy 2001–2004 is a recognition of the new reality. This suggests that the Department is now required to be all things to all men: developing the agriculture and food sectors, while protecting the environment, promoting food safety and animal health, and rural development. There is a real danger that these objectives may prove difficult if not impossible to reconcile; the ghost of the dual-purpose cow lingers in today's agricultural policy. An increasing proportion of farm incomes now comes in the form of payments for not producing crops or livestock, and for caring for the land. The pressures on the Department of Agriculture at the beginning of its second century are infinitely more complex than those facing Horace Plunkett and the Department's founders. Over the past 100 years the Department of Agriculture has devoted considerable effort to creating a modern agricultural sector, but the current structure of farm income supports means that many farmers are now being encouraged to regress to earlier practices, where farming was less an economic enterprise than a way of life.

When the DATI was founded in 1900 it was charged with 'aiding, improving and developing agriculture, fisheries and other industries of Ireland insofar as may be proper to such a Department and in such a manner as to stimulate and strengthen the self-reliance of the people'. With marginal changes this statement could provide an appropriate mission statement for the Department in its second century.

Appendix 1

100 Years of Service
1900–2000

Over the last 100 years generations of men and women working in the Department of Agriculture, Food and Rural Development and its predecessor Departments have served Irish agriculture and rural Ireland well.

Marking a centenary of service, 1900–2000, Irish agriculture salutes the Ministers, Department Secretaries and their staff, who have fostered and led Irish agriculture through good times and bad, working always for the greater good.

Vice-Presidents

Name	Term of Office
Sir Horace Plunkett	1900–1907
Thomas Wallace Russell	1907–1919
Hugh T. Barrie	1919–1921

Ministers

Name	Term of Office
Robert C. Barton	1919–1920
Art O'Connor	1920–1922
Patrick Hogan	1922–1932
Dr Seamus Ó Riain	1932–1947
Patrick Smith	1947–1948

Ministers (Cont'd)

Name	Term of Office
James M. Dillon	1948–1951
Thomas Walsh	1951–1954
James M. Dillon	1954–1957
Frank Aiken	1957
Sean Moylan	1957
Patrick Smyth	1957–1964
Charles J. Haughey	1964–1966
Neil T. Blaney	1966–1970
James Gibbons	1970–1973
Mark Clinton	1973–1977
James Gibbons	1977–1979
Ray McSharry	1979–1981
Alan Dukes	1981–1982
Brian Lenihan	1982
Austin Deasy	1982–1987
Michael O'Kennedy	1987–1991
Dr Michael Woods	1991–1992
Joe Walsh	1992–1994
Ivan Yates	1994–1997
Joe Walsh	1997–

Department Secretaries

Name	Term of Office
Thomas Patrick Gill	1901–1922
Francis J. Meyrick	1923–1933
Daniel Twomey	1934–1946
Sean O'Broin	1947–1955
John Dempsey	1955–1958
John C. Nagle	1958–1971
Michael Barry	1971–1977
James O'Mahony	1977–1988
Donal Creedon	1988–1989
Michael Dowling	1989–1997
John Malone	1997–

NOTES TO CHAPTERS

CHAPTER ONE

1. 'A mere replica of the English Board would not have fulfilled a tithe of the objects we had in view'. Horace Plunkett, *Ireland in the New Century*, (London, 1905 edition), p. 211.
2. Oliver MacDonagh, *Ireland: the Union and its Aftermath*, (London, 1977), chapter 2.
3. Plunkett was the third son of Lord Dunsany of Dunsany Castle, County Meath.
4. Andrew Gailey, *Ireland and the Death of Kindness. The Experience of Constructive Unionism 1890–1905*, (Cork, 1987), p. 34.
5. Gailey, *Ireland and the Death of Kindness*, p. 56.
6. *Departmental Committee on the Department of Agriculture and Technical Instruction (Ireland)*, (hereafter *Departmental Committee DATI*), 1907. Minutes of Evidence, Cd. 3574, para. 1293.
7. For a detailed description of post-Famine agriculture, see Michael Turner, *After the Famine. Irish Agriculture 1850–1914*, (Cambridge, 1996), especially chapter 2.
8. Peter Solar, 'Agricultural productivity and economic development in Ireland and Scotland in the early 19th century', in T. M. Devine and D. Dickson (eds), *Ireland and Scotland, 1600–1850*, (Edinburgh, 1983), p. 81.
9. Turner, *After the Famine*, p. 145. On an index of 1850–4 =100, the index rose to 101.2 in 1855–9; fell to a low of 79.9 during 1885–9; and by 1895–9 stood at 81.7.
10. Mary E. Daly, 'Farming and the Famine', in Cormac Ó Gráda (ed.), *Famine 150*, (Dublin, 1997), pp 29–48.
11. Solar, 'Agricultural productivity', p. 81.
12. Cormac Ó Gráda, *Ireland. A New Economic History 1780–1939*, (Oxford, 1994), pp 261–2.
13. Mary E. Daly, *The Spirit of Earnest Inquiry. The Statistical and Social Inquiry Society of Ireland 1847–1997*, (Dublin, 1997), p. 62.
14. Turner, *After the Famine*, chapter 6.
15. T. P. O'Neill, 'The food crisis of the 1890s', in E. M. Crawford (ed.), *Famine: the Irish Experience 900–1900*, (Edinburgh, 1989), p. 177.
16. Barbara L. Solow, *The Land Question and the Irish Economy, 1870–1903*, (Cambridge, Mass., 1971), pp 149–50.
17. W. L. Micks, *The History of the Congested Districts Board*, (Dublin, 1925).

18. Liam Kennedy, 'The Union of Ireland and Britain, 1801–1921', in Liam Kennedy (ed.), *Colonialism, Religion and Nationalism in Ireland*, (Belfast, 1996), p. 54.
19. *Report of the Recess Committee*, (Dublin, 1896), p. 45.
20. Arthur Young, *A Tour in Ireland*, 2nd edition, (London, 1780).
21. Daly, 'Farming and the Famine', pp 35–6.
22. Sam Clark, *Social Origins of the Irish Land War*, (Princeton, 1979), pp 214–20; K. Theodore Hoppen, *Elections, Politics and Society in Ireland 1832–1885*, (Oxford, 1984), pp 468–9.
23. James Meenan and Desmond Clarke, 'The RDS 1731–1981', in James Meenan and Desmond Clarke (eds), *The Royal Dublin Society, 1731–1981*, (Dublin, 1981), p. 1.
24. Simon Curran, 'The society's role in agriculture since 1800', in Meenan and Clarke, *The Royal Dublin Society*, (Dublin, 1981), pp 88–100.
25. *Report of the Recess Committee*, pp 70–2.
26. John O'Donovan, *An Economic History of Livestock in Ireland*, (Cork, 1940), pp 361–2.
27. W. J. Vaughan, *Landlords and Tenants in Mid-Victorian Ireland*, (Oxford, 1994), pp 117–23.
28. *Ibid.*, pp 99–100.
29. William L. Feingold, *The Revolt of the Tenantry: The Transformation of Local Government in Ireland, 1872–1886*, (Boston, 1984), pp 30–1, 214–15.
30. Paul Bew, *Charles Stewart Parnell*, (Dublin, 1980), p. 33.
31. Carla Keating, 'Sir Horace Plunkett and Rural Reform 1889–1914', PhD thesis, University College, Dublin, 1984, p. 49.
32. Keating, 'Sir Horace Plunkett', pp 102, 107.
33. Cormac Ó Gráda, 'The beginnings of the Irish creamery system 1880–1914', *Economic History Review*, vol. xxx, 1977, pp 284–305.
34. Brian Harvey, 'The Emergence of the Western Problem in the Irish Economy in the Latter Part of the 19th Century and its Persistence into the 20th Century, with Special Reference to the Work of the Congested Districts Board 1891–1923', MA thesis, University College, Dublin, 1986, p. 100.
35. Keating, 'Sir Horace Plunkett', p. 229.
36. Mary E. Daly, *The Buffer State. The Historical Roots of the Department of the Environment*, (Dublin, 1987), p. 25.
37. Pauric Travers, 'The financial relations question, 1800–1914', in F. B. Smith (ed.), *Ireland, England and Australia. Essays in Honour of Oliver MacDonagh*, (Cork, 1990), pp 50–6.
38. *Freeman's Journal*, 28/29 August 1895; *Irish Daily Independent*, 28/29 August, 1895; *Belfast Newsletter*, 28/29 August 1895; *The Irish Times*, 28/29 August 1895.
39. Keating, 'Sir Horace Plunkett', pp 238–40, 249–50.
40. Trevor West, *Horace Plunkett: Co-Operation and Politics, an Irish Biography*, (Gerrards Cross and Washington, 1986), pp 48–9.
41. *Report of the Recess Committee*, pp 72–7.
42. Keating, 'Sir Horace Plunkett', p. 241.
43. Daly, *The Buffer State*, p. 18.
44. Keating, 'Sir Horace Plunkett', p. 247.

45. On the latter topic see David S. Johnson and Liam Kennedy, 'Nationalist historiography and the decline of the Irish economy: George O'Brien revisited', in Sean Hutton and Paul Stewart (eds), *Ireland's Histories. Aspects of State, Society and Ideology*, (London, 1991), pp 11–36.
46. *Report of the Recess Committee*, pp 3–4.
47. For a detailed description see *Departmental Committee DATI*, Minutes of Evidence, Cd. 3573, para. 11.
48. Gailey, *Ireland and the Death of Kindness*, pp 44–5; p. 124.
49. Agricultural rates relief was mainly of benefit to landlords; the reform of local government would mean the abolition of the unelected grand juries, which were dominated by landlords and the creation of elected local authorities. Daly, *The Buffer State*, pp 24–7.
50. Gailey, *Ireland and the Death of Kindness*, pp 81–4.
51. Micks, *History of the Congested Districts Board*.
52. There is almost nothing in print on the Development Commission. Its annual reports are published in the Parliamentary Papers series. On the background to the 1903 Development Commission, see Gailey, *Ireland and the Death of Kindness*, pp 188–9, 196–7, 201– 7. Details of the grants that the DATI received from the Development Commission are given in the annual reports of the DATI.
53. *Departmental Committee DATI*, evidence, para. 14.
54. The Chief Secretary was also president of the Local Government Board of Ireland, although effective power rested with the vice-president, who was a civil servant. Daly, *The Buffer State*, p. 18.
55. Plunkett lost his seat in Dublin South when the unionist vote was split by an independent unionist candidate, Francis Elrington Ball.
56. *Departmental Committee DATI*, evidence, para. 17.
57. *Ibid.*, paras 281–6.
58. The book was first published in 1904.
59. West, *Horace Plunkett*, p. 69.
60. *Ibid.*, p. 75.
61. For details see section later in this chapter, 'The 1906/7 Inquiry into the DATI'.
62. Keating, 'Sir Horace Plunkett', pp 347–8.
63. West, *Horace Plunkett*, pp 78–80.
64. Paul Bew, *Conflict and Conciliation in Ireland, 1890–1910: Parnellites and Agrarian Radicals*, (Oxford, 1987), pp 86–7.
65. Alvin Jackson, *The Ulster Party: Irish Unionists in the House of Commons, 1884–1911*, (Oxford, 1989), p. 156.
66. Bew, *Conflict and Conciliation*, pp 88–91.
67. *Departmental Committee DATI*, evidence, para. 661.
68. Liam Kennedy, 'Farmers, traders and agricultural politics in pre-Independence Ireland', in Kennedy, *Colonialism*, pp 150–1.
69. R. A. Anderson, *With Horace Plunkett in Ireland*, (London, 1935), pp 119–20.
70. *Departmental Committee DATI*, paras 4862–76.
71. Council of Agriculture, Minutes, 19 November 1907.
72. Board of Agriculture, Minutes, 12 September 1900.
73. Board of Agriculture, Minutes, 16 January 1901.

74. Board of Agriculture, Minutes, 16 October 1901, 19 June 1902.
75. Board of Agriculture, Minutes, 26 June 1906.
76. Board of Agriculture, Minutes, 29 August 1902, 5 February 1903.
77. Board of Agriculture, Minutes, 14 June 1900, 6 November 1900; DATI *First Annual Report*, p. 84.
78. Board of Agriculture, Minutes, 22 May 1906.
79. *Departmental Committee DATI*, para. 3198.
80. *Ibid.*, paras 3179–97.
81. *Ibid.*, paras 709–10.
82. *Ibid.*, para. 3316.
83. Kennedy, 'Farmers, traders and agricultural politics', p. 147.
84. Gailey, *Ireland and the Death of Kindness*, p. 59.
85. *Departmental Committee DATI* , para. 708.
86. *Ibid.*, para. 3075. Dr Kelly, bishop of Cloyne, was a close associate of the Irish Parliamentary Party.
87. Board of Agriculture, Minutes, 22 May 1906.
88. Angela Bolster, *The Knights of Saint Columbanus*, (Dublin, 1979), pp 5–9; Lawrence W. McBride, *The Greening of Dublin Castle. The Transformation of Bureaucratic and Judicial Personnel in Ireland, 1892–1922*, (Washington, 1991).
89. National Archives, Department of Agriculture Files, AGI G 6400/1932 Part I, Returns of Salaried Officials in DATI 1902–03; G 6400/1932 Part II, Returns of Salaried Officials in DATI 1902–33.
90. *Departmental Committee DATI*, para. 661.
91. *Ibid.*, para. 301.
92. *Ibid.*, para. 304.
93. Keating, 'Sir Horace Plunkett', p. 295.
94. Daly, *The Spirit of Earnest Inquiry*, p. 99.
95. *Returns Names, etc. of persons appointed without competitive examination to any position in the public service during the period 29 June 1895 to 5 December 1905 with an annual salary of £100 or upwards.* PP 1912–13, lvi, HC paper 454.
96. *Departmental Committee DATI*, para. 1606.
97. AGI G 6400/1932 Part II.
98. P. L. Curran, 'Emergence of a technological agriculture 1592–1972', in P. L. Curran (ed.), *Towards a History of Agricultural Science in Ireland*, (Dublin, 1992), pp 18, 22.
99. Seamus Ó Buachalla, *Education Policy in Twentieth Century Ireland*, (Dublin, 1988), p. 33.
100. John A. Murphy, *The College. A History of Queen's University College Cork*, (Cork, 1995), pp 52, 56–60, 76.
101. Murphy, *The College*, p. 110.
102. Curran, 'Emergence of a technological agriculture', pp 25–9.
103. Sighle Bhreathnach Lynch, 'The Life and Works of Albert G. Power, R.H.A. (1891–1945). A Sculpted Legacy of Irish Ireland', PhD thesis, University College, Dublin, 1992, pp 219–20.
104. Lionel Smith-Gordon and L. C. Staples, *Rural Reconstruction in Ireland. A Record of Co-operative Organisation*, (London, 1917), p. 196.

105. *Departmental Committee DATI*, para. 132.

106. DATI *First Annual Report*, p. 16.

107. Board of Agriculture, Minutes, 26 June 1906; *Departmental Committee DATI*, para. 286.

108. On several occasions, both the minutes of the Board of Agriculture and annual reports of the DATI emphasise the need for secretaries to be well-qualified, e.g. DATI *Annual Report*, (1901–02), p. 11; *Annual Report*, (1902–03), p. 15.

109. *Departmental Committee DATI*, para. 695.

110. *Ibid.*, paras 1293; 2068.

111. *Ibid.*, para. 1307.

112. Board of Agriculture, Minutes, 23 April 1907.

113. Board of Agriculture, Minutes, 6 May 1908.

114. Board of Agriculture, Minutes, 27 April 1910.

115. Board of Agriculture, Minutes, 30 June 1910.

116. O'Donovan, *Economic History of Livestock*, pp 365-6; 372.

117. *Departmental Committee DATI*, paras 15139–55.

118. Board of Agriculture, Minutes, 2 August 1905.

119. *Departmental Committee DATI*, paras 1293; 1307.

120. *Ibid.*, para 7945.

121. *Ibid.*, para 9612.

122. *Ibid.*, para 5235.

123. For example, Board of Agriculture, Minutes, 19 July 1906.

124. Board of Agriculture, Minutes, 19 June 1912.

125. Horace Plunkett, *Memorandum on Agricultural Education for Ireland, Addressed To the Irish Farmer and His Friends*, Appendix in DATI *First Annual Report*, (1902).

126. *Departmental Committee DATI*, para 1494.

127. *Ibid.*, para. 1320.

128. *Ibid.*, para. 1610.

129. *Ibid.*, paras 1629–39.

130. Royal Commission on Congestion, *Fourth Report of the Commissioners*, Dublin, PP 1907, Cd. 3508, paras 19008–972.

131. *Ibid.*, para. 7229.

132. *Departmental Committee DATI*, paras 5235–5615

133. *Ibid.*, paras 15254–55.

134. *Ibid.*, paras. 6491–531.

135. Board of Agriculture, Minutes, 1 December 1909.

136. *Departmental Committee DATI*, paras 7229; 7611; 6531.

137. *Ibid.*, para. 6643.

138. *Ibid.*, para. 5703.

139. *Ibid.*, para. 6644

140. O'Donovan, *Economic History of Livestock*, pp 372–5.

141. *Departmental Committee DATI*, Campbell, para. 1402; Adams, para. 2992

142. *Ibid.*, para. 7279.

143. Patrick McNabb, 'Social structure', in Jeremiah Newman (ed.), *Limerick Rural Survey, 1958–64*, (Tipperary, 1964), p. 213.

144. *Departmental Committee DATI*, para. 1293.

145. *Ibid.*, para. 6311.
146. William Bulfin, *Rambles in Eirinn*, (Dublin, 1907), pp 179–81.
147. Micks, *History of the Congested Districts Board*, pp 25–6.
148. *Departmental Committee DATI*, Campbell, paras 1382–5.
149. Board of Agriculture, Minutes, 13 July 1907; 23 October 1907.
150. *Departmental Committee DATI*, para. 7968.
151. *Ibid.*, Plunkett, paras 632–3.
152. Royal Commission on Congestion, *Third Report of the Commission*, Dublin, PP 1907, Cd. 3413, paras 18269–388.
153. Eunan O'Halpin, *The Decline of the Union. British Government in Ireland 1892–1920*, (Dublin, 1987), p. 20.
154. Royal Commission on Congestion, *Appendices to First Report*, Dublin, 1906, Cd. 3267, paras 4420–22.
155. Board of Agriculture, Minutes, 11 November 1903; 19 July 1906.
156. Royal Commission on Congestion, *Appendices to First Report*, Dublin, 1906, Cd. 3267, paras 4490–91.
157. Board of Agriculture, Minutes, 9 January 1907.
158. Royal Commission on Congestion, *Third Report of the Commission*, paras 18208–263.
159. Micks, *History of the Congested Districts Board*, pp 33–4.
160. Board of Agriculture, Minutes, 25 January 1905.
161. Board of Agriculture, Minutes, 9 January 1907.
162. *Departmental Committee DATI*, 1907, Cd. 3572, xviii.
163. Keating, 'Sir Horace Plunkett', p. 348; West, *Horace Plunkett*, pp 82–3.
164. O'Halpin, *The Decline of the Union*, p. 69.
165. *Departmental Committee DATI*, 1907, Cd. 3575.
166. Cited in Keating, 'Sir Horace Plunkett', pp 325–6.
167. The Conservatives and unionists had a strong parliamentary majority.
168. *Departmental Inquiry DATI*, Plunkett, paras 17313–19.
169. Anderson, *With Horace Plunkett*, pp 117–18.
170. Ó Gráda, 'The beginnings of the Irish creamery system', p. 290.
171. *Departmental Inquiry DATI*, Gill, para. 875; Anderson, paras 14584–85.
172. Board of Agriculture, Minutes, 25 January 1905; 3 February 1906.
173. Board of Agriculture, Minutes, 20 March 1906.
174. Kennedy, 'Farmers, traders and agricultural politics', pp 146–7. On 29 November 1906 W. L. Micks sent John Dillon a detailed breakdown of the votes. Manuscript Room, Trinity College, Dublin, Dillon Papers 6800-01/129.
175. Board of Agriculture, Minutes, 29 November 1906; 27 February 1907; 18 December 1907.
176. *Freeman's Journal*, 21 December 1907.
177. *Freeman's Journal*, letter, 24 January 1908.
178. Rolleston's employment had ended by the time Russell became vice-president of the DATI. *Freeman's Journal*, 22 January 1908.
179. *Freeman's Journal*, 24 January 1908.
180. Council of Agriculture, Minutes, 16 November 1911.
181. For the background to the Development Commission, see footnote 52.
182. Council of Agriculture, Minutes, 16 November 1911.

183. Board of Agriculture, Minutes, 23 January 1912.
184. DATI *Annual Report* (1911–12), p. 19.
185. National Archives, Department of An Taoiseach Files, S 1206 B, IAOS.
186. Kennedy, 'Farmers, traders and agricultural politics', pp 157–66.
187. Council of Agriculture, Minutes, 16 November 1911.
188. Ingrid Henriksen, 'Avoiding the lock-in: cooperative creameries in Denmark, 1882–1903', *European Review of Economic History*, vol. 3, part I, April 1999, p. 76.
189. Cyril Ehrlich, 'Sir Horace Plunkett and agricultural reform', in L. M. Goldstrom and L. A. Clarkson (eds), *Irish Population Economy and Society. Essays in Honour of the late K. H. Connell*, (Oxford, 1981), p. 282.
190. Turner, *After the Famine*, pp 95–125; 129.
191. *Ibid.*, p. 139.
192. Cormac Ó Gráda, *Ireland Before and After the Famine. Explorations in Economic History*, (Manchester, 1988), p. 130.
193. Turner, *After the Famine*, p. 139.
194. Joanna Bourke, 'Women and poultry in Ireland, 1891–1914', *Irish Historical Studies*, vol. xxv, no 99, (May, 1987), p. 308.
195. Turner, *After the Famine*, p. 115.
196. Bourke, 'Women and poultry', pp 301–6.
197. *Report of the Departmental Committee on the Irish Butter Industry*, Dublin, PP 1910, Cd. 5093, viii.
198. O'Donovan, *Economic History of Livestock*, pp 326–7.
199. Council of Agriculture, Minutes, November 1909; 4 December 1912.
200. Board of Agriculture, Minutes, 4 February 1909; Council of Agriculture, Minutes, 4 December 1912; 25 May 1916.
201. DATI *20th Annual Report*, (1919–20), pp 39–42.
202. Vincent McCarthy, *The Formative Years of Seed Testing in Ireland*, (Dublin, 1996).
203. Council of Agriculture, Minutes, 21 January 1913.
204. Peter Solar, 'The agricultural trade statistics in the Irish Railway Commissioners' report', *Irish Economic and Social History*, 6, (1979), pp 24–40.
205. T. P. Linehan, 'The development of official Irish statistics', *JSSISI*, vol. xxvii, pt. 5, (1997/8), pp 50–3.
206. E. J. Riordan, *Modern Irish Trade and Industry*, (London, 1920).

CHAPTER TWO

1. Avner Offer, *The First World War. An Agrarian Interpretation*, (Oxford, 1989).
2. Niall Ferguson, *The Pity of War*, (London, 1998), pp 276–7.
3. Keith A. H. Murray, *Agriculture*, in Keith Hancock (ed.), *History of the Second World War*, (London, 1955), p. 6.
4. The five members were C. F. Bastable, professor of political economy at TCD; John Bagwell, general manager of the Great Northern Railway in Ireland; Robert Downes, JP, a Dublin baker; Joseph O'Connor, Mylerstown, Naas; and Patrick J. O'Neill, chairman of Dublin County Council. Bastable is the most interesting of these names since in 1923 George O'Brien described him as 'a survivor of the

great days of Victorian liberalism when free trade was regarded by British economists as a religion rather than a policy' (James Meenan, *George O'Brien, a Biographical Memoir,* (Dublin, 1980), p. 129).

5. *Departmental Committee on Food Production in Ireland. Report,* Dublin, 1915, Cd. 8946. Minority Report, p. 12.

6. *Departmental Committee on Food Production in Ireland. Minutes of Evidence,* (London, 1916), Cd. 8158, para. 291.

7. Murray, *Agriculture,* pp 6–7.

8. Board of Agriculture, Minutes, 16 February 1916; DATI *Annual Report,* (1916–17).

9. Murray, *Agriculture,* pp 8–9.

10. DATI, *Annual Report,* (1917–18), pp 12–19.

11. Board of Agriculture Minutes, 30 March 1917.

12. DATI, *Annual Report,* (1917–18), pp 14–15.

13. Emmet O'Connor, *Syndicalism in Ireland 1917–1923,* (Cork, 1988), p. 37.

14. T. H. Middleton, *Food Production in War,* (Oxford, 1923), pp 192–3; 240–3; 308–9.

15. DATI, *Annual Report,* (1917–18), p. 14; DATI *Annual Report,* (1918–19), p. 13.

16. Board of Agriculture, Minutes, 23 March 1915.

17. O'Donovan, *Economic History of Livestock,* pp 334–361; *Commission of Inquiry into the Resources and Industries of Ireland Dairying and the Dairy Industry,* (Dublin, 1920), Evidence of R. A. Anderson, pp 15–16.

18. AGI A 31211/19, Agricultural Instructors Association Deputation, 2 November 1915.

19. AGI G 4256/19, Civil Service Commission. Files on Staff.

20. O'Connor, *Syndicalism,* p. 378.

21. David Fitzpatrick, *Politics and Irish Life, 1915–1921,* (Dublin, 1977), pp 72–3.

22. Council of Agriculture, Minutes, 25 May 1916.

23. Dorothy Macardle, *The Irish Republic,* 2nd Revised Edition, (London, 1968), pp 223–5.

24. Fitzpatrick, *Politics and Irish Life,* pp 269–71.

25. O'Connor, *Syndicalism,* p. 74.

26. Fitzpatrick, *Politics and Irish Life,* p. 69.

27. Council of Agriculture, Minutes, 13 November 1918.

28. Emmet O'Connor, *A Labour History of Ireland 1824–1960,* (Dublin, 1992), p. 99.

29. O'Connor, *Syndicalism,* p. 39.

30. AGI A 8786/19, North Kildare Farmers and Compulsory Tillage.

31. O'Connor, *Syndicalism,* pp 39–40.

32. AGI A 8093/19, Irish Oat Control.

33. Council of Agriculture, Minutes, 14 May 1919.

34. AGI G 2863/19, Labour Disputes and Farm Labourers.

35. Board of Agriculture, Minutes, 5 November 1919.

36. Minutes of Proceedings of Dáil Éireann, 2 April 1919, p. 36.

37. Arthur Mitchell, *Revolutionary Government in Ireland. Dáil Éireann 1919–22,* (Dublin, 1995), p. 86.

38. National Archives, DE 2/30, Directorate of Agriculture. Appointment of Art O'Connor.

39. Minutes of Proceedings of Dáil Éireann, 4 April 1919, pp 40–2. The committee

comprised P. O'Malley, Connemara; J. J. Clancy, North Sligo; A. McCabe, South Sligo; L. Ginnell, Westmeath; D. Ó Buachalla, North Kildare; J. MacDonagh, North Tipperary; P. Moloney, South Tipperary; S. Etchingham, East Wicklow; E. J. Duggan, South Meath; J. McGrath, Dublin; and J. A. Burke, Mid-Tipperary.

40. DE 4/3/7, Robert Barton and the Advisory Committee on Land Policy.
41. A payment conceded to tenants under the Land Act of 1881, which took account of the tenants' co-ownership of the soil and which compensated them for improvements carried out to the land.
42. DE 4/3/7, R. Barton and Advisory Committee on Land Policy.
43. Minutes of Proceedings of Dáil Éireann, 17 June 1919, p. 115.
44. *Ibid.*, 18 June 1919, p.121.
45. Land Settlement Commission Papers, Minutes of Agriculture Committee, 30 July 1919. The following signified their intention of serving on the committee: S. Etchingham; Alasdair McCabe; R. Wetteman; R. Barton; P. Ó Gallagáin; T. MacSuibhne; P. Ó Laoidhleis; D. Ceannt; Sean Ó Ceallaigh; C. Ó Coilean; A. Ó Conchubhair; and L. Seers. P. Ó Caoimh, S. MacDonnchada and Father Sweetman were later added.
46. George Gavan Duffy Papers, NLI 15439(7), 19 August 1919. Letter from Robert Barton to each TD.
47. Francis Sheehy-Skeffington, *Michael Davitt*, (London, 1908), p. 75; James Connolly, *Labour in Ireland*, (Dublin, 1917), pp 3–4.
48. Minutes of Proceedings of Dáil Éireann, 20 August 1919, pp 146–8.
49. Land Settlement Commission Papers. Minutes of Agriculture Committee, 10 September 1919.
50. George Gavan Duffy Papers, NLI 15440 (4), October 1919, Report of the Department of Agriculture. (The reports of the Director of Agriculture, and of other Dáil Ministers, were not reproduced in full in the Minutes of Proceedings of Dáil Éireann. A few survive in Dáil Éireann files in the National Archives; others in private papers, such as the George Gavan Duffy Papers.)
51. Minutes of the Proceedings of Dáil Éireann, 27 October 1919, p. 161.
52. Mitchell, *Revolutionary Government*, p. 87.
53. Minutes of Proceedings of Dáil Éireann, 29 June 1920, pp 180–1.
54. Land Settlement Commission Papers, General Correspondence.
55. George Gavan Duffy Papers, NLI 15440 (4), January 1921, Report Director of Agriculture.
56. Mitchell, *Revolutionary Government*, pp 86–9.
57. *Ibid.*, p. 154.
58. Land Settlement Commission Papers.
59. Mary Kotsonouris, *Retreat from Revolution. The Dáil Courts, 1920–24*, (Dublin, 1994), pp 24–5.
60. Minutes of Proceedings of Dáil Éireann, 17 August 1921, pp 66–8.
61. For details of O'Sheil's work in the Land Courts, see 'Memories of my lifetime', a series of articles published in *The Irish Times* in November 1966, especially those of 11–22 November 1966.
62. George Gavan Duffy Papers, NLI 15439 (7), 29 June 1920, Report of Acting Director of Agriculture.

63. Land Settlement Commission Papers, Report, 26 June 1920.
64. Minutes of Proceedings of Dáil Éireann, 29 June 1920, p. 179.
65. *Ibid.*, 6 August 1920.
66. O'Sheil, 'Memories of my lifetime, 6. The Dáil Land Courts', *The Irish Times*, 14 November 1966.
67. Minutes of Proceedings of Dáil Éireann, 6 August 1920, pp 199–202.
68. Conor A. Maguire, 'The Republican Courts', *Capuchin Annual*, 1969, pp 378–89.
69. Land Settlement Commission, Report to 31 December 1920.
70. Minutes of Proceedings of Dáil Éireann, 17 August 1921, p. 54.
71. Land Settlement Commission, Report, May 1921.
72. George Gavan Duffy Papers, NLI 15440 (4), Report, Acting Director of Agriculture to 31 December 1920.
73. Land Settlement Commission Papers. Minutes of Forestry Committee, 30 July – 1 November 1919.
74. Minutes of Proceedings of Dáil Éireann, 17 August 1921, p. 54.
75. Mitchell, *Revolutionary Government*, pp 89–90.
76. Minutes of Proceedings of Dáil Éireann, 17 August 1921, p. 64.
77. George Gavan Duffy Papers, NLI 15440 (4), Report, Acting Director of Agriculture to 31 December 1920.
78. O'Sheil, 'Memories of my lifetime, 6. The Dáil Land Courts', *The Irish Times*, 14 November 1966.
79. Leon Ó Broin, . . *Just Like Yesterday ... An Autobiography*, (Dublin, 1986), pp 43–9.
80. Kotsonouris, *Retreat from Revolution*, p. 32.
81. DE 5/3, Agriculture: staff and salaries, 9 June 1920–24 September 1923.
82. DE 5/1/1, Estimates for Agriculture.
83. Jackson, *The Ulster Party*, (Oxford, 1989), pp 60–1.
84. Council of Agriculture, Minutes, 16 November 1911.
85. Another obvious exception to this generalisation is Joseph Brennan, who became secretary of the Department of Finance in the Irish Free State. Most senior appointments in the Irish administration, including that of Gill, were filled by patronage. Although a greater proportion of these positions between 1906 and 1915 went to candidates who were supported by the Irish Parliamentary Party, when the wartime coalition government was formed in 1915, preference was again given to unionists. Brennan passed the highly-competitive examination for first-division clerkships. Most successful candidates were graduates, like Brennan, of Oxford and Cambridge.
86. DATI, *29th and Final Report*, (1930–31), p. 2.
87. AGI A 35363/19, Prohibition of fairs and markets in certain districts. Letter from Gill to Under-Secretary.
88. AGI A 35363/19, Prohibition of fairs and markets in certain districts.
89. AGI A 7400/21, Attacks on Creameries.
90. *Ibid.*
91. S 946, Irish White Cross Association, Creameries.
92. AGI A 11940/19, Limerick Livestock Schemes 1919–20. Inspectors' Report, 24 August 1918.
93. A press cutting (*Cork Examiner*, 28 February 1919) on AGI A 11182/19, Refusal of Cork County Council to levy agricultural rate.

94. AGI A 11182/19.
95. AGI A 31211/19, Agricultural Instructors Association, Deputations 1905–20.
96. AGI A 9349/19, Security of Tenure of Officers, Minutes of Meeting, 29 March 1919.
97. AGI A 9349/19, Security of Tenure of Officers, Barrie, 29 March 1919.
98. For details see Daly, *The Buffer State*, chapter 2.
99. DE 4/3/6, Attitude of Local Committees towards the DATI – Art O'Connor.
100. Minutes of Proceedings of Dáil Éireann, 17 August 1920.
101. Daniel Hoctor, *The Department's Story. A History of the Department of Agriculture*, (Dublin, 1971), p. 120.
102. DE 4/3/6, Attitude of Local Committees towards the DATI – Art O'Connor.
103. Daly, *The Buffer State*, chapter 2.
104. DE 4/3/6.
105. George Gavan Duffy Papers, NLI 15440 (4), 20 January 1921, Report of Art O'Connor.
106. DATI, *Annual Report*, (1920–21).
107. AGI A 9349/19, Security of Tenure, Barrie, 29 March 1919.
108. AGI A 31211/19, Agricultural Instructors Association, Deputations 1905–20.
109. AGI A 12833/20, Itinerant Instructor in Agriculture. Exemption of Appointment from Annual Review.
110. AGI A 8909/21, Kerry County Committee Agricultural Scheme.
111. For example, AGI/A 11940/19, Limerick Livestock Schemes 1919–20.
112. AGI A 8909/21, Kerry County Committee Agricultural Scheme 1921.
113. DATI, *Annual Report*, (1921–2).
114. AGI A 264561/20, Conference re Marketing of Dead Meat and Eggs in London, 1920.
115. AGI A 7880/21.
116. Ó Broin, *An Autobiography*, pp 43–9.
117. Land Settlement Commission, parcel 1.
118. George Gavan Duffy Papers, NLI 15440 (4).
119. Minutes of Proceedings of Dáil Éireann, 19 June 1919.
120. Land Settlement Commission, Minutes, Committee on Agriculture.
121. Minutes of Proceedings of Dáil Éireann, 17 August 1921, pp 69–70.
122. DE 2/146, Memorandum re potatoes and wheat, 16 November 1920.
123. George Gavan Duffy Papers, NLI 15440 (4), 20 January 1921, Report of the Land Commission and Agricultural Department for period ending 31 December 1920.
124. *Ibid.*, Report of the Land Commission and Agricultural Department to Dáil Éireann, March 1921.
125. Land Settlement Commission Papers.
126. Daly, *The Buffer State*, pp 83-7.
127. Report of the Land Commission and Agricultural Department to Dáil Éireann, August 1921.
128. Land Settlement Commission Papers. Reports by County Committees of Agriculture on the condition of crops in the county, July 1921. Report by J. Scully, instructor, Listowel, County Kerry.

129. DE 2/493, Art O'Connor's Minutes of Meetings of Economic Group of Ministers, 27 October 1921.
130. Land Settlement Commission Papers. Miscellaneous Papers.
131. Land Settlement Commission Papers. Ministry of Economic Affairs; Food Committee, 12 November 1921 and 18 November 1921 .
132. Minutes of Proceedings of Dáil Éireann, 11 March 1921.
133. Art Ó Briain Papers, NLI 8425, Department of Agriculture, Report, May 1921.
134. Council of Agriculture, Minutes, 15 March 1921.
135. Land Settlement Commission Papers.
136. DE 2/418, Attendance by Republicans at meeting of Council of Agriculture.
137. Land Settlement Commission Papers, Council of Agriculture.
138. Redmond Papers, NLI MS 26175. Minutes of meetings between the Irish Party and the Irish Executive over the formation of a Home Rule Government, 1914–15.
139. *Report of the Proceedings of the Irish Convention*, (London, 1918), Cd. 9019.
140. John McColgan, *British Policy and the Irish Administration, 1920–22*, (London, 1983), p. 37.
141. McColgan, *British Policy*, p. 48.
142. AGI G 2750/21, Estimates of Expenditure: Memorandum on it and on Transfer of Services to the New Governments, North and South.
143. AGI G 5172/21, Allocation of Staff between Northern Ireland and South, 1921–22.
144. McColgan, *British Policy*, p. 112.
145. Hoctor, *The Department's Story*, pp 132–3.

CHAPTER THREE

1. DE 4/3/6, Attitude of Local Committees towards the DATI – Art O'Connor.
2. Bhreathnach-Lynch, 'Albert Power', pp 212–20.
3. Commissioners of Public Works, *Reports*, 31 March 1921–31 March 1928.
4. Minutes of Proceeding of Dáil Éireann, 28 February 1922, p. 95; John M. Regan, *The Irish Counter-Revolution 1921–1936*, (Dublin, 1999), p. 50.
5. Regan, *The Irish Counter-Revolution* , p. 89.
6. Maguire, 'The Republican Courts', pp 381–2.
7. PDDE, 16 November 1923, col. 927.
8. Regan, *The Irish Counter-Revolution*, p. 95.
9. Joseph Lee, *Ireland 1912–1985*, (Cambridge, 1989), p. 115.
10. PDDE, 6 July 1928, col. 2270.
11. Ronan Fanning, *Independent Ireland*, (Dublin, 1983), pp 60–1.
12. Register of Establishment and Record of Services for 1901–1922, Library of the Department of Agriculture; Hoctor, *The Department's Story*, p. 131.
13. Leon Ó Broin, who became secretary for Posts and Telegraphs, and who had worked with the Dáil Ministry of Agriculture, was another member.
14. *Blackrock College Annual* 1964. Meyrick died on 6 December 1963 at the age of ninety.

15. AGI G 595/1945, Export Bounties.
16. S 5501, Transferring of Educational Functions from Agriculture to Education, 1927.
17. PDDE, 16 November 1923, cols 928–31; 951.
18. PDDE, 28 November 1923, col. 2351.
19. *Report of the Commission of Inquiry into the Preservation of the Gaeltacht*, R 23/27, 1926.
20. PDDE, 4 June 1925, col. 324.
21. Commission of Inquiry into the Civil Service. *Vol. III. Memoranda of Evidence.* Evidence of D. Twomey, secretary of the Department of Agriculture (Dublin, 1936).
22. S 4355, Winding up of Fund for Congested Districts 1925.
23. Ronan Fanning, *The Irish Department of Finance 1922–58,* (Dublin, 1979), pp 98–105.
24. PDDE, 18 February 1931, col. 124.
25. PDDE, 18 February 1931, col. 125.
26. Patrick Hogan to Horace Plunkett, 20 December 1927, Plunkett Papers, Plunkett Foundation, Oxford University, HOGA/14. My thanks to Dr Carla King for giving me a copy of these letters.
27. Brian Lynch, 'The first agricultural broadcasts on 2RN', *History Ireland*, vol. 7, no 2, Summer, 1999, pp 42–5.
28. Michael Neenan, *A Popular History of Agriculture* (unfinished work). A copy was supplied by the Department of Agriculture.
29. Commission of Inquiry into the Civil Service. *Vol III. Memoranda of Evidence.* D. Twomey.
30. PDDE, 16 November 1923, col. 937; 21 November 1923 , cols 1015–16.
31. PDDE, 16 January 1924, col. 248; 27 February 1924, col. 1483.
32. University Education (Agriculture and Dairy Science) Act, 1926.
33. S 7375, University Education (Agricultural and Dairy Science) Act, 1930.
34. Hoctor, *The Department's Story*, pp 139–42.
35. S 16604, Agricultural Research in Ireland.
36. S 4521, Veterinary Profession in Ireland.
37. S 3502, Operation of the Diseases of Animals Acts.
38. S 3502, Operation of the Diseases of Animals Acts.
39. S 3502, Operation of the Diseases of Animals Acts.
40. S 3502, Operation of the Diseases of Animals Acts.
41. McColgan, *British Policy*, pp 110–20.
42. PDDE, 28 November 1922, col. 2353.
43. Elizabeth R. Hooker, *Readjustments of Agricultural Tenure in Ireland,* (Chapel Hill, 1938), p. 103.
44. Land Settlement Commission Papers. General Correspondence.
45. Minutes of Proceedings of Dáil Éireann, 26 April 1922, p. 276.
46. Land Settlement Commission Papers. General Correspondence, 25 April 1922.
47. Land Settlement Commission Papers. General Correspondence.
48. Minutes of Proceedings of Dáil Éireann, 10 May 1922, p. 389.
49. Land Settlement Commission Papers, Misc No 6, Inspectors' Work Diaries.

50. Kotsonouris, *Retreat from Revolution*, p. 83.
51. Fanning, *Finance*, pp 133–4.
52. Fanning, *Finance*, p. 136.
53. S 3192, Land Act, 1923.
54. S 3192, Land Act, 1923.
55. Hooker, *Readjustments*, p. 93.
56. S 3192, Land Act, 1923.
57. S 3192, Land Act, 1923.
58. S 3192, Land Act, 1923.
59. Hooker, *Readjustments*, pp 98–9.
60. S 3192, Land Act, 1923.
61. Hooker, *Readjustments*, pp 105–6.
62. PDDE, 14 June 1923, cols 1954–66.
63. Hooker, *Readjustments*, pp 163–5.
64. Land Settlement Commission. Inspector's report on executing decrees in Ballycastle and Glenamoy, 23 August 1923.
65. Hooker, *Readjustments*, pp 106–8.
66. PDDE, 4 June 1925, cols 344–50.
67. Fanning, *Independent Ireland*, p. 75.
68. Hooker, *Readjustments*, p. 103.
69. DATI, *23rd General Report 1922–23*, p. 1.
70. The precise terms of reference were 'To inquire into the National Resources and the present condition of Manufacturing and Productive Industries in Ireland, and to consider and report by what means those Natural Resources may be more fully developed, and how those Industries may be encouraged and extended'. The Commission published a series of reports. Those concerning agriculture were, Interim Report on Milk Production (March 1920) R. 10/1; Report on Stock Breeding Farmers for Pure Bred Dairy Cattle (April 1921) R. 10/3; Report on Dairying and Dairy Industry (March 1922), R. 10/9.
71. PDDE, 28 November 1922, col. 2349.
72. S 1778, Commission on Agriculture.
73. PDDE, 28 November 1922, col. 2348.
74. In 1908 James Drew was appointed farm superintendent and lecturer in agriculture at the Albert College, Glasnevin. In 1919 he was appointed to the chair of agriculture, within the Faculty of Science in the College of Science. He held this position in addition to the Albert College position. When the College of Science was absorbed into UCD in 1926, he became dean of the new faculty of agriculture and director of the Albert College and farms. P. L. Curran (ed.), *Towards a History of Agricultural Science in Ireland*, (Dublin, 1922), p. 51.
75. *Reports of the Commission on Agriculture*, (Dublin, 1924), p. 6.
76. First Interim Report, 9 February 1923, Tobacco Growing; Second Interim Report, 22 May 1923, Butter; Third Interim Report, 22 May 1923, Eggs; Fourth Interim Report, 5 September 1923, Agricultural Credit; Fifth Interim Report, 5 September 1923, Licensing Bulls; Final Report,1924.
77. Final Report, pp 27–8.
78. *Ibid.*, pp 29–31.

79. *Ibid.*, pp 31–2.
80. Commission on Agriculture, *Second Interim Report*, pp 11–15; *Final Report*, p. 38.
81. Commission on Agriculture, *Final Report*, pp 31–2; 37.
82. *Ibid.*, pp 33–6.
83. *Ibid.*, p. 32.
84. *Ibid.*, pp 71–2.
85. *Ibid.*, pp 52–5.
86. Commission on Agriculture, *Final Report*, Minority Report, pp 79–80.
87. Mary E. Daly, *Industrial Development and Irish National Identity*, (Syracuse, New York, 1992), p. 44.
88. PDDE, 9 July 1924, cols 892–3; 901.
89. S 3557, Agricultural Situation, Economic Report.
90. Daly, *Industrial Development*, pp 21–3. The committee was asked to report (a) as to the effect of the existing fiscal system, and of any measures regulating or restricting imports or exports, on industry and agriculture in the Saorstát, and (b) as to the effect of any changes therein intended to foster the development of industry and agriculture, with due regard to the interests of the general community and to the economic relations of the Saorstát with other countries.
91. DATI, *24th Annual General Report 1923–26*.
92. R. O'Connor and C. Guiomard, 'Agricultural output in the Irish Free State area before and after Independence', *Irish Economic and Social History*, xii, 1985, pp 79–88.
93. S 3557, Agricultural Situation, Economic Report.
94. For details, see Daly, *Industrial Development*, pp 51–2.
95. Mary E. Daly, 'The economic ideals of Irish nationalism: frugal comfort or lavish austerity?', *Éire-Ireland*, winter 1994, pp 84–5.
96. S 1206A, IAOS and Government Grant 1922–34.
97. Horace Plunkett to Patrick Hogan, 13 November 1925, Plunkett Papers, Plunkett Foundation, Oxford University, HOGA/3.
98. S 1206A, IAOS and Government Grant 1922–34.
99. S 5213, Creamery Reorganisation 1927–31.
100. PDDE, 6 June 1924, col. 2032.
101. The Irish Farmers' Union was running so-called co-operative companies that exported pork and engaged in the purchase and distribution of manure and seed. These were organised as limited liability companies. See Patrick Hogan to Horace Plunkett, 20 December 1927, Plunkett Papers, Plunkett Foundation, Oxford University, HOGA/14.
102. S 3889, Dairy Produce Act 1924.
103. S 5213, Creamery Reorganisation 1927–31.
104. *Ibid.*
105. PDDE, 15 March 1927, col. 1869.
106. S 5213, Creamery Reorganisation 1927–31.
107. S 2352, Creamery Act 1928.
108. S 5213, Creamery Reorganisation 1927–31.
109. PDDE, 9 June 1933, col. 392.
110. S 7543, Redundant Creameries Managers, Compensation, 1935.

111. *Annual Report of the Minister for Agriculture and Fisheries 1975*, p. 48.
112. *Departmental Committee DATI*, evidence, Gill, para. 955.
113. *Ibid.*, Campbell, para. 1716.
114. Board of Agriculture, Minutes, 23 April 1901. For the early history of these co-operative credit societies, see Smith-Gordon and Staples, *Rural Reconstruction*, pp 130–53. They blame the failure of co-operative credit societies on Russell's hostility. However, it is obvious that these societies were unable to survive without substantial financial assistance from the state.
115. DATI, *Report of the Departmental Committee on Agricultural Credit*, 1914, Cd. 7375.
116. S 15465A, Agricultural Credit, General File.
117. Commission on Agriculture, Fourth Interim Report. Agricultural Credit, 5 September 1923.
118. AGI G4818/1932, Agricultural Societies, General File. The Department tried to put pressure on the IAOS to enforce repayment but heavy debts were still outstanding in 1938.
119. S 5213, Creamery Reorganisation 1927–31.
120. S 2685, Agricultural Credit.
121. Irish Banks Standing Committee, Minutes, 24 June 1928.
122. Commission on Vocational Organisation, 1943. *Report*, (1944), R. 76/1, para. 416.
123. Fanning, *Finance*, p. 187.
124. S 2645, Agricultural Credit Acts, 1929–47.
125. Commission of Inquiry into Banking, Currency and Credit, 1934–8. *Reports*, (1938), R. 38, para. 388, paras 396–7.
126. S 15465A, Agricultural Credit, General File.
127. Fanning, *Finance*, p. 188.
128. Commission on Vocational Organisation, *Report*, para. 416.
129. Irish Banks Standing Committee, Minutes, 13 July 1928.
130. PDDE, 28 May 1926, col. 2412.
131. AGI G 5695/1934, IAOS and State Grant, 1934/5.
132. AGI G 5695/1934, IAOS and State Grant, 1934/35.
133. S 6471A, Co-operative Agricultural Societies Bill 1933.
134. S 6471B, Co-operative Agricultural Societies Bill 1933.
135. G. A. Fleming, 'Agricultural support policies in a small open economy: New Zealand in the 1920s', *Economic History Review*, vol. lii, no 2, May 1999, p. 339.
136. David Harkness, *Northern Ireland since 1920*, (Dublin, 1983), p. 32.
137. Sir John Winnifrith, *The Ministry of Agriculture, Fish and Food*, (London, 1962), p. 26.
138. R. J. Hammond, *Food and Agriculture in Britain*, (Stanford, California, 1954), p. 162; Keith A. H. Murray, *Agriculture*, in Keith Hancock (ed.), *History of the Second World War*, (London, 1955), pp 26–7.
139. Joan M. Cullen, 'Patrick J. Hogan, Minister for Agriculture, 1922–32. A Study of a Leading Member of the First Government of Independent Ireland', PhD thesis, Dublin City University, 1993, pp 92–4. This was yet another instance of the hostility between the IAOS and the DATI during Russell's term as vice-president.
140. S 3889, Dairy Produce Act 1924.

141. DATI, *24th Annual General Report 1923–26*, pp 79–81.
142. S 3407, Agricultural Produce (Eggs) Act, 1924.
143. S 3847, Agricultural Produce (Eggs) Act, 1930.
144. S 6102, Agricultural Produce (Potatoes) Bill.
145. Cullen, 'Patrick J. Hogan, Minister for Agriculture', p. 89.
146. S 3029, Regulations Applying to the Importation of Meat into the United Kingdom.
147. DATI, *26th General Report 1927–28*; DATI, *27th General Report 1928–29.*
148. S 3029, Regulations Applying to the Importation of Meat into the United Kingdom; DATI, *28th General Report, 1929–30, 29th and Final General Report, 1930–31.*
149. In addition to acting as Irish trade commissioner, Dulanty was the Irish High Commissioner in London.
150. Department of Agriculture, *Interim Report of the Tribunal to Inquire into the Marketing of Butter,* A 18/1, 1930.
151. Commission on Vocational Organisation, *Report,* para. 206; F. C. King (ed). *Public Administration in Ireland,* (Dublin, 1944), p. 61; DATI, *29th and Final General Report, 1930–31.*
152. Department of Agriculture, *Interim Report of the Tribunal to Inquire into the Marketing of Butter Marketing Tribunal,* para. 7.
153. Fleming, 'Agricultural support policies', p. 350.
154. Cormac Ó Gráda, *A Rocky Road. The Irish Economy since the 1920s,* (Manchester, 1997), p. 145, citing Gerard McKeever, 'Economic Policy in the Irish Free State', PhD thesis, McGill University, 1979, pp 76–9.
155. H. T. Williams, *Principles for British Agricultural Policy,* (Oxford, 1960), p. 14.
156. S 4128, A Sugar Beet Industry in the Saorstát.
157. McGilligan Papers, UCDA, P 35b/25A.
158. PDDE, 24 February 1928, cols 372–82.
159. S 4128, A Sugar Beet Industry in the Saorstát.
160. PDDE, 21 July 1933, cols 410–11.
161. Jacqueline Hayes, 'The Shannon Scheme Strike 1925', MA thesis, University College, Dublin, 1995, pp 26–30; 33–6.
162. Daly, *The Buffer State,* pp 138–41.
163. Daly, *Industrial Development,* pp 3–57.
164. It would appear that O'Brien was pushed into this decision by Professor Bastable, another member of the committee. Meenan, *George O'Brien,* pp 128–9.
165. Daly, *Industrial Development,* pp 17, 23.
166. McGilligan Papers, UCDA, P 36/b/9.
167. Daly, *Industrial Development,* pp 26–7.
168. F 22/57/25, Kildare County Committee of Agriculture.
169. F 22/57/25, Kildare County Committee of Agriculture.
170. Daly, *Industrial Development,* p. 28.
171. Akihiro Takei, 'Business and Government in the Irish Free State: The Case of the Irish Flour Milling Industry 1922–1945', PhD thesis, Dublin University, 1998, pp 87–8. The only evident record of these proposals comes in a file of the Department of Agriculture, G 76/1943.
172. F 39/6/26, Application for Duties in Finance Act.

173. PDDE, 21 April 1925, col. 155.
174. F 22/44/25, Tariff Commission, 29/6/26.
175. Daly, *Industrial Development*, pp 39–46.
176. Takei, 'Business and Government in the Irish Free State', pp 99, 102.
177. S 2502, Tariff on Flour.
178. AG1 G 3233/28, Tariff on Barley.
179. S 5939, Grain Inquiry.
180. Daly, *Industrial Development*, pp 44–5.
181. Economic Committee, *First Interim Report on Wheat Growing*, 1929, R 42.
182. W. J. L. Ryan, 'The Nature of Protective Policy in Ireland, 1932–39', PhD Thesis, Dublin University, 1949, p. 61. Between 1924 and 1928 imports of bacon fell from 455,000 to 342,000 cwt. By 1930 they had risen to 373,000 cwt, and reached 403,000 cwt in 1931.
183. S 6081, Irish Grain Growers' Association.
184. Daly, *Industrial Development*, pp 46–7.
185. George O'Brien, 'Patrick Hogan', *Studies*, vol. xxv, September 1936, pp 360–1.
186. Kieran A. Kennedy, 'Thomas Giblin and Deirdre McHugh', in *The Economic Development of Ireland in the Twentieth Century*, (London, 1988), p. 37.
187. Agricultural Price Index in *Statistical Abstract*, 1932, p. 166.
188. Louis P. F. Smith, 'Recent developments in northern Irish agriculture', *JSSISI*, 1948–49, pp 143–58.
189. AGI A 7880/21, Cheese Marketing.
190. In the early 1920s the banks were almost in a position to determine whether the state would survive. In 1923 they refused to co-operate in promoting the first national loan, until instructed to do so by the British authorities. Fanning, *Finance*, pp 88–98.
191. PDDE, 28 May 1926, col. 2418.

CHAPTER FOUR

1. Extract from a speech made by James Ryan, Minister for Agriculture, on 6 January 1935 at Enniscorthy, County Wexford. AG1 G5893/34.
2. Daly, *The Buffer State*, pp 173–7.
3. AGI G 3172/1932, Compensation for cows sold under value due to the Economic War.
4. Commission of Inquiry into Banking, Currency and Credit, *Reports and Memoranda of Evidence*, (1938), R. 38, paras 92–3.
5. *Ibid.*, para. 393.
6. AGI G 4818/1932, Agricultural credit societies – general file; AGI G 3121/1932, Appeal for assistance from farming woman to tide over the crisis.
7. Daly, *The Buffer State*, pp 173–4.
8. R. Crotty, *Irish Agricultural Production. Its Volume and Structure*, (Cork, 1966), pp 137–8.
9. John O'Hagan, 'An analysis of the relative size of the government sector: Ireland, 1926–52', *Economic and Social Review*, vol. 12, no 1, 1980, pp 23–4.
10. Liam Skinner, *Politicians by Accident*, (Dublin, 1946), pp 145–6.

11. AGI G 1513/1935, The role of the Department of Agriculture in giving effect to the Government's policy of self-sufficiency.
12. AGI G 6537/1933, Aspects of the agricultural situation in Denmark.
13. Northern Ireland had been relieved of these payments under the 1920 Government of Ireland Act.
14. Deirdre McMahon, *Republicans and Imperialists. Anglo-Irish Relations in the 1930s*, (New Haven, 1984), pp 63, 68.
15. 'Irish cattle trade', *Irish Trade Journal*, June 1932.
16. Edith Whetham, *Agrarian History of England and Wales Vol. VIII, 1914–39*, (Cambridge, 1978), pp 230–4; 242–3.
17. *The Economist*, 12 November 1932, cited in P. Canning, *British Policy towards Ireland, 1921–41*, (Oxford, 1987), p. 154.
18. S 9420, The Cattle Industry.
19. For further discussion of these issues, see Mary E. Daly, 'Integration of diversity? Anglo-Irish economic relations 1922–39', in S. J. Connolly (ed.), *Kingdoms United? Great Britain and Ireland since 1500. Integration and Diversity*, (Dublin, 1998), pp 169–80.
20. Cormac Ó Gráda, *Ireland: A New Economic History*, pp 414–15; Kevin O'Rourke, 'Burn everything British but their coal: the Anglo-Irish Economic War of the 1930s', *Journal of Economic History*, vol. li, no 2, 1991, pp 361–2.
21. AGI G6537/1933, Aspects of the agricultural situation in Denmark.
22. PDDE, 3 November 1932, col. 1018.
23. PDDE, 30 May 1934, col. 2105.
24. PDDE, 21 April 1937, col. 1356.
25. S 6511A.
26. S 6274, Economic Committee.
27. Fanning, *Finance*, pp 248-9; F 200/25/37.
28. In the past, when pig prices rose, farmers responded by producing more litters of pigs; when these pigs came on the market, the price of pigs fell, and farmers were discouraged from raising pigs. This in turn led to a rise in pig prices, and the cycle began once more.
29. S 6274, Economic Committee.
30. Fanning, *Finance*, p. 249.
31. AGI G 4372/1932.
32. S 6511A.
33. AGI G 4013/1935, Agricultural Exports Advisory Committee.
34. AGI G 5303/1934, High Commission London: Export of Cattle to Britain 1934–38.
35. S 7342, Agricultural Products (Regulation of Export) Act 1935; amending legislation.
36. AGI G 1385/1936.
37. McMahon, *Republicans and Imperialists*, pp 150–2, 168–9.
38. AGI G 1536/1933, Meeting between Acting Minister and Deputation representing Cattle Industry.
39. AGI G 4372/1032, Bounties on Livestock Exports, 1932–38.
40. *Irish Trade Journal*, June 1932.
41. AGI G 3744/1934, Export Bounty on Beef and Veal 1934–8.

42. Daly, 'Integration of Diversity?', p. 176.
43. McMahon, *Republicans and Imperialists*, p.123.
44. AGI G 3062/1934.
45. AGI G 2033/1936, Supplies of fat cattle.
46. UCDA, FF/439, Minutes of Parliamentary Party Meetings, 27 June 1935.
47. S 2273, Financial position of farmers. General survey.
48. AGI G 1092/1934, Meyrick to Twomey, 24 January 1934.
49. S 2361, Beef – encouragement of home consumption.
50. Annual Reports of the Ministers for Agriculture, 1934/35 and 1935/36.
51. Daly, *The Buffer State*, pp 188–92.
52. AGI G 5893/1934.
53. Commission of Inquiry into Banking, Currency and Credit, *Memoranda of Evidence*, (1938), q. 9900.
54. AGI G 1513/1935, Role of the Department of Agriculture in giving effect to the Government's policy of self-sufficiency.
55. S 2945, Slaughter of defective cattle.
56. S 2912, Slaughter of animals.
57. S 2945, Slaughter of defective cattle.
58. S 6649, Proposed state-owned tinned meat factory.
59. S 8066, Cattle: control of production.
60. PDDE, 17 July 1935, cols 674–5.
61. McMahon, *Republicans and Imperialists*, pp 151–2.
62. Alan Matthews, 'The State and Irish agriculture, 1950 – 1980', in P. J. Drudy (ed.), *Ireland: Land, Politics and People*, (Cambridge, 1982), pp 249–50.
63. S 6310, Free loans for agricultural purposes.
64. AGI G 3644, Creamery Butter Prices 1932–37.
65. PDDE, 17 July 1935, col. 672.
66. PDDE, 26 March 1936, col. 413.
67. S 2408, Milk depot.
68. S 2347, Encouragement of home consumption of milk and oats.
69. O'Donovan, *Economic History of Livestock in Ireland*, p. 353.
70. O'Connor and Guiomard, 'Agricultural production', p. 93.
71. PDDE, 21 April 1937, col. 1356.
72. PDDE, 24 May 1938, col. 1668.
73. AGI G 754/1940.
74. AGI G 11/1933, The continuation of bounties.
75. S 8066, Cattle: control of production.
76. S 7379, Dairy Produce Price Stabilisation Bill, 1935.
77. The Conditions of Employment Act regulated the hours, working conditions and holiday entitlements of factory workers.
78. The question of agricultural wages was raised on several occasions at meetings of the Fianna Fáil parliamentary party during these years. UCDA, FF/439, 21 February 1935 and 28 February 1935. Deputies complained that the Labour party was publicising the government's failure to raise agricultural wages.
79. S 8066, Cattle: control of production.
80. On the relationship between livestock fattening and tillage in Britain, see Edith

Whetham, *Beef, Cattle and Sheep, 1910–1940,* (Cambridge, 1976), pp 21–4.
81. S 8066, Cattle: control of production.
82. AGI G 682/1937, Export bounties.
83. In 1934/5 the export value of creamery butter was 70s, whereas the price paid to Irish creameries was 104s 3d per cwt. In 1935/6 the export value rose substantially to 91s 10d, whereas the price to Irish creameries rose only marginally to 106s 7d. Crotty, *Irish Agricultural Production,* p. 149. On export subsidies, see AGI G 765/1940.
84. AGI G 2256/1934.
85. PDDE, 30 May 1934, cols. 2099–102.
86. FF/439, 28 March 1935, 28 November 1935.
87. S 9636, Small farmers in West Cork, economic conditions.
88. Crotty, *Irish Agricultural Production,* pp 150–2.
89. For example, see S 7379, Comment by Department of Finance, 1935, and S 2356, Creameries, share payments by transferred suppliers.
90. Commission of Inquiry into Banking, Currency and Credit, *Reports,* (1938), para. 87.
91. *Ibid.,* para. 77.
92. D. Twomey, 'Agricultural organisation', in F. C. King (ed.), *Public Administration in Ireland,* (Dublin, 1944), p. 62.
93. Crotty, *Irish Agricultural Production,* p. 148.
94. *Ibid.,* p. 138.
95. Commission of Inquiry into Banking, Currency and Credit, *Reports,* (1938), para. 70.
96. PDDE, 30 May 1934, col. 2102.
97. S 6623, Bacon and Pigs Act 1935.
98. PDDE, 26 March 1936, cols 417–18.
99. AGI G 5373/1933, Agricultural Produce (Fresh Meat) Amending Bills.
100. S 9620, Pigs and Bacon (Amendment) Act 1937.
101. S 11162, Pigs and Bacon Act 1939.
102. Crotty, *Irish Agricultural Production,* p. 153.
103. Economic Committee. *First Interim Report on Wheat-Growing,* (1929), R. 42.
104. The committee was chaired by the Director of Agriculture, J. M. Adams. The other members were J. Dempsey (a future secretary of the Department of Agriculture), D. J. McGrath, P. J. Murray, T. O'Connell, J. R. O'Donnell, E. J. Sheehy, D. Twomey (a future secretary of the Department of Agriculture) and F. M. Walsh (secretary to the committee).
105. S 6306, Interim report on wheat of Committee on Agricultural Production.
106. Takei, 'Business and Government in the Irish Free State', p. 146.
107. S 6306; S 2669, Agricultural Produce (Cereals) Act 1933.
108. S 2664, Committee on Agricultural Production 1932 (Final Report).
109. S 2669, Agricultural Produce (Cereals) Act 1933.
110. S 2669; PDSE, xvi, 15–22 March 1933, cols 697–880.
111. S 2665, Wheat Scheme (proposed advertising campaign), 1933.
112. S 2670, Agricultural Produce (Cereals) (Amendment) Act 1933.
113. S 2670; S 2667, Agricultural Produce (Cereals) Amendment Act 1934; S 6917,

Agricultural Produce (Cereals) Act 1933; and Amending Legislation 1934.
114. S 6917.
115. Takei, 'Business and Government in the Irish Free State', p. 213.
116. Commission of Inquiry into Banking, Currency and Credit, *Reports*, (1938), para. 67.
117. S 10915, Wheat: proposals for increasing home production, 1938.
118. AGI G 62/1938, Red Marvel propagation.
119. PDSE, xvi, 16 March 1933, cols 760–7.
120. AGI G 2411/1933, Maize meal for human consumption: questionnaire.
121. S 8822, Agricultural Produce (Cereals) Act, 1936.
122. AGI G 1126/1933.
123. S 2666, Proposal admixture of oatmeal and flour. Purchase and storing of oats by State.
124. A barrel of wheat was 20 stone; a barrel of barley, 16 stone; a barrel of oats, 14 stone.
125. PDDE, 30 May 1934, cols 2091–2.
126. S 9636.
127. In 1931 there were 182,000 acres of turnips grown, as against 307,000 in 1851 and 212,000 in 1911; by 1937 the figure was 149,000 . The acreage under mangels rose from 24,000 in 1851 to 75,000 in 1911, 84,000 in 1931 and 86,000 by 1937. The overall fall in the acreage under these root crops suggests that maize was being substituted as the preferred animal feed.
128. O'Connor and Guiomard, 'Agricultural production', pp 94–5.
129. S 10616, Agricultural Produce Cereals Amendment Act 1938; S 10914, Agricultural Produce (Cereals) Act 1939.
130. Takei, 'Business and Government in the Irish Free State', pp 228–35.
131. S 4218B, Sugar Industry Interdepartmental Committee Report.
132. S 10434A.
133. DIC, R 212/c 15, Industrial Alcohol.
134. R 212 C 44, Industrial Alcohol Bill.
135. DIC, TID 2/187.
136. S 10392.
137. S 10016, Report of a Special Committee on Home-Grown Tobacco Duties.
138. S 2578, Tobacco Act.
139. S 4218B, Sugar Industry Interdepartmental Committee Report.
140. S 2578, Tobacco Act.
141. TID 11/23, Tobacco industries, 23 January 1934.
142. TID 11/23, 22 May 1934 and 17 June 1934.
143. S 11692, Tobacco, encouragement of home grown production, December 1938.
144. S 11692.
145. PDDE, 25 May 1936, col. 426.
146. S 11692.
147. I have not been able to find details of where tobacco was grown. However, my father recalls that it was grown in counties Kildare, Carlow and Laois, and probably also in County Louth. Donal Creedon suggested that tobacco was also grown in

Wexford and Cork. In the early 1940s tobacco was collected from farms over a wide area and brought to the Greene farm at Kilkea, County Kildare, where it was dried and stripped.

148. Daly, *Industrial Development*, p. 99.
149. S 7901A; Daly, *Industrial Development*, p. 99.
150. McGilligan Papers, UCDA, P35/b/44. Notes on History and Operation of the Anglo-Irish Trade Agreement 1938.
151. This meeting was attended by Ryan and Twomey from Agriculture, and Lemass and Leydon from Industry and Commerce. The British Ministers present were Oliver Stanley, President of the Board of Trade; W. S. Morrison, Minister of Agriculture; five officials from the Board of Trade; two from the Ministry of Agriculture; one from the Home Office; and one from the Mines Department.
152. PRO, T 160/746 /5.
153. PRO, T 160/746 F025/33/3/, 16 February 1938, memorandum by Waley.
154. PRO, BT 11/2833, Negotiations, 19 January 1938.
155. PRO, BT 11/2833, Meeting at House of Commons, 23 February 1938.
156. Commission of Inquiry into Banking, Currency and Credit, *Memoranda of Evidence*, (1938), qs 10280–995.
157. Daly, *Industrial Development*, pp 164–7.
158. AGI G 2105/1937, British agricultural policy.
159. S 10980, Agricultural Commission 1938.
160. S 2773, Financial position of farmers. General survey.
161. Daly, *The Buffer State*, pp 189–96.
162. AGI G 3648/1936, Agricultural Wages Act; AGI G 3678/1936.
163. AGI G 1093/1938.
164. AGI G 1567/1937.
165. AGI G 5502/1932.
166. AGI G 2480/1932, Concession re milk and cream imported from Northern Ireland into Free State creameries.
167. AGI G 5373/1933.
168. PDDE, 26 March 1936, col. 441.
169. PDDE, 26 March 1936, col. 412.
170. Ó Gráda, *Ireland: A New Economic History*, p. 394.
171. Department of the Environment Files, Waterford Box 776. Inquiry into the Dissolution of Waterford County Council.
172. Mike Cronin, *The Blueshirts and Irish Politics*, (Dublin, 1997), pp 135–67.
173. The Irish Beet Growers' Association was founded in Carlow in 1926 to negotiate with the sugar factory. It was funded by a levy on all sugar-beet delivered to the factories. By 1939 it had 27,442 members in twenty-four counties and was representing grain growers in annual talks with the millers. *Report of the Commission on Vocational Organisation, 1943.* P 6743 (1944) R. 77, para. 210.
174. UCDA, FF/439, 8 March 1934.
175. These examples are drawn from the files of the Department of Agriculture.
176. AGI G 4013/1935, Agricultural Exports Advisory Committee.
177. S 7379, Dairy Produce Price Stabilisation Act, 1935.
178. S 2622, Lime subsidy.

179. AGI G 1513/1935, The Role of the Department of Agriculture in giving effect to the Government's policy of self-sufficiency.
180. AGI G 2094/1937, Wheat campaign use of cinema.
181. AGI G 1556/1934, Poultry experiments.
182. AGI G 1376/1934, Meath County Committee of Agriculture Relief Scheme. Some of the payments for poultry houses appear to have been fraudulent.
183. UCDA, FF/439, 11 July 1935.
184. O'Connor and Guiomard, 'Agricultural output', pp 92–3.
185. AGI G 1513/1935.
186. Crotty, *Irish Agricultural Production*, pp 145–6.
187. S 2638 A-C; S 6759; S 8836; S 10700.
188. Richard Bruton and Frank J. Convery, *Land Drainage Policy in Ireland,* (Dublin, 1982), p. 19.
189. S 9636.
190. Commission of Inquiry into Banking, Currency and Credit, *Memoranda of Evidence,* (1938), qs 10285–995.
191. Ó Gráda, *Ireland. A New Economic History*, pp 392–5.
192. Commission of Inquiry into Banking, Currency and Credit, *Report* (1938), para. 76.

Chapter Five

1. James Meenan, *The Irish Economy since 1922,* (Liverpool, 1970), p. 103.
2. Crotty, *Irish Agricultural Production,* p. 158.
3. This includes the value of turf drawn by farmers, but not the much larger output by the Turf Development Board and the local authorities.
4. S 11762A, Dairy produce: supplies and prices.
5. PDDE, 20 October 1943, cols 683–4; 21 March 1944, cols 115–16.
6. AGI G 931/1945, Food production.
7. AGI G 931/1945, Food production.
8. AGI G 1542/1942, Food production. Transcripts of the radio talks during the Emergency are printed in the *Journal of the Department of Agriculture* for the appropriate years.
9. AGI G 498/1942, Traffic organisation and food supply.
10. S 11466A, European War: Government economic policy.
11. AGI G21/1941, Regional commissioners and the supply of food.
12. Takei, 'Business and Government in the Irish Free State', pp 341–2.
13. S 11402A, Agricultural Production: maintenance and increase in time of war.
14. AGI G 750/1940, Impact of war.
15. S 11466A, European War: Government economic policy.
16. R. J. Hammond, *Food,* in Keith Hancock (ed.), *History of the Second World War,* (London, 1955), pp 64–9.
17. Meenan, *The Irish Economy*, p. 102.
18. Murray, *Agriculture*, pp 57–8.

19. S 11405, Livestock exports to Great Britain in the event of war.
20. S 11466A, European War: Government economic policy.
21. Hammond, *Food*, pp 115–17.
22. The words in square brackets were added in pencil, apparently by de Valera.
23. S 11846A, Trade discussions with Britain.
24. Cabinet Minutes, 30 April 1940; S 11846A.
25. S 11846A.
26. For details see John Bowman, *De Valera and the Ulster Question 1917–1973*, (Oxford, 1982), pp 217–37.
27. Hammond, *Food*, p. 90.
28. S 11846A.
29. Dermot Keogh, *Twentieth-Century Ireland*, (Dublin, 1994), p. 117.
30. S 11466A.
31. S 11762A.
32. AGI G 639/1940, Dairy Produce 1939–57.
33. S 11762A.
34. S 12533, Discussion with the British Government: Inter-Departmental Committee.
35. S 13347 A/1, Eggs and poultry.
36. Commission on Vocational Organisation, 1943, *Report*, (1944), R. 76/1, para. 363.
37. S 11627A, Flax growing during the Emergency.
38. Report of the Minister for Agriculture for 1941/42, p. 123.
39. PDDE, 1 May 1941, cols 2170–82.
40. Murray, *Agriculture*, pp 118–20; p. 157.
41. PDDE, 15 April 1942, col. 589.
42. PDDE, 1 May 1941, cols 2173–4.
43. AGI G 1139/1940, Cattle Exports.
44. AGI G 2014/1941, Export of stores.
45. S 10121A, Flour and Bread Prices.
46. Table 5 – Agricultural Statistics; Table 6 – *Census of Industrial Production 1938–44*, I.77/8, p. 85.
47. The Irish Farmers' Federation was founded in 1937 in an attempt to establish a general non-political farmers' organisation. It was a federation of the Dublin Farmers' Association, the Association of Milk Producers (Dublin Sales Area) and the Cavan Farmers' Trade Union. In the early 1940s it claimed a membership of 13,500 farmers and 1,000 farm labourers. Commission on Vocational Organisation, *Report*, (1944), para. 213. This is the earliest reference to the Farmers' Federation in the Department's files.
48. AGI G 1568/1939, Farmers' Conference with Taoiseach.
49. A barrel of wheat was 20 stone or 2½ cwt.
50. S 11402A.
51. S 11402B.
52. S 10121A, Bread and flour prices.
53. S 11 402B.
54. Richard Dunphy, *The Making of Fianna Fáil Power in Ireland 1923–48*, (Oxford, 1991), p. 225.

55. On parish councils, see Daly, *The Buffer State*, pp 305–11.
56. Beet was grown under contract with guaranteed prices.
57. S 11402B.
58. UCDA, FF/440, May 1940–May 1942.
59. S 11402B.
60. S 12335A, Collection and distribution of 1941 cereal crop.
61. Takei, 'Business and Government in the Irish Free State', pp 357, 364.
62. UCDA, FF/440.
63. *Irish Press*, 13 January 1942.
64. Gerard Fee, 'The effect of World War II on Dublin's low-income families', PhD thesis, University College, Dublin, 1996, p. 68.
65. S 11402C.
66. S 12335A.
67. Fee, 'The effect of World War II', pp 69–70; J. E. Counihan and T. W. Dillon, 'Irish tuberculosis death rates', *JSSISI*, xviii, 1943–44, p. 169.
68. S 11402A, 21 September 1939.
69. S 11466.
70. S 11402B, 23 December 1940.
71. PDDE, 15 April 1942, cols 591–2.
72. S 12335A, Grain supplies and prices.
73. PDDE, 15 April 1942, cols 591–2.
74. S 12335A.
75. S 11402C.
76. S 12335A, 5 January 1944.
77. AGI G 749/1940, Commission on Agriculture.
78. AGI G 750/1940, Impact of war.
79. S 10434, Sugar and sugar beet prices.
80. S 10434B.
81. S 11402C.
82. AGI G 1944/1941, Default re tillage.
83. S11402B.
84. S 12868A, Breaches of emergency powers orders. Stating of cases by Circuit Court judges.
85. PDDE, 20 October 1943, col. 685.
86. S 11402C.
87. PDDE, 20 October 1943, col. 685.
88. S 12335A.
89. S 12962A, Threshing sets: hiring charges.
90. S 11402A.
91. PDDE, 15 April 1942, col. 590.
92. S 11402C.
93. S 12508, Agricultural machinery suspension of duty; S 12768A, Agricultural appliances and materials: suspension of duty.
94. AGI G 1542/1942, Increased food production, 1942–51.
95. G 498/1942, Traffic organisation and food supplies.
96. Murray, *Agriculture*, p. 53.

97. S 11402B.
98. AGI G 749/1940.
99. AGI G 1162/1939, Fertiliser scheme, 1938–58.
100. PDDE, 15 April 1942, col. 593. It consisted of 20 per cent soluble phosphate, 2 per cent citric soluble phosphate, 2 per cent insoluble phosphate, with 1 per cent nitrogen and 1 per cent fertiliser.
101. S 13122B, Supplies of lime.
102. S 11466, European War: Economic Policy of the Government.
103. Fanning, *Finance*, pp 319–21.
104. S 11466.
105. Daly, *The Buffer State*, pp 263–70.
106. For example, AGI G 1885/1941, Army and the harvest. This was also regularly mentioned in the newspapers.
107. AGI G 1551/1941, Harvest labour.
108. S 11582A, Irish Labour. Emigration to Great Britain and Northern Ireland 1940–44.
109. Department of the Environment, Roads Section, T 308, Conference, 6 November 1941.
110. S 13029A, Agricultural and turf workers. Formation of reserve pool of labour.
111. S 13029A.
112. Department of the Environment, Box 743 TA 161 G, Wages and conditions for turf workers.
113. AGI G 989/1943.
114. Daly, *The Buffer State*, p. 268.
115. AGI G 764/1946, Supply of agricultural labour, 1943–51.
116. AGI G 145/1943, Supply of agricultural labour. On 18 August the *Irish Press* reported that six men were charged with intimidating workmen, in an attempt to prevent them working for the proprietor of the charcoal-burning plant. One of the men was charged with possession of a revolver. The charges were dismissed when witnesses refused to testify. However, the men were re-arrested under the Offences against the State Act, 1939. The incident appears to have been prompted by allegations of land-grabbing rather than by shortage of agricultural labour.
117. AGI G 145/1943.
118. AGI G 145/1943.
119. AGI G 145/1943.
120. *Irish Press*, 25 October 1943, cutting on AGI G 764/1946.
121. AGI G 764/1946.
122. S 11052B, Rates relief on agricultural land.
123. AGI G 764/1946.
124. AGI G 244/1946, Harvest labour scheme.
125. Agricultural Statistics, 1939–46.
126. *Census of Industrial Production 1938–44*, I. 77/8.
127. AGI G 639/1940, Dairy produce 1939–57.
128. AGI G 639/1940, Dairy produce 1939–57.
129. S 11762A.
130. AGI G 639/1940, Dairy produce 1939–57.

131. S 11762A.
132. S 12546.
133. AGI G 529/1942, Butter shortage.
134. S13001A, Milk supply: maintenance during the Emergency.
135. *Census of Industrial Production 1938–44.*
136. S 13001A.
137. S 11762A.
138. S 11762A.
139. S 12846A, Bacon and pork: Control of production and distribution 1941.
140. The membership consisted of J. Griffin and T. F. Coakley, Department of Supplies; P. O'Connor and P. A. Rogan, Department of Agriculture; J. O'Dwyer, Department of Industry and Commerce; and M. J. O'Brien, the chairman of the Pigs and Bacon Commission.
141. S 12846A, Bacon and pork: Control of production and distribution 1941.
142. This required that any proposal entailing additional expenditure should be submitted to the Department of Finance in advance of the Cabinet meeting.
143. S 12846A, 16 October 1942.
144. S 12846B, Bacon and pork: Control of production and distribution 1941.
145. S 13347A/1, Eggs and poultry.
146. S 13347A/2.
147. Cormac Ó Gráda and Kevin O'Rourke, 'Irish economic growth, 1945–88', in Nicholas Crafts and Gianni Toniolo, 'Postwar growth: an overview', in Nicholas Crafts and Gianni Toniolo (eds), *Economic Growth in Europe since 1945*, (Cambridge, 1996), p. 400.
148. Michael Murphy, 'Financial results on sixty-one West Cork farms in 1940–41', *JSSISI*, xvi, 1941/2, p. 60.
149. S 12670, National Ploughing Association state assistance.
150. S 10121A, Price of Flour.
151. *Ibid.*
152. S 12888A, Agriculture Post-emergency planning.
153. AGI G 275/1942, Soil fertility. This organisation was founded in 1937 as a central body to unite existing farmers' organisations, with the general aim of making life on the land more attractive and remunerative for both farmers and workers. Commission on Vocational Organisation, *Report*, (1938), para. 213.
154. Commission on Vocational Organisation, *Report*, (1938), para. 222; NLI, Commission on Vocational Organisation, Minutes, vol. 20, Document 184.
155. Commission on Vocational Organisation, *Report*, (1938), para. 222.
156. NLI, Commission on Vocational Organisation, Evidence, vol. 9, Ms 930, para. 18737.
157. PDDE, 20 October 1943, col. 692.
158. Commission on Vocational Organisation, *Report*, (1938), para. 214.
159. AGI G 711/1945, Post-Emergency agricultural policy. This file includes press-cuttings, e.g. *Irish Independent*, 15 September 1942.
160. See note 159.
161. Dublin Diocesan Archives, McQuaid Papers, Minutes of the meeting of the Catholic Hierarchy, 22 June 1942.
162. Crotty, *Irish Agricultural Production*, p. 158.

CHAPTER SIX

1. Nicholas Crafts and Gianni Toniolo, 'Postwar growth: an overview', in Nicholas Crafts and Gianni Toniolo (eds), *Economic Growth in Europe since 1945*, (Cambridge, 1996), p. 2.
2. *Annual Report of the Minister for Agriculture, 1945/6.*
3. PDDE, 4 June 1946, col. 1268.
4. Ireland held all its foreign exchange in the form of sterling. In the summer of 1947 Britain suspended the convertibility of sterling; this meant that Ireland could not buy dollars or other foreign currencies.
5. AGI G 637/1945.
6. *Irish Press*, 8 February 1946; *The Irish Times*, 9 February 1946.
7. S 13907, Harvest, 1946, damage caused by bad weather.
8. S 13907.
9. S 12335B, Grain Supplies and Prices.
10. S 10121B, 23 June 1949.
11. PDDE, 19 March 1947, col. 2397.
12. S 14065A, Livestock Losses, 1947: Special Loan Schemes for Farmers.
13. S 14065A.
14. S 14203, Slaughter of Calves for Veal.
15. PDDE, 9 July 1948, col. 2588.
16. The Committee on Post-Emergency Agricultural Policy consisted of de Valera, Lemass, who was Minister for Industry and Commerce and Supplies, and Sean T. O'Kelly, the Minister for Finance. For details see Lee, *Ireland 1912–1985*, pp 229–32; Daly, *The Buffer State*, pp 283–95.
17. S 12888A, Agriculture, Post-Emergency Planning.
18. S 12888A.
19. S 12888B, Agriculture, Post-Emergency Planning.
20. Committee of Inquiry on Post-Emergency Agricultural Policy, *(First) Interim Report – Cattle and Dairy Industries*, (1943), A. 31/1; *Second Interim Report – Poultry Production*, (1944), A 31/2.
21. S 12888B.
22. S 13101A, Full Employment.
23. S 13101A.
24. It has been suggested that Sheehy had a major influence on Fianna Fáil's agricultural policy. He wrote on agriculture in the *Irish Press* under a pen-name. Further information on this is to be found in a biographical note on Sheehy by Matt Hyland in Curran, (ed.), *Agricultural Science in Ireland*, pp 153–4.
25. *Final Report of the Committee of Inquiry on Post-Emergency Agricultural Policy*, 1945, A 31/4, P. 7175.
26. *Irish Independent*, 18 February 1946.
27. S 12888C, Agriculture, Post-Emergency Planning.
28. S 12888C.
29. AGI G 73/1946, Reorganisation of Pig Industry.
30. AGI G 73/1946, Reorganisation of Pig Industry.
31. S 12846B, Department of Agriculture, memo to government, 8/8/1947.

32. Department of Agriculture, *Policy in Regard to Crops, Pastures, Fertilisers and Feeding Stuffs,* 1946, P. no. 7597.
33. S 12888C.
34. S 12888C.
35. AGI G 928/1946. The Industrial Efficiency Bill proved highly controversial and it never became law.
36. PDDE, 8 October 1947, col. 33.
37. AGI G 928/1946, Agricultural Costs Commission.
38. For a comprehensive account see Bernadette Whelan, 'Ireland and the Marshall Plan', *Irish Economic and Social History,* xix, (1992), pp 49–70 and Bernadette Whelan, *Ireland and the Marshall Plan 1947–1957,* (Dublin, 2000).
39. Hoctor, *The Department's Story,* p. 232.
40. *Ibid.,* p. 233; *Kilkenny People,* 21 July 1956.
41. S 2472 C, Appointment of Secretary to Department of Agriculture. This file cites S 15897, a file that has not been released to the public. Most establishment files are not released for 100 years.
42. S 2472 B and S 2472C, Appointment of Secretary to Department of Agriculture.
43. PDDE, 12 May 1949, col. 1095.
44. Cited on S 12888D, Agriculture, Post-Emergency Planning.
45. PDDE, 15 June 1950, col. 1791.
46. S 12335C/2, Grain Supplies.
47. S 13101D, Full Employment.
48. S 13875 C/1, Food and Agricultural Organisation.
49. For example, Walsh, PDDE, 16 July 1952, col. 1060.
50. PDDE, 16 July 1952, col. 1073.
51. Whelan, *Ireland and the Marshall Plan,* pp 230–1. Fanning, *Finance,* pp 405–7, suggests this was something of a cosmetic exercise to qualify for Marshall Aid.
52. G. A. Holmes, *On the Present State and Methods for Improvement of Irish Grasslands,* 1949, A. 38.
53. Maurice Manning, *James Dillon. A Biography,* (Dublin, 1999), p. 238.
54. Whelan, *Ireland and the Marshall Plan,* p. 298.
55. National Archives, Washington, ECA Program Coordination Division Position Paper Ireland. The Marshall Aid Programme was introduced under the Economic Cooperation Act; the Economic Cooperation Administration was the office responsible for the programme. Thanks to Dr Deirdre McMahon for giving me copies of these papers.
56. Ó Gráda and O'Rourke, 'Irish economic growth, 1945–88', p. 400.
57. Whelan, *Ireland and the Marshall Plan,* p. 128.
58. Whelan, *Ireland and the Marshall Plan* , p. 316.
59. Whelan, *Ireland and the Marshall Plan,* pp 241–2.
60. Whelan, *Ireland and the Marshall Plan,* p. 95.
61. *Annual Report of the Minister for Agriculture, 1949/50,* p. 128.
62. Eithne MacDermott, *Clann na Poblachta,* (Cork, 1998), pp 61–2.
63. S 11198B, Drainage Commission.
64. Whelan, *Ireland and the Marshall Plan,* pp 269–71.
65. *Irish Independent,* 2 June 1949.

66. This site was still featuring in a list of proposed investment projects in 1959.
67. S 14477B, Land Reclamation Scheme.
68. PDDE, 16 July 1953, col. 1352.
69. S 14477B.
70. PDDE, 16 July 1952, col. 1058.
71. S 14477B and C.
72. S 14777C, Land Reclamation Scheme. Government expenditure was cut and additional taxes and import restrictions were imposed on three occasions during 1956.
73. S 14477D.
74. Thanks to William Murphy for this observation.
75. *Third Programme. Economic and Social Development, 1969–72*, 1969, Prl. 431, pp 75–6.
76. Annual Report of the Minister for Agriculture and Fisheries, 1973/4 and 1977.
77. M. Neenan, 'Agriculture in the new state', in Curran (ed), *Towards a History of Agricultural Science in Ireland*, pp 115.
78. Murray, *Agriculture*, p. 24.
79. De Valera was guest of honour. He used the occasion to launch his plan to build dower-houses on farms. For further information on this dispute see P. L. Curran (ed), *Towards a History of Soil Science in Ireland*, (Dublin, 1992), pp 55–9.
80. S 13493, Soil Science. Walsh had appeared as an expert witness for a group of Wexford farmers who mounted a successful challenge to a compulsory tillage order. Neenan, 'Agriculture in the new state', p. 116, suggests this may have contributed to the dispute.
81. S 16804, Agricultural Research in Ireland. E. P. Cunningham, 'Dr Thomas Walsh MAGrSC, PhD, DSc, ScD, MRIA', *Agricultural Record*, 1988.
82. T. Walsh, P. F. Ryan and J. Kilroy, 'A half century of fertiliser and lime use in Ireland' *JSSISI*, vol. xix, 1956/7, p. 118.
83. S 14473, Disposal of lime from Tuam beet factory.
84. Walsh, Ryan and Kilroy, 'A half century of fertiliser and lime use in Ireland', p. 114.
85. *Economic Development*, chapter 2, para. 15. This section of *Economic Development* was based on the paper by Walsh, Ryan and Kilroy.
86. S 7901C, Fertiliser Production.
87. S 12888D.
88. S 7901C, Fertiliser Production.
89. S 7901D.
90. 96/6/182 Fertiliser.
91. S 13101B, Full Employment.
92. Whelan, *Ireland and the Marshall Plan*, p. 272.
93. T. K. Whitaker, *Economic Development*, F. 58, 1958, pp 124–5.
94. Richard Bruton and Frank Convery, *Land Drainage Policy in Ireland*, (Dublin, 1982), pp 62–3.
95. *Report by the Inter-Departmental Committee on the Problems of Small Western Farms*, 1962, A. 52.
96. For further details see the annual reports of the Department of Agriculture.

97. BT 11/4246, Anglo-Irish Trade Negotiations, 13 May 1946.
98. BT 11/4246, Anglo-Irish Trade Negotiations.
99. S 14042A, Trade Negotiations.
100. S 14042A, 23 October 1947.
101. T 236/775, Anglo-Irish Trade Negotiations.
102. BT 11/8221.
103. S 14211A, Cattle and Dead Meat Exports and Prices; T 236/776, Anglo-Irish Trade Negotiations.
104. S 14042B, Trade Negotiations.
105. BT 11/8821.
106. PDDE, 15 June 1948, col. 933.
107. Manning, *James Dillon*. pp 235–6.
108. S 14042B.
109. S 14042C, Trade Negotiations.
110. *The Statist*, 3 July 1948; *Irish Press*, 17 July 1948; *The Irish Times*, 22 June 1948.
111. PDDE, 5 August 1948, col. 2151.
112. PDDE, 9 July 1948, col. 2589.
113. The group was chaired by Roy Geary of the Central Statistics Office. The other members were T. K. Whitaker (Finance); M. S. de Barra (Agriculture); E de Buirca (Industry and Commerce); and Con Cremin (External Affairs).
114. Whelan, *Ireland and the Marshall Plan*, p. 229.
115. Whelan, *Ireland and the Marshall Plan*, p. 151.
116. T 236/778, Anglo-Irish Trade Negotiations.
117. David Harkness, *Northern Ireland since 1920*, (Dublin, 1983), p. 112.
118. IBEC Technical Services Corporation, *An Appraisal of Ireland's Industrial Potential*, (Dublin, 1952); Department of Industry and Commerce, I 98, p 11.
119. My thanks to Jimmy O'Mahony for this observation.
120. S 14211B, Cattle and Dead Meat Exports and Prices.
121. IBEC, *An Appraisal of Ireland's Industrial Potential*, p. 76.
122. The Department of Agriculture was responsible for granting export licences under the 1940 Control of Exports Order and the 1947 Agricultural and Fishery Products (Regulation of Exports) Act.
123. IBEC, *An Appraisal of Ireland's Industrial Potential*, p.74.
124. Whelan, *Ireland and the Marshall Plan*, pp 345–6.
125. S 14211B, Cattle and Dead Meat Exports and Prices.
126. D/A 10/10/1/1 Part II, Open-Pack Meat Products.
127. Daly, ' "An Irish-Ireland for Business"? The Control of Manufactures Acts 1932 and 1934', *Irish Historical Studies*, vol. 24, no 94, November 1984, pp 246–72.
128. These figures are taken from the Annual Reports of the Minister for Agriculture.
129. S 14211B, Cattle and Dead Meat Exports.
130. *Irish Press*, 29 January 1953.
131. S 14042F, Minutes of Foreign Trade Committee Meeting, 18 October 1952.
132. S 14042F.
133. S 14211B.
134. *Irish Press*, 29 January 1953.
135. D/A 10B/1/1.

136. S 14042G, Trade Negotiations.
137. S 13089D, Diseases of Animals.
138. S 14211B.
139. S 14042H, Trade Negotiations.
140. S 14042I, Trade Negotiations.
141. *Report of the Advisory Committee on the Export of Agricultural Produce. The export of livestock and meat*, 1959. A. 46. Pr. 5224.
142. S 14042J; S 14211I, Trade Negotiations.
143. *Statistical Abstract*, 1957, p. 129.
144. S 14042J; S 14211I.
145. *Report of the Advisory Committee on the Export of Agricultural Produce. The export of livestock and meat*, 1959. A. 46. Pr. 5224.
146. Sources for Tables 8 and 9: for 1952–3, *Statistical Abstract*; for 1954–8, *Report of the Advisory Committee on the Marketing of Agricultural Produce*, and *Report on the Export of Livestock and Meat*.
147. S 15730, Levy on Cattle Exports. PDSE, 19 June 1952, cols 1574–1649; PDDE, 30 June 1954, cols 835–7; 1 July 1954, cols 1044–6; 10 November 1954; *Irish Press*, 29 November 1954.
148. S 15428A, Agricultural Policy 1953: Report by Seán Moylan.
149. S 11762B, Dairy Produce: Supply and Price.
150. S 11762C/1, Dairy Produce: Supply and Price.
151. S 14627A/1, Dairy Industry: Proposed Re-Organisation.
152. This pattern of repeated postponement was quite a common feature of the first and second inter-party governments; it was much less common under Fianna Fáil.
153. S 14627A/1, Dairy Industry: Proposed Re-Organisation.
154. David McCullough, *A Makeshift Majority. The First Inter-Party Government, 1948–51*, (Dublin, 1998), pp 239–41.
155. S 11762/C1, Dairy Produce.
156. S 14627 A/2, Dairy Industry: Proposed Re-Organisation.
157. Murphy had published several studies of costs and output on dairy farms: M. Murphy 'Financial results on mixed dairy farms in 1937–38', *JSSISI*, vol. xvi, 1938–9, p. 105; 'Financial results on mixed dairy farms in 1942–43 as compared with 1938–39', *JSSISI*, vol. xvii, 1943–4, p. 269; 'Financial results on sixty-one West Cork farms in 1940–41', *JSSISI*, vol. xvi, 1941–2, p. 60.
158. S 13930B, Agricultural Produce Prices: Cabinet Committee, 1952.
159. S 11762C.
160. S 11762D, Dairy Produce.
161. PDDE, 16 July 1952, cols 1058–9. Kieran Kennedy and Brendan Dowling, *Economic Growth in Ireland. The Experience since 1947*, (Dublin, 1975), p. 215.
162. S 11762/C1.
163. S 11762D.
164. PDDE, 16 July 1952, col. 1061.
165. S 11762D.
166. S 11762C/1.
167. S 11762D.

168. *Irish Press*, 13 May 1954 and 14 May 1954; *Irish Independent*, 4 May 1954.
169. PDDE, 8 May 1957, cols 946–7.
170. S 11762G, Dairy Produce.
171. S 15255B, Committee on Milk Production Costs.
172. My thanks to Donal Creedon for this observation.
173. PDSE, 6 February 1963, col. 187.
174. S 13936A, Live Stock (Artificial Insemination) Act, 1947.
175. E. P. Cunningham, 'The genetic improvement of the Irish cattle population', *JSSISI*, vol. xxi, pt. 4 (1965/6), p. 106; *Annual Report of the Minister for Agriculture, 1950/51.*
176. S 11762E, Dairy Produce.
177. PDDE, 9 July 1949, cols 2603–4.
178. S 15428A, Improvement of Cattle Breeding.
179. S 11762E, Dairy Produce.
180. S 15428A.
181. S 15428A.
182. S 11762E.
183. Department of Finance, *Economic Development*, p. 71; Department of Agriculture, *Report of Two-Tier Milk Price Study Group*, (1968), A. 60, p. 16.
184. S 12888D, Post-Emergency Agricultural Policy.
185. S 15428A.
186. S 13101 C/1, Full Employment.
187. S 13089D, Diseases of Animals.
188. S 13089E.
189. S 13347B, Eggs and Poultry.
190. Manning, *James Dillon*, p. 236.
191. *The Irish Times*, 24 December 1949. My thanks to Owen Dudley Edwards for the description of the Abbey pantomime.
192. S 13447B, Eggs and Poultry Exports.
193. S 13347B.
194. S 12888E, Report of Advisory Committee on the Marketing of Agricultural Produce. Report on Shell Eggs and Liquid Eggs.
195. S 12846C/1, Pork and Bacon.
196. S 12846/C/2, Pork and Bacon.
197. S 12846/D/1, Pork and Bacon.
198. Advisory Committee on the Marketing of Agricultural Produce, *Report on the Export of Bacon and other Pigmeat*, (1958), A. 41.
199. S 12846/D/1, Pork and Bacon.
200. Crotty, *Irish Agricultural Production*, pp 170–1.
201. S 10121C, Flour and Bread Prices.
202. S 12335 C/1, Grain Supplies and Prices.
203. PDDE, 9 July 1948, cols 2589–94.
204. S 14413 A/1, Transfer of Functions from Minister for Agriculture.
205. S 12335 C/1.
206. S 12335 C/2, Grain Supplies and Prices.
207. S 12335C/2.

208. S 15282A, County Committees of Agriculture.
209. S 15282A.
210. GIS 1/357, Speech on 3 May 1952.
211. S 12335C/2, Grain Supplies and Prices.
212. S 12335C/2.
213. S 10121D, Flour and Bread Prices.
214. *Irish Independent*, 10 May 1954; *Irish Press*, 11 May 1954 and 13 May 1954.
215. S 12335 C/2.
216. S 10121E, Flour and Bread Prices.
217. S 10121F, Flour and Bread Prices.
218. PDDE, 16 June 1953, col. 1345.
219. Crotty, *Irish Agricultural Production*, pp 168–9.
220. S 12335C/2.
221. Kennedy *et al.*, *Economic Growth in Ireland*, p. 207.
222. Michael Tracy, *Government and Agriculture in Western Europe 1880–1988*, (London, 1989), pp 215–29. The Organisation for European Economic Co-Operation was established in 1948 as a permanent organisation representing the sixteen countries that were participating in the Marshall Aid Programme. Participating countries undertook to promote increased production; to develop the maximum possible interchange of goods and services by relaxing restrictions on international trade and international payments; to achieve currency stability and source rates of exchange; and to make the fullest and most effective use of available manpower by providing full employment.
223. Peder J. Pederson, 'Post-war growth of the Danish economy', in Crafts and Toniolo (eds), *Economic Growth in Europe since 1945*, pp 541–2.
224. S 16283D/63, Improved Marketing of Agricultural Produce.
225. S 14638I, Proposals by the OEEC for the Liberalisation of European Trade.
226. S 15011A, Green Pool Conference Notes for information of Irish ambassador in Paris. 1952.
227. S 15011A, Green Pool.
228. S 15011B, Green Pool.
229. Belgium, the Netherlands, Luxembourg, France, Germany and Italy had already embarked on the process of establishing the EEC.
230. D/A 6/29/31 (part v), Revision of Anglo-Irish Trade Agreement.
231. Denis Maher, *The Tortuous Path. The Course of Ireland's Entry into the EEC 1948–73*, (Dublin, 1986), pp 55–67
232. D/A 6/29/31 (part v).
233. D/A 6/29/31 (part v).
234. D/A 6/29/31 (part v).
235. D/A 6/29/31 (part v).
236. Belgium, France, Germany, Italy, Luxembourg and the Netherlands formed the EEC. The EFTA member countries were Austria, Britain, Denmark, Norway, Portugal, Sweden and Switzerland.
237. S 15281/U, European Free Trade Area.
238. Capital Investment Advisory Committee, *Third Report*, (1958), F. 53/3, Table 4.
239. Kennedy *et al.*, *Economic Growth in Ireland*, p. 202.

240. The Commission, which was chaired by J. P. Beddy, was asked to investigate 'the causes and consequences of the present level and trend in population; and to examine, in particular, the social and economic effects of birth, death, migration and marriage rates at present and their probable course in the near future; to consider what measures, if any, should be taken in the national interest to influence the future trend in population; generally, to consider the desirability of formulating a national population policy'.

241. Commission on Emigration, 1948–54, *Report*, (1955), R. 84, pp 146–9, paras 338–49; Minority Report by Dr Cornelius Lucey, pp 343–8, paras 338–49.

242. S 14249C, Commission on Emigration.

243. S 15428A, Improvement of Cattle Breeding.

244. S 13101B, Full Employment.

245. Kennedy *et al.*, *Economic Growth in Ireland*, pp 214–18; Lee, *Ireland 1912–1985*, pp 303–13; 321–8.

246. Central Statistics Office, *National Farm Survey 1955/56–1957/58*, (1962), I. 110.

247. PDDE, 17 May 1945, col. 657.

248. S 15011A.

249. Michael Shiel, *The Quiet Revolution; The Electrification of Rural Ireland, 1946–1976*, (Dublin, 1984); Diarmaid Ferriter, *Mothers, Maidens and Myths. A History of the ICA*, (Dublin, 1996), pp 37–40; Mary E. Daly, ' "Turn on the Tap": the state, Irish women and running water', in Maryann Valiulis and Mary O'Dowd (eds), *Women and Irish History*, (Dublin, 1997), pp 206–19.

250. Jim Miley, *A Voice for the Country. Fifty Years of Macra na Feirme*, (Dublin, 1994), pp 1–33.

251. Miley, *A Voice for the Country*, pp 40–1.

252. S 13875A, Food and Agricultural Organisation.

253. S 13875 B/1, Food and Agricultural Organisation.

254. S 13875 C/1, Food and Agricultural Organisation; *Annual Report of the Minister for Agriculture and Fisheries, 1965/66*, pp 153–4.

Chapter Seven

1. Department of Finance, *Programme for Economic Expansion*, (1958), F. 57, paras 1–3.

2. John F. McCarthy, 'Ireland's turnaround: Whitaker and the 1958 Plan for Economic Development', in John F. McCarthy (ed.), *Planning Ireland's Future. The Legacy of T. K. Whitaker*, (Dublin, 1999), pp 11– 73.

3. John Horgan, *Seán Lemass. The Enigmatic Patriot*, (Dublin, 1997), pp 191–2.

4. Horgan, *Seán Lemass*, p. 192.

5. S 16405.

6. S 2472 B and C, Appointment of Secretary to Department of Agriculture.

7. Hoctor, *The Department's Story*, p. 236.

8. MAF 379/33. My thanks to Paul Rouse for providing me with this quotation.

9. S 12888E, Post-Emergency Agricultural Policy, Cabinet Minutes, 26 April 1957.

10. Department of Finance, *Economic Development*, (1958), F. 58, p. 12.
11. *Ibid.*, pp 59–69.
12. *Twenty-Eighth Annual Report of the Minister for Agriculture, 1958–59*, p. 25.
13. S 7901D, Fertiliser Production.
14. S 16541A, Programme for Economic Expansion.
15. *Economic Development*, pp 59–69.
16. S 12888E, Post-Emergency Agricultural Policy.
17. Annual Price Index Numbers of Certain Farm Materials. James McGilvray, *Irish Agricultural Statistics*, (Dublin, 1968), p. 68.
18. PDDE, 11 June 1959, col. 1400.
19. PDDE, 13 July 1961, col. 946.
20. R. O'Connor, 'An analysis of recent policies for beef and butter', *JSSISI*, vol. xxii, pt. 2, (1969–70), p. 67.
21. Annual Price Index Numbers of Certain Farm Materials. McGilvray, *Irish Agricultural Statistics*, p. 68.
22. PDDE, 12 July 1960, cols 379–80.
23. *Twenty-Ninth Annual Report of the Minister for Agriculture, 1959–60*, p. 93.
24. PDDE, 12 July 1962, col. 2303.
25. Robert O'Connor, 'Implications of Irish agricultural statistics', in I. F. Baillie and S. J. Sheehy (eds), *Irish Agriculture in a Changing World* , (Edinburgh, 1971), p. 42.
26. Fred W. Gilmore, *Survey of Agricultural Credit in Ireland*, (1959), A. 44.
27. *Twenty-Eighth Report of the Minister for Agriculture, 1958–59*.
28. PDDE, 12 July 1960, cols 1387–8.
29. PDDE, 13 July 1961, cols 940–1.
30. E. P. Cunningham, 'The genetic improvement of the Irish cattle population', *JSSISI*, vol. xxi, pt. 4, (1965–6), p. 105.
31. S 15428B/61, Improvement of Cattle Breeding.
32. *Thirty-Second Annual Report of the Minister for Agriculture, 1962–63*.
33. S 15428B/63, Improvement of Cattle Breeding.
34. S 15428 B/95, Improvement of Cattle Breeding.
35. PDDE, 29 April 1965, col. 411.
36. S 17468/63, Gift of Aberdeen Angus Bull to Pope.
37. S 16405.
38. PDDE, 14 May 1958, col. 159.
39. PDDE, 13 July 1961, col. 941.
40. S 2392A, Diseases of Animals.
41. S 2392 B/1, Diseases of Animals.
42. S 14815 A/2, Agriculture and Veterinary Science Institute: Proposed Establishment.
43. S 2392 B/1, Diseases of Animals.
44. S 2392 B/2, Diseases of Animals.
45. S 2392 B/1.
46. S 2392 B/2.
47. Hoctor, *The Department's Story*, p. 250.
48. S 12888D.
49. S 2392B/2.

50. *Economic Development*, chapter 7.
51. S 2392C, Diseases of Animals.
52. S 12888E, 24 June 1959; S 2392 C.
53. S 12888E, 24 June 1959; S 2392 C.
54. S 2392 E/61, Diseases of Animals.
55. S 2392 E/62, Diseases of Animals.
56. S 2392 D/94, Diseases of Animals.
57. S 2392 E/62.
58. PDDE, 11 May 1966, col. 1511.
59. R. C. Watchorn, *Bovine Tuberculosis Eradication Scheme 1954–65*, (Department of Agriculture and Fisheries, 1959).
60. S 16674J/63, Trade Relations with Britain.
61. S 12888E.
62. S 16283A, Improved Marketing of Agricultural Produce, 1957. The full list of organisations represented on the committee included the NFA; the ICMSA; the IAOS; the Irish Bacon Curers' Association; the National Executive of the Irish Livestock Trade; the Co-operative Poultry Products, Cootehill; Irish Eggs Ltd; Irish Cheese Exporters' Association; Irish Cream Exporters' Association; Irish Fresh Meat Exporters' Society; the Beef Canners' Advisory Association; the Irish Exporters' Association; Incorporated Sales Managers' Association; and CTT.
63. Advisory Committee on the Marketing of Agricultural Produce, *Report on the Export of Pigmeat*, (1958), A. 41; *Shell Eggs and Liquid Egg*, (1959), A. 42; *The Export of Turkeys*, (1959), A. 43; *The Export of Dairy Produce*, (1959), A. 45; *The Export of Livestock and Meat*, (1959), A. 46.
64. Advisory Committee on the Marketing of Agricultural Produce. *Report on General Aspects of Irish Export Trade in Agricultural Produce*, 1959, A. 47. Signed August 1959.
65. *Export Marketing of Irish Agricultural Produce. Statement of the Government's Policy on the Recommendations of the Advisory Committee*, (1959), A. 49.
66. S 16283 A, Improved Marketing of Agricultural Produce.
67. S 16283C, Improved Marketing of Agricultural Produce.
68. S 16283C.
69. S 16283C.
70. S 17007/61, Agricultural Produce (Eggs) Bill 1961.
71. PDDE, 12 July 1962, col. 2301.
72. S 11762G, Dairy Produce: Supply and Price.
73. S 11762G.
74. PDDE, 11 May 1966, col. 1505; PDDE, 29 April 1965, col. 411.
75. S 16541A, Programme for Economic Expansion
76. S 16451B, Programme for Economic Expansion.
77. S 17032A, Small Farms: Inter-Departmental Committee.
78. S 11762H, Dairy Produce.
79. S 17005A, Dairy Produce Marketing Act 1961.
80. Maher, *The Tortuous Path*, p. 99
81. S 16674 K 1/95. This contains a summary of Anglo-Irish discussions in 1959/60 on closer economic relations. Maher, *The Tortuous Path*, pp 94–9.

82. Maher, *The Tortuous Path*, pp 102–6.
83. Maher, *The Tortuous Path*, pp 105–6.
84. This term crops up repeatedly in memoranda on Anglo-Irish trade; e.g. D/A 6/ 29/33, 1960.
85. S 16674 I/63, Trade Relations with Britain.
86. D/A 6/29/33.
87. GATT came into force on 1 January 1948. At the time twenty-three countries, mainly the industrial countries of Europe and North America, contracted into the agreement. GATT provided a framework for negotiating reductions in barriers to trade. Ireland did not become a member until 1967. Maher, *The Tortuous Path*, p. 11.
88. S 11762J/61, Trade Relations with Britain.
89. S 11762K/63, Trade Relations with Britain.
90. Britain indicated as much to Irish officials during talks in December 1961. S 16674 J/63, Trade Relations with Britain.
91. S 12846D/2/61, Pork and Bacon.
92. PDDE, 12 July 1960, col. 1389.
93. S 11762L/62.
94. S 11762/L62, Dairy Produce Supplies and Price.
95. S 11762L/62.
96. PDDE, 20 July 1960, cols 1918–22.
97. S 16877A.
98. S 16877C, *The Irish Farmers' Journal*, 23 July 1960.
99. D/A 6/29/33, Anglo-Irish Trade Agreement.
100. S 16877D, European Free Trade Area.
101. S 16877G, European Free Trade Area.
102. S 16877I/61, European Free Trade Area.
103. Maher, *The Tortuous Path*, pp 128–30.
104. S 17313 A/62.
105. S 16877I/61.
106. S 16877 I/61.
107. S 16877P/61, European Economic Community.
108. S 16877O/61, European Economic Community.
109. S 16877 I/61, European Free Trade Area.
110. S 16877L, European Economic Community.
111. S 16877M, European Economic Community; S 16877 T/61, European Economic Community.
112. S 17246 F/62, European Economic Community.
113. S 17246 M/62, European Economic Community.
114. S 16877 X/62, European Economic Community.
115. S 16877V/62, European Economic Community.
116. S 17246C/62, European Economic Community.
117. S 17246 E/62, European Economic Community.
118. S 17246A/62, European Economic Community.
119. S 17246C/62, European Economic Community.
120. S 17246 F 62, European Economic Community.

121. S 17246D /62, European Economic Community.
122. S 17246 E/62.
123. S 17246 E/62.
124. S 17246 H/62, European Economic Community.
125. S 17246B/62, European Economic Community.
126. S 17246C/62.
127. S 17246 L/62, European Economic Community.
128. S 17246 R/62, European Economic Community.
129. S 17246 U/62, European Economic Community.
130. S 17246 V/62, European Economic Community.
131. S 17246 T/62, European Economic Community.
132. S 17246 X/63, European Economic Community.
133. S 17246 K/62, European Economic Community.
134. S 17426 M/62, European Economic Community.
135. S 17246 L/62, European Economic Community.
136. S 17246 V/62, European Economic Community.
137. S 17246 W/62, European Economic Community.
138. S 17246 X/63, European Economic Community.
139. Maher, *The Tortuous Path*, pp 163–4.
140. S 3291A/2, Livestock Trade.
141. S 13291A/2.
142. S 16674 J.63, Trade Relations with Britain.
143. Tracy, *Government and Agriculture in Western Europe*, p. 234.
144. Horgan, *Seán Lemass*, p. 230.
145. S 16877 X/62, European Economic Community.
146. S 17313 A/62, State Aid to Agriculture.
147. S 16105C/61, Farm Apprenticeship.
148. S 17303/62, State Aid to Agriculture.
149. S 12846E/95, Pork and Bacon.
150. S 11563C/63, National Incomes: NFA Claim.
151. S 17032/A/61–A/62, Small Farms: Inter-Departmental Committee.
152. S 12888E, Post-Emergency Agricultural Policy.
153. S 2392 E/61, Diseases of Animals.
154. Department of Agriculture, *Report of the Survey Team established by the Minister for Agriculture on the Dairy Products Industry*, (1962), A. 53.
155. Daly, *The Buffer State*, pp 483–8; Daly, '"Turn on the Tap"', pp 206–19.
156. S 16405.
157. S 16405.
158. S 16666.
159. S 16719, NFA seeks Financial Assistance to attend Conferences.
160. S 16405.
161. S 12888E, Post-Emergency Agricultural Policy.
162. S 11563C/62, National Incomes: NFA Claim.
163. Louis Smith and Seán Healy, *Farm Organisations in Ireland. A Century of Progress*, (Dublin, 1996), p. 172.
164. S 11563/C 63, National Incomes: NFA Claim.

165. S 11762/O63, Dairy Produce.
166. S 11762L/62, Dairy Produce.
167. S 11762L/62.
168. S 11563C/63, National Income and Agricultural Income.
169. S 11563 C/63.
170. S 17246 E62, European Economic Community.
171. S 17313 A/62, State Aid to Agriculture.
172. FitzGerald was the Irish correspondent for *The Economist.*
173. S 17246F/62, European Economic Community.
174. *Irish Press*, 22 February 1963; *Sunday Telegraph*, 3 March 1963.
175. PDDE, 21 March 1963, col. 315.
176. S 11762 N/63, Anglo-Irish Trade.
177. S 17303/62, NFA Application for Technical Assistance.
178. Patrick Smith, PDDE, 11 June 1959, col. 1397.
179. Garret FitzGerald, *Planning in Ireland*, (Dublin, 1968), pp 45–9.
180. S 16283D/63, Improved Marketing of Agricultural Produce.

CHAPTER EIGHT

1. *Economic Development*, chapter 11.
2. Henry Spain, 'Agricultural education and extension', in Baillie and Sheehy (eds), *Irish Agriculture in a Changing World*, p. 159.
3. S 13101A, Full Employment.
4. S 12888B, Agriculture, Post-Emergency Planning.
5. S 14815A/2, Agricultural and Veterinary Science Institute: Proposed Establishment.
6. Miley, *A Voice for the Country*, p. 54.
7. Annual Reports of the Minister for Agriculture, 1947–58.
8. Miley, *A Voice for the Country, passim*; Ferriter, *Mothers, Maidens and Myths*, pp 34–7.
9. *FAO: The First 40 Years*, (Rome, 1985).
10. S 16804, Agricultural Research in Ireland.
11. S 14815A/2.
12. S 14815/A 2.
13. S 14815A/1.
14. McCullough, *A Makeshift Majority*, pp 56–62. The decision to exclude Maurice Moynihan, secretary to the government, from Cabinet meetings meant that long-established procedures were not observed and many important decisions were taken at informal meetings where no minutes were kept.
15. S 14815A/1.
16. The Fine Gael party incorporated the former Cumann na nGaedheal party.
17. S 14815A/2.
18. S 14815A/2.
19. The committee was chaired by W. Fay of the Department of External Affairs. It included representatives of the departments of the Taoiseach, Agriculture, Finance and Industry and Commerce.

20. S 14815A/2.
21. Whelan, *Ireland and the Marshall Plan*, pp 304–5; S 14815A/2.
22. S 14815A/2.
23. S 14815A/2.
24. S 4521B, Veterinary Profession. The Agricultural Science Association's view that the new College should be controlled by an academic council was probably coloured by the difficult relationship that existed between advisers and the administrative staff of the Department. See Martin McDonald, 'The work of the ASA from 1949 to 1972', in Curran (ed), *Agricultural Science in Ireland*, pp 157–66.
25. This was a critical issue in the catholic church's opposition to the proposal to provide comprehensive health services for mothers and children, which was known as the Mother and Child scheme.
26. S 15428A, Cattle Breeding Improvement.
27. S 15893, Proposals for an Agricultural Faculty in UCG.
28. S 10816A, Muintir na Tíre.
29. S 12888D, Agriculture: Post-Emergency Planning.
30. PDDE, 6 November 1957, col. 545; 20 November 1957, col. 822; 21 November 1957, col. 861; 27 November 1957, col. 1044; 4 December 1957, cols 1387–1401; PDSE, 12 December 1957, col. 1257.
31. *Twenty-Eighth Annual Report of the Minister for Agriculture, 1958/59.*
32. Smith and Healy, *Farm Organisations in Ireland*, pp 45, 54.
33. S 16647A, An Foras Talúntais: Relations with the Department.
34. S 12888D, Agriculture: Post-Emergency Planning.
35. S 16647A.
36. S 16647A.
37. S 16647A.
38. S 16647B/61.
39. TCD students attended the College of Science and the Albert College until 1926 and when these institutions became part of the faculty of agriculture at UCD it was agreed that this arrangement would continue.
40. S 16647A.
41. 98/6/508, An Foras Talúntais, Relations with the Department.
42. Thomas Walsh, 'Research and future agricultural developments', in Baillie and Sheehy (eds), *Irish Agriculture in a Changing World*, pp 151–4.
43. 98/6/508, An Foras Talúntais, Relations with the Department.
44. *Annual Report of the Minister for Food and Agriculture 1997*, p. 46.
45. *Annual Report of the Minister for Agriculture 1963/4*, p. 31; Annual Report of An Foras Talúntais 1959/60, p. 13.
46. Public Services Organisation Review Group, *Report of the Public Services Organisation Review Group, 1966–1969*, (Dublin, 1969), Prl. 792.
47. S 10816A, Muintir na Tíre; P. L. Curran, Pat Finn and M. Neenan, 'The Parish Plan', in Curran (ed), *Agricultural Science in Ireland*, pp 187–9.
48. On parish councils and parish-based organisations see Daly, *The Buffer State*, pp 305–11.
49. Commission on Vocational Organisation, 1943. *Report*, (1944), R. 76/1, paras 544–56.

50. Manning, *James Dillon*, p. 303.
51. S 10816A; Manning, *James Dillon*, pp 302–4.
52. Curran, Finn and Neenan, 'The Parish Plan', pp 203–6; Manning, *James Dillon*, p. 305.
53. S 10816A; Curran, Finn and Neenan, 'The Parish Plan', pp 191–202.
54. PDDE, 17 July 1952, col. 1100.
55. S 14815A/2.
56. S 15428A, Improvement of Cattle Breeding.
57. S 13101C1, Full Employment.
58. S 13831 F/2, State and Local Authorities: Financial Position.
59. *Economic Development*, chapter 11.
60. Department of Agriculture (W. Emrys Jones and Albert J. Davies), *A Review of the Irish Agricultural Advisory Service*, (1967), A. 59, p. 12.
61. *Economic Development*, chapter 11.
62. S 12888D.
63. S 15893, Proposal for an Agriculture Faculty in UCG.
64. Hoctor, *The Department's Story*, pp 244–5.
65. S 4521 B/1.
66. Commission on Higher Education 1960–67. *Report I*, Vol. II, E 59/1, (1967–68), chapter 7.
67. Commission on Higher Education 1960–67. *Presentation and Summary of Report*, Vol. I, E. 59.
68. Jeremiah Newman (ed.), *Limerick Rural Survey, 1958–64*, (Tipperary, 1964), pp 213–4.
69. Annual Reports of the Minister for Agriculture. The Munster Institute ran two courses every year and the figures are the combined attendance at two sessions. It may be possible that some students attended both sessions.
70. OECD Survey Team, *Investment in Education*, (1965), pp 15, 97.
71. Spain, 'Agricultural education and extension', p. 159.
72. *Economic Development*, chapter 11.
73. Spain, 'Agricultural education and extension', pp 161–2.
74. For details of some of the agricultural classes that were provided by VECs during the 1950s see Mary Bernadette Clarke, 'Vocational Education in a Local Context 1930–1998', PhD thesis, University College, Dublin, 1999.
75. Miley, *A Voice for the Country*, pp 5–21.
76. S 17437D/95, Second Programme for Economic Expansion.
77. Arnold Marsh Papers, Commission on Emigration, Evidence, Ms 8307/20. Department of Education.
78. UCDA, Fianna Fáil Archives, Minutes of the National Executive, 1955–58; Ms 344 and 345.
79. S 16105A, Agistment and Conacre: Provision of Farms for Young Farmers; Farm Apprenticeships.
80. S 17437D/95, Second Programme for Economic Expansion.
81. S 17437B/63, Second Programme for Economic Expansion.
82. S 17437D/95.
83. S 17032/B/62, Inter-Departmental Committee on Small Western Farms.

84. Commission on Emigration, *Report*, (1955), R. 84, paras 150–65; 430–444.
85. Arnold Marsh Papers, Commission on Emigration, Evidence. Ms 8305/4. Leitrim VEC.
86. Daly, '"Turn on the tap"', pp 206–19.
87. Newman (ed), *Limerick Rural Survey*, p. 195.
88. Ferriter, *Mothers, Maidens and Myths*, pp 38–9.
89. S 17318/62, Rural Home Economics Advisory Service.
90. S 17032A/61, Small Farms: Interdepartmental Committee.
91. S 17318/62.
92. S 170432 D/62, Small Farms: Interdepartmental Committee.
93. S 17318/62, Rural Home Economics Advisory Service.
94. Department of Agriculture (Jones & Davis), *A Review of the Agricultural Advisory Service*, (1967), A. 59, p. 12.
95. S 17318/62, Rural Home Economics Advisory Service.
96. S 17318/62.
97. S 17318/63.
98. S 17318/62.
99. S 17318/63.
100. Department of Finance, *Third Programme. Economic and Social Development, 1969–72*, (1969), F. 57/7, pp 72–3.
101. S 13431A and B, Early Marriage. Encouragement of Young Farmers.
102. S 16105A, Provision of Farms for Young Farmers and Farm Apprenticeship Scheme.
103. Commission on Emigration, *Report*, (1955), R. 84, para. 372.
104. D/A 24/24/1, Farm Apprenticeship Scheme.
105. S 16105A.
106. A group that debated social problems in contemporary Ireland.
107. S 16105A. O'Connor later became a research professor at the Economic and Social Research Institute. He was the author of many articles and reports on Irish agriculture.
108. D/A 24/24/1, Farm Apprenticeship Scheme.
109. S 16105A.
110. S 16105A.
111. D/A 24/24 I Part II.
112. S 16105B.
113. S 16105C/61.
114. S 16061C/62.
115. S 16061C/62.
116. 98/6/400, Farm Apprenticeship Scheme.
117. S 15161 A and B; S 15161C/61, Glass-House Crops. In 1961 the Cabinet decided to write off the loans that had been made under this scheme.
118. S 15160A and B, Production of Grass-Meal.
119. Central Statistics Office, *National Farm Survey*, (1962), I. 110, Table 5.
120. S 17032A/61, Small Farms Committee.
121. S 17032 F/62.
122. Department of Agriculture, *Report of the Inter-Departmental Committee on the Problems of Small Western Farms*, (1962), A. 52, pp 34–5.

123. S 17032 A/62.
124. Department of Agriculture, *Report of the Inter-Departmental Committee on the Problems of Small Western Farms*, p. 11.
125. S 17032A/62.
126. S 17032 A/62.
127. S 17032 B/62.
128. S 17032/F/62.
129. PDDE, 26 March 1963, col. 353.
130. S 17032 D/62.
131. S 15160 A and B, Grass-Meal Factory.
132. Department of Agriculture (Jones & Davis), *A Review of the Irish Agricultural Advisory Service*, (1967), A. 59, Table II. Their figures relate to 1966; the disparity between western counties and those cited would have been even greater in 1960.
133. Daly, *The Buffer State*, pp 501–2.
134. Department of Agriculture (Jones & Davis), *A Review of the Irish Agricultural Advisory Service*, (1967), A. 59, p. 21.
135. Rosemary Fennell, *Industrialisation and Agricultural Development in the Congested Districts*, An Foras Talúntais Economic Research Series, No 2, (Dublin, 1962).
136. E. A. Attwood, 'Agriculture and economic growth in western Ireland', *JSSISI*, vol. xx, pt. 5, (1961/2), p. 172.
137. S 17032/E/62.
138. PDDE, 12 November 1963, cols 1358–9.
139. The county development teams brought together the senior officers of the main government agencies in the county: the county manager, the chief agricultural officer, the chief executive officer of the VEC, the county engineer and the chairman of the county council and the county engineer, to promote economic development.
140. S 17032A/61.
141. 96/6/269, Small Farms, Interdepartmental Committee.
142. S 17032E/62.
143. See press-cuttings on 98/6/712, Government and NFA.
144. *The Western People*, 25 January 1964.
145. *The Western People*, 16 November 1963.
146. S 17032/H/95.
147. The committee included representatives from the departments of Agriculture, Local Government, Industry and Commerce. It was chaired by a senior official in the Department of Finance.
148. Department of Agriculture, *Report on Pilot Areas Development (by) the Inter-Departmental Committee on the Problems of Small Western Farms*, (1964), A. 52/1.
149. S 17032I/95.
150. S 17032I/95.
151. 96/6/269, Small Farms, Interdepartmental Committee.
152. This was noted by Department of Agriculture (Jones & Davis), *A Review of the Irish Agricultural Advisory Service*, (1967), A. 59, p. 19.
153. 96/6/269.
154. 98/6/594, Small Farms, Interdepartmental Committee.

155. John J. Scully, *Agriculture in the West of Ireland. A Study of the Low Farm Income Problem*, (1971), A. 67.
156. PDDE, 11 May 1966, cols 1516–17.
157. Public Services Organisation Review Group, *Report of Public Services Organisation Review Group, 1966–69*, (1969), p. 284.
158. S 16451A, Programme for Economic Expansion.
159. Department of Agriculture (Jones & Davis), *A Review of the Irish Agricultural Advisory Service*, p. 47.
160. J. B. Ruane, 'The farmer in a changing industry', in Baillie and Sheehy (eds), *Irish Agriculture in a Changing World*, p. 170.
161. Spain, 'Agricultural education and extension', pp 160–1; 171.
162. Newman, *Limerick Rural Survey*, p. 213.
163. S 17032 I/95, Small Western Farms.

Chapter Nine

1. FitzGerald, *Planning in Ireland*, p. 191.
2. S 17543B/95, National Farmers' Association.
3. FitzGerald, *Planning in Ireland*, p. 95.
4. S 17437A/63, Preparation of the Second Programme.
5. S 17437A/63, Preparation of the Second Programme.
6. S 17437E/95, Preparation of the Second Programme.
7. Department of Finance, *Closing the Gap (Incomes and Output)*, (1963), F. 64.
8. The Employer-Labour Conference was formed in November 1961 in an attempt to prevent workers from demanding and securing higher wage increases than what had been agreed during the wage-rounds. Kieran Allen, *Fianna Fáil and Irish Labour*, (London, 1997), p. 116.
9. S 17419D/63, National Industrial and Economic Council.
10. FitzGerald, *Planning in Ireland*, pp 163–4; Catherine Brock, *The Work of the NIEC (1963–1966)*, (September 1966), NIEC Occasional Publication No 2, Pr. 9090.
11. S 17419E/63.
12. S 17419F/63.
13. *The Irish Times*, 10 October 1963.
14. S 17419B/63 and C/63. This phrase recurs on many occasions in speeches by Lemass and by various ministers for Agriculture including Smith, Haughey and Blaney.
15. S 17419F/63.
16. S 17006B/61, Pigs and Bacon (Amendment) Act 1961.
17. S 17543A/95, National Farmers' Association.
18. S 16450B/63; Smith and Healy, *Farm Organisations in Ireland*, p. 170.
19. S 17543A/95.
20. S 16450B/63, Agricultural Produce (Cereals) Acts; National Farmers' Association.
21. S 17543A/63.
22. S 17543A/63.
23. Horgan, *Seán Lemass*, p. 236.

24. When the ICMSA was first established in the early 1950s, government ministers denounced its extremist tactics, but by the 1960s the relationship between the ICMSA and the government seems to have been amicable, although the documents relating to the ICMSA are much fewer than those relating to the NFA. There is an irony in Smith's friendlier attitude towards the ICMSA, given that Walsh, the Minister for Agriculture, had criticised their extremist tactics in 1952, and Seán MacEntee drew comparisons between the behaviour of the ICMSA and Hitler and Stalin.
25. S 17543A/95.
26. 98/6/853, National Agricultural Council.
27. S 17419F/95, National Industrial and Economic Council.
28. S 17543A/95.
29. S 17543C/95.
30. S 17543C/95.
31. S 17543 C/95.
32. PDDE, 14 April 1964, cols 1344–6.
33. Horgan, *Seán Lemass*, p. 235.
34. This was the necessary figure if agricultural output was to rise at an annual rate of 2.9 per cent for the decade.
35. E. A. Attwood, 'Future prospects for agriculture', in Baillie and Sheehy (eds), *Irish Agriculture in a Changing World*, p. 226.
36. PDDE, 29 April 1965.
37. S 17543C/95.
38. PDDE, 11 June 1964, cols 1163–5.
39. PDDE, 29 April 1965, col. 406.
40. PDDE, 11 June 1964, cols 1163–5.
41. Allen, *Fianna Fáil and Labour*, p. 119.
42. Horgan, *Seán Lemass*, pp 233–4.
43. S 15848B/95, Agricultural Wages.
44. Allen, *Fianna Fáil and Irish Labour*, p. 120.
45. *Irish Press*, 9 October 1964; *Irish Independent*, 9 October 1964.
46. Smith and Healy, *Farm Organisations in Ireland*, p. 161.
47. PDDE, 5 January 1966, col. 1291.
48. S 17246/Z/1/63, European Economic Community.
49. S 17427F/63, European Economic Community.
50. S 16674M/95, Trade Relations with Britain.
51. S 16674K/95, Trade Relations with Britain.
52. S 17247B/63, European Economic Community.
53. S 17247C/63, European Economic Community.
54. Denmark exported substantial quantities of agricultural produce to Germany and this market would be severely restricted when the CAP came into operation.
55. S 17247C/63.
56. S 17427D/63.
57. S 11762N/63, Dairy Produce.
58. Maher, *The Tortuous Path*, pp 170–5.
59. S 16674K/95, Trade Relations with Britain.

60. S 16674L/95.
61. Maher, *The Tortuous Path*, pp 170–5.
62. S 16674L/95.
63. 96/6/677, Economic Relations with Britain.
64. My thanks to Jimmy O'Mahony, who participated in the talks, for these observations.
65. 96/6/677.
66. Information supplied by Jimmy O'Mahony.
67. S 16674M/95.
68. S 16674N/95.
69. S 16674N/95.
70. S 16674L/95.
71. S 16674N/5.
72. S 16674O/95.
73. S 16674Q/95.
74. S 16674Q/63.
75. 96/6/777, Economic Relations with Britain.
76. *Annual Report of the Minister for Agriculture, 1962/63*, p. 27. My source for the involvement of John F. Kennedy is Jimmy O'Mahony.
77. 96/6/777.
78. These provided for restrictions to be imposed in order to safeguard a country's balance of payments, or to protect human, animal or plant life.
79. 96/6/779, Economic Relations with Britain.
80. 96/6/779.
81. 96/6/780, Economic Relations with Britain.
82. 96/6/782, Economic Relations with Britain.
83. 97/6/471, Economic Relations with Britain.
84. PDDE, 5 January 1966, col. 1288.
85. Robert Savage, *Seán Lemass*, (Dublin, 1999), p. 60.
86. 97/6/471.
87. 98/6/712, National Farmers' Association.
88. 97/6/102, National Farmers' Association.
89. 97/6/102.
90. PDDE, 29 April 1965, col. 443.
91. PDDE, 11 May 1965, cols 961–1002. The only additional expenditure announced was £400,000 to pay for the 1d a gallon quality bonus for creamery milk that was announced during the annual discussions between the government and the NFA.
92. 97/6/102.
93. 97/6/103, National Farmers' Association.
94. 97/6/102.
95. 96/6/103.
96. Department of Finance, *Second Programme for Economic Expansion, Review of Progress, 1964–67*, (1968), F. 57/6, p. 41.
97. *Ibid.*, p. 35.
98. Kennedy and Dowling, *Economic Growth in Ireland*, pp 233–5.
99. 96/6/103.

100. Kennedy and Dowling, *Economic Growth in Ireland*, pp 233–5.
101. *Ibid.*, pp 233–5.
102. PDDE, 11 May 1965, col. 1496.
103. PDDE, 26 May 1965, cols 2444–6.
104. 97/6/102.
105. PDDE, 11 May 1966, cols 1497–9.
106. Smith and Healy, *Farm Organisations in Ireland*, p. 175.
107. Martin Mansergh (ed), *The Spirit of the Nation: Speeches and Statements of Charles J. Haughey (1957–86)*, (Dublin, 1986).
108. Kennedy and Dowling, *Economic Growth in Ireland*, p. 235.
109. Department of Agriculture, *Report of the Study Group on Store Cattle*, (1968), A. 62, p. 32.
110. 97/6/103.
111. 97/6/102.
112. 97/6/102.
113. Horgan, *Seán Lemass*, p. 331.
114. Keogh, *Twentieth-Century Ireland*, p. 282; Allen, *Fianna Fáil and Irish Labour*, pp 127–32.
115. Keogh, *Twentieth-Century Ireland*, pp 291, 441.
116. 97/6/102. The Department subsequently calculated that the Minister had met the NFA on twenty-eight occasions during 1965, and on twenty-six occasions between January and June 1966. Officials in the Department of Agriculture held separate meetings with representatives of the NFA on at least thirty-two occasions in 1964 and at least twenty-nine occasions in the first half of 1966. 98/6/712.
117. 98/6/102.
118. 98/6/853, National Agricultural Council.
119. 98/6/853, National Agricultural Council.
120. 98/6/712.
121. 2000/6/6000, Department of Agriculture. Government relations with NFA and ICMSA. Brief Summary of Developments.
122. 98/6/712.
123. 98/6/712.
124. Daly, *The Buffer State*, p. 509.
125. 98/6/712.
126. 98/6/853, National Agricultural Council.
127. 99/1/489, National Agricultural Council.
128. *Irish Press*, 22 January 1969.
129. 2000/6/343, National Farmers' Association.
130. 96/6/345.
131. Department of Finance, *Second Programme, Review of Progress*, (1968), pp 36–7.
132. 98/6/647, Government Assistance to Agriculture.
133. 98/6/654, Press Criticism of Government Departments.
134. 98/6/654.
135. FitzGerald, *Planning in Ireland*, p. 189.
136. Department of Finance, *Second Programme, Review of Progress*, (1968).
137. PDDE, 10 December 1968, col. 2317.

138. *Annual Report of the Minister for Agriculture 1964/5*, p. 30.
139. PDDE, 11 June 1964, col. 1168.
140. PDDE, 11 May 1966, col. 1504.
141. Robert O'Connor, 'Implications of Irish agricultural statistics', in Baillie and Sheehy (eds), *Irish Agriculture in a Changing World*, pp 29–31.
142. Department of Agriculture, *Report of the Study Group on Store Cattle*, (1968), A. 62.
143. Kennedy and Dowling, *Economic Growth in Ireland*, pp 119–21.
144. *Annual Report of the Minister for Agriculture and Fisheries 1967/68*, pp 111–12; 117.
145. R. O'Connor, 'An analysis of recent policies for beef and milk', *JSSISI*, vol. xxii, pt. 2, (1969–70), p. 35.
146. *Statistical Abstracts*, 1965–70.
147. Annual Reports of the Minister for Agriculture and Fisheries, 1968–73.
148. PDDE, 10 December 1968, col. 2324.
149. E. P. Cunningham, 'The genetic improvement of the Irish cattle population', *JSSISI*, vol. xxi, (1965/6), pp 99–130.
150. Annual Reports of the Minister for Agriculture and Fisheries, 1970–73.
151. The phrase was used by Charles Haughey, the Minister for Agriculture, during a speech introducing the estimate for the Department of Agriculture for 1965/6. PDDE, 29 April 1965, col. 429.
152. Central Statistics Office, *National Farm Survey 1955/56–1957/58, Final Report*, (1962), I. 110.
153. O'Connor, 'Recent policies for beef and milk', p. 51.
154. Department of Agriculture, *Report of the Survey Team Established by the Minister for Agriculture, on the Dairy Products Industry*, (1962), A. 53.
155. *Ibid.*
156. S 1206/63, Knapp Report.
157. Department of Agriculture, *An Appraisement of Agricultural Co-Operation in Ireland* by Joseph G. Knapp, (1964), A. 54.
158. S 1206C/95, Agriculture: Co-Operative Organisation: Knapp Report.
159. PDDE, 1 July 1964, col. 1332.
160. 96/6/11, Reactions to the Knapp Report.
161. Hugh L. Cook and Gordon W. Sprague, *Irish Dairy Organisation*, (1968), A. 61.
162. 96/6/269.
163. *Annual Report of the Minister for Agriculture and Fisheries, 1972/73*, pp 48–9.
164. *Annual Report of the Minister for Agriculture and Fisheries, 1971/72*, p. 53.
165. PDDE, 11 May 1966, cols 1505–7.
166. Department of Agriculture, *Report of Two-Tier Milk Price Study Group*, (1967), A. 60. The terms of reference were 'To consider all aspects of a two-tier system of payment for milk delivered to creameries, including the advantages and disadvantages of such a system for the agricultural industry, the national economy and the Exchequer and to report thereon to the Minister for Agriculture and Fisheries'.
167. *Annual Report of the Minister for Agriculture and Fisheries, 1968/69*, p. 123.
168. PDDE, 10 December 1968, col. 2325.
169. 2000/6/600, NFA/Government Relations.
170. 2000/6/368, Economic Relations with Britain.

171. 2000/6/368, Economic Relations with Britain. The primary purpose of Lynch's trip to London was to protest at the import deposit scheme; the meeting with Cledwyn Hughes was added to the original agenda.
172. 2000/6/368.
173. 2000/6/617.
174. PDDE, 10 December 1968, col. 2230.
175. 2000/6/369, Economic Relations with Britain.
176. 2000/6/370, Economic Relations with Britain.
177. *Annual Report of the Minister for Agriculture and Fisheries, 1970/71*, pp 25–26; *ibid., 1971/72*, p. 27.
178. The Study Group was appointed in April 1966 by Charles Haughey, at a time when the NFA was demanding the establishment of a meat marketing authority. It was chaired by M. J. Bruton, a prominent member of the NFA. The seven members represented producers, exporters, the Agricultural Institute, the Department of Agriculture, and also included Seamus Sheehy of the Faculty of Agriculture at UCD. The original terms of reference were 'To examine all aspects of the store cattle trade and to make recommendations'. These were expanded in September 1966 to include '(a) investigating promotional possibilities for Irish store cattle in Britain, and (b) examining possible European and other outlets for Irish cattle.'
179. Throughout the 1960s the annual reports of the Minister for Agriculture carry reports of such activities.
180. 99/1/510, Second Programme
181. Tracy, *Government and Agriculture in Western Europe*, p. 267. The Mansholt Plan is discussed in greater detail in chapter 10.
182. 99/1/510, Second Programme.
183. 2000/6/399, Second Programme.
184. O'Connor, 'An analysis of recent policies for beef and milk', pp 37; 67.
185. 2000/6/611, Dairy Produce; *Estimates for the Public Services 1970/1*.
186. O'Connor, 'An analysis of recent policies for beef and milk', pp 37–41; 67.
187. Robert O'Connor, 'Implications of Irish agricultural statistics', in Baillie and Sheehy (eds), *Irish Agriculture in a Changing World*, p. 33.
188. 2000/6/611.
189. Department of Agriculture and Fisheries, *Report of the Committee on the Review of State Expenditure in Relation to Agriculture*, (1970), A. 65.
190. *Annual Report of the Minister for Agriculture and Fisheries, 1966/67*.
191. *Irish Agriculture and Fisheries in the EEC*. Report of Study Group, (1970), A. 64.
192. *Annual Report of the Minister for Agriculture and Fisheries, 1970/71*, p. 27.
193. *Annual Report of the Minister for Agriculture and Fisheries, 1971/72*, p. 28.
194. Public Services Organisation Review Group, *Report of Public Services Organisation Review Group, 1966-69*, (Dublin, 1969), Prl. 792, pp 278–97.
195. *Ibid.*, pp 278–97.
196. 'Postscript' in Baillie and Sheehy (eds), *Irish Agriculture in a Changing World*, p. 233.
197. 2000/6/176, Grain Supplies and Prices.
198. *Report of the Minister for Agriculture and Fisheries, 1971/72*; Rosemary Fennell, 'The

domestic market for Irish agricultural produce', in Baillie and Sheehy (eds), *Irish Agriculture in a Changing World*, p. 99.
199. *Annual Report of the Minister for Agriculture and Fisheries, 1973/4*, p. 14.
200. 2000/6/343.
201. PDDE, 30 May 1967, cols 1670–1700
202. E. A. Attwood, 'The development of an agricultural incomes policy', *JSSISI*, vol. xxii, pt. 2, (1969/70), p. 100.
203. Tracy, *Government and Agriculture in Western Europe*, p. 267.

CHAPTER TEN

1. The term EEC, or European Economic Community was used until 1988, when the Community began to describe itself as the EC – European Community, a change that reflected its wider role. When the Maastricht Treaty came into force in November 1993 the name was changed to the European Union. I have generally used the term that applied at the particular time.
2. S 11563 C/63
3. Alan Matthews, *Farm Incomes. Myth and Reality*, (Cork, 2000), p. 77.
4. Tony McNamara, 'A conversation with Donal Creedon, Secretary, Department of Agriculture and Food (1988–89)', *Administration*, vol. 38, no. 1, (1970), pp 81–2.
5. Agriculture, Department of, 'A Century of Service. Celebrating 100 Years of the Department of Agriculture', a supplement issued with the *Farmers' Journal*, December, 2000.
6. Department of Agriculture and Food, *Agriculture and Food Policy Review*, December, 1990, p. 6.
7. Tracy, *Government and Agriculture in Western Europe*, p. 272.
8. See above p. 364.
9. Brigid Laffan, *Organising for a Changing Europe: Irish Central Government and the European Union*, (Dublin, 2001), p. 66.
10. *Annual Report of the Minister for Agriculture and Food, 1992*, p. 18.
11. Laffan, *Organising for a Changing Europe*, pp 65–6.
12. Matthews, *Farm Incomes*, p. 85.
13. Laffan, *Organising for a Changing Europe*, p. 65.
14. At an informal Council, held in Echternach (Luxembourg), on 8–9 September 1997. Minutes of Council Meeting supplied by the Department.
15. PDSE, 30 March 1999, cols 1286–8.
16. *Annual Report of the Minister for Agriculture, 1977*, p. 10.
17. *Annual Report of the Minister for Agriculture and Food, 1987*, p. 24.
18. Department of Agriculture and Food, *Agriculture and Food Policy Review*, p. 64.
19. Seamus Sheehy, 'Agricultural policy', in Jim Dooge & Ruth Barrington (eds), *A Vital National Interest. Ireland in Europe, 1973–1998*, (Dublin, 1999), p. 246.
20. Between 1968 and 1972 creamery prices increased by 40 per cent, cattle prices

by over 60 per cent, and calf prices by 135 per cent. R. O'Connor & P. Keogh, *Crisis in the Irish Cattle Industry*, (Dublin, ESRI, 1975), pp 15–17.

21. *Annual Report of the Minister for Agriculture and Fisheries, 1972/3*, pp 68–9.
22. *Annual Report of the Minister for Agriculture and Fisheries, 1973/4*, p. 55.
23. The only exception to this was for commodities where an import quota had been agreed through GATT.
24. *Annual Report of the Minister for Agriculture and Fisheries, 1972/3*, pp 26–8.
25. Tribunal of Inquiry into the Beef Industry, *Report of Tribunal of Inquiry into the Beef Professing Industry*, (1994), A. 91. Statement by Michael Dowling, Secretary of the Department of Agriculture and Food, p. 710.
26. O'Connor & Keogh, *Crisis in the Irish Cattle Industry*, p. 17.
27. *Annual Report of the Minister for Agriculture and Fisheries, 1973/4*, pp 48, 58, 80, 87.
28. Agriculture, Department of, 'A Century of Service', p. 6.
29. *Annual Report of the Minister for Agriculture and Fisheries, 1974*, p. 35.
30. Department of Agriculture and Food, *Agriculture and Food Policy Review*, p. 35.
31. Tribunal of Inquiry into the Beef Industry, *Beef Tribunal*, Statement by Michael Dowling, pp 704–8.
32. Agriculture, Department of, 'A Century of Service', pp 6–7.
33. Tribunal of Inquiry into the Beef Industry, *Beef Tribunal*, p. 35.
34. *Annual Report of the Minister for Agriculture, 1977*, p. 49.
35. Tribunal of Inquiry into the Beef Industry, *Beef Tribunal*, Statement by Michael Dowling, p. 704.
36. *Annual Report of the Minister for Agriculture and Fisheries, 1976*, p. 59.
37. *Annual Report of the Minister for Agriculture, 1977*, p. 57.
38. *Annual Report of the Minister for Agriculture, 1979*, p. 54.
39. Department of Agriculture and Food, *Agriculture and Food Policy Review*, pp 13, 51.
40. Tribunal of Inquiry into the Beef Industry, *Beef Tribunal*, pp 1–3; 18–30.
41. Tribunal of Inquiry into the Beef Industry, *Beef Tribunal*, Evidence of Michael Dowling, p. 706.
42. Tribunal of Inquiry into the Beef Industry, *Beef Tribunal*, p. 703.
43. Tribunal of Inquiry into the Beef Industry, *Beef Tribunal*, p. 709. Fintan O'Toole referred to the 'ambivalent' relationship between the Department and the beef industry in *Meanwhile Back at the Ranch: The Politics of Irish Beef*, (London, 1995), pp 266–7.
44. Tribunal of Inquiry into the Beef Industry, *Beef Tribunal*, p. 716. This was the practice in some other member states.
45. Tribunal of Inquiry into the Beef Industry, *Beef Tribunal*, pp 706–8.
46. Tribunal of Inquiry into the Beef Industry, *Beef Tribunal*, p. 710.
47. Tribunal of Inquiry into the Beef Industry, *Beef Tribunal*, pp 714–17.
48. The Irish pound was pegged to sterling until Ireland joined the European Monetary System (EMS) in 1979.
49. Annual Reports of the Minister for Agriculture, 1975–78.
50. Alan Matthews, 'The economics of 1992: agriculture and food', in ESRI, *The Economics of 1992. A Symposium on Sectoral Issues*, (Dublin, 1989), pp 74–5.
51. *Annual Report of the Minister for Agriculture and Food, 1992*, pp 15–16.

52. *Annual Report of the Minister for Agriculture and Fisheries, 1975,* pp 25–6.
53. Department of Agriculture and Food, *Agriculture and Food Policy Review,* p. 17.
54. Tracy, *Government and Agriculture in Western Europe,* p. 302.
55. The Non-Marketing of Milk and Milk Products was a five-year scheme introduced in 1977; another scheme, scheduled to run for four years, the Conversion of Dairy Herds Scheme, encouraged dairy farmers to convert to beef. Department of Agriculture, Food and Rural Development, 'Outline of the Milk Quota/ Superlevy System in Ireland', unpublished memorandum, 2001.
56. PDDE, 8 February 1984, cols 2022– 4.
57. Garret FitzGerald, *All in a Life,* (Dublin, 1992), pp 582–6.
58. An increase in output was permitted in Mediterranean countries with a low output of milk, such as Greece.
59. Hugo Young, *One of Us,* (final edition, London, 1993), p. 472.
60. Department of Agriculture, Food and Rural Development, 'Outline of the Milk Quota/Superlevy System in Ireland', unpublished memorandum.
61. *Ibid.*
62. Brian MacDonald, *Lakeland Dairies. The Triumph of Co-Operation,* (Killeshandra and Tullynahinera, 1996), p. 149.
63. Smith, Louis & Healy, Seán, *Farm Organisations in Ireland. A Century of Progress,* (Dublin, 1996), p. 266.
64. Sheehy, 'Agricultural policy', p. 246; Tracy, *Government and Agriculture in Western Europe,* pp 267, 326.
65. *Annual Report of the Minister for Agriculture and Fisheries, 1973/4,* pp 103-5.
66. Richard, Bruton & Frank J. Convery, *Land Drainage Policy in Ireland,* ESRI Policy Research Series No. 4, (Dublin, 1982), p. 61.
67. *Annual Report of the Minister for Agriculture and Fisheries, 1973/4,* p. 34.
68. *Annual Report of the Minister for Agriculture, 1982,* p. 87.
69. Bruton & Convery, *Land Drainage Policy,* pp 61, 79.
70. Sheehy, 'Agricultural policy', p. 246.
71. *Annual Report of the Minister for Agriculture and Fisheries, 1975,* p. 38.
72. *Annual Report of the Minister for Agriculture and Fisheries, 1976,* p. 86.
73. Bruton & Convery, *Land Drainage Policy,* pp 24–5; 62.
74. *Annual Report of the Minister for Agriculture, 1981,* pp 85–6.
75. Tracy, *Government and Agriculture in Western Europe,* p. 295.
76. *Annual Report of the Minister for Agriculture, 1985,* p. 76; Tracy, *Government and Agriculture in Western Europe,* p. 327.
77. *Annual Report of the Minister for Agriculture, 1986,* p. 79.
78. Department of Agriculture and Food, *Agriculture and Food Policy Review,* p. 60.
79. Department of Agriculture and Food, *Agriculture and Food Policy Review,* pp 59, 62.
80. Tracy, *Government and Agriculture in Western Europe,* p. 326.
81. National Economic and Social Council, *Ireland in the European Community: Performance, Prospects and Strategy,* (Dublin, 1989), p. 462.
82. National Economic and Social Council, *Ireland in the European Community,* p. 93.
83. Smith & Healy, *Farm Organisations,* p. 243.
84. *Annual Report of the Minister for Agriculture and Food, 1988,* p. 24.

85. Sheehy, 'Agricultural policy', p. 248.
86. Statement on CAP reform by the Minister for Agriculture and Food, Joe Walsh, PDDE, 27 May 1992, col. 802.
87. Ray MacSharry, 'Reform of the CAP', in Barrington & Dooge (eds), *A Vital National Interest*, p. 303.
88. *Annual Report of the Minister for Agriculture and Food, 1991*, p. 13.
89. PDDE, 27 May 1992, cols 802–4. Irish objectives were to protect the role of agriculture as the most important sector of the Irish economy; to safeguard farm incomes; to promote policies that would result in the maintenance of the maximum number of families on the land; to protect the vital commercial element of Irish agriculture; to prevent discrimination against grass-based extensive methods of production; to ensure adequate and lasting budgetary resources of the EU farm programme; and to ensure that any reform package would be secure in the context of a GATT agreement.
90. MacSharry, 'Reforming the CAP', pp 303–4.
91. Sheehy, 'Agricultural policy', p. 249.
92. Matthews, *Farm Incomes*, pp 17–20.
93. *Annual Report of the Minister for Agriculture and Food, 1996*, pp 51–2.
94. PDDE, 27 May 1992, cols 802–4.
95. Matthews, *Farm Incomes*, p. 10; Sheehy, 'Agricultural policy', p. 249.
96. Laffan, *Organising for a Changing Europe*, p. 68. The Department contends that its record on payments is better than that of most other ministries of agriculture.
97. Barry Desmond, 'The European Court of Auditors', in Dooge & Barrington (eds), *A Vital National Interest*, pp 117–19.
98. Agriculture, Department of, 'A Century of Service,' pp 7–9.
99. Matthews, *Farm Incomes*, p. 13.
100. *Annual Report of the Minister for Agriculture and Food, 1996*, p. 9.
101. *Annual Report of the Minister for Agriculture and Food. 1998*, p. 9.
102. *Annual Report of the Minister for Agriculture, Food and Rural Development, 1999*, pp 11–12.
103. *Annual Report of the Minister for Agriculture, Food and Rural Development 1999*, pp 9-10, and Appendix 2. The delay in paying export refunds for beef was due to the transfer of staff to Wexford.
104. Meeting of Informal Council (Agricultural) in Echternach (Luxembourg), 8/9 September 1997; EU Commission, *Agenda 2000. The Future for European Agriculture*, (18 March 1998), pp 2–3.
105. PDSE, 30 March 1999, cols 1289–90; Speaking Notes for the Minster for Agriculture and Food, EU Agriculture Council, 17–19 November 1997, as delivered at Council. Supplied by the Department.
106. PDSE, 30 March 1999, cols 1286–95.
107. *Report of AFT/ACOT Review Group*, (1986), A.84, p. 15.
108. Department of Agriculture, *A Review of the Irish Agricultural Advisory Service* (W. Emrys Jones and Albert J. Davis), (1967), A. 59; Public Services Organisation Review Group, 1966–69. *Report of the Public Services Organisation Review Group, 1966–1969*, (Dublin, 1969), Prl. 792.
109. PDDE, 26 October 1978, col. 1308, Statement by John Bruton.

110. PDDE 9 Feb 1977 col. 1086.

111. PDDE, 26 October 1978, cols 1302–3.

112. *Report of AFT/ACOT Review Group*, pp 19–20;41–4; Department of An Taioseach, *Building on Reality 1985–1987: A Summary*, (Dublin: The Stationery Office, 1987), pp 42–3; PDDE, 18 February 1988, col. 322.

113. *Report of AFT/ACOT Review Group*, p. 19.

114. Department of Agriculture and Food, *Agriculture and Food Policy Review*, p. 75.

115. *Report of AFT/ACOT Review Group*, pp 15–16, and Appendix IV.

116. G. E. Boyle, 'An exploratory assessment of the returns to agricultural research in Ireland 1963–1983', *Irish Journal of Agricultural Economics and Rural Sociology*, 11 (1986), pp 58, 71.

117. G. E. Boyle & Mary C. Ryan, 'Technological progress in Irish agriculture: the role of the state', (National University of Ireland, Maynooth, Department of Economics, 1992), p.2.

118. *Report of AFT/ACOT Review Group*, p. 9.

119. *Ibid.*, pp 52–5.

120. Figures taken from the Institute of Public Administration Yearbooks, 1987–90.

121. PDDE, 18 February 1988, col. 322.

122. PDDE, 18 February 1988, cols 315–20; 327.

123. PDDE, 4 June 1987, cols 778–9.

124. Department of Agriculture and Food, *Agriculture and Food Policy Review*, pp 76–8.

125. Department of Agriculture and Food, *Agriculture and Food Policy Review*, p. 78.

126. MacDonald, *Lakeland Dairies*, p 130.

127. *Annual Report of the Minister for Agriculture, 1987*, p. 34.

128. *Annual Report of the Minister for Agriculture and Food, 1988*, p. 84.

129. R. O'Connor, *A Study of the Bovine Tuberculosis Eradication Scheme*, (Dublin, ESRI, 1986), p. 29.

130. *Annual Report of the Minister for Agriculture, 1985*, p. 83.

131. *Annual Report of the Minister for Agriculture, 1988*, p. 84.

132. Department of Agriculture, Food and Rural Development, Agri Food 2010, *Main Report*, (2000), A.104, pp 8, 23.

133. This is disputed by some senior officials in the Department.

134. *Annual Report of the Minister for Agriculture and Fisheries, 1972/3*, pp 29–30.

135. *Annual Report of the Minister for Agriculture, 1983*, p. 20.

136. *Annual Report of the Minister for Agriculture, 1989*, p. 22

137. *Annual Report of the Minister for Agriculture, 1973/4*, p. 21.

138. PDDE, 9 February 1977, cols 1075–6.

139. John Stapleton, 'Civil service reform 1969–87', *Administration*, vol. 38, no. 4, (1991), p. 332.

140. Industrial Development Authority/Department of Agriculture, *A Future for Food: Strategy for the Food and Drink Industry 1988–1992*, (Dublin, 1987).

141. National Economic and Social Council, *Ireland in the European Community*, p. 214.

142. National Economic and Social Council, *Ireland in the European Community*, p. 97.

143. Department of Agriculture and Food, *Agriculture and Food Policy Review*, p. 32.

144. Alan Matthews, 'The economics of 1992: agriculture and food', in ESRI, *The Economics of 1992. A Symposium on Sectoral Issues*, (Dublin, 1992), p. 72.

145. Department of Agriculture and Food, *Agriculture and Food Policy Review.*
146. *Annual Report of the Minister for Agriculture, 1995,* pp 60–1.
147. Matthews, 'The economics of 1992', pp 79–80; John FitzGerald, '1992: the distribution sector', in ESRI, *The Economics of 1992. A Symposium on Sectoral Issues,* (Dublin, 1992), pp 59–68.
148. FitzGerald, '1992: the distribution sector', p. 48.
149. Rory O'Donnell, 'Manufacturing', in ESRI, *The Economics of 1992. A Symposium on Sectoral Issues,* (Dublin, 1992), p. 39.
150. MacDonald, *Lakeland Dairies,* pp 123–38.
151. Smith & Healy, *Farm Organisatiosn,* p. 171.
152. Boyle, 'Modelling the Irish agricultural and food sectors', pp 129–30.
153. MacDonald, *Lakeland Dairies,* pp 134–6.
154. *Ibid.,* p. 138.
155. PDDE, 18 February 1988, col. 318.
156. Department of Agriculture and Food, *Agriculture and Food Policy Review,* pp 65-8.
157. Tracy, *Government and Agriculture in Western Europe,* p. 325. Tracy cites no supporting evidence for this statement.
158. MacSharry, 'Reform of the CAP', p. 297. Objective 1 was to promote cohesion – to reduce the gap between average incomes in the less-developed regions, where per capita incomes were below 75 per cent of the EC average. All of Ireland qualified under Objective 1. Objective 2 provided special assistance for frontier regions and regions that were seriously affected by industrial decline. Objective 3 was designed to combat long-term unemployment. Objective 4 promoted the training and education of young people. Almost two-thirds of the CSF budget was devoted to Objective 1.
159. Matthews, 'The economics of 1992: agriculture and food', pp 84–5.
160. John Bradley, John Fitz Gerald and Ide Kearney, 'The role of structural funds: analysis of consequences for Ireland in the context of 1992', in ESRI, *The Economics of 1992. A Symposium on Sectoral Issues,*(Dublin, 1992), pp 53–4.
161. Patrick Honohan (ed.), *EU Structural Funds in Ireland: A Mid-Term Evaluation of the CSF 1994–99,* (ESRI, 1997), pp 25–6.
162. Honohan (ed.), *EU Structural Funds in Ireland,* p. 90.
163. Bradley *et al.,*'The role of structural funds', pp 56–9, 90.
164. Honohan (ed.), *EU Structural Funds in Ireland,* p. 90.
165. Speaking Notes for the Minister for Agriculture and Food, Joe Walsh, for Informal Meeting of the Council of Ministers, 7–9 September 1997.
166. EU Commission, *Agenda 2000,* p. 3.
167. PDSE, 30 March 1999, col. 1293.
168. *Report of the Minister for Agriculture,1976,* p. 18.
169. McNamara, 'A conversation with Donal Creedon', p. 83.
170. Department of Agriculture and Food, *Agriculture and Food Policy Review,* pp 31–2.
171. Department of Agriculture, Food and Rural Development, Agri Food 2010, *Main Report,* (2000), A. 104, pp 20–1.
172. *Ibid.,* pp 11, 21.
173. *Ibid.,* p. xi.
174. Smith & Healy, *Farm Organisations,* p. 239.

175. Department of Agriculture, Food and Rural Development, Agri Food 2010, *Annexes*, (2000), p. 1.
176. Department of Agriculture, Food and Forestry, *Summary Statement of Strategy, 1995–2000*, p. 12.
177. Department of Agriculture, Food and Rural Development, Agri Food 2010, *Main Report*, p. 9.
178. Department of Agriculture, Food and Rural Development, Press Release, 161/99.
179. Matthews, *Farm Incomes*, p. 22.
180. Seamus Sheehy, 'Agricultural policy', in Dooge & Barrington (eds), *A Vital National Interest. Ireland in Europe 1973–1998*, (Dublin, 1999), p. 245.
181. Matthews, *Farm Incomes*, p. 3.
182. Department of Agriculture, Food and Rural Development, Agri Food 2010, *Main Report*, p. 6. Poverty was defined as below 50 per cent of the national average income.
183. Honohan (ed.), *EU Structural Funds in Ireland*, p. 100.
184. PDSE, 30 March 1999, cols 1293–4, Statement by Joe Walsh, Minister for Agriculture, Food and Rural Development.
185. Denis Brosnan, 'The new challenges for agriculture and food: Responding to the demands of the market', Centenary Conference, Department of Agriculture, Food and Rural Development, 30 March 2000. Unpublished.

CHAPTER ELEVEN

1. Estimating the numbers engaged in farming is becoming increasingly difficult with the rising number of part-time farmers. In the interests of consistency, the figures cited all come from the Census of Population. As statistics relating to women in farming have been even less reliable in the past I have omitted them in this instance.
2. *Report of the Recess Committee*, pp 145, 164.
3. *Ibid.*, p. 48.
4. Henri Mendras, *The Vanishing Peasant: Innovation and Change in French Agriculture*, (Cambridge Mass., 1970), pp 4–37.
5. Suzanne Berger, *Peasants against Politics. Rural Organization in Brittany, 1911–1967*, (Cambridge Mass., 1972), pp 85–9.
6. Daly, *Industrial Development and Irish National Identity*, pp 46–7.
7. S 6306, Interim report on wheat of Committee on Agricultural Production.
8. S 10980, Agricultural Commission 1938.
9. R. Jarrell and A. O'Sullivan, 'Agricultural education in Ireland' in Norman McMillan (ed.), *Prometheus's Fire*, (Kilkenny, 2001), p. 394.
10. Seamus Ó Buachalla, *Education Policy in Twentieth Century Ireland*, (Dublin, 1988), p. 62. The 1936 School Attendance Act amended the 1926 School Attendance Act to permit children aged 12 and over to be absent from school from 17 March to 15 May, and from 1 August to 15 October, in order to carry out 'light agricultural work' on the family farm. PDDE, 12 February 1936, col. 458.

11. Jarrell and O'Sullivan, 'Agricultural education in Ireland', p. 394. This reluctance was not confined to Ireland. Mendras, *The Vanishing Peasant*, p. 175.
12. The only reference to agricultural education is to some brief factual details concerning the agricultural colleges. OECD Survey Team, *Investment in Education*, (1966), E. 58, Pr. 8311, p. 15.
13. Agri Food 2010, *Main Report*, (2000), p. 45.
14. Plunkett, *Ireland in the New Century*, p. 238.
15. Efforts to track down the records of the county committees of agriculture have proved fruitless.
16. *29th and Final General Report of the DATI 1930/31*, p. 15
17. *Report of the Minister for Agriculture 1955/6*, p. 19; *Report of the Minister for Agriculture 1958/9*, p. 23.
18. S 14154A, Agriculture Acts, amending legislation.
19. AGI G 2033/1936, Supplies of fat cattle; UCDA, Fianna Fáil Archives, FF/439, Minutes of Parliamentary Party Meetings, 27 June 1935.
20. Douglass North, *Institutions, Institutional Change and Economic Performance*, (Cambridge, 1990), p. 87.
21. Mendras, *The Vanishing Peasant*, pp 181–2.
22. B. A. Holderness, *British Agriculture since 1945*, (Manchester, 1985), p. 155.
23. Daly, *Industrial Development and Irish National Identity*, pp 128-30.
24. Smith and Healy, *Farm Organisations in Ireland*, p. 161.
25. Department of Agriculture, Food and Forestry, *Summary Statement of Strategy 1995–2000*, pp 7–8.
26. Richard Dunphy, *The Making of Fianna Fáil Power in Ireland 1923–1948*, (Oxford, 1995), p. 83.
27. This directive is included among the Directive Principles of Social Policy, which were intended for 'the general guidance of the Oireachtas. Article 45.v states 'That there may be established on the land in economic security as many families as in the circumstances shall be practicable'.
28. Crotty, *Irish Agricultural Production*, pp 233–60.
29. Ronan Keane, 'Property in the Constitution and in the Courts', in Brian Farrell (ed), *De Valera's Constitution and Ours*, (Dublin, 1988), p. 137.
30. Newman (ed), *Limerick Rural Survey, 1958–64*.
31. Agri Food 2010, *Main Report*, p. 37.
32. Agri Food 2010, Plan of Action. August 2000, p. iv.
33. Department of Agriculture, Food and Forestry, *Summary Statement of Strategy 1995–2000*, p. 10.

BIBLIOGRAPHY

Manuscript Sources

BANK OF IRELAND
Minutes, Irish Banks Standing Committee.

DUBLIN DIOCESAN ARCHIVES, ARCHBISHOP'S HOUSE, DRUMCONDRA
McQuaid Papers.

LIBRARY OF THE DEPARTMENT OF AGRICULTURE, FOOD AND RURAL DEVELOPMENT
Board of Agriculture, Minutes 1900–1921.
Council of Agriculture, Minutes, 1900–1921.
Michael Neenan, *A Popular History of Agriculture* (unfinished work; typescript, no date).
Register of Establishment and Record of Services for 1901–1922.

NATIONAL ARCHIVES, DUBLIN
Dáil Éireann Files, DE 2, 3, 4 and 5 Series.
Dáil Éireann. Land Settlement Commission Papers, 1919–23. Unlisted.
Department of Agriculture Files, AGI Series and G Series.
Department of Agriculture and Technical Instruction Files, AGI Series.
Department of the Environment Files.
Department of Finance Files, F Finance Series and S Supply Series.
Department of Industry and Commerce Files, R Series and TID Series.
Department of An Taoiseach Files, S Series.
Government Information Service Files, GIS.

NATIONAL LIBRARY OF IRELAND
George Gavan Duffy Papers.
Art Ó Briain Papers.
Redmond Papers.
Commission on Vocational Organisation, Minutes and Evidence.

PLUNKETT FOUNDATION, OXFORD UNIVERSITY
Hogan/Plunkett Correspondence in Plunkett Papers (copies supplied by
    Dr Carla King).

PUBLIC RECORD OFFICE, LONDON
Treasury Files, T Series.
Board of Trade Files, BT Series.
Ministry of Agriculture and Fisheries Files, MAF.

TRINITY COLLEGE DUBLIN, MANUSCRIPT ROOM
Dillon Papers.
Arnold Marsh Papers, Commission on Emigration, Evidence.

UNIVERSITY COLLEGE DUBLIN ARCHIVES (UCDA)
Fianna Fáil Archives: Minutes of Parliamentary Party Meetings; Minutes of
    the National Executive.
McGilligan Papers.

NEWSPAPERS AND PERIODICALS

Belfast Newsletter
Blackrock College Annual
The Economist
Farmers' Journal
Freeman's Journal
Irish Independent
Irish Press
Kilkenny People
Irish Trade Journal
The Irish Times
The Statist
Sunday Telegraph
The Western People

Printed Parliamentary Debates

Minutes of Proceedings of Dáil Éireann, 1919–22.
Published Debates Dáil Éireann (PDDE).
Published Debates Seanad Éireann (PDSE).
United Kingdom, Parliamentary Debates, House of Commons.

Irish Government Publications (in chronological order)

Commission of Inquiry into the Resources and Industries of Ireland, 1920–22:
Interim Report on Milk Production, (March 1920), R. 10/1.
Report on Stock Breeding Farms for Pure Bred Dairy Cattle, (April 1921), R. 10/3.
Report on Dairying and Dairy Industry, (March 1922), R. 10/9.
Fiscal Inquiry Committee, *Reports,* (1923), R. 20.
Commission on Agriculture:
First Interim Report – Tobacco Growing, (9 February 1923).
Second Interim Report – Butter, (22 May 1923).
Third Interim Report – Eggs, (22 May 1923).
Fourth Interim Report – Agricultural Credit, (5 September 1923).
Fifth Interim Report – Licensing Bulls, (5 September 1923).
Final Report, (1924), R. 25.
Commissioners of Public Works in Ireland, *Reports for Years 31 March 1921– 31 March 1928,* W.1/1–W.1/7.
Gaeltacht Commission, *Report of the Commission of Inquiry into the Preservation of the Gaeltacht,* (1926), R. 23/27.
Economic Committee, 1928. *First Interim Report on Wheat Growing,* (1929), R. 42.
Department of Lands and Agriculture, *Interim Report of the Tribunal to Inquire into the Marketing of Butter,* (1930), A. 18/1.
Commission of Inquiry into the Civil Service, 1932–35. *Reports and Memoranda of Evidence,* (1936), R. 54/2–5.
Commission of Inquiry into Banking, Currency and Credit, 1934–8. *Reports and Minutes of Evidence,* (1938), R. 38.
Commission on Vocational Organisation, 1943. *Report,* (1944), R. 76/1.
Department of Trade and Industry, *Census of Industrial Production, 1938– 44,* I.77/8.
Committee of Inquiry on Post-Emergency Agricultural Policy:

[First] Interim Report – Cattle and Dairy Industries, (1943), A. 31/1.

Second Interim Report – Poultry Production, (1944), A. 31/2.

Final Report, (1945), A. 31/4.

Department of Agriculture, *Policy in regard to Crops, Pastures, Fertilisers and Feeding Stuffs,* (1946), A. 36.

Department of Agriculture, *Report on the Present State and Methods for Improvement of Irish Grasslands,* (Holmes, G. A.), (1949), A. 38.

IBEC Technical Services Corporation, *An Appraisal of Ireland's Industrial Potentials,* (1952), I. 98.

Commission on Emigration and Other Population Problems, 1948–1954. *Report,* (1955), R. 84.

Department of Finance, Capital Investment Advisory Committee, *Third Report,* (1958), F. 53/3.

Department of Finance, *Programme for Economic Expansion,* (1958), F. 57.

Department of Finance (T. K. Whitaker), *Economic Development,* (1958), F. 58.

Advisory Committee on the Marketing of Agricultural Produce:

Report on the Export of Bacon and other Pig-meat, (1958), A. 41.

Report on Shell Eggs and Liquid Egg, (1959), A. 42.

Report on the Export of Turkeys, (1959), A. 43.

Survey of Agricultural Credit in Ireland by Fred. W. Gilmore, (1959), A. 44.

Report on the Export of Dairy Produce, (1959), A. 45.

Report on the Export of Livestock and Meat, (1959), A. 46.

Report on General Aspects of Irish Export Trade in Agricultural Produce, (1959), A. 47.

Export Marketing of Irish Agricultural Produce. Statement of the Government's Policy on the Recommendations of the Advisory Committee, (1959), A. 49.

An Foras Talúntais, *Annual Report for 1959/60,* published as an appendix to the *Report of the Minister for Agriculture, 1959–60.*

Central Statistics Office, *National Farm Survey 1955/56–1957/58, Final Report,* (1962), I. 110.

Department of Agriculture, *Report of the Survey Team Established by the Minister for Agriculture on the Dairy Products Industry,* (1962), A. 53.

Department of Agriculture, *Report of the Inter-Departmental Committee on the Problems of Small Western Farms,* (1962), A. 52.

Department of Finance, *Closing the Gap (Incomes and Output),* (1963), F. 64.

Department of Finance, *Second Programme for Economic Expansion, Part I,* (1963), F. 57/1; *Second Programme for Economic Expansion, Part II,* (1964), F. 57/2; *Second Programme for Economic Expansion, Review of Progress 1964–67,* (1968), F. 57/6.

Department of Agriculture, *Agriculture and the Second Programme for Economic Expansion,* (1964), A. 55.

Department of Agriculture, *An Appraisement of Agricultural Co-Operation in Ireland* by Joseph G. Knapp, (1964), A. 54.

Department of Agriculture, *Report on Pilot Areas Development (by) the Inter-Departmental Committee on the Problems of Small Western Farms,* (1964), A. 52/1.

Department of Education, *Investment in Education: Report of the Survey Team appointed by the Minister for Education in October 1962,* (1966), E. 56.

Brock, Catherine, *The Work of the NIEC (1963–1966),* (September 1966), NIEC Occasional Publication No 2, Pr. 9090.

Department of Agriculture, *A Review of the Irish Agricultural Advisory Service* (W. Emrys Jones and Albert J. Davis), (1967), A. 59.

Department of Agriculture, *Report of the Store Cattle Study Group,* (1969), A. 62.

Department of Agriculture and Fisheries, *Irish Dairy Industry Organisation,* (Hugh L. Cook & Gordon W. Sprague), (1968), A. 61.

Department of Agriculture, *Report of Two-Tier Milk Price Study Group,* (1967), A. 60.

Commission on Higher Education, 1960–67. *Presentation and Summary of Report,* (1967), E. 59; *I Report,* 2 vols, (1967), E. 59/1–2.

Department of Finance, *Third Programme. Economic and Social Development, 1969–72,* (1969), F. 57/7.

Public Services Organisation Review Group, 1966–69. *Report of the Public Services Organisation Review Group, 1966–1969,* (Dublin, 1969), Prl. 792.

Department of Agriculture and Fisheries, *Report of the Committee on the Review of State Expenditure in Relation to Agriculture,* (1970), A. 65.

Irish Agriculture and Fisheries in the EEC, *Report of Study Group,* (1970), A. 64.

Scully, John J., *Agriculture in the West of Ireland. A Study of the Low Farm Income Problem,* (1971), A. 67.

Report of AFT/ACOT Review Group, (1986), A. 84.

Department of An Taoiseach, *Building on Reality 1985–1987: A Summary,* (Dublin: The Stationery Office, 1987).

Industrial Development Authority/Department of Agriculture, *A Future for Food: Strategy for the Food and Drink Industry 1988–1992,* (Dublin, 1987).

Department of the Taoiseach, *Programme for National Recovery,* (Dublin, 1987), Y. 19.

National Economic and Social Council, *Ireland in the European Community: Performance, Prospects and Strategy,* (Dublin, 1989).

Department of the Taoiseach, *National Development Plan, 1989–93*, (Dublin, 1989), Y. 22.

Department of Agriculture, *Agriculture and Food Policy Review*, (December, 1990).

Tribunal of Inquiry into the Beef Processing Industry, *Report of Tribunal of Inquiry into the Beef Processing Industry*, (1994), A. 91.

Department of Agriculture, *Summary Statement of Strategy, 1995–2000* (1995).

Department of Agriculture and Food, *White Paper on Rural Development: Ensuring the Future – A Strategy for Rural Development in Ireland*, (Dublin, 1999), A. 99.

Department of the Taoiseach, *Programme for Prosperity and Fairness*, (Dublin, 2000).

Department of Agriculture, Agri Food 2010, *Main Report*, (2000), A. 104.

Department of Agriculture, Agri Food 2010, *Annexes*, (2000).

Agricultural Statistics (included in the *Statistical Abstract*, published annually since 1931).

Journal of the Department of Agriculture 1900 –
Annual Reports of the DATI, 1921–31.
Annual Reports of the Minister for Agriculture, 1931–65.
Annual Reports of the Minister for Agriculture and Fisheries, 1965–76
Annual Reports of the Minister for Agriculture, 1977–87.
Annual Reports of the Minister for Agriculture and Food, 1988–94.
Annual Reports of the Minister for Agriculture, Forestry and Food, 1995–97.
Annual Report of the Minister for Agriculture and Food, 1998.
Annual Report of the Minister for Agriculture, Food and Rural Development, 1999.

EUROPEAN UNION PUBLICATIONS

European Commission, *The Future of Rural Society*, (Luxembourg, 1988).

Euro Commission, *Agenda 2000: The Future for Europeture*, (Brussels, 1998), DG VI.

BRITISH GOVERNMENT PUBLICATIONS
(IN CHRONOLOGICAL ORDER)

Royal Commission on Congestion, *Appendices to First Report*, (1906), Cd. 3267, vol. xxxii, paras 4420–22.

Departmental Committee of Inquiry into the Provisions of Agriculture and Technical Instruction (Ireland) Act, 1899 [referred to in 'Notes to Chapters' as Departmental Committee DATI], *Report*, (1907), Cd. 3572, vol. xvii; *Evidence*, (1907), Cd. 3574, vol. xviii; *Appendix*, (1907), Cd. 3573, vol. xviii.

Royal Commission on Congestion, *Third Report*, (1907), Cd. 3413, vol. xxxv.

Royal Commission on Congestion, *Fourth Report*, (1907), Cd. 3508, vol. xxxvi.

Departmental Committee on the Irish Butter Industry, *Report*, (1910), Cd. 5092, vol. vii; Evidence, Appendices and Index, (1910), Cd. 5093, vol. viii.

Returns Names, etc. of persons appointed without competitive examination to any position in the public service during the period 29 June 1895 to 5 December 1905 with an annual salary of £100 or upwards, (1912–13), vol. lvi.

Departmental Committee on Agricultural Credit in Ireland, *Report*, (1914), Cd. 7375, vol. xiii.

Departmental Committee on Food Production in Ireland, *Report*, (1914–16), Cd. 8046, vol. V; Evidence and Appendices, (1914–16), Cd. 8158, vol. v.

Report of the Proceedings of the Irish Convention, (1918), Cd. 9019, vol. x.

Annual Reports of the DATI:
1900/1, (1902), Cd. 838, vol. xx.
1901/2, (1902), Cd. 1314, vol. xx.
1902/3, (1904), Cd. 1919, vol. xvi.
1903/4, (1905), Cd. 2509, vol. xxi.
1904/5, (1906), Cd. 2929, vol. xxiii.
1905/6, (1907), Cd. 3543, vol. xvii.
1906/7, (1908), Cd. 4148, vol. xiv.
1907/8, (1908), Cd. 4430, vol. xxii.
1908/9, (1910), Cd. 5128, vol. viii.
1909/10, (1911), Cd. 5611, vol. ix.
1910/11, (1912–1), Cd. 6107, vol. xii.
1911/12, (1912–13), Cd. 6647, vol. xii.
1912/13, (1914), Cd. 7298, vol. xii.
1913/14, (1914–16), Cd. 7839, vol. vi.
1914/15, (1916), Cd, 8299, vol. iv.

1915/16, (1917–18), Cd. 8574, vol. iv.

1916/17, (1918), Cd. 9016, vol. v.

1917/18, (1919), Cmd. 106, vol. ix.

1918/19, (1920), Cmd. 929, vol. ix.

1919/20, (Dublin, Stationery Office), A. 1.

1920/21, (Dublin, Stationery Office), A. 2.

SECONDARY WORKS

BOOKS

Allen, Kieran, *Fianna Fáil and Irish Labour*, (London, 1997).

Anderson, R. A., *With Horace Plunkett in Ireland*, (London, 1935).

Baillie, I. F. & Sheehy, S. J., *Irish Agriculture in a Changing World*, (Edinburgh, 1971).

Berger, Suzanne, *Peasants against Politics. Rural Organization in Brittany 1911–1967*, (Cambridge Mass., 1972).

Bew, Paul, *Charles Stewart Parnell*, (Dublin, 1980).

Bew, Paul, *Conflict and Conciliation in Ireland, 1890–1910: Parnellites and Agrarian Radicals*, (Oxford, 1987).

Bolger, Patrick, *The Irish Co-Operative Movement. Its History and Development*, (Dublin, 1977).

Bolster, Angela, *The Knights of Saint Columbanus*, (Dublin, 1979).

Bowman, John, *De Valera and the Ulster Question 1917–1973*, (Oxford, 1982).

Bruton, Richard & Convery , Frank J., *Land Drainage Policy in Ireland*, (Dublin, 1982).

Bulfin, William, *Rambles in Eirinn*, (Dublin, 1907).

Canning, P., *British Policy towards Ireland, 1921–41*, (Oxford, 1987).

Clark, Sam, *Social Origins of the Irish Land War*, (Princeton, 1979).

Connolly, James, *Labour in Ireland*, (Dublin 1917).

Crafts, Nicholas & Toniolo, Gianni (eds), *Economic Growth in Europe since 1945*, (Cambridge, 1996).

Crotty, R., *Irish Agricultural Production. Its Volume and Structure*, (Cork, 1966).

Cronin, Mike, *The Blueshirts and Irish Politics*, (Dublin, 1997).

Curran, P. L. (ed.), *Towards a History of Agricultural Science in Ireland*, (Dublin, 1992).

Daly, Mary E., *Industrial Development and Irish National Identity*, (Syracuse, New York, 1992).

Daly, Mary E., *The Buffer State. The Historical Roots of the Department of the Environment*, (Dublin, 1997).

Daly, Mary E., *The Spirit of Earnest Inquiry. The Statistical and Social Inquiry Society of Ireland 1847–1997,* (Dublin, 1997).

Dooge, Jim & Barrington, Ruth (eds), *A Vital National Interest. Ireland in Europe, 1973–1998,* (Dublin, 1999).

Drudy, P. J. (ed.), *Ireland: Land, Politics and People,* (Cambridge, 1982).

Dunphy, Richard, *The Making of Fianna Fáil Power in Ireland 1923–48,* (Oxford, 1995).

ESRI, *The Economics of 1992. A Symposium on Sectoral Issues,* (Dublin, 1989).

Fanning, Ronan, *The Irish Department of Finance 1922–58,* (Dublin, 1979).

Fanning, Ronan, *Independent Ireland,* (Dublin, 1983).

FAO: The First 40 Years, (Rome, 1985).

Farrell, Brian (ed.), *De Valera's Constitution and Ours,* (Dublin, 1988).

Feingold, William L., *The Revolt of the Tenantry: The Transformation of Local Government in Ireland, 1872–1886,* (Boston, 1984).

Ferguson, Niall, *The Pity of War,* (London, 1998).

Fennell, Rosemary, *Industrialisation and Agricultural Development in the Congested Districts,* An Foras Talúntais Economic Research Series, No 2, (Dublin, 1962).

Ferriter, Diarmaid, *Mothers, Maidens and Myths. A History of the ICA* (Dublin, 1996).

FitzGerald, Garret, *Planning in Ireland,* (Dublin, 1968).

FitzGerald, Garret, *All in a Life,* (Dublin, 1992).

Fitzpatrick, David, *Politics and Irish Life, 1915–1921,* (Dublin, 1977).

Gailey, Andrew, *Ireland and the Death of Kindness. The Experience of Constructive Unionism 1890–1905,* (Cork, 1987).

Hammond, R. J., *Food. The Growth of Policy,* (London, 1951), in Keith Hancock (ed.), *History of the Second World War* (London, 1955).

Hammond, R. J., *Food and Agriculture in Britain,* (Stanford, California, 1954).

Hancock, Keith (ed.), *History of the Second World War,* (London, 1955).

Harkness, David, *Northern Ireland since 1920,* (Dublin, 1983).

Hoctor, Daniel, *The Department's Story. A History of the Department of Agriculture,* (Dublin, 1971).

Honohan, Patrick (ed.), *EU Structural Funds in Ireland: A Mid-Term Evaluation of the CSF 1994–99,* (Dublin, 1997).

Holderness, B. A., *British Agriculture since 1945,* (Manchester, 1985).

Hooker, Elizabeth R., *Readjustments of Agricultural Tenure in Ireland,* (Chapel Hill, 1938).

Hoppen, K. Theodore, *Elections, Politics and Society in Ireland 1832–1885,* (Oxford, 1984).

Horgan, John, *Seán Lemass. The Enigmatic Patriot,* (Dublin, 1997).

Jackson, Alvin, *The Ulster Party: Irish Unionists in the House of Commons, 1884–1911,* (Oxford, 1989).

Kennedy, Kieran & Dowling, Brendan, *Economic Growth in Ireland. The Experience since 1947,* (Dublin, 1975).

Kennedy, Kieran A., Giblin, Thomas & McHugh, Deirdre (eds), *The Economic Development of Ireland in the Twentieth Century,* (London, 1988).

Kennedy, Liam (ed.), *Colonialism, Religion and Nationalism in Ireland,* (Belfast, 1996).

Keogh, Dermot, *Twentieth-Century Ireland,* (Dublin, 1994).

King, F. C. (ed.), *Public Administration in Ireland,* (Dublin, 1944).

Kotsonouris, Mary, *Retreat from Revolution. The Dáil Courts, 1920–24,* (Dublin, 1994).

Laffan, Brigid, *Organising for a Changing Europe: Irish Central Government and the European Union,* (Dublin, 2001).

Lee, Joseph, *Ireland 1912–1985,* (Cambridge, 1989).

Macardle, Dorothy, *The Irish Republic,* 2nd Revised Edition, (London, 1968).

McBride, Lawrence W., *The Greening of Dublin Castle. The Transformation of Bureaucratic and Judicial Personnel in Ireland, 1892–1922,* (Washington, 1991).

McCarthy, John F. (ed.), *Planning Ireland's Future. The Legacy of T. K. Whitaker,* (Dublin, 1990).

McCarthy, Vincent, *The Formative Years of Seed Testing in Ireland,* (Dublin, 1996).

McColgan, John, *British Policy and the Irish Administration, 1920–22,* (London, 1983).

McCullough, David, *A Makeshift Majority. The First Inter-Party Government, 1948–51,* (Dublin, 1998).

MacDonagh, Oliver, *Ireland: the Union and its Aftermath,* (London, 1977).

MacDermott, Eithne, *Clann na Poblachta,* (Cork, 1998).

MacDonald, Brian, *Lakeland Dairies. The Triumph of Co-Operation,* (Killeshandra and Tullynahinera, 1996).

McGilvray, James, *Irish Agricultural Statistics,* (Dublin, 1968).

McMahon, Deirdre, *Republicans and Imperialists. Anglo-Irish Relations in the 1930s,* (New Haven, 1984).

McMillan, Norman (ed.), *Prometheus's Fire. A History of Scientific and Technological Education in Ireland,* (Kilkenny, 2001).

Maher, Denis, *The Tortuous Path. The Course of Ireland's Entry into the EEC 1948–73,* (Dublin, 1986).

Manning, Maurice, *James Dillon. A Biography*, (Dublin, 1999).

Mansergh, Martin (ed.), *The Spirit of the Nation: Speeches and Statements of Charles J. Haughey (1957–86)*, (Dublin, 1986).

Matthews, Alan, *Farm Incomes. Myth and Reality*, (Cork, 2000).

Meenan, James, *The Irish Economy since 1922*, (Liverpool, 1970).

Meenan, James, *George O'Brien, A Biographical Memoir*, (Dublin, 1980).

Meenan, James & Clarke, Desmond (eds), *The Royal Dublin Society, 1731–1981*, (Dublin, 1981).

Mendras, Henri, *The Vanishing Peasant: Innovation and Change in French Agriculture*, (Cambridge Mass., 1970).

Micks, W. L., *The History of the Congested Districts Board*, (Dublin, 1925).

Middleton, T. H., *Food Production in War*, (Oxford, 1923).

Miley, Jim, *A Voice for the Country. Fifty Years of Macra na Feirme*, (Dublin, 1994).

Mitchell, Arthur, *Revolutionary Government in Ireland. Dáil Éireann 1919–22*, (Dublin, 1995).

Murray, Keith A. H., *Agriculture*, in Keith Hancock (ed.), *History of the Second World War*, (London, 1955).

Murphy, John A., *The College. A History of Queen's University College Cork*, (Cork, 1995).

Newman, Jeremiah (ed.), *Limerick Rural Survey, 1958–64*, (Tipperary, 1964).

North, Douglass, *Institutions, Institutional Change and Economic Performance*, (Cambridge, 1990).

Ó Broin, Leon, *… Just Like Yesterday… An Autobiography*, (Dublin, 1986).

Ó Buachalla, Seamus, *Education Policy in Twentieth Century Ireland*, (Dublin, 1988).

O'Connor, Emmet, *Syndicalism in Ireland 1917–1923*, (Cork, 1988).

O'Connor, Emmet, *A Labour History of Ireland 1824–1960*, (Dublin, 1992).

O'Connor, R., *A Study of the Bovine Tuberculosis Eradication Scheme*, (Dublin, 1986).

O'Connor, R. & Keogh, P., *Crisis in the Irish Cattle Industry*, (Dublin, 1975)

O'Donovan, John, *An Economic History of Livestock in Ireland*, (Cork, 1940).

Offer, Avner, *The First World War. An Agrarian Interpretation*, (Oxford, 1989).

Ó Gráda, Cormac, *Ireland Before and After the Famine. Explorations in Economic History*, (Manchester, 1988).

Ó Gráda, Cormac, *Ireland. A New Economic History 1780–1939*, (Oxford, 1994).

Ó Gráda, Cormac, *A Rocky Road. The Irish Economy since the 1920s*, (Manchester, 1997).

O'Hagan, John (ed.), *The Economy of Ireland*, (Dublin, 1995).

O'Halpin, Eunan, *The Decline of the Union. British Government in Ireland 1892–1920*, (Dublin, 1987).

O'Hara, Patricia, *Partners in Production? Women, Farm and Family in Ireland,* (Oxford, 1998).

O'Toole, Fintan, *Meanwhile Back at the Ranch: The Politics of Irish Beef,* (London, 1995).

Plunkett, Horace, *Memorandum on Agricultural Education for Ireland, Addressed To the Irish Farmer and His Friends,* Appendix in DATI First Annual Report, (1902).

Plunkett, Horace, *Ireland in the New Century,* (London, 1905 edition).

Regan, John M., *The Irish Counter-Revolution 1921–1936,* (Dublin, 1999).

Report of the Recess Committee, (Dublin, 1896).

Riordan, E. J., *Modern Irish Trade and Industry,* (London, 1920).

Savage, Robert, *Seán Lemass,* (Dublin, 1999).

Sheehy-Skeffington, Francis, *Michael Davitt,* (London, 1908).

Shiel, Michael, *The Quiet Revolution; The Electrification of Rural Ireland, 1946–1976,* (Dublin, 1984).

Skinner, Liam, *Politicians by Accident,* (Dublin, 1946).

Smith, Louis & Healy, Seán, *Farm Organisations in Ireland. A Century of Progress,* (Dublin, 1996).

Smith-Gordon, Lionel & Staples, L. C., *Rural Reconstruction in Ireland. A Record of Co-operative Organisation,* (London, 1917).

Solow, Barbara L., *The Land Question and the Irish Economy, 1870–1903,* (Cambridge Mass., 1971).

Tracy, Michael, *Government and Agriculture in Western Europe 1880–1988,* (London, 1989).

Turner, Michael, *After the Famine. Irish Agriculture 1850–1914,* (Cambridge, 1996).

Vaughan, W. J., *Landlords and Tenants in Mid-Victorian Ireland,* (Oxford, 1994).

Watchorn, R. C., *Bovine Tuberculosis Eradication Scheme 1954–65,* (Department of Agriculture and Fisheries, 1965).

West, Trevor, *Horace Plunkett: Co-Operation and Politics, An Irish Biography,* (Gerrards Cross and Washington, 1986).

Whelan, Bernadette, *Ireland and the Marshall Plan 1947–1957,* (Dublin, 2000).

Whetham, Edith, *Beef, Cattle and Sheep, 1910–1940,* (Cambridge, 1976).

Whetham, Edith, *Agrarian History of England and Wales, Vol. VIII, 1914–39,* (Cambridge, 1978).

Williams, H. T., *Principles for British Agricultural Policy,* (Oxford, 1960).

Winnifrith, Sir John, *The Ministry of Agriculture, Fish and Food,* (London, 1962).

Wylie, Laurence (ed.), *Chanzeaux. A Village in Anjou*, (Cambridge, Mass., 1966).

Young, Arthur, *A Tour in Ireland*, 2nd edition, (London, 1780).

Young, Hugo, *One of Us*, (London, 1989).

ARTICLES

Agriculture, Department of, 'A Century of Service. Celebrating 100 Years of the Department of Agriculture', a supplement issued with the *Farmers' Journal*, December, 2000.

Attwood, E. A., 'Agriculture and economic growth in western Ireland', *Journal of the Statistical and Social Inquiry Society of Ireland*, vol. xx, pt 5, (1961/62), pp 172–95.

Attwood, E. A., 'The development of an agricultural incomes policy', *Journal of the Statistical and Social Inquiry Society of Ireland*, vol. xxii, pt 2, (1969/70), pp 100–19.

Attwood, E. A., 'Future prospects for agriculture', in I. F. Baillie & S. J. Sheehy (eds), *Irish Agriculture in a Changing World*, (Edinburgh, 1971), pp 216–32.

Beddy, J. P., 'A comparison of the principal economic features of Éire and Denmark', *Journal of the Statistical and Social Inquiry Society of Ireland*, vol. xvii, (1943/4), pp 189–220.

Bourke, Joanna, 'Women and poultry in Ireland, 1891–1914', *Irish Historical Studies*, vol. xxv, no 99, (May, 1987), pp 293–310.

Boyle, G. E., 'An exploratory assessment of the returns to agricultural research in Ireland 1963–1983', *Irish Journal of Agricultural Economics and Rural Sociology*, 11 (1986), pp 57–71.

Boyle, G. E. & Ryan, Mary C., 'Technological progress in Irish agriculture: the role of the state', (National University of Ireland, Maynooth, Department of Economics, 1992).

Boyle, G. E., 'Modelling the Irish agricultural and food sectors', in John Bradley, John FitzGerald & Ide Kearney (eds), *The Role of the Structural Funds. Analysis of Consequences for Ireland in the Context of 1992*, (Dublin, 1992), pp 123-54.

Bradley, John, FitzGerald, John & Kearney, Ide (eds), 'The Role of the Structural Funds: Analysis of Consequences for Ireland in the Context of 1992', in ESRI, *The Economics of 1992. A Symposium on Sectoral Issues*, (Dublin, 1989).

Brosnan, Denis, 'The new challenges for agriculture and food: responding to the demands of the market', Centenary Conference, Department of

Agriculture, Food and Rural Development, 30 March 2000. Unpublished.

Commins, P., 'Land policies and agricultural development', in P. J. Drudy (ed.), *Ireland: Land, Politics and People*, (Cambridge, 1982), pp 217–40.

Counihan, J. E. & Dillon, T.W., 'Irish tuberculosis death rates', *Journal of the Statistical and Social Inquiry Society of Ireland*, vol. xviii, (1943/44), pp 169–88.

Cunningham, E. P. 'The genetic improvement of the Irish cattle population', *Journal of the Statistical and Social Inquiry Society of Ireland*, vol. xxi, pt 4, (1965/66), pp 99–130.

Cunningham, E. P., 'Dr Thomas Walsh MAGrSC, PhD, DSc, ScD, MRIA', *Agricultural Record*, 1988.

Curran, P. L., 'Emergence of a technological agriculture 1592–1972', in P. L. Curran (ed.), *Towards a History of Agricultural Science in Ireland*, (Dublin, 1992), pp 11–62.

Curran, P. L., Finn, Pat & Neenan, M., 'The Parish Plan', in P. L. Curran (ed.), *Towards a History of Agricultural Science in Ireland*, (Dublin, 1992), pp 187–210.

Curran, Simon, 'The Society's role in agriculture since 1800', in Meenan, James & Clarke, Desmond (eds), *The Royal Dublin Society*, (Dublin, 1981), pp 88–100.

Daly, Mary E., ' "An Irish-Ireland for business"? the Control of Manufactures Acts 1932 and 1934', *Irish Historical Studies*, vol. 24, no 94, (November 1984), pp 246–72.

Daly, Mary E., 'The economic ideals of Irish nationalism: frugal comfort or lavish austerity?', *Éire-Ireland*, (Winter, 1994), pp 77–100.

Daly, Mary E., 'Farming and the Famine', in Cormac Ó Grada (ed.), *Farming 150: Commemorative Lecture Series*, (Dublin, 1997), pp 29–48.

Daly, Mary E., 'Integration of diversity? Anglo-Irish economic relations 1922–39', in S. J. Connolly (ed.), *Kingdoms United? Great Britain and Ireland since 1500. Integration and Diversity*, (Dublin, 1998), pp 169–80.

Daly, Mary E., ' "Turn on the tap": the state, Irish women and running water', in Maryann Valiulis & Mary O'Dowd (eds), *Women and Irish History*, (Dublin, 1997), pp 206–19.

Desmond, Barry, 'The European Court of Auditors', in Jim Dooge & Ruth Barrington (eds), *A Vital National Interest. Ireland in Europe, 1973–1998*, (Dublin, 1999), pp 113–25.

Ehrlich, Cyril, 'Sir Horace Plunkett and agricultural reform', in L. M. Goldstrom & A. Clarkson (eds), *Irish Population Economy and Society*.

Essays in Honour of the late K. H. Connell, (Oxford, 1981), pp 271–86.

Fennell, Rosemary, 'The domestic market for Irish agricultural produce', in I. F. Baillie & S. J. Sheehy (eds), *Irish Agriculture in a Changing World*, (Edinburgh, 1971), pp 98–117.

Fitz Gerald, John, '1992: The distribution sector', in ESRI, *The Economics of 1992. A Symposium on Sectoral Issues*, (Dublin, 1992), pp 59–68.

Fleming, G. A., 'Agricultural support policies in a small open economy: New Zealand in the 1920s', *Economic History Review*, vol. lii, no 2, (May, 1999), pp 334–54.

Henriksen, Ingrid, 'Avoiding the lock-in: cooperative creameries in Denmark, 1882–1903', *European Review of Economic History*, vol. 3, part I, (April, 1999), pp 57–78.

Jarrell, R. & O'Sullivan, A. 'Agricultural education in Ireland' in Norman McMillan (ed.), *Prometheus's Fire. A History of Scientific and Technological Education in Ireland*, (Kilkenny, 2001), pp 376–404.

Johnson, David S. & Kennedy, Liam, 'Nationalist historiography and the decline of the Irish economy: George O'Brien revisited', in Sean Hutton & Paul Stewart (eds), *Ireland's Histories. Aspects of State, Society and Ideology*, (London, 1991), pp 11–36.

Keane, Ronan, 'Property in the Constitution and in the Courts', in Brian Farrell (ed.), *De Valera's Constitution and Ours*, (Dublin, 1988), pp 137–51.

Kennedy, Liam, 'The Union of Ireland and Britain, 1801–1921', in Liam Kennedy (ed.), *Colonialism, Religion and Nationalism in Ireland*, (Belfast, 1996), pp 35–74.

Kennedy, Liam, 'Farmers, traders and agricultural politics in pre-Independence Ireland', in Liam Kennedy (ed.), *Colonialism, Religion and Nationalism in Ireland*, (Belfast, 1996), pp 135–66.

Linehan, T. P., 'The development of official Irish statistics', *Journal of the Statistical and Social Inquiry Society of Ireland*, vol. xxvii, pt 5, (1997/8), pp 50–3.

Lynch, Brian, 'The first agricultural broadcasts on 2RN', *History Ireland*, vol. 7, no 2, (Summer, 1999), pp 42–5.

McCarthy, John F., 'Ireland's turnaround: Whitaker and the 1958 Plan for Economic Development', in John F. McCarthy (ed.), *Planning Ireland's Future. The Legacy of T. K. Whitaker*, (Dublin, 1990) pp 11–73.

McDonald, Martin, 'The work of the ASA from 1949 to 1972', in P. L. Curran (ed.), *Towards a History of Agricultural Science in Ireland*, (Dublin, 1992), pp 157–66.

MacSharry, Ray, 'Reform of the CAP', in Jim Dooge & Ruth Barrington (eds), *A Vital National Interest. Ireland in Europe, 1973–1998*, (Dublin, 1999), pp 295–311.

McNamara, Tony, 'A conversation with Donal Creedon, Secretary, Department of Agriculture and Food (1988–89)', *Administration*, vol. 38, no 1, (1970), pp 70–86.

Maguire, Conor A., 'The Republican Courts', *Capuchin Annual*, (1969), pp 378–89.

Matthews, Alan, 'The State and Irish agriculture, 1950–1980', in P. J. Drudy (ed.), *Ireland: Land, Politics and People*, (Cambridge, 1982), pp 241–70.

Matthews, Alan, 'The economics of 1992: agriculture and food', in ESRI, *The Economics of 1992. A Symposium on Sectoral Issues*, (Dublin, 1989), pp 71–87.

Matthews, Alan, 'Agricultural competitiveness and rural development', in John O'Hagan (ed.), *The Economy of Ireland*, (Dublin, 1995), pp 328–62.

Meenan, James & Clarke, Desmond, 'The RDS 1731–1981', in James Meenan & Desmond Clarke (eds), *The Royal Dublin Society, 1731–1981*, (Dublin, 1981), pp 1–55.

Murphy, Michael, 'Financial results on mixed dairy farms in 1937–39, *Journal of the Statistical and Social Inquiry Society of Ireland*, vol. xvi, (1938/9), pp 105–30.

Murphy, Michael, 'Financial results on sixty-one West Cork farms in 1940–41', *Journal of the Statistical and Social Inquiry Society of Ireland*, vol. xvi, (1941/2), pp 60–87.

Murphy, Michael, 'Financial results on mixed dairy farms in 1942–43 as compared with 1938–38, *Journal of the Statistical and Social Inquiry Society of Ireland*, vol. xvii, (1943/4), pp 269–308.

Neenan, M., 'Agriculture in the new state', in P. L. Curran (ed.), *Towards a History of Agricultural Science in Ireland*, (Dublin, 1992), pp 83–130.

O'Brien, George, 'Patrick Hogan', *Studies*, vol. xxv, (September, 1936), pp 353–68.

O'Connor, R., 'Financial results on twenty farms in mid-Roscommon in 1945–46', *Journal of the Statistical and Social Inquiry Society of Ireland*, vol. xviii, (1948/9), pp 79–108.

O'Connor, R. 'Financial results on twenty-five farms in mid-Roscommon in 1948–49', *Journal of the Statistical and Social Inquiry Society of Ireland*, vol. xviii, pt 3, (1949/50), pp 270–92.

O'Connor, R., 'An analysis of recent policies for beef and milk', *Journal of the Statistical and Social Inquiry Society of Ireland*, vol. xxii, pt 2, (1969/70), pp 28–80.

O'Connor, Robert, 'Implications of Irish agricultural statistics', in I. F. Baillie & S. J. Sheehy, *Irish Agriculture in a Changing World*, (Edinburgh, 1971), pp 16–43.

O'Connor, R. & Guiomard, C., 'Agricultural output in the Irish Free State area before and after Independence', *Irish Economic and Social History*, vol. xii, (1985), pp 79–88.

O'Donnell, Rory, 'Manufacturing' in ESRI, *The Economics of 1992. A Symposium on Sectoral Issues*, (Dublin, 1989), pp 5–42.

Ó Gráda, Cormac, 'The beginnings of the Irish creamery system 1880–1914', *Economic History Review*, vol. xxx, (1977), pp 284–305.

Ó Grada, Cormac & O'Rourke, Kevin, 'Irish economic growth, 1945–88', in Nicholas Crafts & Gianni Toniolo, 'Postwar growth an overview', in Nicholas Crafts & Gianni Toniolo (eds), *Economic Growth in Europe since 1945*, (Cambridge, 1996), pp 388–426.

O'Hagan, John, 'An analysis of the relative size of the government sector: Ireland, 1926–52', *Economic and Social Review*, vol. 12, no 1, (1980), pp 17–35.

O'Neill, T. P., 'The food crisis of the 1890s', in E. M. Crawford (ed.), *Famine: the Irish Experience 900–1900*, (Edinburgh, 1989), pp 176–97.

O'Rourke, Kevin, 'Burn everything British but their coal: the Anglo-Irish Economic War of the 1930s', *Journal of Economic History*, vol. li, no 2, (1991), pp 357–66.

O'Sheil, Kevin, 'Memories of my lifetime', *The Irish Times*, 11–22 November 1966.

Parlon, Tom, 'Responding to the demands of the market', Address to the Department of Agriculture, Food and Rural Development Centenary Conference, Dublin Castle, 30 March 2000. Unpublished.

Pederson, Peder J., 'Post-war growth of the Danish economy', in Nicholas Crafts & Gianni Toniolo (eds), *Economic Growth in Europe since 1945*, (Cambridge, 1996), pp 541–75.

Ruane, J. B., 'The farmer in a changing industry', in I. F. Baillie & S. J. Sheehy, *Irish Agriculture in a Changing World*, (Edinburgh, 1971), pp 130–43.

Sheehy, Seamus, 'Agricultural policy', in Jim Dooge & Ruth Barrington (eds), *A Vital National Interest. Ireland in Europe, 1973–1998*, (Dublin, 1999), pp 244–56.

Smith, Louis P. F., 'Recent developments in northern Irish agriculture',

Journal of the Statistical and Social Inquiry Society of Ireland, vol. xviii, (1948/9), pp 143–58.

Solar, Peter, 'The agricultural trade statistics in the Irish Railway Commissioners' Report', *Irish Economic and Social History*, vol. 6, (1979), pp 24–40.

Solar, Peter 'Agricultural productivity and economic development in Ireland and Scotland in the early nineteenth century', in T. M. Devine & D. Dickson (eds), *Ireland and Scotland, 1600–1850*, (Edinburgh, 1983), pp 70–88.

Spain, Henry, 'Agricultural education and extension', in I. F. Baillie & S. J. Sheehy, *Irish Agriculture in a Changing World*, (Edinburgh, 1971), pp 176–96.

Stapleton, John, 'Civil service reform 1969–87', *Administration*, vol. 38, no 4, (1991), pp 303–35.

Travers, Pauric, 'The financial relations question, 1800–1914', in F. B. Smith (ed.), *Ireland, England and Australia. Essays in Honour of Oliver MacDonagh*, (Cork, 1990), pp 50–6.

Twomey, D., 'Agricultural organisation: Marketing and grading of agricultural produce' in F. C. King (ed.), *Public Administration in Ireland*, vol. 1, (Dublin, 1944), pp 55–66.

Walsh, Thomas, 'Research and future agricultural developments', in I. F. Baillie & S. J. Sheehy, *Irish Agriculture in a Changing World*, (Edinburgh, 1971), pp 144–56.

Walsh, T., Ryan, P. F. & Kilroy, J., 'A half century of fertiliser and lime use in Ireland', *Journal of the Statistical and Social Inquiry Society of Ireland*, vol. xix, (1956/7), pp 104–36.

Whelan, Bernadette, 'Ireland and the Marshall Plan', *Irish Economic and Social History*, vol. xix, (1992), pp 49–70.

UNPUBLISHED THESES

Bhreathnach Lynch, Sighle, 'The Life and Works of Albert G. Power, R.H.A. (1891–1945). A Sculpted Legacy of Irish Ireland', PhD thesis, University College, Dublin, 1992.

Clarke, Mary Bernadette, 'Vocational Education in a Local Context 1930–1998', PhD thesis, University College, Dublin, 1999.

Cullen, Joan M., 'Patrick J. Hogan, Minister for Agriculture, 1922–32. A Study of a Leading Member of the First Government of Independent Ireland', PhD thesis, Dublin City University, 1993.

Fee, Gerard, 'The Effect of World War II on Dublin's Low-Income Families', PhD thesis, University College, Dublin, 1996.

Harvey, Brian, 'The Emergence of the Western Problem in the Irish Economy in the Latter Part of the 19th Century and its Persistence into the 20th Century, with Special Reference to the Work of the Congested Districts Board 1891–1923', MA thesis, University College, Dublin, 1986.

Hayes, Jacqueline, 'The Shannon Scheme Strike 1925', MA thesis, University College, Dublin, 1995.

Keating, Carla, 'Sir Horace Plunkett and Rural Reform 1889–1914', PhD thesis, University College, Dublin, 1984.

Ryan, W. J. L., 'The Nature of Protective Policy in Ireland, 1932–39', PhD thesis, Dublin University, 1949.

Takei, Akihiro, 'Business and Government in the Irish Free State: The Case of the Irish Flour Milling Industry 1922–1945', PhD thesis, Dublin University, 1998.

REFERENCE WORKS

Institute of Public Administration Yearbooks

Thom's Directory

INDEX

Royal Irish Constabulary (RIC), 50, 55,
56, 102
Royal Veterinary College, 50
Rugby, Lord *see* Maffey, Sir John
Rumbold, Mr (official, Board of Trade),
362
rural development, 477, 530–2, 551
Rural Environment Protection Scheme
(REPS), 520, 521, 534, 535
rural home economics, 401, 408, 409,
412–15
rural industries, 11–12, 14, 24, 35–6, 103,
104, 121
Russell, T. W.
and Agricultural Wages Board, 58
and Board of Agriculture (DATI), 21,
45
and Council of Agriculture (DATI), 18
and county committees of agriculture,
31, 79
and Easter Rising (1916), 62
and IAOS, 41–3, 45, 54–5, 75
vice-president of DATI, 16–17, 38, 50,
75
and World War One, 53, 54–55, 57
Ruttledge, P. J., 91–2
Ryan, James
after Emergency, 264, 265, 267, 268,
269
and agricultural education, 387–8, 392
and agricultural policy, 268, 269, 271–
2, 339, 455
and agricultural subsidies, 177, 375
and agricultural wages, 200
and Anglo-Irish trade, 359
and Anglo-Irish Trade Agreement
(1938), 196–7
and Co-operative Organisation Bill, 137
and Department of Agriculture, 204
and Economic War, 164, 171, 172
and Emergency, 212, 222, 259
agricultural labour, 240, 243, 245
compulsory tillage, 227, 229, 230, 232,
236
dairy industry, 248, 250, 251
fertiliser, 238
trade negotiations, 217–18
western farmers, 239–40

and Food and Agricultural Organisation (FAO), 341
and foot and mouth, 223
and free beef scheme, 173
international trade, 168
and marketing, 166–7
Minister for Agriculture, 160–1, 162,
274
and Northern Ireland, 202
and pig industry, 272
and Pilot Area Programme, 432
and *Second Programme for Economic
Expansion* (1963), 443–4
and small farmers, 207
and small western farms, 422, 423
and soil fertility, 287
and sugar industry, 190–1, 193
and tillage, 183, 187, 188, 193, 506
and tobacco, 193–4

S
Salisbury, Lord, 17
Sandys, Duncan, 363
Saunderson, Colonel, 2
sausages, 301
Science and Art Museum, Dublin, 25
Scotland
agricultural expertise, 4, 7, 23, 29, 31,
51
Board of Health in, 139
cattle and beef in, 170
during World War One, 53, 55, 56, 58
Scott, Thomas, 77
Scully, Dr John, 433, 434–5, 437
Scully, J.J., 491
seed
after Emergency, 293
before the DATI, 8
the DATI and, 49–50
during Emergency, 229, 237
during 1920s, 127
during 1930s, 160, 186, 205, 208
during World War One, 53, 56
self-help *see* co-operative movement, Pilot
Area Programme
self-sufficiency
after Emergency, 268
during Emergency, 224